THE CHRIST IN THE BIBLE COMMENTARY
Volume Six

THE
CHRIST IN THE BIBLE
COMMENTARY

Volume Six

First and Second Thessalonians
First and Second Timothy
Titus
Hebrews
James
First and Second Peter
First, Second and Third John
Revelation

Dr. Albert B. Simpson

CHRISTIAN PUBLICATIONS
CAMP HILL, PENNSYLVANIA

Christian Publications
3825 Hartzdale Drive, Camp Hill, PA 17011

The mark of ✝ vibrant faith

ISBN: 0-87509-503-8
LOC Catalog Card Number: 92-70937
© 1994 by Christian Publications
All rights reserved
Printed in the United States of America

94 95 96 97 98   5 4 3 2 1

Cover Design: Step One Design

CONTENTS

First and Second Thessalonians

First and Second Timothy

Titus

Hebrews

James

First and Second Peter

First, Second and Third John

FIRST AND SECOND THESSALONIANS

CHAPTER 1

THE EPISTLES OF THE ADVENT

At the coming of our Lord Jesus Christ. (1 Thessalonians 5:23)

The New Testament epistles have, as a rule, some specific quality or characteristic by which they are known: Romans is the epistle of gospel truth; Corinthians of the Church; Galatians of grace; Ephesians of the highest Christian life; Philippians of the sweetest Christian life; Colossians of the Christ life, etc. The letters to the Thessalonians are the advent epistles. The one theme that runs throughout the two letters like a sort of golden thread and appears in every chapter in connection with some important and practical doctrine, is the blessed hope of the Lord's coming. So prominently did this subject occupy the preaching of Paul during his visit to Thessalonica, that when his enemies brought charges against him before the rulers of the city, they made this the point of their accusation, that "these men who have caused trouble all over the world have now come here, . . . all defying Caesar's decrees, saying that there is another king, one called Jesus" (Acts 17:6–7).

It is evident from this that the general impression received from his preaching in Thessalonica was that the Christ to whom he bore witness was a real King, and was coming again to establish a kingdom on the earth. Otherwise there would have been no possible grounds for jealousy on the part of Caesar's friends. Indeed, we know from the very first chapter of his epistle that he began with this theme in his first messages to the unconverted, and it was this that awakened their consciences while still heathen, and led them to turn "to God from idols to serve the living and true God, and to wait for his Son from heaven" (1 Thessalonians 1:9–10).

The fact that the letters to the Thessalonians were Paul's earliest epistles, and that this subject occupies so prominent a place in them, makes it very plain that the doctrine of the Lord's coming is not an advanced truth that can only be understood by deeply spiritual Christians. It is one of the

1

primary doctrines of the gospel, and is part of the very essence of the gospel of the kingdom.

CONVICTION AND CONVERSION

This doctrine is presented as a means of conviction and a motive to conversion. "For they themselves report what kind of reception you gave us. They tell how you turned to God from idols to serve the living and true God, and to wait for his Son from heaven, whom he raised from the dead—Jesus, who rescues us from the coming wrath" (1:9–10).

It is evident from this passage that it was the truth of the Lord's coming that led the Thessalonians to turn from heathen idols to the Lord Jesus Christ. It is, therefore, a most appropriate message to preach to the unsaved and to proclaim to the heathen. It was a similar message carried by Jonah to the people of Nineveh that brought them to repentance, and awakened profound and universal conviction throughout the empire of Assyria. Our missionaries tell us that when they announce to the most wicked chiefs of pagan tribes that there is another Sovereign to whom they are accountable, and who is soon to appear to call them to account, there is an instinct in the human heart that seems to respond to such a message, and they are often led by it to deep conviction and awakening. Surely this is the meaning of "the good news of the kingdom" (Matthew 9:35), which the Lord has commissioned us to give to the world as a witness before His coming. We are sent forth not merely as heralds to individual Christians, but as ambassadors to all nations, and we are to proclaim the King who is coming to call them to judgment as well as to deal with every individual conscience and life. May God give us wisdom as Christian workers and missionaries to understand and fill our great commission. If any reader of these lines is still unsaved, let us appeal to you by all the powers of the world to come to prepare for that great day! "Since, then, we know what it is to fear the Lord, we try to persuade men. . . . Be reconciled to God" (2 Corinthians 5:11, 20).

A MOTIVE TO FAITHFUL MINISTRY

The Lord's coming is a motive to faithful ministry. "For what is our hope, our joy, or the crown in which we will glory in the presence of our Lord Jesus when he comes? Is it not you? Indeed, you are our glory and joy" (1 Thessalonians 2:19–20). Here the apostle bears witness that the Lord's coming was a motive in his own ministry and the inspiring hope of his own loving service for the souls of men. As he tells us elsewhere, he expects to present his beloved people to the heavenly Bridegroom as a delightful trust, and to find in their joy his joy and crown. Our service for Christ is to receive both wages and fruit. The wages are paid now, but the fruit we shall share with Him. To the faithful elders Peter says in this connection. "And when the Chief

Shepherd appears, you will receive the crown of glory that will never fade away" (1 Peter 5:4). A still more ancient promise declared that "those who lead many to righteousness, [will shine] like the stars for ever and ever" (Daniel 12:3). There is one sense in which the souls we win for Christ shall be eternally linked with our happiness and reward, and be as jewels in our crowns of rejoicing. Are there any who are reading these lines who will wear a starless crown? Have you been accumulating blessings only for yourself, and will it be your sad record, as a man once cabled across the sea to his friends at home after an awful shipwreck in which his family had all perished by his side, "Saved alone"? "Your heaven," Rutherford used to write, "will be two heavens for me; your salvation will be two salvations to me."

A MOTIVE FOR CHRISTIAN LOVE

The Lord's coming is a motive for Christian love. "May the Lord make your love increase and overflow for each other and for everyone else, just as ours does for you. May he strengthen your hearts so that you will be blameless and holy in the presence of our God and Father when our Lord Jesus comes with all his holy ones" (1 Thessalonians 3:12–13).

In the beautiful series of parables of the kingdom (Matthew 13) there is a progression in the parable of the treasure and of the pearl from the individual to the body. In the first of these two parables the Church is viewed as made up of innumerable persons, but in the second as one beautiful pearl. The unity of the Church must be accomplished before the Lord's coming. He is to meet not a number of virgins, but the Bride. The divisions of Christendom hinder His coming. It may be we shall never see all the denominations united as one organic body, but we do see something coming to pass which is perhaps God's substitute for this; that is, a gathering together of the spiritual elements of the Church of God in a deeper unity of heart and holy fellowship. They are being drawn to Christ as a mystical and spiritual body. As such we meet in our great conventions forgetting our denominational names, and it is this company whom Christ is calling out and training for the hour of His *parousia*.

Of course, it goes without saying that all individual bitterness, strife and uncharitableness is an offense to Jesus Christ and a hindrance to His coming. You cannot expect Him to call you to the meeting in the air if there is anyone in that assembly with whom you stand in strained relations. There can be no adjustments and reconciliations there. You must be "found . . . at peace with him" (2 Peter 3:14) and must love all men. Are we ready in this regard for the coming of the Lord Jesus Christ with all His saints?

SOURCE OF COMFORT

The Lord's coming is a source of comfort to the afflicted and bereaved.

"Therefore encourage each other with these words" (1 Thessalonians 4:18). This entire passage (4:13–18) contains the most comforting and tender picture of the Lord's coming in the Scriptures. Even the briefest enumeration of the point is full of instruction and consolation.

1. Living Still

We are here most plainly reminded that those who sleep in Jesus are living still, for it is said: "God will bring with Jesus those who have fallen asleep in him" (4:14). If God is to bring them with Him they must be somewhere. They cannot be mere dust and ashes in the grave, for He is to bring them to the earth. They must be real persons, or how can He bring them? And they must be with Him now in their disembodied state in order that He may bring them to meet their resurrected bodies.

2. Reunion of Long-Parted Friends

Next, there is a beautiful provision for the reunion of long parted friends. The dead in Christ are first raised, and then the living believers changed. But there is a little time before the meeting with the Lord for mutual recognition and fellowship. They are caught up together and on the way what happy greetings, what mutual explanations, what tales there will be to tell of the years that rolled between and the blended experiences of earth and heaven! Then when all tears are wiped away and all longing satisfied, will come the meeting with the Lord in the air.

3. The Meeting with the Lord

The meeting with the Lord in the air and all lesser love will for a time be lost sight of in the rapture of His presence and the welcome from His voice.

A MESSAGE AND A WARNING

The Lord's coming is a message of warning and a call to watchfulness. "But you, brothers, are not in darkness so that this day should surprise you like a thief. . . . So then, let us not be like others, who are asleep, but let us be alert and self-controlled" (5:4, 6). We are here reminded that the saints of Christ shall know enough of the time of His coming to be ready. The world will be surprised, but the Bride of the Lamb will know early enough to be in the attitude for translation. At the same time, there must be no carelessness, but a spirit of vigilance and a habit of constant preparedness.

AN INCENTIVE TO HOLINESS

The coming of the Lord is a powerful incentive to holiness. "May God himself, the God of peace sanctify you through and through. May your whole spirit, soul and body be kept blameless at the coming of our Lord

Jesus Christ. The one who calls you is faithful and he will do it" (5:23–24).

"Without holiness no one will see the Lord" (Hebrews 12:14), and doubt-less this means at His coming. In the parable of the 10 virgins, they were vir-gins who were pure in a sense, and even expecting their Lord, but who were not fully prepared to enter into the marriage because of the lack of the Holy Spirit. First Thessalonians 5:24 contains a prayer for the entire sanctification of the believers at Thessalonica in order that they might be fully prepared for the Lord's coming. The word translated "unto" in the King James should be translated "at," implying not that we are to grow into sanctification in view of the Lord's coming, but we are to receive it as a gift of the God of peace, and then be preserved in it by His grace so that we shall be in a constant state of preparedness whenever the Lord may come, and we shall be "found spotless, blameless and at peace with him" (2 Peter 3:14). This preparation must be very thorough and complete, embracing our whole spirit, soul and body, and including our abiding in Him so that we shall be "kept blameless" (1 Thessalonians 5:23) and presented "before his glorious presence without fault and with great joy" (Jude 24). Such a high degree of grace is beyond human attainment, and therefore it is divinely provided and promised to those who will receive it. "The one who calls you is faithful and he will do it" (1 Thessalonians 5:24). By all the hopes and fears of the coming age, let us receive this grace and be clothed in the fine linen, clean and white, which is the righteousness of the saints (Revelation 19:8).

DIFFERENT FOR THE RIGHTEOUS AND THE WICKED

The Lord's coming will have a very different aspect for the righteous and the wicked. In the second epistle, chapter 1, verses 7 to 10, we have the vivid picture of the other side of the advent—the coming of the day of God as it will appear to the unbelieving and ungodly. It shall be rest with us "on the day he comes to be glorified in his holy people and to be marveled at among all those who have believed" (2 Thessalonians 1:10), but for "those who do not know God and do not obey the gospel of our Lord Jesus Christ" (1:8), it will be "everlasting destruction . . . shut out from the presence of the Lord and from the majesty of his power" (1:9). This doubtless describes the latter phase of the Lord's coming when He shall be revealed and openly manifested to all the world. This is not His coming for His saints, but His coming with His glorified Bride and His mighty angels to judge the nations and establish His kingdom on the millennial earth. It is in view of the terrors of that day that God's mercy now pleads with men to meet Him as a Savior and Friend, and not as a sovereign Judge.

APOSTASY AND SIGNS

The Lord's coming in connection with the development of the apostasy and the immediate signs of the times is the subject of the second chapter of Second Thessalonians. There the apostle endeavors to correct some false impressions that had gone abroad among the disciples through false teachers, to the effect that the day of Christ had already come and that they had been left behind. These false impressions had been diligently circulated by forged letters as from him, and pretended revelations in the Spirit, and they were causing much distress and disturbance of mind to the brethren. Paul, therefore, takes occasion to tell them that the day of Christ will not come until some precedent events occur, and one particularly shall be fully developed. This one he calls the apostasy. It is interesting to note some special features of this great movement of evil in order that we may be able to identify it in our own time, and be preserved from the disturbing influences of false views ourselves.

1. An Apostasy

It is an apostasy. It is not an infidel movement. It is not a political combination of ungodly men. It is not some organized form of latter day evil, such as Spiritualism, Nihilism, Socialism, Fanaticism. But it is something that was originally Christian and has become perverted.

2. A Religious Movement

It is still professedly a religious movement, for we are here told that, "he sets himself up in God's temple, proclaiming himself to be God" (2:4). It is Antichrist not in the sense of being opposed to Christ, but rather being a substitute for Christ, a usurper on His throne. It claims miraculous powers, and signs, and lying wonders, and appears to be a great religious system claiming supernatural authority and power, a sort of vicar of Christ on earth.

3. Already at Work

This apostasy was already working in the days of Paul, and needed only the removal of certain external restraints to work out its full development of evil. It was in the churches in the form of pride, ambition, worldly policy, human selfishness and all the evils of the carnal mind. Even before the death of Paul and John we find the spirit of ecclesiastical pride shutting them out from their own churches and disciples, and claiming assumptions which already received the severest rebukes of the ascended Lord in His letters to the churches of Asia. Quite early in the history of Christianity we find the very ministers of Jesus Christ contending with each other about their respective rank and dignity, until finally the supreme question was which of the bishops should be the pope; and then the pope demanded a power supreme even above the emperor and the state. This spirit, however, of ambition and pride was restrained as long as the Roman emperor retained his supremacy, but when Rome fell, the last barrier in the way of ecclesiastical pride was removed, and then there rose up in the place of the Caesars a spiritual power more despotic and even more universal and resistless than theirs, and for half the Christian age that power sat in the temple of God, showing itself as God, and it sits there still.

4. The Spirit of Wickedness

Behind all its religious claims is the spirit of wickedness, a system of unrighteousness. "The coming of the lawless one will be in accordance with the work of Satan displayed in all kinds of counterfeit miracles, signs and wonders, and in every sort of evil that deceives those who are perishing" (2:9–10). It is the very mystery of iniquity. It even claims the right to call evil good and good evil. It assumes such infallibility that its dictums and decrees possess all the authority of the Word of God. Even the Scriptures must be interpreted by its canons and must be suppressed at its will. The grossest sins on the part of its members and officials are condoned by specious and plausible pretexts and canonized as virtues. It issues authorized indulgences to sin. It opens the gates of hell and of heaven. It adapts itself to every age and clime, and when it cannot rule the king upon his throne, it can use a democracy, a political boss, just as effectually. It thrives on ignorance, and the illiterate and profligate are its favorite constituency and are its most effectual allies and agents. Our readers have already anticipated its name. It is that system of iniquity which has grown out of a perverted Christianity, and has for more than a thousand years been the greatest menace to the liberties of the world and the rights of man. Its form has changed today, but not its spirit. There remains but one more development.

5. A Man of Sin

It will finally head up in a man of sin, the son of perdition. Some brilliant and perverted genius will yet grasp the reins of its worldwide power and organize it into the last great enemy of God and man, and then it will receive its death blow: "The Lord Jesus will overthrow with the breath of his mouth and destroy by the splendor of his coming" (2:8).

But the last blow is to be struck only when Christ shall come in His glorious epiphany, not in His *parousia*. It will still go on after He has caught away His saints, evolving its most dreadful forces and forms of evil, and therefore, as far as the apostasy is concerned, it may be that all the conditions that must precede the coming of Jesus have already been fulfilled and that nothing may remain except that which is to be precipitated to its rapid ripening by the exciting conditions of the tribulation times. If this apostasy was in the days of Paul a reason for not immediately expecting the Lord to come, today it surely is the opposite, a reason for believing that that great event is near, even at the doors.

NOT FANATICAL EXCITEMENT

Finally, the practical preparation for the Lord's coming is not a fanatical excitement. This preparation for His coming does not lead us to neglect any of life's duties, but rather leads to a simple, faithful attitude of righteousness and fidelity to every trust. As the apostle expresses it so finely: "May the Lord direct your hearts into God's love and Christ's perseverance" (3:5).

In the days of Paul a class of men had risen up who have never been without their successors, who abused his doctrine by turning it into an occasion for all sorts of irregularity in life and conduct. They neglected their families. They gave up honest work. They fell into fanatical practices, and they disturbed all religious social order. We have them still. Longhaired, loudmouthed talkers, too sanctified to live with their families, too spiritual to defile themselves with the touch of a handsaw or claw hammer, a dustpan or a washtub. The gospel of the kingdom has no sympathy with such rubbish. The best preparation for Christ's coming is to be faithful in your calling, whatever it may be, and to be found at your post.

The three classes of people whom the Lord singles out for translation (Matthew 24:36–51; Luke 17:30–35) are all engaged in ordinary things. One woman is grinding grain; one man is plowing or harvesting in the field, and both go up instantly at the signal without needing to go home to change their clothes. The third is in bed, where honest people ought to be at that hour, and is translated just as readily as if he had been at an all-night prayer meeting. The idea seems to be that Christ expects us to be always ready, and then everything that comes in the way of life's duties is equally sacred and heavenly.

The old Massachusetts senator was right when he refused to vote to adjourn the legislature, because the awful darkness that had come on seemed to portend the day of judgment. Said he, "If this is not the day of judgment there's no need for all this fuss; and if it is, I for one, prefer to have the Judge find me at my post."

CHAPTER 2

THE CHRISTIAN LIFE IN THESSALONIANS

May God himself, the God of peace, sanctify you through and through. May your whole spirit, soul and body be kept blameless at the coming of our Lord Jesus Christ. The one who calls you is faithful and he will do it. (1 Thessalonians 5:23–24)

We have traced the golden thread of Advent truth through the letters of Paul to his early converts at Thessalonica. It will be interesting next to trace the teaching of the apostle in the same epistles concerning the true preparation for Christ's coming—personal holiness. Especially is it interesting to note the manner in which this prince of teachers introduced the subject to comparatively young disciples, for, as we have already seen, the Thessalonians were among his earliest converts, and the Thessalonian epistles were the first of his inspired letters. We shall see that no convert can be too young to be profoundly taught the doctrine of entire sanctification.

We sometimes find that a skillful scientist can restore, from a few fragments of fossil bones, the entire anatomy of some extinct animal that ages ago roamed the primitive earth. So from the few fragments of apostolic teaching that are left to us we may reconstruct the ideal of Christian life in the early Church, and find a high and perfect standard of Christian experience of holy living fitted to instruct, attract and inspire us to holy imitation.

GENUINE CONVERSION

The experience of these Thessalonian Christians began with a genuine Holy Spirit conversion. "Because our gospel came to you not simply with words, but also with power, with the Holy Spirit and with deep conviction. You know how we lived among you for your sake. You became imitators of us and of the Lord; in spite of severe suffering, you welcomed the message with the joy given by the Holy Spirit" (1 Thessalonians 1:5–6). This was no mechanical revival gotten up by sensational excitement, but a powerful work of the Holy Spirit, producing conviction so deep and conversion so thorough that no affliction or persecution could intimidate them; but they joyfully faced the afflictions of the gospel and took their stand on the side of Christ and His apostle with boldness and unreserved decision. Their conversion was accompanied with much deep feeling, and especially with joy in the Holy Spirit and full assurance of faith. These men and women knew that they were saved, and they let everybody else know it, too. It is a great thing to be well saved and to have the strong, full tides of a deep spiritual work carry us from the outset to the high level of an out-and-out salvation.

FOUNDED ON THE WORD OF GOD

The Thessalonian Christians had an experience that was founded on the Word of God and established on thoroughly scriptural lines. "When you received the word of God, which you heard from us," he reminds them, "you accepted it not as the word of men, but as it actually is, the word of God, which is at work in you who believe" (2:13). Theirs was a Bible experience and a scriptural holiness. They had not accepted a system of theology or series of opinions from the teaching of Paul. But behind the messenger they had heard the Master's voice, and accepted, without hesitation or equivocation, the authority of the Word of God as the supreme law of their life.

It is a great thing to have an experience founded directly upon the Scriptures. Don't get your theories of holiness from the best of human books or biographies. Go direct to the fountainhead, and let the first principle of your faith and obedience be, "Thus saith the Lord." Then your convictions, your joys, your hopes, your impulses and all your experience will be steadfast, abiding and effectual. You will be saved from the drift and uncertainty of a mere emotional experience, and your life will become "stedfast, unmoveable, always abounding in the work of the Lord" (1 Corinthians 15:58, KJV).

A LIFE OF FAITH

The life of the Thessalonian Christians was a life of faith. So we find Paul praying for them that God "by his power . . . may fulfill every good purpose of yours and every act prompted by your faith" (2 Thessalonians 1:11), and speaking of the Word of God which "effectually worketh also in you that believe" (1 Thessalonians 2:13, KJV). They had learned that the secret of a happy Christian experience is not emotional feeling, but simple faith, and that all the graces of the Spirit and the comfort of the Holy Spirit must be the work of faith. It is a great thing to get established on this solid ground and learn to walk by faith and not by sight.

THE LIFE OF LOVE

The Thessalonians had also been taught the life of love. The apostle reminds them with evident pleasure, that

> Timothy has just now come to us from you and has brought good news about your faith and love. He has told us that you always have pleasant memories of us and that you long to see us, just as we also long to see you. Therefore, brothers, in all our distress and persecution we were encouraged about you because of your faith. For now we really live, since you are standing firm in the Lord. . . .
> May the Lord make your love increase and overflow for each other and for everyone else, just as ours does for you. (1 Thessalonians 3:6–8, 12)

They were not hard or formal Christians, but simple and affectionate children of one dear family, intensely devoted to Paul, their spiritual father, as he was to them; and loving one another with tender, simple-hearted affection. The deepest Christian life must always be a life of love. It is through the cultivation of the natural and spiritual affections that the heart is opened for God's richest impartings of grace, and it is only in fellowship "with all the saints, to grasp how wide and long and high and deep is the love of Christ, and to know this love that surpasses knowledge" (Ephesians 3:18–19).

THE LIFE OF JOY AND CHEER

The ideal life of this epistle is a life of joy and cheer. "Be joyful always; pray continually; give thanks in all circumstances, for this is God's will for you in Christ Jesus" (1 Thessalonians 5:16–18). This is the apostle's ideal for them and doubtless they lived up to it. There is nothing that makes our Christian influence so effective as a spirit of cheerfulness, thankfulness and holy gladness. A happy disposition and a shining face are a heritage of unspeakable blessing to the possessor and everybody with whom he comes in contact. And a taciturn, moody, discontented spirit and manner repel us like the nightshade and the east wind. The most wholesome, helpful people are the happy people. How we thank God for a few such friends! If you can't do anything else for God and a suffering world, be bright and glad and full of good cheer at least. God help us to "be joyful always," and to "give thanks in all circumstances, for this is God's will for you in Christ Jesus" (5:16, 18).

A LIFE OF PRAYER

Their life was a life of prayer. "Pray continually" (5:17). There is a great difference between prayer and a life of prayer. Almost everyone prays, but very few pray without ceasing. This is the habit of devotion. This is the altar of incense ever burning in the Holy Place. This is the fragrance of a heart that lives in the presence of the Holy One, and breathes the very life of God. This is the deep undertone of a sanctified life. It is from this that the sweetness, the gladness, the holiness and the helpfulness come. Lord, teach us the habit of prayer, the prayer that springs spontaneously from the heart, and which neither secular duty, satanic temptation nor the waves of sorrow can interrupt, but which is only stimulated by the things that try us, until every experience becomes transformed into an occasion for communion and fellowship with God.

A LIFE OF HOLINESS

The life of the Thessalonian Christians was a life of holiness. This brings us to the heart of our subject—entire sanctification as taught in these epistles.

1. The Will of God

The Thessalonians were taught that sanctification was the will of God for them. "It is God's will that you should be sanctified" (4:3). With them the holy life was not an option, but an obligation. Sanctification was not the experience of a few exclusive and *elite* saints, but the normal standard for every age and every Christian. "Shall we go on sinning so that grace may increase? By no means!" (Romans 6:1–2). God forbids you to continue in sin. God commands you to be holy, and He provides what He commands. At the same time there is a sweet modesty about the teaching of these epistles concerning holiness. There is no boasting of their own perfection, but it is held up as a standard to accept and press forward to something which, if not yet fully attained, is never to be lost sight of or lowered to suit their failures and imperfections. If they have not yet experienced it they are to be ever as the Methodist book of discipline expresses it, "groaning after it," and pressing forward until they have claimed it.

2. The Work of God

They were taught that sanctification is the work of God. "The very God of peace [*himself*] sanctify you," is the fine force of the original here (1 Thessalonians 5:23, KJV). It is God's work, not ours. And this is still further strengthened by the next verse. "The one who calls you is faithful and he will do it" (5:24). It is part of the provision of grace, and God is bound to fulfill it to us in our experience if we will follow up our redemption rights and the full claims of the inheritance of faith. Just as Isaac's bride was provided with her wedding array and only had to put it on to meet her lord, so it is granted to the Bride of Christ that she should be arrayed in "fine linen, bright and clean,/ . . . (Fine linen stands for the righteous acts of the saints.)" (Revelation 19:8). Christ is "become for us wisdom from God— that is, our righteousness, holiness and redemption" (1 Corinthians 1:30). Let us accept the great provision of faith and put on the Lord Jesus.

3. Entire Sanctification

God has provided entire sanctification for His people. "The God of peace sanctify you through and through" (1 Thessalonians 5:23). The word "sanctify" has three meanings—to separate from, to dedicate to and to fill with; and all these three are necessary to constitute entire sanctification.

There is a work of separation. There are things we cannot consecrate to God but must surrender and leave outside the camp—our sinful habits, our old self-life, the things which the light of the Holy Spirit will surely condemn if you let them in.

There is but one inexorable course to take here. You cannot give them to God; you may not be able to cleanse yourself from them; but you can consent to be cleansed. You can pass the sentence of death on them. You can dare to say "No" to them. You can give God the right to destroy them. It is here that the great decisive act is usually performed; and it is here that the coward heart usually fails. Is God speaking to you, my brother, my sister? Dare to obey. Dare to say to yourself a brave, eternal "No," and to God an everlasting "Yes"; and you will find that He has a way of making real the death warrant that you dare to sign.

Then comes the work of dedication. You give to God your surrendered life, your will and all the possibilities of your being. You choose to belong to Him. You say by one great act of your will, "I am henceforth not my own. I belong to Him." You hand yourself over in every power of your being to be His property, to obey His will and to live to please Him. This is consecration. "Therefore, I urge you, brothers, in view of God's mercy, to offer your bodies as living sacrifices, holy and pleasing to God" (Romans 12:1).

But when all this is done you are still but an empty vessel. God has the vessel, but He must fill it with His own grace and goodness by the Holy Spirit and the life of Christ. And so the third and chief stage of sanctification is union with Jesus and the incoming and indwelling of the Holy Spirit as the continual source of our new life with all its graces and victories. Hence it is a life of dependence on Him in which He is made unto us sanctification, and all the goodness and sweetness of our experience is but the fruit of the Spirit working in us "love, joy, peace, patience, kindness, goodness, faithfulness, gentleness and self-control" (Galatians 5:22–23). Thus sanctification is the work of the Spirit and the life of Jesus and the gift of God's grace. Our part in it is to receive of His fullness grace for grace, and live out His life step by step as He dwells in us and walks in us.

How simple, how scriptural and how complete is this philosophy of the life of holiness! Have you received it? Will you enter in? Will you separate yourself from all that His Word, His Spirit, and your own quickened conscience forbid? Will you dedicate yourself unreservedly to Him and count yourself His, and His alone, and begin to live on His fullness and walk in His Spirit?

But there is a further and fuller specification of entire sanctification in the next clause, "Your whole spirit, soul and body" (1 Thessalonians 5:23). Here we get a little inventory of the properties that we are handing over. It is a great empire, a human life. First, there is the spirit, our highest nature: that which knows right and wrong; that which knows God and enjoys His presence; that which is immortal and capable of union with the vine; that which may be either good or evil as it is possessed by God or Satan. This must be separated, dedicated and filled with the Holy Spirit.

Then there is the soul, the intellectual and emotional part: that which thinks, feels, loves; that which has its tastes, it passions, its desires. This must be separated from all that is impure, earthly, selfish. This must be dedicated to God, to desire, to love, to think at His bidding and according to His will. And this must be filled by the Holy Spirit so that He shall control our thoughts, direct our affections and possess and use all the powers of our mind and affections of our heart.

And then the body with all its members is counted in and must be held under the control of a sanctified will, separated from every sordid, gross, sensual and unnatural use, dedicated to God and filled with the life of Christ. This will lead to an individual and explicit transaction in which eyes, ears, lips, hands, feet and heart—every member—will be turned over to Him and become the subject of this blessed indwelling. For He, too, has a body like our own, and He is the head of the body. "The body is . . . for the Lord, and the Lord for the body" (1 Corinthians 6:13). He can take these members and cleanse them from unholy appetites and selfish indulgences, and even the humors and infirmities of disease. He can make them strong and pure through the touch of His life, and then give them double power to speak, to work, to walk on His errands and in the ministries of His love. This is entire sanctification; and oh, what a great and glorious possibility it is!

4. Preserved Blameless

Here again we come to an important doctrinal teaching. Our sanctification is not a crystallized and self-centered state, but a condition of constant dependence upon Him who is its Author and Finisher. We must be preserved moment by moment and "through faith [be] shielded by God's power until the coming of the salvation . . ." (1 Peter 1:5). This introduces us to the life of abiding, and compels us to watch constantly and walk closely with our living Lord. But He is "able to keep you from falling and to present you before his glorious presence without fault and with great joy" (Jude 24). He does not say that we are preserved spotless, for holiness is relative and none is absolutely holy but God. But we can be blameless.

Your little child just beginning to write may make many a crooked scrawl, but if he is doing his best with a true heart and a watchful hand, you count him blameless and reward him because he did his best. And so we may walk worthy of God unto all pleasing, even though the eye of infinite holiness might discover many a flaw in our work.

It is a blessed thing to walk in the constant sense of His acceptance, and it is most depressing to be constantly condemning yourself and living in bondage and self-depreciation. It is possible to come to the place where we find out once for all that God expects nothing of us, and we are to expect nothing of ourselves. But taking Him as our all-sufficiency and throwing upon Him the responsibility of our life, we just draw upon His boundless grace and live in His perfect love. This will lift us to a higher plane than all our morbid self-reproaches, which do not please Him and certainly only drag us down. Let us rise to the blameless life and dwell in the perfect love that casts out fear.

5. A Practical Holiness

The holiness of the Thessalonian Christians was intensely practical. It was not a theory or a sentiment merely, but it led to such results as these:

> For you know that we dealt with each of you as a father deals with his own children, encouraging, comforting and urging you to live lives worthy of God, who calls you into his kingdom and glory. (1 Thessalonians 2:11–12)

> And so you became a model to all the believers in Macedonia and Achaia. The Lord's message rang out from you not only in Macedonia and Achaia—your faith in God has become known everywhere. Therefore we do not need to say anything about it. (1:7–8)

What a beautiful testimony! What a splendid witness for God! This is better than all our preaching. Oh, for lives that will sound out the gospel so widely and so wisely that our preaching will be needless!

The Thessalonian Christians lived their holiness. Their lives were not self-bound, but unselfish, and reached in blessing to the utmost confines of their influence. And so the truly sanctified disciple will always be an active, useful and missionary force. Is God enabling us to reproduce the ancient type, and to live this sweet and holy life of faith and love, of joy and gladness, of prayer and power, of practical goodness and missionary service, of entire sanctification in our spirit and soul and body unto the coming of our Lord Jesus Christ? "The one who calls you is faithful and he will do it" (5:24). He is calling you, my brother. He is calling you, my sister. He is calling you today. Like the old prophet who dropped his mantle on the shoulders of the young ploughman in the summer fields of Abel Meholah (and henceforth Elisha never could be the same again), the Holy Spirit is dropping on you the mantle of a higher calling. Rise to meet Him. Burn up, as Elisha, the things that hinder and hold you back. Lay yourself and everything on the altar and go forth to prove what God can do with a single consecrated life.

CHAPTER 3

A PATTERN WORKER AND MINISTER

You know, brothers, that our visit to you was not a failure. (1 Thessalonians 2:1)

On the contrary, we speak as men approved by God to be entrusted with the gospel. We are not trying to please men but God, who tests our hearts. (2:4)

A man's character is revealed by his correspondence. Much more was this the case in the days that are past, before the modern typewriter and stenographer had come in between the full heart and the written page. Then you could read between the lines many a shade of feeling and many a touch of character which now become lost in transmission through our artificial mediums of correspondence. The best biographies are compiled from the heart to heart letters of confidential friendship. Paul's first letters to the Thessalonians are full of such touches, and we can trace without much difficulty a personal portrait of the man behind the message.

First of all, let us remember that it is a man speaking to us from our own level. This is not the traditional priest in his conventional robes high upon the steeple, but this is the man among his fellow men "down among the people," and speaking to them from their own class and their own level. It is Paul working for daily wages at his loom and web of haircloth, and then preaching in his moments of leisure without canonical robes or ecclesiastical titles, but just because a joy and love made him preach the message that had filled his own heart. This is a message for the reader, whoever you may be or whatever may be your calling, reminding you that as you toil at the workbench, the plow, the washtub or the laundry table, you may be as truly a minister and a messenger of the glorious gospel as the man in the pulpit and the woman in the rescue mission. The charm of Paul's ministry was its unconventional freedom. Put him on board a storm-tossed vessel as a

17

prisoner, and you soon find him working for the salvation of all on board, and by sheer force of character taking command both of captain and of crew. Put him in a Roman barracks chained between two soldiers, and you soon find the whole praetorium in a great revival meeting. Bring him up before Agrippa, Felix and Caesar on trial for his life, and he turns the tables on his judges and preaches the gospel to them till they tremble before him. Set him loose in Philippi among strangers, and he will first get a job at the factory to make a living for himself and his companions, and then find his way on Sabbath morning to the little open air meeting by the riverside, and have the leader of the meeting converted before the day is over. Put him down in the deepest, darkest dungeon in the Philippian prison, and before morning you will find the prison broken up, the jailer converted and the magistrates begging him to leave and help them out of the dilemma into which his arrest has brought them. In fact there was no possible situation where Paul did not manage to find service and turn the situation into an opportunity to witness for Jesus Christ.

Let us look a little more closely at the spirit of his ministry.

HIS AIM AND MOTIVE

His aim and motive were single and supreme consecration to God. "We speak as men approved by God to be entrusted with the gospel. We are not trying to please men but God, who tests our hearts. . . . We were not looking for praise from men, not from you or anyone else" (2:4, 6). He had but one Master to please and one purpose to fulfill, like the railroad employee who had refused to accommodate a lot of passengers by suspending one of the rules of the company for their accommodation, and when told by the crowd that there was no danger of his being spoiled by popularity, answered, "The only man with whom I wish to be popular is the man who employs me." This was the secret of Paul's courage and faithfulness. He tried to please God only.

We are living in an age when it is very difficult for the ministers of Christ to be true to God and popular even with the religious world. No man can stand in a pulpit today and bear faithful testimony against the social, political and commercial wrongs represented in the average congregation, without becoming a bore and an offense and sacrificing his worldly advantages. But Paul had died to all these things, and so he could afford to speak of God whether men would hear or forbear. May the Holy Spirit make us true to our testimony and to our Master.

HIS PERSONAL LIFE

His personal life was pure and blameless, and he could appeal to them and say, "You are witnesses, and so is God, of how holy, righteous and blameless we were among you who believed" (2:10).

Our life is more powerful than our eloquence and wisdom. We can give to others only that which we have personally lived. Men soon detect the professional talker and the unreal life. They make burning glasses out of pieces of ice, but you cannot set fire to human hearts until you yourself are first on fire.

> Thou must thyself be true
>   If thou the truth wouldst teach;
> It needs the overflowing heart
>   To give the lips full speech.

The most eloquent address will be neutralized by one flash of angry temper or one fall into sin. Living epistles, "known and read by everybody" (2 Corinthians 3:2) are the messages which each of us can hold forth before a world that often reads no other message and hears no other gospel. God help us so to live that "in every way [we] will make the teaching about God our Savior attractive" (Titus 2:10).

INDEPENDENCE OF ALL MERCENARY METHODS

Paul gloried in but one thing in his ministry, and that was that he could preach the gospel without charge and say to his fellow disciples, "nor did we eat anyone's food without paying for it. On the contrary, we worked night and day, laboring and toiling so that we would not be a burden to any of you. We did this, not because we do not have the right to such help, but in order to make ourselves a model for you to follow" (2 Thessalonians 3:8–9).

Many people are tempted to think that they should give up business and go into what they call mission work, where somebody else would support them while they give all their time to direct religious service. It would be well for these friends to take a good look at the example of Paul, and remember how many of his servants God has used without taking them from the vocations of secular life. Think of Daniel, the statesman of Babylon; Nehemiah, the courtier of Persia; Barnabas, the consecrated merchant; and Paul, the weaver, who just found a pulpit in their ordinary business life. They all preached the gospel to their fellow men from their own level. It is a blessed advantage to look in the face of the world and say no man has hired me to preach. "These hands have ministered to my necessity." Such a testimony has a dignity and a force that even the world can fully appreciate. There is nothing wrong in receiving a salary in the ministry of the gospel if God has called you to that place. But if God has placed you in a business station, think well before you fly from it to a more conventional ministry, and remember the words of the apostle in another place, "Each one should remain in the situation which he was in when God called him. . . . Brothers, each man, as responsible to God, should remain in the situation God called him to" (1 Corinthians 7:20, 24).

In the midst of the trials, temptations and conflicts of business life you get in touch with men as the professional preacher never can. You understand their needs, and they can feel that you understand them. You can speak with an authority born of experience, and help them heart to heart and hand in hand as mere preaching never could.

The methods of financial support in some lines of Christian work are a great reproach to the cause of Christ. It is always painful to see the Christian worker going around with his hat soliciting help for the Mighty One who owns the cattle upon a thousand hills and says that the silver and gold are His. There are so many ways of doing this and so many temptations to do it, that we cannot be too careful in maintaining our dignity and independence. Often have I been humiliated to see some modest girl obliged to go to coarse and godless men of the world in the business offices of India, and beg for a few coins to help spread the gospel. The coins were often given, but with a leer and a jest which must have gone with a pang to the Master's heart. It is all right for God's people to give to the support of the gospel, but they should do it voluntarily as a debt which no gift ever can repay, and never put the ministry of Christ in the humiliating position of asking for charity.

In these last days when God wants messengers on irregular lines, let us not be surprised if He often takes people just as He finds them, and makes use of the rod of Moses, the ox goad of Shamgar, the needle and thread of Dorcas, and the loom of Paul, as instruments for his boldest and most effective messages to a world that is itself absorbed in business cares and seldom goes off the secular plane to hear the conventional message. Thank God for the laymen of our age whom the Holy Spirit has ordained to a higher ministry than even the touch of human hands could have bestowed.

PRAYER AND POWER

The secret of Paul's power as a Christian worker and minister is found in the closet. He was always praying for his converts and getting them to pray for him. "We always thank God for all of you, mentioning you in our prayers. We continually remember before our God and Father your work produced by faith, your labor prompted by love, and your endurance inspired by hope in our Lord Jesus Christ" (1 Thessalonians 1:2–3). "Night and day we pray most earnestly that we may see you again and supply what is lacking in your faith" (3:10). And so on the other hand he begs them to pray for him, "that the message of the Lord may spread rapidly and be honored, just as it was with you. And pray that we may be delivered from wicked and evil men" (2 Thessalonians 3:1–2).

If we turn to the 18th chapter of Acts we shall see how this prayer was marvelously fulfilled in the deliverance of Paul from the persecutions of the Jews, even after he had been dragged before the judgment seat of Gallio by Sosthenes and the Jewish mob of his persecutors. Gallio dismissed the charge with contempt and drove the accusers from his judgment seat, while the mob, ever ready to turn upon the beaten party, attacks Sosthenes instead of Paul. And to complete the revenge of the apostle we find him writing to these very Corinthians a few years later and including Sosthenes with himself in the dedication of the epistle as "our brother Sosthenes" (1 Corinthians 1:1). That looks as though he were no ordinary brother, but there was a history behind him. What a splendid revenge of love it would be if after his failure and his beating, Paul became his protector and friend, and led him to the Savior that once he opposed, and accepted him as the fellow-worker in the church at Corinth! Surely this would be an answer to the prayers of the Thessalonians worthy of the things God loves to do for those that trust Him. This must ever be the deep secret of spiritual power. Our work must be born in prayer, watered by prayer, guarded and protected by prayer, and the worker himself ever steeped in prayer, and hidden behind the supernatural working of an almighty hand.

THE SPIRIT OF GENTLENESS AND LOVE

The preeminent charm of Paul's ministry, as illustrated in these letters, is the spirit of gentleness and love. "We were gentle among you, like a mother (nurse, KJV) caring for her little children" (1 Thessalonians 2:7). This is not a hired nurse or nanny, but a mother nurse, for the original emphasizes the fact that it is her own children. This is the right sort of nursing, and God forgive the mothers and help the children where they are left exclusively to the care of some hired nurse. These were Paul's own children, and how tenderly he nursed them! Then a little later we have the figure of the father as well as the mother. "You know that we dealt with each of you as a father deals with his own children" (2:11). And yet even more tender was the sacrifice of a love that gave himself to his spiritual children. "We loved you so much that we were delighted to share with you not only the gospel of God but our lives as well, because you had become so dear to us" (2:8). The true worker must give himself to his work and put his life into it if it is to tell.

"How did you succeed in bringing up such a lovely family?" was asked of a mother whose children had become her crown and reward. "I gave myself to them," was her answer. "I shared in all their trouble and their joys, held my leisure at their command, counted no sacrifice too great, and poured out my life for them as well as in them, and I have, indeed, my great reward today." We cannot win souls without love. A harsh theology will not bring them to

Christ. Alfred Tennyson says that he had an old Calvinistic aunt that used to say every time she met him. "Alfred, whenever I see you I am led to think of that verse, 'Depart ye cursed into everlasting fire prepared for the devil and his angels.' " It is a wonder that under such circumstances the poet ever had as much religion and love as he attained. The wise Spurgeon used to say to his students, "Ye are the salt of the earth, and, boys, the sugar, too." It is the sweetness that draws. What a blessed quality a genial, kindly spirit is in Christian work! How often a smile, a playful word, or a grain of love will prevent a painful crisis and heal an incipient strife!

In one of the meetings of a New Jersey Presbytery, at a little village called Cranberry, the brethren were almost coming to the boiling point of some local trouble which they were trying in vain to settle from the opposite sides of the question, when a good brother from Princeton, noted for his blandness as well as his wholesome humor, arose and said, "Mr. Moderator, I propose that we put a little sugar into this Cranberry tart." The effect was electric, and even the good doctors of divinity were unable to get up to the plane of conflict again after their humiliating fall.

But it is especially in the work of soul-winning that love tells. It is said the first incident in the Christian work of the late Mrs. Catherine Booth occurred while she was but a child. A poor fellow was being dragged to prison by two policemen, and the jeering, hooting crowd were following him along the street, while his face was blazing with shame and anger. The little child was deeply touched, and pressing through the crowd to his side she gently put her hand upon his arm and told him that she was going to walk with him as far as they would let her. And so all the way to the jail the little one tramped beside the criminal, cheering him by her loving sympathy and standing by him in his trying hour. Little wonder that in later years she was able to draw the hearts of lost men and women to her with a power that has left its impress on one of the noblest religious movements of the Christian age.

GLIMPSES OF THE GOSPEL PAUL PREACHED

We have some glimpses of the gospel that Paul preached to the Thessalonians, for besides the spirit of the man we must ever emphasize the power of the Word. It is the man of God and the Word of God together that the Holy Spirit uses. Paul's gospel was large and complete. It was a gospel to attract men and save them to the uttermost. He was not a social reformer wasting his strength and time on a thousand little negative efforts to fence men round, but he just trusted to the truth in all its largeness and fullness to lift them to a higher plane and carry them with a controlling impulse.

The difference between man's moral system and God's great salvation is that man is always trying to dig up the rocks and remove the snags from the river, while God is aiming to pour a floodtide into the channel that will lift the little boat above the snags and rocks. They tell of an old weather-beaten pilot who once pulled himself up to the desk of a ship owner in New Orleans and asked for a job to run one of the river steamers up the Mississippi. Of course, the ship owner immediately asked him if he knew the river. He said he did know something about it, but added, "That's not saying that I know much about the snags in the river." "Well," said the owner, "I don't see much sense in my employing you as pilot if you don't understand where the snags are." "Well," said he, with an impressive look, "I reckon I know where the snags ain't, and that's where I expect to do my sailing." The ship owner did not need much shrewdness to see the qualities behind this weather-beaten but keen old man, and he soon closed the contract. Far better to know where the snags ain't than where they are.

God's great salvation is intensely positive. It has one thing for us, and that one thing is all we need to know. For the rest the Holy Spirit will care from day to day. Paul's great gospel gave to his disciples salvation, sanctification, deliverance for the body as well as for the soul and spirit, the blessed hope of the Lord's coming, and the Holy Spirit Himself to lead and teach. God has given us such a gospel. Let it be our joy and pride to give it in all its fullness to a perishing world.

THE SPIRIT OF PAUL'S MINISTRY

Finally the spirit of Paul's ministry was the Holy Spirit. "Because our gospel came to you not simply with words, but also with power, with the Holy Spirit and with deep conviction" (1:5). All personal qualities, all ministerial training, and even the most full and glorious message will fail to reach men's hearts and lives without the direct power of the Holy Spirit. As the Master did not begin His ministry until after the baptism at Jordan, and the disciples also waited for Pentecost, so we must tarry before we go, and learn that it is not our eloquence or unction, but the direct working of a mightier Person through which all fruit must come. It is not only that we are conscious of the power, but if we are truly working in dependence on the Spirit we shall find that He is working along with us in the hearts of the hearers, and witnessing to our message with an authority and power altogether apart from our personal influence or conscious blessing. He will convict the world of sin and righteousness and judgment. This is not our convicting but His. This is a power that we can claim only by faith, and as we believe in Him we will find it coworking with us, and our work will cease to be ours and become His, for as Jesus said, "anyone who has faith in me will do what I have been doing. He will do even greater things than these, because I am going to the Father" (John 14:12).

May God make us such ministers and workers for Christ and our fellow men as God has taught us in the beautiful example which we have gathered from the letters of Paul to the disciples at Thessalonica.

CHAPTER 4

GOD'S BEST

With this in mind, we constantly pray for you, that our God may count you worthy of his calling, and that by his power he may fulfill every good purpose of yours and every act prompted by your faith. (2 Thessalonians 1:11)

There is a good, a better and a best. It is a good thing to be sanctified and consecrated unto the Lord; but there is a best and highest life into which we may enter, even all the good pleasure of His goodness and the highest possibilities of faith and love.

There is such a thing as graduating from college after passing the required subjects and receiving your diploma; but there is also an honor class and a prize awaiting the successful competitors and the students who reach the highest proficiency.

Paul wanted to be the best. "All the runners run," he says, in this great conflict,

> but only one gets the prize. . . . Therefore I do not run like a man running aimlessly; I do not fight like a man beating the air. No, I beat my body and make it my slave so that after I have preached to others, I myself will not be disqualified for the prize. (1 Corinthians 9:24, 26–27)

Paul did not want to be lost or cast away from the presence of God, but rather he wanted "a crown that will last forever" (9:25). In another place he tells us, "Forgetting what is behind and straining toward what is ahead, I press on toward the goal to win the prize for which God has called me heavenward in Christ Jesus" (Philippians 3:13–14). The day came when the prize was won, and he could say, "I have fought the good fight, I have finished the race, I have kept the faith. Now there is in store for me the crown of righteousness" (2 Timothy 4:7–8).

This was the prize to which James and John aspired, and Jesus did not discourage them or tell them that it was unattainable. He told them it was dependent upon their willingness and ability to be baptized with His baptism and to drink of His cup. It was not His to give, except to those for whom it was prepared—the heroes, the conquerors, the highest and the best.

This principle of hope is an element of human nature, and God appeals to it in the promises of His Word and the recompenses of His kingdom. God is not looking for great quantities today, but for high qualities.

THE CLOSING DAYS

We are in the closing days of the New Testament dispensation, and we may expect the same things that marked the last days of the old economy. Then God had to turn from communities to individuals for the accomplishment of His great purposes. The kingdom of Judah failed to fulfill His expectation and stand as His witness against an evil world; and so He had to reject Israel and Judah and let them go into captivity, and even allow His own glorious temple to fall because His people would not be true to Him.

Then He picked out a woman named Esther, and a young man called Daniel, and three Hebrews in Babylon; and through these weak instruments He compelled the proud Babylonians to acknowledge His power and bow to His glory, and He wrought in a single generation more for His great name than all the dynasties of Israel had accomplished in centuries.

So again the day is approaching when even His own Church may fail Him. The pure apostolic church of John and Polycarp became the apostasy of Rome. We need not wonder if the church of the Reformation should have begun already to resemble the picture of Laodicea, rich and wealthy, and saying, "[I] do not need a thing" (Revelation 3:17), and about to be rejected with disgust because of its lukewarmness.

God forbid that we should utter aught against its true spirit, but every earnest and true Christian knows that, at best, we have today a small minority for fidelity to the truth, and no sort of approximation of Christian living up to the standard of His Word and the power of His Spirit. It is the old story of Gideon once more, not only the 30,000 picked out of Israel, but the 300 picked out of the 30,000.

God is looking today for pattern men and women; and when he gets a true sample, it is very easy to reproduce it in a thousand editions and multiply it in other lives without limitation.

All the experiences of life come to us as tests; and as we meet them, our loving Father is watching, with intense and jealous love, to see us overcome; and if we fail, He is deeply disappointed, and our great adversary is filled with joy and triumph. We are a gazing stock continually for angels and principalities, and every step we take is critical and decisive for something in our eternal future.

When Abraham went forth that morning to Mount Moriah, it was an hour of solemn probation; and when he came back, he was one of God's tested men, with the stamp of His eternal approbation. God could say, "I have chosen him, so that he will . . . [do] what is right and just, so that the LORD will bring about for Abraham what he has promised him" (Genesis 18:19).

God is looking for such men today. He is longing to say of us; "I know him. I can depend upon him. I have tried him, and he has not been found wanting."

THE HIGHEST CHRISTIAN LIFE

What is the highest Christian life? What is the life that God is trying to reproduce in the lives of His saints? Is it the repair of wrecked humanity? Is it simply the restoration of Adamic purity? Is it only the bringing back of the human soul to the condition in which it was before the fall? This would be a poor result for such tremendous cost as the death of the Lord Jesus Christ. And what guarantee have we that, if this were accomplished tomorrow, the wreck would not be repeated next day, and the race as lost as ever?

No, God has accomplished something very much higher; nothing less, in fact, than the new creation of a new race, patterned not after the human, but the divine.

> The first man was of the dust of the earth, the second man from heaven. (1 Corinthians 15:47)

> The first man Adam became a living being; the last Adam a life-giving spirit. (15:45)

> As was the earthly man, so are those who are of the earth; and as is the man from heaven, so also are those who are of heaven. And just as we have borne the likeness of the earthly man, so shall we bear the likeness of the man from heaven. (15:48–49)

God is now aiming to reproduce in us the pattern which has already appeared in Jesus Christ, the Son of God. The Christian life is not an imitation of Christ, but a direct new creation in Christ; and the union with Christ is so complete that He imparts His own nature to us, and lives His own life in us. It is not an imitation, but simply an outgrowth of the nature implanted within.

We live Christlike lives because we have the Christ life. God is not satisfied with anything less than perfection. He required that from His Son. He requires it from us. And He does not, in the process of grace, reduce the standard, but He brings us up to it. He counts us righteous in justification, and then He makes us righteous in sanctification, and says of the new creation, "He who does what is right is righteous, just as he is righteous" (1 John 3:7). "Through Christ Jesus the law of the Spirit of life set me free from the law of sin and death" (Romans 8:2), for this very purpose "that the righteous requirements of the law might be fully met in us, who do not live according to the sinful nature but according to the Spirit" (8:4). He requires of us a perfect faith, and He tells us that if we believe and doubt not, we shall have whatsoever we ask. The faintest touch of unbelief will neutralize our trust.

But how shall we have such perfect faith? Is it possible for human nature? No, but it is possible to the divine nature; it is possible to the Christ within us. It is possible for God to give it, and God does give it. But Christ is the Author and Finisher of our faith, and He bids us to have the faith of God; and as we have it through the imparting of the Spirit of Christ, we believe even as He.

We pray in His name and in His very nature, and we "live by the faith of the Son of God, who loved me, and gave himself for me" (Galatians 2:20, KJV). The love that He requires of us is not mere human love, nor even the standard of love required in the Old Testament, but something far higher. The new commandment is "Love one another," not as yourselves, but "as I have loved you" (John 13:34).

How shall such love be made possible? "In this way love is made complete . . . because in this world we are like him" (1 John 4:17). Our love is simply His love wrought in us and imparted to us through His own indwelling Spirit.

There is no place in life to which we ever come that is so delicate, so difficult and so critical, as the place where God requires of us some exercise of love which is contrary to nature, and we find ourselves utterly inadequate to it. When we have to meet an enemy with divine forgiveness and with what seems a perfect adjustment of spirit, not ignoring, perhaps, their gross and inexcusable wrongs, but, at the same time seeing them as He sees them, loving them as He loves them, meeting them without resentment, but with a pure divine benevolence—at such points as these we are thrown upon Christ, and without Him we should sink in despair.

It is here that the life of Christ reveals itself, and the heart is lifted up into a divine sweetness impossible to the natural man, and filled with praise and wonder at the riches of Christ's glorious grace.

This is also the secret of all true service and of all victorious suffering. Someone has expressed it in this striking way: "We can do more than we can." God is constantly calling us to situations where human nature is utterly unequal to the pressure, just that we may show the infinite resources of His grace. Therefore, it is not the patience of the suffering one, but the power of Christ which enables us to bear it, so that we shall be stronger for the very suffering. This was Paul's experience with the thorn in the flesh. The thorn was not removed, but there came to him through it such an influx and afflux of divine strength that he was really better off than if the thorn had not been there; and the spectacle of his victorious spirit brought infinite glory to the name of his divine Lord.

So again our service for Christ is not the best that we can do, for God most frequently uses the weakest instruments, and uses them at their weakest, that the glory may be given to Him, and that it may be manifestly His working and not ours.

How shall we glorify God? By doing something for Him that will make Him our debtor, and show how loving, faithful and capable we are? That would glorify us, not Him. God needs no addition to His happiness from our little store. He is richer by far than we, and all we call our own belongs to Him. The true way to glorify God is for God to show His glory through us, to shine through us as empty vessels reflecting His fullness of grace and power. The sun is glorified when it has a chance to show its light through the crystal window, or reflect it from the spotless mirror or the glassy sea.

There is nothing that glorifies God so much as for a weak and helpless man or woman to be able to triumph, through His strength, in places where the highest human qualities fail us. When carried in divine power, through every form of toil and suffering, a spirit that is naturally weak, irresolute, selfish and sinful, is transformed into sweetness, purity and power, and stands victorious amid circumstances for which its natural qualities must utterly unfit it, a mind not naturally wise or strong, directed by divine wisdom, and carried along the line of a great and mighty plan—this is what glorifies God.

He does not want to see us reflecting our own glory; but, like the heavenly blue and the celestial constellations reflected from the glassy bosom of the lake, He wants to see His own face and His own grace shining through our lives and saying to the world, "I can do everything through him who gives me strength" (Philippians 4:13).

So the highest possibilities of Christian life are put within the reach of the feeblest and the most helpless lives. It is all of God; and if it is all of God, it is possible for the weakest of men. And, therefore, in a sense, it is easier to live a high life than to drag along upon the lower plane.

It is easier to stand on a higher plane than below. It is easier to stand on the mountaintop than to stand with one foot on the heights of grace while with the other we are dragging our life along the lower levels. It is easier for a car to run on a track than off, and it is easier to be always on the track than to be sometimes dragged along the pavement stones.

If we are but willing to trust God utterly, and belong to Him unreservedly, He is waiting for vessels "useful to the Master and prepared to do any good work" (2 Timothy 2:21).

The Potter has the clay before Him for a beautiful vase, to be embellished with every touch of loveliness, to stand in His palace for the highest and holiest use. But, alas, through no fault of the Potter, but because the clay will not suffer His hand to mold it as He would, it is marred in the hands of the potter, and unfit for His highest destination. One little scratch will cause a hopeless blemish. The highest things must be the most unspotted. The more costly the dress, the more it shows the ink spot. The whiter the muslin, the more easily it takes a stain. The more perfect the French glass, the more quickly does it show a flaw. It may be used for some other purpose, but it is unfit for the higher place. It must be set aside, and its highest use be ever unfulfilled.

Oh, how very, very sad the disappointments that heaven will reveal; the might-have-beens that will pass before our vision and then vanish forever away; the crowns we might have worn; the high callings we might have won!

The Potter may take up the clay again and make another vessel. So God takes up our broken lives and does the best He can with them.

May God inspire us to choose His highest choice, and let nothing hinder all the good pleasure of His goodness, or keep us from what the Apostle John has said, "Watch out that you do not lose what you have worked for, but that you may be rewarded fully" (2 John 8).

> Give me, Lord, Thy highest choice;
>   Let others take the rest;
> Their good things have no charm for me
>   For I have got Thy best.

FIRST AND SECOND TIMOTHY

INTRODUCTION

The letters of Paul to Timothy show what a tender bond there was between them, and how solicitous the aged apostle was for his son in the gospel. They warn the young man of many perils to faith and life that lurked in his pathway. They prophesy that "evil men and impostors will go from bad to worse, deceiving and being deceived" (2 Timothy 3:13). They foretell a time when there will be an almost universal departure from the faith, and an outburst of demonism. They call for eternal vigilance and dogged perseverance, and challenge to a calm trust in Him against the day of Christ. They leave no room for overconfidence or carelessness.

The expressions, "sound words," "sound doctrine," and "good doctrine" appear repeatedly in these letters. A casual glance will persuade the thoughtful reader that the apostle has something more in mind than a logical statement of truth or a correct creed. When he would have us know what things are "contrary to the sound doctrine" (1 Timothy 1:10), he mentions such gross sins as lying, stealing, murder, and immorality. He warns the household slave to count his master worthy of honor that the "doctrine be not blasphemed" (6:1, KJV). He emphatically decreed that men might not be appointed to official positions in the Church unless they commended themselves for public ministry by an unimpeachable private life. He begged Timothy to keep close to the Scriptures squaring his life with the Word, so that no sin might have dominion over him. He gave explicit instructions in many practical duties of daily life.

The warnings are enforced by placing before Timothy the example of some who had departed from the faith, a sort of rogues' gallery of traitors to the cause, all of whom were but examples, for in that period of stress many had slipped from their moorings and landed on the rocks of infidelity and impurity.

Backsliding and apostasy are never necessary. The cause lies deep in the human heart that is rooted in the world and minds earthly things. The secret and method of victory is given in the command. "Guard the good deposit that was entrusted to you—guard it with the help of the Holy Spirit who lives in us" (2 Timothy 1:14).

CHAPTER 1

CHRIST IN THE EPISTLES TO TIMOTHY

Let us examine the teachings of the epistles to Timothy respecting the Lord Jesus Christ and the glorious gospel to which the apostle refers so frequently in these letters.

A REVELATION OF GOD

First there is the importance of the gospel as a revelation of God. The apostle announces the great theme of the gospel in the profound passage, "Beyond all question, the mystery of godliness is great: He appeared in a body,/ was vindicated by the Spirit,/ was seen by angels,/ was preached among the nations,/ was believed on in the world,/ was taken up in glory" (1 Timothy 3:16). Like the mysteries of ancient philosophy, the gospel, too, has its profound mysteries. The one here mentioned is "the mystery of godliness." A mystery in the Bible means something unknown until divinely revealed. This mystery the gospel alone could reveal. It is the great mystery of the incarnation. It embraces six statements.

1. Appeared in a Body

God appeared in a body—"was manifest in the flesh" (3:16, KJV). This is the incarnation of the Lord Jesus Christ as the "image of the invisible God" (Colossians 1:15), " 'Immanuel'—which means 'God with us' " (Matthew 1:23). He who lay in Mary's arms and died on Calvary's cross was none other than "the Lord of Glory."

2. Vindicated by the Spirit

He was vindicated by the Spirit—"justified in the Spirit" (1 Timothy 3:16, KJV). This undoubtedly refers to the resurrection of the Lord Jesus Christ as the divine proof of His deity. It is the same thought expressed in Romans 1:4, "who through the Spirit of holiness was declared with power to be the Son of God by his resurrection from the dead." The Holy Spirit justified the claim of Christ's death by this especial proof to which the Lord Jesus Himself appealed before His crucifixion, and which the Holy Spirit through the apostles constantly used after His resurrection as the attestation of His deity.

3. Seen by Angels

He was "seen by angels" (1 Timothy 3:16). This refers to the angelic witnesses of His resurrection. Their presence and their testimony are frequently referred to in the New Testament story of the resurrection.

4. Preached among the Nations

He was "preached among the nations" (3:16). This also is part of the great mystery which the apostle tells the Colossians had been hid for ages and generations (see Colossians 1:26–27), that the Gentiles should be fellow heirs of the gospel and the grace of God (see Ephesians 3:4–6).

5. Believed on in the World

He was "believed on in the world" (1 Timothy 3:16). This, too, is one of the attestations of the Lord Jesus, the testimony of human hearts to His deity. When Thomas beheld Him after His resurrection, he needed no tangible proof that Jesus was his risen Lord, but his own heart bore witness, and he cried in adoration, "My Lord and my God!" (John 20:28). And how many myriads since have borne the witness of their living and dying faith, that Jesus is the Son of God, the Savior of the world, a living, bright reality, and the satisfying portion of the soul that trusts Him.

6. Taken up into Glory

He was "taken up in glory" (1 Timothy 3:16). This is the climax of the mystery, except we add that still greater revelation which will be the seventh and crowning stage of the mystery of godliness, His appearing in glory, and which the apostle in this epistle a little later introduces as the climax of divine revelation. That Jesus Christ has really been received up into glory and is now there at His Father's right hand, is sufficiently evident from the descent of the Holy Spirit and the mighty working of His power on earth since His ascension.

A REVELATION OF JESUS CHRIST

The gospel was a revelation of Jesus Christ as the Mediator and Redeemer. "For there is one God and one mediator between God and men, the man Christ Jesus, who gave himself as a ransom for all men—the testimony given in its proper time" (2:5–6). This is a magnificent declaration of the great theme of the gospel, following in logical order upon the previous declaration of Christ's incarnation. The reason He became incarnate is that, as "the man

Christ Jesus," He might be the "mediator between God and men." Christ's mediatorial work includes His sacrificial death for us upon the cross; therefore, it is added, "[He] gave himself as a ransom for all men—the testimony given in its proper time" (2:6). The word "ransom" suggests the whole plan of redemption, the central idea of which was that He purchased us by His precious blood, and offered His own life as the ransom by which we are set free. Blessed Redeemer and glorious redemption!

> He gave me back my bond,
>   It was a heavy debt.
> And as He did, He smiled and said:
>   "Thou wilt not Me forget."
> He gave me back my bond,
>   The seal was torn away:
> And as again He smiled, He said:
>   "Remember Me alway."

His mediation also includes His intercession for us as our Great High Priest in the presence of the Father, and all the work of grace which He is accomplishing until the whole number of His elect shall have been completed and gathered home.

Let us not forget that there is but one Mediator between God and men. "There is no other name under heaven given to men by which we must be saved" (Acts 4:12). There is no other way than the Living Way. Oh, have we come through Him who "is able to save completely those who come to God through him, because he always lives to intercede for them" (Hebrews 7:25)?

A REVELATION OF THE LOVE AND GRACE OF GOD

The gospel was a revelation of the love and grace of God toward all classes and degrees of sinners. "This is good, and pleases God our Savior, who wants all men to be saved and to come to a knowledge of the truth" (1 Timothy 2:3–4). How wide this mercy is no human tongue can tell, or reason dare to limit. There is no doubt that God's will is that all men should be saved and come to the knowledge of the truth. There is no hindrance in the will or purpose of God to the salvation of the most lost of human souls. Broad and clear let the message stand, God our Savior "wants all men to be saved, and to come to a knowledge of the truth." With such a gospel how dare we hold back the message from one of our ruined race?

But the apostle gives us a still more touching and personal illustration of the grace of the gospel.

The grace of our Lord was poured out on me abundantly, along with the faith and love that are in Christ Jesus.

Here is a trustworthy saying that deserves full acceptance: Christ Jesus came into the world to save sinners—of whom I am the worst. But for that very reason I was shown mercy, so that in me, the worst of sinners, Christ Jesus might display his unlimited patience as an example for those who would believe on him and receive eternal life. (1:14–16)

After Paul, anybody; after the chief of sinners, what sinner need hesitate to come? Oh, the grace that has sought us and brought us to the fold! Sinner, if you are reading these lines, is not that grace large enough and free enough for you? Christian, with such a gospel, how can you lose a single opportunity to say to sinful men, "Here is a trustworthy saying," a true saying, "that deserves full acceptance"; that is, worthy that all should accept it. "Christ Jesus came into the world," for no other cause than for this: "to save sinners," even "the worst of sinners."

A REVELATION OF GOD'S GOODNESS

The gospel is a revelation of God's goodness even to unsaved men. For He is "the Savior of all men, and especially of those who believe" (4:10). In what sense is God the Savior of all men in distinction from them that believe? Surely this refers to the secondary results that come from Christ's redemption and have covered the world with blessings for the present life, even where they have not reached the higher plane of salvation. How Christ has elevated human society! How Christianity has transformed almost all earthly conditions! How much womanhood, childhood, misfortune and suffering owe to the beneficent influence of the gospel! It has given freedom to the slave. It has given liberty to the oppressed. It has quickened the human mind, stimulated all the forces of modern civilization and brought a thousand blessings to the men and women who never mention the Savior's name except in blasphemy.

Like the glorious sun, the gospel pours its radiance wherever there is an open window to let in the light or a dark cavern to be illuminated by its beams. God is love, and He loves every human being as much as men will let Him.

THE FRUITS OF THE GOSPEL

Next we look at the fruits of the gospel in the practical life of its followers.

"These are the things you are to teach and urge on them. If anyone teaches false doctrines and does not agree to the sound instruction of our Lord Jesus Christ and to godly teaching" (6:2–3), "from such withdraw thyself" (6:5, KJV). Thus the apostle describes the practical results of the

principles of the gospel. It is a doctrine "according to godliness" (6:3, KJV).
A little later he adds, referring to the spirit of worldliness and selfishness,
"But you, man of God, flee from all this, and pursue righteousness, godliness, faith, love, endurance and gentleness" (6:11). Here we have a splendid
group of Christian graces which represent the true results of faith in the
Lord Jesus Christ and obedience to the gospel of His grace.

In the opening of the first epistle Paul is careful to point out that the law
was not made for a righteous man,

> We also know that law is made not for the righteous but for
> lawbreakers and rebels, the ungodly and sinful, the unholy and
> irreligious; for those who kill their fathers or mothers, for murderers, for adulterers and perverts, for slave traders and liars and
> perjurers—and for whatever else is contrary to the sound
> doctrine that conforms to the glorious gospel of the blessed God,
> which he entrusted to me. (1:9–11)

The gospel assumes that men will avoid these things, not because they are
afraid of the law, but because they are animated with a higher spirit of love
and grace. I am not kept from murder by the fear of the electric chair, but by
something in me that lifts me above the desire to take another's life. And so
the gospel of Jesus Christ inspires men with motives and principles which
lead them to fulfill the righteousness of the law, not because of the fear of
the law, but because of the law of love.

A REVELATION OF THE FUTURE LIFE

The gospel is a glorious revelation of the future life.

> I charge you to keep this command without spot or blame until
> the appearing of our Lord Jesus Christ, which God will bring
> about in his own time—God, the blessed and only Ruler, the
> King of kings and Lord of lords, who alone is immortal and who
> lives in unapproachable light, whom no one has seen or can see.
> To him be honor and might forever. Amen. (6:13–16)

> . . . who has saved us and called us to a holy life—not because of
> anything we have done but because of his own purpose and
> grace. This grace was given us in Christ Jesus before the beginning of time, but it has now been revealed through the appearing
> of our Savior, Christ Jesus, who has destroyed death and has
> brought life and immortality to light through the gospel. (2
> Timothy 1:9–10)

These passages unfold the blessed hope of His appearing, and the life and immortality which Christ has brought in through the gospel. How dark the future would have been but for this light! How little men could know from human reasoning about the immortality of the soul and the certainty of the future life at all. How glorious the revelation Christ has given to us, not only of life after death, but of the resurrection of the body, the reunion of parted friends in glory and the inheritance of the saints in light!

How much more is to be brought to us at "the appearing of our Lord Jesus Christ, . . . the blessed and only Ruler, the King of kings and Lord of lords" (1 Timothy 6:14–15). He who was God manifest in the flesh is yet to be manifest in His glory as King of kings and Lord of lords. The prospect of this glorious day was the inspiration of Paul's own faith and hope in the midst of all his trials and discouragements, and in view of it he could utter that magnificent boast, "I know whom I have believed, and am convinced that he is able to guard what I have entrusted to him for that day" (2 Timothy 1:12). "That day" was to him the day of days, the day on which all accounts should be balanced, all losses regained, all wrongs righted, all sacrifices repaid, and all tears forever wiped away.

Such is the gospel which Paul and Timothy preached and loved. Such is the glorious message which has brought us life and hope, and the only gospel that can save and cheer lost and dying men. A minister, who was practically Unitarian in his belief and preaching, was called in to see a poor sinful woman who was dying. He told her of the beautiful life, the loving ministries and the noble example of Jesus. He urged her to follow Him, but she shook her head hopelessly, saying: "That is not for the like o' me; I'm a sinful woman, and I'm dying." "It flashed upon me," said the preacher, "that I had a message of help and hope for that dying woman, and like lightning I leaped in mind to the gospel my mother taught me. I told her of Jesus Christ, the Son of God, dying on the cross that such as she might be saved, of His blood poured out for the remission of sins, and all the blessed truths of the old, old story, and she professed saving faith in the Lamb of God that taketh away the sin of the world."

Such is the glorious trust which God has given to us for all our race. God help us to receive it in all its fullness, and then give it in all its blessed power to that great constituency of which this epistle has said that God "wants all men to be saved and to come to a knowledge of the truth" (1 Timothy 2:4). "Who gave himself as a ransom for all men—the testimony given in its proper time" (2:6). Oh, is it not the proper time that that testimony should be given to all? God forgive us that we have so shamefully failed! God help us to tell it to all our race!

CHAPTER 2

THE GOSPEL IN THE EPISTLES TO TIMOTHY

(The Church)

The first thing which the apostle teaches us about the Church in these pastoral epistles is its calling and purpose.

CALLING AND PURPOSE

These are expressed in the 15th verse of the third chapter of the first epistle and have a threefold meaning.

1. The House of God

It is the house of God. The first time we meet with this expression in the Bible is at Bethel, where Jacob had just met with God and declares, "This is none other than the house of God; this is the gate of heaven" (Genesis 28:17). It does not refer to a building, for there was no building at Bethel, and there were no church buildings in the early centuries other than upper rooms and private homes which sheltered "the church that meets at their house" (Romans 16:5). It does not so much mean a place as a fellowship of people in whom God has His habitation. The house of God today is a living temple of human hearts where God Himself is already residing. "And in him you too are being built together to become a dwelling in which God lives by his Spirit" (Ephesians 2:22).

The Church, therefore, consists of those who have been already baptized by one Spirit into one body, and in which the Lord is dwelling. It is of this company that the Lord Jesus has said, "For where two or three come together in my name, [or as it is translated, 'into my name'] there am I with them" (Matthew 18:20). "The Most High does not live in houses made by men" (Acts 7:48), but wherever purified and consecrated human souls worship God, there He is present just as really as in the highest heaven.

41

2. The Church of the Living God

It is called "the church of the living God" (1 Timothy 3:15). The word "church" means "called out" and denotes the company of believers who have been separated from the world to be His peculiar people. Here again it is not a church building that is referred to, but a body of holy people. The Church had its best days when it had no churches to meet in. Its piles of splendid architecture, its gilded crosses and its spires that seem to point to heaven, have often been but the ministers of idolatry and the shrines of worldliness, pride and sin. By the Church of the living God, Paul emphasizes the contrast between the dead idols of paganism and the one true God revealed in the Lord Jesus Christ and dwelling in the hearts of Christians.

3. The Pillar and Foundation of the Truth

It is described as "the pillar and foundation of the truth" (3:15). This evidently means the pillar which supports the truth, even as the foundation and the pillar support the arch of the building. It is as though the truth were inscribed upon the front of the arch, and the Church holds up the message and exhibits it to the world. The business of the Church, therefore, as here expressed, is to be a witness to the world of God's truth, a revealer of His will, a light to those that sit in darkness, and a message from heaven to the children of men. We have already seen what the message of heaven is. The very next verse expresses it. "He appeared in a body,/ was vindicated by the Spirit,/ was seen by angels,/ was preached among the nations,/ was believed on in the world,/ was taken up in glory" (3:16). If the Church fails to be true to her testimony, she is the pillar and foundation, not of the truth, but of error. Therefore, it is most important that she should maintain true doctrine as well as life, and be a faithful witness to Jesus Christ in His divine glory and His death and resurrection. Not only is the Church to witness to it by her testimony, but she is to manifest it in her life and to be a living object lesson to the world around her of the life and grace of the Lord Jesus Christ.

THE GOVERNMENT OF THE CHURCH

The apostle gives us in these pastoral epistles a good many glimpses of church government in the early Church. It is evident that the principal official ministers in the church of Ephesus were elders and deacons. It is also evident that the words "elder" and "bishop" were used interchangeably and that they both denote an office of spiritual oversight. A little later there is a distinction in First Timothy 5:17 between two classes of elders, the one that seems only to have exercised authority and rule, the other class whose "work is preaching and teaching." In other words, the one was a ruling elder, the other a teaching elder. There appears to have been no extremely rigid rule in the New Testament about church government further than that a certain body of spiritual overseers were appointed out of every church, and they were called elders or bishops. Some of them, who had the requisite qualifications, exercised the ministry of teaching, while others simply took pastoral oversight over the flock. Out of these general conditions gradually arose Presbyterianism on one hand, and Episcopacy on the other, but neither has exclusive warrant of sufficient strength to justify bigotry or controversy. It is a safe rule to recognize all these various forms of church government as sufficiently scriptural to furnish a frame for the gospel and the Church of God, which is the really essential thing.

There was a second class of officers, called deacons. The word denotes a minister; that is, one who ministers—a servant to the Church. This sufficiently covers the office of deacon as it is usually exercised today in Christian churches, the ministry of hospitality and welcome, fellowship, sympathy, kindness to the sick, the stranger and the sufferer, and relief to the poor and needy. These ministries are so important that the office of deacon was the first to be filled in the Apostolic Church. The apostle puts great emphasis upon this part of the ministry and evidently regards it as a steppingstone to a higher service in the Church, for he adds: "They must keep hold of the deep truths of the faith with a clear conscience. They must first be tested; and then if there is nothing against them, let them serve as deacons" (3:9–10).

The epistles to Timothy recognize the ministry of women, but with very great restrictions. The woman is not allowed to teach or usurp authority over the man, but to maintain her place of subjection. But there was evidently some sisterhood described as widows indeed, into whose number worthy widows were to be taken and cared for by the Church, and who were to devote their lives to ministries to their brethren and the Church of God (1 Timothy 5:5). It would seem that the form of government in the early Church gradually developed and adjusted itself to conditions, and there would seem to be, as far as church government is concerned, no great principle at stake which need hinder the organic union of almost all evangelical denominations of Christians on some simple basis of compromise and concession with each other.

THE SUPPORT OF THE MINISTRY

The passage already quoted in First Timothy 5:17, "the elders who direct the affairs of the church well are worthy of double honor, especially those whose work is preaching and teaching," evidently refers to the support of a certain part of the eldership; namely, those who labor in the Word and doctrine. This is the "double honor" meant by the text. Our honorarium, which means the payment of a complimentary fee for literary or special service, conveys the same idea. While Paul himself claimed freedom to preach the gospel without charge, he nowhere imposed this on his brethren as a law, but defended their right to receive adequate support from the churches to which they ministered. This is the law of giving and receiving which the Lord everywhere enjoins, that they who minister to their spiritual needs should receive from those to whom they minister, of their material things. And any Christian who is content to receive the privileges of the gospel without liberal and loving recompense to those who minister to him or her, is spiritually dishonest and will surely lose some blessing for his unfaithfulness.

THE CARE OF THE NEEDY

There was evidently special care exercised in looking after the poor, the widowed and the needy. "The poor you will always have with you" (Matthew 26:11) was the Lord's own intimation of the sacred and representative character which this class always was to have in the Church of Christ. As we minister to them, we minister to God; and as we neglect and forget them, we let our Master suffer in their person, and someday we will hear Him say, "I was in need and you ministered not unto Me." Let us not think it a small service to be permitted to care for God's poor, and let us not complacently enjoy our temporal blessings if we have not distributed to the necessities of saints, and shared our abundance with God's poor.

DISCIPLINE

We find the apostle giving several directions about guarding the Church from false teachers and unfaithful brethren. Of the former, he says, "have nothing to do with them" (2 Timothy 3:5), and concerning the latter, he gives several directions: "Those who sin are to be rebuked publicly, so that the others may take warning" (1 Timothy 5:20). This was to be in extreme cases, undoubtedly of open and flagrant and probably unrepented sin. In another place he says,

> And the Lord's servant must not quarrel; instead, he must be kind to everyone, able to teach, not resentful. Those who oppose him he must gently instruct, in the hope that God will grant them repentance leading them to a knowledge of the truth, and that they will come to their senses and escape from the trap of the devil, who has taken them captive to do his will. (2 Timothy 2:24–26)

We are to be tender and gentle to the erring, if haply we may win them back; and where this is impossible, we must be stern and faithful for the sake of the truth and honor of the Lord, testifying against bold and impenitent sin in the Church of God. "Do not be hasty in the laying on of hands, and do not share in the sins of others" (1 Timothy 5:22), may have reference to the hasty calling of men into sacred offices before they have been fully proved, or it may have reference to hastily taking up evil reports against people and laying our hands upon them in judgment. The wise servant of Christ will avoid both extremes.

THE PERILS OF THE CHURCH IN THE LAST DAYS

The apostle gives a very solemn picture in both epistles of the teachers that are to develop in the Church of Christ before the end. The first passage is First Timothy 4:1–3.

> The Spirit clearly says that in later times some will abandon the faith and follow deceiving spirits and things taught by demons. Such teachings come through hypocritical liars, whose consciences have been seared as with a hot iron. They forbid people to marry and order them to abstain from certain foods, which God created to be received with thanksgiving by those who believe and who know the truth.

These errors arise from seducing spirits and doctrines of demons. It was clearly intimated by the Lord that the enemy would sow tares among the wheat, and these are some of the tares. They were to look very much like wheat; indeed, the error was in the guise of truth and an overstraining of the good, until it became all bad. The spirit of asceticism which afterwards developed in the Roman Catholic Church, with all its attendant errors and crimes, is clearly hinted at in the words, "they forbid people to marry and order them to abstain from certain foods" (4:3)—an unnatural and strained severity and self-denial, posing as a higher kind of holiness, and leading to the depths of sin. Christianity is natural and normal and simple.

In Second Timothy 3, Paul gives another picture of these latter-day apostates. These two pictures have reference to the days in which we are living, and give a very solemn view of the perils that are sweeping around the Church of Christ like a flood.

They are of Satanic origin. The apostle distinctly refers to seductive spirits and doctrines of demons. Again he refers to Jannes and Jambres, who withstood Moses, as types of these latter-day false prophets. In the book of Revelation John tells us of a flood of demons, "evil spirits that looked like frogs" which are "spirits of demons performing miraculous signs" (Revelation 16:13, 14), which are to break loose in the last days and lead their victims on to the battle of Armageddon. We may, therefore, look for supernatural manifestations in our time of the most seductive and misleading character which are not of God, but from the wicked one. There is a true and holy supernaturalism which will always be recognized by its humility, self-control, holiness, love and good fruits. But there is a loud, arrogant, presumptuous and disorderly fanaticism, which scoffs at all restraints and scatters its anathemas against all that oppose it and, if possible, would "deceive even the elect" (Matthew 24:24).

The special apostasy to which Paul refers in Timothy is marked by a flood of human wickedness as well as devilish delusion. Its first feature is selfishness, leading to covetousness, the love of pleasure, pride and arrogance, licentiousness, neglect of home, loss of natural affection, evil speaking, and hardness and cruelty towards others. One of its special features is the multitudes of weak women who are carried away by it. Its leaders "worm their way into homes and gain control over weak-willed women, who are loaded down with sins and are swayed by all kinds of evil desires, always learning but never able to acknowledge the truth" (2 Timothy 3:6–7). These persons are troubled about their sins and burdened with an evil conscience, and they are ready to turn to any teacher who will give them rest. And yet they never find rest and never get anywhere. These are in every age at once dupes and the deceivers of others.

Again it will be noticed that this apostasy is "having a form of godliness but denying its power" (3:5). It claims superior sanctity and is characterized by the strain that marks almost all false teaching. "They forbid people to marry and order them to abstain from certain foods" (1 Timothy 4:3), and as someone has said, standing so straight that it really falls over backwards. We are in the beginnings of these things. Let us watch and pray, and keep very humble, very simple, very practical and very near to the Master's feet.

THE SECURITY OF THE CHURCH

"Nevertheless," Paul assures us, "God's solid foundation stands firm" (2 Timothy 2:19). The foundation means that which God has founded, the Church which He has already spoken of as the house of God. He then proceeds to give several reasons for its security.

The first is God's foreknowledge and infinite wisdom. "Sealed with this inscription: 'The Lord knows those who are his' " (2:19). God will keep His own and they shall never perish, and "no one can snatch them out of [his] hand" (John 10:28).

The next reason for the Church's security is "Everyone who confesses the name of the Lord must turn away from wickedness" (2:19). Our personal holiness is the best proof we are His, and against the breastplate of righteousness the assaults of hell can never prevail. The third condition of the Church's security is given in the fine passage, Second Timothy 2:20–22.

In a large house there are articles not only of gold and silver, but also of wood and clay; some are for noble purposes and some for ignoble. If a man cleanses himself from the latter, he will be an instrument for noble purposes, made holy, useful to the Master and prepared to do any good work.

Flee the evil desires of youth, and pursue righteousness, faith, love and peace, along with those who call on the Lord out of a pure heart.

1. The Church of Christ

The great house here referred to is the Church of Christ, which we have already seen is the house of God, here compared to some courtly mansion with a great variety of servants, vessels and ministries.

2. Its Various Vessels [KJV]

We have its various vessels. There are vessels of gold and silver; there are also vessels of wood and earth; there are vessels unto honor, and there are vessels unto dishonor. The idea is not that some are good, but some are of higher rank than others. There are lower and higher ministries in the Church of God. There are ordinary Christians and there are choice ones. Some Christians spend all their lives in the scullery and the cellar. They are not gold and silver vases in the chambers of the king to hold rich perfume, but slop-pails to empty out the refuse in the waste pipes. There are some lips that would not condescend to gossip and frivolity. There are others from whom it pours like an eave-trough or a waterspout on a wet day. The Lord cannot use such people much in His higher service, or to bear His holy messages. You would not want to drink out of a slop-pail, and the Lord does not greatly enjoy the worship of those who allow themselves to be defiled by all the flotsam of life's murky stream. Paul says that we should purge ourselves from these. He does not mean purge ourselves from the sinful sins of the world outside, but from the common things that may be loved in a way, but are not the highest things. Be not content to be always in the kitchen, but let the Lord make you a vessel of gold to be used at the altar of incense and as a minister to feed His people at the table of His grace.

CHAPTER 3

PAUL, TIMOTHY AND THEIR FELLOW WORKERS

The epistles to Timothy contain many sidelights upon the personal character of Timothy himself and his fellow-workers, and especially of Paul the great apostle.

TIMOTHY

We have in these epistles:

1. A Reference to His Family

"I have been reminded of your sincere faith, which first lived in your grandmother Lois and in your mother Eunice and, I am persuaded, now lives in you also" (2 Timothy 1:5). He was happy in being born of a godly mother and a pious ancestry. His mother Eunice and his grandmother Lois are described as women of unfeigned faith. The reference is probably to their life before their conversion; even as Jewish believers they had genuine faith in God and were His true people, and their little son Timothy was brought up to fear and trust their God. Let us thank God if we have the same great privilege, and let us be careful to transmit to our children the same benediction.

2. A Reference to His Call

Paul next refers to Timothy's call to the ministry and his enduement with the Holy Spirit for His sacred work. "For this reason I remind you to fan into flame the gift of God, which is in you through the laying on of my hands. For God did not give us a spirit of timidity, but a spirit of power, of love and of self-discipline" (1:6–7). He had been set apart by the apostle himself, and had received in connection with his ordination the special gift of the Holy Spirit as the "Spirit of power, of love and of self-discipline [a sound mind, KJV]." This enduement is indispensable to true and effectual ministry in every age, and the blended gifts of wisdom, love and power in Timothy's experience are well worthy of our emulation and ambition. But we see that even this precious gift had been in some measure neglected, and the apostle calls upon his son in the faith to rekindle the fire that was burning low. Let not the message be lost upon any of us, but let us stir up the gift of God that is in us. We have the Holy Spirit, but we may not have the fullness of His gifts and energies, and He is waiting to respond to our faith, our prayer and our earnest waiting upon Him for a great revival in our own hearts.

3. His Relation to Paul

Paul describes Timothy as his own son. "Timothy, my dear son" (1:2) and again "Timothy my true son in the faith" (1 Timothy 1:2). He had been converted during Paul's first missionary journey in Asia Minor, and the apostle had adopted him as a spiritual son, and felt toward him an affection and confidence which no other shared. "I have no one else like him," he writes to the Philippians,

> who takes a genuine interest in your welfare. For everyone looks out for his own interests, not those of Jesus Christ. But you know that Timothy has proved himself, because as a son with his father he has served with me in the work of the gospel. (Philippians 2:20–22)

4. His Special Ministry at Ephesus

Paul had left Timothy at Ephesus in charge of the great work which for three years he had carried on in that important city, the metropolis of the East. There were dangerous errors creeping up in the young church, and the apostle says: "As I urged you when I went into Macedonia, stay there in Ephesus so that you may command certain men not to teach false doctrines" (1 Timothy 1:3). Already some of the leading disciples had turned away, even from Paul, and still later John writes that the church at Ephesus had refused to receive him because of the jealousy of a leader who was more concerned for his own interest than for the cause of Christ (see 3 John 9–11).

5. His Personal Characteristics

The picture which stands out from Paul's letters to his son is not altogether free from blemishes. The Holy Scriptures do not flatter in their photographs of men and women. There is no form of literature that more impartially reveals both the strength and weakness of a man than his correspondence. We can read between the lines in Paul's letters to Timothy a good many things which show he was indeed human. In the first place he was in feeble health and appears to have been a dyspeptic. Note the direction of Paul: "Stop drinking only water, and use a little wine because of your stomach and your frequent illnesses" (1 Timothy 5:23). Evidently Timothy was in that unhappy class whose physical condition colors with a somber hue almost everything in their character and life. Perhaps you say he should not have continued to be an invalid, but should have taken the Lord for healing. But it is very doubtful whether Timothy's spiritual character had yet reached that maturity which brings the faith of perfect healing, for the apostle had to admonish him about a number of things in terms which would scarcely seem necessary if he were living a wholly victorious life. "Don't let anyone look down on you because you are young" (4:12), he says in one place. Then he adds, "Flee the evil desires of youth, and pursue righteousness, faith, love and peace, along with those who call on the Lord out of a pure heart" (2 Timothy 2:22).

Again he warns him against haste in dealing with people, and partiality in relation to his flock. There appears to have been strains of softness and self-indulgence in the young minister, and Paul calls upon him to "endure hardship . . . like a good soldier of Christ Jesus" (2:3), to avoid entanglements with the world, to flee the love of money, and not to be "ashamed to testify about our Lord, or ashamed of me his prisoner. But join with me in suffering for the gospel, by the power of God" (1:8).

THE COMPANIONS OF PAUL

1. Luke

We have a number of touching and graphic allusions to the men and women who stood nearest to the great apostle. One of these is Luke, who was with him at Rome in his imprisonment and loneliness. Luke was his constant companion in all his ministry among the Gentiles, and the historian of his missionary work. It was not given to him to be an apostle, or perhaps a great preacher, but to use a consecrated pen, and to be a true and helpful friend. How much we owe to the Gospel of Luke, the Acts of the Apostles, and the ministry of this modest writer, who has forever set the seal of God's mighty blessing upon every consecrated pen.

2. Mark

Mark is the next in the group. And a touching force is added to Paul's appeal to bring Mark with him "because he is helpful to me in my ministry" (4:11), when we remember that Paul himself had turned Mark down in the beginning of his career because he had deserted them in the hour of danger. Barnabas stood by Mark at that time and led him back to the path of faithfulness; and Paul, now, by a beautiful play upon his name which means *profitable*, intimates that the erring one has been forgiven, and that his fellowship in the Lord's work will once more be welcomed and appreciated.

3. Priscilla

The next name that shines out in this list is Priscilla (2 Timothy 4:19), the wife of Aquila. No comment is needed upon the new order of the names of these two faithful friends of the apostle of the Lord. It used to be Aquila and Priscilla, but now it is Priscilla and Aquila; and as she usually does, she has gone far ahead of her husband and fellow-worker.

4. Onesiphorus

"The household of Onesiphorus" (4:19) is deemed worthy of special mention and loving commendation in contrast with the others who have turned away from the old apostle.

> May the Lord show mercy to the household of Onesiphorus, because he often refreshed me and was not ashamed of my chains. On the contrary, when he was in Rome, he searched hard for me until he found me. May the Lord grant that he will find mercy from the Lord on that day! You know very well in how many ways he helped me in Ephesus. (1:16–18)

Here is the picture of a Christian friend whose ministry was that of comfort, love and charity to a suffering servant of the Lord, both at Ephesus and at Rome. The labor of love is to meet some great reward "on that day."

5. Trophimus

We have met with Trophimus before as one of Paul's faithful friends in the hour of his peril in Jerusalem. He is not with the apostle now, for he says, "I left Trophimus sick in Miletus" (4:20). What a blending of light and shade we have in this holy volume! Here is no rose-colored teaching even of divine healing as an immediate and unfailing remedy for all diseases. Even Paul was not authorized to heal everybody, and there may have been something in Trophimus himself which delayed his immediate restoration and made it necessary that God should lay him upon his back and deal with him for a little season. This is no argument against the promises of God and the faith that claims healing, but a wise balancing of truth which always has reference to our spiritual condition quite as much as to our physical needs.

6. Demas

The next picture is a sad one. "Demas, because he loved this world, has deserted me" (4:10). Alas, for all the Demases that have since followed in his wandering footsteps, let us hope that even Demas at last saw his error and came back before it was too late.

7. The False Teachers

Finally we have a group of false teachers and enemies of the truth as typical of the future history of the Church as these brighter examples of fidelity that have just been named. There are Alexander, Hymenaeus, Philetus, Hermogenes, Phygellus, whose heresies and oppositions were but typical of the story of the Church to the end. The apostle looks upon them with sorrow, not with vindictiveness. Second Timothy 4:14 should be translated, "The Lord will reward him according to his works." It is not a prayer for the punishment of this man, but a prophecy. The true spirit of Paul toward his enemies comes out in the 16th verse, "May it not be held against them."

THE PICTURE OF PAUL

This stands out bright and clear above all the other personalities of the letter.

1. His Commission

We have a reference to his own commission and high calling. He is an apostle "by the command of God our Savior and of Christ Jesus our hope" (1 Timothy 1:1), "by the will of God, according to the promise of life that is in Christ Jesus" (2 Timothy 1:1) and also a "teacher of the Gentiles" (1:11, KJV).

2. His Conversion and Testimony

Next we have a reference to Paul's conversion and his testimony to the grace of the Lord Jesus Christ. He does not forget the pit from whence he was dug and the rock from whence he was hewn. Rather, he bears testimony to his own unworthiness and the great mercy of God in saving and using him.

> Even though I was once a blasphemer and a persecutor and a violent man, I was shown mercy because I acted in ignorance and unbelief. The grace of our Lord was poured out on me abundantly, along with the faith and love that are in Christ Jesus.
> Here is a trustworthy saying that deserves full acceptance: Christ Jesus came into the world to save sinners—of whom I am the worst. But for that very reason I was shown mercy so that in me, the worst of sinners, Christ Jesus might display his unlimited patience as an example for those who would believe on him and receive eternal life. (1 Timothy 1:13–16)

How he loved to lie low at the foot of the cross, and glory in the grace of his Redeemer, using even his own shame for the encouragement of other poor sinners.

3. His Sufferings

Next we get a glimpse of Paul's afflictions, persecutions and sacrifices that he suffered for Christ's sake. He calls himself the prisoner of the Lord (2 Timothy 1:8). He speaks of his chains (1:16). He tells us that all who are from Asia have deserted him (1:15). He complains that at his first defense no one stood by him, but all deserted him, and yet he prays that it would not be held against them (4:16). We hear him saying, "This is why I am suffering as I am" (1:12). And again, we find him a prisoner at Rome, begging Timothy to bring the cloak and scrolls that he left at Troas, and to be sure to come to him before winter (4:13, 21). And finally we catch a glimpse of him facing bloody Nero himself and barely escaping the cruel lions of the Colosseum (4:17).

4. His Personal Characteristics

We have also a glimpse of his patient, faithful, and holy life. "You, however, know all about my teaching, my way of life, my purpose, faith, patience, love, endurance" (3:10). He could appeal to his most intimate friends as witnesses of his conversation and conduct among men, as well as his ministry for God.

5. His Triumphant Faith and Hope

Above all, we see his triumphant faith and hope in the Lord Jesus, his heavenly Master, and the certainty of his final triumph and glorious reward. Where shall we find anything finer than the noble confession: "That is why I am suffering as I am. Yet I am not ashamed, because I know whom I have believed, and am convinced that he is able to guard what I have entrusted to him for that day" (1:12). Glorious watchword for every servant of Jesus Christ and every sufferer for the Lord

And where in all literature is there a more magnificent climax to any career than the triumphant shout with which he approaches the hour of martyrdom and cries,

> For I am already being poured out like a drink offering, and the time has come for my departure. I have fought the good fight, I have finished the race, I have kept the faith. Now there is in store for me the crown of righteousness, which the Lord, the righteous Judge, will award to me on that day—and not only to me, but also to all who have longed for his appearing. (4:6–8)

At length his course is finished, his fight is well fought, his trust fulfilled; and he is ready to lie down as a bleeding sacrifice on the altar where he has already sacrificed his glorious life. The future has no clouds for him, the martyr's fate no terror; his crown is already won, and even in the hour of its realization, his great loving heart goes out in the longing to share it with his brethren as he tells them it is not for him only, but for all who love the Lord's appearing.

Perhaps the very finest touch in all the epistle is the picture of his standing solitary and forsaken before the tribunal of Nero while he could hear the growling of the lions that had been prepared for his martyrdom. But thinking nothing of his own fate, his sole concern was to preach the gospel to the wicked men before him, and all that vile court. His one thought was that, "the message might be fully proclaimed" (4:17), and he adds as a casual and less important matter, "I was delivered from the lion's mouth" (4:17). He was not thinking of his deliverance, but of his message, and the Lord took care of him until his work was done, so that he closes his message with this triumphant assurance: "The Lord will rescue me from every evil attack and will bring me safely to his heavenly kingdom. To him be glory for ever and ever. Amen" (4:18).

This was his last public message, his parting word to the Church of God. Surely his great ambition was fulfilled which he expressed many years before in his charge to the elders of the church at Ephesus, "However, I consider my life worth nothing to me, if only I may finish the race [the course with joy, KJV] and complete the task the Lord Jesus has given me—the task of testifying to the gospel of God's grace" (Acts 20:24). God help us to be as true to our trust, and to finish our course with joy.

CHAPTER 4

THE TRUE MINISTER OF JESUS CHRIST

A good minister of Christ Jesus. (1 Timothy 4:6)

T he epistles to Timothy give us the divine ideal of the "good minister of Christ Jesus."

THE FOUNDATION

1. The foundation of the minister is the Word of God. We read,

> From infancy you have known the holy Scriptures, which are able to make you wise for salvation through faith in Christ Jesus. All Scripture is God-breathed and is useful for teaching, rebuking, correcting and training in righteousness, so that the man of God may be [perfect, KJV] thoroughly equipped for every good work. (2 Timothy 3:15–17)

The Bible which Timothy possessed was a much smaller one than ours, but nonetheless it was essential that he should thoroughly know it, faithfully preach it and wisely practice it in all his work. Only through the Scriptures can the man of God be perfect, thoroughly equipped for all good works. Other learning is valuable in so far as it trains the mind better to understand and rightly divide the Word of truth. To the apostle's conception, these Scriptures were "given by inspiration of God" (KJV); literally, "God-breathed," and they had an authority and value which put them in an absolutely distinctive class from all human literature. We are living in an age when as never before it needs to be emphasized that the one business of the Christian ministry is to know, to believe, to preach, to teach and to live the Word of the living God.

THE POWER

2. The power of the ministry is the Holy Spirit. Therefore, we find the apostle exhorting the young minister at Ephesus, "Fan into flame the gift of God, which is in you through the laying on of my hands. For God did not give us a spirit of timidity, but a spirit of power, of love and of self-discipline" (2:6–7). Timothy has received the Holy Spirit, but the fire is burning low and needs to be rekindled. And the rekindling is to be along distinctive and definite lines; not a one-sided emotional excitement, but a happy blending of love and power and practical wisdom, constituting a well-poised and sober mind, a sanctified judgment, supernatural wisdom, and yet a divine enthusiasm and the mighty and effectual power of the Holy Spirit.

There is no hint given here, notwithstanding Timothy's deficiency and possible declension, that he should seek a new baptism of the Holy Spirit; but that he should stir up the Spirit that was already within him, and by heart-searching, earnest prayer, and living faith, should open all his being to be filled and fired with the mighty power of God. There is such a thing as receiving the Holy Spirit at a definite moment, and there is such a thing as being filled in the present tense by a continuous experience in which we are to be workers together with God, and thus increase the one pound which the Master gives to all His servants until it is five pounds. Surely, as never before in these days of perplexity and strain, we may well go back to the wholesome, practical ideals of the great apostle for every true minister and servant of Jesus Christ.

THE CULTURE

3. The culture of a true minister is not forgotten. In First Timothy 4:13–16 we have this suggestive exhortation:

> Until I come, devote yourself to the public reading of Scripture, to preaching and to teaching. Do not neglect your gift, which was given you through a prophetic message when the body of elders laid their hands on you.
>
> Be diligent in these matters; give yourself wholly to them, so that everyone may see your progress. Watch your life and doctrine closely. Persevere in them, because if you do, you will save both yourself and your hearers.

Here we find the true minister a diligent student, giving attention to reading, meditating upon these things, and giving himself wholly to them that his progress may be apparent to all. God does not place indolence in any department of life. The gifts of the Spirit do not depreciate our diligence in making the most of the natural talents that God has bestowed upon us. The fact that God may in His sovereign pleasure bestow by a miracle some foreign language upon some of His servants, does not excuse the ordinary missionary from the diligent study of the language in which he is to minister the gospel to the heathen. The fact that the Holy Spirit has promised to give us utterance in preaching the Word does not in the least degree preclude the same Holy Spirit giving us light and quickening while we are quietly preparing our message in the study.

SOUND DOCTRINE

4. The doctrine of a good minister should be sound. He should be "brought up in the truths of the faith and of the good teaching that you have followed" (1 Timothy 4:6). To the same purpose the apostle appeals to Timothy in the second epistle, "What you have heard from me, keep as the pattern of sound teaching, with faith and love in Christ Jesus" (2 Timothy 1:13). Error is falsehood, and falsehood is the stock in trade of the devil who is the father of lies. It is, therefore, most important that the minister of Christ should be established in the truth and not easily led away by "every wind of doctrine" (Ephesians 4:14, KJV) and every new theory of the age.

THE PREACHING

5. The preaching of the good minister is the Word.

> Preach the Word; be prepared in season and out of season; correct, rebuke and encourage—with great patience and careful instruction. For the time will come when men will not put up with sound doctrine. Instead, to suit their own desires, they will gather around them a great number of teachers to say what their itching ears want to hear. They will turn their ears away from the truth and turn aside to myths. (2 Timothy 4:2–4)

I have often recalled the pungent reproof once administered to me by a good Scotch elder in my early ministry. The well-known Harry Morehouse had just completed a series of evangelistic meetings in my church, and the people had been deeply stirred by his simple, scriptural messages. Some of the brethren were discussing the secret of his power when this quiet Scotchman ventured the remark, "You brethren are always preaching about the gospel, but Harry Morehouse preaches the gospel." There is a great difference in preaching about the Word and preaching the very Word itself, and letting God's own sharp sword cut its way into the consciences and hearts of men.

WHAT OTHERS ARE PREACHING

6. The good minister lets a lot of things alone which others are constantly preaching about.

The apostle intimates in the passage already quoted that the time will come when people with itching ears for new and strange things will turn them away from the simple gospel unto fables, and "gather around them a great number of teachers" (4:3) who will minister to their false appetite and taste. What great numbers of them there are today! One has but to read the titles of the majority of Sunday sermons announced in our Saturday papers to feel that the deluge is already on. The true minister will let these things safely alone. Listen, "Have nothing to do with godless myths and old wives' tales; rather, train yourself to be godly" (1 Timothy 4:7). "Timothy, guard what has been entrusted to your care. Turn away from godless chatter" (6:20), for "those who indulge in it will become more and more ungodly. Their teaching will spread like gangrene" (2 Timothy 2:16–17). "Don't have anything to do with foolish and stupid arguments, because you know they produce quarrels. And the Lord's servant must not quarrel" (2:23–24). If the apostle had been writing today, he would throw in a few more kindred topics, including Washington's and Lincoln's birthdays, the latest criminal trial, the presidential election and the newest novel or play.

CAREFUL PREPARATION

7. Careful preparation of his messages will characterize the good minister. "Do your best to present yourself to God as one approved, a workman who does not need to be ashamed and who correctly handles the word of truth" (2:15).

In His parable of the wise householder, the Lord Himself taught that the faithful minister will study to give to each of the guests at his Master's table "their food allowance at the proper time" (Luke 12:42), and will bring "out of his storeroom new treasures as well as old" (Matthew 13:52).

If the successful literary man thinks it worth his while to give his best thoughts, phrases and ideas to his generation, why should the student of God's holy Word not think it worth his while to bring out from this inexhaustible mine of spiritual treasures, the silver, the gold and the precious gems which God has given us in His holy Word, and which are found not at random, but by prayerful and assiduous study and meditation.

AN EVANGELIST AND TEACHER

8. The good minister will be an evangelist as well as a teacher. The apostle especially emphasizes this in his message to Timothy, "Do the work of an evangelist" (2 Timothy 4:5). We should never get beyond the love of souls

and the holy art of seeking and finding them.

A PERSONAL WORKER AND PASTOR

9. The good minister is a personal worker and pastor. "Be prepared in season and out of season; correct, rebuke and encourage—with great patience and careful instruction" (4:2). This is personal dealing with men. It is often a great deal harder to speak to a man face to face, than to pour a broadside from the pulpit. We must go to our brethren one by one, not only in season, but often out of season, and bring them the Master's message in love and tenderness; and the more it costs us to do it, the more often it will be blessed to them.

I remember a stormy night when I was impelled by the voice of God to call upon an old man of high social position at a late hour when it seemed inappropriate, to speak to him about his soul. The old man broke down and said, "If it was worth your while to come out this awful night to speak to me about my soul, it is worth my while to turn to God."

WORLDLY ENTANGLEMENTS

10. The good minister will keep out of worldly entanglements. "No one serving as a soldier gets involved in civilian affairs—he wants to please his commanding officer" (2:4). He will not get mixed up with political parties, with social clubs and with fashionable society, but will stand apart from doubtful influence, so that he may speak his Master's message impartially and fearlessly.

HIS DEPORTMENT

11. The good minister will be careful of his deportment. Timothy was a young man and needed to be the more guarded in his social relations and his personal example. Therefore, the apostle exhorts him, "Don't let anyone look down on you because you are young, but set an example for the believers in speech, in life, in love, in faith and in purity" (1 Timothy 4:12). Our life should speak for God louder than our words; and if we fail in this, our words are as "a resounding gong or a clanging cymbal" (1 Corinthians 13:1).

HIS SELECTION OF WORKERS

12. The good minister is careful in his selection of workers. "And the things you have heard me say in the presence of many witnesses entrust to reliable men who will also be qualified to teach others" (2 Timothy 2:2). "Do not be hasty in the laying on of hands," the apostle says in another passage. "And do not share in the sins of others" (1 Timothy 5:22). We need to be very careful in committing the Master's work to untried instruments. In

speaking of candidates for the eldership, the apostle warns him against accepting "a recent convert" (3:6); that is, one newly come to the faith, "or he may become conceited and fall under the same judgment as the devil" (3:6).

A THOROUGHLY DISCIPLINED SOLDIER

13. A good minister must necessarily be a strong character—a brave, self-denying and thoroughly disciplined soldier of Jesus Christ. "Endure hardship with us like a good soldier of Christ Jesus" (2 Timothy 2:3). If we want luxury, ease, popularity, a comfortable life, let us seek it in some other calling. God save us from men who seek the ministry as a lucrative profession and a calling offering the prize of distinction and success to human ambition. But if there is a man whose heart aspires to follow the Master without the camp, bearing His reproach, to stand alone for God amid misunderstanding, and perhaps neglect and poverty, all hail to such a candidate for the honors and sacrifices of this holy war.

HIS ACCOUNTABILITY TO GOD

14. The true minister of Jesus Christ will love and labor under the solemn sense of his accountability to God. How thrilling are the parting messages of Paul to Timothy, "I charge you, in the sight of God and Christ Jesus and the elect angels, to keep these instructions without partiality, and to do nothing out of favoritism" (1 Timothy 5:21). "In the sight of God, who gives life to everything, and of Christ Jesus, who while testifying before Pontius Pilate made the good confession, I charge you to keep this command without spot or blame" (6:13–14).

CHAPTER 5

THE MAN OF GOD

But you, man of God, flee from all this, and pursue righteousness, godliness, faith, love, endurance and gentleness. Fight the good fight of the faith. Take hold of the eternal life to which you were called when you made your good confession in the presence of many witnesses. (1 Timothy 6:11–12)

There is something striking and suggestive in the name here given to Timothy—"man of God." They used to give it to the ancient prophets, but why should it not belong to every true follower of Jesus Christ? To belong to God, to be in fellowship with God, to be like God, to be serving God, and to be looking forward to spending eternity with God—surely this is enough to constitute any child of earth a man of God.

Someone has defined a man of God as "God's man doing God's glory." The apostle uses the expression in this epistle with reference to others than Timothy: "That the man of God may be thoroughly equipped for every good work" (2 Timothy 3:17). Human leaders have their devoted followers, ready to lay down their lives for the hero they worship. Why should not God have His men whose one business is to represent Him?

A stirring message came once from a poor Kroo to the missionary who had led him to Christ years before. Finding an Englishman who was acquainted with his old teacher, he sent him this word: "Tell him that I was God's man then, and I am God's man still."

The epistles to Timothy give us some fine glimpses of the man of God.

A MAN OF FAITH

1. A Man of Faith

This is the foundation of all Christian character, of confidence in God. The man of God must know that God is for him before he can be for God.

Where shall we find sublimer confidence than in the testimony of Paul: "I know whom I have believed, and am convinced that he is able to guard what I have entrusted to him for that day" (1:12)? First, he believed in God, literally trusted in God. It is a glorious thing to simply, fully trust God, and rest without a quiver of doubt and fear, in His mighty and everlasting arms.

2. Come to Know God

"I know whom I have believed." There is a faith that comes from receiving the simple Word of God, and there is a deeper confidence that comes from closer intimacy with Him. It is of this that the Psalmist says, "Those who know your name will trust in you" (Psalm 9:10). This intimacy with God grows up through the trials and deliverances which test His faithfulness, and bind Him to our hearts by 10,000 cords of memory and love.

3. Committed Everything to God

"What I have entrusted to him" (2 Timothy 1:12) literally means, "my deposit." It is the figure of a deposit in the bank. We put our treasures where we have assurance of safety; we make our deposits where we have confidence in the stability of the bank. Paul had committed everything to one great investment. Everything that was dear to him was in the hands of Christ and bound up with His coming and the prospects of "that day." He had kept nothing back; he had no other resources. These are the lives that God loves to honor and use. Have we thus committed ourselves and all we hold dear—spirit, soul, body, friends, fortune, life—to His hands as One we know and trust, and are we persuaded that He is able to guard us for that day?

There is nothing in the compass of human experience to be compared with the value of such a confidence as this. It will keep your heart secure amid every conflict and danger, and leave your soul at leisure to make the most of life for God and your fellowmen, because your interests are safe, and your cares are all cast on Him who cares for you and who has promised that you shall "live in safety/ and be at ease, without fear of harm" (Proverbs 1:33).

OTHER-WORLDLINESS

One of the strongest features brought out in the contrast of our text is what might be called other-worldliness. It began with a picture of worldliness, "Men of corrupt mind, . . . who think that godliness is a means to financial gain" (1 Timothy 6:5). Then comes a twofold picture of the worldling. The first is a frightful description of the confirmed and utter devotee of mammon. "People who want to get rich" (6:9) is the description of such men. They have set their minds on the acquisition of money at any cost; scruples have been thrown away; risks have been taken, and all sails are set for the port of wealth. The results are next described. They "fall into temptation and a trap and into many foolish and harmful desires" (6:9). Oh, the temptations, the snares, the follies and the lusts that accompany the pursuits and acquisition of wealth! But this is not all; the end is an eternal tragedy which culminates in "ruin and destruction" (6:9). That is the sure end of every man who sets out with the determination that he will be rich. We have no right to set our hearts upon any supreme choice but God; and covetousness, which is idolatry, makes the world its god and finds its own place at last. It is the curse of our age, and the wrecks that it has flung on the shores of time are surely enough, as they look back on us with their ghastly faces, to make us "flee from all this" (6:11).

But the apostle gives us a second picture of the worldling, not quite so desperate and determined, but one of tremendous peril. He proceeds to say, "The love of money is a root of all kinds of evil. Some people, eager for money, have wandered from the faith and pierced themselves with many griefs" (6:10). These men have not determined to be rich at any cost, but they are hankering after it; it really has touched their hearts with its fascinating peril. They "have wandered from the faith." Oh, the compromises of principle that men are tempted to make for the sake of position and gain! And they pierce "themselves with many griefs." Oh, the wrecked fortunes, the ruined constitutions, the broken hearts, the backslidden lives that come from sailing too close to the mouth of the pit! Oh, men of today, "Watch out! Be on your guard against all kinds of greed" (Luke 12:15). "But you, man of God, flee from all this" (2 Timothy 6:11).

But it is not all a matter for men alone. The women, too, have their word of warning. Listen, "[She] who lives for pleasure is dead even while she lives" (1 Timothy 5:6). "They bring judgment on themselves, because they have broken their first pledge. Besides, they get into the habit of being idle and going about from house to house. And not only do they become idlers, but also gossips and busybodies, saying things they ought not to" (5:12–13). There is your fashionable woman for you, with her fashions, her five o'clock teas, her theater parties, her formal calls, and her wretched gabbling, gossiping waste of life and ruin of peace, reputation and home. What is it all worth when the end comes, for "we brought nothing into the world, and we can take nothing out of it. But if we have food and clothing, we will be content with that" (6:7–8). The spirit of other-worldliness is a spirit of simplicity in dress, in domestic life, and in all the tastes and habits of our life.

But it is even more than that. It has a more valuable use for wealth than selfish aggrandizement or gain.

Command those who are rich in this present world not to be arrogant nor to put their hope in wealth, which is so uncertain, but to put their hope in God, who richly provides us with everything for our enjoyment. Command them to do good, to be rich in good deeds, and to be generous and willing to share. In this way they will lay up treasure for themselves as a firm foundation for the coming age, so that they may take hold of the life that is truly life. (6:17–19)

The idea of this splendid passage is that a man or woman of wealth can invest his or her means in the work of God so that they shall be laid up in the coming kingdom and shall meet them with an eternal fortune there. This was what the Lord meant when He said, "Use worldly wealth to gain friends for yourselves, so that when it is gone, you will be welcomed into eternal dwellings" (Luke 16:9). Use your earthly fortune for God, and you will find it awaiting you yonder. Surely, this is a sane and attractive sort of other-worldliness which holds out to the men and women of today a splendid ambition and a glorious and enduring prize.

COURAGE, FORTITUDE AND CHRISTIAN SOLDIERSHIP

Another feature of the man of God so strongly emphasized in this passage is courage, fortitude and Christian soldiership. "Fight the good fight of the faith" (1 Timothy 6:12), our text says. The Christian life is a fight as well as flight; we are to run away from some things, but we are to face others. "I have fought the good fight" (2 Timothy 4:7) is the apostle's splendid testimony, as he closes his noble career. "Endure hardship . . . like a good soldier of Christ Jesus" (2:3). "You then, my son, be strong in the grace that is in Christ Jesus" (2:1). How much we need this quality of moral courage, of spiritual daring, of the faith that knows no fear. "God did not give us a spirit of timidity" (1:7), is the apostle's first mark of discernment of the Holy Spirit. The enemy will try to intimidate you if he can; and if he can make you a timid weakling, your usefulness is practically done. We need today a confidence that has no fear for itself, and dares to claim all that God has promised, and stand for all that he has commanded.

The exhortation of the Apostle Peter in another epistle is of preeminent importance. "Make every effort to add to your faith goodness [virtue, KJV] [courage, author's translation]" (2 Peter 1:5). The word means virility. The baptism of the Holy Spirit always gives holy boldness. Shame on the men and the women who are afraid to hear their own voices witnessing for Christ, and who hide their teaching when their Master's name is dishonored in polite society by profane language, Sunday newspapers and suggestive innuendoes which scoff at His holy Word and other sacred things.

PASSIVE VIRTUES

But the man of God is characterized by the passive virtues of meekness, gentleness, patience and love. How they shine out in this picture. "Pursue righteousness, godliness, faith, love, endurance and gentleness" (1 Timothy 6:11). And again, "The Lord's servant must not quarrel; instead he must be kind to everyone" (2 Timothy 2:24), and again, "At my first defense, no one came to my support, but everyone deserted me. May it not be held against them" (4:16).

FAMILY LIFE AND DUTY

The man of God is true to the claims of family life and duty. The head of every home is to provide industriously and honestly for his own household; and "if anyone does not provide for his relatives, and especially for his immediate family, he has denied the faith and is worse than an unbeliever" (1 Timothy 5:8). The ethics of Paul have no place for the religious idler or tramp. Woman also comes in for her due need of admonition and reproof. The gadabout, the busybody, the tattler, were a trouble to Paul and Timothy as well as to us today. The true matron, wife and mother who guides her house, rears her children and loves her husband, giving no occasion to the adversary to speak reproachfully, is held up as the simple and practical ideal of the average woman,

> A creature not too great or good
> For human nature's daily food.

Perhaps the apostle's teaching in the second chapter of First Timothy respecting feminine fashions may be difficult to harmonize with modern ideals, but the spirit of his counsels and admonitions is equally becoming to woman in every age whatever the outward form of her dress may be. "I also want women to dress modestly, with decency and propriety, not with braided hair or gold or pearls or expensive clothes, but with good deeds, appropriate for women who profess to worship God" (2:9–10).

Servants also are remembered in the apostle's directions. "All who are under the yoke of slavery should consider their masters worthy of full respect, so that God's name and our teaching may not be slandered" (6:1) And if their masters are believers, the servants in turn are commanded to "not show less respect for them because they are brothers. Instead, they are to serve them even better, because those who benefit from their service are believers, and dear to them" (6:2).

When we remember that the servant of Paul's time was an absolute slave, how much it does add to the force of this right relationship between employers and employees in the Church of God. Christianity is the true socialism, and in contrast with its sober peace-making and heavenly principles, the conflicts of the classes and the masses in our day present a very dark picture, a very different picture of confusion and selfishness.

PRAYER

Prayer is emphasized as one of the supreme duties and ministries of the man of God. "I want men everywhere to lift up holy hands in prayer, without anger or disputing" (2:8). The prayer which God accepts must be a prayer of faith, of love, of holiness. The apostle specifies the objects of prayer and the wide range of our intercession.

> I urge, then, first of all, that requests, prayers, intercession and thanksgiving be made for everyone—for kings and all those in authority, that we may live peaceful and quiet lives in all godliness and holiness. This is good, and pleases God our Savior, who wants all men to be saved and to come to a knowledge of the truth. (2:1–4)

This ministry of intercession is recognized as a real spiritual force, promoting peace, quietness, godliness and honesty, and contributing to the great end which God ever has in view, to have all men saved and come to the knowledge of the truth.

THE RESOURCES

There are three resources of the man of God.

1. The Faithfulness of Christ in Trial and Suffering

> Here is a trustworthy saying:
>
> If we died with him,
>   we will also live with him;
> if we endure,
>   we will also reign with him.
> If we disown him,
>   he will also disown us;
> if we are faithless,
>   he will remain faithful,
>   for he cannot disown himself.
>   (2 Timothy 2:11–13)

It is not our faith, but His faithfulness that guarantees our stability. Even if we do not believe, yet He stays faithful; He cannot deny Himself. And the measure of our suffering is the measure of our glory. The further the pendulum swings downward, the loftier will be the reversion; and it will be found that "our light and momentary troubles are achieving for us an eternal glory that far outweighs them all" (2 Corinthians 4:17).

2. The Promises Cover Both Present and Future Life

The promises cover the present life as well as the life to come, for "godliness has value for all things, holding promise for both the present life and the life to come" (1 Timothy 4:8). God's goodness takes in the whole circumstance of our present life. His providence is ever protecting us, and His promise is sure. "He who did not spare his own Son, but gave him up for us all—how will he not also, along with him, graciously give us all things?" (Romans 8:32).

3. Divine Deliverance in Every Extremity

The man of God is provided with divine deliverance in every extremity. "The Lord will rescue me from every evil attack and will bring me safely to his heavenly kingdom. To him be the glory for ever and ever. Amen" (2 Timothy 4:18). This promise is as true for us as it was for Paul. And Paul himself seems still to say to us from the battlements of glory, "My God will meet all your needs according to his glorious riches in Christ Jesus" (Philippians 4:19).

THE EXPECTATIONS

Next come the expectations of the man of God. The blessed hope that inspired Paul's closing hours he has bequeathed to us also, "Now there is in store for me the crown of righteousness, which the Lord, the righteous judge, will award to me on that day—and not only to me, but also to all who have longed for his appearing" (2 Timothy 4:8). That will make amends for all, and in its prospect we may well say, "I reckon that the sufferings of this present time are not worthy to be compared with the glory which shall be revealed in us" (Romans 8:18, KJV). As we quoted in the beginning of this chapter, what else do we need if we can say, "I am convinced that he is able to guard what I have entrusted to him for that day" (1:12)? To Paul there was but one day that counted; it was "that day." What will it matter then if we have had a stormy passage, a hard and bloody fight, a long and weary waiting, so long as we are home at last, safe at last, satisfied at last, crowned at last? Then let us

Wait, only wait;
  God is working—trust, and only wait;
Wait, and ev'ry cloud will brighten,
Wait, and ev'ry load will lighten,
Wait, and ev'ry wrong will righten,
  If you only wait.

CHAPTER 6

OUR TRUSTEESHIP

That conforms to the glorious gospel of the blessed God, which he entrusted to me. (1 Timothy 1:11)

Guard the good deposit that was entrusted to you—guard it with the help of the Holy Spirit who lives in us. (2 Timothy 1:14)

Almost everyone is familiar with the idea of trusteeship. The figure is frequently used in the Scriptures to illustrate our responsibility as individuals and as bodies of Christians.

THE TRUTH

First we are trustees for the truth. The epistle of Jude tells us of "the faith that was once for all entrusted to the saints" (Jude 3). This was a great committal and commission which involved a corresponding trust. In his epistle to Timothy Paul tells us the Church is "the pillar and foundation of the truth" (1 Timothy 3:15); that is, it upholds, as pillars in a great architectural front, the arch on which God has inscribed His message to the world. As trustees for the truth we should uphold the integrity and authority of the Bible, and work for its wide and universal circulation. More especially should we stand for the emphatic and special lines of spiritual teaching which God has made so real and significant to us, and has literally inscribed upon our own lives and incarnated in our own very bodies. God has given to us a message for His people, and we cannot afford to be lax in it without losing our own peculiar blessing and being set aside from our high calling as His witnesses.

OUR OWN AGE AND TIME

Next we are trustees for our own age and time. It is said of David that he served his own generation by the will of God. The men of Issachar had understanding of their times to know what Israel ought to do. God wants us to live in this century and to know its spiritual conditions, to meet its peculiar perils and opportunities, and to be true to the emergency work which belongs to our age. "Therefore do not be foolish, but understand what the Lord's will is" (Ephesians 5:17). "Be very careful, then, how you live—not as unwise but as wise, making the most of every opportunity, because the days are evil" (5:15).

THE FUTURE

We are also trustees for the future. We are all heirs of the past and have received a heritage of truth, privilege, and responsibility from our fathers. It is a costly heritage, and we are not only to be true to its improvement, but to pass it on undiminished and enlarged to those who follow us. David did not build the temple, but he had the privilege of preparing the materials for the work of Solomon, his son. We also are laying foundations and working for the ages to come. What a glorious thing if we should be permitted to do things that will last till Jesus comes! Is not this the meaning of that great promise, "I have . . . covered you with the shadow of my hand—/ I who set the heavens in place,/ who laid the foundations of the earth" (Isaiah 51:16)? Let us be true to this holy trust.

OUR COUNTRY AND COMMUNITY

We are also trustees for our country and our local community. In this land, citizenship is a sovereign right and solemn responsibility for every man and woman. We may not necessarily mingle in the noisy and unholy arena of present-day politics, but we can be loyal to the highest interests of the nation; and if we are watchful, we shall find God laying many burdens of prayer upon us for conditions in public affairs that greatly affect His kingdom. In this respect we can be the salt of the earth, and the 10 righteous persons who would have saved Sodom and Gomorrah. Especially is this true of our local community. Perhaps we have done a little to meet that responsibility, but we ought to have a larger ministry, a wider and deeper influence for the gospel.

OUR BRETHREN IN THE CHURCHES

We are also to be trustees for our brethren in the churches. As our Lord looked out upon the multitude that fainted and were scattered abroad like sheep without a shepherd, His heart was moved with compassion. What multitudes of hungry hearts there are around us today. How many are starving for bread and getting a stone! Perhaps God has scattered us that we might be as a light in a dark place. We cannot do this by being harsh, self-important and out of sympathy with those around us. We may so commend

Christ that though they may not believe all that we believe, and have all that
we possess, yet at least they will be attracted and drawn to the Master by the
light of His life which we reflect. The apostle said that he was glad to make
manifest the sweet savor of Christ in every place. Are we fulfilling this delicate and divine trusteeship?

OUR CHILDREN

We are the trustees for our children. The future of the rising generation
is the most serious question before the Church today. The spirit of independence has largely destroyed family discipline. The atmosphere of our
schools is largely materialistic and hostile to the Bible. Our textbooks represent a standard of scientific teaching which wholly leads toward evolution and the worst forms of modern philosophy and psychology. The
amusements of our young people are perilous, and the moral conditions of
both sexes, even of the most tender years, have recently been shown to be
appalling.

All this has created a great necessity. The first remedy, of course, is prayer
and faith in God for our own children, a constant reliance upon His
covenant promise for us and our seed. Along with this is the maintenance of
family discipline on the part of parents notwithstanding the spirit of the age
and the difficulty of holding the reins of authority. Let it not be harshness,
but the nurture and admonition of the Lord. And there must be a holy and
courageous separation in our social life from the world and its associations
and pleasures.

THE EVANGELIZATION OF THE WORLD

We are the trustees for the evangelization of the world. This is the ultimate
goal of all our plans and preparations. We have been put in trust with the
gospel for the whole heathen world. This is peculiarly our trust as a people.
This work has brought to us a greater blessing than we have ever brought to
it. It is the true outlet of the spiritual forces which God is developing among
His people. It is the only thing that is large enough for the message He has
given us and the Spirit He is pouring upon us.

A MISSIONARY TRUST

What constitutes a missionary trust?

1. The Missionary Idea

What is God's thought for the evangelization of the world? Is it the conversion of everybody everywhere? If that were so, we might well confess
that Christianity is a failure, and that God has been baffled in His purpose. There is no more prospect of the conversion of the race than 2,000

years ago. The prospects are growing dimmer every day for the conversion of the people of Christian lands. It surely would be a forlorn hope to look for more in the blackness of heathen night. No, God has a more practicable program. It is the gathering out of a few as samples of the race from every clime and tongue, to form the Bride of the Lamb and the people for His name who shall constitute the leaders of the new dispensation which His coming is to bring. This is the outlook of every scriptural scheme of foreign evangelization, and this is the keynote of our Christian missions, not the conversion but the evangelization of the world in the present generation.

2. The Missionary Conscience

Having caught the divine idea, we need to have it become the center of our moral nature and the conviction of our conscience. Henceforth evangelization is not merely a passion but an obligation, a necessity, and a debt. "I am debtor" (Romans 1:14, KJV), says the apostle; and a debtor is one who has something which belongs to somebody else. That is a very awkward place for a consistent Christian to stand. An unpaid debt, when you are able to pay it, means sin, and calls for conviction, repentance and restitution. When the Church of God and the conscientious Christian deal with missions in this way, something will come to pass.

3. The Missionary Heart

This means the love of Christ. It is not mere charity, but the passion of God, the love that moves us as God's love moved Him to give and sacrifice; not only the divine passion, but the divine passion for perishing men, that sees them and pities them as Christ Himself would. It is the heart of Christ within, loving and giving as He Himself loved and gave.

This will lead to sacrifice. "For God so loved . . . that he gave" (John 3:16), and divine love never stops short of giving to the point of living sacrifice. This will also lift us to the plane of divine enthusiasm. The missionary heart is an intense heart—a heart that glows and burns. A heart that exclaims like Paul, "Christ's love compels us" (2 Corinthians 5:14). Literally, he means it is like a great mountain torrent, cleaving its way in spite of every obstacle and becoming the overflowing, resistless river. That is the true secret of the missionary movement which the world needs today.

4. Missionary Feet

It will lead some of us to go. It will lead all of us to be willing to go. It will make the obligation so personal and overpowering that we shall not need a divine commission to go so much as a divine permission to stay.

5. Missionary Hands

It will become missionary hands, the hands that are lifted up in intercession, definitely, systematically, perseveringly and believingly. Unselfish
prayer, prayer that moves us and moves the hand that moves the world. It
means the hands that toil, for our missionary money will not drop from
heaven upon us, but will be the fruit of painful labor, the sweat of brawn
and brain, and the sacrifice of many an hour of leisure and comfort. It
means the hands that give. The ministry of giving is as much a grace as faith
and love and prayer. If you do not love to give, it is because you have not
received the full baptism of the Holy Spirit. Christian stewardship means
more than Jewish tithes. You do not give under restrictions or requisitions,
but you give in holy freedom, the liberty of love; and liberty and love ought
to mean much more than law and necessity. You can live a selfish life if you
please. You can use your money for your own indulgence and let the crowd
of the perishing pass away. God may send no judgment upon you. He may
not withdraw His presence from you, for there are selfish and stingy Christians who may get to heaven. He may not take away your means as a judgment upon your unfaithful stewardship. He may let you pass smoothly
through life to its last chapter. It may be with you as with the rich man who
fared sumptuously everyday, and perhaps looked kindly at the beggar who
lay festering at his door, and who certainly never said a rough word or did
an unkind act. He simply lived for himself and was not rich toward God.
But oh, what a change when the tables were turned and the dreadful revelation came! In hell he lifted up his eyes in torment and begged for a single
drop of water from the man on whose misery and poverty he had looked
down upon through all his earthly life. God make us to understand and to
be true to our holy trust, and to answer back to Him:

> Lord, Thou hast given to me a trust,
>   A high and holy dispensation,
> To tell the world, and tell I must
>   The story of Thy great salvation.
>
> Thou mightest have sent from heav'n above
>   Angelic hosts to tell the story,
> But in Thy condescending love
>   On men Thou hast conferred the glory.
>
> We all are debtors to our race;
>   God holds us bound to one another.
> His gifts in providence and grace
>   Were given thee to give thy brother.

We owe to every soul on earth
　One chance of life and hope and heaven:
Oh, by the love that brought us in.
　Let help and hope to them be given.

TITUS

CHAPTER 1

THE GOSPEL IN TITUS

The letter of Paul to Titus, appointed by him overseer of the church of Crete, contains about 50 sentences, and 750 words. It is less than one quarter the size of a short sermon, could easily be printed on four pages of a small leaflet, and written on six pages of note paper, or two pages of typewriting, thus comprising about as much matter as a very ordinary personal letter. But within this little space there is compressed a body of doctrinal and practical teaching outweighing volumes of sermons, and full enough to be expanded into an immense library, so concise and so pregnant with living truth are the words of the Holy Spirit.

Let us look at the teachings of this epistle as they relate to doctrine, to practical duty, and to Christian hope. Verses 11–14 in the second chapter are a very good compendium of the whole letter, and almost every phrase is laden with suggestive and comprehensive truth.

THE DOCTRINES OF GRACE

It contains a plea for sound doctrinal teaching on the part of the Christian minister. "You must teach what is in accord with sound doctrine" (Titus 2:1). It comprises every doctrine of grace within the brief space of its 46 verses.

1. The Glory and Dignity of Jesus

It begins with the glory and dignity of the Lord Jesus Christ who is named side by side with God. "Paul, a servant of God and an apostle of Jesus Christ" (1:1). Then he adds, "by the command of God our Savior" (1:3). Next, his benediction includes the Lord Jesus with the Father in glory, honor and worship: "Grace and peace from God the Father and Christ Jesus our Savior" (1:4). Again in the second chapter and the 13th verse, the correct reading is, "The glorious appearing of our great God and Savior, Jesus Christ." Once more the familiar phrase, "God our Savior," is used in the third chapter. "When the kindness and love of God our Savior appeared"

(3:4). The testimony of this epistle, therefore, to the Lord Jesus Christ is that He is equal with the Father, our divine Savior and Lord, to whom, with the Father and the Holy Spirit, be glory everlasting. Amen.

2. Recognizes Man's Fallen Condition

This epistle also recognizes man's fallen condition. "At one time we too were foolish, disobedient, deceived and enslaved by all kinds of passions and pleasures. We lived in malice and envy, being hated and hating one another" (3:3). There is no rose-colored humanitarianism here. It is crimson sin and crimson blood, utter ruin and divine redemption.

3. God's Electing Love

Paul's apostleship, he says, "is according to the faith of God's elect" (1:1, KJV). He further says in the next verse that it is "resting on the hope of eternal life, which God, who does not lie, promised before the beginning of time, and at his appointed season he brought his word to light through . . . preaching" (1:2). Salvation, therefore, is not an afterthought, but was always in God's thought and plan and was even formulated in His mind and promised to His beloved Son as our Representative in that eternal covenant, which is very clearly referred to in other Scripture. We were given to Christ by the Father before we were ever born, in consideration of His promise to redeem us in due time by His precious blood. This is the meaning of that mysterious, but gracious word, "All that the Father gives me will come to me, and whoever comes to me I will never drive away" (John 6:37).

4. Divine Mercy and the Grace of God

The doctrine of the divine mercy and grace of God is most clearly expressed in at least two passages in this short epistle. "The grace of God that brings salvation has appeared to all men" (Titus 2:11). "But when the kindness and love of God our Savior appeared, he saved us, not because of righteous things we had done, but because of his mercy" (3:4–5). Salvation is a stream of grace that has flowed to men from the foundation of the Father's love. We have done nothing to deserve it; we can do nothing apart from Him to affect it. It is the gift of God's love, freely bestowed, freely received for Jesus' sake.

5. Redemption through the Sacrifice of Jesus Christ

The doctrine of redemption through the sacrifice of the Lord Jesus Christ is presented. "While we wait for the blessed hope—the glorious appearing of our great God and Savior, Jesus Christ, who gave himself for us to redeem us from all wickedness and to purify for himself a people that are his very own, eager to do what is good" (2:13–14). This is the same old Pauline gospel, the gospel of the cross, the great atonement, the precious, precious blood. Without that blood there can be no gospel and no salvation. It is the distinguishing mark which identifies the divine currency of truth and grace, and without this crimson sign all else is vanity and lies.

6. Justification through the Righteousness of Christ

Next comes the doctrine of justification through the righteousness of Christ. "So that, having been justified by his grace, we might become heirs having the hope of eternal life" (3:7). This again is the old, old story which we hear so often in Romans and the other Pauline letters. It is the fundamental message of the gospel. There are some who tell us that we are saved by feeling, by experience, by a clean heart, and by a sanctified soul. These are "things that accompany salvation" (Hebrews 6:9), but the sinner is justified by a sovereign act of God the moment he turns from his sin and accepts the Lord Jesus Christ as his righteousness and salvation.

> Could my zeal no respite know,
>   Could my tears forever flow,
> All for sin could not atone,
>   Thou must save, and Thou alone.

7. The Doctrine of Regeneration

"He saved us, . . . because of his mercy. He saved us through the washing of rebirth and renewal by the Holy Spirit" (Titus 3:5). Regeneration is not justification; it is the effect of it. "Yet to all who received him, to those who believed in his name, he gave the right to become children of God— children born [that is, regenerated] not of natural descent, nor of human decision or a husband's will, but born of God" (John 1:12–13). God gives a new heart to every soul that He justifies, but we cannot make this new heart—we can simply believe for it. And as we accept His grace by faith, we receive His quickening life by conscious experience.

8. The Doctrine of the Holy Spirit

Titus presents the doctrine of the Holy Spirit. "The washing of rebirth and renewal by the Holy Spirit, whom he poured out on us generously through Jesus Christ our Savior" (Titus 3:5–6).

This is something more than regeneration; this is the filling of the Spirit. It is recognized here as the privilege of every regenerated person. It is also intimated that it is a repeated experience, and one capable of great variety of degrees. We receive the Holy Spirit by one definite act of faith, but God gives us new or renewed outpourings of His grace and power as we come into closer fellowship and become responsive to His touch. The command of the apostle in Ephesians is best expressed in a continuous present tense and imperative mood: "Be being filled with the Spirit" (see Ephesians 5:18). That is, be continually receiving more and more fully the influences of the Holy Spirit, and opening your being more completely to His indwelling control. And so it will be true of us, as our text expresses it, that He will be shed on us abundantly through Jesus Christ our Savior.

9. The Doctrine of Holiness

Titus provides us with a doctrine of holiness. "Who gave himself for us to redeem us from all wickedness and to purify for himself a [peculiar, KJV] people that are his very own, [zealous, KJV] to do what is good" (Titus 2:14). The ultimate purpose of Christ's redemption was not so much to save us from judgment as from sin, and to make us a separated people, as the word "peculiar" here means, and on fire, as the word "zealous" means, to serve and glorify God. Here then is a body of Christian doctrine as complete, clear and simple as perhaps no similar portion of Scripture contains in such condensed form: God's everlasting and electing love, God's free and boundless grace, Christ's great redemption, justification by faith, regeneration by the Spirit, the baptism and filling of the Holy Spirit and the life of separation and sanctification. Blessed be God for all this precious truth, this glorious gospel of the grace of God.

THE DUTIES OF THE CHRISTIAN LIFE

The apostle in this epistle emphasizes the side of practical duty quite as much as heavenly doctrine. He speaks in the very first verse of "the truth that leads to godliness." The Lord's own test is "by their fruit you will recognize them" (Matthew 7:20).

1. It Embraces Practical Righteousness

The teaching of the gospel and the grace of God embraces practical righteousness in all its departments. "For the grace of God that brings salvation has appeared to all men. It teaches us to say 'No' to ungodliness and worldly passions, and to live self-controlled, upright and godly lives in this present age" (Titus 2:11–12). The word "teaches" here literally means, disciplines. Salvation is a discipline in the practice of godliness. It has a certain negative quality, "[saying] 'No' to ungodliness and worldly passions." That is, we must say "no" to everything that comes to us from without or from within that would lead us away from God or into sinful indulgence. A very large part of character and conduct consists of what we do not do. Without the power to say "no," we shall be as "a reed swayed by the wind" (Matthew 11:7).

But there is a positive side to the discipline of grace. We should "live self-controlled, upright and godly lives in this present age" (Titus 2:12). The first word includes what we owe to ourselves, and carries with it the idea of self-restraint and temperance in all things. The second word, "upright," covers our duties to others, and requires that we should deal justly with all our fellow beings. The third sweeps the mightier circle of the heavens. It is not the horizontal line of duty, but the vertical. It includes supreme love, obedience, confidence and faithfulness toward God in all things. Where shall we find a finer compendium of practical Christian living?

The word "teaches" should be translated "disciplines," as we have already seen. The idea is that not all at once do we learn to live this practical Christian life. We get the principle of it in a moment, but the practice of it is like the learning of some fine art, like stenography and painting, and everything depends upon proficiency and practice. How patiently our great Teacher bears with us and takes us over the same lesson again and again, until at last we are made perfect in obedience, and the lesson of meekness, forbearance, silence or submission is fully learned. "I am instructed," (KJV) Paul had to say, "I have learned the secret" (Philippians 4:12). So let us learn and receive the discipline of the Holy Spirit.

2. Do What Is Good

Again he enjoins the disciples of Christ that they should be "careful to devote themselves to doing what is good" (Titus 3:8). In the third chapter and eighth verse he says that Titus must constantly affirm this. It is one of the things of which God's children must be ever reminded, and one of the things which must be guarded with sedulous vigilance and care. Evil, it has been truly said

> . . . is wrought
>   By want of thought
> More than by want of heart.

3. Conduct of the Elders and Officers

Next he comes down to the specific conduct of the elders and officers of the Church of Christ. Their Christian deportment is quite as important as their teaching.

> Since an overseer is entrusted with God's work, he must be blameless—not overbearing, not quick-tempered, not given to drunkenness, not violent, not pursuing dishonest gain. Rather he must be hospitable, one who loves what is good, who is self-controlled, upright, holy and disciplined. He must hold firmly to the

trustworthy message as it has been taught, so that he can encourage others by sound doctrine and refute those who oppose it. (1:7–9)

And he emphasizes this by insisting upon Titus himself maintaining an example of great carefulness and uprightness in his own life. "In everything set them an example by doing what is good. In your teaching show integrity, seriousness and soundness of speech that cannot be condemned, so that those who oppose you may be ashamed because they have nothing bad to say about us" (2:7–8).

4. Words for Older Men

Again he comes down to the aged men and gives them a word of wholesome counsel in six significant terms. "Teach the older men to be temperate, worthy of respect, self-controlled, and sound in faith, in love and in endurance" (2:2).

5. Words for Young Men

He does not forget the young men, but has a word directly for them. "Encourage the young men to be self-controlled" (2:6). He emphasizes self-controlled, because youth is apt to be impetuous and ill-balanced, and the work of Christ requires that the intense enthusiasm of the young should be controlled by the "spirit . . . of love and self-discipline" (2 Timothy 1:7).

6. Words for Women

Then he turns to the women, and, having given them much wholesome counsel for their own conduct, he commits to older women the oversight of the younger women. Here he devotes two whole verses and holds up a standard of sweetness, discretion and true home life—that were never needed more than they are today in Christian families—a picture and realization of which would save many a heartbreak and many a wrecked family.

> Likewise, teach the older women to be reverent in the way they live, not to be slanderers or addicted to much wine, but to teach what is good. Then they can train the younger women to love their husbands and children, to be self-controlled and pure, to be busy at home, to be kind, and to be subject to their husbands, so that no one will malign the word of God. (2:3–5)

7. Words to Servants

Nor does he overlook the servants who were indeed the slaves in the families of Crete. They were exhorted to obedience, zeal, meekness, silence, even under rebuke, strict honesty, and such fidelity as would even on the part of a poor slave "make the teaching about God our Savior attractive" (2:10). This beautiful expression is used only of the servants. When the Lord would choose some jewel of special beauty to adorn His crown, He looks for it not in a royal palace, but in some lowly kitchen. It is not a mighty preacher or an illustrious statesman that is to shine with brightest luster, but some humble maid in an American family or some patient slave in a Roman palace. I remember more than one humble servant in this work who has been used of God, by a sweet, transformed life in the kitchen or laundry, to bring her proud mistress to these meetings to find the secret which made her maid's life so changed and blessed.

8. Our civil and social duties.

Finally, he completes his sketch of Christian virtue by a fine reference to our civil and social duties. "Remind the people to be subject to rulers and authorities, to be obedient, to be ready to do whatever is good, to slander no one, to be peaceable and considerate, and to show true humility toward all men" (3:1–2). Here is the true Christian socialism even under a cruel, despotic Roman tyrant. This is the ideal of the Christian state; and such living transformed ancient Rome, and today would be mightier than all the ravings of demagogues and the politics of Democrats and Republicans.

THE OUTLOOK OF FAITH AND HOPE

The circle of truth would not be complete without this precious verse. "While we wait for the blessed hope—the glorious appearing of our great God and Savior, Jesus Christ" (2:13). This is the incentive of all true living and the consummation of faith and hope. Not death but glory. Not to get away from the turmoil and trouble of life, but to fight a good fight and to share by and by the victory and the crown. For this blessed hope Paul lived, suffered and labored. How much nearer it is to us today. Let it fire our dying love and zeal. Let it inspire our sacrifice and service. "He who testifies to these things says, 'Yes, I am coming soon.' Amen. Come, Lord Jesus" (Revelation 22:20–21).

It will give largeness, loftiness and sublimity to our lives if we live under the power of this blessed hope. It is said that a number of sculptors once brought their statues of Minerva to surmount a lofty tower; but as one by one they were reared aloft, they appeared so small in the distance that not a single feature could be distinguished. At last one artist brought a colossal figure, roughly outlined, but nobly planned. It had little beauty when looked at near at hand. But when it was placed on its lofty pedestal, the distance lent enchantment to the view, and every detail of form and feature stood out in such noble relief that a great shout of approval went up from the witnessing company. So our little lives are too small to fit this magnificent hope. Let us make them larger, grander and more in keeping with the mighty mold and inspiring motive which comes from the expectation of that glorious day.

What a day it will be! "Gather together all the treasures of sight, all that is beautiful. Gather together all the treasures of sound, of sweet harmonies. And to these all the treasures of the heart, of dear loves, holy friendships, and happy fancies. Ransack the treasures of time. Pile them all in one. Then double them. Then treble them. Then quadruple them. Then multiply them a hundredfold. Then multiply them a thousandfold. Then multiply them by thousands of thousands. Then multiply them by all the arithmetic of all the ages."

> And still the soul a far off glory sees,
>   Strange music hears.
> As something not of earth, borne on the breeze.
>   The sun and stars
> Point to some land of endless, endless truth
>   Of light and life.
> Where souls renewed in an immortal youth
>   Shall know the Infinite.

HEBREWS

INTRODUCTION

This section on the epistle to the Hebrews was formerly published by the author under the title, *Within the Veil.* It consists of messages delivered by Dr. Simpson in the Gospel Tabernacle in New York City in the course of his regular ministry, at a time when he was at the zenith of his popularity as an exponent of the Word of God. For many years it has been out of print, so that we esteem it a great privilege to make it available to another generation.

Andrew Murray called the epistle to the Hebrews "The Holiest of All," and so it is. However, not only is it one of the finest devotional books of the entire Scriptures, but it is also the counterpart of Leviticus in the Old Testament. That book and the Levitical system of offerings take on new meaning when interpreted by this great epistle.

In originally publishing these sermons Dr. Simpson wrote: "These messages will be found to aim not at profound thought, deep scholarship, or originality of phrase or illustration, but rather at the spiritual unfolding of the mind of the Holy Ghost, and the comfort and edification of the average Christian. We trust that they will be as abundantly blessed to those who read them as they have been to the heart of the writer and speaker.

"We have found that this beautiful epistle gives the richest and most varied picture of the Lord Jesus Christ in His ascended life and glory to be found within the inspired Word, and as Andrew Murray has so well said in his admirable book on the Epistle to the Hebrews, the secret of a holy and victorious life is to see and constantly realize the Person and glory of Jesus Christ in His ascended life at God's right hand. May the following pages add something to the revelation of Christ in the hearts of many, and be used for the glory of His blessed name."

THE PUBLISHERS

CHAPTER 1

THE APOSTLE OF OUR PROFESSION

Fix your thoughts on Jesus, the apostle and high priest whom we confess. (Hebrews 3:1)

God . . . in these last days . . . has spoken to us by his Son. (1:1–2)

The epistle to the Hebrews in importance stands side by side with Romans and Corinthians as one of the major messages of the Holy Spirit to the Church after Pentecost. At the same time it has a unique place not only on account of the special people to whom it was addressed, but of the great wealth of Old Testament allusion and illustration which it contains, throwing as it does a flood of light upon the ancient types, and more fully than any other New Testament writing unfolding the intimate connection between the Old and New Testaments.

THE AUTHORSHIP

The authorship of this epistle is in doubt. Popularly it bears the name of Paul, but the style and internal evidence are all against his authorship. In any case if he wrote it he must have written it in Hebrew, and some other hand translated it into Greek, thus dropping the peculiarities of his style in the translation. The most probable alternative suggested is that it was written by Apollos, the learned Jew of Alexandria, who was mighty in the Scriptures and who was led into deeper spiritual truth by Aquila and Priscilla, who themselves were disciples of Paul. The uncertainty, however, of the human channel through which it came makes it all the more the message of the Holy Spirit to the people of God. While addressed to the Hebrew Christians it is no less the heritage of the whole Church than the other epistles that were also addressed to particular churches or individuals, but meant for the whole household of faith.

THE PLAN

The plan of the epistle is very simple. Its chief design is to exalt the Lord Jesus Christ and show His superiority to Moses, Joshua, the angels and all other beings, as the Son of God and the divine Head of redeemed humanity. This is done in three distinct sections representing Christ in various offices and aspects:

1. Christ the Apostle of our profession, or the divine Messenger by whom God hath spoken in these last days to His people (Hebrews 1:1 to 4:13).
2. Christ our Great High Priest (4:14 to 10:34).
3. Christ the Author and Finisher of our faith (10:35 to 13:25).

CHRIST OUR APOSTLE

The word apostle means "one sent, a messenger." The first section of this epistle is devoted to the consideration of Christ as God's last messenger to humankind.

The opening sentence of this epistle is most impressive, standing out like an inscription cut in stone over the entrance to some majestic building, or, like the frontispiece of some great volume. Two words compose this majestic message: "God spoke." (1:1). "[God] has spoken to us by his Son" (1:2).

Long and vainly had the world waited for some message from above. Nature had spoken, but her message was too confused and vague to tell us what we needed to know. Written on the glowing skies and the verdant earth the dullest eye could read the two words, "God is." But there the sentence ended with a note of interrogation, and another voice was needed to complete the sentence and write it out fully, "God is love." Philosophy had sought to penetrate the mysteries of truth and from human intuition and natural reasoning find out the unknown God; but the best that philosophy could find was the dead, cold, abstract trinity of Plato, "The True, the Beautiful, the Good." This, however, had no power to lift humanity from its wretchedness and sin. Idolatry had spoken, but its gods were monsters of cruelty and corruption, and it had no light or help for hopeless humanity. Sorcery and spiritualism pretended to speak, and they brought some messages from the darkness of the unseen and the future world, but their words were idle and unsatisfying and only *ignis fatuus* gleams that left us in deeper darkness.

But "God spoke." "At many times and in various ways" (1:1) He had previously "[spoken] to our forefathers through the prophets," but now "in these last days he has spoken to us by his Son" (1:2). He has given us at length His greatest, fullest, latest word, and it is the living Word Himself—

Jesus, who is not only the Messenger of the truth, but is Himself "the way and the truth and the life" (John 14:6). The gulf between earth and heaven is spanned. The mystery of the unknown is unsealed. The will of God is revealed, and "God spoke." How solemn, how thrilling, how important to know that the Sovereign of the universe has condescended to make Himself known to the inhabitants of this remote and insignificant world, and that we have in this sacred book and this holy gospel the word and will of eternal God!

But the weight of the message is infinitely enhanced by the dignity of the Messenger. In a previous Chino-Japanese war an attempt was made two or three times through some subordinate officials of the Chinese government to negotiate a peace. But no attention was paid to the message because of the unimportance of the messenger. But when at last the Chinese government expressed their earnestness and sincerity by sending to Japan their Plenipotentiary, their most distinguished citizen, the Viceroy himself, the government of Japan treated the matter with due consideration and steps were taken to meet the embassy and arrange an amnesty. And so God has shown His deep sincerity and profound interest in our race and the great question of reconciliation between man and God by sending to us as His Ambassador and Apostle no less a person than His own beloved Son.

The difficulty with the Hebrew people in receiving the gospel of Christ was their profound veneration for Moses and the prophets, and their unwillingness to admit any other to a place of equal authority, and therefore the author of this epistle takes special pains to prove to them that the Lord Jesus Christ in His own right and by His Father's recognition is superior in dignity and importance to Moses and the prophets.

THE DIGNITY AND GLORY OF THE MESSENGER

1. The Son of God

"For to which of the angels did God ever say, 'You are my Son;/ today I have become your Father?'/ Or again, 'I will be his Father,/ and he will be my Son'?" (Hebrews 1:5). God's last Messenger to men is His own well-beloved Son. This is finely set forth in the parable of the vineyard (see Matthew 21:33-45). The husbandman sent his servants one by one, but they took them and beat them and killed them. "Last of all, he sent his son to them. 'They will respect my son,' he said. But when the tenants saw the son, they said to each other, 'This is the heir. Come, let's kill him and take his inheritance.' So they took him and threw him out of the vineyard and killed him" (21:37-39). Foreknowing all this, "God so loved the world that he gave his one and only Son, that whoever believes in him shall not perish but have eternal life" (John 3:16).

2. The Heir of All Things

It is for Him that all things were made and planned. He is the end as well as the beginning of the universe of God. "All things were created by him and for him" (Colossians 1:16). In Him at last shall be summed up all the glory of nature and all the government of the new heaven and earth. "For God was pleased to have all his fullness dwell in him" (1:19). It is this glorious and dignified Person who has come to us from the heavenly world as the bearer of God's last message to men. He is the Viceroy of the universe and the Vice Regent of God Himself.

3. The Image of God

He is "the radiance of God's glory and the exact representation of his being" (Hebrews 1:3). This stronger language expresses His equality and unity with God. He is the effulgence and outflow of the Father's glory and the very counterpart of His person. Two persons of equal dignity and glory and yet distinct personality are here described. Therefore all that the Father is He is, and He can truly say, "Anyone who has seen me has seen the Father," for "I am in the Father, and . . . the Father is in me" (John 14:9–10). Would you know the character of God, the will of God, the thoughts of God, the plan of God for men? Look at Jesus, listen to His words, accept His teachings.

4. The Creator of All Things

"Through whom he made the universe" (Hebrews 1:2) (or more literally, the aeons or ages). He is the Creator therefore, not only of space, but of time; not only of matter, but of all the cycles, dispensations and ages to come. His wisdom has planned the unfolding stages of God's mighty purpose down to the latest ages of eternity. His hand has formed and poised every circling planet and every central sun amid the constellations, and as you look up into the shining firmament and think of the infinite wisdom and grandeur of God's works and ways turn sweetly to the gentle Presence that is filling all your heart with peace, and say, "This is my Redeemer and my Friend."

5. The Sovereign Lord

He is the sovereign Lord and the Almighty Creator "sustaining all things by his powerful word" (1:3). He is the God of providence as well as nature, controlling all events and circumstances from the fall of a sparrow to the conquest of an empire.

6. The Mediatorial King

"After he had provided purification for sins, he sat down at the right hand of the Majesty in heaven. So he became as much superior to the angels as the name he has inherited is superior to theirs" (1:3–4).

This is not the same authority referred to in the last paragraph. This is a new kingdom given to Him in consideration of His completed redemption and accomplished atonement. This is the place of ascension glory on the right hand of the Majesty on high where He sits enthroned as King of saints and King of nations, and in a little while to be the Lord of the millennial world.

7. Greater Than the Angels

The apostle enters into a very elaborate argument to prove Christ's superiority to all angelic beings. Mighty beings they doubtless are. A single one of them by a touch destroyed an army of 185,000 men. A single one sitting on the stone of the sepulcher frightened away the whole Roman guard. But Christ is mightier than all the angels. They are but His obedient servants, nay, the servants of His disciples, "ministering spirits sent to serve those who will inherit salvation" (1:14).

8. Witnessed to by the Father

"But about the Son he says, 'Your throne, O God, will last for ever and ever,/ and righteousness will be the scepter of your kingdom./ . . . / In the beginning, O Lord, you laid the foundations of the earth,/ and the heavens are the work of your hands" (1:8, 10). This is the language of the Father to the Son. With the deepest reverence the eternal God addresses Jesus Christ as God and Lord. How can any reverent heart ever doubt again the deity of Jesus? Rather should we in humble fellowship with the Father's testimony bow at His feet and cry, "My Lord and my God."

9. Witnessed to by the Holy Spirit

"God also testified to it by signs, wonders and various miracles, and gifts of the Holy Spirit distributed according to his will" (2:4). The miracles of Christ were all testimonies by His Father and by the Holy Spirit to His divine character. The forces of nature, the powers of hell, the germs of disease, the dread monster Death itself, were all subject to His command, and His mighty works give emphasis to His authoritative words and seem to say, "This is my Son, whom I love. Listen to him" (Mark 9:7).

10. The Head of Redeemed Humanity and Lord of the Millennial Age

It is not to angels that he has subjected the world to come, about which we are speaking. But there is a place where someone has testified:

> "What is man that you are mindful of him,
>   the son of man that you care for him?
> You made him a little lower than the angels;
>   you crowned him with glory and honor
>   and put everything under his feet."

> In putting everything under him, God left nothing that is not
> subject to him. Yet at present we do not see everything subject to
> him. But we see Jesus, who was made a little lower than the an-
> gels, now crowned with glory and honor because he suffered
> death. (2:5–9)

That is, man as a race has not yet attained his lordship over the world, but
the Son of man has. We see Jesus exalted as Lord of all, and we know that
His people will share the glory which He has achieved. He is already
crowned King of the millennial earth, and is waiting only until all the many
sons that have been given Him shall be brought unto glory for the final
manifestation.

11. The Conqueror of Death and Satan

By the grace of God He tasted death for every man, and "since the
children have flesh and blood, he too shared in their humanity so that by his
death he might destroy him who holds the power of death—that is, the
devil—and free those who all their lives were held in slavery by their fear of
death" (2:14–15). He who speaks to us as our great Apostle has not only
come from above and dwelt on earth with man, but He has also penetrated
the underworld of death and hell and brought back its spoils. Therefore, He
can now speak with authority as He gives to us eternal life and declares, "I
am the Living One; I was dead, and behold I am alive for ever and ever! And
I hold the keys of death and Hades" (Revelation 1:18). Satan has no power
to resist the authority of His Word, and death is spoiled of its awful sway.

12. Greater Than Moses

"Jesus has been found worthy of greater honor than Moses, just as the
builder of a house has greater honor than the house itself. . . . Moses was
faithful as a servant in all God's house, . . . But Christ is faithful as a son
over God's house. And we are his house" (Hebrews 3:3–6).

13. Greater Than Joshua

He is greater than Joshua, their victorious leader into the Land of Promise,
for He, too, is leading them into a better rest, and as the Captain of their salvation bringing many sons unto glory. "For if Joshua had given them rest,

God would not have spoken later about another day. There remains, then, a Sabbath-rest for the people of God; . . . Let us, therefore, make every effort to enter that rest" (4:8–9, 11).

14. The Living Word

"For the word of God is living" (4:12). Not only is He the Messenger of the truth, but He is Himself the Truth. Therefore He is called by the disciple who was nearest His heart, the Word of God. God has not merely spoken to us in articulate sentences but by a living Personality. Like the ancient prince who begged for the freedom of his captive queen, and the conqueror sent him not a written answer to his plea but his very queen herself with the message, "This is my word of reply," God has given us Jesus as His highest, sweetest, last Word; and when we receive Him we have within us as part of our very mind, the heart, the will, the thought of God. This mighty Word is here described as "living and active. Sharper than any double-edged sword, it penetrates even to dividing soul and spirit, joints and marrow; it judges the thoughts and attitudes of the heart" (4:12). Will we receive Him as God's Word to us? Will we hear Him say, "Today, if you hear [my] voice,/ do not harden your hearts" (3:7)? And will we follow Him as the Captain of our salvation until He leads us into all the fullness of the Land of Promise, the rest of faith and the will of God?

CHAPTER 2

OUR RESPONSE TO GOD'S MESSAGE

We must pay more careful attention, therefore, to what we have heard, so that we do not drift away. (Hebrews 2:1)

See to it, brothers, that none of you has a sinful, unbelieving heart that turns away from the living God. (3:12)

Today, if you hear his voice,
  do not harden your hearts
  as you did in the rebellion. (3:15)

Therefore, since the promise of entering his rest still stands, let us be careful that none of you be found to have fallen short of it. (4:1)

Let us, therefore, make every effort to enter that rest, so that no one will fall by following their example of disobedience. (4:11)

God has spoken. This is the first message of Hebrews. But what response does He expect from us? That is our present message, and it is answered in the passages quoted above.

PAY CAREFUL ATTENTION

"We must pay more careful attention" (2:1), or as the King James puts it: "we ought to give the more earnest heed." The word "heed" is derived from "head," and it means that we should give our most earnest and careful attention and consideration to the great Messenger whom God has sent from the throne to bear His last word to men. How little attention we give to His Word! Preoccupied with a thousand other things when we hear it, and distracted afterward by the whirl of the world's cares, pleasures and temptations, it scarcely finds a lodgment in our minds, and birds of the air bear away the fallen seed from the trodden wayside. "Consider carefully how you listen" (Luke 8:18). If God has sent His only Son as His last Messenger to men, He expects us at least to listen to His message. "This is my Son, whom I love," He says; "Listen to him" (Mark 9:7).

But not only does He demand attention, but retention. "So that we do not drift away [slip, KJV]" (Hebrews 2:1). The word means "to leak out as from a broken vessel." How much leakage there is in our recollection of sacred things! How soon we forget! The word is also translated by some "lest we should slip away from them." How soon forgetfulness leads to backsliding! It is not enough that we should have hold of the truth, but we want the truth to have hold of us.

Beloved, we are living in a day when men and women easily slip away from the authority of the words of Christ. To do this is to drift from all the moorings of safety and find yourself afloat at last on the downward tide of ruin. Cling to the Word of God. Believe it, and let it keep you from the perils of time's last days.

SEE TO IT

"See to it" (3:12) or let us "take heed" as the King James translates it. And to what shall we see to? That we not only hold to the Word, but that we believe it. "See to it . . . that none of you has a sinful, unbelieving heart that turns away from the living God" (3:12). The Bible must not only be understood but believed. It is not given for speculation, but for simple, absolute, implicit faith. The word unbelief is translated in the margin "disobedience," and the connection between faith and obedience is indeed very close. The old Saxon word "believe" originally meant by a simple inversion "to live by," and we will always find that we live by that which we believe. The only secret of a right life is a true faith, and the only proof of a true faith is a life committed to our creed and reflecting it in our conduct. Do we believe the Word of God and are we living by it, putting our whole weight upon it and making it the standard, the safeguard, and the guide of our whole life?

HEAR HIS VOICE

We must hear His voice. Or to use a word common in the King James: Let us *hearken.* "If you hear his voice,/ do not harden your hearts" (3:15). As we have seen, it is not only the spoken and the written Word, but it is the living Word in the heart, and His voice is often so still that we will fail to hear it unless we have the hearkening ear. The first condition of hearing is the desire to hear, the readiness to listen to the Master's voice, and to know and to do His will for us in everything. God's covenant with His people was, "If you listen carefully to the voice of the LORD your God and do what is right in his eyes, if you pay attention to his commands and keep all his decrees, I will not bring on you any of the diseases I brought on the Egyptians" (Exodus 15:26). It was not enough to obey what they knew already, but it was essential that they should be watching and waiting to know His voice in everything and at all times. It was the failure to do this that lost Saul his kingdom and brought upon him the solemn warning and reproof, "To obey is better than sacrifice,/ and to heed is better than the fat of rams" (1 Samuel 15:22). God will always be ready to speak if we are ready to listen, but if we close our ears and refuse His counsel He may leave us in silence to our ignorance and folly. Let us listen to the Holy Spirit. Let us be in touch with the Shepherd, and we shall know His voice and follow Him in perfect safety through every dangerous path of life.

LET US FEAR

"Since the promise of entering his rest still stands, let us be careful [let us therefore fear, KJV] that none of you be found to have fallen short of it" (Hebrews 4:1). This is founded especially on the typical connection between Joshua, the ancient leader of Israel, and the Lord Jesus Christ, the great Captain of our Salvation. The word "Jesus" here used in the King James (4:8) undoubtedly refers to Joshua, which was the Old Testament name of Jesus. The Land of Promise into which Joshua brought the people of God was simply the type of the better inheritance into which Christ the great Captain of our salvation is bringing His people. Certainly it did not refer to our future heaven, for there, there will be no Canaanites and no conflicts. It was the type of the present rest into which Christ is bringing His willing people. It is of that He says in this passage, "Since the promise of entering his rest still stands" (4:1), and we who have believed do enter into rest. There is for us in Christ an inheritance of reality, of victory and of peace as different from the condition of the average Christian as the Land of Promise was different from the weary wanderings of the wilderness. Now there is a promise left us of entering into this rest. That promise is repeated over and over again in God's Word. "You will keep in perfect peace/ him whose mind is steadfast" (Isaiah 26:3), is the ancient Hebrew form of the promise. "Come to me, all you who are weary and burdened, and I will give you rest" (Matthew 11:28), is Christ's new edition of the promise turned into a great request. "The peace of God, which transcends all understanding, will guard your hearts and your minds in Christ Jesus" (Philippians 4:7). This is the bequest divided among the children, and proved in the actual experience of life.

Now if this is left to us it becomes a very serious thing for us to fail to receive it. It would be a very serious thing to allow your father's will to go by default and waste the great inheritance which amid sacrifice and toil he spent his life accumulating for his loved ones. And how much worse is it to waste the purchase of the precious blood of Christ and allow to be of no effect His costly sacrifice and His infinite gift of love! "How shall we escape if we ignore such a great salvation?" (Hebrews 2:3). How serious it is even to seem to come short of it! It is not the danger of a life of open wickedness that is here pointed out; it is a life that just barely misses God's best. It only comes short, but loses it just the same.

Was there ever a more pathetic story than that of the tribes that marched behind the pillar of cloud and flame, that came right up to the gates of Canaan, and yet right there at the very threshold failed to enter in? Was there ever a sadder spectacle than those ancient millions turning back into the desert day after day and year after year, in that endless round of fruitless wandering, until at last they sank and perished in the sands? They just came short, that was all. They reached the borders of the land. One day more and they would have been across. But they hesitated, they doubted, they feared, they disobeyed and they failed. They were willing enough next day to go, but God refused to let them. They had missed their opportunity. They had come too late. Well may we fear this coming short of entering into His rest. Well may we "make speed" to enter in.

It marks the difference between two classes of Christians—the one, the wanderers in the wilderness, the other, victors of the Land of Promise; the one ever learning and never able to come to the knowledge of the truth, ever seeking and never obtaining, with just enough religion to make them wretched, just enough light to know how much they have lost. But the saddest part of it is not merely its influence upon themselves, but its influence upon others. Not only do they lose, but their work suffers, their testimony for Christ is in vain, their prayers are unanswered, and their lives are a reflection upon their Lord as well as a disappointment to themselves and everybody else.

MAKE EVERY EFFORT

"Let us, therefore, make every effort [labor, KJV] to enter that rest" (4:11). There is such a thing as laboring for rest. The struggle of war is necessary to bring the victory of peace. The toil of busy years is the prelude to affluence, retirement and repose. The full surrender in which we die to some strong self-will is the pathway through which we rise to a new and better life. There are some things that we must let go in order to keep. There are crisis moments through which a soul must pass in the throes of a great conflict ere it can find lasting peace. And so there is a moment in every life when we meet God, and by a supreme surrender enter into His sovereign will and His perfect peace.

John Bunyan tells us of his significant dream when his soul was struggling to enter into the better life. He saw a company of happy women dwelling in a region of celestial light, and bearing upon their faces the expression of infinite rest and blessedness. Many of them were faces that he knew among the saints of God. But he was not among them. A great wall rose between, shutting him out in the cold and cheerless darkness. He wept and struggled to find some entrance, until at last he discovered the secret passage under the wall, but so narrow that he could not get through with all his belongings. But then he heard their voices calling him and telling him that if he was willing to part with all, he, too, could pass within the narrow gate and enter in. At length after a painful struggle he was able to leave his impediments and possessions, and slowly pressing through the narrow passage he awoke to find himself in this Land of Light. "Let us, therefore, make every effort to enter that rest" (4:11). God has been leading you up to it all your days. There is some decisive act, some supreme surrender, some great letting go or taking hold which He will show you, which probably He has shown you, and in which you will find the problem solved, the die cast, the door opened and the land possessed. So may He help you to labor to enter into His rest.

But the word translated "labor" has a slightly different literal meaning. "Make speed," is its exact force. It calls to instant action, and thus it harmonizes with the previous message, "Today, if you hear his voice,/ do not harden your hearts" (3:15). There are some things which in their very nature must be done quickly or they lose their effect. There are processes that will bear slow, deliberate action, but there are great decisions that must be instantly made, and advance movements that must be carried forward as the walls of the fortress are stormed by swift and sudden assault. When God is calling to some great decision there is no time for Paul to confer with flesh and blood, for Elisha to go home and bid his friends farewell or for the young disciple to wait until he has buried his father. It is today, "As was said before:/ 'Today, if you hear his voice,/ do not harden your hearts' " (4:7). It is the moment when God is speaking. It is the moment when the resources of grace are waiting to carry you through. That is the time, the only time for action, and God will not brook delay. Is He so calling you today? The moment to answer is the moment He speaks. Oh, then, "Today, if you hear his voice" make speed to enter into His rest. Go forward, step out into the Jordan of death to do all His will: step out into the act of obedience which is calling you on; step out to trust Him in the dark and stand waiting for Him to vindicate you and to carry you through.

Therefore, beloved, since God "in these last days . . . has spoken to us by his Son" (1:2), let us "pay more careful attention . . . to what we have heard, so that we do not drift away" (2:1).

Let us take heed "that none of you has a sinful, unbelieving heart that turns away from the living God" (3:12).

Let us today if we would hear His voice harden not our hearts (3:15).

"Therefore, since the promise of entering his rest still stands, let us be careful that none of [us] be found to have fallen short of it" (4:1).

And, finally, let us make speed "to enter that rest, so that no one will fall by following their example of disobedience" (4:11).

CHAPTER 3

OUR GREAT HIGH PRIEST

Therefore, since we have a great high priest who has gone through the heavens, Jesus the Son of God, let us hold firmly to the faith we profess. For we do not have a high priest who is unable to sympathize with our weaknesses, but we have one who has been tempted in every way, just as we are—yet was without sin. Let us then approach the throne of grace with confidence, so that we may receive mercy and find grace to help us in our time of need. (Hebrews 4:14–16)

After Moses, Aaron. After the great leader and messenger of God to Israel, the Great High Priest. After Jesus as the Apostle of our profession, the writer of this beautiful epistle proceeds to represent Him as our Great High Priest. This is the second theme of the epistle to the Hebrews. Although there were two brief references to His priesthood in previous passages (2:17, and 3:1), yet the regular discussion of this subject commences with our text, Hebrews 4:14, and continues until near the close of the 10th chapter.

There was no figure more impressive in all the imposing ritual of ancient Judaism than the high priest when arrayed in his magnificent official robes. Every part of his garments had a special typical significance. His inner robe of white linen expressed the perfect purity of the Great High Priest of whom he was the type. His outer garments of blue, purple and scarlet were all significant of His high character and lofty functions. The blue signified His heavenly and divine character. The purple proclaimed His royalty; the scarlet His atoning blood. The priest's brow was crowned with a flashing mitre on which were inscribed in jeweled letters, "HOLY TO THE LORD" (Exodus 28:36). His shoulders bore two epaulets, each composed of a massive jewel inscribed with the names of the tribes of Israel. On his bosom blazed 12 many-tinted gems, each bearing in the crystal stone deeply engraved the name of one of Israel's tribes. These jewels on his shoulders and his breast proclaimed at once the power and tenderness of the great High Priest bearing His people in the place of strength and in the place of love.

As he passed into the holy place on the Day of Atonement, having offered the sacrifices of that momentous occasion and bearing the precious blood and the holy incense into the innermost chamber where the Shekinah shone and God manifested His living Presence, awful suspense fell upon the people as they stood waiting outside, for they knew that the fate of the nation hung upon his acceptance. Solemnly and silently he passed within the veil, sprinkled the blood upon the mercy seat, made intercession for the sins of the people, stood for a moment in the awful and immediate presence of Jehovah and then came forth with the signal of divine acceptance. With hands uplifted, he stood at the door of the tabernacle and pronounced upon the waiting congregation the great benediction of the ancient ritual, and then they knew they were accepted in their high priest, and that for another year the cloud of Jehovah's presence would rest upon them still, and the pillar of His guidance lead them forth in safety and victory.

It is not difficult for us to understand how hard it was for the Hebrew mind for one moment to think that any other could usurp a place so sacred and lofty, or claim higher honor and authority than their venerated high priest. And when the author of this epistle proceeds to show them that even Aaron was but the figure of a greater, and that the Lord Jesus Christ whom they had crucified, was the true Mediator and Antitype of Aaron, no wonder that they listened with the gravest questionings and needed the most powerful arguments to persuade them that He could be worthy of such honor. This is the subject of his argument in the epistle to the Hebrews, and it is needless to say that it is as powerful and convincing as the inspired Word of the Holy Spirit might be expected to be, and presents one of the sublimest and sweetest pictures of the Lord Jesus Christ in all the sacred volume. Let us as we follow it "consider the Apostle and High Priest of our profession, Christ Jesus" (Hebrews 3:1, KJV).

HIS FUNCTIONS

These are explicitly defined in chapter five, verse one: "Every high priest is selected from among men and is appointed to represent them in matters related to God, to offer gifts and sacrifices for sins." And again, "That he might become a merciful and faithful high priest in service to God, and that he might make atonement for the sins of the people" (2:17). He was ordained for men in things pertaining to God. He was man's Representative to God just as the apostle was God's representative to men. He was especially the Mediator between God and men in dealing with sin. The ministry of the high priest was specifically on account of sin. His business was to open and maintain relations of friendship and fellowship between an offended God and a sinful people. This involved two ministries.

1. Sacrifice

This our Great High Priest has accomplished by offering Himself as the great Sacrifice. The entire ritual of Aaron and the entire teaching of the New Testament proceeds on the recognition of the necessity of satisfaction to the justice of God through vicarious suffering on account of sin. The primary work of the Lord Jesus Christ was to die in the room and stead of guilty men. "The LORD has laid on him/ the iniquity of us all" (Isaiah 53:6). "Christ died . . . the righteous for the unrighteous, to bring you to God" (1 Peter 3:18). "God made him who had no sin to be sin for us, so that in him we might become the righteousness of God" (2 Corinthians 5:21). There is no ambiguity about these statements. Let there be none about our faith or testimony. The only ground of a sinner's justification is through the precious blood of Christ. "God presented him as a sacrifice of atonement, through faith in his blood . . . to be just and the one who justifies those who have faith in Jesus" (Romans 3:25–26). Salvation is not merely the forgiveness of the sinner; it is the justification of the sinner. It is not mere pardon; it is righteousness. It is not overlooking our account; it is settling our account in full.

2. Intercession

Having accomplished His sacrifice He passed within the veil and there for 18 centuries He has been engaged in our behalf as our Advocate and Representative. His work as our High Priest in heaven is just as unselfish as His work on earth. He is not there for His pleasure, but for our interests. He belongs to us and His one occupation is to represent us, befriend us and help us in time of need. His intercession involves in the first place His presenting to the Father His accomplished sacrifice and claiming on the ground of His finished work for His people all the blessings of the covenant of grace.

Next it involves His constant representing of their interests before the throne as expressed a little later in this epistle: Christ "entered heaven itself, now to appear for us in God's presence" (Hebrews 9:24). "Therefore he is able to save completely those who come to God through him, because he always lives to intercede for them" (7:25). Not only has He secured for us the forgiveness of past sins, but He is constantly securing for us forgiveness and grace for every fault and every need. Therefore we read, "If anybody does sin, we have one who speaks to the Father in our defense—Jesus Christ, the Righteous One" (1 John 2:1), and "If we confess our sins, he is faithful and just and will forgive us our sins and purify us from all unrighteousness" (1:9). His advocacy includes the receiving and presenting of our prayers before the throne, and the mingling with our imperfect petitions of the sweet incense of His merits and righteousness through which we find continual acceptance. He is the strong Angel before the throne who presents much incense with the prayers of all the saints upon the golden altar which is before the throne (Revelation 8:3). Thus we are kept in constant fellowship and can say with holy boldness, "Who is he that condemns? Christ Jesus, who died—more than that, who was raised to life—is at the right hand of God and is also interceding for us" (Romans 8:34).

HIS QUALIFICATIONS

1. He Is Divine

"We have a great high priest who has gone through the heavens, Jesus the Son of God" (Hebrews 4:14). In seeking an attorney to conduct some important case in court it is usual that men should endeavor to secure some person of high standing and superior influence, a great name in the legal profession, one who has access at headquarters and influence in places of authority. Our Advocate is the Judge Himself, the most potent name in heaven and all the universe. His pleas are all demands. His petitions are always claims. The Father always hears Him (John 11:41–42). He has never lost a case, and He is your Advocate. You do not need to retain Him by some enormous fee. You do not need to fear that He will ever be retained by your adversary. His one business is to attend to your interests and represent your case. There is emphatic force in the phrase, "We have a great high priest" (Hebrews 4:14). You have Him. He is yours.

2. He Is Human

He is as human as He is divine. He is committed to the interests of our race. He is one of us. He wears our nature and stands before the throne a Man. "For surely it is not angels he helps, but Abraham's descendants. For this reason he had to be made like his brothers in every way, in order that he might become a merciful and faithful high priest in service to God, and that he might make atonement for the sins of the people" (2:16–17).

3. He Has Passed through the Heavens

He represents not merely the natural life, but the resurrection life. He has entered into the world of the unseen. He has traversed the realms of death. He represents the future life as well as the present. He is able to carry us not only through, but beyond the present sphere and stage of our existence. He has passed not only into the heavens, but through the heavens; as it is expressed in another passage, "[He] ascended higher than all the heavens" (Ephesians 4:10). There is no part of the universe that is not beneath His feet and under His control. He is supreme in authority, infinite in influence and all-powerful in His advocacy and resources. What confidence we may have in confiding all our interests to His almighty hands!

4. He Can Sympathize

He is able to sympathize with us to the fullest possible extent, "for we do not have a high priest who is unable to sympathize with our weaknesses, but we have one who has been tempted in every way, just as we are—yet was without sin" (Hebrews 4:15). "Because he himself suffered when he was tempted, he is able to help those who are being tempted" (2:18).

a. He is able to sympathize with us in our temptations. He has felt the keen pressure, and while He has not yielded to it He knows all the pain, the strain and the horrible contact with the powers of darkness. There is no form of temptation which He has not experienced, and in the hour of painful pressure He is near at hand and "able to help those who are being tempted" (2:18).

b. He is able to sympathize with us in our weaknesses. He knows what it is to be peculiarly susceptible to temptation. He remembers the long fast days, when, exhausted and hungry, the enemy tried to take advantage of His infirmity and make Him eat forbidden bread. And so when you are pressed above measure, in sore extremities, nervous, tired and susceptible to evil influence, He understands. He makes allowance and He will give supernatural help and deliverance if you will but look to Him and never be discouraged.

c. He is able to sympathize with us even in our failures. He can have compassion on the ignorant and on them that are out of the way. He does not judge harshly even the sinner so long as he is willing to forsake his sin and receive the help of the Savior. His one business is to deal with sin and save the erring, and we can come boldly to Him not only when we are right but when we are wrong, for mercy to pardon as well as grace to help.

d. He is able to sympathize with us in our sorrows. There is no form of affliction which He has not shared. Have you mourned in bitter bereavement? He, too, wept at Bethany. Have your felt the keen pang of a false and faithless friend? He, too, was denied by the disciple for whom He had done the most. Have you been betrayed by those whom you had harbored and who had accepted your friendship only that they might have a better opportunity for deception? He, too, felt the kiss of Judas and "knew what was in a man" (John 2:25). Have you been poor and homeless? He had nowhere to lay His head. Have you ever felt the anguish of spiritual desertion and vainly sought your Father's face? He, too, once cried in darkest agony, "My God, my God, why have you forsaken me?" (Matthew 27:46). There is no step on the dark path of human sorrow, not even the last deep plunge of death itself, through which the Forerunner has not passed and in which He does not come back to your side and whisper, "Fear not, for I am with you."

Once, it is said, a timid prisoner was sentenced for some breach of discipline to spend the night in a dark and lonely cell so terrible in its isolation and its gloom that it was the one horror of the prison, and was dreaded almost worse than death itself. He was borne away in chains to his dark and dreary dungeon, and at last flung in upon the damp floor while he felt the loathsome air creep over his vitals and almost choke out his life. As he heard door after door close behind him, and knew that he was there for one hopeless night, far removed from every human voice or ear, buried underground in a living tomb, he sank upon the floor with a gasp of despair and his very reason for a moment seemed to fail him. Then suddenly he thought he heard above him the sound of footsteps, and as he listened he knew that someone was pacing the floor above with measured steps. It was an infinite relief, although he knew not who might be there. And as he listened the steps ceased and a low voice was heard speaking through the floor to him, and saying, "Fear not, I am here; I am the chaplain of the prison. I heard of your terrible fate. I learned that you were here. I knew you could not stand it alone, and want you to remember that I will be here as long as you remain." Instantly that dark vault was transformed into a place of rest. He was no longer afraid. He was no longer alone. Another heart was throbbing by his side. A friend was near with love and sympathy. Beloved, listen in the darkest hour and the loneliest night and you, too, will hear Him softly saying, "And surely I am with you always, to the very end of the age" (28:20); and you will answer back, "Even though I walk/ through the valley of the shadow of death,/ I will fear no evil,/ for you are with me" (Psalm 23:4).

e. He is able to sympathize with us in our physical sufferings and conflicts. The word infirmities is often applied to physical disease, and our Savior was tested in His body as well as in His spirit, and learned in more than one conflict to take divine strength for His physical frame. In the wilderness, when weak and faltering the enemy pressed Him to accept forbidden bread, He left us the lasting message that for man, as well as the Son of man, physical strength may be received not from bread alone but from the mouth of God.

But this epistle tells us of another conflict, "During the days of Jesus' life on earth, he offered up prayers and petitions with loud cries and tears to the one who could save him from death, and he was heard because of his reverent submission" (Hebrews 5:7). This seems undoubtedly to refer to that conflict in the garden when the devil tried to take His life before the time, and He cried to the Father that the cup might pass from Him. We have been accustomed to be taught that His prayer was not heard. But we are told in this passage that "he was heard because of his reverent submission." His life was preserved. There appeared an angel unto Him strengthening Him, and He was able to go through the awful strain of the judgment hall and the

cruel cross, fulfilling every Scripture, finishing every task, and then voluntarily yielding up His own life, and saying, "It is finished" (John 19:30) as
He bowed His head and gave up His Spirit. So He still understands your
disease and pain, your fight for life, your faith that overcomes disease and
lives till your work is all complete through His almighty life and strength.
Let us, therefore, come boldly to His throne for physical help in every time
of need.

f. He is able to sympathize with us in all the steppings and painful discipline of our Christian life. He was made "perfect through suffering"
(Hebrews 2:10). He "learned obedience from what he suffered" (5:8). And
having been made perfect He now comes to perfect us and lead us to glory
by the same path through which He, the Captain of our salvation, went
before. Christ's perfection had no suggestion in it of moral imperfection. It
simply means completeness and full growth. He did not come upon the
scene like Adam, full grown, to bring to us a cast-iron example of holy character, but He was born a little babe and His whole life unfolded in perfect
naturalness and simplicity like ours. And so His trials, temptations and
various situations all came to Him in the course of a perfectly human life,
and He met each of them in detail, just as we meet ours, developing day by
day all those traits of patience, unselfishness and obedience which at last left
the record complete and yet perfectly human. He had learned obedience by
a long and painful discipline, and His life was symmetrical and perfect. So,
now, He comes to walk with us in all the details and teach us step by step
and day by day to finish our course and complete our life-pattern even as
His.

THE PRACTICAL LESSONS OF CHRIST'S PRIESTHOOD

1. Hold Firm

"Let us hold firmly to the faith we profess" (4:14). Let us be true to Him
who is so true to us.

2. Approach with Confidence

"Let us then approach the throne of grace with confidence, so that we may
receive mercy and find grace to help us in our time of need" (4:16). Literally, "Let us draw near." We have perfect access; let us accept it. Let us enter
into our holy privileges and heavenly rights in Him. Let us do it with boldness; let us have perfect assurance of His love and our acceptance, and
without fear or faltering let us come boldly to the throne of grace. Let us
come in the time of need, for He is ready to give us instant help. It is grace
for timely need. We need not wait. The telephone line is always open. The
door is always open. As someone has said, "He is such a handy God." There

need not be one lost link or one instant of failure. Let us make more of the privilege of prayer and come boldly to the throne of grace.

3. Become Mature

"Let us leave the elementary teachings about Christ and go on to maturity" (6:1). Let us follow Him in obedience until the Captain of our salvation shall have made us also perfect through sufferings, and brought us unto glory even as Himself (2:10).

CHAPTER 4

OUR GREAT HIGH PRIEST SUPERIOR TO AARON

But the ministry Jesus has received is as superior to theirs as the covenant of which he is mediator is superior to the old one, and it is founded on better promises. (Hebrews 8:6)

Having shown that our Great High Priest is divine and human, and thus able at once to sympathize with and help us, the author of this epistle next proceeds to show His superiority to Aaron and all the priests of his line. It was very difficult for a pious Hebrew to believe that anyone could succeed or supersede the imposing figure of the great high priest. And so the writer devotes several chapters to a masterly argument to prove the superiority of the Son of God as the One to whom Aaron was but the type and forerunner. In the course of this argument he brings out many points of profound interest and instruction, illustrating the connection between the Old and New Testaments, and showing with great beauty and power the blessed character of our Advocate in the heavens.

A SUPERIOR ORDER OF PRIESTHOOD

Our Great High Priest belongs to a superior order of priesthood. He is not a priest of the Levitical line, but "in the order of Melchizedek" (Hebrews 7:11). This is expounded and expanded with great fullness in Hebrews 7:1–17. This ancient figure looms out of the gray mists of the patriarchal age with a strange dignity and importance. He comes upon the stage of time, as the writer expresses it, "Without father or mother, without genealogy" or pedigree, "without beginning of days or end of life, like the Son of God he remains a priest forever" (7:3). Perhaps it is only meant that Melchizedek's descent is unrecorded, and yet there are many who believe that he was none other than the Son of God Himself anticipating His incarnation, and as Dr. Andrew Bonar once expressed it, "trying on the garments of His humanity a little in advance of the time."

His very name is typical and significant, King of Righteousness. His very office as priest of the Most High God set him forth as the forerunner of Him who came to bring in everlasting righteousness. His very capital was emblematic of his great Antitype. King of Salem, which means peace, foreshadowed the coming Prince of Peace. Meeting Abraham on his return from a glorious campaign, he blessed him in the name of the Most High God whom he represented, and received from him tithes in acknowledgment of his high official character as God's representative on earth. The most striking feature of his priesthood was that he was both priest and king, which was true of no one else in the whole history of the priesthood, except of Jesus only, of whom it was said that He will "sit and rule a priest . . . on his throne" (Zechariah 6:13). Christ as our Great High Priest is also a King with power to answer His own petitions and guarantee to us the blessings for which He intercedes. Now, this is a dignity far higher than any of the priests of Aaron's line enjoyed, and the apostle uses it to demonstrate the inferiority of Aaron to Melchizedek; for when Abraham acknowledged Melchizedek, Aaron and his sons who were then "still in the body of [their] ancestor" (Hebrews 7:10) virtually acknowledged him too as their superior, for as the writer well expresses it, "the lesser person is blessed by the greater" (7:7). If Aaron was inferior to Melchizedek he must, of course, be inferior to Christ, and so the apostle's argument is demonstrated by an inevitable conclusion, while at the same time the picture of our Great High Priest is exalted on the highest possible sublimity.

A SUPERIOR TRIBE

Our Great High Priest belongs to a superior tribe. Aaron and his sons were of the tribe of Levi, but Christ was born of the tribe of Judah, "For it is clear that our Lord descended from Judah, and in regard to that tribe Moses said nothing about priests" (7:14). Judah was the royal tribe bearing the scepter of domination, of which it was said, "The scepter will not depart from Judah,/ nor the ruler's staff from between his feet,/ until he comes to whom it belongs" (Genesis 49:10). Judah always marched first among the tribes of Israel, and Christ's peculiar preeminence is that He is the Lion of the tribe of Judah. In this alone consists a distinct preeminence as well as a line of demarcation separating Him wholly from the whole line of Aaronic priesthood. Indeed, He could not lawfully belong to the Hebrew priesthood, and "if he were on earth, he would not be a priest" (Hebrews 8:4), because they all necessarily belonged to the tribe of Levi. Therefore His priesthood is of a heavenly order and belongs to the great sanctuary in the heavens and the relations of God with sinful men of every race and time.

A HIGHER CALLING AND APPOINTMENT

Our Great High Priest has a higher calling and appointment. The Aaronic priests were set apart by ceremonies of peculiar sacredness, which are described in the 29th chapter of the book of Exodus. But Christ was appointed by far more sacred authority, even by the oath of Jehovah Himself (see Hebrews 7:21). Back of the work of redemption and the gospel of salvation there is a great divine transaction known as the covenant of redemption between the Father and the Son. And this is the source and foundation of all the blessings of grace far back in the ages before the angels sang or sinner fell. The Father and the Son, foreseeing the ruin of the human race, entered into an eternal covenant by which the Son agreed to fulfill all the conditions of the broken law by His obedience and death, and the Father swore that in consideration of this He would give the Son to the people whom He redeemed, and all the blessings which He purchased by His sacrifice. Therefore when He was finishing His earthly work our Lord appealed to His Father in His final prayer, claiming the fulfillment of this covenant, "I have brought you glory on earth by completing the work you gave me to do. . . . Holy Father, protect them by the power of your name—the name you gave me" (John 17:4,11). It was in connection with this covenant that the Father pronounced the solemn oath constituting Christ our Great High Priest. In the 110th Psalm we find David referring to this covenant and oath, saying, "The LORD has sworn/ and will not change his mind:/ 'You are a priest forever,/ in the order of Melchizedek' " (110:4). Our Savior's priesthood and our salvation rest upon a foundation as strong and sure as the Rock of Ages and the everlasting throne.

A BETTER TENURE

Our Great High Priest holds His office by a better tenure. "There have been many . . . priests, since death prevented them from continuing in office; but because Jesus lives forever, he has a permanent priesthood" (Hebrews 7:23–24). With every human generation there was a new family of official priests. Some, like Aaron, were true to God. Some, like the sons of Eli, were sinful men. But our High Priest remains unchanged through the eternal years. He, on whose bosom John leaned, is just as near to us. He, whom your father and mother trusted, is still as real to you. He, who is your Friend today, will be your Friend forever. When the sun has ceased to glow and the heavens have passed away He will remain your everlasting Friend.

A HIGHER AND HOLIER CHARACTER

Our Great High Priest bears a higher and holier character than the priests of Aaron's line. "Such a high priest meets our need—one who is holy, blameless, pure, set apart from sinners, exalted above the heavens" (7:26). He is absolutely spotless, while they were sinful men. He has no guilt to atone for, while they had to offer first for their own sins. While so perfectly human that He can fully represent us, He is so perfectly sinless that all His merits become available for our unrighteousness and sin. Not only does His death expiate our guilt, but the obedience of His perfect life is credited to our account and we become invested with His merits and righteousness and stand in the same place as if we, like Him, had kept God's holy law. At the same time His greatness adds immeasurable worth to His goodness, for He is made higher than the heavens.

MINISTERS IN A BETTER SANCTUARY

Our Great High Priest ministers in a better sanctuary. Aaron's place of service was the tabernacle in the wilderness, but "Christ did not enter a man-made sanctuary that was only a copy of the true one; he entered heaven itself, now to appear for us in God's presence" (9:24). That ancient tabernacle was shifted day by day, and after awhile it perished and passed away. But the heavenly tabernacle is a greater and more perfect tabernacle, "not man-made" (9:11), "eternal in the heavens" (2 Corinthians 5:1, KJV). Not only so, but when He brings us near, He Himself becomes to each of us "a little sanctuary," and the heart of the believer becomes a holy place where God meets him as of old He met the people, and we understand the meaning of such mighty words as these: "He who dwells in the shelter of the Most High/ will rest in the shadow of the Almighty" (Psalm 91:1). "Remain in me, and I will remain in you" (John 15:4). "I will put my dwelling place among you, . . . I will walk among you and be your God, and you will be my people" (Leviticus 26:11–12). In our very heart of hearts we may still come to the altar of sacrifice, the laver of cleansing, the golden lamps with their perfect light, the Living Bread, the sweet incense, nay, even the innermost chamber of the personal presence of God within the veil.

THE MEDIATOR OF A BETTER COVENANT

Our Great High Priest is the mediator of a better covenant. This part of his argument commences at chapter 8:6–13 and is repeated in chapter 10:15–16, so important does he deem it. It draws a striking contrast between the message of the old covenant and the new. Four particulars are specially emphasized. The first is the promise of sanctification. "I will put my laws in their minds/ and write them on their hearts" (8:10). God does not demand of us external obedience merely, but He puts in us the nature, the principle, and disposition to obey. He makes His law the law of our being, and we as naturally follow it as a material body falls to the ground by the law of gravitation, or, as an acorn develops into an oak because the law of the oak is in the heart of the acorn. So He puts His will into our heart as the new constitution and impulse of our nature, and it becomes second nature for us to love it, to will it and to do it.

The second promise of the covenant is His guarantee to give us Himself first, and then to make us His people. "I will be their God," he says, "and they will be my people" (8:10). He does not condition His relationship upon ours, but ours upon His. He takes the initiative and gives Himself to us, and in consequence we give ourselves to Him.

The third promise is His fellowship, intimacy and the personal revelation of His will to us. "No longer will a man teach his neighbor,/ or a man his brother, saying, 'Know the Lord,'/ because they will all know me,/ from the least of them to the greatest" (8:11). He reveals Himself by the Holy Spirit to the simplest child, the most illiterate mind, and to the most humble saint, so that we are not dependent on earthly priesthoods and secondary channels for our knowledge of His will, but we know Him for ourselves as our Father, our Teacher and our Friend.

And finally, the promise of full forgiveness, constant friendship and deliverance from even the consciousness of sin is added: "I will forgive their wickedness/ and will remember their sins no more" (8:12).

A BETTER OFFERING AND SACRIFICE

Our Great High Priest brings a better offering and sacrifice. This great truth occupies a large part of the ninth and 10th chapters (9:12–14; 10:1–14). The sacrifices of Aaron's office were dumb and soulless brutes. The sacrifice of our Great High Priest is His own precious life. The sacrifices were involuntary. They were dragged as victims to the altar. His was voluntary. "Here I am," was His glad cry, as He plunged from the heights of heaven to give Himself to save ruined man. His heart was in it. His love was in it. His will was in it. "By that will, we have been made holy through the sacrifice of the body of Jesus Christ once for all" (10:10). Their sacrifices had no personal merits. His was the life of the holiest Being in the universe, who had no sins of His own to atone for and whose merits are all availing for others. It was the life also of the greatest and noblest Being in the universe and it represents the infinite value which suffices to make atonement even for the sins of the whole world. "The blood of goats and bulls and the ashes of a heifer sprinkled on those who are ceremonially unclean sanctify them so that they are outwardly clean. How much more, then, will the blood of Christ, who through the eternal Spirit offered himself unblemished to God, cleanse our consciences from acts that lead to death, so that we may serve the living God!" (9:13–14).

And finally His sacrifice was once for all completed. Theirs were constant-ly renewed because they never were effectual except as figures of His greater sacrifice which was to come. "But now he has appeared once for all at the end of the ages to do away with sin by the sacrifice of himself" (9:26). It is final and complete and now we are going to enter into all the fullness of its glorious fruition.

THE EFFICACY OF CHRIST'S SACRIFICE

Finally, the efficacy of Christ's sacrifice is greater than that of the ancient priesthood. "(For the law made nothing perfect), and a better hope is introduced, by which we draw near to God" (7:19). "Because by one sacrifice he has made perfect forever those who are being made holy" (10:14). Their sacrifices could not take away from the conscience the sense of sin, but His sacrifice is able to "cleanse our consciences from acts that lead to death, so that we may serve the living God!" (9:14; also see 10:2). Their ministrations brought only temporary blessing and needed to be constantly repeated; His priesthood brings us the promise of eternal inheritance and settles every question forever (9:15). There is no limit to the blessings of His priesthood, but "he is able to save completely those who come to God through him" (7:25). What this uttermost salvation means none of us has fully fathomed. It reaches down to the lowest depths of unworthiness, helplessness and misery. It reaches out to the widest range of sinful men and the farthest circle of human experience and spiritual need. It reaches on to the remotest age of eternity, and it will not have been fully interpreted until the Millennium shall have ended and the ages of glory begun to roll. It reaches to our temporal affairs, to our physical needs, to the outermost extremity of our being, and the innermost need of our heart and life. It is an infinite, everlasting, complete salvation of spirit, soul and body for all time and all eternity. Blessed be His holy name!

Such then is an imperfect picture of the work of our Great High Priest. Saved by His death, how much more are we saved by His life! Not only did He plunge for us to the depths of death and Hades, but He has thrown His glorified life across the gulf that separated us from God and heaven.

An incident in the early life of the late Louis Agassiz, the distinguished naturalist, has been published. When he was a little boy in Switzerland, his mother once sent him with a younger brother across a frozen lake to carry some message to his father on the other side of the lake. After they had started she observed that in the middle of the lake was a great crack in the ice, over which Louis might be able to leap, but which she was quite sure the little brother could never pass, and she tried in vain to call them back, but the wind was unfavorable and she could not make them hear. All she could do was to pray and watch. At length the little fellows came to the crack, and Louis took a long look at it and seemed to be measuring the distance and the ability of his little brother to get over. Then after giving some careful instructions he threw himself across the gulf on his face, forming a living bridge over which his little brother safely passed, and then he gathered himself up and leaped across.

There is One who has for us become the living Ladder that leads from earth to heaven, the living Bridge that spans the great abyss, the Way that carries us through every dark and strange and impossible place. He has saved us by His life. Let us take His uttermost salvation and let us go forth to carry it and to represent Him to the world, which so sorely needs Him, each of us in turn a living bridge over which our helpless brothers may pass to Him.

CHAPTER 5

THE AUTHOR OF OUR FAITH

Let us fix our eyes on Jesus, the author and perfecter of our faith. (Hebrews 12:2)

And without faith it is impossible to please God. (11:6)

So do not throw away your confidence; it will be richly rewarded. (10:35)

Having unfolded the first two themes of the epistle, Christ our Apostle and Christ our Great High Priest, the writer now proceeds to the third—Christ, the Author and Finisher of our faith. Christ our Apostle comes from God to us. Christ our Great High Priest goes from us to God. Christ the Author and Finisher of our faith brings us with Him to God in actual touch and fellowship. Faith is the point of contact, the organ of the spiritual life, the sixth sense by which we come into connection with the unseen spiritual realm all around us. The last portion of the epistle is devoted to a discussion of the nature and effects of faith, and a full unfolding of its influence in the lives of all the long array of holy witnesses who fill the pages of sacred story.

THE NATURE OF FAITH

A very clear and comprehensive definition is given of it in the first verse of the eleventh chapter, "Now faith is being sure of [substance, KJV] what we hope for and certain of what we do not see" (Hebrews 11:1). Many expositions and various versions of this important passage have been given, but the following points sum up substantially the meaning of this definition.

1. A Substantial Reality

Faith is not a mere sentiment, but a substantial reality. The word "substance" carries with it the idea of solidity and reality. Faith is not a mere subjective state of mind, but there is corresponding to it an actual fact of which the confidence faith gives is as a shadow cast by the substance. There are in fact two realities in every instance of true faith. There is first an inward consciousness and confidence which gives to the soul a realizing and satisfying sense of the blessing claimed, and there is secondly an actual blessing, a real fact corresponding to the inward conviction and coming into our personal experience according to our faith. The man who believes in God is not therefore an idealist and a theorist building castles in the air, but he has something reliable to count upon and he can be counted upon to meet our expectations and prove the reality of his confidence. In fact, the only men that have made their mark on the religious history of the world are the men who definitely believed in God and ventured all the weight of their life upon Him.

2. A Present Fact

Faith is not a future hope, but a present fact. It is the substance of things once hoped for, but now not hoped for but believed. The difference between faith and hope is that hope is always in the future, and faith always in the present. Hope is expecting, faith is accepting. The language of the one is, "He will bless"; the language of the other, "He does bless." In the first great object lesson of faith in the Word of God we find God leading Abraham through three tenses: the future, the present and the past. First He says, "I will bless"; next "I do"; and finally, "I have made you a father of many nations." All this, it will be remembered, was said long in advance of the actual fulfillment, and yet God counted it and Abraham had to count it the same, as if it were already accomplished. It is thus that faith takes salvation and exclaims: "The blood of Jesus, his Son, purifies us from all sin" (1 John 1:7). Thus we receive the Holy Spirit and begin to act as if He were abiding in us. It is thus we take the answer to our prayers. "Whatever you ask for in prayer, believe that you have received it, and it will be yours" (Mark 11:24). It is thus we may take His healing and His help, and count upon Him literally as He speaks to us, "Your faith has healed you" (Matthew 9:22). It was thus He gave the Land of Promise to Joshua, saying to him, "Get ready to cross the Jordan River into the land I am about to give to them—to the Israelites" (Joshua 1:2); "I will give you every place where you set your foot" (1:3). And so it is true still that "we who have believed enter that rest" (Hebrews 4:3). This is, perhaps, the most vital and supernatural feature about faith—its power to anticipate the future and call "the things that are not as though they were" (Romans 4:17).

Some years ago a little woman used to attend our meetings in the Tabernacle [Simpson's New York Gospel Tabernacle] very regularly, and she was always giving bright and encouraging testimonies of God's wonderful help and her confidence in Him. She had a very hard life. Her husband was blind and helpless, her family large, and she the only breadwinner among them all.

But she would get up at four in the morning and finish her washing in time to get to the Friday meeting, and she would always have a shining face and a bright, glad message. Her husband was an old soldier and they were entitled to a pension, for which she was steadily praying and believing. One day she came rushing into my office with both hands extended, crying out with exuberant joy: "Oh my dear pastor, I want to tell you the good news. We've got our pension. We've just had a telegram from Washington that it has passed." She could hardly restrain herself for joy as she talked about the change that it was going to bring, the help and comfort for her husband, the leisure for her, for her Christian work, and the means to give to the cause she loved. After she got somewhat through I asked her if the money had come. "Oh, no," she cried, "we may not get the money for a year, but we've got the pension all the same." And so it came to pass. It was a long time that the case went through the slow forms of the department, but all the time she counted the money just the same as if it were already in her hand, and she was planning for the future without a particle of question. She was simply counting on the government and discounting its promises, so that to her the future was substantially present. How much more should we count upon our God and overleap the intervening spaces by that faith which Abraham had, "in whom he believed—the God who gives life to the dead and calls things that are not as though they were" (4:17).

3. It Lives in the Unseen

Faith is not vision, but it lives in the unseen. Its watchword is: "We live by faith, not by sight" (2 Corinthians 5:7). It can step out in the dark and people the barren wastes with creations that have not yet come into being. It can look at the most unfavorable conditions and see them transformed until the wilderness blossoms as the rose. Like Abraham, without being discouraged, it can consider its own body as good as dead, and "against all hope" believe (Romans 4:18). It is the proving of things not seen. Seeing is not believing. Seeing is the material demonstration. Faith is confidence in the word of another, and against its own senses. As we have formerly said, it is a new sense that sees what others cannot see, and hears what others cannot hear, and lives in the world beyond the ken of man's material senses. So Moses believed as seeing Him who is invisible. So David set the Lord always before Him and said: "Because he is at my right hand,/ I will not be shaken" (Psalm 16:8). So the Lord Jesus Christ as He walked through the world could say: "the one who came from heaven—the Son of Man" (John 3:13); "The one who sent me is with me; he has not left me alone" (8:29). So Peter could write: "Though you have not seen him, you love him; and even though you do not see him now, you believe in him and are filled with an inexpressible and glorious joy" (1 Peter 1:8).

4. Faith Is Certainty

Faith is not probability, but certainty. It "is being . . . certain of what we do not see" (Hebrews 11:1), or as some have translated it, it is the "assurance," or the "proving" of things not seen. This brings us to the fact that the word usually used for faith in this epistle is a stronger term, denoting not merely faith, but the boldness of faith. It is the term employed in the 35th verse of the 10th chapter, "Do not throw away your confidence." There are some things which if done at all must be done audaciously. A cavalry charge cannot be made with caution or timidity. When once the order is given it must be all charge and nothing else. The faintest hesitation would defeat the whole movement. The very element of its strength is its abandon. When Peter went out to walk on the water it was too late to feel his way or to resort to the alternative of swimming if he failed to walk successfully. He must either walk or sink, and when afterwards he tried to swim he actually did sink. It must be the natural or the supernatural. And so when we come to deal with God, if it be God at all it is an infinite God. It is as easy for Him to do the hardest thing as the easiest. It is said of Abraham that he "did not waver through unbelief regarding the promise" (Romans 4:20). The Greek is a little finer: he "faltered not." He did not even quiver, but steadfastly pressed forward "being fully persuaded that God had the power to do what he had promised" (4:21)—not only able but abundantly "able to also perform" (4:21, KJV). The difference between believers consists entirely in this element of assurance of faith.

> There are some who believe the Bible,
>   And some who believe a part;
> Some trust with a reservation,
>   And some with all their heart.

It is these who reach the throne and move the world. This is the grain-of-mustard-seed faith which lifts the sycamore tree and levels the mountain. There is power in it. It is the boldness of faith. It is the only faith that is worthy of God or equal to man's emergencies. Let us ask Him for it. Let us cultivate it. Let us exercise and use it. It is the one victorious weapon of our spiritual warfare. It is the one link of connection between helpless man and the infinite resources of God. "Do not throw away your confidence," your boldness, for it "will be richly rewarded" (Hebrews 10:35).

THE IMPORTANCE AND VALUE OF FAITH

1. Partakers of Christ

It makes us partakers of Christ. "We have come to share in Christ if we hold firmly till the end the confidence we had at first" (3:14). It brings us into partnership with our Lord and puts at our command all His resources. The difference between faith and works is that in the one case we do it, and in the other God does it. This was what Christ meant when He said: "Anyone who has faith in me will do what I have been doing. He will do even greater things than these, because I am going to the Father" (John 14:12). There are two in this partnership. They are working together. We are doing His works because He is doing them in us, and this is only while we believe in Him. It is just the same as when the belt is applied all the power of the engine passes into the machine, and when the belt is disconnected the power ceases. Faith is the belt; and while we use it, it brings all the strength of Christ into our being and work.

2. Brings Us into Rest

Faith brings us into rest. "We who have believed enter that rest" (Hebrews 4:3). This denotes that state of victorious rest, that Land of Promise into which we pass when we turn from our own strength and will, and enter into the fullness of Christ. It is a land of rest. It is a life of victory. And so at every step faith alone brings rest and peace. Thus only can the anxious, troubled heart grow still. "You will keep in perfect peace/ him whose mind is steadfast,/ because he trusts in you" (Isaiah 26:3). "All joy and peace" come "as you trust in him" (Romans 15:13). Would you know His perfect rest? "Commit your way to the LORD;/ trust in him" (Psalm 37:5). "Rest in the LORD" (37:7, KJV).

3. Inherits the Promises

Faith inherits the promises. "Those who through faith and patience inherit what has been promised" (Hebrews 6:12). You may give me a check and it may be good, but it is practically useless to me if I keep it in my pocketbook; but if I endorse it, come into personal relations with it, and deposit it in my bank, it becomes available for actual things. But even then I must draw upon it, giving my check for perhaps a score of little needs in detail, and each one will be honored up to the full value of that check. I have simply converted it into coal, food, rent, clothing and the actual necessities of life. It is thus that we take the promises of God. They are blank checks, all signed and endorsed by the potential name of Jesus Christ; but we must put our endorsement on each one, and we must send in our definite check for the things we actually need, and thus the promises become converted into the currency of life, the blessing of every day, the pardon, peace, comfort, strength and help in time of need, which each covers as we claim it. There are tens of thousands of these "very great and precious promises" (2 Peter 1:4). But they must be appropriated, applied and inherited or they become dead letters and drafts that have gone by default. Thus let us inherit the promises and turn them into glorious victories and living experiences.

4. A Rich Reward

Faith has a rich reward (Hebrews 10:35). It has glorious rewards here, but these are nothing compared with the rich reward of which this epistle speaks a little later (11:26). The highest place in heaven today is given to a man who never preached a sermon, built a church or organized a mission. He simply believed God. And Abraham, the father of the faithful, sits at the head of the table, and we behold the translated souls who pass above carried to Abraham's bosom. The first that entered paradise after Christ's ascension was a poor sinner whose hands were stained with crime, but who, in the brief moment before his spirit was torn from his suffering body, sent up one little prayer of faith to the crucified Redeemer hanging by his side, and received the instant response, "Today you will be with me in paradise" (Luke 23:43); and so he passed through those gates as the first ransomed spirit to claim the purchase of the Redeemer's blood, all because he simply trusted Christ and committed his future unreservedly to His mercy. "The work of God is this: to believe in the one he has sent" (John 6:29), and it will bring to us the recompense of the reward. If you can do nothing else for God you can, at least, be like Abraham, who was "strengthened in his faith and gave glory to God" (Romans 4:20).

5. Faith Pleases God

Faith pleases God. "Without faith it is impossible to please God, because anyone who comes to him must believe that he exists and that he rewards those who earnestly seek him" (Hebrews 11:6). Our trust expresses confidence in God, and there is nothing so offensive as to be doubted.

The great Lord Shaftesbury related in Exeter Hall a little before his death a personal incident full of beautiful significance. He said that once crossing the crowded streets of London on a slippery day, a little girl was standing at a crossing in evident perplexity, looking up and down the street and eagerly scanning the faces of the passersby. She gave a keen look at the old statesman, and then with simple frankness stepped up to him and politely asked him if he would help her across the crowded street. He did so with great courtesy and care, and after he had landed her safely on the other side he ventured to ask her why she had selected him. She looked up simply and said: "Why I looked into your face and felt I could trust you." He was very much gratified, took her name and address, and afterwards remarked that although he had often been honored by his queen and his country he had never been so highly honored as when that little girl put her hand in his and told him that she would trust him. How must our Father feel when we doubt Him! Let us please Him by trusting Him more.

6. Our Life Is Sustained

Faith is the principle by which our very life is sustained. "My righteous one will live by faith" (10:38). Not only are we saved by faith, but it is our vital breath and the channel of our constant communion with the sources of our spiritual strength. "The life I live in the body, I live by faith in the Son of God" (Galatians 2:20). The moment we cease trusting we cease receiving, and our life begins to die. It is only as we abide in Him that we live, for He says, "apart from me you can do nothing" (John 15:5).

7. The Secret of Life

Faith is the secret of the life of every saint that has passed on before, and the one testimony of all the cloud of witnesses is: Let us "imitate those who through faith and patience inherit what has been promised" (Hebrews 6:12). We shall take this up more fully later.

PRACTICAL APPLICATION

1. "See to it, brothers, that none of you has a sinful, unbelieving heart that turns away from the living God" (3:12). Let us guard against the evil heart of unbelief.

2. Let us "hold firmly till the end the confidence we had at first" (3:14).

3. Let us "hold on to our courage and the hope of which we boast" (3:6). We must keep our joy or we shall lose our faith.

4. Let us give "diligence to the very end, in order to make your hope sure," and do not "become lazy, but . . . imitate those who through faith and patience inherit what has been promised" (6:11–12). This is earnest work and needs vigilance, diligence and faithfulness.

5. "Let us hold unswervingly to the hope we profess" (10:23). Let us not only cherish it, but proclaim it, and as we tell it to others it will strengthen our own hearts.

6. Let us have patience in the exercise of our faith. "You need to persevere so that when you have done the will of God, you will receive what he has promised" (10:36). God will keep us waiting until He has proved to us and all others that we really do believe Him.

7. Let us be careful of the little shrinkages of faith. "If he shrinks back,/ I will not be pleased with him" (10:38). These are the little soft-winged moths that cut holes in our garments. Let us not wait till the mischief is done, but check the first approaches of doubt and unbelief.

8. Let us look back often and "remember those earlier days" (10:32), and all we have already suffered, and not lose our victory now by casting away our confidence.

9. Let us look forward and remember the rich reward so soon to come, and hold fast our confidence (10:35).

10. Let us look "on Jesus, the author and perfecter of our faith" (12:2) and trust Him to keep it to the end.

CHAPTER 6

THE PATRIARCHS OF FAITH

This [faith] is what the ancients were commended for. (Hebrews 11:2)

That is to say, the men of old, the patriarchs of ancient times, made a record and obtained witness to their high character and achievements only through faith.

The 11th chapter of Hebrews is a star cluster in the firmament of inspired biography. It is more: it is a whole Milky Way crowded with constellations of light and glory. Think a moment of the difference between the heroes of mythology and ancient secular history and the characters of this inspired cluster, and you will be struck with the self-evidencing power of the Bible. Just as the character of Jesus Christ is the supreme evidence of the divinity of His teachings, so these ancient lives bear witness to a source of power and goodness infinitely higher than mere human virtue. Look for a moment at the divinities of heathen religions: the coarse and brutal Ram, the household god of India; the cruel Kali, their supreme female divinity; or even their venerated Buddha himself, who was but a dreamer. Look at the heroes of Greek and Roman history: Aeneas, Romulus, Achilles, Hercules; or at their fabled deities: the imperious Jupiter, the licentious Venus, or any of the real or ideal figures that loom out of the gray antiquity of the world's traditions. Then contrast with them the humble faith of Abel, the holy walk and glorious translation of Enoch, the magnificent spiritual courage of Noah, the overshadowing grandeur of Abraham's life, the triumphant fortitude and splendid coronation of Joseph's sufferings. Note how the very ideals themselves transcend the characters of human history and tradition as high as heaven is above the earth, and prove to us that back of these conceptions there must have been some greater reality that inspired them and some supernatural power that impelled them.

And this really is the secret of the difference: Man's ideals are but human and reflect the imperfection of the human; back of these lives there is divine power, and they are but reflections of God's goodness and God's strength.

In fact this is the essential difference between the heroes of human history and the examples of the Bible. The character of a Washington, a Dewey or a Lincoln stands out in bold relief, and men hold up to the rising generation the virtues and achievements of these distinguished examples as patterns of what we can attain by energy, patience, courage and genius. But the characters of Holy Writ stand forward in the light of something greater and better than themselves. They make no claim to personal superiority. They tell us at the outset that they were but weak and fallible men without strength or virtue, and that all they became and all they accomplished was due to a power behind them.

Take, for example, Jacob in the Old Testament. The one lesson of his life was unlearning, undoing and suppressing his own self-confidence and self-sufficiency. Take the character of Paul in the New Testament. The very watchword of his experience is: "I have been crucified with Christ and I no longer live, but Christ lives in me" (Galatians 2:20). These men exhibit not themselves but the grace of God through which they overcame. Thus they became examples of faith, for faith is just that organ that touches God and brings Him into our life, enabling us to cease from our own strength and draw our life and strength from Him alone.

Let us look at this galaxy of holy character and victorious faith, and as we do so we shall find that it consists of a series of groups each complete in itself, and rising to a climax by successive stages.

The first of these groups consists of the eight witnesses taken from the book of Genesis and reaching from Abel to Joseph. We shall find that these eight patterns cover a complete series of progressive steps in religious experience.

ABEL, OR THE FAITH THAT SAVES

"By faith Abel offered God a better sacrifice than Cain did. By faith he was commended as a righteous man, when God spoke well of his offerings" (Hebrews 11:4). Abel began at the beginning. This is more than a great many are willing to do today. Rather they are learning to climb up some other way and get into the life of Christ a little beyond the cross. The other day a clergyman in the old orthodox Southland flung aside a hymn book with a gesture of impatience because of the hymn, "There Is a Fountain Filled with Blood," which he said was coarse and unfit for refined ears. The idea of a bath of blood was an outrage on good taste. Happily there was another minister present who was brave enough to get up and read a passage in Zechariah speaking of a "fountain . . . opened . . . to cleanse them from sin and impurity" (Zechariah 13:1).

The first thing about Abel's faith was that it recognized his sin. He came as a guilty sinner needing atonement, and bringing a sacrifice. Cain came as a gentleman to exchange compliments with God and present some fruits and flowers as a visitor on equal terms. But God would have nothing to do with him. Faith always takes the sinner's place and then claims the sinner's Savior.

The next thing about Abel's faith was that it brought a bloody sacrifice as the type of the dying Lamb of God. This must always be faith's first acceptable act, to present the blood of Christ as the settlement for our sin and the ground of our acceptance. It was for the sake of this that Abel was accepted, God testifying not of him but of his gifts. God did not look at Abel, but He looked at the lamb, and he, like us, was "accepted in the beloved" (Ephesians 1:6, KJV).

The third thing that happened to Abel was his justification. He was declared righteous. He was recognized as standing in exactly the same relation to God as his great Sacrifice and Representative. And so God pronounces us righteous and treats us as if we were as righteous as His Son and had obeyed every commandment of the law even as He.

And finally Abel received all this by faith. He did not feel it or wait to feel it, but he claimed it simply because it was God's prescribed way. He counted upon it. He took his stand upon it and God made it good to him. And so he was saved in exactly the same way as every poor sinner is today, by coming in simple faith as a sinner, claiming the promise, putting his weight upon it, and going out to act as if it were true for him. There is no finer illustration of the faith that saves than the simple testimony of Hedley Vicars the moment he accepted the blood of Christ to cleanse him from all sin and went forth saying: "If this be true for me I act from this moment as a man who has been cleansed from all sin in the blood of Christ."

ENOCH, OR THE FAITH THAT SANCTIFIES

This is the natural order. Having found Christ as a Savior we next want to walk with Him as our Sanctifier and very life. And so we find the second step of faith in Enoch's life. The first thing we see about him is his walk. He has begun, now he is going on. This takes in every department of our life, our inner experiences and our outward conduct. It is all to be by faith and under the influence of God.

Next we see Enoch's companion. We are not told so much about Enoch as we are about the One with whom he walked. It was not his holiness that was so marked, but that of his Friend. This is the New Testament conception of holiness: fellowship with Jesus, union with God, Christ in the heart, "Remain in me, and I will remain in you" (John 15:4). There is no simpler, deeper, higher definition of the life of faith unless it be the Pauline edition of that truth: "Just as you received Christ Jesus as Lord, continue to live in him" (Colossians 2:6). Sanctification is the Christ life; it is to know Him, to be with Him, to have Him in us, to look to Him every moment and to lean upon Him for everything, drawing our life moment by moment entirely from Him.

Next we are told that he pleased God. The will of God was the rule of his life. The divine acceptance was his constant aim and joy. His supreme purpose was his Master's example, his Master's Word. We can please God too. The best part of it is to want to please Him. A little child full of imperfection can have a perfect heart to please its mother, and even amid all our errors of judgment and stumbling steps our hearts can still turn to Him as the needle to the pole and say: "Lord . . . you know that I love you" (John 21:16).

And finally we are told how Enoch pleased God and walked with God and had the testimony that God accepted and loved him. It was by faith. He just believed in the love of God. He walked with Him in confidence. He looked to Him as a little child. He leaned hard upon His presence and dwelt in the very love-life of his Lord. So let us by faith realize the Master's precious words: "As the Father has loved me, so have I loved you. Now remain in my love" (15:9).

NOAH, OR THE FAITH THAT SEPARATES

"By faith Noah, when warned about things not yet seen, in holy fear built an ark to save his family. By his faith he condemned the world and became heir of the righteousness that comes by faith" (Hebrews 11:7). The difference between Noah and the people of his age is this, that they were living for the present world, building their houses, investing their money, forming their attachments as though the existing order of things was to go on forever, while Noah believed that his present age was condemned and soon to pass away, and all his plans and works had reference to the age beyond on the other side of the flood. They were "eating and drinking, marrying and giving in marriage" (Matthew 24:38), but Noah was building that house of refuge that was to bear him across to his true inheritance on the shores of the new world which faith continually saw before. Thus Noah's was a separated life and it was separated by his belief in the great fact which God told him respecting the destruction of the world by the flood and the new age that was to follow.

So, beloved, our lives must be separated from this present age.

> What I mean, brothers, is that the time is short. From now on those who have wives should live as if they had none; those who mourn, as if they did not; those who are happy, as if they were not; those who buy something, as if it were not theirs to keep;

those who use the things of the world, as if not engrossed in
them. For this world in its present form [that is, the stage show
which is merely being acted for an hour] is passing away. (1
Corinthians 7:29–31)

The only power that can lift us into this and keep us there is the blessed
hope of Christ's coming believed and realized. It will make the next age so
real that the present age will lose its power of attraction and we shall live
under the "power of the age to come." It is one thing to hold the theory of
the Lord's coming; it is another to believe and realize it and constantly live
under its power. This can only be effected through a realizing faith, a faith
that condemns the world as unworthy of our affection and confidence, and
gives us our inheritance in the age to come.

When the old city of Rome was abandoned as the capital of the great
Roman Empire, and Constantinople was selected as the new site, then every
man who was in on the secret would doubtless hasten to exchange his old
possessions in the ancient city of the Caesars, for a little strip of barren sand
on the shores of the Bosphorus, for he knew that in a little while the value of
the latter would infinitely surpass and supersede the former. And so if we are
truly believing in the Lord's return we will be turning all things into the currency of the coming age and investing our lives above. Are we doing so, and
have we the faith that separates us from this present evil age and leads us like
them to live as strangers and pilgrims and "looking forward to the city with
foundations, whose architect and builder is God" (Hebrews 11:10)?

ABRAHAM, OR THE OBEDIENCE OF FAITH

"By faith Abraham, when called to go to a place he would later receive as
his inheritance, obeyed and went, even though he did not know where he
was going" (11:8). In a sense Abraham combines in his own life all the other
qualities already represented. He is the overshadowing figure of ancient faith
and holy character, the father of all who believe, and, as someone has said,
the Christopher Columbus who first stepped out into the new realms of the
spiritual world and discovered new continents of faith and blessing. The first
thing about Abraham's faith is that he obeyed God. Here we see faith not
trying to get God to do something for us, but faith doing something to
please God. If you stop and think you may find that the reason you do not
get more from God is because God has been waiting a good while to get
something from you. Have you learned the obedience of faith? Have you
responded to the call of Abraham's God? Let us take in some of the meaning
of this great act of faith. Modern research has taught us that Ur of the Chal-
dees, where Abraham dwelt, was no semi-barbarous haunt, but a cultivated,
wealthy and important city in ancient Chaldea. In fact, it was a great univer-

sity town, and to this day there are remains to attest its importance and its culture. Here Abraham had dwelt in the midst of every earthly attraction. Probably he had a position of influence, for everything about his subsequent history attests the dignity of the Arab chief, the man of weight and culture. But he was called in a moment to part from all this and go out into a dismal desert across more than 400 miles of barren sands, without even knowing the land to which he was to go, or one step of the way. All he knew was that God had said: "I will be with you." But that was all he asked to know, for the next thing about Abraham's faith that we should note is the fact that he believed God. It was not merely the promise of God, the attraction God held out to him to recompense him for his obedience, but it was God Himself he believed. To him God was a personal reality, and it was enough for him to have God's Word, God's presence, God's guiding hand. Then when he trusted God it was easy to trust His Word. Back of true faith there is more than a truth, more than a promise, more than a creed. There must also be the living personality and the conscious presence of God Himself. This was what satisfied Abraham's faith and made it easy for him to go out, not knowing where he was going, so long as he was going out with God. This is faith. Beloved, is it your faith?

But again, Abraham had next to learn to believe God's Word, for the promise grew more definite and explicit, and soon it became the promise of a country and the promise of a child. But even then it was a promise that, humanly speaking, seemed impossible. The promised child was to be born in his old age contrary to nature, and yet Abraham believed and waited even when men laughed him to scorn, and his faith certainly seemed the wildest fanaticism. He even dared to assume the new name of Abraham, "the father of a multitude," when it would only make him the jeer of all his friends. But still he trusted God and waited for the fulfillment of His Word, and in due time the promise was fulfilled. But once again his faith had to be tested in the severest way, and the very thing that God had given him to be surrendered and given back, although it seemed that it was necessary for the very honor of God Himself that it should be retained. Isaac, through whom the promised seed was to come, had to be laid on the sacrificial altar and God's very own Word appears to become a contradiction. But still he wavered not until every test was confirmed and Abraham stood before the ages the supreme example of faith in God and the father of all that believe.

SARAH, OR THE FAITH THAT TAKES SUPERNATURAL STRENGTH EVEN FOR THE BODY

"Through faith also Sara herself received strength to conceive seed, and was delivered of a child when she was past age" (Hebrews 11:11, KJV). There is something very emphatic in the language here. The pronoun "herself" seems to imply that Sarah was the very last who might have been expected to believe, for indeed she had begun by laughing to scorn the promise of the seed. But the time came when even Sarah herself could not only believe, but could take into her body a supernatural power that, like Mary, in later times gave her a glorious part in the lineage of the coming Savior. We are not told of the struggle through which she passed until at last she came to believe the word which once she had laughed to scorn, but we know that God had transformed her doubts into supernatural trust and given through her to the ages the first object lesson of that faith that can take the life of God into our mortal frame and renew our youth like the eagle's. This is the lesson which Samson's life afterwards taught and which the great apostle expresses when he says, "so that his life may be revealed in our mortal body" (2 Corinthians 4:11). This is divine healing in its truest lesson, the very life of God Himself lifting us above the human and anticipating even here the coming resurrection.

ISAAC, OR THE FAITH THAT SUFFERS

The patience of faith is one of the largest sections of every true Christian experience. God has given us the story of Isaac to illustrate it. His was the faith that could yield up his own life at his father's command and lie down without a rebellious word on the altar of Moriah. His was the faith that could let another choose for him the object of his dearest affections, and the wife of his bosom. His was the faith that could give up his wells as the Philistines pressed upon him and pushed him from place to place. His was the faith that could renounce his choice of his favorite Esau and give the blessing to Jacob at God's command. All through it was a life of self-renouncing faith and love, the love that "is patient, . . . is kind" (1 Corinthians 13:4), that "always protects, always trusts, always hopes, always perseveres" (13:7), and "never fails" (13:8). Beloved, it is only faith that can teach us patience. It is only when we know that we have something better that we can let the present good go by and the present wrong be forgotten, and wait for God to vindicate and recompense.

JACOB, OR THE DISCIPLINE OF FAITH

Jacob stands before us as the type of a life that began with poor materials and had to be cut and polished at every point by keen affliction until at last "he learned obedience from what he suffered" (Hebrews 5:8), and the man of earth was transformed into the Israel of God. There is no place where we need faith so much as when God is chastening us and the heart grows discouraged and we are tempted to think that He is against us. It is then that we need to believe in His everlasting love and lie like plastic clay in the potter's hand, or like the gold in the consuming crucible and say: "When he has tested me, I will come forth as gold" (Job 23:10). Are you there today? Trust Him. Let your eyes see your teachers (Isaiah 30:20). Take the lesson He is so severely teaching. Thank Him that He loves you with inexorable love and will not let you go astray, and some day you will bless Him most of all for the things that hurt you most keenly now. It was not Abraham, it was not Isaac, it was not Joseph, but it was Jacob, the chief of sinners and the meanest of men, that became God's patriarchal prince, the head of Israel's tribes and the one who gave his own new name of Israel to the race that shall endure when dynasties and empires shall have passed away.

JOSEPH, OR THE FAITH THAT OVERCOMES SORROW AND TURNS THE CURSE INTO A BLESSING

Space will not permit us to dwell on this illustrious prince further than to say that through all the depths of his humiliation and anguish which were not, like Jacob's, on account of his own sin and folly, but simply through the wrongs of others, there was one golden ray of light that illuminated every dark place. And it was this: that God was in it and above it all. "You intended to harm me," he could say to these wicked men, "but God intended it for good" (Genesis 50:20). Only when our faith can see His overruling hand, His ultimate and victorious purpose, shall we also be able to rise above our sorrows and glorify Him even in trials.

Standing once on the banks of the St. Lawrence during a summer holiday, I threw my little ships of paper and of pine into the stream beside me, and I noticed that they all flowed upward against the stream. At first I wondered, and said, "Am I mistaken, does the river run the other way?" Then I looked into the center of the stream and saw a great log sweeping down toward the rapids a little below. "Why no," I said, and I looked again and then I understood. "Ah, this is but an eddy on the shore and things are not what they seem." And so, beloved, if you look at the things immediately around you they may often appear to be going in the wrong direction, but if you will look up to God and fix your faith upon the great midcurrent of His love and faithfulness, you will find that one unvarying purpose of blessing is running through it all and you will know that "in all things God works for the good of those who love him, who have been called according to his purpose" (Romans 8:28).

God give us the faith of Abel that saves; the faith of Enoch that sanctifies; the faith of Noah that separates; the faith of Abraham that obeys; the faith of Isaac that endures; the faith of Jacob that learns; and the faith of Joseph that overcomes wrong and sorrow and turns every midnight into morning; and finally, above all the faith of Jesus, "the author and perfecter of our faith, who for the joy set before him endured the cross, scorning its shame" (Hebrews 12:2).

CHAPTER 7

THE SEVEN TYPES OF FAITH

By faith Moses' parents hid him for three months after he was born, because they saw he was no ordinary child, and they were not afraid of the king's edict. (Hebrews 11:23)

This passage (Hebrews 11:23–31) contains a separate cluster of stars in the firmament of faith. The last group was taken from the book of Genesis. This includes seven types of faith selected from the next period of Bible history, from Moses to Joshua. This also forms a complete group and, like the other, reaches a climax. It covers a period of trial and conflict as the story of faith ever does. The night is necessary for the stars, and it is out of the darkness of trial that the brightest examples of divine grace and human trust shine forth in every age. Just as it is true that the golden age of a nation's literature is often an age characterized by stirring and trying events, so in Christian experience and Bible story the most illustrious examples of holy character, high achievement and lofty faith are wrung from the bosom of anguish and forged in the flames of affliction.

FAITH FOR THE FAMILY

Here we see the germ of Moses' future life and Israel's history in the breast of a humble mother and a godly father. They were two slaves in the brick fields of Egypt, and all that has come down to us from them is their name and the record of this mother's faith. But there was a spark of celestial fire in those lowly breasts, which kindled all the flames of faith and power that afterwards consumed the hosts of Pharaoh and lighted the torches of Israel's marvelous revelation. Eternity alone will reveal how often the life-story of some illustrious man started in a mother's bosom, and grew out of a little germ of maternal trust even as the mighty oak out of the little acorn.

The cruel law had gone forth that every baby boy should die; but as this mother looked on her little one she saw he was a beautiful child. What mother ever saw anything else in her babe? But her faith saw deeper than even a mother's love. And although it might be death to her as well as to her babe to conceal it, yet she dared to defy the king's commandment, and when she could no longer conceal her treasure God led her to devise the little ark of bulrushes, and then to wait beside the stream until she was called to exchange the place of mother for that of nurse, and bring up the little life that she had committed in faith to the hands of God. Blessed privilege indeed to have the strength of a father's faith and a mother's prayers behind us. Blessed resource for a parent's heart to have the same God still to whom we may confide the lives that are dearer than our own, and the tasks that are too hard for us. Beloved, have you covered the heads of your precious ones with the sheltering wing of a covenant God?

Once, it is said, Audubon, the great naturalist, while collecting specimens in South America, saw a little bird fluttering in great excitement over its nest. He soon discovered the cause. A huge black snake was slowly climbing up the tree to devour the little birdlings and the mother was vainly struggling to beat him off. Suddenly she shot into the forest and soon afterwards returned with a trailing vine in her beak which she softly spread over the nest, and then went back for more, until she had securely covered the little ones and tucked them in beneath the leaves of this strange plant. Then she sat over on a branch and watched the issue. The snake still crawled steadily up, but when he reached the vine there was something in it that evidently distressed and repelled him. He shrank from it as from a poisonous breath. Again and again he tried to crawl around the tree and approach the nest without touching this thing. But it was all in vain, and at last, disgusted and angry, he dropped from the tree and coiled himself up in despair upon the ground, while the little bird chattered out its joy and praise and seemed to thank the heavenly powers for their protection. So God has given to us not only our salvation, but for the protection of our homes and our loved ones, the leaves of the tree of life which we place about their defenseless heads and defy the serpent's sting.

There is a promise in the New Testament which many of us read only half way through: "Believe in the Lord Jesus, and you will be saved." But there is another clause: "you and your household" (Acts 16:31). Why should this be true only of our salvation? You have taken that promise for yourself; take it for your child; take it for your brother; take it for every unsaved member of your household. Claim it and hold fast to it until, a reunited family above, you thank Him that His Word is just as true for you as for the little family of old in Egypt's bondage and on the shores of the Nile.

FAITH FOR OUR INDIVIDUAL CHOICE

"By faith Moses, when he had grown up, refused to be known as the son of Pharaoh's daughter. He chose to be mistreated along with the people of God rather than to enjoy the pleasures of sin for a short time" (Hebrews 11:24–25). There comes a time when even the mother's prayers cannot be a substitute for our personal responsibility. Then we must act and choose for ourselves. Moses had the benefit of a mother's teachings as well as a mother's faith, and when the crisis hour came he was true to the convictions that she had instilled into his youthful mind, and he stepped out and assumed for himself the full responsibility of faith.

His religious life began as every life really does, in a true purpose, in a right choice. It is the will that is the helm of life. It is our choice that determines our destiny. Two lives opened before the young Hebrew standing out in clear relief and separated as far from each other as pole from pole. One was a life of honor, luxury and power; in fact, all that the world at its best could offer, for he was the heir to Egypt's throne, and there was nothing within the scope of human ambition which he might not have claimed. The other was a life of danger, affliction, sacrifice, possibly violent death through the vengeance of those whose kindness he refused; and yet withal the blessing of God and the fellowship in suffering, and reward of God's people. But the prospects and the recompenses were all in the distance. The allurements were all at hand, and only the eye of faith could make real the overbalancing value of the things of God and eternity. But Moses had that higher vision which makes the distant and the unseen more real than the present. He had respect unto the recompense of the reward, and without a moment's hesitation he made his choice. He said one eternal "No" to the world, and one everlasting "Yes" to God. He gave up a throne and a crown, and he chose his lot among the afflicted people of God, regarding "disgrace for the sake of Christ as of greater value than the treasures of Egypt" (11:26). This is the very essence of faith. This is the first principle of consecration. This is the root of piety. This is the fear of the Lord which is the beginning of wisdom. This is the crisis of every soul. This was the great temptation in the wilderness when the Master refused the devil's splendid bribe and chose instead the will of God alone. There are two sides to this great decision. There is a choosing; there is a refusing. There is a "Yes," there is a "No." Beloved, have you spoken the decisive word? Have you said "Yes" to God without reserve? Have you said "No" to the world and self and sin?

FAITH SEPARATING FROM THE WORLD AND MAKING GOOD ITS CHOICE

"By faith he left Egypt, not fearing the king's anger; he persevered because he saw him who is invisible" (11:27). The time came when the will must become the deed, and the choice must be translated into action. That time came when the preparations were complete for the departure of the children of Israel from the house of bondage. It was a step of the most serious danger. Pharaoh had bitterly refused and opposed it, and his reluctant consent had been slowly wrung from him; but Moses knew at the last that consent would be withdrawn and that all the power of Pharaoh's armies would be used to draw them back, but "by faith he left Egypt, not fearing the king's anger," and bravely marched forth until he found himself with Pharaoh's chariots behind him and the rolling flood before. And so, beloved, your decision must be proved. God will take you at your word. He will put you to the test and He will help you, like Moses, to persevere "because he saw him who is invisible."

And yet it is just this that renders many a decision abortive. There are thousands of souls in heathen lands who believe the gospel and have lost all faith in their old traditions, but they dare not step out and confess their faith and risk the sacrifices that are sure to be involved; the grief and anger of their heathen friends, the loss of influence, reputation, employment, family and sometimes of life itself. And there are thousands in the homeland whose decision for God is rendered comparatively impotent by the compromises they make with the world, and their failure to be out and out for God, to forsake Egypt like Moses and stand unequivocally on the side of Christ. Unless you dare to confess your Lord and let your former associates know just where you stand, you will be sure to be entangled once more and drawn back perhaps to a life of sin.

It is interesting to notice how Pharaoh tried to keep them back from leaving Egypt. He was willing for anything but this. First, he said they might sacrifice to the Lord, but they must do it in the land. And so the devil is willing that we should have all the religion we want, but we must not leave the world. Next, when beaten from this position he said they might go out of the country, but they must not go very far away. And so the enemy tries to compromise again and lead us to give up the evil things of the world but hold the harmless idols. Baffled in this, he made a third compromise. He was willing that they should go, but they must leave their children. And so the devil's next move, if he cannot get us to the theater and the dance, is to take our children. We begin to lower the standard of Christian life for the young and consent to a license that we would not claim for ourselves. Finally, Pharaoh fought his last compromise battle on the ground that they and their children might go, but they must leave their property. If the devil cannot have us, he wants our business, our investments, our money. We can have the Sunday, but he must have the six days of the week, the bank book and the safe, the stock exchange and the spirit of Mammon. And so millions today have made the compromise, and the result is that every year in this so-called Christian country 200 million dollars are spent for whiskey and tobacco and about 10 million for the spread of the gospel [editor's note: this was originally written in March of 1900]; 200 dollars given to the devil for every dollar given to the Lord. What the Church of Christ needs today is what Dr. Chalmers used to call an "oot and oot" religion, that is the broad Scotch for "out and out."

FAITH APPROPRIATING THE BLOOD OF CHRIST

"By faith he kept the Passover and the sprinkling of blood, so that the destroyer of the firstborn would not touch the firstborn of Israel" (11:28). All our choices, separations and sacrifices are vain until we come to Calvary and reach the sprinkled blood. "What would Jesus do?" is not the question until first we have understood what Jesus has done, and accepted it for our salvation. It is this alone that gives us acceptance with God. It is this alone that takes away the paralyzing blight of guilt and sin. It is this that puts us to death in His dying and brings us the new life of His resurrection. It is this that not only atones for the past but, by feeding on the flesh of the Lamb of God, gives us divine strength for the future. Never let us get away from the blood. Never let us cease to feel the heartthrob which those precious words should bring to every ransomed soul,

> Dear dying Lamb, Thy precious blood
> Shall never lose its power.

A silly minister sitting beside a dying saint forgot himself enough to say to her that it must be a great comfort to her in her dying hour to be able to reflect on a well-spent life. "Yes," she said, "it is." And then with a little twinkle even in her dying eye she looked hard at him and said: "But, my dear pastor, the well-spent life on which I am reflecting is not mine, but that of Jesus Christ, my Savior; and I am occupied in putting my good works in one bundle and my bad works in another, and turning from both to Christ."

FAITH STEPPING OUT AND GOING FORWARD ON THE WORD OF GOD

"By faith the people passed through the Red Sea as on dry land; but when the Egyptians tried to do so, they were drowned" (11:29). This is a fine description of the act of faith—stepping out on the word of God and acting as if it were true. Their way apparently was utterly closed. Behind them was the pursuing foe, before them, the pathless flood. There was no way of escape, and yet the word came: "Go forward." Whither? There was no other way but into the darkness and into the depths of the sea, and it was not until they had stepped forth into the very margin of the flood that the waters rolled apart and opened a pathway for their trusting and obedient feet. So faith must not only accept, but also act. It must take its stand upon the Word of God. It must venture on it. It must count it true and simply step out as if it were an accomplished fact.

"Thank you, Captain," said a grateful general to the private soldier who had saved his life by a sudden act of heroism. He was not a captain, but his general's word was enough for him, and looking up quietly answered, "Thank you, General. Of what company?" He simply went forward and acted according to his master's word, and he found it good. So not only at the entrance, but all along the way of faith we must act upon the Word of God, put our weight upon it, risk our life upon it, face impossibilities upon it and then find the sea divided, the stone rolled away, the mountain become a plain and the darkness and shadow of death turned into the morning.

FAITH OVERCOMING AND ENTERING INTO THE FULL INHERITANCE OF PROMISE

"By faith the walls of Jericho fell, after the people had marched around them for seven days" (11:30). Here we pass at a bound over 40 years of Hebrew history, and from the Red Sea to the other side of the river Jordan. The wilderness is passed, the Land of Promise is before them, the realization of their grandest hopes is about to begin, the inheritance of faith is awaiting their grasp. But it must be taken also by faith.

There is a formidable barrier lying across their path. There always is when God has some new and glorious experience for us, something too hard for us, some crisis hour, some midnight conflict, some towering Jericho which we cannot leave behind us. It is then, like Jacob, that we must get alone with God, and through the narrow place of trial come into a large place of exalted blessing and life-long victory. Perhaps some reader of these lines is there today. The struggle through which you are passing is to decide your whole religious future. It is God's opportunity for your spiritual triumph. God can bring you through, but only by faith can the walls of your Jericho fall down. The first thing is to believe that it is possible, that it is for you, that it is for you today. And then take the place of faith and stand fast through all the seven days and the sevenfold test, until the shout of victory shall ring, and prayer shall be turned to praise. Beloved, have you taken this higher step of faith? Have you not only left Egypt but entered Canaan? Will you take God for it, and will you press on until it becomes for you, as for them, a glorious realization?

You will notice that all the interval including the 40 years in the wilderness is omitted in this record. There was no faith in it and it did not count. And so all your years are lost and you have only your pains for your labor until you believe God and enter into the rest of faith and the fullness of your victory and your inheritance.

THE FAITH THAT LIFTS AND SENDS

Hebrews tells us about the faith that lifts and sends the vilest sinner into the highest place of blessing and sends us forth from the fullness of our blessing to save the lost.

"By faith the prostitute Rahab, because she welcomed the spies, was not killed with those who were disobedient" (Hebrews 11:31). The story of Rahab is strangely interwoven with the victory of Joshua. The book that tells us of the highest Christian life quickly reminds us of the mercy of God for the vilest sinner, and bids us blend the work of salvation with the higher work of sanctification. The heart of God is as much concerned in seeking and saving the lost as in leading His people into a higher blessing. Let us, like Him, ever be found close to the publicans and sinners. The very best proof that we have reached the Land of Promise will ever be that we are found seeking to save the Rahabs all around and plant the Cities of Refuge for the manslayer and sinner. How beautiful to know that He who raised poor Rahab from the ranks of deepest sin to be the mother of our Lord in His human lineage still waits to lift the most lost and helpless to the very highest place of blessing!

"What are these and whence came they?" we might ask as we look upon the radiant clouds that gather about the setting sun, and the answer would be: "These were the foul and fetid miasmas that came from the swamps and marshes, but yonder sun has transformed them into the glorious forms that wait upon the chariot of his ascension." "What are these and whence came they?" we might ask about the shining pages on which the beautiful words of inspiration are printed, and the answer might be: "These were filthy rags trodden by the passing throng, reeking with uncleanness, but they have been cleansed and purified until they became the very messengers of God and leaves from the Tree of Life." "What are these and whence came they?" will be asked some day by the visitors from distant worlds as they gaze upon the faces and forms of ransomed saints around the throne, and a voice will answer: "These were Rahab the harlot, and the dying malefactor; these were vile and sinful men, but they 'have washed their robes and made them white in the blood of the Lamb' (Revelations 7:14)."

This is God's great laboratory of grace, God's living miracle of love, God's sweetest, highest, most enduring work. He lets us have a part in it. Saved ourselves, let us live to save and serve, and let us remember that the secret of all our power to save is the same old secret by which we were saved ourselves—faith and faith alone.

> Lord, give us such a faith as this,
>   And then whate'er may come,
> We'll taste e'en here the hallowed bliss
>   Of an eternal home.

CHAPTER 8

LIGHTHOUSES OF FAITH

And what more shall I say? I do not have time to tell about Gideon, Barak, Samson, Jephthah, David, Samuel and the prophets. (Hebrews 11:32)

Lighthouses indeed they were, these men of faith that illuminated the darkest periods of Old Testament history from the time of the Judges to the great reformation under Samuel. Sad as was the story of the wilderness when Israel wandered for 40 years, it was not half so sad as the declension after Joshua's conquest of Canaan and the glorious inheritance of the Land of Promise, which was not for 40, but for 400 years. But the lighthouse is not kindled for placid seas and sunlit skies, but for starless nights and raging storms. And so these troublous times brought out the highest and noblest types of faith and character in all the story of the past. In like manner it will be found that in our own experience faith is born not of favorable circumstances and comfortable surroundings, but of deep afflictions, temptations and sorrows.

Out of this humiliating chapter of Israel's history, the apostle selects half a dozen unique examples of the highest faith and the noblest achievement. Each is a distinct type, and all together form a third series and reach a still higher climax.

GIDEON, OR FAITH FINDING STRENGTH THROUGH WEAKNESS

1. Gideon's Call

We see this illustrated in Gideon's call. Hiding from the Midianites in his threshing floor, and trying by stealth to thresh a little grain for his daily supply, Gideon is visited by the angel of the Lord and greeted with this surprising message: "The LORD is with you, mighty warrior" (Judges 6:12). Never was mortal more startled and mortified by such a message. It seemed as if even God was mocking him. He, a mighty man of valor, indeed! Rather might he be called a miserable coward. And very naturally he began to remonstrate and tell of his own insignificance and the overwhelming trials that had fallen upon his people. But God quickly reminded him that it was not his might, but the might of Jehovah in which he was to go, and that taking this by faith he was, notwithstanding all his insignificance, a mighty man of valor. "Go in the strength you have," said God, "and save Israel out of Midian's hand. Am I not sending you?" (6:14). And so Gideon put on the strength of God by faith, and a little later we find this striking expression regarding him: "Then the Spirit of the LORD came upon Gideon" (6:34), and henceforth the feeble coward was the mighty man of valor.

2. Gideon's Company

We see this illustrated in Gideon's company. At his summons 32,000 men gathered from Israel to fight the battle of freedom. But God told him that he could not use so many. And so the sifting process began. Reduction is not always loss. When that diamond is cut back from 600 carats to less than 100, its value is multiplied 10 times over, and every new facet cut in its form adds to its glorious luster. And so when God would strengthen His work He often reduces its apparent proportions. First, He allowed them to sift themselves as He still often does with us. Gideon was ordered to tell all the timid ones that they might go home, and soon 22,000 men were marching back. In like manner, still, God often frightens away from a work the people that are in the way. He makes the reproach so heavy and the sacrifices so great that they cannot stand it, and they leave to find something easier and more honorable.

But there are still too many. It is necessary that they be sifted again. As they drink from the brook all those are set aside who drink with weariness and caution, dipping up the water like a dog from hand to mouth and watching meanwhile against surprise, while the rest, who go down upon their knees and drink with reckless abandon as though there were no danger and no foe to watch are sent away. These men will not do for the Lord's work. He wants hearts that are alert, minds that are wide awake, and soldiers that He can depend upon. Let us not think that faith means dullness. God does not need a great many men, but He must have the right kind. So Gideon's 300 are all that are left, but these are enough, and with this little host Midian's myriads are hurled back in disaster and destruction.

3. Gideon's Conflict and Victory

Again we see this principle illustrated in Gideon's conflict and victory. The battle must be fought by faith as well as the army prepared. First, Gideon must get his token from the Lord and know that it will be victory. With a single companion he is sent to Midian's hosts to reconnoiter, and as the two listen on the borders of the camp, lo! a Midianite has awakened from his sleep and is telling his comrades the dream he has just had of Gideon's cake of barley tumbling into the host of Midian. That is enough. It is God's token of coming victory. Gideon hastens back to prepare for the assault. Surely the weapons of that warfare are weapons of faith: fragile pitchers, useful only when they are shivered into broken fragments; flaming torches and rude trumpets proclaiming the name of God and the sword of Gideon—this is all. And these still are weapons of our victorious warfare. We, ourselves, must become as broken vessels, and then the light will shine through our displacement, and the message which we ring out will become the power of God to the salvation of men and the destruction of the enemy. It is still as true as ever that the greatest hindrance to God's working is dependence on human genius, wealth, influence and power, and that the men whom God is using today are the men that have learned to say with Paul, "Therefore I will boast all the more gladly about my weaknesses, so that Christ's power may rest on me" (2 Corinthians 12:9).

When tens of thousands were thronging Mr. Moody's meetings in London, the leading journal of England sent an experienced reporter to find out the secret of his power. He listened for several days and then declared that he could see nothing in the manner or the matter of the evangelist's addresses to interest such multitudes of people or to explain this movement. When Mr. Moody heard of it he laughed quietly and said: "Why that is the very secret of the movement, that there is nothing in it that can explain it but the power of God." It is " 'Not by might nor by power, but by my Spirit,' says the LORD Almighty" (Zechariah 4:6).

BARAK, OR THE PRESENT TENSE OF FAITH

Barak had gone forth at the call of Deborah, willing to take second place to a woman in the work of the Lord, and to receive from her lips the keynote of his victory. Very finely does she give it in Judges 4:14. Her name signifies a bee, and there is a wholesome sharpness in her words that might well wake him up from his languor and delay. "Go!" she cries, "This is the day the LORD has given Sisera into your hands. Has not the LORD gone ahead of you?" Here we have the very essence of faith. It is stepping out to meet a God that has already stepped out in front of us. It is not waiting for something to turn up, or hoping for something to happen, but it is instant action, accepting and not expecting.

One day I listened to a very humble African-American as he told the wonderful story of his experience and the way God had used him, which I knew to be true. He told us that all this had begun by his one day taking literally a single verse in the eleventh chapter of Mark: "Whatever you ask for in prayer, believe that you have received it, and it will be yours" (11:24), or, as he put it: "Believe that you take them and you've got them." Sinner, Christ meets you as He met the paralytic at Capernaum, saying, "Your sins are forgiven" (2:5). If you believe it this moment it is true for you. Discouraged and defeated one, He meets you as He met Gideon, and He says: "The LORD is with you, mighty warrior" (Judges 6:12). If you take Him at His word it becomes a living fact in your experience as it was in Gideon's. Sinful, struggling soul, He says to you: "You are already clean because of the word I have spoken to you" (John 15:3). If you take it, it is true for you and you go forth cleansed through His precious blood. Sick one, this is the secret of your healing. "The prayer offered in faith will make the sick person well; the Lord will raise him up" (James 5:15). And this is the prayer of faith: "Believe that you receive and you have." God is always speaking in the present tense. He lives in one "eternal now," and this is where faith must also dwell with Him, moment by moment taking Him for each new deed and having only what we take. Oh you who are lingering, leaning, and losing your blessing, "Go! This is the day the LORD has given [your enemy] into your hands. Has not the LORD gone ahead of you?" (Judges 4:14).

SAMSON, OR THE FAITH THAT BRINGS PHYSICAL STRENGTH

If Samson had lived today he would have been the leading man in all our college clubs, and no price would have been too high to secure him for the football team, and the athletic tournaments that so rapidly are turning American brains into heels, hands, punching bags and prize fights. But Samson's strength was not that of physical brawn, but a far more subtle and supernatural power. It came to him through the touch of faith and the Spirit of God. Away back in those Old Testament times we have three people who provide object lessons of this kind of strength that even a material age can appreciate: the strength that enabled Abraham and Sarah to defy the decaying power of age and natural infirmity, and claim the fulfillment of the great promise of a child when naturally it was impossible, and the strength that clothed Samson with more than Herculean power when probably his own frame was not physically stronger in himself than any of his fellows. Samson's strength could not have come from gigantic stature or exceptionally developed muscle, for we know that in a single moment he lost it, and yet he had probably not lost an ounce of weight, but had touched the forbidden earth and lost the secret of the Lord. Samson's physical strength was a vital principle that came to him from the unseen world and the living One, and it came to teach us that there is for our mortal frame a life and strength in God which we may claim as surely as the power that quickens our soul. For One has lived on earth since Samson's day who contained in His own human frame the power that could raise the dead and heal the sick, and who has become for us, in His resurrection life, the second head of redeemed humanity and the living Source from which we can take our perfect life for body and for brain. "We are members of his body" (Ephesians 5:30), of His flesh, and His bones, and His life is revealed in our mortal body.

But Samson teaches us one lesson more; namely, that the supernatural life of God in the human body is dependent upon our separation from the world and sin. We can retain it only while we live in His holy will, and we lose it whenever we touch the forbidden world of evil. There is nothing that is so sanctifying as the life of Christ in your mortal flesh. There is nothing else that so holds you to a life of separation and dedication. If Christ is dwelling in your body that body must be used as His holy temple and for the things that Christ Himself would do if He were living in your place. This then, beloved, is one of the providences of faith, to take the Lord for supernatural strength, and give it back to Him in living sacrifice and loving service.

JEPHTHAH, OR THE FAITH THAT KEEPS FAITH WITH GOD

Jephthah was an outcast. He was born under discouraging circumstances, repudiated by his father's house, and covered with a stigma of reproach from his mother, for which he was not responsible. But instead of giving up to discouragement, he turned to God for help, and God always loves to take up the cause of the wronged one. Is there a soul within reach of this message whose life has been crushed by some misfortune, wrong or hereditary entailment for which you were not to blame? Beloved, Jephthah's God will be your Vindicator and your almighty Friend. Even if there has been wrong and fault and folly, and you are suffering from the effects of your own mistake, still there is One that will "repay you for the years the locusts have eaten" (Joel 2:25), and undo the bitter past. And so the time came when Jephthah's brethren turned to him to lead the forlorn hope of their country's struggle, and with his brave freebooters to give them back their freedom. Jephthah was not slow to respond, and in due time his courage was crowned with victory. As he prepared for the battle he vowed to give to God the first thing that he should meet, and the sequel gave a singular opportunity for illustrating another of the highest qualities of faith. It was his one and only daughter that he met leading the triumphal dance of Israel's maidens in celebration of his victory. "Oh! My daughter!" he cried, as he rent his clothes, "You have made me miserable and wretched, because I have made a vow to the LORD that I cannot break" (Judges 11:35). We do not believe that this sacrifice meant the literal immolation of his child on an altar of blood, but rather the dedication of her life in perpetual virginity to the service of God. This is confirmed by the later references (11:37, 40). What all this meant to Jephthah and his daughter can only be understood by one who realizes all that posterity meant to an Israelite, especially to a ruler like Jephthah, who longed for an heir, and more especially to every Hebrew woman, who felt herself the possible mother of the coming Messiah.

But Jephthah was true to his pledge. Not for a moment did he falter in his purpose of obedience, and so he stands to latest ages a type of the man who not only can count upon God, but a man upon whom God can depend.

If you expect God to keep faith with you, how can you forget that God expects as much of you? Therefore, faith and obedience go hand in hand. Oh, to live so that God can say of us as He said of Abraham, "I know him." I can depend upon him, I can fulfill to him all that I have promised.

DAVID, OR THE FAITH THAT CAN WAIT GOD'S TIME AND STILL CLAIM GOD'S PROMISE

David was anointed king over Israel years before he ever sat upon his throne. Indeed the very first result of his anointing was a long period of persecution, trial and the apparent defeat and defiance of all that God had given. For nine years he wandered a refugee in the mountains of Judah, hunted for his life by the hate of Saul; and still through it all, he counted himself God's anointed king and held himself with the lofty dignity of an heir of promise.

So faith on our part can discount the future, and while the promise seems to tarry, still hear His voice whispering: "Though it tarry, wait for it; because it will surely come, it will not tarry."

Next we see the faith of David strengthening his hands for battle and girding him with power in the conflict with his foes. Speaking of this in the Psalms he says, "It is God who arms me with strength" (18:32). "He trains my hands for battle;/ my arms can bend a bow of bronze" (18:34). It was faith that fought the battle with Goliath. It was faith that went into every conflict asking God, "Shall I go and attack them? Will you hand them over to me?" It was faith that took the victory before the battle began and gave God the glory. So still we fight the good fight of faith, and like David may exercise the faith by which God's heroes "whose weakness was turned to strength; and who became powerful in battle and routed foreign armies" (Hebrews 11:34).

But the last and perhaps the highest exercise of David's faith was in the dark hour of its eclipse, when through subtle temptation he sank into his double crime and fell under the judgment of his God. That is the darkest hour in the history of the soul, and only faith can save it from utter despair. It was then that David's faith reached up from the depths and the darkness until it found God and put on record its simple and sublime confidence in that tender penitential Psalm, in which deeply conscious of His guilt and sin he still could cry in his confidence in the power of divine grace: "Wash me, and I will be whiter than snow" (Psalm 51:7). To believe that God could thus save him from the uttermost to the uttermost was indeed a faith that reaches down to the deepest experiences of New Testament times.

SAMUEL AND THE PROPHETS, OR THE FAITH THAT HEARKENS AND THEN SPEAKS FOR GOD

It was Samuel that began his life of faith by the simple response: "Speak, for your servant is listening" (1 Samuel 3:10). This is the first attitude for all that would be messengers and voices for God. They must first hearken and be good listeners before they learn to speak. The true watchword of every effectual witness for God must ever be: "The Sovereign LORD has given me an instructed tongue,/ to know the word that sustains the weary./ He wakens me morning by morning,/ wakens my ear to listen like one being taught" (Isaiah 50:4).

And having learned to hear, Samuel next was as faithful in repeating the message and giving forth the word of God. Therefore he became the prophet of the Lord and founder of the school of the prophets which remained through all succeeding times the truest body of men among all the classes of ancient Israel. When kings and priests and princes failed, still the prophets were true to God. The prophetic office has been continued in the New Testament Church. It does not consist merely of men who can foretell future events, but is thus defined: "Everyone who prophesies speaks to men for their strengthening, encouragement and comfort" (1 Corinthians 14:3). He, then, who speaks to men to edify, exhort and comfort is a true prophet of the Lord. God wants men in this and every age who can thus represent Him, who can catch the message from above and echo it out around the world. But our words are weak and vain unless we get them first from God. Our messages must be burned into our souls. Our texts must take us before we take them. Our preaching must be the giving out of our very life. We must get the Word at His mouth and warn them from Him. Then the least message that we speak by the wayside, in the inquiry room, in the hospital, in the prison or from the pulpit will be a prophetic word. It will go just as far as the height from which it comes. God will go with it and "it will not return to [him] empty,/ but will accomplish what [he] desires/ and achieve the purpose for which [he] sent it" (Isaiah 55:11).

A man may speak ever so eloquently; he may prepare his address with scholarship and rhetoric and polished sentences; he may give it with the most impressive elocution; and yet it may be the voice not of a prophet, but of a parrot. He is simply repeating something that he has heard from man. It is the message of God the world wants, and it is the men of God that must give it. Oh, for the faith that knows how to get from Him His word for the age in which we live, His message to the men of today, and give it to all the world.

CHAPTER 9

THE CLOUD OF WITNESSES

Therefore, since we are surrounded by such a great cloud of witnesses, let us throw off everything that hinders and the sin that so easily entangles, and let us run with perseverance the race marked out for us. (Hebrews 12:1)

The writer has already given us three distinct star clusters in the firmament of faith, and now he sums up a great multitude, of whom the time would fail to tell individually, in one mighty cloud of witnesses, identified rather by their achievements than by their names. His mind becomes lost in a cloud of light, a great Milky Way, as it were, of countless stars spanning the sky of his holy vision. But there is no confusion. The examples fall into distinct classes, and stand for definite lessons of faith and obedience.

THE CLOUD ITSELF

Let us look at the cloud itself. It contains four classes of witnesses representing first, the achievements that spring from faith, or what faith can do; next, the personal qualities that spring from faith, or what faith can be; third, the sufferings of faith, or what faith can endure; and finally, the blessings that faith can claim from God, what faith can receive.

1. The Achievements of Faith

"Who through faith conquered kingdoms, . . . shut the mouths of lions, quenched the fury of the flames, and escaped the edge of the sword;. . . who became powerful in battle and routed foreign armies" (Hebrews 11:33–34). Three classes of achievements are here described. The subjugation of kingdoms refers to Joshua and David; it was by faith that they won their great inheritance. Let us not think that there are no kingdoms left for us to conquer. There are mightier victors still than Alexander or Tamerlane. "Better a patient man than a warrior,/ a man who controls his temper than one who takes a city" (Proverbs 16:32).

There are kingdoms of self-conquest that cost more than a cavalry charge or a bombardment from besieging armies, and there are kingdoms of glorious service for God and the world which are being won by the heroes of faith in every age. When Robert Moffat entered South Africa as a physical and moral wilderness and left it not only one of the richest provinces of the British Empire, but one of the most successful of modern mission fields, a kingdom was subdued more valuable than the empires of the Caesars. When David Livingstone fought and won the battle of his own education and preparation for the ministry, and then went forth to traverse all the heart of Africa and win it from barbarism to civilization, commerce and Christ, and to leave upon the hearts of the natives the memory of his own high character and stainless goodness, so that for his sake the white man is still treated with kindness and reverence in the regions through which he passed, Livingstone subdued a kingdom whose worth can never be told. When William Duncan sat down amid the inhospitable regions of northern Canada and out of the wild forest and wilder Indian tribes slowly built up a settlement and a colony of civilized and Christian natives, who can be seen today in the village of Metlakatlah—an object lesson of Christian civilization, with their industries, schools, chapel and happy homes—surely it is a kingdom for which earthly heroes might well lay down their crowns. When John Geddie passed up to his great reward from the New Hebrides and left upon his tombstone this simple epitaph telling the story of 30 years of self-denying triumph: "When he came there were no Christians, when he left there were no heathen," surely it was a triumph for which angels would gladly leave their thrones. And there are such kingdoms still left in the wide field of this sinful world, if only we have the faith and love to win them for God. As Joshua said to the men of Ephraim when they asked him for a larger inheritance: "Go to the mountains and conquer for yourself all you want. You can have as much as you will subdue" (author's paraphrase of Joshua 17:17–18). So still God is saying to every aspiring soul: "I will give you every place where you set your foot" (Joshua 1:3). You may conquer your own kingdom. You may forge your own crown. You may win as much as you will dare. Never was there an age with such possibilities of heroic faith and self-denial as today.

> The Son of God goes forth to war,
>   A kingly crown to gain,
> His blood-red banner streams afar,
>   Who follows in His train?

Next he speaks of those who through faith achieved deliverance from dangers. Three kinds of dangers are mentioned; namely, wild beasts, the elements of nature, such as fire, and the sword of cruel men. Of course, this includes the story of Daniel in Babylon, of his three companions who passed unscathed through the fiery furnace, and of Peter who was rescued at the last moment from the sword of Herod in answer to the faith and prayers of the disciples. But the story of divine deliverance did not end with the age and the page of inspiration. Still the heroic servant of the cross can tell of the tiger of the jungle shrinking away from the fearless eye of the undaunted missionary; of the stormy wind becoming a calm, or the becalmed vessel being saved by the breeze that came in answer to the prayer of the suppliant missionary, and bore them safely from the cannibal shore; and of the oft-repeated story of the Covenanters in Scotland, of the Waldenses in Italy, and of missionaries in pagan lands, who were saved from the cruel hatred of their persecutors by providential interpositions supernatural and divine. Dr. Paton tells of a night when the savages had surrounded his cottage and determined to have his life. But afraid to venture into his immediate presence, they set fire to the outbuildings of his home, and the wind was fiercely driving the flames to the house itself. But the good man calmly prayed to God, and lo, the wind was changed to the opposite direction and the flames were swept back into the faces of the foes, who fled in dismay, pursued by the missionary as he shouted to them the warnings and threatenings of his God; and they flew as from an avenging angel.

When the story of our individual lives is all told in the light of eternity, and we see the hidden dangers from which the hand of love has oft delivered, how we will wonder and adore the God of faith, and praise Him for the faith of God!

There is still a third class of achievements; namely, victory over adverse circumstances and armies—"routed foreign armies" (Hebrews 11:34). Doubtless he was thinking when he wrote these lines of David's triumphs over the Philistines and the later victories of Abijah, Asa, Jehoshaphat, Josiah, and Hezekiah, and of the legions who tried in vain to capture Elijah and found themselves outwitted, stricken with blindness or with death; or, of Elisha, surrounded by heavenly horses and chariots. But the story of victory over difficulties and enemies is not yet ended. Every great work for God has to face opposition and attack, and our strongest weapon still is to believe and wait, and to see our God triumph, until instead of fearing and hating our foes, we shall pity them from the depths of our hearts and pray for them in tender compassion, as we behold their humiliation and ruin.

Beloved, shall we claim our place among the conquerors of faith and count all the difficulties and foes that surround us this very hour as only God's challenges to win a crown, and God's opportunities to enable us to prove the possibilities of faith and the power of God?

2. The Personal Qualities Which Faith Gives

"Who through faith . . . administered justice . . . whose weakness was turned to strength" (11:33–34). This is what faith can be. Spiritual righteousness and both spiritual and physical strength—these are its personal fruits. There is no greater miracle in Bible history than the personal characters of the men of faith. See Daniel in Babylon, against whom his foes were obliged to say: "We will never find any basis for charges against this man Daniel unless it has something to do with the law of his God" (Daniel 6:5). Note the three men who could answer Nebuchadnezzar's threat with the lofty defiance: "O Nebuchadnezzar, we do not need to defend ourselves before you in this matter. . . . We want you to know, O king, that we will not serve your gods or worship the image of gold you have set up" (3:16–18). These men were a greater stumbling block and wonder to the heathen world than even the miracle of their deliverance. There is nothing mightier than personal goodness and virtue, and it is today the strongest proof of the power of faith and the grace of God.

The London *Christian,* in publishing a sermon of Rev. F.B. Meyer, related the following incident concerning it. Among the hearers was a very rough and ill-tempered man, of whom his wife and family had often cause to be much afraid. That morning as he returned from church his wife met him with terror, for she had just had the misfortune to drop the cage containing his favorite canary, killing the bird, and she expected as usual a violent storm and a cruel beating; but to her amazement he simply smiled when she told him, and said, "Never mind, Mary, I am glad it was not you." Her little boy was looking on behind the scene, and afterwards came up to his mamma and said: "What's the matter with papa? I thought he'd nearly kill you, but he didn't do nuffin'." Yes, it was the other side of the sermon. It was the faith that "works righteousness" which tamed his wild and savage heart into gentleness, and made the desert blossom like the rose. It has done it, beloved, for you and for me, and it can do it for any temperament, in the face of any situation, and it can do it this moment if you will only believe and receive.

Then faith is just as effectual for physical as for spiritual strength. The faith that strengthened Sarah to become the mother of the seed of promise, that made Samson mightier than the giants of Philistia, can still heal the sick and bring the life of Jesus to "quicken our mortal bodies" (Romans 8:11, KJV) and still make it true of us as of our fathers: "Who through faith . . . whose weakness was turned to strength; and who became powerful in battle and routed foreign armies" (Hebrews 11:33–34).

3. The Sufferings of Faith

Its supreme power appears in the hour of trial. Every variety of suffering is here described. There is pain, shame, privation, temptation and even death itself. But faith not only enabled them to endure, but even to triumph over persecution, pain, reproach and death. "What can your Christ do for you?" they asked the little martyr of Antioch as they beat him before the judges and the soldiers until he was almost insensible. "My Christ," he said, "can make me so happy that I scarcely feel your blows." And when they stretched him on the rack until life was almost gone, they brought him back and asked him again: "What can Christ do for you now?" "He can make me love my enemies," the hero answered, "and pray for those who despitefully use me and persecute me." Once more the awful ordeal was renewed and once more they brought him back from death to torture him with the same question, and he meekly breathed out his last breath with the sweet reply: "My Christ can take me to Himself where I shall never suffer pain again." Such was the story of ancient martyrdom 10,000 times repeated by noble children, heroic maidens, venerable fathers, insulted mothers and a great cloud of witnesses of whom the world was not worthy. No longer are we compelled to prove our faith at such a cost, but there are daily martyrdoms, there are little annoyances, there are ceaseless fires of humiliation, temptation and pain that are often harder than one great sacrifice, but still the grace that comes to faith can suffer long and be kind, can endure all things, and even count it pure joy when we face trials (James 1:2). It is not merely suffering that God asks, but triumphant suffering, suffering that keeps its love, its sweetness, its shining face and triumph song, and for the joy set before us "endure the cross, scorning its shame" (Hebrews 12:2).

4. The Promises and Blessings of Faith

The last class of witnesses in this catalog includes those who through faith "gained what was promised" (11:33), and received blessings from the hand of God. This is the highest province of faith. It is not so much what we do, what we suffer, what we are, as what we take from Him. Faith is just an open hand and all its power comes from outside itself. It brings us into contact with God and receives His all-sufficiency, for He gives what He commands and supplies what He requires. Therefore the chief business of faith is not so much to be as not to be. Its very weakness is its strongest plea. Therefore we find that those who took most from God through faith were not strong men but feeble women. The very height of its achievements is this: "Women received back their dead, raised to life again" (11:35). Still faith can take from God as much as it will dare to claim. The treasure house is as full, the promise as large, and the need is as vast as in the days of old. Still there are "given [to] us his very great and precious promises" (2 Peter 1:4), and "everything we need for life and godliness" (1:3), and still we may "[receive] a faith as precious as ours" (1:1) to claim these promises and receive this fullness of His power. This is today the great province of faith, and the men who know how to use this victorious weapon are the men who as in the days of old shall once more prove what faith can do, can suffer, by what faith can receive. So let us take the fullness of our inheritance that we may give it back in service to God and blessing to the race.

THEIR WITNESS TO US

What is the message of this cloud of witnesses to us? What is our relation to them?

1. They Encompass Us

Somehow we are closely related to them. They have preceded us in the race and perhaps they are watching us now as spectators from the galleries. There is an inspiration in a noble past telling us that what man once did man may do again. "Soldiers," said Napoleon to his little band at the battle of the Pyramids, "from yonder pyramids 40 centuries are watching you to see you do your duty." But this cloud of witnesses covers more than 40 centuries. The good of all the ages are perhaps surveying us as we follow on; at least we may survey their glorious example and follow in their footsteps.

2. They Call Us

But they call us to run the race ourselves. This is not a mere play that we are looking at for our entertainment. It is for us a tremendous and a living reality. We are standing in the arena. We are in the dust and heat of the conflict. Our crown is still at stake. Our very life is hanging in the balance. For us it means the most strenuous endurance. It is not a dream of sentiment, and it is not a piece of fine art, but it is a sober and awful reality involving the stake of every interest that the heart can hold most dear.

3. It Means Careful Preparation

It means the most careful preparation for the contest. "Let us throw off everything that hinders and the sin that so easily entangles" (Hebrews 12:1). In the athletic contests of today we find the competitors are willing to sacrifice every appetite and indulgence while training for the course, and in this heavenly race there are things to be laid down, sacrifices to be made, self-denials to be proved without which we cannot hope to win the prize. The sin which so easily entangles us must be laid aside, whether this be some easily entangling habit into which we are most likely to fall, or simply the sin of unbelief against which the whole force of this epistle has been directed, the one sin which leads to all other sins. But not only so, there are also weights as well as sins that must be laid down, things not necessarily wrong in themselves, but things that hinder us in our course, which each heart must learn from its own experience and the voice of a sensitive con-science. " 'Everything is permissible'—but not everything is beneficial. 'Everything is permissible'—but not everything is constructive" (1 Corinthians 10:23). The question is how does it affect our spiritual life, our love to Christ, our readiness for service, our power in prayer? It is by this that we must decide the question of what is best. The prize is too precious, the issue too vast, and eternity too long to be weighed in the balance with any bauble of earthly pleasure or earthly gain.

4. Run with Patience

We must run the race with patience. Not by paroxysms of sudden enthusiasm, but by the slow and steady plod of a life of patient endurance shall the struggle be won and the victory be made complete. Faith must learn to stand as well as to run, and having done all, at last to stand approved and crowned.

5. Receive the Fullness of the Promise

But after all that has been said the apostle adds that these glorious witnesses failed to receive the fullness of the promise. "God had planned something better for us so that only together with us would they be made perfect" (Hebrews 11:40). What is this better thing wherein we possess the advantage over them? Surely it is in this, that we have the Holy Spirit and the living Christ, of which they had but the promise and the occasional visitation. To us the Spirit has come to abide. In us the living Christ dwells not only as the Example, but as "the author and perfecter of our faith" (12:2). Not only are we called to look up the shining way whither the Forerunner has gone in—but He comes back to hold our hand and lead us up the steps of faith until we reach our coronation too—but all that He has won we also may claim, and where He has entered in, there we may follow.

A bright and intelligent young lad from a very poor family had been received to a position of confidence and responsibility not only in the business but also in the family of his employer.

One night he had been invited to spend the evening at a social gathering in this home of wealth and luxury. Of course he never took his family with him for they were wretchedly poor, and all that he could do was just to keep them from destitution. But late that evening a gentle tapping was heard on the door of the mansion and when opened two little tots were standing there clothed in rags and as dirty as little animals, and they timidly said: "Please may we come in? Our elder brother is in there." It is needless to say that they were very cordially welcomed, and yet it would not be strange if that elder brother flushed with shame and hurried away with his little wards as soon as possible. But there is one palace home where the poorest sinner may come with boldness, and knocking at the door may say: "May I come in? My Elder Brother is there." The doors will swing wide open. The Elder Brother will meet us with a welcome which will have in it no flush or reproach or shame, for "Jesus is not ashamed to call [us] brothers" (2:11), and all that He has shall be ours. This is the next vision that comes before us in the cloud of witnesses. And so as the witnesses pass by let us lift up our eyes and see no man except Jesus only, and go forth to run the race "[fixing] our eyes on Jesus, the author and perfecter of our faith" (12:2).

CHAPTER 10

THE FINISHER OF OUR FAITH

Let us fix our eyes on Jesus, the author and [finisher, KJV] of our faith, who for the joy set before him endured the cross, scorning its shame, and sat down at the right hand of the throne of God. (Hebrews 12:2)

The epistle to the Hebrews is the working out of three magnificent thoughts. First, Jesus Christ our great Apostle, coming from God to us. Second, Jesus Christ our great High Priest, going back from us to God. Third, Jesus Christ the Author and Finisher of our faith and the Captain of our salvation, taking us back with Him to God. It is the last of these thoughts that the writer is now expounding. He has already explained the nature and province of faith, and given us four groups of examples from the Old Testament, and now he brings the series to a lofty climax by introducing the Lord Jesus Christ as the crowning witness of faith both as an example of its power and as its Author and Finisher in the hearts and lives of His people.

CHRIST IS THE PATTERN OF OUR FAITH

The expression in this verse has been translated more literally in some versions "the Prince Leader," or "Forerunner" of our faith. Christ was Himself a great believer. In the earliest glimpse which we have of the life of His boyhood we find Him studying the Word of God and asking questions as well as answering them. It was through the Scriptures of truth that He reached the profound conviction which enabled Him to say: "I had to be in my Father's house" (Luke 2:49).

Later the Holy Spirit brought to Him the more direct and personal witness of His divine Sonship when at His baptism in the Jordan the voice of the Father proclaimed: "You are my Son, whom I love; with you I am well pleased" (3:22). In His first temptation in the wilderness it was His faith that was directly assailed. "If you are the Son of God" (4:3), said the tempter; as much as to say, "You, the Son of God, and in this deserted and desolate condition? It cannot be! It is some great delusion. You are mistaken."

But Christ held steadfastly to His faith, and trusting in His Father's care, rejected the tempter's prescription and met him with the sword of the Spirit, "It is written." All through His life we find Him expressing the most complete and constant dependence upon His Father for His life, strength and even His very messages. "I do nothing on my own" (John 8:28), He says. "These words you hear are not my own; they belong to the Father who sent me" (14:24). "The one who sent me is with me; he has not left me alone" (8:29). "Just as the living Father sent me and I live because of the Father, so the one who feeds on me will live because of me" (6:57). This is the language of faith in its deepest essence, the very element of trust and dependence.

Then in the crisis hours of His life it was faith that sustained Him. In this very epistle we find the writer quoting from the Old Testament and applying to Him the language of trust and confidence in God, "And again, 'I will put my trust in him'" (Hebrews 2:13, quoted from Psalms 18:2). Again in Isaiah 50:6–9, we have a fine exhibition of His faith in the hour of trial.

> I offered my back to those who beat me,
>   my cheeks to those who pulled out my beard;
> I did not hide my face
>   from mocking and spitting.
> Because the Sovereign LORD helps me,
>   I will not be disgraced.
> Therefore have I set my face like flint,
>   and I know I will not be put to shame.
> He who vindicates me is near.
>   Who then will bring charges against me?
>   Let us face each other!
> Who is my accuser?
>   Let him confront me!
> It is the Sovereign LORD who helps me.
>   Who is he that will condemn me?

But the finest exhibition of our Savior's faith in the hour of trial is in the 22nd Psalm, the inspired Psalm and portraiture of our Redeemer's last sufferings. "My God, my God," He cries, "why have you forsaken me?/ Why are you so far from saving me" (22:1). But still in that dark and dreadful hour when even His Father's face was averted, He continued to trust. The very taunt of His enemies is "He trusts in the Lord; let the Lord rescue him."

And so he cries, "You brought me out of the womb;/ you made me trust in you/ even at my mother's breast./ . . ./ Do not be far from me,/ for trouble is near" (22:9, 11). And soon His cry of agony is changed to a song, "From you comes the theme of my praise in the great assembly;/ before those who fear you will I fulfill my vows" (22:25). "For he has not despised or disdained/ the suffering of the afflicted one;/ he has not hidden his face from him/ but has listened to his cry for help" (22:24).

Again in His ministry the secret of His power was faith in God. When the disciples wondered at the withering of the fig tree He simply answered, "Have faith in God" (Mark 11:22), as much as to say, "This is the work of faith and if you will have the same faith which I have exercised, you, too, may accomplish the same works." It was in this spirit of faith that He stood at Lazarus' grave and cried, "Father, I thank you that you have heard me. I knew that you always hear me" (John 11:41); and then the grave was opened and the dead came forth obedient to the power of faith.

It is delightful to think of our blessed Redeemer as fighting the good fight of faith just like us. For while He was the Son of God and is forevermore the equal of the Father, yet we never should forget that during His earthly life He voluntarily suspended the exercise of His independent rights and powers, and placed Himself in the same attitude of dependence upon God and trust in God as He requires of us, His disciples.

CHRIST THE AUTHOR OF OUR FAITH

Here the parallel between Him and all others ends. Abel and Abraham are patterns, but each had to live for himself and they cannot share with us their faith. But Christ, having traversed all the pathway of life and having won the crown of victory, comes back to take us with Him up the ascent of faith till we reach the throne. There are three ways in which Christ is the Author of our faith.

1. By His Words

He has given to us the precious promises which are the foundation of faith. How much His own personal words have contributed to the faith of His disciples! There is something in the utterance of the Lord Jesus which in their very manner and terms are peculiarly fitted to inspire confidence. Take that single promise, "Whoever comes to me I will never drive away" (6:37). How could language be more explicit, simple and encouraging to a timorous and troubled heart? There is no possibility of evading its sweet and reassuring force. It wakens in us its own response and makes it so easy for us to come. Or again take the words: "Do not let your hearts be troubled. Trust in God; trust also in me" (14:1). It seems as if a fond and tender face were looking into ours and saying, "Won't you trust Me?" and everything within us answers back, "Lord, I will believe in You."

2. His Work

Back of His gracious words is the finished work of redemption which has made them possible and guaranteed their fulfillment. The promise of forgiveness means infinitely more when we know that behind it is the precious blood that has atoned for our sins and opened the way for our acceptance with the Father. The promise of answered prayer has tenfold meaning when we realize that behind it is His own name in which we may come, and His intercession for us at the Father's right hand, so that all His words are guaranteed to us by His glorious redeeming work. He has given us the standing and the rights of faith. He has clothed us with His own righteousness, and placed at our credit His infinite merits, and so faith has its firm foundation not only in the words, but also in the greater works which have guaranteed His exceeding great and precious promises.

3. He Inspires Our Faith

But Christ is the Author of faith in a more direct sense, inasmuch as He inspires our faith and by the Holy Spirit puts in us the Spirit of trust and confidence. For our faith is just as much the work of Christ as our holiness, our love or any of the graces of Christian life. When He comes to abide within us He simply imparts to us His own nature and Spirit, and puts into our heart the very same sentiments of trust toward His Father which He Himself ever cherished. There is nothing so delightful as this consciousness of the very life and heart of Christ within us, the trust that springs spontaneously within our breast, the prayer that prays itself, and the song that sings its joyous triumph even when all around is dark and strange. God help us to understand this deepest secret of the Lord and to be able to say in a literal sense, "The life I live in the body, I live by faith in the Son of God, who loved me and gave himself for me" (Galatians 2:20).

CHRIST THE FINISHER OF OUR FAITH

There is nothing more touching in the life of the Master than the incident in which He tells Peter of the great temptation that is coming to Him. "Simon," He says, "Satan has asked to sift you as wheat. But I have prayed for you, Simon, that your faith may not fail" (Luke 22:31–32).

The difference between Simon and Judas was not in the intensity of their sorrow, but in the fact that Simon's faith failed not. At the last moment there was just one cord left that held him and brought Him back to His Lord—his confidence in Christ. This was really one of Christ's own heartstrings. It was the prayer that kept the faith of Peter. And so He keeps us. Again and again in the darkest hour of life all else had failed us, but the heart could still trust. Christ was keeping our faith.

But not only does He keep it, He educates it. He lets the trial come to strengthen it and establish it. He puts us into situations where we must have more faith or be overwhelmed, and He gives us the faith in the hour of need and leads us on from strength to strength and grace to grace. Just as the eagle teaches her young to fly by hurling them from their downy nests, and compelling them to strike out with their own feeble pinions and learn to soar upon the pathless air, so Christ puts us into impossible situations that He may prove to us that all things are possible to Him that believes, and that with God nothing is impossible. Sometimes in this process He even hides His face from us, as once the Father's was hidden from Him, and teaches us to trust where we cannot trace, and walk with Him in the dark. Thus by various means He is preparing us for some future day when by faith we may perhaps be able like Him to create a world and prove the full meaning of His own mighty Word, "Everything is possible for him who believes" (Mark 9:23). Be not discouraged, tried and suffering child of God, "though now for a little while you may have had to suffer grief in all kinds of trials. These have come so that your faith—of greater worth than gold, which perishes even though refined by fire—may be proved genuine and may result in praise, glory and honor when Jesus Christ is revealed" (1 Peter 1:6–7).

OUR ATTITUDE TOWARD THE AUTHOR AND FINISHER OF OUR FAITH

"Let us run with perseverance the race marked out for us" (Hebrews 12:1).

1. Our Example

Let us look to Him as our Example, and as He endured the cross, despising the shame for the joy set before Him, so let us look over every seeming trial, and in view of the glorious reversion by and by, let us rise above our trials and triumph over all their pain and shame.

2. The Guarantee of our Victory

Let us look to Him as the guarantee of our victory. He has overcome. He has sat down upon the right hand of the throne of God. His trials are over forever. His triumph has begun. And as surely as He has overcome, so shall we. Not for Himself did He enter in, but for us. He passed through the gates of suffering and death that He might record our names on yonder thrones and hold possession for us until we come. So let us look to the glorious end, and count nothing too dear if we may finish our course with joy and sit down with Him on His throne.

3. He Is There to Help Us

Let us keep looking to Him for help as we run the race, for He is there for the very purpose of helping us. His one business is to uphold and succor us and see us through. Every moment, every breath, we may be in communication with Him and drawing strength and help from above.

A little newsboy was complaining of his discouragements, and a Christian friend was trying to tell him how to bring them to Jesus. But the little fellow could not easily comprehend the mystery of prayer. Putting his finger on the boy's forehead the gentleman said, "What do you do in there?" "I think," said the little fellow. "Well, now," said the other, "God can look down and see your thought. Suppose therefore that you just think a little wish or prayer every time you are in difficulty; God will look down and read it, and it will become a telegram to heaven and bring you an answer." The next time the gentleman met his little friend he hardly knew him, he looked so bright. "Oh," said he, as quickly as they met, "it's all right since I began sending them sky telegrams. Everything is different, and I sell twice as many papers as I used to." So let us keep looking unto Jesus, and when too tired or busy to formulate a prayer, let us think it, and the Holy Spirit will flash it to heaven.

4. Looking Brings Life

There is in the eye a strange power to bring the object into contact with us. Looking at the sun the sun comes into my brain. The photographic plate exposed to the camera receives the very impress of the object before it. Attached to a telescope a photographic plate will absorb in the course of a night the whole circle of the heavens exposed to view, and in the morning the finest stars will have written their impress on that sensitive surface. So also the microscope will reveal minute worlds the human eye never saw. This is the secret of the strange power of hypnotism which through a look lets one mind control another. So as we look at Christ He becomes a living act in our consciousness and in our heart. And just as the dying Hebrew gazing on the brazen serpent felt life and power flowing through all his being, so looking unto Jesus we are healed, we are comforted, we are filled with His life and power and we become partakers of His very nature and being.

5. Looking Off or Looking Away

But the expression means not only looking, but looking off, or looking away. It has an obverse and negative side.

a. We are to look away from others, from their failures, yes, and even their attractions, if they distract us from Him.

b. We are to look away from ourselves undiscouraged by our shortcomings, expecting nothing from self, and moment by moment looking away from our work and our best to Him.

c. We are to look away from the world's attractions and illusions to Him. He is the only power that can break the spell of earth's enchantments. I have seen a child from whose careless hands no power could wrest the razor which it held without danger of its wounding itself to death, drop it instantly when some counter-attraction was held before it, and the little hands reached out for the beautiful picture or the more attractive candy.

d. Let us look away from our trials to Him. There is power in care and sorrow to mesmerize the soul until everything else is absorbed in one corroding sense of vexation and discouragement. We must look away from all this. Christ will not give you strength to carry your cares. You must drop them and look on the brighter side. There is always a bright side, and as happy Nancy said: "It is always sunshine where Jesus is." "You see, Sir," she said to her troubled boss, "when I see the dark cloud coming and it appears like it was just crushing down on me, I just whisk around on the other side and I find Jesus there. Then all is bright and clear. The bright side is always where Jesus is." But the dark side has a strange fascination for some minds. Like the astronomer who had spent a day watching one of the sun spots, and when his friend called and remarked what a beautiful sunshiny day it had been, he looked up surprised and answered, "I thought it was rather dark today, but now you mention it, the sun does seem very bright." The poor fellow had been watching a speck all day and it had eclipsed the sun. Let us look away from all this into the eternal light of His unchanging love and our sun will no more go down, but God will be our everlasting light and the days of our mourning shall be ended.

Finally, let us not only look, but run, for there is an intensely practical side of faith. Let us run while we look and let us look while we run. Let us take our inspirations and exultations with us, and live them out in the quiet plod of daily duty, and become better workmen, better businessmen, better husbands, wives, and children because we are living in heaven while our feet are still treading the pathways of earth.

"I suppose John is your best weaver," said a clergyman to the foreman of a factory, where one of his people was employed, a man who was always talking about his religion. "Well, no," said the foreman, "John is a good fellow, but he has yet to learn that while it is all right to talk about religion in its place, yet in the workshop a man's religion should come at his fingers and not at his mouth."

> So let our lips and lives express
> The holy Gospel we profess;
> So let our works and actions shine
> To prove the doctrine all divine.

CHAPTER 11

THE SCHOOL OF FAITH

No discipline seems pleasant at the time, but painful. Later on, however, it produces a harvest of righteousness and peace for those who have been trained by it. (Hebrews 12:11)

The mystery of suffering is deeply interwoven with every thread and fiber of the web of nature and of life. Not a blossom breathing its sweet fragrance on the air of spring but it came from a buried seed or a bursting bulb. Not a shining pearl but it was evolved from the suffering of the life that gave it birth. Not a human life but it came into being through travail and sore agony. The world's oldest poem is a deep discussion of the mystery of suffering. The book of Job is the inspired drama which seeks to fathom the meaning of sorrow and affliction. Every heroic page in human history was gilded by some sacrifice or deed of daring or suffering. The glorious galaxy of Bible characters that have just been set forth in these verses as witnesses and types of faith were all evolved out of circumstances of severest trial, and reached their high achievements and splendid triumphs through such scenes and circumstances as these:

> Some faced jeers and flogging, while still others were chained and put in prison. They were stoned; they were sawed in two; they were put to death by the sword. They went about in sheepskins and goatskins, destitute, persecuted and mistreated—the world was not worthy of them. They wandered in deserts and mountains, and in caves and holes in the ground. (Hebrews 11:36–38)

It was thus they reached the heights of victory and won the great rewards of faith.

And He who marks the climax of this series, Christ Himself, the Author and Finisher of our faith, reaches His place at the "right hand of the throne of God" by "[enduring] the cross, scorning its shame" (12:2), and suffering the "opposition from sinful men" (12:3). It is suffering all the way through, but suffering transformed and glorified by victorious faith.

And so this chapter takes up the mystery of suffering and links it with the education of our faith. It is quite remarkable that immediately after the profound discussion which the apostle has just given of the subject of faith, the very first theme that he should introduce to us should be trial. And yet this is always God's order; after faith trial, after trial more faith. God never leads us into the 11th chapter of Hebrews without also bringing us into the 12th. I once heard George Müller say, when asked by a friend how one could have more faith, "My beloved brother, by having more trial."

THE NAME HERE GIVEN TO TRIAL

It is translated "chastening" in the King James Version. Rotherham renders it "discipline," but the original means "son training." The training of a child; this is the beautiful phase of affliction which the Holy Spirit would impress upon every troubled heart. It is not judgment. It is not punishment. It is not even chastisement. It is not even the education of a school, but it is the education of a father or of a mother. There are some children who have had the great privilege of being educated by a loving mother, and it is a peculiar privilege where the mother has been fitted for her sacred task. There is a touch of tenderness in such a schooling that no conventional discipline can ever give. It is not as our schoolmaster, but as our loving Father; nay, as our very mother God, that the Holy Spirit teaches us and trains us for our future destiny. What a difference it makes when a trial comes, to see in it not the hand of an avenger, but the loving discipline of a father and the gentle admonition of a mother! God would not have us feel even the shadow of His anger. Judgment hardens the spirit and God never wants to break the spirit of His obedient child, but to win us by His love and transform us by His gentleness. Beloved, let us ever look upon our trials in the tender light of the Father's love. It is not the token of His displeasure, but the very pledge of His jealous love, a love so inexorable that it will not let us miss His holiest and best.

THE PRESENT EFFECT OF TRIAL

Not now "pleasant, . . . but painful" (12:11). We must not be disappointed if the blow is keenly felt and the trial is hard to endure. We must not wonder if the heart sinks in depression and every feeling and instinct is crushed for the time, and we must "consider it pure joy" (James 1:2) when we cannot feel a throb of joy in our actual consciousness. It is true often that for the time "you may have had to suffer grief in all kinds of trials" (1 Peter 1:6). There came an hour when even the Lord Himself had to say, "My soul is overwhelmed with sorrow to the point of death" (Mark 14:34). It is not a sign of unbelief, rebellion or an unsanctified heart if the iron should enter the soul and the chastened spirit should cry like Him, "My God, my God, why have you forsaken me?" (15:34).

It is hard to feel the blow of sharp disease and excruciating pain. It is hard to see your loved ones suffer and be unable to relieve them. It is hard to see the grave close over our fondest treasures. It is hard to be scorched and blistered with the fiery heat of temptation and feel the very breath of hell upon our souls. It is hard to be wronged, misrepresented, betrayed by those whom we have trusted and benefited, and like the Master, to meet the kiss of Judas and the denial of Peter. It is still harder to suffer the deep spiritual silences of God and find that even He has withdrawn the light of His countenance and the shining of His face. He knows how hard it is for He has felt the same, and He tenderly reminds us that He is not grieved with us when the fiery trial comes if it does seem strange, and is not joyous but grievous.

THE FRUIT OF TRIAL

"Later on, however, it produces a harvest of righteousness and peace for those who have been trained by it" (Hebrews 12:11). It is afterward that it comes. Give it time to appear. The bleeding plant cut back by the gardener to a single bud might well seem to say, "How cruel! How harsh!" But wait a little until that single bud has burst into a rich hanging cluster and the purple grapes of autumn bear witness to the wisdom and the kindness of the gardener's knife. The lawn might well cry out against the sharp scythe and the crushing mower, as they leave the little plants bleeding and crushed. But wait until the soft velvet of that lawn carpets the ground with a glory that no upholsterer could imitate, and then compare it with the dry and withered stalks on yonder common, where the same grass has been allowed to grow untrained and run to seed, and you will not question the wisdom or the beneficence of the process. The precious gold might well cry out against the crushing roller, and the consuming flame. But wait a little, until the rough and rugged lump of ore has become the shining jewel, or the glistening chain of burnished gold, and you need no one to explain the crucible and the fire.

So God is putting His children through the ordeal of trial with a hand of infinite wisdom and perfect love, and the very trial of our "faith—of greater worth than gold, which perishes even though refined by fire" (1 Peter 1:7) will be "proved genuine and may result in praise, glory and honor when Jesus Christ is revealed" (1:7).

It is called the "harvest of righteousness and peace" (Hebrews 12:11). It is both righteousness and peace. It corrects and directs our life into His perfect will. It shows us the weak places in our character and leads us to put on His righteousness and strength, and then it gives us the deeper peace and rest, the chastened tenderness, the mellow and subdued depth which you can always trace in those that have passed through God's deepest testings, and learned all the lessons in the school of heavenly discipline. It is all so different from the callow, crude and shallow profession of souls that have learned it by rote, but have not yet lived it in the school of sorrow or had it burned into their inmost being in the very crucible of God. Such souls have entered into a rest which never can be moved. Sorrow has burned out all that is combustible and only that is left which, like the pure gold, even trial cannot consume but only purify the more.

THE PROCESS THROUGH WHICH ALL THIS IS ACCOMPLISHED

"For those who have been trained by it" (12:11). Trial is not always a blessing. There are souls that suffer and are not sanctified, sweetened and mellowed. There are trials that are wasted and thrown away. There are bitter tears that leave only desolation behind. There are lives that are scorched, soured and crushed by their trials, and only driven farther from God and righteousness. Suffering in itself cannot sanctify; else Satan and his angels would long ago have been purified. Punishment is not a purifying process. Everything depends upon our attitude to the trial and our being "trained by it." What does this mean?

1. Don't Make Light of Discipline

"Do not make light of the Lord's discipline" (12:5). We are not to think too lightly of it. We are not to regard it as a mere accident or incident, and plan for its removal by our own counsels or the advice of others. God means that we shall feel it. It has a message for us, and He wants us to understand it and take it deeply to heart and hear what God the Lord will say.

2. Don't Lose Heart

On the other hand, we must "not lose heart when he rebukes [us]" (12:5); rather when we are "reproved" of Him, we must not take it too much to heart. We must not let it discourage us or break our spirit. We must never look on the dark side. We must never see God's anger, but always His love. If we lose heart we shall be sure to miss the meaning of our trial, to fail to get our true lesson and to fly from God instead of sweetly turning to Him in the hour of trial. It was thus that Israel lost their blessing. God was chastening them, but in the chastisement He was there to meet them and to help them, and His gentle message was, "In repentance and rest is your salvation,/ in quietness and trust is your strength" (Isaiah 30:15). But they would not. They fell into a panic. They said, "We will flee on horses" (30:16). And they fled. But their pursuers flew faster, and God looked on and said, "Yet the

LORD longs to be gracious to you" (30:18). In the time of trouble our greatest danger is that we will become alarmed and run away from God instead of running into His everlasting arms. Therefore remember, no matter what the nature of your trial, no matter though you may yourself be to blame for it, do not give up your trust, do not give way to fear, do not become discouraged, faint not.

3. Don't Grow Weary and Lose Heart

"Consider him who endured such opposition from sinful men, so that you will not grow weary and lose heart" (Hebrews 12:3). Remember how much more severely He suffered. Remember how triumphantly He maintained His courage and His joy, how He endured the cross and despised the shame for the joy set before Him; and remember that what He once accomplished in His lone conflict He can still enable you to accomplish through Him.

4. Take a Firm Hold

"Strengthen your feeble arms" (12:12). That is, take a firmer hold by the hand of faith. The time of trial is faith's opportunity. As someone once said, "When God tests me I always turn around and test Him." Take more because you need more through His providence, and the trial that He has permitted. Tell Him that He has brought you into this hard place, and He must see you through. Stir up yourself to take a hold of His strength, and you will find that He will never be displeased with the boldness of your faith and the largeness of your believing claim.

5. Weak Knees

Besides strengthening our feeble arms there is a reference to our weak knees. The knees may stand for prayer as the hands for faith, and if they do, it is needless to say that the time of trial is the time for prayer. It is God's challenge to ask more from Him. "Call upon me," He says, "in the day of trouble;/ I will deliver you, and you will honor me" (Psalm 50:15). "Call to me and I will answer you and tell you great and unsearchable things" (Jeremiah 33:3). Hard places are God's very challenges to prayer. Or the knees may stand for courage, the courage that strengthens itself to stand firmly upon His promises and upon the ground that faith has claimed. The feeble knees represent perhaps the paralysis of fear, when the knees smite together and the frame trembles with alarm. This is the effect of sorrow on the natural heart. But faith can give courage and take away our fear, and enable us to triumph in the darkest hour and shout before the ramparts fall. It is not our courage. It is the courage of faith. And so we are exhorted to add courage to our faith. It is God's courage, not ours. He will clothe us with it in the time of need.

6. Press through the Obstacles

"Make level paths for your feet, so that the lame may not be disabled, but rather healed" (Hebrews 12:13). This seems to mean that we are not to turn aside from the obstacles of faith, but to press on through and above them, and take strength from God to enable us to do so. The feeble and the lame would naturally be tempted to go round the mountain, and the enemy would say you are not able for this hill of difficulty and this rugged height of danger. But faith takes God to heal the lame, and then it marches forward boldly and victoriously through every obstacle, and keeps right on its way rejoicing. Of course, this may literally be applied to the healing of bodily disease. Many a time through physical infirmity it seems almost unavoidable that God's servants should turn back from some task of difficulty and take the easy way of escape. But God will give us faith and strength to claim His healing power and go right on in the path of service and of duty, finding His grace sufficient from moment to moment, and His strength made perfect in our weakness.

But it also applies to difficulties of every sort, and inspires us with a faith that presses forward in the face of every discouragement and obstruction. So Israel pressed on at the Red Sea, refusing to turn aside, and the floods divided and the way was opened for their escape and for the destruction of their foes. So Daniel pressed forward when he knew that his life was hanging in the balance and a little subterfuge might have saved him from the den of lions. But no; when he knew that the decree was passed, and that the spies were already skulking under his window and watching for him to fall into the snare, he went quietly home and, entering his house, he set his face steadfastly toward Jerusalem and prayed unto his God "just as he had done before" (Daniel 6:10). There is a sublime heroism in those words, "just as he had done before." There was no advertising of his courage for the sake of showing it off. But he just went on as before in the consistent course of implicit faith and inexorable fidelity.

7. Live in Peace

"Make every effort to live in peace with all men and to be holy; without holiness no one will see the Lord" (Hebrews 12:14). This is the great end of all our trials, to lead us to be right with God and with our fellowmen. In the hour of trial it is a great comfort to feel that our relationships with one another are right, and there is no unseemly strife or wrong. And above all else, trial comes to deepen our holiness and lead us to that sanctification, without which no man shall see the Lord. The reference here seems to be to the Lord's coming. Holiness is the preparation for that glorious meeting in the air, and without it we shall not see Him when He comes, nor can we hope to share the welcome of His glorious Bride. But He does not expect us to work up this holiness by our own exertions. He tells us that we are to "share in his holiness" (12:10). Therefore trial comes to show us where our holiness is at fault that we may put on His righteousness and receive His grace and all-sufficiency. We shall be so glad some day when the supreme test comes that we have been already tried by fire and not left to go through the final conflict with armor unproved and weapons that may fail us in the crisis hour.

CHAPTER 12

THE GOAL OF FAITH

You have not come to a mountain that can be touched and that is burning with fire; to darkness, gloom and storm; to a trumpet blast or to such a voice speaking words that those who heard it begged that no further word be spoken to them, because they could not bear what was commanded: "If even an animal touches the mountain, it must be stoned." The sight was so terrifying that Moses said, "I am trembling with fear."

But you have come to Mount Zion, to the heavenly Jerusalem, the city of the living God. You have come to thousands upon thousands of angels in joyful assembly, to the church of the firstborn, whose names are written in heaven. You have come to God, the judge of all men, to the spirits of righteous men made perfect, to Jesus the mediator of a new covenant, and to the sprinkled blood that speaks a better word than the blood of Abel. (Hebrews 12:18–24)

We have seen in our former studies in the epistle to the Hebrews, the Captain of our salvation bringing many sons unto glory along the pathway of faith. Now in this sublime passage we have presented to us the final goal to which He is bringing them. The figure is a strong antithesis, presenting in striking contrast the difference between the Old Testament and the New. The whole epistle has been richly laden with Old Testament allusions and quotations. The writer has taken us back to Abel and Enoch, Noah and Abraham, Isaac and Jacob, Melchizedek and Joseph, Moses and Joshua, Gideon and Barak, Samuel and David, the Old Testament prophets and the ancient high priest. The tabernacle in the wilderness and its imposing ritual, and indeed all the ordinances and types of the ancient Scriptures have been laid under contribution to unfold the richness of Jesus Christ in whom they are all fulfilled. Now he gathers up the substance of all these ancient types and figures in one magnificent contrast between the law and the gospel, the

Old Testament and the New.

He had already told us in the close of the 11th chapter that "God had planned something better for us so that only together with us would they be made perfect" (Hebrews 11:40). In the present passage he shows us by this striking antithesis how much better the thing that God has provided is, and how lofty and sublime are the immunities and privileges to which we have been introduced by the gospel and the grace of our Lord Jesus Christ.

NO CONDEMNATION

He tells us that we "have not come to a mountain that can be touched and is burning with fire; to darkness, gloom and storm" (12:18). All this is descriptive of the terrors of the ancient law. This was the dispensation of judgment. We are not under it now. We have been delivered from it, and there is "now no condemnation for those who are in Christ Jesus" (Romans 8:1). Not by the sanctions of fear and the threatenings of judgment, but by the gentle constraint of love are we held to our sacred obligations. Let us not get under the law or back to bondage, but stand firm—"it is for freedom that Christ has set us free" (Galatians 5:1). We are under the law of faith and not of works, and the law of faith is the law of love, and the reign of grace.

COME TO MOUNT ZION

Mount Zion is the antithesis of Mount Sinai. It is the mount of mercy as the other was of judgment. Therefore the ark of God was set up on Mount Zion and the symbol of God's covenant and mercy was established there and it became significant of divine grace. The ark and the tabernacle were symbols of God's mercy and types of Jesus Christ, who came to fulfill the law and deliver us from its curse and condemnation; therefore Mount Zion stands for the grace of God in contrast with the terrors of Sinai. Let us ever remember this and dwell in the light of its mercy and so "keep [ourselves] in God's love as [we] wait for the mercy of our Lord Jesus Christ to bring [us] to eternal life" (Jude 21).

THE HEAVENLY JERUSALEM

We come unto "the heavenly Jerusalem, the city of the living God" (Hebrews 12:22). The earthly Jerusalem was the center of God's earthly people; the heavenly Jerusalem is the home of God's spiritual people. It is a city which He is preparing out of spiritual realities, and of which His holy people are the materials and elements which He is building together, and which shall one day be seen descending from heaven as a vision of transcendent glory, more radiant than the rainbow, more precious than all the gems of earth. We have come to this city now. We are members of its glorious society. Our citizenship is in heaven and our names are written in its civic records. Faith claims our high position even here,

> And hope foredates the joyful day
> When these old skies shall cease to sunder
> The one dear love-linked family.

THOUSANDS OF ANGELS

We are come "to thousands upon thousands of angels" (12:22). These celestial beings are also inhabitants of the city of God and attendants upon the heirs of salvation. Already we are compassed about with them as ministering spirits, and although we see them not yet, doubtless their interposing love often rescues us from hidden dangers and snares. Undoubtedly they are the spectators of our earthly course, and are watching our conflicts and our victories with intense interest. We are to them object lessons of the government of God and the wonders of redeeming love, and they are doubtless our protectors and guardians and often the unseen messengers of answered prayer and divine blessing. Let us realize the honor of our glorious associations and walk worthy of such high companionships.

THE CHURCH OF THE FIRSTBORN

We have come "to the church of the firstborn, whose names are written in heaven" (12:23). Literally this means, "the firstborn ones." This description includes the whole company of the redeemed, the great assembly of the saints of God from every age and clime. They are all called firstborn ones; that is, they share the inheritance of the firstborn, and they stand in exactly the same position as Christ, the only begotten Son of God, and the Elder Brother in the divine family. Our inheritance as God's children is not that of a younger son, but is the same as the Elder Brother's. Jesus, the Firstborn, shares with us all His privileges, and reminds us that God is "[his] Father and [our] Father; [his] God and [our] God" (John 20:17). In what sense have we come to this general assembly and heavenly Church? Our names are written there. We are recognized already as if we also were there. We are counted one with the ransomed saints above.

> One family we dwell in Him,
>   One Church above, beneath;
> Though now divided by the stream,
>   The narrow stream of death.
> One army of the living God
>   At His command we bow,

Part of the host have passed the flood,
And part are crossing now.

THE JUDGE OF ALL MEN

We have come "to God, the judge of all men" (Hebrews 12:23). The idea of this reference seems to be that through the redemption of Jesus Christ we have been brought back to the Father, and have been restored to our original place as His children. "For Christ died for sins once for all," we are told, "the righteous for the unrighteous, to bring [us] to God" (1 Peter 3:18). We were "without God in the world" (Ephesians 2:12). We were strangers and enemies to God. We were far away from God; but Christ has brought us home, and now we are back in the Father's house. He came from God to seek us and to bring us the message of His love. He went back to God as our High Priest to present His offering and sacrifice for our salvation, and now He has taken us back to God with Him. And so once more it is true that God is our home and our dwelling place, and we are restored to that place for which He interceded in His last prayer by Kidron's brook, "That all of them may be one, Father, just as you are in me and I am in you. May they also be in us" (John 17:21). Union with God in the blessed beatific fellowship of His eternal love—this is the goal of faith and the consummation of redemption.

THE SPIRITS OF RIGHTEOUS MEN

We have come "to the spirits of righteous men made perfect" (Hebrews 12:23). This is almost synonymous with the previous statement that we have come to the general assembly and the Church of the firstborn. But it seems to refer to the individual spirits of the glorified, rather than to the collective body of the whole general assembly and Church above. Perhaps it suggests the precious hope and consoling thought that we are standing in close fellowship with the glorified dead whom we have known and loved on earth. Is there not back of the lie of spiritualism a truth somewhere, perhaps but dimly revealed, but not forbidden to our clinging, longing hearts—that those who have left us are not, perhaps, so far away as we sometimes deem? And although they cannot speak to us and we must not attempt by the arts of sorcery to open communications with the world beyond through them, yet through Him in whose presence they dwell, and to whom we may freely come in prayer, they have a very close connection with our earthly life. It may be that they are conversant with our struggles, joys and triumphs. Perhaps they are permitted in some sense to minister to us still, and are undoubtedly allowed to keep alive the love that still binds our hearts together, and are waiting with joyful expectation to the time when we shall meet them again at His glorious coming. How much there may be hidden behind those gentle words of Christ, "If it were not so, I would have told you" (John 14:2).

JESUS THE MEDIATOR

We have come "to Jesus the mediator of a new covenant" (Hebrews 12:24). Perhaps this was inserted here to keep us from thinking for a moment that our beloved dead could in any sense be mediators between us and God. There is but one Mediator, and that is Jesus Christ. Through Him alone we have access to the eternal world, and through Him all our interests and relationships are maintained. We are come to Him, but in coming to Him He brings us to all that He represents on the heaven side. He brings us to the Father and to the family. He secures for us the help and strength we need from moment to moment. He keeps open to us all the resources of divine sufficiency. He presents our prayers before the throne and sends the answer from above. He represents us continually to the Father, and through Him we are accepted every moment even as He. And by and by, should His public advent be delayed, He will be the Mediator through whom our spirit will pass from the earthly to the eternal world and we be translated, in the arms of His love, into that heavenly city and society, for He says: "I am going there to prepare a place for you. And if I go and prepare a place for you, I will come back and take you to be with me that you also may be where I am" (John 14:2–3).

THE SPRINKLED BLOOD

We have come "to the sprinkled blood that speaks a better word than the blood of Abel" (Hebrews 12:24). The blood of sprinkling refers to the constant provision of Christ's priesthood for our acceptance and full salvation. The blood shed was the figure of Christ's life offered to atone for our sins, but the blood sprinkled refers to the constant application of Christ's grace to our souls in sanctifying and keeping us from the power of sin. It speaks better things than that of Abel inasmuch as Abel's blood cried out for judgment against his murderer, but Christ's blood cries out for pardon even for His murderers and enemies. Perhaps also the better things may refer to the fact that while Abel's blood availed for justification, Christ's blood avails for sanctification, cleansing us from both the guilt and power of sin.

HIM WHO SPEAKS

"See to it that you do not refuse him who speaks" (12:25). On account of these high and glorious dignities and distinctions that belong to the gospel of Jesus Christ and our standing in Him, there arises a corresponding responsibility on our part, much greater than even under the ancient law.

Therefore the apostle adds, "See to it that you do not refuse him who speaks. If they did not escape when they refused him who warned them on earth, how much less will we, if we turn away from him who warns us from heaven?" (12:25). Let us not imagine that because the spirit of the gospel is more beneficent than that of the law, our transgression against its grace and love will be suffered with impunity. The very gentleness of that grace will but aggravate our guilt and increase our punishment. He who can despise such mercy and trifle with such love can only look for the severest punishment. The God of the New Testament, not less than the God of the Old, is a consuming fire. Only the fire seeks now to consume the sin rather than the sinner, but if the sinner refuses to part with the sin it must consume him too.

SHAKING THE EARTH

"At that time his voice shook the earth" (12:26). The goal of faith will not be fully reached until the coming of that more glorious day of which this passage speaks in the concluding verses when Christ shall come in all His glorious power. "At that time his voice shook the earth, but now he has promised, 'Once more I will shake not only the earth but also the heavens.' The words 'once more' indicate the removing of what can be shaken—that is, created things—so that what cannot be shaken may remain" (12:26–27). That is to say, in a little while this dispensation is to reach its close in a grand upheaval and convulsion of both earth and heaven, and in a tragedy more tremendous than Mount Sinai ever saw. Then everything that is shakable shall be shaken to pieces and disappear with the dissolving world. And so God is testing us now that He may shake out of us the things that are transient and temporal, and that we may be established in the things which cannot be shaken and which shall remain. This is the meaning of all the tests and trials of life. Christ the Author and Finisher of our faith is searching and proving our faith, and bringing to light every weakness and defect so that we may be established, and settled and prepared for the testing day. Whatever is subject to change, let it change and pass away. Let us not fear the fire. Let us not shrink from the sifting and shaking process. Let us be thankful that we have One who loves us with such inexorable love that He will not let us go into judgment unprepared, but is giving us armor proved and tried before that testing day. Let us welcome the ordeal and echo the prayer:

> Burn on, O fire of God, burn on,
>   Till all my dross is burned away,
> Burn up the dregs of self and sin,
>   Prepare me for the testing day.

BE THANKFUL

"Therefore, since we are receiving a kingdom that cannot be shaken, let us be thankful, and so worship God acceptably with reverence and awe" (12:28). Let faith claim her kingdom in all its fullness and glory, and let her also claim the grace and power to be worthy of it. It is all grace from first to last, and the grace that prepared the kingdom can prepare us for it and keep us true to it until the final consummation. Glory be to God, and thanks and praise for the riches of grace and the possibilities of faith!

CHAPTER 13

"LET US"

In the study of the epistle to the Hebrews our attention has been chiefly confined to the unfolding of the great doctrinal plan of the writer, the revelation of Jesus Christ as our Apostle, our great High Priest, and the Author and Finisher of our faith. But there is no portion of the New Testament more intensely practical and whose argument is more frequently broken up with brief and pungent interjections of exhortation and appeal addressed to the conscience and the heart. These are mostly expressed in a uniform phrase commencing with the two little words, "Let us." There are no less than 12 of these appeals in the course of the epistle, and they constitute together a very complete series of practical homiletics and personal application. The number 12 is particularly appropriate to this great epistle which is based on the connection between the Old and New Testaments, and it is scarcely necessary to say that 12 is the symbolical number of God's covenant people suggested by the 12 tribes of Israel and the 12 apostles of the Lamb.

"LET US BE CAREFUL"

"Therefore, since the promise of entering his rest still stands, let us be careful that none of you be found to have fallen short of it" (Hebrews 4:1).

The point of his appeal lies in the phrase "fallen short," or still finer, "seem to come short." In fact the very feature of the whole epistle consists not in emphasizing the more common qualities of the Christian character, but in bringing out the finer points of the life of faith and holiness. It is not faith that the writer emphasizes as much as the boldness of faith, the confidence of trust. So it is not salvation that is presented to us so much as the "great salvation," the deeper fullness of Christ, the test of faith and the Land of Promise. Here we are exhorted not so much to fear lest we should lose our souls, as that we should miss something of God's best and come short of the fullness of our inheritance, or even seem to come short of it. A single degree in the physical world constitutes the boiling or the freezing point, and one

185

step less or more marks the line of demarcation between the life of failure and the life of victory. It is so sad to be almost there and yet to lose our victory and our crown. We may well fear the faintest seeming and symptom of it, and be on our guard lest we seem to come short of all that God has so abundantly provided at such cost, and so jealously guards from our indifference and neglect.

"LET US ENTER THAT REST"

"Let us, therefore, make every effort to enter that rest, so that no one will fall by following their example of disobedience" (4:11).

The word "effort" literally means, "let us make speed to enter into that rest." Here again the point lies not so much in entering into that rest as in entering at once and making it the supreme business of life to enter in now. In the ancient story on which this appeal is based, we read that they were willing a little later to enter in, but they were too late. The opportunity had passed and the Lord would not allow them to renew it. For a whole night He waited while they parleyed and questioned, and then the irrevocable sentence went forth that sent them back to traverse the sands of the desert for 40 years until all the unbelieving generation had passed away. And so we may come too late. There are souls along the path of life who reach the crisis hour of some great decision. Every leading of God's providence has converged to that point, and at last the Holy Spirit, with solemn urgency, is pleading: "Today, if you hear his voice,/ do not harden your hearts" (Psalm 95:7–8). Tomorrow will not do. Oh, if God is speaking through these lines to any undecided soul, make speed this moment to say, "Yes, Lord, forever yes."

"LET US HOLD FIRMLY"

"Therefore, since we have a great high priest who has gone through the heavens, Jesus the Son of God, let us hold firmly to the faith we profess" (Hebrews 4:14).

This may be perhaps better translated "our confession." It is not so much our faith we are to hold as the confession of our faith. After we enter into His rest and receive any deeper blessing from the Lord there is always a time of testing, and the adversary will try his best to make us abandon our confidence and give up our high claim. Even God cannot fully bless us, and make real to us what we have taken by faith, until we have been proved and tried. After Jesus received the Holy Spirit, He was led by the Spirit into the wilderness 40 days to be tempted of the devil. Let us not count it strange concerning the fiery trial that tests our faith, and let us remember that the weapon is, "standing firm in the faith" (1 Peter 5:9). But our faith must be exercised and established by our testimony. If we hide it in our heart, and are afraid to commit ourselves to it, it will die of strangulation. But if we boldly take our stand upon it and proclaim it in the face of the enemy, it will grow by the very conflict, and when we have proved true to our testimony God will make the reckoning real, and "make your righteousness shine like the dawn,/ the justice of your cause like the noonday sun" (Psalm 37:6).

LET US COME IN OUR TIME OF NEED

"Let us then approach the throne of grace with confidence, so that we may receive mercy and find grace to help us in our time of need" (Hebrews 4:16). Our struggle is not in our own strength. In our conflict we are not left to our own resources. Our great High Priest has gone to the headquarters of the universe for the one business of succoring and sustaining us; and now the way is open, the throne of grace is accessible, and there is mercy for the sinful, grace for the helpless, and instant succor for the moment of need. We cannot only come, but come again and yet again, and keep coming for continual supply. We never can exhaust either His grace or its resources. We never can find Him too busily engaged to hear our cry and send us help. We need not wait for the long-deferred response, but before we call He will answer, and while we are yet speaking He will hear. It is grace for timely aid. He is a very present help in time of trouble. Thus let us come, and come boldly, and take His fullness to meet His highest claims upon us.

"LET US GO ON"

"Therefore let us leave the elementary teachings about Christ and go on to maturity" (6:1).

Having entered in, becoming established and finding the source of all-sufficient grace, let us now advance, let us make progress, let us grow in grace, let us not be easily satisfied with present attainments, for, unless we go on we shall surely go back. It is not safe to lose an inch of ground. "We are not of those who shrink back and are destroyed" (10:39). The faintest drawing back may land us in perdition. There is no portion of the holy Scriptures so filled with impressive warnings against backsliding as this. In two of its leading chapters (6,10) we are told of the peril of the soul that falls away, and the only remedy against falling away is to go forward. Are we going on? And are we going unto perfection? Is our goal the very highest? Are we aiming at nothing less than the highest possibilities of a life of faith and service for God? Nothing less is safe, and nothing less is worthy of our high calling and our exceeding great and precious promises.

"LET US DRAW NEAR"

Therefore, brothers, since we have confidence to enter the

Most Holy Place by the blood of Jesus, by a new and living way opened for us through the curtain, that is, his body, and since we have a great priest over the house of God, let us draw near to God with a sincere heart in full assurance of faith, having our hearts sprinkled to cleanse us from a guilty conscience and having our bodies washed with pure water. (10:19–22)

This marks a still deeper nearness. Having gone on in our Christian progress, God calls us along the way at various times to still deeper fellowship and closer intimacy. There are depths and heights in the Christian life, and new stages of Christian experiences through which the Captain of our salvation loves to lead His obedient followers. Just as in the structure of the crust of this world we often find the different geological periods marked by successive strata, and these in turn separated by great masses of conglomerate rock, showing that there was for a time a regular deposit of stratified matter, and then a great upheaval and a new layer of rock, so God marks our experience by successive blessings; but there is beyond this more and more for all who will enter in. The nearness described in this passage is accomplished through the Redeemer's crucified flesh and, of course it follows, our crucifixion with Him. As we pass through new and deeper surrenders we pass into closer fellowship with Him. As we die deeper deaths we rise to higher planes of resurrection life. But let us remember that it is neither through our dying or our efforts at rising, but through the new and living way of Jesus Himself, that we must enter in. It is by our first entering into His death, and then receiving His life to dwell within us, that we pass in where He already dwells, and our life is hid with Christ in God through Him our Living Way.

"LET US HOLD UNSWERVINGLY"

"Let us hold unswervingly to the hope we profess, for he who promised is faithful" (10:23). This is the second time that this language is employed and this appeal made. After deeper experience in the life of God it is necessary for us to have a new establishing, and therefore God again tests us, and settles us in the closer place into which we have entered, before He sends us forth once more to service and testimony. This time we are not only to hold fast, but we are to hold fast without wavering. We have reached a deeper, stronger place and henceforth we become "stedfast, unmoveable, always abounding in the work of the Lord" (1 Corinthians 15:58, KJV).

LET US HELP OTHERS TO ENTER IN

"And let us consider how we may spur one another on toward love and good deeds. Let us not give up meeting together, as some are in the habit of doing, but let us encourage one another—and all the more as you see the Day approaching" (Hebrews 10:24–25).

Every new experience is a preparation for a higher ministry. We can only give to others the Christ that we ourselves know. After coming closer to God we shall always find some hungry heart waiting for our message and ready for our assistance. Let us go out of ourselves as soon as we can, and find our blessings in blessing one another. There is special reference in the following verse to the approaching day of the Lord's coming, and the ministry referred to has doubtless reference to the gathering out and preparation of the Bride to meet her Lord. This, indeed, seems to be the great work which the Holy Spirit has for the disciples of Christ today, not so much the conversion of sinners, although that is not to be forgotten, but the purifying and preparing of the Lord's own people to meet Him in the air. We shall find as we endeavor to give our blessing to others that it grows in the exercise, even as the traveler who found that he had saved himself from death by the warmth that came into his freezing limbs while he rubbed and chafed the limbs of a fellow-traveler who was dying in the snow. So let us "consider how we may spur one another on toward love and good deeds" (10:24).

LET US RUN THE RACE

"Therefore, since we are surrounded by such a great cloud of witnesses, let us throw off everything that hinders and the sin that so easily entangles, and let us run with perseverance the race marked out before us" (12:1). We are not spectators in a great amphitheater. We are competitors for a prize. For us the contest is immensely practical and solemnly real. The life of faith is a life of holy activity and yet of patient endurance. So let us run "in such a way as to get the prize" (1 Corinthians 9:24).

LET US RECEIVE GRACE

"Therefore, since we are receiving a kingdom that cannot be shaken, let us be thankful, and so worship God acceptably with reverence and awe" (Hebrews 12:28). This verse comes at the close of a splendid contrast which the writer has drawn between the law and the gospel. There all was darkness. Here all is light. There terror was the strong but insufficient sanction. Here love is the mighty and all constraining motive. While more is demanded than under the ancient law, yet grace gives what it demands. The exhortation to us is not to try harder or do or suffer more, but to receive and take from Him the grace, the divine supply through which we shall be able to render the service demanded, and rise to the height of the kingdom into which we have been introduced. God is not calling upon us for more strenuous endeavors, or more severe sacrifices, but for simpler faith, for larger confidence, for the spirit that takes more that it may give it back in better service and larger love. So let us receive that we may give, and say like the poet of old, "Of Thine own, O Lord, have we given Thee."

LET US GO

> And so Jesus also suffered outside the city gate to make the people holy through his own blood. Let us, then, go to him outside the camp, bearing the disgrace he bore. For here we do not have an enduring city, but we are looking for the city that is to come. (13:12–14)

Here we enter upon the sufferings of Christ. We are not only to share His grace but His cross, and bear His reproach, but we are to bear it gladly because this world is not our place of recompense, but the city that is to come. Therefore we are to be willing to be misunderstood, not only by the secular world but even by the religious world. The camp outside of which He had to go was the camp of religious professors and leaders of His day. Christ was cast out by what was accounted the best society in His time. Need we wonder if in following Him in the life of faith and holiness, we, too, should be misunderstood by the public opinion of the large majority even of the people of God? We are not encouraging a spirit of rashness and criticism, but no thoughtful observer can deny that today there is a great mass of lukewarm and merely professing Christians, and inside this multitude there is a little flock of humble followers of the lowly Jesus, who are learning what it is to go forth unto Him without the camp, bearing His reproach. Let us not deserve criticism by open wrong, but let us not fear reproach if it comes for the name of Jesus. Let us be content to be unpopular and stand with the minority for the fullness of Christ, the power of the Holy Spirit, the separate life and the religion of service and sacrifice.

LET US PRAISE AND SERVE

"Through Jesus, therefore, let us continually offer to God a sacrifice of praise—the fruit of lips that confess his name. And do not forget to do good and to share with others, for with such sacrifices God is pleased" (13:15–16)

Two things are here required of the soul that has entered into the fullness of Christ and passed within the veil. First, we are to come forth with shining faces, rejoicing and praising; and secondly we are to go forth and bless the world. The sacrifice of praise is a life of thanksgiving. Our first duty is to God, and that is the habit of continual worship, praise and thanksgiving. It is more than service, more than testimony, more than any work we can do for our fellowman. It is the sweet ointment of Mary poured upon His head and His feet, while service is busy-handed Martha ministering in loving activity. He asks both, but the love and the praise have the higher place. Let us not, however, forget the other. There are two ways of doing, one by our own personal efforts, the other by the gifts of our money, supporting those who work as our substitutes. This is included in the meaning of the word "share." It means to give of our substance for the support of the gospel and the sending forth of laborers, and even to give until it becomes a real sacrifice, for with such sacrifices God is well pleased.

Beloved, let us not forget these holy ministries. It is all vain to talk of our deeper experiences, if our outward services and sacrifices do not express them. Money today is the measure of value, and tells how much we care for things and how highly we estimate them. What we give and what we sacrifice for the cause of Christ is the true test of how much we love.

I remember a very rich man who on his deathbed longed to live to serve God, but although reminded of it, utterly failed to leave a penny to support a substitute to work for him when he was gone, but held on to every dollar to the last, and then left it to relatives to whom it became not a blessing but a curse. How much happier had he laid up his treasure in heaven.

CHAPTER 14

CONCLUDING MESSAGES

May the God of peace, who through the blood of the eternal covenant brought back from the dead our Lord Jesus, that great Shepherd of the sheep, equip you with everything good for doing his will, and may he work in us what is pleasing to him, through Jesus Christ, to whom be glory for ever and ever. Amen. (Hebrews 13:20–21)

W e have now reached the close of the doctrinal portion of this great epistle, and the last chapter is occupied with a number of practical applications, and a final benediction and doxology, followed by a few parting salutations.

PRACTICAL APPLICATION

Hebrews 13:1–19

1. Love

The great theme of this epistle has been faith, but faith ever works by love. And so four kinds of love are here enjoined:

a. Love to the brethren. "Keep on loving each other as brothers" (13:1).

b. Love to the stranger. "Do not forget to entertain strangers, for by so doing some people have entertained angels without knowing it" (13:2).

c. Love to the suffering, a love that leads us to make common cause with them, and take upon us in practical sympathy their very burdens and bonds. "Remember those in prison as if you were their fellow prisoners, and those who are mistreated as if you yourselves were suffering" (13:3).

d. Domestic love and personal purity in the relationships of the home (13:4).

2. Contentment and Freedom

Contentment and freedom from the restless and inordinate desire for earthly things. "Keep your lives free from the love of money and be content with what you have" (13:5).

It will be noticed here that this virtue is founded upon faith and springs from a spirit of confidence in God's protecting and providing care, for it is added, "Because God has said, 'Never will I leave you;/ never will I forsake you'" (13:5). But our faith must be very positive, and meet God's promise with full confession and perfect confidence. Therefore it is added, "So we say with confidence, 'The Lord is my helper; I will not be afraid./ What can man do to me?'" (13:6). There is a beautiful correspondence here between what He has said and what we should say. Faith should take up and echo back the Word of God, and only as it does this will the promise be made good, and the reckoning become real.

3. Constancy

"Do not be carried away by all kinds of strange teachings. It is good for our hearts to be strengthened by grace, not by ceremonial foods, which are of no value to those who eat them" (13:9). The Hebrew Christians were in great danger, like the disciples of Galatia, of being disturbed by false teachers, especially those that sought to persuade them to go back to the law and give up their simple faith for a religion of ceremonialism. The apostle seems to connect this exhortation with the two preceding verses, seven and eight, the one reminding them of the example of their teachers, the other recalling to them the unchangeable character of the Lord Jesus Christ. This is one of the most beautiful verses in the whole Bible, "Jesus Christ is the same yesterday and today and forever" (13:8), and while it stands in splendid isolation in this chapter, apparently disconnected from the context, there can scarcely be a question that there was a latent connection in the mind of the writer between the unchangeableness of Jesus and our stability as Christians. This is the only way for us to hold fast our constancy, by having in us as the source and strength of our life the heart of the unchangeable Christ. If Jesus Christ is in us in every thought and feeling, word and action, we, too, shall be the same yesterday and today and forever, and all our moods and tenses will be resolved into one blessed present tense of immovable peace and victorious joy.

4. Fellowship of Sufferings

"Let us, then, go to him outside the camp, bearing the disgrace he bore" (13:13). We have already referred to this verse in the former chapter, and it is necessary here only to notice that it is connected with the blessed hope of the coming kingdom and the city which God is preparing for His separated and suffering people. In the assurance of that blessed hope, it should not be hard to give up the earthly camp and the prizes of human ambition and success.

5. Service

"Through Jesus, therefore, let us continually offer to God a sacrifice of praise—the fruit of lips that confess his name. And do not forget to do good and to share with others, for with such sacrifices God is pleased" (13:15–16). Here, as we have seen in the last chapter, there is a double service, thanksgiving to God and blessing to our fellowmen, both by our personal acts and our liberal gifts.

6. Submission

Next the apostle makes reference to submission to one another in the Lord, especially to our spiritual teachers and leaders. "Obey your leaders and submit to their authority. They keep watch over you as men who must give an account. Obey them so that their work will be a joy, not a burden, for that would be of no advantage to you" (13:17).

7. Mutual Prayer

The need for mutual prayer, especially for the Christian ministry, is presented. "Pray for us. We are sure that we have a clear conscience and desire to live honorably in every way. I particularly urge you to pray so that I may be restored to you soon" (13:18–19). This is the highest of all service—our ministry at the throne of grace. This is a blessed work from which nothing need ever debar us, and if we are hindered from personal activity we can pour out the strength of our lives through those for whom we pray. So let us love, so let us be content, so let us stand steadfast, so let us enter into the fellowship of His sufferings, so let us serve, submit ourselves and pray for one another in the blessed household of faith and family of God.

PARTING BENEDICTION

But now the full heart of the writer turns from didactic speech and personal exhortation, and pours out one burning prayer and benediction, in which he gathers up the deepest teachings of this whole blessed epistle. "May the God of peace, who through the blood of the eternal covenant brought back from the dead our Lord Jesus, that great Shepherd of the sheep, equip you with everything good for doing his will, and may he work in us what is pleasing to him, through Jesus Christ, to whom be glory for ever and ever. Amen" (13:20–21).

1. The God of Peace

This beautiful expression sums up in a single phrase the spiritual results of the great redeeming work with which the epistle to the Hebrews has been occupied. We have already seen that the first great thought was the coming of Jesus Christ from God to bring us the message of His will. The next was the going back of Jesus Christ to God as our great High Priest. But the consummation of the writer's thought was the bringing of us back to God in full reconciliation and perfect fellowship, as the Author and Finisher of our faith. This is the idea expressed by the "God of peace." Jesus Christ has brought us back to God, and now He steps back from the foreground of the picture, and leaves us in the Father's house, and in direct relations with God Himself. There is no cloud between us and the eternal Father. He is to us the very God of peace.

2. The Shepherd of the Sheep

But while we recognize our reconciliation to the Father, not for a moment can we forget the blessed Mediator through whom it has been accomplished and is still maintained. Here a new figure is introduced, although it is used to express an old fact. It is the figure of the shepherd, and back of it there rises the vision of the lost and wandering sheep, of the long and loving search, of the midnight, the wilderness and the terrible cost, the glad homebringing and the peace and safety of the heavenly fold. But while this is a new figure in the epistle to the Hebrews, it is not a new figure in the Old Testament from which this beautiful epistle is so largely drawn. Indeed, it is the oldest, sweetest and most frequent image under which the grace of God has been portrayed, from Abel down to Christ Himself. And so it adds a delightful touch of tenderness and completeness to the whole epistle, to represent our Lord Jesus, in the last picture of His person and work, under the figure of the great Shepherd of the sheep.

3. The Everlasting Covenant

This expresses the security of our salvation and the solid and permanent foundation on which our relationship to God through the work of Jesus Christ has been established. It is the result of an arrangement as stable as the throne of God. Every condition of justice and equity has been met. Every possible cause of failure has been anticipated. And the interests of Christ's redeemed people are guaranteed by an everlasting covenant between the Father and the Son, in which all the conditions have been fully met, and all the contracts and promises ratified so completely that, as David expresses it, it is "arranged and secured in every part" (2 Samuel 23:5). This is one of the most helpful truths brought out in the epistle to the Hebrews, that we are saved not through the work of the law, but through a new covenant in which Christ has met and fulfilled all the conditions and bequeathed to us all the promises. As the writer expressed it in a former passage, "by two unchangeable things in which it is impossible for God to lie, we who have fled to take hold of the hope offered to us may be greatly encouraged. We have this hope as an anchor for the soul, firm and secure" (Hebrews 6:18–19).

4. The Precious Blood

"Through the blood of the eternal covenant" (13:20). This covenant has been ratified by blood, and the blood runs as a crimson thread all through this evangelical epistle. It is perhaps the most prominent thought in the central portion of the letter. There is no ambiguity about the teaching of this portion of the Scriptures respecting the cross of Christ. It is the blood that purchases our redemption. It is the blood that puts away our sin. It is the blood that seals and ratifies the covenant. It is the blood that sanctifies and keeps us. It is the blood that opens the way into the holiest of all. It is the blood that pleads for us, and claims the answer to our prayers. Over every page of this beautiful book we might well write the caption, "The Precious Blood of Christ."

5. The Practical Outworking

Next there is the practical outworking of this great redemption. "Equip you with everything good for doing his will" (13:21). It is not a mere treatise on systematic theology; it is not a mere intellectual diversion; but it leads to the very highest standard of holy living. His will becomes our rule of action, perfect conformity to it our goal of attainment, and every good work our mode of reaching this lofty standard and heavenly aim. The life of faith, if genuine and sincere, will always lead to the life of holy activity and practical righteousness. But here it is more than an ordinary standard of righteousness. It is nothing less than the highest perfection that the apostle asks for his readers. Just as the faith required in this epistle is the highest confidence, so the holiness presented as our ideal is entire conformity to the will of God "with everything good." This would be impossible for us, but it is not impossible when we remember the crowning thought of the whole epistle, that Jesus Himself is the Author and Finisher of our faith, and this truth is not forgotten in the closing benediction, for in the very next clause he reminds us of the divine inworking.

6. The Divine Inworking

Then there is mention of the divine inworking which is to bring about the practical outworking. This high and holy standard is not to be reached by our most strenuous exertions, but by God's "work in us what is pleasing to him, through Jesus Christ" (13:21). It is union with Christ, abiding in

Christ, the heart and life of Christ within us, the realization of that fine expression which we find in Colossians 1:29: "To this end I labor, struggling with all his energy, which so powerfully works in me," and which we find yet again in Philippians 2:12–13: "Work out your salvation with fear and trembling, for it is God who works in you to will and to act according to his good purpose."

7. The Doxology

And so the benediction ends in a sublime doxology: "To whom be glory for ever and ever. Amen" (Hebrews 13:21). Instead of being crushed with discouragement, and paralyzed with a sense of the impossibility of our task, we are lifted up to sublime confidence and praise by the delightful fact that it is not our working, but His, and duty is transformed into delight and the heart can only sing:

> Once it was my working,
>   His it hence shall be,
> Once I tried to use Him,
>   Now He uses me.

Well may we say of such a Savior and such a salvation, "to him be glory for ever and ever. Amen."

JAMES

CHAPTER 1

THE PRACTICAL DISCIPLINE OF LIFE

Consider it pure joy, my brothers, whenever you face trials of many kinds. (James 1:2)

Blessed is the man who perseveres under trial, because when he has stood the test, he will receive the crown of life that God has promised to those who love him. (1:12)

Rotherham slightly changes the translation of these verses, as does also the Revised Version. "My brethren, count it all joy when we fall in with divers temptations" (1:2). "Blessed is the man that endureth temptation (or testings), for when he is *approved*, he shall receive the crown of life, which the Lord hath promised to them that love him" (1:12).

The epistles of Paul and John represent the interior, the experiential, and spiritual side of Christian life, while that of James represents the practical. God makes His mosaics of many different pieces and the blending of all together makes the perfect whole. There is room for James as well as for Paul and John. Paul is the apostle of faith, John of love, Peter of comfort; but James is the apostle of good works, the apostle of practical living. He stands in the New Testament very much as the book of Proverbs stands in the Old. It has been said that the reason the Scotch are such a practical and prosperous race is because every Scotchman used to be brought up with the book of Proverbs in his vest pocket. It would be well to have some cheap editions of Proverbs and more pockets to hold them.

This conservative old minister in the church of Jerusalem, James, deals with the practical discipline of life from two sides.

THE DISCIPLINE THAT COMES TO US THROUGH TEMPTATION

1. Not an Unmingled Evil

He first tells us that temptation is not an unmingled evil. By temptation he means undoubtedly evil; not trouble, but the solicitation of evil, the battle for right with the power of the tempter and our evil heart. "Consider it pure joy, my brothers, whenever you face trials [temptations, KJV] of many kinds" (1:2). "Blessed is the man who perseveres under trial [temptation, KJV]" (1:12). While it is evil, it has a good side, and it becomes an agency in the education of our spiritual character and the strengthening of all the better elements of our nature.

2. Overruled by God

While temptation is not directly from God, yet it is overruled by God, and made one of His instrumentalities of blessing to us. "God cannot be tempted by evil, nor does he tempt anyone" (1:13), yet God permits us to be tempted. God put our first parents into temptation and He made it possible for them either to choose or refuse; He gave them a nature subject to temptation, and while it might overcome them, it might also be overcome. God does not tempt any man, yet He does allow this to be one of the classes in the school of faith and holiness. He even led Jesus Christ, His own Son, into the wilderness by the Spirit to be tempted of the devil. Think it not a strange thing then, dear friends, if your life is called to pass through the ordeal of the conflict—evil from within and from without, not merely things that grieve, afflict and distress you, but things that tend to make you do wrong and draw you from the path of righteousness, truth and godliness. They will come. God wants you to be forewarned and forearmed, and to know it is better that they should come to you, if you but take the panoply of God and come through in victory.

3. The Source of Temptation

We should never forget where the source of temptation comes from. "Each one is tempted when, by his own evil desire, he is dragged away and enticed" (1:14). Temptation comes from your own heart. There are innumerable tempters: men, women and fallen spirits of wickedness. But none have any power unless we have ourselves a traitor in the citadel of the heart. The enemy cannot get in unless you let him in. You hold the key of the fortress. Therefore it is in your own heart that the crucial battle is fought, the secret foe is hidden—your own lust, your own desire or "coveting," which is the literal translation, the thing in you that wants to do the wrong, your wish for it, even if it is not yet your will. This is the starting place of temptation. It is that blossom of sin. And this is where God wants to bring His sanctifying grace and take away the very desire.

Just as the sea fowl plunging in the miry water comes up undefiled because its wing is oiled and burnished and the filth around cannot adhere to it, so the Lord Jesus passed through the powers of darkness and the allurements of the world and all the evil that was around Him and was proof against it. He could say "the prince of this world is coming. He has no hold on me" (John 14:30). It is in the heart that temptation has its starting point. Ask God to give you a true and holy desire to please Him, and an instinctive repugnance and recoil from evil; and so long as you have this, you shall not fall into temptation.

4. The Blessedness of Resisting and Enduring Temptation

Then we have the blessedness of resisting and enduring temptation. "Consider it pure joy, my brothers, whenever you face trials [temptations, KJV] of many kinds, because you know that the testing of your faith develops perseverance. Perseverance must finish its work so that you may be mature and complete, not lacking anything" (James 1:2–4). "Blessed is the man who perseveres under trial [temptation, KJV]" (1:12). The battle does you good. The conflict educates you, strengthens you, establishes you, and is necessary for you that you may be grounded and settled and finally approved and rewarded. One of the best results of temptation is that it shows you what is in your own heart. It reveals yourself. Until temptation comes, you feel strong and self-confident; but when the keen edge of the adversary's weapon has pierced your soul, you have more sympathy with others and less confidence in your own self-sufficiency. You are humiliated and broken at His feet, a poor, helpless thing; and this is the best thing that can happen to you. God wants to disarm you and lay you low, and then He can lift and save you and give you His strength. It makes you humble and doubtful of yourself. You find you must not take the aggressive, but fly to your refuge in Christ. "He will also provide a way out so that you can stand up under it" (1 Corinthians 10:13). Like the little conies that hide in the rock and do not face their enemies, but fly for shelter, you will find your only safeguard is Jesus Christ. He is the shield to cover you, and you will be safe not by fighting, but by hiding behind the cross and in the bosom of your Savior. If you have had much spiritual conflict, it has humbled you, shown you your helplessness, and taught you sympathy for others.

Temptation exercises our faith and teaches us to pray. It is like military drill and a taste of battle to the young soldier. It puts us under fire and compels us to exercise our weapons and prove their potency. It shows us the resources of Christ and the preciousness of the promises of God. It teaches us the reality of the Holy Spirit, and compels us to walk closely with Him and hide continually behind His strength and all-sufficiency. Every victory gives us new confidence in our victorious Leader, and new courage for the next onset of the foe, so that we become not only victors, but more than conquerors, taking the strength of our conquered foes and gathering precious spoil from each new battlefield. Temptation strengthens what we have received and establishes us in all our spiritual qualities and graces.

You will find the forest trees which stand apart, exposed to the double violence of the storm, are always the sturdiest and strike their roots the deepest in the soil. And so it is true in the spiritual world, as the Apostle Peter expressed it: "The God of all grace, who called you to his eternal glory in Christ, after you have suffered a little while, will himself restore you and make you strong, firm and steadfast" (1 Peter 5:10).

At the same time temptation teaches us to watch as well as pray, to avoid the things that bring temptation, and to keep off the enemy's ground. It is only the inexperienced Christian that plays lightly with evil. Luther used to say "He must needs have a long spoon who sups with the devil." "Pray," says Bishop Hamlin, "from God's side of the fence." Don't jump over into the devil's garden and then ask God to help you, but keep on God's side, and watch and pray that you enter not into temptation. Often our overconfidence betrays us. Like the man who had escaped the bailiff who tried to serve him with a warrant for arrest, and had just got across the state line, where the law protected him, when his pursuer, exchanging guile for force, laughed and said, "You have the best of me. And now let us shake hands and part friends." The foolish fellow reached out his hand, and in a moment the bailiff had pulled him over to his side of the line and clapped the handcuffs on him. So if Satan cannot beat us fairly, he will allure us so near the borders of danger that we will be caught by his wiles. Some people sail so near the lake of fire that they get their sails scorched and find it impossible to get away. The maturest Christian is always the humblest and most watchful. Let us be not high-minded, but fear, and learn to combine the two blessed safeguards of hope and fear, which God has so wisely blended in these two passages: "If you think you are standing firm, be careful that you don't fall!" (1 Corinthians 10:12), and then in the 13th verse, "God is faithful; he will not let you be tempted beyond what you can bear." And yet once more, in the 14th verse, he returns to the language of warning and caution, "Therefore, my dear friends, flee from idolatry."

Temptation also teaches us patience. "Perseverance must finish its work so that you may be mature and complete, not lacking anything" (James 1:4). This implies that patience is the finishing grace of the Christian life. Therefore, God usually puts His children through the school of suffering last. It is the graduation class in the discipline of Christ. Let us not, therefore, be surprised if God puts us through the hottest of all furnaces, namely, that which is fired with the devil's brimstone, before He makes us vessels for his glory.

5. Temptation Brings a Reward

Temptation brings a glorious recompense of reward, for "because when he has stood the test, he will receive the crown of life that God has promised to those who love him" (1:12). There is a reward for the soul-winner. There is a reward for the Christian pastor and worker. But there is also a special reward for the man or the woman who has had no great service, and perhaps has won no single soul, but who has stood in the hard place, has kept sweet in the midst of wrong, and in the face of temptation, pure amid the allurements of the world, and simply withstood in the evil day, and having done all, stood at last approved.

On the field of Waterloo, there was a regiment which stood under fire through all that awful day and was not once suffered to charge upon the enemy. It held the key to the position, and as again and again permission to advance was asked, the answer came, "Stand firm." When they had nearly all fallen, the message came back for the last time from their commander, "You have saved the day," and the answer was returned, "You will find us all here." Sure enough they lay a heap of slain on that fatal, yet glorious hill. They had simply stood, and history has given them the reward of valor and the imperishable fame of having turned the tide of the greatest battle of the 19th century. So God is preparing crowns for quiet lives, for suffering women, for martyred children, for the victims of oppression and wrong, for the silent sufferers and the lonely victors who just endured temptation. Tempted brother, be of good cheer. Some day you will wonder at the brightness of your crown.

THE DISCIPLINE OF PROVIDENCE

In the striking parable of the potter and the wheel, Jeremiah has taught us that while God is disciplining the heart by the touch of His Spirit, He is turning round the clay on the wheel of providence and bringing us into new situations for the exercise of new graces and the teaching of new lessons with every alternation of life's conditions. So His providence cooperates with His Holy Spirit in the education of our spiritual character, and we are to recognize the things that happen to us as in no sense accidents, but simply divine methods of dealing with us and teaching and blessing us. So James proceeds to bring out the relation of God's providence to our spiritual discipline: "The brother in humble circumstances ought to take pride in his high position. But the one who is rich should take pride in his low position" (1:9–10).

1. The Discipline of Prosperity

We have the discipline of prosperity. This is not a hard or uncongenial experience to the natural heart, but it often is the hardest of all experiences for the soul. "I have learned," says Paul, "to be content whatever the circumstances. I know what it is to be in need, and I know what it is to have plenty [abound, KJV]" (Philippians 4:11–12). But how few Christians really know how to abound. How frequently prosperity changes their temper and the habits and fruits of their lives! To receive God's blessing in temporal things, to have wealth suddenly thrust upon us, to be surrounded with the congenial friends, to be enriched with all the happiness that love, home, the world's applause and unbounded prosperity can give, and yet to keep a humble heart, to be separated from the world in its spirit and in its pleasures, to keep our hearts in holy indifference from the love and need of earthly things, to stand for God as holy witnesses in the most public station, and to use our prosperity and wealth as a sacred trust for Him, counting nothing our own, and still depending upon Him as simply as in the days of penury—this, indeed, is an experience rarely found, and only possible through the infinite grace of God. And yet God calls His children in greater or less measure to pass through the test of blessing.

It may not be a great fortune, but a joy in your humble life worth more to you than millions. Now He does not ask us to refuse it, to be harsh, narrow and monkish, and think to make ourselves better by asperities and penances. No, "The brother in humble circumstances ought to take pride in his high position" (James 1:9). Open your heart to the love and joy He is bringing. Bask in the sunshine of His smile. But do it with a humble and unselfish heart. Let your blessing only make you more sensitive to the sufferings of others, more grateful to Him, and more ready to make sacrifices and render services to your Master and your fellow men. Then can God rejoice over you to do you good with all His heart and with all His soul.

2. The Discipline of Adversity

Then comes the other side of the revolving wheel, the discipline of adversity. The brother of high degree is made low. Wealth takes wings and flies away. Friends prove false, and even the downy nest of love and home breeds viper's eggs and bitter heartbreaks. But we must still rejoice. God is testing us in the crucible. We have a witness for Him that only the dark shadows can bring out. Let us be true to our testimony. Let us glorify Him in the fires. Let us look over the head of all our trouble to Him, and still believe that "in all things God works for the good of those who love him" (Romans 8:28). Then nothing can be against us.

And sorrow touched by God grows bright

With more than rapture's ray,
As darkness shows us worlds of light
We never saw by day.

Adversity often has to come to save us from the loss of eternal life. Then only when all other things fail us, can we fully find the all-sufficiency of God, and learn that within ourselves we may possess the resources of perfect happiness by having Him. It was thus that the Hebrew Christians could take joyfully the spoiling of their goods, knowing in themselves that they had a better and more enduring substance (Hebrews 10:34).

It is a rare secret in the alchemy of grace to be able thus to transmute a seeming flaw into an eternal touch of grace and glory.

A lapidary once purchased a beautiful stone, but found afterwards that there was a hidden flaw of iron rust beneath the surface. At first he was disposed to throw it away as worthless. Then there came to him the conception of a rich design, in which a female figure was cut in the stone, and the strong tint of the iron vein was carved into a rich robe whose drapery and color added a beautiful adorning to the exquisite figure. Thus the flaw became the fairest charm in all the fine creation of his genius. And so God would have us take the things that seem to be against us and so transmute them by the power of His grace that "instead of the thornbush will grow the pine tree,/ and instead of briers the myrtle will grow" (Isaiah 55:13).

In conclusion let us learn to find in God the secret of blessing and victory under all conditions and circumstances, and even to turn the hate of Satan into an occasion of victory and blessing. Thus shall the curse be made a blessing, sorrow turned into joy, and even sin so conquered that grace shall much more abound.

CHAPTER 2

PRACTICAL FAITH

If any of you lacks wisdom, he should ask God, who gives generously to all without finding fault, and it will be given to him. But when he asks, he must believe and not doubt, because he who doubts is like a wave of the sea, blown and tossed by the wind. That man should not think he will receive anything from the Lord. (James 1:5–7)

There is nothing in the world more practical than faith. It may seem to the naturalist a very dreamy, speculative thing, but when we stop to think, we will readily see that the most practical thing in life is confidence. Like the law of gravitation which holds the universe together, the principle of cohesion that binds human society is confidence between man and man. Take it away from the home, and where would the family be? Take it away from business, and where would your bank and stock exchanges be? Take it away from the State, and we have revolution, anarchy, socialism and the uprooting of the foundations of society.

A few months ago a certain stock went up from 16 points to 160 points. When the manipulation was sufficient to make several millionaires, then confidence failed. We were told in the newspapers of yesterday that 50 million dollars were waiting for a certain financial scheme. The moment a franchise was secured, a mighty structure would be spanned across the Hudson River, and all our complicated lines of transportation directly connected with New York. The money is ready for this, but all that is necessary is confidence. If confidence is a fortune in business, how much more in the higher realm?

The scientist believes, and risks everything for his beliefs. The Prince of Wales was standing beside Professor Playfair once, near a cauldron of boiling lead at white heat. The professor said: "I am going to ask you to put your hand in that cauldron and ladle out a handful of that lead." "Do you tell me to do it?" asked the Prince. "Yes, but wait a moment." He then washed the

Prince's hand with ammonia that there might be no oil on his flesh. The Prince put his hand in the cauldron and poured out some of the boiling lead without injury. He believed the word of the scientist and risked his life upon it, just because he had confidence.

We owe this continent to the fact that a humble Italian believed in a great West—to him a great East—and he plodded on in his faith. He met rebuffs and refusals, but his vessels were at last launched, and Christopher Columbus discovered America, because he believed in it.

Palissy worked a long time to develop the secrets of his exquisite art. His wife reviled him, and his children pleaded with him to give up his foolishness and settle down to honest work. He saw only this mighty secret, he believed in it and he worked it out; his faith became a fact and in consequence was crowned with triumph and success.

So it is that everything that is of value in the world has come from the confidence of some great soul who pressed on till triumph was achieved and his efforts were crowned with success.

And so in the higher world, the mightiest force is faith. It is the law of Christianity. Paul calls it the "law of faith" (Romans 3:27, KJV). It is just as mighty a law in the spiritual world as gravitation is in the material world. It binds us to God, and then to one another. So Abraham goes out, leaving the culture and wealth of that ancient civilization, out into the wilderness, an emigrant, and God gives him a new kingdom, and all our hopes have sprung from that old pioneer believer who dared to risk everything upon God.

Thus Joseph goes down and down for years, until his life is crushed and "the iron enters his soul." But he believes through it all in the vision of his youth, and he comes up again, as every true believer does at last, and becomes the lord of Egypt, and transforms the destiny of two nations.

We find the Old and the New Testament full of the triumphs of faith, until at last Jesus Himself becomes the "Prince Leader" of our faith, and achieves His miracles and works His mighty deeds by faith in God. When asked why the fig tree withered, He said faith had caused it. At the grave of Lazarus he said, "Father, I thank you that you have heard me. I knew that you always hear me" (John 11:41–42). It was faith. He never doubted God. He always expected the thing to come to pass that He claimed.

So He has left to us the secret. Paul has told us we may "have the faith of the Son of God" (Galatians 2:20, KJV), the very same touch that He had; we may link with Omnipotence just as He did. There are just two things that are almighty, God and faith. The man that believes God just comes into partnership with God and shares His all-sufficiency. We know that in the natural world the mightiest forces are those we do not see—not the mountains, but the principle that holds them together; not the worlds, but the law that moves them; not the things we touch, but the hidden forces that control them. And we are being taught by the progress of our age to believe in nature's forces and to use them as levers to lift our loads and as motors to move our engines. So in the spiritual world faith is the power to attach ourselves to God.

There are two ways to do things—faith and works; one to do them yourself, the other to let God do them. The power of faith is not how much can I do, but how much can God do? Faith saves us just because it puts us into God's hands. It drops us into the salvation that He has already finished, and we have only to accept. Faith sanctifies us, not because it would have us do better, but it brings the power to do it. So faith heals, not by slowly building up the tissues and blood, but by putting a new electric fountain of vitality in your frame that makes an old man young, and although ready to drop into the grave keeps you by a second life. Faith brings the answers to your prayers, because it takes God's prayers instead of yours, and then they must be answered, because they are His asking, claiming and commanding. Faith puts us out and brings God in, and our life becomes a supernatural one. Faith is, therefore, a practical force, the secret of all real power, and a secret which can be applied to everything in our life. Let us now examine the exposition of faith as we find it in the Epistle of James.

THE PRINCIPLE OF FAITH

We are taught the principle of faith—what it is and how it comes.

It must be absolute and unwavering. You cannot have a half faith. It must be not doubting. The element of uncertainty destroys the vitality of faith just as much as a scratch defaces a mirror, and as a little chip in the side of your grain of corn kills the germ. The faith which accomplishes omnipotent results is confidence, boldness and the full assurance of faith.

Next we are told that faith is the receiving organ of the soul, that without it we cannot receive anything of the Lord. "God . . . gives generously to all without finding fault" (James 1:5), or "of course," as Alford translates it. God always gives. But the unbelieving heart cannot receive. It is fettered and paralyzed by its doubts, and like the sensitive plant shrinks helplessly, and misses the blessing that His love would gladly have bestowed. "That man should not think he will receive anything from the Lord" (1:7).

FAITH AND WISDOM

"If any of you lacks wisdom, he should ask God . . . But when he asks, he must believe and not doubt" (1:5–6). Wisdom is that quality which enables us to suit the right means to the end in view. It is wholly practical and concerned not with theories and ideas, but with actual conditions and the way to meet them. It teaches us how to live, and enables us to meet every emergency rightly and successfully. It does not mean that we are infallible. It is not the wisdom of our common sense and level-headedness. It presupposes our ignorance and fallibility, and takes God's wisdom instead of our own. Even when we cannot understand His leading, faith still can trust Him that it will be right in the end. Even when we err, God's wisdom can still over-rule our mistake and bring blessing out of it in the end.

Spurgeon used to tell about a weather vane which had the text inscribed above it, "God is love." When he asked the old miller why he put the verse on top of it, he said that it might speak to the people at all points of the compass and say to them, "God is love, whichever way the wind blows." So faith in God's wisdom counts upon His goodness and faithfulness in the face of all conditions and in spite of all hindrances.

John Vassar used to say that he doubted whether our so-called mistakes were mistakes always. Knocking at a door one day in quest of a woman with whom he wished to speak about her soul, a different person met him, and told him that he had made a mistake, and that she did not live there. The good man answered, "I guess it is not a mistake after all, but the Lord wants me to talk to you instead." And so tactfully breaking through the barrier of her strangeness, he reached her heart, and ended by leading her to the Savior.

I recall an incident in the early history of this work through which I was strangely led to lease as my residence for a year the dwelling in which all the Alliance work began in this city. I had been offered the house by a friend who owned it, and after much prayer had decided that it was the Master's will that I should take it. But on almost the last day of the season I was in-formed that the house had just been sold to a neighbor who was determined to live in it himself. All efforts to induce this man to consent to my occupy-ing the house were vain, and the only thing left was to accept the house that the man was leaving instead, as the season was late, and moving day came within 24 hours. Against every inclination I became convinced that it was the Lord's will for me to consent to this arrangement. After a great struggle I called to sign the lease for the unwelcome house, which was most unattrac-tive in every way. To my surprise, however, the gentleman came out to greet me, and immediately explained that he had changed his mind and decided to stay where he was, and that he would be glad to lease the other house that he had just purchased, as we desired. The strange reason of it all was that that very day he had attended the funeral of an old friend in the country, and that he and his wife had come home with the feeling that if they moved something might happen to them. It was a mere superstition, but God had allowed it to come in order to change his mind and accomplish the purpose to which He had been leading all the time.

There is nothing in the whole circle of our commonplace life that we may not bring to God in faith, and thus find a hundred Ebenezers every day all along the path of life.

FAITH AND WORKS

In the second chapter of James the apostle takes up the practical side of faith, and shows that it is not idle dreaming, but stepping out and acting according to our convictions. There are works that are not the works of faith, but the works of fear, doubt and human dependence. But there are works which must follow faith, if it is genuine and vital. When the nobleman believed the word that Jesus had spoken for the healing of his boy, he was bound to stop his praying, and go back to meet the answer that had been promised. When the cripple at Lystra believed the gospel which Paul preached, immediately he rose up and leaped and walked. "If I believed," said an infidel, "as you say you do, that the world was perishing and that Christ alone could save it, I would abandon every interest and fly to the ends of the earth to tell men the story of salvation." As poor crippled Tom used to say, "Knowin' is lovin' and lovin' is doin'; and if we're not a doin' on it, we don't love Him, that's all."

FAITH AND HEALING

"And the prayer offered in faith will make the sick person well; the Lord will raise him up" (5:15). Surely this is practical faith, a faith that comes down to the level of our daily life and all our physical needs. This was the sort of faith that James believed in. And was he not right? If God cannot help us in the things we see, how can we expect Him to help us in the world of the future and the unseen?

In these days of materialism and unbelief on one hand, and fanaticism on the other; when the supernatural and scriptural conceptions of divine healing are in danger of being confounded with the vagaries of Christian Science and the extravagances of modern "apostles" and faith healers, it is more important than ever that a sober and conservative, yet bold and uncompromising testimony be given to the true doctrine of the Lord's healing. While this truth has not the first place in our testimony, it has a very important place; and the experience which it has brought us has become a turning point in the life and work of multitudes whom God has used in the teaching of deeper truth and the work of missions. While we do not go forth to be the special apostles of divine healing, yet we owe much of our ministry on the higher and more spiritual planes to this truth and its blessed influence.

It is most distinctly promised here to the prayer of faith. What the prayer of faith is the Apostle James has already told us in the first chapter. It is the prayer of the man who believes, nothing wavering, that he receives the things he asks. It involves three steps. First, to believe that divine healing is provided for us in the Word of God and in the work of Christ. Second, to come to God and actually claim it for ourselves by a definite act of committal. And third, to act as if we had it, and step out and prove our faith by our works.

Over in Flamborough, Ontario, there lives a young farmer named Patterson, whose parents are well known to me, and whose brother is one of our most prominent official workers. A few years ago he broke his leg, and the village doctor came and set it, showing the family beforehand how serious the compound fracture was, so that the father told afterwards how he had with his own hand felt the great void between the broken bones. The limb was tied with splints as usual and stretched out in a horizontal position, and the patient told to keep in that position for several weeks. Next morning to the surprise of the family, young Patterson was out feeding the cattle at the usual hour and doing his work as if nothing had happened. The explanation was this: During the night the Lord had spoken to him something on this wise, "Have I not healed you often before, and can't you trust Me now? Then, if you trust Me what are you going to do about it?" The young man knew the Lord and had proved Him. And so he quietly got up, took off the splints, and lay down again until daylight, and then arose and dressed himself and went about his work, and has been going about it ever since. That is the prayer of faith.

FAITH AND SERVICE

Higher than healing, infinitely more important than helping people out of their troubles, is the climax to which James conducts us in the closing verses, after having told us that "The prayer of a righteous man is powerful and effective" (5:16). Here is faith's highest triumph and its noblest ministry. "My brothers, if one of you should wander from the truth and someone should bring him back, remember this: Whoever turns a sinner from the error of his way will save him from death and cover over a multitude of sins" (5:19–20). How is this to be accomplished? It is given to the ministry of faith, the faith that works by love. How will your children be saved? "Believe in the Lord Jesus, and you will be saved—*you and your household*" (Acts 16:31, italics added). Read the story of Jerry McAuley and you will find that after his conversion, he often "erred from the truth" and had to be re-converted, or, rather, brought back to the fold; and but for the patient, untiring love of a humble missionary, who used to pursue him, when he tried to slip out of the meeting unobserved, and hold him back from the river thieves, and was always saying to him, "Jerry, keep on trying, keep on trying, and it will be all right at last"—but for this, the story of his wondrous life and his harvest of precious souls would never have been told.

In a wretched attic in London there lived a lad named Tom Reed, a poor cripple, who was sometimes able to drag himself to the corner and sweep the street crossing for a penny, and sometimes even to find his way to the little mission round the corner, where they told about Jesus and His love. His only earthly friends were his grandmother, who gave him a scant living, and Jack Lee, his pal. One day Jack called to say good-bye, as he started to the country for a new field of operations in his humble trade. And he brought Tom a shilling as his parting gift, telling him that he must use it for something he "wanted partikler." Then Tom told him that what he wanted "most partikler" was a Bible. Jack tried to laugh him out of it, for "these here books," he said, were only for scholars, and not for such as they. But Tom begged hard, and at last Jack went out and got the Bible, adding as he left him that the bookseller had told him that the book was all right and might make his fortune yet. It wasn't long till Tom had devoured it, and was so full of it that he felt he must do something for his Savior and his fellow sinners. So he denied himself his daily mug of milk to buy some paper and a pencil, and began to write verses of his Bible on bits of paper. After praying over them and watering them with his tears, he would address the outside, "Passerby, please read," and drop them out of the window. One day a handsome gentleman climbed the rickety stairs and asked if he was the boy who dropped the papers out of the window. And then he told Tom with much feeling that he had come to thank him for the blessing he had brought him, and how his own son in the country, a suffering and dying boy, had pleaded with him to find some service to do for God, so that he would not go empty-handed to meet his Master. The verse that he had picked up was this: "I must work the works of him that sent me, while it is day" (John 9:4, KJV), and it had changed his whole purpose and life. Tom did not want any thanks. "I only do the writin'," he said, "He does the blessin'." But the gentleman undertook the care of Tom henceforth in his little attic, and went to live out his lesson. He built a mission chapel for his boy, and souls were saved, and Tom's warning message to him was faithfully lived out. "Tell your rich friends that if they are not workin' for Him they don't know Him, for workin' is lovin', and lovin' is doin'." One day there came a little parcel to the mission. It was Tom's old Bible, underlined and stained with many a tear, for Tom had gone above, where "their deeds will follow them" (Revelation 14:13). And for many a day the old Bible continued to live out its owner's life, and "he still speaks, even though he is dead" (Hebrews 11:4). God give us the faith that knows and loves and does for Jesus' sake. Amen.

CHAPTER 3

PRACTICAL OBEDIENCE

Do not merely listen to the word, and so deceive yourselves. Do what it says. Anyone who listens to the word but does not do what it says is like a man who looks at his face in a mirror and, after looking at himself, goes away and immediately forgets what he looks like. But the man who looks intently into the perfect law that gives freedom, and continues to do this, not forgetting what he has heard, but doing it—he will be blessed in what he does. (James 1:22–25)

Practical obedience naturally follows the subject of practical faith. Trust and obey are the two wings which maintain the equilibrium of our flight, the two oars which keep us steadily in the channel of our course. This paragraph unfolds some of the profoundest ethical principles of the New Testament.

THE WILL OF GOD

First, there is the will of God as the supreme authority of right and duty.

"The Father of the heavenly lights, who does not change like shifting shadows. He chose [of his own will, KJV] to give to us birth through the word of truth" (James 1:17–18). Here our very conversion is referred back to the will of God as its supreme source. And God Himself is recognized as the Sovereign Being who sits enthroned in His eternal, unchangeable and infallible authority and righteousness as the Sovereign of our being and of all being. The figure here involved in the beautiful original phrase is that of the parallax by which the astronomer measures the distance of the remotest stars. The parallax is the angle formed by two points on the earth's surface from which an observation is taken of a distant star according to the angle made. From these two points we measure the distance of the star by the acuteness of the angle. But with God, James says there is no parallax. Looking at Him from every standpoint He is eternally the same and His will is forever the same. Therefore, there is a fixed standard of right and wrong, and duty is not a mere accommodation to circumstances, sentiments or human opinions, but conformity to the will of God.

THE WORD OF GOD

This passage presents the Word of God as the standard of right and wrong. For this supreme Lawgiver has given us a law, and has revealed to us His will concerning our conduct. That law is here called "the perfect law that gives freedom" (1:25). It is a perfect law. There is no greater miracle in the Bible than its revelation of righteousness. Even the Decalogue itself, although not nearly so perfect in its primal edition at Sinai as it has become through the teachings of the Son of Man, and as reissued and reenacted by Him through the Sermon on the Mount and His wise and holy teachings, is a marvelous monument of the wisdom and righteousness of God. One of our American Justices, it is said, was converted from infidelity to Christianity by studying the Mosaic Law. "Where did Moses get that Law?" he asked himself after carefully reading and analyzing it. There is nothing in the literature of Egypt, Chaldea or Greece from which he could have derived its profound and comprehensive principles of jurisprudence. Everything is there in the most condensed and comprehensive form. Under two great tables he classifies our duty to God and to one another, and covers all ethical questions with sublime simplicity and completeness. He must have got it from heaven. And so he did. And as we read it in its larger edition in the spiritual teachings of the New Testament, it claims the subjection of our conscience, the homage of our will, the obedience of our life, and we are constrained to say of it, as Jehovah said of His ancient commandments, that it is "for our good always" (Deuteronomy 6:24, KJV).

THE LAW OF LIBERTY

Here in James it is described by a new phrase, "the perfect law of liberty" (James 1:25, KJV). This is the New Testament law, the law of love. As it came to us from Sinai, it was not the law of liberty, but of condemnation. But now with its penalty met in the person of Christ, and its motive power supplied by His Holy Spirit and His indwelling life in our heart, it becomes to us not the authority of necessity, but the constraint of love. It is the law in our heart becoming part of our nature so that we keep it, not because we have to, but because we love to. As citizens of the State we do not avoid the crime of murder because we fear that we will be electrocuted if we murder, but because our nature lifts us above it. We do not want to murder. We are under the law of liberty. We make the law ourselves, and so long as we keep it, we are free from it, for the "law is made not for the righteous but for lawbreakers and rebels" (1 Timothy 1:9). The obedient are lifted above it, and are free from its condemnation and its bondage.

THE GRAFTED WORD

A new figure is here introduced (James 1:21, KJV). The principle of grafting is very simple and suggestive. On a common root or stock a cultivated bud or branch is fastened and trained to grow into its new trunk and stem until all its vegetable organism has become connected with the new fountainhead. And then it begins to bear, not the fruit of the old stem, which is but a common crab or wild vine, but the cultivated fruit in all its mellowness and delicacy of flavor. It is really drawing upon the life of the old root, but crowning it with new beauty and richest fruitfulness. So upon the stem of our natural life God engrafts His Word, and so infuses and inworks that Word into our very life that it becomes the element of our being and the second nature of all our habits, controlling us without arbitrary constraint and making it our delight to do His will. Thus it becomes to us a law of liberty. We do right because we want to. We serve God because we love Him. Obedience becomes as natural as sin was before, and the heart is spontaneous and free in all its spiritual affections and actions. Obedience, therefore, is not a matter of outward authority, but inward impulse. Character is not built as you would build a house, by adding plank and timber to timber from the outside, but as God builds a tree, by throwing out life from the inside, and adding each new layer from the heart out.

This is the secret of liberty and power in all the natural and spiritual world. Take the laws of the physical realm and get them incorporated into your industrial art, and what power they exercise! Take the law of electricity and put it in your house as a telephone, and it will carry your messages for hundreds of miles. Put it in your towns and cities as a telegraph system, and it will traverse continents and oceans with its messages of fire. Put it in your vehicles, and it will carry your trolleys and your automobiles. Put it in your factories, and it will become the motive power of all business, transportation and commerce. But let it get beyond your control, disobey it, and it will strike you lifeless with the lightning's awful blaze. So the Word of God must be received, incorporated, engrafted and assimilated into our spiritual being, and then it becomes the motive power of our being and the guide of our life.

THE MORAL CONDITIONS

The passage presents the moral conditions which hinder the free operation of the Word of God in our lives.

"Therefore, get rid of all moral filth and the evil that is so prevalent and humbly accept the word planted in you, which can save you" (1:21). Just as the electric current must be insulated before it can be operated, so the Word of God cannot work freely in a soul that willingly indulges in sin. Two forms of evil are here classified, one the impure, the other the malignant. Filthiness includes all forms of sensual indulgence; naughtiness all forms of bitter and malicious feeling. Either of these will cloud the spiritual vision and interrupt the life of God in the heart. Just as the compass on shipboard can be deflected from its true direction by a counter-attraction through some piece of metal thoughtlessly left on deck, so conscience, though sincere, may be warped and misdirected by the influence of unholy desire of indulgence, and the soul perverted even when flattering itself that it is acting with the deepest sincerity and doing that which it believes to be right. There must, therefore, be a spirit of surrendered self-will and holy meekness, if we would receive the engrafted word. The Apostle Peter expresses the same truth in almost identical terms, "Therefore, rid yourselves of all malice and all deceit, hypocrisy, envy, and slander of every kind. Like newborn babies, crave pure spiritual milk, so that by it you may grow up in your salvation" (1 Peter 2:1– 2). Therefore it has come to pass that this same Word of God has been used to defend the most unholy teachings by men whose judgment was biased by a wrong heart, and whose conscience was perverted by an unsanctified spirit.

THE SELF-REVEALING POWER

James talks about the self-revealing power of the Word of God. It is here compared to a mirror, and the ordinary hearer of the Word to a man beholding his natural face in the glass. But the hasty glance passes, and he "immediately forgets what he looks like" (James 1:24). The true hearer is represented by the man who takes a nearer view of himself in the sacred mirror, and becomes not a forgetful hearer of the Word, but a doer. Literally translated, this should read, "But the man who looks intently into the perfect law that gives freedom, and continues to do this, not forgetting what he has heard, but doing it—he will be blessed in what he does" (1:25). The beginning of all self-improvement is self-knowledge, and the most wholesome knowledge we can have of ourselves is to know our faults. "Blessed are the poor in spirit,/ for theirs is the kingdom of heaven" (Matthew 5:3). Blessed are they that are dissatisfied, for they shall be satisfied, so this has been happily translated. It is thus that the Word of God sanctifies us by showing us first our need, and then leading us to Christ for the supply. We look into the picture of love first in the 13th chapter of First Corinthians, and we see how little we have of the love that "is patient [and] is kind" (13:4). Humbled by a sense of our failure, we take Christ for the grace of love. We bring our strifes and quarrels to the teaching of Jesus in the 18th and 19th chapters of Matthew, and we begin to settle our disputes according to the Word.

Thus we "discern ourselves," and by true self-judgment we escape the divine judgment and rise to a higher righteousness, taking Christ as our sanctification over against our self-condemnation. The willingness to see ourselves in our true light is the very highest proof of a true heart. "The fear of the LORD is the beginning of wisdom" (Proverbs 9:10). And the best evidence that there is no hidden sin covered up in our heart is our readiness to say, "Search me, O God, and know my heart;/ test me and know my anxious thoughts./ See if there is any offensive way in me,/ and lead me in the way everlasting" (Psalm 139:23–24).

THE BLESSEDNESS OF DOING

"He will be blessed in what he does" (James 1:25). Having seen our fault and also the vision of God's highest will for us, now follows the responsibility of practical obedience. James is a thorough believer in good works. He is no musty ascetic living in pensive cloisters and dreaming his life away in self-centered introspection, but a man of wholesome action carrying his religion into the light of day and the field of human life and helpful duty. It is in the doing that the blessing comes.

1. The Secret of Faith

This is the remedy for doubt and the secret of faith. "If anyone chooses to do God's will, he will find out whether my teaching comes from God or whether I speak on my own" (John 7:17). Don't argue with your skeptic. Say to him as Christ used to say, "Come and see." Prove Christianity by testing it. Go to God with even the little faith you have, or if you have nothing but doubt to bring, go with your doubt. Tell Him the worst. If you can only pray, "O God, if there be a God, help me," He will hear that cry.

I once knew of an intelligent infidel being converted by what might be called an unconscious prayer. His Christian wife had just died, and in the remembrance of her beautiful life and still more beautiful death, his heart was bursting with agony. Before he realized it, he had uttered a sob of prayer to her God for comfort and help. Instantly he remembered that he did not believe in her God; but before he had time to recall his prayer by an act of reasoning, it had reached heaven through an impulse of his heart, and the answer had come back to him in a new consciousness such as he had never felt before. From that moment he knew there was a God. He had proved Him by the practical test.

2. The Way to Find Salvation

This is the best way to find salvation. Take it as Christ has freely offered it, and then begin to act as if you had it, and you will be blessed in your doing. The best formula for beginning a Christian life that we have ever heard is the simple resolution of Hendly Vivars the night in which he turned away from a life of ungodliness to follow Christ, "If this be true for me, I will live from this moment as a man that has been cleansed from all sin by the blood of Christ." That decision put him on salvation ground, and from that moment he was a Christian. The most happy and useful Christian I have ever known was a gentleman who struggled for months for a religious experience without any result, and then quietly walked into the woods one day and made this resolution, "From this moment I will serve Christ as my Master whether I am lost or saved. My business is to follow Him. The responsibility of my salvation rests with Him." Before 24 hours had passed, that man was rejoicing in the experience that he had stopped seeking, and was blessed in his doing.

3. Realizing the Experience and the Baptism

This is the way to realize the experience of Christ's indwelling and the baptism of the Spirit. Simply yield yourself to God and claim the promise of the Spirit. And then begin to act as if you had Him as your Sanctifier, Keeper and indwelling Life, and He will answer to your expectation and meet your faith. If you venture on Him, He will be there every time. It is the doing that brings the blessing.

4. The Action in Healing

Are you seeking for healing? Christ never healed anybody on his back or his bed. "Stretch out your hand" (Matthew 12:13), was His prescription to the man with the withered hand. "Get up! Pick up your mat and walk" (John 5:8), was His command to the paralytic. "Go, show yourselves to the priests" (Luke 17:14), He said to the lepers, and "as they went they were cleansed" (17:14). "You may go. Your son will live" (John 4:50), He told the anxious father, and as he was obeying, the message met him that the healing had come. It was in doing something they all received the blessing. And so still we must show our faith by our works, and find strength in stepping out even in our weakness, and throwing ourselves upon the strength of God for life's duties and demands.

5. The Key to Finding Happiness

Would you find joy and happiness? Again it will meet you in doing the will of God. "Well done, good and faithful servant!" (Matthew 25:21), is the significant benediction of the Master, "come and share your master's happiness!" (25:21). It is duty well done that brings the joy of the Lord.

"What is heaven?" said one of our eccentric preachers. "I'll tell you what heaven is. It's out yonder in that little back street where a poor widow is weeping over her roofless children and sitting on her boxes and furniture on the street. Go to her with a basket of groceries, a load of coal and a good-sized bank note for her unpaid rent, and you will soon find what heaven is."

And the hard-fisted hearer came next day to tell Mr. Jones that he had been in heaven the last 24 hours, ever since he had found that poor widow and helped her out of her distress.

I remember a New Year long ago in my own experience when I dedicated a whole month, beginning with the week of prayer, to wait in my musty old study for a fuller baptism of the Spirit. I had received the Spirit, but I was straining after something more. Day after day I prayed, and left my duties largely undone. Thicker grew the murky air, and darker the visions of my troubled brain. More intense became my sensations and temptations, and more terrible the struggle with my feelings and my spiritual foes. But still I persevered, expecting surely some mighty blessing. At last one day when my brain was almost bursting with the strain, I turned to my Bible with a cry for direction and help. Before me in letters of light I read, "He is not here, He is risen. He goeth before you into Galilee. There shall ye see Him. Go ye and teach all nations" (see Matthew 28, KJV). In a moment the message was plain. Not dreaming, but doing. And as I went forth from that cloister to the bedsides of the sick and the pressing duties of a sad world, lo, the light returned, the sky cleared, the Master was revealed, the Lord drew nigh, and a blessing came which has never ceased through all these years to meet me still, as I go forth in self-forgetting love to bless others, to pray for others and to find the fellowship of the Master in doing His perfect will.

6. The Things That Count the Most

Finally, in the work of the Lord and the ministry of our Christian service we shall find that what we do and what we are count for more than what we say. Missionary Richards preached for many years with little effect to the savages of the Congo, until one day he began to live the Sermon on the Mount in their midst, and told them he was going to act according to all its precepts. Before the day was over they had taken him at his word, and the last stick of his furniture was gone. But before the next sun went down they had felt that they, too, must live according to the Sermon, and they brought back his furniture with compound interest. Before many months were passed hundreds of them were saved, and today (1901) the largest congregation on the Congo stands there at Banza Mateke as the monument, not of saying, but of doing the Word of God.

In the last months of the Civil War there was a soldier in Andersonville prison named Frank Smith. The day came for the exchange of prisoners. Six Northern soldiers were to be released for six Confederates, and Frank Smith heard with delight his name read. But a poor fellow with a wife and children came and pleaded so hard that Frank gave up his ticket of release, and let the other be his substitute and go home to the little family that needed him more. The months rolled round, and again there was a release of prisoners, and once more Frank Smith heard his name called and dreamed of home and liberty. But he remembered an infidel whom he had often talked to in the prison, and he said, "I cannot go till I make one more appeal to him to accept Christ." But the infidel laughed him to scorn, and told him that talk was cheap. Then Frank breathed a prayer and made a great resolution. Taking his little ticket of release from his pocket he said, "Take this, and in my place tomorrow walk out into freedom." The infidel started and looked hard at him "What made you do this?" he asked. "The love of Christ," he said. "The Christ that you will not receive." Then the proud heart broke; sobbing and kneeling beside him, he asked forgiveness for his hard heart, and gave himself to the Savior whose love could make such sacrifice possible. "It was not what you said that convinced me," he explained, "but it was what you did."

Once again there came a day when a little company walked forth from that awful dungeon into liberty, and for the third time Frank Smith's name was on the roll. He went to a lad who was dying of consumption. The poor fellow wept bitterly and said: "Oh, Frank, I had hoped that you could be with me at the last. I have nobody else to pray with me or point me to the Savior. How shall I ever die alone?" Again Frank closed his eyes, lifted his heart to God, and formed another big resolution. He gave his ticket of liberty for the third time to someone else, and he went back, and throwing his arms around the dying boy, he said, "I'll not leave you till He comes to take you." And he held the hand of the sinking lad until the gates of light opened, and with blessings on his lips a ransomed soul passed in.

Then on the dark storm clouds of war burst the rainbow of peace. The gates of Andersonville prison swung open forever, and this Christian hero went forth to well-earned liberty with a record of Christian heroism and blessed doing mightier than libraries of books or sermons.

So may we be blessed in our doing.

CHAPTER 4

PRACTICAL LOVE

If you really keep the royal law found in Scripture, "Love your neighbor as yourself," you are doing right. (James 2:8)

Speak and act as those who are going to be judged by the law that gives freedom. (2:12)

W e now come to practical love as set forth in this plain, matter-of-fact manual for daily life.

We will call it practical love, for there is another kind of love. No word has been so prominent in song and story all through the history of human life and literature as this old word "love." But the best kind of love is not the most prominent in song and story. There, sitting in that home, is a beautiful girl full of sentimental love, her mother's hope, her father's darling, the idol of her social circle and of herself. She is an example of sentimental love. But there is that old mother, wrinkled and worn by a lifetime of toil for that ungrateful child. That is the love that has sacrificed, suffered and forgotten itself to minister to another's comforts and luxuries. That is practical love.

Standing in that pulpit is a minister who can speak about love in glowing terms. In front is a poor unlettered Christian, who, when they asked about the doctrines of the creed and confession, was unable to answer the questions that were necessary to make him a member of the Church of Christ. They are about to drop him, when he breaks out into a great sob and cries, "I canna' speak for Him, but I could die for Him." Ah, that is love more eloquent than words! It is the love that Jesus talks about, the love that does things for Christ's sake and for our fellow man.

THE ROYAL LAW OF LOVE

"If you really keep the royal law, . . . 'Love your neighbor as yourself,' you are doing right. . . . Speak and act as those who are going to be judged by the law that gives freedom" (James 2:8, 12). Undoubtedly it is the law of love that he is thinking about when he speaks of the royal law. It is a royal law because:

1. The Law of the Kingdom

It is the law of the kingdom. It is the one great law that He had laid down, and the Decalogue is but the amplification of two thoughts, " 'Love the Lord your God with all your heart' . . . 'Love your neighbor as yourself.' All the Law and the Prophets hang on these two commandments [which are but one]" (Matthew 22:37–40). Love is therefore the law of the kingdom and the law of the King.

2. The Law by Which the King Lives and Acts

But not only so, it is also the law by which the King Himself lives and acts. It is the royal law because God makes it His own law, and God is not above the law of love. "God is Love" (1 John 4:16), and everything He does is according to the divine law of love. "Carry each other's burdens, and in this way you will fulfill the law of Christ" (Galatians 6:2). This law of Christ is love. The Father's love from eternity reached out beyond Himself in blessing. And from that came this wondrous universe so full of goodness and loving kindness; every object of it proclaiming not only His wisdom and power but His thoughtful kindness and loving regard for the happiness of His creatures. He might have made the earth a dazzling white or a crimson glow and thus blinded you; but He has made it an exquisite green, adjusted to your optical organs. He might have given us food without the sense of taste and without the variety of supply. But He has given us 10,000 sources of gratification through our senses. He made earth a ministering paradise even amid the ruins of the Fall, and fitted us to enjoy it. Everything might have contributed to our pain where now it ministers to our pleasure. "The earth is full of thy riches" (Psalm 104:24, KJV), and "You open your hand/ and satisfy the desires of every living thing" (145:16). Thus we see that love is the law of creation.

But how much more is love the law of the new creation in the gift of His Son! And when He was received back, there came the gift of the Spirit, and all the ministries of His love and grace. Then the love of Jesus Christ Himself, His example of unselfishness, His constant ministry to others, and the love of the Holy Spirit all proclaim to us that God Himself is ruled by His own law of love. Therefore it is the royal law, the law of the kingdom, and should be the gladly accepted law of every child of that kingdom.

3. Supreme above All Laws

It is supreme above all other laws. "The greatest of these is love" (1 Corinthians 13:13). It is royal in the sense that it stands higher than all other laws and qualities. It is the supreme beauty and excellency of all character and being, and the blending of every virtue and grace.

4. The Mightiest and Strongest Power

It is royal because it is the mightiest and strongest power in the universe of God. You talk of the law of gravitation, but nothing draws like love. Nothing lies behind the story of human history like love. It has inspired all the heroism of the battlefield. It is the secret of all that is highest in literature and the story of mankind. It alone can inspire the martyr's sacrifice, the hardships, toils and privations of Christian service, in the mission field, the hospital, the rescue work and the whole story of the service of Christ and our fellow men. It is a kingly force, the power that moves men. God has incorporated it in the spiritual economy as the force that leads to obedience and every sacrifice and service that honors God and blesses mankind.

5. The Law of Liberty

It is called "the law of liberty." It is a law that is not enforced, but is spontaneous. It is of no value if it is compelled, but you choose it and live up to it because it is your own instinctive nature. You are not compelled to serve Christ and sacrifice for Him. You can be selfish, if you will. But the law of liberty appeals to the best in you, and makes you generous and noble, and brings you the recompense for it in a higher nature and deeper satisfaction.

Yet the reward is not your motive. It is a blessed law of spontaneous love, your second nature a law of liberty, as God puts it in us by His Holy Spirit and makes it a part of our being. This is the great law of Christ's kingdom, love. Have we understood it, accepted it, adopted it by our own choice, and is it to us now a glorious privilege to be like Him who came "not . . . to be served, but to serve, and to give his life as a ransom for many" (Matthew 20:28)?

THE APPLICATION OF THE LAW OF LOVE

1. The Social Questions of Life

He applies it to the social questions of life. He shows us that where this law is lived up to it does away with respect of persons. "My brothers," he says, "as believers in our glorious Lord Jesus Christ, don't show favoritism" (James 2:1). There is a blessed application of the great law of divine socialism, not man's socialism, but Christ's love.

> Suppose a man comes into your meeting wearing a gold ring and
> fine clothes, and a poor man in shabby clothes also comes in. If

you show special attention to the man wearing fine clothes and say, "Here's a good seat for you," but say to the poor man, "You stand there" or "Sit on the floor by my feet," have you not discriminated among yourselves and become judges with evil thoughts?

Listen, my dear brothers: Has not God chosen those who are poor in the eyes of the world to be rich in faith and to inherit the kingdom he promised those who love him? But you have insulted the poor. Is it not the rich who are exploiting you? Are they not the ones who are dragging you into court? Are they not the ones who are slandering the noble name of him to whom you belong?

If you really keep the royal law found in Scripture, "Love your neighbor as yourself," you are doing right. But if you show favoritism, you sin and are convicted by the law as lawbreakers. (2:2–9)

These social questions have been practically the same in all ages, and James introduces an element into human life that has been at war with selfishness, exclusiveness and caste, from the earliest times.

The caste system of India is the one barrier against all progress. It shuts away the wretched lower caste in hopeless isolation, and paralyzes every hope and ambition, consigning them to drudgery, and hopelessness. Perhaps the most sorrowful feature of the life of India, and the greatest hindrance to the progress of the gospel of Jesus Christ, is caste. It is the more aggravated form of a principle which we find in all lands, and which sometimes comes into the very Church of Jesus Christ itself. For example, we have our pew rent system, which gives the wealthy man the choice of the more advantageous sitting, and leaves the poor man to take what is left. The principle is wrong, and I believe most unscriptural. Another form is that of uptown and downtown churches. The home church should be a mission church too, and all class distinctions forgotten there. The Duke of Wellington once sat at the communion table, while a poor man passed the cup for him to drink first. Wellington said, "No, my friend, after you. We are all one here."

There is a place for social differences, and they exist in the nature of things. God does not come with an iconoclastic hand to sweep away all differences and bring a hopeless socialism. There are differences. They grow out of successful lives, they can be maintained with sweetness, and the door can be left open for ambition to rise to the highest possibilities. But let there be no harshness. Let the doors be wide open, and the spirit of love and sympathy meet from both sides. God recognizes this, and bids us "Give everyone what you owe him" (Romans 13:7). Impudence and insolence are not part of the gospel of Jesus Christ. Courtesy and respect to all classes and in all places are qualities of true Christian humility. But this is very different from exclusiveness and pride. The true church should be a mission, too. So in our family, social and business life, let us carry out this law of love—proper respect and honor for all—and yet loving consideration, a spirit of considerateness for those in humbler places, the graciousness that in every way covers our social differences by Christ's own law of love.

2. The Judging of One Another

He applies the law of love to the judging of one another harshly. "Because judgment without mercy will be shown to anyone who has not been merciful. Mercy triumphs over judgment!" (James 2:13). Again, "Brothers, do not slander one another. Anyone who speaks against his brother or judges him speaks against the law and judges it. When you judge the law, you are not keeping it, but sitting in judgment on it" (4:11). The spirit of criticism, fault finding, and censoriousness are all condemned by this law of love. Ask God for the love that "always trusts, always hopes" (1 Corinthians 13:7), and *dares to think the best both of others and of yourself.* God wants you to look on the brightest side in your own heart and life and then in others. You will find the one who is harsh and censorious gets the worst of it. Like the scorpion which after stinging others ends by stinging itself to death, that one gets the retribution of a bitter spirit in the misery it brings.

God puts us in the place of trial to give us the opportunity of rising to the spirit of Christian love, just as He placed Christ in the judgment hall in order that He might stand before us as an example of long-suffering love. He lets people hurt and wrong us that we may be more like Him. When God in His providence calls you to these trying conditions, it is that you may have your education completed and enter into the sweetness of the Lord Jesus Christ, and be merciful even as you expect him to be merciful to you.

The unpardonable sin of the New Testament is that of unforgiveness, "Because judgment without mercy will be shown to anyone who has not been merciful" (James 2:13).

A Christian worker said that he once became satisfied that the worm at the core of much of the work in his field was this petty spirit of faultfinding, this readiness to see wrong. He set his face against it and got his people to set their faces against it by prayer and watching. The result was wonderful in the blessing that had come to the work. The work had grown and prospered since they had put these weeds out of the garden and destroyed the worm at the roots. This curse grows unconsciously. Shall we resolve by God's grace that if we cannot speak well, we will not speak ill of one another?

"Speak and act as those who are going to be judged by the law that gives freedom" (2:12). How do you expect to be judged? Do you suppose God is going to reveal all your sins before the throne, and you stand in shame of that revelation? "Therefore judge nothing before the appointed time; wait till the Lord comes. He will bring to light what is hidden in darkness . . . At that time each will receive his praise from God" (1 Corinthians 4:5). In that day of final assize, your Judge is going to bring out every hidden motive that could shed a generous light upon your conduct and character. He is going to bring out the praise, and not the blame. We have not been living up to our expectations. Let us ask God not to deal with us as we have dealt with one another. Lord, help us so to act "as those who are going to be judged by the law that gives freedom" (James 2:12).

3. The Question of Practical Beneficence

James applies this royal law of love to the question of practical beneficence, our kindly help to one another. "Suppose a brother or sister is without clothes and daily food. If one of you says to him, 'Go, I wish you well; keep warm and well fed,' but does nothing about his physical needs, what good is it?" (2:15–16). It is doing things to relieve and help the temporal needs of our suffering fellowmen. He came to heal as well as to save, to help the multitudes and to practice His own precepts, as well as to point the way to heaven. Our acts of love and help may be His links in bringing them to see the attraction of His love and to listen to the gospel of His grace. One of the most beautiful kinds of service is the service lost in its own shadow. A saint was told to ask the greatest good he could claim, and as the angel waited, who brought the message, the answer came, "That I may do the largest amount of good without it ever being known." It was granted. It was so ordered that wherever his shadow fell, somebody would be restored, comforted or saved. Thus his shadow always brought blessing. He never saw it; the world never knew it; but God knew it. It was a life of love hidden until the great revealing day.

God wants us to be practical in blessing others. Very quaintly did an old pioneer Methodist preacher answer some friends to whom he had been preaching. "God bless you," they said, "God will surely bless you; God will reward you for this in the resurrection." But the poor preacher did not have much money in his bag, and he had a long way before him, and he thought their love was rather cheap, so he said, "I am much obliged for your good wishes for the resurrection. It will do very nicely for me, but not for my old mare, for she is not going to have a resurrection; don't forget her, if you please, before the resurrection."

4. A Gentle and Peaceful Spirit

Love will manifest itself in a gentle and peaceful spirit. "But the wisdom that comes from heaven is first of all pure; then peace-loving, considerate, submissive, full of mercy and good fruit, impartial and sincere" (3:17). The children of love are peacemakers, and "peacemakers who sow in peace raise a harvest of righteousness" (3:18). Among all "the fruit of the Spirit" there is none more precious than a gentle, meek and quiet disposition. "The unfading beauty of a gentle and quiet spirit" is indeed "of great worth in God's sight" (1 Peter 3:4). Like an oasis in a desert, like a fragrant blossom on the air of spring, like a cool breeze on a sultry day, like a mother's kiss or gentle breast to a tired child, so is the spirit of gentleness in this rude world of strife and sorrow. Good temper, better still, the Christian temper, is the charm of character and the solace of life. It is but another name for practical love.

5. Expressed in Practical Religion

Practical love expresses itself in practical religion, for James has already told us that "religion that God our Father accepts as pure and faultless is this: to look after orphans and widows in their distress and to keep oneself from being polluted by the world" (James 1:27). Practical love can never stop short of the highest of all service, the spiritual help and blessing of our fellow beings. To lead the unsaved to Christ, to restore the backslider, to comfort the broken hearted, to rescue the tempted, "to look after orphans and widows in their distress" (1:27), this is Christian service, this is heavenly love. Beyond your routine of daily duty and your consistent endeavor to carry your religion into common life, are you also doing something definitely for the spiritual help of your fellow creatures? Are you ministering to their souls and bearing their burdens? "I was sick and you looked after me, I was in prison and you came to visit me" (Matthew 25:36). These are His own tests in the great final day of love and discipleship. How much often comes from such simple ministry! The visits of a clergyman to a poor dairyman's daughter led to a little story which became the instrument of God in the conversion of such illustrious lives as William Wilberforce and Thomas Chalmers.

How many lonely women and neglected children crowd the tenement houses of the block on which you live, whom a little thoughtful kindness might find out in their isolation and comfort in their loneliness!

On a stormy New Year's day a loving Christian girl made her way to a widow's home instead of to some grand social function, and, after cheering the heart of the lonely mother, gave her boy an illustrated almanac with a verse for every day in the year. As she left him she said, "Mind, Harry, that you learn your verse every day and that you live it, too." And as the verse for the day was, "Choose you this day whom ye will serve" (Joshua 24:15, KJV), Harry took it as his watchword for the New Year, and promised to serve the Lord. Harry had a roommate called Tom Short who worked in a sugar factory, and after a little sneering and jesting, Tom also promised to learn the verses. The next day when Tom arrived at the shop, his neighbor asked him what was the latest news. "Oh," said Tom, "I cannot tell you the news, but I can tell you the verse." And so Tom repeated it amid a shower of profane jests and scoffs. But one man listened with a different spirit, and when he went home, he repeated to his poor dying wife each day Tom's texts. The second day was, "For the wages of sin is death" (Romans 6:23). All that day and all that night the words rang in her startled ear, until at last she called her husband, and told him she was dying, because the wages of sin was death, and she had lived in sin and knew not how to be saved. But the next night her husband brought her a new text and oh, how eagerly she listened! "The blood of Jesus Christ his Son cleanseth us from all sin" (1 John 1:7, KJV). And all through that night of weakness and sinking agony, again and again she repeated it, until once more she called her husband to her and told him how the past had all come back to her—the teachings of her childhood, the lessons of her Sunday school, the gospel she once heard so often—and with it the peace of forgiveness and joy of salvation, and in that peace and joy she passed from her troubled life into the rest above. All the fruit of a little ministry of unselfish love. So let us love and serve our Master and our fellowmen.

CHAPTER 5

THE PRACTICAL USE OF THE TONGUE

We all stumble in many ways. If anyone is never at fault in what he says, he is a perfect man, able to keep his whole body in check. (James 3:2)

Speech is one of the supreme distinctions between man and the lower animals. The power of expressing thought in articulate language and written speech, and giving it an incarnate body and a tangible immortal life, is one of the high prerogatives of rational beings. Science through the phonograph is putting upon the tablets which will endure through time the very tones of our voice. God is emphasizing the power and importance of the tongue, and it may be that we will find some day that every whisper that ever emanated from our life has been recorded on phonographic plates in yonder sky. We may find that the witnesses of the judgment will be the records that we ourselves have made, and we will realize that by our words we will be justified and by our words we will be condemned, and "I tell you that men will have to give account on the day of judgment for every careless word they have spoken" (Matthew 12:36).

The Apostle James considers it worthwhile to devote a whole chapter to the subject of the tongue and the practical use of our little member of speech.

THE TEST OF CHARACTER

James tells us that the control of the tongue is the test of character. A man's conversation is the real test of his character, and a man that "does not keep a tight rein on his tongue, he deceives himself and his religion is worthless" (James 1:26). An unbridled tongue is a sure sign of an unsanctified, undisciplined and perhaps unsaved soul. On the other hand, "If anyone is never at fault in what he says, he is a perfect man, able to keep his whole body in check" (3:2). It is a sign that he is under the government of his conscience, his will and the Holy Spirit. This is a most heart-searching test. Let us take it home. Can we stand it? It was a foolish word, a hasty word, a word of doubt and irritation that lost Moses the Land of Promise. He would have taken it back if he could, but it was recorded. It had gone upon the record, and it had to stand, and for that one little speech Moses lost the hope of a lifetime. While he was taken to heaven, he could not lead Israel into the land which was the type of a victorious life.

When Isaiah was called to his ministry, it was his lips that were first sanctified. The live coal was applied to these members, and the word spoken, "See, this has touched your lips; your guilt is taken away and your sin atoned for" (Isaiah 6:7). His tongue had to be purified before God could use him.

On the day of Pentecost, it was cloven tongues, tongues of fire that came, tongues possessed by the Holy Spirit. If you have received the baptism of the Spirit, your tongue has received the first touch. You will never talk as you used to talk, you will never have the same unlicensed freedom, but your language will be under the control of a watchful spirit. Our words are God's touchstones by which He is showing us to ourselves and to the world.

We find even in common life, that if a man has sense enough to hold his peace, "even a fool is thought wise if he keeps silent" (Proverbs 17:28). Quiet, self-contained people are often taken for more than they really are, while many a man of capacity and many a woman of beautiful qualities wreck their whole lives by an uncontrolled tongue. If it settles our influence and character here, then how much more in the sight of Him who said, "For by your words you will be acquitted, and by your words you will be condemned" (Matthew 12:37).

THE INFLUENCE AND THE POWER OF THE TONGUE

The apostle next proceeds to illustrate the tremendous influence and power of the tongue. He uses a number of illustrations. He says "We put bits into the mouths of horses" (James 3:3), because it is their mouths that determine their action. Just as a man's mouth is the test of character, so the horse's mouth is the place to control him. We put bits in their mouths, and by these turn about their whole body, so that a little bit of steel and a little thong of leather will hold a fiery steed, and turn it at the touch of a woman's hand. So the tongue is like a bridle, which can be put upon us. With a fiery horse you put a curb in its bit. The idea is to hurt it, if it pulls against the bit. So God has given to us checks upon our tongue, making it hurt us, if we speak unadvisedly. If you are a spiritual Christian and walking watchfully, you will find that He will curb you tremendously when you speak hastily. If you succeed in speaking unadvisedly, the curb will hurt you so much you will have to go and take it back. He wants it to hurt us, so we will not do it again. Don't try to get out of it easily, but let God's discipline be as hard as He pleases, and go honestly and manfully and have it out. Tell the injured person you are sorry, and ask his forgiveness. You will soon cease doing it, if you will be brave enough to let it hurt you. Speak against another, and God will hold you to it sooner or later. You may get over it easily now. But some day when health is gone, your brain weak, your nerves shattered and the grave seems near, the devil will drive you to it by an evil conscience or a sinking life; and you will wish you had gone and made restitution in better days, when God would have made it easy and used it to save and sanctify you and bless all concerned.

Again, James uses the figure of the helm. He says we put rudders in ships, and a very small rudder turns about a very great ship. The tongue is as little as the rudder, but as mighty. It turns round your life and the lives of others. How great the power of a single word spoken at the marriage altar! It changes two lives. A single word spoken in criminal court brings judgment. The single word spoken by the foreman of the jury means death. A single word spoken as a false testimony consigns some poor fellow to an undeserved doom. The single word of a true witness saves a life. A reckless word stops some blessing that might have reached a soul. That slander that you fired, as a hunter would wing a bird in midair, has shot to the heart some messenger of God that could have brought blessing to countless souls, but for your fiery dart. A word has tremendous power for good or for evil.

Again, he speaks of the tongue as the forest fire. "Consider what a great forest is set on fire by a small spark" (3:5). Sometimes a spark will set a whole county on fire, and sweep away homes, factories, towns and scores of lives. So the "tongue also is a fire" and a "world of evil" (3:6). It is an awful figure. If you were to go to a powder magazine, you would find the place guarded for miles around, and within the enclosure matches are not allowed and each party is searched, for the least combustible thing in that world of combustibles would send thousands of lives into eternity and destroy millions of dollars of property. That is what James means here. We are going through a world of combustion. The air is full of destructive elements, and we must keep the fiery darts away.

On the Oriental steamers the passengers are not allowed to carry matches other than the patented safety ones which cannot be lighted without striking them upon the box. A passenger would be fined for carrying an ordinary match. God says "Don't carry anything but safety matches in the world of iniquity." All around is danger and destruction. You can set it off by a hasty word.

Going through the Alps sometimes a whisper will bring down an avalanche, and the guide cautions every one to silence. The air is so sensitive that the least vibration would loosen the rocks and glaciers and hurl destruction on the pathway. So as we go through life let us say, "I will put a muzzle on my mouth/ as long as the wicked are in my presence" (Psalm 39:1). "I was silent and still" (39:2). "I said, 'I will watch my ways/ and keep my tongue from sin'" (39:1). "Let your conversation be always full of grace, seasoned with salt, so that you may know how to answer everyone" (Colossians 4:6).

ITS POWER FOR EVIL

There is a dark side to the picture. James likens the tongue to poison: "full of deadly poison" (James 3:8). It is the poison of a viper, a subtle poison that contaminates even the good, and mingles with our worship and all our Christian work. "It is a restless evil, full of deadly poison" (3:8).

"All kinds of animals, birds, reptiles and creatures of the sea"—the whole inanimate creation—"are being tamed and have been tamed by man, but no man can tame the tongue" (3:7–8). It is more terrible than the lion; it is more wily than the serpent. It is *incorrigible, and like the carnal mind*, it must be crucified, given up to die; and we must get a new tongue from the Spirit of Pentecost.

Again it is a destructive and consuming element, "a fire." It is a contaminating element, for it contaminates the good as well as works in the bad. If it would only stick to its own livery, if it would only come in the garment of evil and the livery of Satan, we would know how to recognize it. It comes as an angel of light. "With the tongue we praise our Lord and Father, and with it we curse men, who have been made in God's likeness. Out of the same mouth come praise and cursing" (3:9–10). Praying and singing today, swearing, evil-speaking, gossiping tomorrow. "Can both fresh water and salt water flow from the same spring?" (3:11). James tells us the tongue will be used one moment in the service of God and the next in the employ of the wicked one. So it mingles with our best words and works, and coming in the disguise of good defiles and contaminates all our ways. If you want to find the practical side of a wholesome as well as an evil tongue, read the book of Proverbs. It was written by a man who had suffered much from its fiery shafts and subtle wiles, and he tells us there is nothing worse beneath the sky than to be the victim of a bitter and unwholesome tongue. There are four or five kinds of evil tongues.

1. The Foolish Tongue

The foolish tongue, vain and idle. The tongue that talks thoughtlessly, bores you to death and seems never to know its own weakness; a tongue that will go from the house of God and talk all day about worldly follies, and waste God's holy day and your precious life. "Count yourselves dead to sin but alive to God in Christ Jesus" (Romans 6:11). Bring up your tongue and sentence it to death, and then hand it over to die, count it dead, and give it back to God as alive from the dead, and say, "Lord, henceforth my tongue is yours and yours alone." It is to speak only as the Holy Spirit wants to use it. It is to be under guard, and to recognize itself as a soldier that waits for orders. Then you will be watchful in your speech, and all this idle, vapid, empty talk will cease. It is "idle words" that are to be given account of in the day of judgment. Think perhaps that they are being recorded now on heavenly tablets for the day of the great Assize, and ask God to hold your tongue, to so control it that you will be glad to recognize it as the instrument of Christ.

2. The Profane Tongue

How easy it is to speak the words that are irreverent, flippant and profane without meaning to be profane. The worst kind of profanity is that which uses slang, jest and innuendo, other than coarse blasphemy; phrases that have gradually worn smooth like the pebbles, until the edges are taken off, and now seem innocent and harmless, but really are profanity in disguises. These are not the habits of the tongue that is under the control of the Holy Spirit. How easy it is to fall into the light jesting pun on the Scriptures, the criticism of the sermon, forgetting that these idle words may arrest the conviction of your companion, and the impression that may have been made upon some other heart, and so be the turning point of a soul's ruin! All these things will be brought to a sensitive conscience by the Holy Spirit, if you really have yielded your members to God.

3. The False Tongue

Then comes the false tongue, whether it be the deliberate lie, the direct misrepresentation of the truth or the milder form that you call "white," the suppression of truth, the intentional deceiving of another, the innumerable forms of subtle and flattering deceit which men and women use in the business and society of today. You are not obliged to tell everybody about all your business, but if you are reserved, be reserved truthfully. You have the right of silence and the right of speech but whether you recognize the one or the other, let it always be with the guard upon your lips, with the thought upon your heart, "I cannot do this thing and sin against the Lord."

4. The Impure Tongue

Then we have the impure tongue, the unclean tongue, the salacious story, the spicy anecdote that men will tell to each other when ladies are not present, and the innumerable forms of double speech which may be capable of a right or a wrong interpretation, which evil men can use to such unworthy advantage, shielding themselves behind the better sense when they fail to reach the mark of their infamous purpose. Here is where women's empire should be supreme, and where her severest judgment should refuse in any way to sanction it by her toleration. A lady is always justified in refusing the company of any gentleman, if she has to be compromised either by doubtful speech or profane expressions. She will be much more respected and honored, even by the one she is compelled to rebuke, for honoring her Savior, her conscience and her womanhood.

5. The Malignant Tongue

The malignant tongue, the unkind tongue is perhaps the worst of all; the tongue of slander, the backbiting tongue, the criticizing tongue, the fault-finding tongue, the sarcastic tongue, the thousand forms of evil speaking, which work such bitterness and misery in our home life, and worst of all in our own heart and character. Men have been driven to the saloon and the pit by unwise tongues and bitter speech and by the lack of a tenderness and love that might have won and saved. There may be provocation, but love can triumph over this.

The worst of all is its dreadful influence on your own heart—the reflex action of unkindness, harshness and the loss of gentleness and victory.

Ask God to save you from an evil tongue, an irreverent tongue, an impure tongue, a foolish tongue, a false tongue and above all a bitter and malignant tongue.

How shall we speak of the malignant fruits of the tongue—the reputation it has ruined, the homes it has blasted, the hearts that it has torn asunder, the desolation and wreck that it has left behind, the servants of God that it has crippled in their work for Him, the wrongs that it has done in time and eternity, too late to recall even when we find our fatal mistake? God give us a wholesome tongue, and send us forth to watch our words and to ask God to "keep the door of our lips."

I have heard of a man cruelly wronged by such a tongue, and called upon by the one who had injured him after the evil had done its cruel work. The poor man, a minister of God, who had been crippled and hindered in a noble work was broken down under the accumulated miseries that had come upon him and his family through slander and misrepresentation. Too late the guilty one found her mistake and came to ask his pardon with bitter tears. "Yes, I will pardon, gladly pardon you. What else can I do as a servant of God? But you will not refuse me two simple requests." And she said, "No, I would do anything to undo my folly." "Take this pillow, then," he said, and wrapped up a pillow in a parcel. "Take it to yonder church tower where we have been used to worship together, and just open it and scatter the feathers to the winds." She took the pillow, mounted the stairs of the church tower, opened the pillow and scattered the feathers. They went north, south and in every direction. She came back and said, "I did as you asked me, what else?" "Now will you go," he said, "and pick up the feathers and bring them back to me." "Ah, that is more than I can do. They are gone." "Yes, my friend," replied the man, "they have gone and you cannot take them back. And the words you have spoken have gone and you cannot undo them—the words, the looks, the evil speaking, the misrepresentation, the cruel wrong. You know them now, but you cannot undo them. They are irreparable. They have hurt me, but I am sorry that they will follow you forever."

"The tongue also is a fire, a world of evil among the parts of the body. It corrupts the whole person, sets the whole course of his life on fire, and is itself set on fire by hell" (James 3:6).

THE GOOD TONGUE

There are also holy tongues, yielded to the Holy Spirit and under the control of the fire of Pentecost. The good tongue is often a silent tongue. We all talk too much. Hand your tongue over to God; ask Him to take it and help you to remember it is not your own. What will we use our tongue for?

1. For Praise and Prayer

Praise God and pray to God. This will be its eternal employ, the worship of our King. Accustom it to it now. Learn the notes of praise. When it is not praise, let it be prayer, "Lord Jesus, help," or "Lord Jesus, I take You for this." Let it become natural. You can form habits of your tongue. It is natural to the swearer to say his blasphemous word. It has grown upon his tongue. It is part of his physical frame. It has entered into the tissues and nerves. You can learn God's praise so that it will be as natural as breathing.

2. For the Word of Kindness

Then our tongue is for the word of kindness, help and cheer to those around us—the kindly tongue in the home, the business and the social circle. As you go along the path of life, ask God to give you loving messages, not too high or strained "for human nature's daily food." But, to have a tongue always kind, always wise! How blessed is a wholesome tongue! When you come down in the morning, do not forget to say some kindly thing. As you meet people in business or on the street, have a kind and cheering word. Have it for the clerk in your employ, who is toiling hard and wondering if it will be noticed and appreciated. How it will oil the machinery just to speak a little word of encouragement and approval! As you go along the path of life, just lift the little burdens, take the little stumbling blocks out of the way, and scatter kindness as you go.

3. For Witnessing and Seeking to Bless

Finally, the tongue is for witnessing and seeking to bless and save your fellow men—the *consecrated tongue, the tongue that bears the message of God,* the tongue charged with the story of a Savior's love and watching for opportunities to speak "the word that sustains the weary" (Isaiah 50:4). It needs not the lofty pulpit or the learned degree. The simple, heartfelt message of a little child or humble laborer has often been more eloquent than the studied discourse. Meeting at a wayside pump Brainerd Taylor said a single word to a young countryman that led him to become a Christian and a missionary. It was not until years afterward, when the missionary happened to read the life of this saintly man, and saw his portrait on the first page of the volume, that he recognized the man that had led him to Christ.

You have probably heard the story of the little drummer boy, whose simple message led to the conversion of an army surgeon who was a bitter enemy of Christianity and a determined Jew. It is published by the American Tract Society, and the lad is said to have been a member of the Sands' Street Church, Brooklyn, converted in the Sunday school and known as the son of a Christian mother. Terribly wounded on the battlefield, an arm and a leg had to be amputated. But he refused to take either chloroform or brandy, and told the surgeon that he would never break his promise to his mother on any account to taste intoxicating liquor. When the doctor began to saw off the bone, he took the pillow in his mouth, set his teeth, breathed out a low cry of prayer and did not utter a groan. The doctor greatly wondered, and when a few days later the chaplain told him that the lad was dying and wanted to speak to him, he bent over his bed while the boy said, "Doctor, when you were sawing off my leg, I was asking Jesus to convert your soul."

That message the proud Jewish physician never could forget, and it led him at last to Christ. One day in that church in Brooklyn he met the mother unexpectedly at a prayer meeting and heard from her lips the story of her boy's last message, and gladly told her that his prayer had been fulfilled and that his soul was now a star in that little crown. So let us speak for Christ.

> Take my lips and let them be
> filled with messages for Thee.

CHAPTER 6

PRACTICAL SANCTIFICATION

*Do you think Scripture says without reason that the spirit he caused
to live in us envies intensely? But he gives us more grace. That is why
Scripture says:*

> *"God opposes the proud
>   but gives grace to the humble." (James 4:5–6)*

Let no one think that because James demands from us the practical out-
living of our religion in a very real, matter-of-fact way, that he has no sympathy with the deeper experiences of the Christian life and the emotions of
true Christian feeling. On the contrary we will find, as we follow him in his
treatment of this subject of sanctification, that he leads us down into the
very depths of holy mysticism and the most exquisite touches of divine love.
But first he begins at the dark side of the subject and comes to the very root
of the matter.

THE CARNAL HEART OR THE OLD AND SINFUL NATURE

"What causes fights and quarrels among you? Don't they come from your
desires that battle within you?" (James 4:1). This is the root of all our sorrow
and sin, the evil heart. There is no use in trying to put on new garments till
you get the old body cleansed. Nor must the cleansing stop at the skin. It
must reach the heart and the very marrow of the bones. There is no use in
filtering your water with the most improved methods, so long as that old
dead horse is up in yonder reservoir. Get him out, and your filtering will be
to some purpose. It is no use to apply your medical treatment to mere
symptoms, and try invigorating air and good nourishment, so long as that
cancer or ulcer is feeding on the vital organs. Get the root of the evil
removed, then your hygiene will be of some value. There is no use trying to
get the best sort of captain, engineer and crew for that vessel, if the hull is

rotten and worm-eaten. You will flounder at sea with the best captain, engineer and crew. You may have the best plan in the world for your building and the best architects, but if your material is poor, it will fall to pieces in your hands, and the ruin will come in spite of all your ingenuity.

So God comes to the deep secret of all our trouble, this fallen nature, this dead heart, the "desires that battle within you" (4:1). What is lust? It is the desire and inclination to sin. It is the wrong love of anything, love perverted, love turned from God to self-gratification. The last of the commandments, that seems to sum up the whole spirit and essence of morality, strikes at this evil heart, "Do not covet" (Romans 7:7). It means you should not desire to do wrong. The principle of all ethics is to reach the will, the choice, the thing in you that desires. You may put a man in a straitjacket and make it impossible for him to do wrong, but if he wants to do wrong, he is as bad as the other man who is free to do it and does it. What God plans is to take away the root principle of an evil heart.

James tells us that this evil desire enters into our very religion, and even our prayers. "When you ask, you do not receive, because you ask with wrong motives, that you may spend what you get on your pleasures" (James 4:3). So the great mass of human religion is a matter of sinful desire. It is just an accommodation to man's sinfulness, another method of gratifying his evil heart. All pagan religions are founded on sin, and their public rites are usually of the most obscene and abominable character. Even a great deal of the religion of nominal Christians is an effort to electroplate and gild their sinful desires. The ministry becomes a profession and an open door for ambition, and the strife of ministers for honor is as selfish and sinful as the competitions of the world for political preeminence. Religion itself is a convenience to keep people out of hell and make them comfortable through a life of self-indulgence here.

But the difficulty is an evil heart. No matter how it is repressed, until it is taken away, sanctification has not even begun. Sanctification deals with the perverted will, the wrong desire, the evil inclination, the old Adam that is stronger than young Melancthon still. Your best efforts will be baffled until you get him crucified.

This Christ provides for. The first thing to do is to surrender yourself to be crucified with Jesus Christ. Sanctification is not improving your habits by culture, nor is it cleansing your heart; but it is handing the natural life over to death as a useless thing, so bad that you can never make it good, and getting instead something entirely new through union with Jesus Christ. Sanctification is receiving Him to dwell within you, to work through you, to be your Substitute, and to give you His Holy Spirit instead of your old heart.

The beginning of sanctification, therefore, is to see that you are utterly wrong in your desires and choices. The very helm of life is wrong. You must surrender, get out of the way, and die. "Offer yourselves to God, as those who have been brought from death to life" (Romans 6:13), and then let your life be all new and divine. "I have been crucified with Christ and I no longer live, but Christ lives in me" (Galatians 2:20). May God help us to see this truth lived out and died out in all our hearts.

THE FORBIDDEN WORLD

We must deal with the forbidden world, the evil world, the world which stands for the environment of the natural and self-life.

Not only are you wrong, but you are encompassed with a world that is wrong, and you must get out of the world as well as out of yourself. This is separation which must always accompany sanctification. Sanctification is seeing that you are wrong and handing yourself over to Christ by His Holy Spirit to make you right. Separation is pronouncing sentence of death on the world as well as on yourself, and entering into a new world—the world of the unseen, the world of the coming kingdom, the world in which God is supreme and you are "hidden with Christ in God" (Colossians 3:3), waiting for the day of manifestation, when your true world will appear in its fullness and glory.

"You adulterous people, don't you know that friendship with the world is hatred toward God? Anyone who chooses to be a friend of the world becomes an enemy of God" (James 4:4). The true reading here should be "You adulteresses." It is not literal adultery James is talking about, but spiritual adultery. It is the adultery of the Bride of the Lamb who is leaving her Husband for the world. She is the wife who is faithless to her Lord by going into the arms of the world. If you are Christ's, you are His alone. He claims you for Himself and He is jealous of any rival. So James is exclusive, that the world must be crucified unto you and you unto the world, just as the old carnal life is recognized and laid over on Christ Jesus.

What is the world? It does not mean that we must cease eating, working and being good citizens. It means that the love of the world must die, and that we must cease to live for and belong to the present age, and become children of the coming age and the kingdom of our Lord and Savior Jesus Christ which is soon to be revealed.

John tells us all about this forbidden world. "For everything in the world—the cravings of sinful man, the lust of his eyes and the boasting of what he has and does—comes not from the Father but from the world" (1 John 2:16). Here is a trinity over against the Triune God.

1. "The Cravings of Sinful Man"

This means the gratification of your senses, appetites, passions; sensual indulgence for its own sake, whether it is within the law or outside the law; the desire to enjoy the pleasures of the senses, and the making of these the aims and motives of your being.

You have to eat to live, but you do not need to live to eat. It is right to take sustenance, and to have a reasonable enjoyment in it, for God gave us our sense of taste. But these are mere circumstances of life and pass quickly away. If they are in any sense the aim of your being, you are a worldling. They are to be but accompaniments. So every appetite and gratification which God in His beneficence has given is always to be a servant, the hand-maid of a higher purpose, and not the object and aim for which we live.

2. "The Lust of His Eyes"

This includes the whole pageant of worldly display whether it be the love of dress, the love of equipage, the love of palatial furniture, the love of beauty. When these become controlling, and especially when centered upon yourself and ministering to your self-conceit and pride, they are the forbidden world. God makes things beautiful, and we can thank Him for them, but we are not to rest in the thing itself, but rise from everything to God, and make all tributary to His glory and lay them in homage on His altar and at His feet.

3. "The Boasting of What He Has and Does"

"The boasting of what he has and does" is a higher form of worldliness—pride of family, pride of culture, pride of talent or of any personal quality that leads you to make ambition and success in life objects of idolatry. Perhaps today the most dangerous of all is pride of commercial power, for the men that rule the world today are our commercial kings, and the passion that is hardening men's hearts and demonizing human nature is the love of power that money bestows. It is like the pride of Lucifer, and will bring men into close alliance with him. It was this thing that made Nebuchadnezzar call himself a god and set up his image on the plains of Dura. God is letting it be manifested in these last days.

You can have it in your small world just as much as the multimillionaire in his world. The fire and tinder must both be put out of the way. The world is the tinder. The lust is the fire. God wants to separate us from both by open-ing up to us His world of love, purity and hope and the coming kingdom where Jesus reigns and is preparing magnificence immeasurably beyond the richest prize that earth can bestow. This will counteract the present evil world.

THE ANTIDOTE

The antidote to the lust of the flesh and the love of the world is the love of God.

The Holy Spirit that dwells in us loves us jealously. Here, over against the world and its attractions, God shows us another attraction, a higher charm that counteracts and counterbalances the lower. Down through the ages there has come a golden thread of romance that has given its charm to everything beautiful in art, poetry, history and the story of time. That golden thread is just the old romance of love. Whether it comes down to us from Helen of Troy, or Penelope waiting for Ulysses, or the heroines of later times, it is the old, old story; something in the human heart that will give up family, fortune and every earthly thing for the charm of love. If you catch that sacred fire of truehearted love, and there is always something beautiful in it that seems to have come from heaven, it lifts to heroism, sacrifice and nobility of life such as no other earthly motive can supply.

Now the secret of redemption is just the same old story of love. Long before the ages that story began in the heart of God and the love of Christ. He is the heavenly Bridegroom seeking to win His poor lost Bride, and raise her to His glory and His throne. In the 16th chapter of Ezekiel He gives us the picture of the love that found her in her blood, and said unto her, "Live!" (16:6). And then, washing her, arraying her in garments of spotless beauty and adorning her with every precious jewel, He adds, "you became mine" (16:8). Like Eliezer, the servant of Abraham, who went forth to a distant land to find a bride for Abraham's heir, and winning her consent gave to her a splendid trousseau of raiment and precious gems, and then brought her home to her waiting husband, so the Holy Spirit has come forth to call the Bride of Jesus to accept His love and then to prepare her for His coming. His voice throughout the ages is, "Listen, O daughter, consider . . ./ Forget your people and your father's house./ The king is enthralled by your beauty;/ honor him, for he is your lord" (Psalm 45:10–11). The new world of love and hope which awoke in Rebekah's heart gave her strength to forget her father's house and the home of her childhood. Just as today many a gentle maiden, awaking to the new charm of the old attraction, can leave the scenes of her girlhood and the home of her earliest and fondest affections, and go forth to brave the perils of the wilderness, the ocean, the military camp or the toils and hardships of a life of poverty for the sake of one she loves better than all beside; so the love of Christ, when once it takes possession of the soul, is the antidote to selfishness and worldliness, and becomes the master passion of a devoted life. It is to this that the Holy Spirit appeals. His jealous love cannot bear that any inferior claim should absorb our heart or displace the supremacy of Jesus Christ. And so He loves us jealously, and His jealousy burns like a consuming fire.

In connection with the subject of sanctification, it is very interesting to notice that in Paul's treatise on this subject in the seventh chapter of Romans, he represents it under the figure of the marriage union. The believer is represented under the image of a wife unable to obey and please her former husband, and finally slain by him for her disobedience. That old inexorable husband was the law. As she lay bleeding and lifeless at his feet, lo, another passed by, a form of loveliness, gentleness and grace. It was Jesus, the Risen One, and as He passed, He touched her and raised her from the dead, and then took her to His bosom and made her His Bride. And now He says, "So, my brothers, you also died to the law through the body of Christ, that you might belong to another, to him who was raised from the dead, in order that we might bear fruit to God" (Romans 7:4).

Holiness is just the fruit of a marriage to Christ. Just as spontaneously as the offspring comes from the union of two loving lives, just as naturally as the fruit grows from the living vine; so the faith, the holiness, the patience, the good works of the believer, all spring from the love life of the Lord. They are not put on by effort, but they are put forth by vital energy, and prompted by the motive power of life and love. It is to our love that the Holy Spirit appeals. It is by love that He works the work of grace within us. It is the "expulsive power of a new affection" that drives out the world. Just as that selfish girl when her heart is won is willing to give up her little world of indulgence and flattery, and sacrifice luxury, comfort, home, friends and every earthly prospect for the one she loves—suffering for him, toiling for his children and sharing all the hardships of his life with infinite delight, so the love of Christ is the motive power that lifts us above selfishness, ambition and the power of the present age, and makes it a joy to suffer and serve in the interests of so dear a Master, and for the hope of so great a recompense. Would you, therefore, dear friend, know the secret of living above the world and bring forth much fruit? Open your heart to the love of Christ. Yield to the approaches of His wooing and learn to live in His love. So shall your being be filled with the fruits of the Spirit,

> And all your life be lost in love,
> A heaven below, a heaven above.

THE PLACE OF GRACE

There is the place of grace in the life of holiness.

"He gives us more grace" (James 4:6). That is, the more inexorable His love and jealousy in holding us up to the highest standard, the more abundant is His grace in enabling us to meet it. Grace gives what love demands, and love is always asking more.

Strange as it may seem, Christ needs our love and claims our tenderest devotion. But our dull, cold hearts often feel unable to respond, and we cry, "I am laid low in the dust" (Psalm 119:25). But it is here that grace comes to our relief, and the Holy Spirit undertakes to supply the love on our part as well as to reveal the greater love on His. Do you want a tenderer devotion? Take it from Him by faith through grace. Do you want a moving sense of His love, a joy in prayer, a love for His Word, a delight in His service, an experience of deep and tender joy? "He gives us more grace" (James 4:6). "From the fullness of his grace we have all received one blessing after another" (John 1:16). He does not expect us to produce it from the soil of our old natural heart. It must come from heaven, and His grace is waiting to supply it just as fully as you realize your need and are willing to claim His fullness. Lord, give us grace to take the "more grace" from You.

THE SECRET OF RECEIVING

How shall we maintain the attitude through which we will be enabled to meet the expectations of His love and to receive the fullest measures of His grace?

1. Submit yourselves to God. Unconditional surrender is the first condition of sanctification—a yielded will, a spirit prostrate at His feet, crying continually, "Lord, what will You have me to do?" This is the condition of all deeper blessing.

2. We must be as positive against evil as we are passive in the hands of God. "Resist the devil, and he will flee from you" (James 4:7). There is danger that in cultivating the habit of self-renunciation at a certain stage in our spiritual experience, we may lose that willpower which is necessary for strength of character. The true attitude is an everlasting "yes" to God, and an inexorable "no" to evil. For the inevitable experience of the life of holiness is temptation, and the secret of victory is a fearless courage and an inflexible will, quite as much as a victorious faith.

3. We must make a habit of humility. "[He] gives grace to the humble" (4:6). "Humble yourselves before the Lord, and he will lift you up" (4:10). As the valleys receive the fertilizing streams, so it is the lowly heart that claims the more abundant grace of God; and the habit of constantly discounting ourselves is but the reverse side of the faith that always counts upon God.

4. There must be nearness to God, the life of communion, intimacy with our heavenly Father. This is the very essence of the life of holiness. "Come near to God and he will come near to you" (4:8). It is thus we walk with God, until dwelling in His fellowship we catch by intuition His very thought and walk spontaneously in His steppings. So may He "equip you with everything good for doing his will, and may he work in us what is pleasing to him, through Jesus Christ, to whom be glory for ever and ever. Amen" (Hebrews 13:21).

CHAPTER 7

THE PRACTICAL HOPE OF THE LORD'S COMING

Be patient, then, brothers, until the Lord's coming. See how the farmer waits for the land to yield its valuable crop and how patient he is for the autumn and spring rains. You too, be patient and stand firm, because the Lord's coming is near. (James 5:7–8)

With pungent, prophetic words, reminding one of the ancient prophets of Israel, James has just been pointing out the signs and sins of the last days, and summoning earth's children of pride to the tribunal of the coming King.

Now he turns to the suffering disciples of Christ, and tells them of the remedy for their wrongs, and the recompense for their sorrow which that blessed hope holds out to the children of promise. "Be patient, then brothers, until the Lord's coming. See how the farmer waits for the land to yield its valuable crop and how patient he is for the autumn and spring rains. You too, be patient and stand firm, because the Lord's coming is near" (5:7–8). That blessed hope, the glorious appearing of the Lord Jesus, has many precious applications in the Scriptures, but none is more precious than its application to the practical duties and trials of our common life. It is not only a theme for the theologian to discuss, the poet to sing and the saint to dream of, but it is a weapon for life's warfare—a staff for life's journey, a comfort for life's every trial, something for the housewife amid the poverty of her home, something for the laborer under the scorching sun of the harvest field, something for the workman robbed of his wages and tempted to fight for his rights, something better than our modern socialism, than our Utopian dreams—a living hope for living and dying men, and a practical remedy for all earth's wrongs and sorrow. First, however, let us look with James to the terrible social conditions which he describes, and which well might be copied from some photographic picture of our own times. As we read his graphic sketch of the struggle of human selfishness for gold and pleasure, we can almost imagine the author looking upon one of the scenes in our Stock Exchange, or sitting in the gallery of a modern theater, or watching the carnival of pleasure in some social function or society banquet.

THE SPIRIT OF GODLESS SECULARISM AND GREED OF GAIN

> Now listen, you who say, "Today or tomorrow we will go to this or that city, spend a year there, carry on business and make money." Why, you do not even know what will happen tomorrow. What is your life? You are a mist that appears for a little while and then vanishes. Instead, you ought to say, "If it is the Lord's will, we will live and do this or that." (4:13–15)

This is a picture of modern business in its worst form. The one idea of these people is to get gain and to do business. There is no doubt about the value of money, but we may surely say that the pursuit of money for its own sake is no proper object to any Christian man. As a means to a higher end it is perfectly legitimate to pursue business and acquire wealth; but to make it the end of life is selfish and degrading. But these men are not only intent on getting gain, but utterly regardless of God in their means of seeking it. They form their plans without any recognition of His authority and will. They determine what they will do each day, as if their lives were their own. Instead of saying, "If it is the Lord's will, we will live and do this or that," they ride roughshod over divine providence and remind one of the old farmer in the Savior's parable who had made all his plans and settled all questions in that famous interview with himself, without ever thinking of consulting God, until another form was thrown across this vision and another voice insisted upon taking part in the conference. "But God said." Ah, he had not thought of this. God was not in it, "God was not in all his thoughts," until that dreadful message came, "You fool! This very night your life will be demanded from you" (Luke 12:20).

There are two capital letters which I like to interpose in all my appointments, D.V., or translated into reverent English, "If the Lord will," and I should be afraid to make any program without that little parenthesis. God save us from the worldliness and godlessness of what men call up-to-date business methods. "In all your ways acknowledge him,/ and he will make your paths straight" (Proverbs 3:6).

THE SPIRIT OF GREEDY HOARDING

> Now listen, you rich people, weep and wail because of the misery that is coming upon you. Your wealth has rotted, and

moths have eaten your clothes. Your gold and silver are corroded. Their corrosion will testify against you and eat your flesh like fire. You have hoarded wealth in the last days. (James 5:1–3)

Here we have another picture of our times; namely, the sudden accumulation of enormous fortunes. Here we have not only the millionaires, but the multimillionaires, that have grown up like mushrooms in a night, and who rise like colossal figures by the score all along the vista of our modern commercial life. They are features and signs of the times. They are full of ominous significance. They have "hoarded wealth in the last days" (5:3). They are God's signs of the near approach of the Lord's coming. Half a century ago great fortunes were not unknown, but they had chiefly descended as hereditary legacies from ancient houses. But the colossal fortunes of today have grown up in a single generation. The other day the income of a single merchant was estimated at 40 million dollars. This enormous sum would support 100,000 missionaries for one year [originally written in 1901], and would multiply tenfold the missionary agencies of today and put the gospel within the reach of every human being immediately. What an awful responsibility to have such wealth!

Would to God that the men might be prepared to whom the Master could safely entrust vast resources and possibilities. But alas, the holders of the enormous fortunes are here addressed as men to whom they are of little use. "Your gold and silver are corroded," he says, "and their corrosion will testify against you." Money unused is really wasted, and the possessor owns it only in name. The rust of their unused treasure is a witness against them, and tells how little their trust has been spent for God.

Indeed, poor Lazarus at the rich man's gate is truly richer than Dives in all his luxury. Once, it is said, there came in a dream an awful message to a man of selfish wealth, that at a certain hour the richest man in the town was to die. As the day drew near he was prostrated with nervous spasms and overwhelming terror; he felt sure that it was the knell of his doom. Vainly did the physicians administer their opiates. Sleep fled from his eyelid and peace from his mind, and a great horror hung over him night and day. At last the fatal day and hour drew near. With almost insane solicitude he watched the face of the clock as the fateful moment came, and indeed it seemed as it approached that he must surely die. But at length it passed, and he had not succumbed. Gradually the reaction came and the terror passed, and he said, "Perhaps it was but a dream." But a few days later he learned that at that very hour and moment an old man had passed away, a village beggar, who was known to all as a veritable saint. The old miser began to wonder what it meant. Was it indeed true that he was not the richest man in the village, and that this poor old tramp who did not even own a grave, had passed on to the possession of treasures which he could never own? It all seemed to him a bitter irony. Surely it was.

Thank God for a few of the world's rich ones who have learned that "a man's life does not consist in the abundance of his possessions" (Luke 12:15). The other day one of our greatest capitalists declared that no man ought to die immensely rich, and he is setting the example by the liberal distribution of wealth in his last days.

THE SPIRIT OF LUXURIOUS EXTRAVAGANCE AND SELF-INDULGENCE

"You have lived on earth in luxury and self-indulgence. You have fattened yourselves in the day of slaughter" (James 5:5).

Here we have a picture which recalls the banquets of Lucullus and Tiberius, in which every costly luxury was brought from every realm for the gluttonous gratification of a Roman reception. But such scenes are not confined to Roman pride or Roman luxury. Our daily journals tell us of social functions and costly banquets held every night in the season where thousands and even tens of thousands of dollars are offered in vainglorious display and sensual pleasure, and the shameful accessories that often accompany these coarse feasts and "bachelor dinners" are suggested but too plainly by the significant language, "You have lived on earth in luxury and self-indulgence" (5:5).

These exhibitions of godless luxury were associated with the fall of ancient Babylon and Rome, and they are, alas, the signs of the closing days of modern civilization. Surely, as we behold them, their dark shadows are fringed with the light of the better dawning.

THE PICTURE OF INJUSTICE AND OPPRESSION

For the darker shadow of wrong and crime heightens the picture of selfishness and luxury with which the apostle's fearful impeachment of a godless people reaches its climax.

"Look! The wages you failed to pay the workmen who mowed your fields are crying out against you. The cries of the harvesters have reached the ears of the Lord Almighty" (James 5:4). It is not necessary for us to take the side of either capital or labor in the social or political strikes of today, in order to show that this picture of oppression of the poor is not an obsolete one. Go to the sweat shops of our manufacturing cities; see the poor, attenuated women and children that are toiling for a pittance in suffocating workrooms with long hours of half remunerated toil. Read the sickening story, that has sometimes come to us, of struggling girls that have been told to their face that they cannot expect to earn a living merely by honest toil, but must also expect to sell themselves, as well as the labor of their hands, to eke out a sufficient livelihood or help those who are so often dependent upon them. Occasionally the bitter cry of the poor reaches the ears of humanity as well as of the Lord God of Sabaoth, and we get a lurid gleam upon the wrong and sorrow that is done "under the sun," and we say like Solomon,

> Again I looked and saw all the oppression that was taking place under the sun:
>
> I saw the tears of the oppressed—
>   and they have no comforter;
> power was on the side of their oppressors—
>   and they have no comforter.
> And I declared that the dead,
>   who had already died,
> are happier than the living,
>   who are still alive. (Ecclesiastes 4:1–2)

THE DIVINE FORBEARANCE

"You have condemned and murdered innocent men, who were not opposing you" (James 5:6). This is undoubtedly a reference to the murder of our Lord Jesus Himself by proud and wicked enemies, of whom these worldly men are but the successors and representatives. The apostle means to suggest to the suffering disciples whose wrongs he has already referred to, that they are but following in the steps of their Master. The patience which they are expected to manifest was first shown by Him who stood amid the shame and suffering of the judgment hall and the cruel cross of Calvary. He exposed His unresisting body to all their murderous cruelty, and bore in silence all the wrong and shame of wicked men. He let Pilate, Herod and the Scribes and Pharisees have their own way. Yes, they might spit in that gentle face and crown with the mocking thorns at will; it was their day, and well they took advantage of that awful liberty, until they had wrought their wicked will to the full. And so still, in the suffering members of that blessed Master the same wicked world has its way. It is a fearful thing to have our liberty and use it without consulting God. You can hoard your wealth if you please; you can enjoy the banquet and the song if you will; you can grind the face of the poor and compel them to toil on your hard terms; you can do all this for a little while, and God will not resist you; you have your way and your little day, but remember that God is bringing you to judgment. The great Assize is coming on, and all the witnesses will meet you face to face some day, and then how you will wish that you could live your life once more.

Do not too hastily judge that God has forgotten to be just, because He gives you such a long reprieve. "When the sentence for a crime is not quickly carried out, the hearts of the people are filled with schemes to do wrong" (Ecclesiastes 8:11).

HUMAN PATIENCE

The divine forbearance is to be our example, and we are to meet the wrongs of men with the same patience and gentleness. Yes, there is wrong. The hire of the laborer is kept back. The hours are hard and long, the compensation insufficient, the whole system harsh and selfish to the core, but it is not harder than Gethsemane. It is not more shameful or painful than the judgment hall and the cruel cross He bore for you. You are but following in His footsteps; you are but filling up that which is behind of the sufferings of Christ. Do not go and fight your battle; do not get up a strike or a political party. Leave your vindication to Him; "be patient . . . until the Lord's coming" (James 5:7).

THE GREAT INCENTIVE

The coming of the Lord is a great incentive to our patience under suffering and wrong. What a practical aspect this blessed hope assumes in this message! How it comes down to the level of our common life, and sheds its light of hope upon our earthly toil! How it goes with us to the factory and the harvest field and sets to music the task of the toiler! That day will bring us the righting of our wrongs. That day will pay us the long deferred hire. That day will put us in our right place and displace the sons of pride, who have so long trampled on the rights of others. That day will make up for toil and bitter loss. That day will put us in the place for which our talents and merits have fitted us, and from which others have excluded us so long. That day will bring the punishment of our oppressors so terribly that our compassion could wish and plead for mercy. That day will confer upon us, if we are true, rewards so precious and so priceless that we will remember our misery only as a vanished dream. "Be patient, then, brothers, until the Lord's coming" (5:7).

But not only is this hope presented as the remedy and recompense for wrong and suffering, but as a great motive in all the trials and duties of our Christian life. Especially is it suggested as the goal of Christian work, and the harvest time of all our seed sowing. "See how the farmer waits for the land to yield its valuable crop and how patient he is" (5:7).

The suggestion here is for our Christian work and our Christian faith. We must not expect the answer and the fruition too soon. The seed must have time to germinate, the rains must water, both the early and the late rain. Many a waiting day must pass before we shall see "the full corn in the ear"

(Mark 4:28, KJV), and for this we must look away even unto the coming of the Lord. Not always shall we see the results of our labors in the present life. Like Solomon's temple builders we are but gathering materials for the great edifice, timbers from Lebanon, stones from the quarry, jewels and gold from the mine. But the workers in Lebanon did not see the timbers placed in Jerusalem immediately; other hands bore them to Joppa and Jerusalem, other workmen mounted them to their appointed place. The temple that we are building will not appear in its complete glory until He shall come. Our work is fragmentary, not final. Many a prayer that we breathe upon the air shall meet us at His coming. Many a message that seemed to fall in vain shall come back to us in some ransomed soul in that glad day. Many a plan which we left half completed on earth shall appear then like the rainbow about the throne, a finished circle. That is the crowning day; that is the time of the great reward. Then shall the sacrifices made for Him come back with their hundredfold. Then shall the victor receive the unfading crown. Then shall they that "lead many to righteousness, [shine] like the stars for ever and ever" (Daniel 12:3).

Then let us fix our goal on the heights of the advent hope. Let the point of view of every prayer and plan, every sacrifice and service, every enterprise and investment be "until the Lord's coming" (James 5:7). Yes, and if even much still remains unanswered and unfinished here, remember that this is but half the circle, and the rest will appear on the other side. He may keep you waiting long, and He may hold back much from your view, but though He tarry, wait for Him, for He will surely come, He will not tarry too long (Habakkuk 2:3).

On one of the battlefields of Pennsylvania a dying lad lay on the ambulance. The surgeon's instruments were ready for the sudden operation that was necessary, but he paused, as he noticed the stupor on the face of the lad, and he said, "No." It was useless and cruel to arouse him for such agony, he could not save his life, let him die in peace. But his comrade said that he must send for his mother. They remonstrated, for they said, "The excitement will but arouse him to feel his agony, but cannot save his life."

But the lad insisted that he must keep his promise both to the mother and to the boy, and they bore him to the hospital, and they soon brought that mother to his side. But they forbade her to speak to him or arouse him to consciousness, and only suffered her to stand in silence and hold his dying hand. But as she stood beside his cot, and gently held that hand, his lips began to move. The eyes were sealed already for their long sleep, but softly he murmured, "Mother," while a gentle light fell upon his face, and a sweet smile wreathed his lips, and he still murmured, "Mother, mother! I knew she would come, I knew that she would come."

And so the waiting Bride of Christ has waited long, and has often been perplexed and seemingly abandoned, and darker days are yet to come, when her enemies will glory in their triumph, but "will not God bring about justice for his chosen ones, who cry out to him day and night? Will he keep putting them off? I tell you, he will see that they get justice, and quickly" (Luke 18:7–8).

Will we write as our watchword and our hope, over against life's darkest trials and hardest toils, the bright inscription and blessed hope, "Until the Lord's coming"?

CHAPTER 8

PRACTICAL PRAYER

Therefore confess your sins to each other and pray for each other so that you may be healed. The prayer of a righteous man is powerful and effective. (James 5:16)

P ractical prayer. This is the kind that James describes: something to lift us up; something that comes down to the level of our everyday life; something that helps us in our business, that heals us in our sickness, that reaches beyond our need to others, and leads us to convert the sinner from the error of his way, and save a soul from death, and hide a multitude of sins.

THE COMMON AND EVERYDAY AFFAIRS OF LIFE

First, we must look at the place of prayer in connection with the common and everyday affairs of life.

"If any of you lacks wisdom, he should ask God, who gives generously to all without finding fault, and it will be given to him" (James 1:5). This is the ministry of prayer in the ordinary affairs of life. Wisdom just means the ability to do the right thing, to suit the means to the end in view. And so it has to deal with all the things that concern our life. The housewife needs it to make ends meet. The skilled artisan needs it to give a finer touch to his hand. The businessman needs it to meet the difficulties and emergencies of his office, to take advantage of opportunities, to be prudent and farseeing, and make the best of things as they come in his life. We need it in our domestic life in the training of our children. We need it in our spiritual work in rightly handling God's Word and dealing with the souls that come to us. And in our whole life we need a superintending hand, a wisdom greater than our own to suggest the right thing and to overrule our erring judgment and cause the best thing to come about, even if we ourselves did not choose it, making all things work together for good.

Surely this is intensely practical. We are to pray for wisdom. We are to bring to God everything that comes up in our life, and count nothing too small for His interest and interposing hand. The incense which was the type of prayer, was beaten very small, teaching us that nothing is too small to mingle with the cloud of prayer that goes from our closet to the throne of grace, and is presented by our Savior to His Father for acceptance.

So as we look through the Word of God, we find that secular matters and everyday interests are constantly made the turning points of greatest events. A young farmer looking for his father's donkeys led to the establishment of the kingdom of Israel. A lad coming up to see his brothers from Bethlehem led to the selection of David as king. In reading the story of Daniel, we find an emergency too hard for him and his companions becoming the occasion through prayer of all his future history. They were in peril because they could not interpret the king's dream. Daniel and his companions prayed for wisdom to make known this dream and thus deliver them, and it was through this incident that all the mighty future of Daniel, affecting the history of two great kingdoms, came about. He simply asked for wisdom, and his prayer was answered; he and his friends were delivered, and the way was opened for the highest possible service.

So we find Ezra on his way back to Palestine suddenly losing his way in the Syrian desert. How did he act? He says, "I proclaimed a fast, so that we might humble ourselves before our God and ask him for a safe journey . . . I was ashamed to ask the king for soldiers and horsemen to protect us from enemies on the road, because we had told the king, 'The gracious hand of our God is on everyone who looks to him, but his great anger is against all who forsake him' " (Ezra 8:21–22). Nor did he pray in vain. The wisdom was given, the way was made plain, and the pilgrim caravan crossed the desert in safety, and restored the city and temple of the Lord.

So, again, we find David in his first campaign against the Philistines, after he had been crowned, inquiring of the Lord, "Shall I go and attack the Philistines? Will you hand them over to me?" (2 Samuel 5:19). Of course such a beginning was followed by victory. But a year later the enemy returned. Now naturally we would expect David to do just as he did before. But that is not the way of faith. It does not count on experience, but upon God; and notwithstanding all that God had told him and done for him hitherto, he returned implicitly to the oracle of prayer, as though he had never fought a battle before. And happy for him that he did so, for now the direction is entirely different from the former occasion. "Do not go straight up," is the divine command, "but circle around behind them and attack them in front of the balsam trees. As soon as you hear the sound of marching in the tops of the balsam trees, move quickly, because that will mean the LORD has gone out in front of you to strike the Philistine army" (5:23–24). So prayer waits upon God and takes the instructions directly from the throne, even as the eyes of a servant wait upon the hand of her mistress.

It is said of Jotham that he became mighty because "he walked steadfastly before the LORD" (2 Chronicles 27:6). And the wisest of ancient teachers has told us, "Trust in the LORD with all your heart/ and lean not on your own understanding;/ in all your ways acknowledge him,/ and he will make your paths straight" (Proverbs 3:5–6).

I recall an incident in my ministry, a quarter of a century ago, when struggling with a great debt upon the house of the Lord which should never have been put there, I begged my people to unite with me in prayer, and promised them that if they would do so sincerely, God would surely remove it. They told me that it was no use to pray about such a debt for it was too big—$65,000. It was all right to pray about things, but this thing was an impossibility, and beyond their power. It was in vain for me to say that those were just the things to pray about, that we did not need a God for the things that were within our power, but for the difficult and impossible tasks. Finally, however, the senior elder of the church very firmly said to me, "My dear pastor, we esteem you very highly, but we do not at all agree with your extreme views about prayer."

Acting from a conscientious impulse, I refused to dedicate the church until the debt should be removed, but consented to preach in it. After a few months I was so strongly called to my present pastorate that I felt reluctantly constrained to leave the scene of so many prayers and labor, and to commit to God the things yet unfinished. A few months after my arrival in New York, a telegram came one Sabbath morning, inviting me to go the next Sabbath and dedicate the old church in the West, adding that the debt had been paid that week, and that the old elder who had so strongly objected to my view of prayer, had answered those prayers himself by giving 50,000 dollars. Of course the response was "Yes." The church was dedicated. The elder's house was my hospitable home for the next 10 days, and when I thanked him for his noble gift, the modest reply that came with many tears, was, "Don't thank me, it was the Lord." It is needless to add that the dear old saint had revised his view about prayer, and had no question now that God could do the hardest things and that there was nothing too difficult for prayer to ask in Jesus' name for the Father's glory.

IN CONNECTION WITH TRIAL

"Is any one of you in trouble? He should pray" (James 5:13). The book of Psalms is the prayer book of the afflicted. There is no form of trial which cannot find its appropriate expression in this sublime and simple liturgy. The experience of David was in accord with his poetry. He had learned to go to God in every dark and trying hour. In that supreme trial, just before his coronation, when he returned to Ziklag to find it burned with fire, and all his loved ones captives in the hands of the enemy, while his truest followers even threatened mutiny, and talked of stoning him, we are told that "David found strength in the LORD" (1 Samuel 30:6). Turning to the oracle of prayer again he sought direction, and soon had the joy not only of recovering all that he had lost, but of seeing his waiting years crowned with triumph, and his throne at last established. Such is the story of all the saints. When Rabshakeh sent his impious challenge to Hezekiah, and Sennacherib's army invested Jerusalem with a hopeless cordon, the good king called Isaiah to his counsels and spread the matter before the Lord. That was all. They just prayed about it, and lo, before another sun had risen that mighty host lay dead beneath the blighting wing of God's angel of judgment.

Even when our troubles are our own fault, and have come to us through folly or disobedience, even then it is not too late to pray. When Jehoshaphat found himself, through his sinful alliance with Amaziah, the wicked king of Israel, without water in a desolate wilderness, and three armies were threatened with destruction, Amaziah, true to the spirit of wicked unbelief, turned from God and cried, "Has the LORD called us three kings together only to hand us over to Moab?" (2 Kings 3:10). It was the despair of the sinner in the dark hour of calamity. But that was just the time when Jehoshaphat thought of God and turned to prayer, and soon through the hand of Elisha the valley was flowing with water, and deliverance and victory came. Even Jonah, when he found himself in the "belly of hell," did not forget to pray, and out of the depths of despair the cry of faith met the hand of deliverance. "When my life was ebbing away,/ I remembered you, LORD,/ and my prayer rose to you,/ to your holy temple./ . . ./ But I, with a song of thanksgiving,/ will sacrifice to you./ What I have vowed I will make good./ Salvation comes from the LORD" (Jonah 2:7–9).

Yes, even the wicked Manasseh, after half a century of bloodshed, when overtaken by just retribution in Babylon, lifted his heart to God even amid his chains, and God heard his prayer, and restored him to his kingdom and his home. "In his distress he sought the favor of the LORD his God and humbled himself greatly before the God of his fathers. And when he prayed to him, the LORD was moved by his entreaty and listened to his plea; so he brought him back to Jerusalem and to his kingdom. Then Manasseh knew that the LORD is God" (2 Chronicles 33:12–13).

And so the promise remains for all the tried ones, "Call upon me in the day of trouble;/ I will deliver you, and you will honor me" (Psalm 50:15). "Is any one of you in trouble? He should pray" (James 5:13). Is this what we are doing, beloved? Are we meeting God in our trials, or are we running to every expedient that our own minds suggest, and coming to Him only when every other resource has failed? How true to our experience is the reproof of God to Israel, "This is what the Sovereign LORD, the Holy One of Israel, says:/ 'In repentance and rest is your salvation,/ in quietness and trust is your strength,/ but you would have none of it' " (Isaiah 30:15). Instead of trusting Him to work for them, they resolved to make alliance with the world, and borrow the swift horses of Egypt. "You said, 'No, we will flee on horses.'/ Therefore you will flee!/ You said, 'We will ride off on swift horses.'/ Therefore your pursuers will be swift!/ . . . Yet the LORD longs to be gracious to you;/ . . . Blessed are all who wait for him!" (30:16, 18). Alas, how often have we delayed our blessing until we were through with all our earthly expedients and had learned to look to God alone! "Is any one of you in trouble? He should pray" (James 5:13).

IN CONNECTION WITH JOY AND BLESSING

"Is anyone happy? Let him sing songs of praise" (5:13). This is not so much prayer as praise, but praise is the better half of prayer. It is the amen of faith. It is the echo of confidence. It is the clinching of the nail that prayer has driven. It is prayer overflowing into praise. After Paul and Silas had prayed in the dungeon of Philippi, they just had to praise. And so all true prayer becomes praise, when it reaches its fullness.

The book of Psalms is much more a book of praise than of prayer, and it may well put to shame the unbelieving grumbling devotion of the modern saint. If we would praise more, we should have more to praise for.

IN SICKNESS

"Is any one of you sick? He should call the elders of the church to pray over him and anoint him with oil in the name of the Lord. And the prayer offered in faith will make the sick person well; the Lord will raise him up. If he has sinned, he will be forgiven" (5:14–15).

The careful reader will not fail to note the distinction between affliction and sickness. In affliction we are to pray, but it may be for grace to endure the affliction quite as much as deliverance from it. But in the case of sickness prayer is described as a definite remedy, and we are commanded to claim positive deliverance. The promise is, "The Lord will raise him up" (5:15). This is very remarkable, and should not be overlooked. It seems to imply that disease is a special hindrance of the adversary from which we should claim the Lord's protection. This is not only the prayer of the sufferer, but united prayer, and, of course, the prayer of faith.

Prayer and healing for the sick is no new teaching of James. Way back in the Old Testament we find Abraham praying for Abimelech, and Abimelech was healed. We find Moses interceding for Miriam, and her leprosy was taken away. We find David telling of God who healed all his diseases, and redeemed his life from destruction. We find Job receiving the healing touch of Jehovah's hand, and Elihu unfolding the principles of the New Testament with reference to God's healing love and power. We find Hezekiah receiving back even his forfeited life, when he prayed to God in the darkest hour of his existence. And we find the life of Jesus crowded with answers to the helpless cries of those who came to him for healing.

Beloved, are you thus walking in the footsteps of the flock? Are you looking to God first in the hour of sickness and pain? Are you honoring Him with your trust, and making even the attacks of the enemy an occasion for victory and glory to His name? "Is any sick? let him pray."

FOR OTHERS AND THE WORK OF GOD

Next we see the importance of the ministry of prayer for others and for the work of God.

"The effectual fervent prayer of a righteous man availeth much" (James 5:16, KJV). And then he tells us of the prayer of Elijah, and the sinner converted from the error of his way, so that a soul is saved from death, and a veil is cast over a multitude of sins. This is the highest ministry of prayer, not for ourselves, but for others and for God. But such prayer is no idle play. The apostle calls it the "effectual fervent prayer." Rotherham translates it "the supplication of a righteous man availeth much, working inwardly." The idea is that of intense energy, a paroxysm of internal force working out corresponding results. The illustration is Elijah on Mount Carmel. The vivid description of the sacred narrative presents us the picture of the prophet on his face with his head between his knees. It is a picture of strenuous inward conflict. Every nerve and muscle is intensely wrought to the highest strain. A mighty struggle is going on within. He is getting hold of God for something stupendous; and, lo, in a little while we see that inward conflict reproduced in the outer world, in the swift hurricane, the gleaming lightning, the reverberating thunder, the terrors of the tempest. This is but the outcome of the forces that had been working within, and that had touched the springs of omnipotence and let loose the powers of heaven. The literal translation of the passage about Elijah is "Elijah prayed a prayer." He did not pray a phrase or a form, or a paragraph, but a prayer. It was a living force. It had momentum in it. It was like the sure projectile that speeds from that piece of artillery. It reached somewhere. It accomplished something.

You have heard of the Boer hunter who went out with an American sportsman to shoot antelope. The American took his belt full of cartridges. The Boer took just one. "Why," said the other, "don't you intend to take some cartridges?" "Oh," said he, "I have taken my cartridge." "Yes, but," replied the other, "don't you want more?" "Oh no," said he. "I just want one antelope." The Boer meant that he expected to hit his target the first shot, and saw no use in wasting ammunition. The American probably expected one antelope too, but a score of spent shots. This is not a bad illustration of the different kinds of prayer. Most of our petitions go up like soap bubbles, vanishing as we gaze. True prayer is pointed, real and expects to reach the ear of God, and bring the answer from above every time. There is no higher service for the Master than to stand in such holy priesthood, and bear the burdens of other souls and the kingdom of our Lord.

"I am one of 11 children," said an old lady. "My brothers and sisters were all smarter and stronger than I. I am a poor shrunken cripple. I have no talent or influence. But I know how to pray, and God has let them all die; and it seems as though He needed me more than all." This old lady used to lie upon her bed and have her attendant read the letters of friends, or the newspapers of the day, while she would stop between sentences, and take hold of God for each need, waiting until she had claimed the answer and recorded it in the Lord's book of remembrance. Need we doubt that the answer came? These are the forces that are making the history of eternity. God help us to be among them.

Lord, teach us to pray!

FIRST AND SECOND PETER

CHAPTER 1

WORDS OF COMFORT FOR TRIED ONES

In this you greatly rejoice, though now for a little while you may have had [if need be, KJV] to suffer grief in all kinds of trials. These have come so that your faith—of greater worth than gold, which perishes even though refined by fire—may be proved genuine and may result in praise, glory and honor when Jesus Christ is revealed. (1 Peter 1:6–7)

Peter was to be the special target of Satan's assaults just because Christ had chosen him for so high a ministry. But even his very trials were his best preparation for that ministry, and the Master here intimates that when through the discipline of temptation he shall have himself become transformed, it will be his special calling to comfort and confirm his tried and tempted brethren.

How marvelously has he been transformed since that dark night of the denial! One has only to read his tender and lovely messages in his two epistles to see how truly he had taken up his Master's cross, and how deeply he had learned the lesson of his humiliating fall. One has only to read further his messages of consolation to the tried and tempted to see how faithfully he has fulfilled his commission, "Strengthen your brothers" (Luke 22:32). The first epistle of Peter is the best commentary on this text, and we can find no more comforting and helpful message for those who are passing through fiery trials than these letters of hope and comfort.

Peter is indeed the apostle of hope, as Paul is the apostle of faith, and John the messenger of love. The keynote of his first epistle is this word trials, which reappears in every chapter and forms the pivot of almost all his messages of comfort and encouragement. We have but to read the following passages to find that this one thought is sustained through the entire epistle:

Though now for a little while you may have had to suffer grief in all kinds of trials. These have come so that your faith—of greater worth than gold, which perishes even though refined by fire—may be proved genuine and may result in praise, glory and honor when Jesus Christ is revealed. (1 Peter 1:6–7)

For it is commendable if a man bears up under the pain of unjust suffering because he is conscious of God. But how is it to your credit if you receive a beating for doing wrong and endure it? But if you suffer for doing good and you endure it, this is commendable before God. To this you were called, because Christ suffered for you, leaving you an example, that you should follow in his steps. (2:19–21)

But even if you should suffer for what is right, you are blessed. "Do not fear what they fear; do not be frightened." But in your hearts set apart Christ as Lord. Always be prepared to give an answer to everyone who asks you to give the reason for the hope that you have. But do this with gentleness and respect, keeping a clear conscience, so that those who speak maliciously against your good behavior in Christ may be ashamed of their slander. It is better, if it is God's will, to suffer for doing good than for doing evil. (3:14–17)

Dear friends, do not be surprised at the painful trial you are suffering, as though something strange were happening to you. But rejoice that you participate in the sufferings of Christ, so that you may be overjoyed when his glory is revealed. If you are insulted because of the name of Christ, you are blessed, for the Spirit of glory and of God rests on you. If you suffer, it should not be as a murderer or thief or any other kind of criminal, or even as a meddler. However, if you suffer as a Christian, do not be ashamed, but praise God that you bear that name. (4:12–16)

Resist [Satan], standing firm in the faith, because you know that your brothers throughout the world are undergoing the same kind of sufferings.

And the God of all grace, who called you to his eternal glory in Christ, after you have suffered a little while, will himself restore you and make you strong, firm and steadfast. (5:9–10)

Let us gather out of these passages Peter's special messages of consolation to the tried and troubled.

1. The Vision of Hope

He begins by giving them the vision of hope and heaven before he says a single word about trial. He tells them of the inheritance that is incorruptible, undefiled, unfading and reserved in heaven for them, before he draws the dark picture of persecution and suffering. When the sea captain sees the sailor boy growing white as he climbs the mast, he always shouts to him, "Look up!" and his nerves grow cool and his fears are assuaged. So the Lord on that dark night, when He was bidding His disciples not to let their hearts be troubled, told them of the Father's house of many mansions and the place prepared. Let us begin every trial with the thought of heaven and the hope of His coming and the joy set before us, and we, too, shall be enabled to endure the cross, despising the shame, and often sing:

> When I can read my title clear
>   to mansions in the skies,
> I'll bid farewell to every fear,
>   And wipe my weeping eyes.
>
> Let cares like a wild deluge come,
>   And storms of sorrow fall,
> May I but safely reach my home,
>   My God, my heaven, my all.

2. The Length of Time

It is only "for a little while" (1 Peter 1:6). Compared with that long and happy eternity, the longest trial is short indeed. Our light affliction, which is but for a moment, is not worthy to be compared with the glory which shall be revealed in us. Remember, suffering child of God, it will be over soon, and faith and hope can hear the whisper in an undertone, "It is but a little while."

3. Always a Reason

There is a "need be" for every trial. It does not come by chance. There is a divine purpose in it all. It is necessary for your spiritual education, and some day you will thank God that He loved you well enough to let you learn to "endure hardness, as a good soldier of Jesus Christ" (2 Timothy 2:3).

"You may have had to suffer grief," he says, "in all kinds of trials" (1 Peter 1:6), and there is a "need be" even for this. How true it is that trouble never comes alone! When the adversary gets your body under, he loves to strike your soul and inject the fiery darts of discouragement and doubt. And you must not wonder if sometimes the trial strikes into the very depths of your being, and you even lose your joy and spring, and fall into heaviness of spirit. This is the hardest of all temptations. "A crushed spirit who can bear?" (Proverbs 18:14). We are so apt to conclude at such a time that the Holy Spirit has left us or we should not be so depressed. This is simply not so! There was a time when the Master "began to be sorrowful and troubled" (Matthew 26:37). There was a time when Paul had to say, "this body of ours had no rest, but we were harassed at every turn—conflicts on the outside, fears within" (2 Corinthians 7:5). Do not wonder, therefore, if your heart may sink sometimes in deep and long depression. There may be a "need be" even for this. Perhaps the Lord is crucifying you to your natural exuberance of spirit and teaching you to take your joy by faith from the Holy Spirit, and so find an everlasting joy which the world can neither give nor take away.

4. Your Trial Is Precious

Your trial is "of greater worth than gold, which perishes even though refined by fire" (1 Peter 1:7). That is to say, the trial, not the faith, is precious. We really possess nothing but that which has become part of our being. Outward conditions and circumstances will all pass away, but the experience that God burns into us will be part of our life forevermore. Therefore trial is precious because it makes Christ real to us and fixes the spiritual character which the Holy Spirit imparts. Remember, suffering one, that your trial is very precious to Him. He is watching it with anxious and ceaseless solicitude. He will not suffer it to go too far or last too long, but the very moment that the end has been accomplished, He will withdraw the vessel from the flames and give you rest from your sorrow.

5. It Will Result in Praise

It will result in "praise, glory and honor when Jesus Christ is revealed" (1:7). "Praise," for we shall thank Him for His faithful love in not excusing us from the hardest and highest classes in the school of experience. "Honor," for it will entitle us to rank in the school among the veterans and to wear our battle scars as marks of highest honor amid the overcomers yonder. And "glory," for in no other way can we earn the rewards of heaven and the glory which is superadded to the grace except by sacrifice and suffering. Salvation is a gift of grace, all grace, and we have nothing to pay or do to win it. But glory is gained by giving up our will, by taking up the cross, by letting go our rights, by standing in the hard place now, as we share the sufferings of Christ, "so that you may be overjoyed when his glory is revealed" (4:13).

6. It Is Commendable

"For it is commendable if a man bears up under the pain of unjust suffering because he is conscious of God" (2:19). Literally this means God will say, "I thank you." This passage is addressed especially to the slaves at Rome, not ordinary servants, but actually bondslaves, the property of their masters, and compelled to do and endure the most trying things at their will. The apostle comforts them in their trial by telling them that someday God Himself will stoop from the throne to thank them before the universe for their patient and faithful sufferings for His sake. What a proud day that was for Admiral Dewey when the nation thanked him for his great exploit! What a supreme honor it was when Lord Roberts knelt at the feet of his queen to receive her acknowledgments for his victorious campaign! But, oh, what a day it will be when some lowly servant maid shall be taken from the kitchen and seated by the side of the King of glory, while He shall tell the world how she suffered for His sake, and perhaps accomplished a higher ministry in her lowly place than the tongue of eloquence or the gifts of fortune of those who had much higher opportunities.

7. Suffering Innocently

Be comforted by the consciousness that you are suffering innocently. "But if you suffer for doing good and you endure it, this is commendable before God" (2:20). And yet some people are always going about telling how wrongfully they have been accused, how cruelly they have been misrepresented, how unjustly they have suffered. One would think that they were ashamed of that which the apostle considers the highest glory. The fact that you are innocent ought to take all the sting out of your trial and make you rejoice that you are counted worthy to be silent in the hour of misrepresentation, to let God vindicate you, and to "commit themselves to their faithful Creator and continue to do good" (4:19).

8. It Is Your Business

Remember that it is your business to suffer for Christ. "To this you were called, because Christ suffered for you, leaving you an example, that you should follow in his steps" (2:21). What would you think of a soldier complaining because he had been fired at? It is a soldier's business to be fired at. And so it is your calling to suffer for Jesus' sake. If you do not like it you should retire from the business of being a Christian. But if you intend to be true to your calling, you must not shrink from trial for Jesus' sake, nor be as eager to get out of the trial as to glorify Him in it. The apostles recognized their persecutions and summons before courts and magistrates as just so many pulpits to preach the gospel, and they were not half as anxious to escape from their enemies as to have every situation turn to them for a testimony.

Your humble station, your menial task may afford the very opportunity necessary for some special service which another could not do. An ancient legend tells us that one day a lad in Galilee was about to go out with his morning basket of buns and fish to sell for their scanty living. "Mother," he cried, "is the bread all ready?" And the mother answered impatiently, "Oh, I am so tired of the everlasting drudgery. Will it never end?" But at last the little basket was filled, and the lad had sold all but five of the loaves and two of the fishes and just then, boylike, he began to follow the crowd that was streaming over the hills. Before he realized how far he had gone, he was out in the wilderness, close up to the great Teacher and one of His disciples whom he had come to know, good Andrew, whom he had doubtless met on his village rounds. They were looking for bread for that great multitude of perhaps 20,000 people, counting the women and children, and they had nothing but this lad's little basket. But as he told his wondering mother how the Prophet had taken his loaves and fishes and blessed them, and given them out to the multitude in pieces until every one had eaten enough, and there were still left 12 baskets, she listened with strange interest, and her tears fell fast, and she said, "Did He really take my loaves and use them? Then never again will I be weary or discouraged of baking bread, so long as I know that I am making it for Him." Someday, dear one, you shall find that it was indeed for Him, and that instead of being a servant for some earthly and stingy taskmaster, you were ministering to Jesus and winning a crown of glory that shall never fade away.

9. An Opportunity for Witness

Trial affords us a fine opportunity to witness for Christ by our example. Nothing speaks for Him so emphatically as a patient, gentle spirit bearing in silent meekness the abuse and wrong which others may heap upon us; and often we will find that when we are right with people God makes them right with us.

A good woman in Stockholm had started a nursery for friendless and helpless children, but one of the little inmates was a constant trial to her. His body was diseased, his temper was intolerable. He seemed to have no gratitude or appreciation for any kindness shown him, but was always cross and discontented, while in addition his face was covered with sores, his form distorted and repulsive, and everything about him utterly forbidding. At last one day she had been telling the Lord that her burden was too hard to bear. Just then came to her a vision of her Lord, and she seemed to see Him bending over her with a look of great love and saying to her, "My dear child, I have loved and borne with you for more than half a century. Cannot you for My sake love and bear with this wretched child?" Her soul was thrilled with such a sense of His love that the very joy awoke her, and there before her eyes was the miserable child. But her heart was so filled with the Savior's love that she seemed to love everything else for His sake, and bending down she gently kissed the child. All at once her own spirit seemed to have passed into him, and the little one looked up with a smile that she had never seen before and threw his arms around her neck and began to caress her. From that time the disposition of the child was changed. The Savior's love had touched her heart and she had just passed it on to the little heart to whom she was in the place of God, and she had her reward in the beautiful transformation she saw from that time in her little charge. From that day forward the little one was completely changed, and became gentle, affectionate and even beautiful; and that which had been to her an insupportable burden became an unceasing joy. So our gentleness and sweetness will speak to others and awaken in them the response which our words can never call forth; while on the other hand our petulance and temper will often mar in a single moment the efforts of our lips and lives for many years to bring some soul to Christ.

> So let our lips and lives express
> The holy Gospel we profess.

10. Partakers of Christ's Sufferings

It will comfort and sustain us in trial to remember that we are partakers of the sufferings of Christ. Remember when any cross confronts you that it is His cross, that it is not yours, but His, and that it is just part of the load that He has left behind for you to bear for Him. The question is, Will you or He carry it?

The apostle speaks of "filling up that which is behind of the sufferings of Christ for his body, the Church." The Lord Jesus has left behind something for us to bear, something of His sufferings. Will we take it up and carry it for Him, or shall we leave Him to bear the burden alone? Has He not borne enough already, and shall we not consider it a privilege and a joy to be partakers with Him of the burden that some day is to bring so great a blessing and reward?

Doubtless you have heard the ancient legend which has been immortalized in the Polish romance, *Quo Vadis.* It tells us that when the fearful persecution of Nero arose against the Christians at Rome, to which this epistle undoubtedly refers when it speaks of the fiery trial, or more literally, "The trial of burning which is to try you," when Christians were soaked in oil, set on fire and tied to stakes in the Roman squares to light the streets by night—that Peter himself, with a little band of fugitive Christians, was leaving Rome late one night, when he met his Master with a sorrowful face walking back to the city and about to enter that gate through which he had just escaped. "Whither goest Thou?" he asked. And the Lord answered, "I am going to Rome to be crucified again because My servant Peter has fled from the cross." And Peter fell at his Master's feet and cried, "Nay, Lord, I will go back again, and gladly die for Thee." And so with head downward he let them nail him to the cross, counting it too high a privilege even to suffer with as much honor as his dying Lord.

Beloved, who shall bear the cross that meets you in your life? Your Lord or you? God help you to rejoice in your sufferings for Him and fill up that which is behind of the sufferings of Christ for His body, the Church.

11. The Spirit of Glory Will Rest on You

"The spirit of glory and of God rests on you" (4:14) in the hour of trial. When Israel of old came through the depths of the sea, then the cloud moved and came through the camp, baptizing them in its folds and making them to realize that God comes nearest to the heart, and often fills it with wonder and praise, when the "peace of God, which transcends all understanding, will guard your hearts and your minds in Christ Jesus" (Philippians 4:7). We look back upon such seasons as the sunlit memories of life and often say of them, "for you saw my affliction/ and knew the anguish of my soul" (Psalm 31:7). Let us claim the promise and "glory in tribulation also," and when God puts us most severely to the test let us put Him most fully to the test also, and we shall find that "For just as the sufferings of Christ flow over into our lives, so also through Christ our comfort overflows" (2 Corinthians 1:5).

12. Trial Will Bring a Reward

Trial borne for Christ will bring us a great reward, for "rejoice that you participate in the sufferings of Christ, so that you may be overjoyed when his glory is revealed" (1 Peter 4:13). Man loves to keep the memorials of heroic deeds, but, oh, how much more will God treasure up on high the monuments of His people's victories! And some day we shall find our tears transformed to jewels in the crown that we shall lay at Jesus' feet.

In one of the anniversary meetings of the British societies, a wealthy and distinguished layman told this incident in the life of his mother and father, both widely known throughout the Christian world for their splendid gifts to the cause of Christ. He said that when his father came to London, he was a poor lad with his fortune yet to be made. But in passing a certain house one morning, he was attracted by a girl who was washing the stone steps, and with a very bright, happy face, was singing snatches of religious hymns. From morning to morning the lad continued to come that way and often saw the fair vision of this happy face. One day he made bold to ask her to direct him to some Christian church as he was a stranger in the city. Naturally she directed him to her own, and they gradually got better acquainted until that friendship ripened into love and marriage. But he never forgot the vision of his first acquaintance with her and the beautiful spectacle of that humble girl so happy in her life of toil. When his great fortune was made and the time came to build a splendid mansion, he bought the house where she used to work as a servant, and took the stone steps bodily from its front and put them in his new mansion, that he might have a permanent memorial of the beautiful young life that had won him by its patient dignity and sweetness. And so we will doubtless find in our heavenly home, such memorials of sacrifice and service—perhaps some old broom or washtub preserved, as the relics of the saints are kept today on earth, but bearing some blessed memorial of the Master's grace and the disciple's victory.

13. You Are Not Alone

Remember in your darkest hour of trial that you are not alone, for He tells you that "your brothers throughout the world are undergoing the same kind of sufferings" (5:9).

Finally, the issue of your trials. "And the God of all grace, who called you to his eternal glory in Christ, after you have suffered a little while, will himself restore you and make you strong, firm and steadfast" (5:10). So, beloved, may we let Him establish, strengthen and settle us, and thus bring us to His eternal glory by Christ Jesus, to whom be glory both now and forever, Amen.

CHAPTER 2

HE IS PRECIOUS

Now to you who believe, this stone is precious. (1 Peter 2:7)

T he last question the Master asked His disciple, Peter, was, "Simon son of John, do you love me?" (John 21:17). And his beautiful letters leave us in no doubt as to the answer. It is summed up in our emphatic text, "He is precious."

But Peter tells us a great deal about Christ, and he tells it very completely. His picture of the Master leaves no lineament out, and it dwells most fully on the cruel thorns that marred his face, and the sufferings which Peter himself had once refused to hear about.

CHRIST'S SUFFERINGS

This is his first picture of the Lord. There was a time when Christ began to say unto His disciples that the Son of man must suffer many things and be delivered into the hands of the Gentiles, who should falsely condemn and crucify Him, and on the third day He should rise again from the dead. But Peter took Him and began to rebuke Him, and said, "Never, Lord! . . . This shall never happen to you" (Matthew 16:22). Then Jesus turned and with terrible rebuke, He answered Peter, "Get behind me, Satan! You are a stumbling block to me; you do not have in mind the things of God, but the things of men" (16:23). Peter never forgot that rebuke, and he makes full amends for his unitarianism in this epistle. Six times he tells us about the suffering Christ.

1. Our Example

He goes so far with the Unitarian as to hold up the suffering Master as our example that

you should follow in his steps.

"He committed no sin,
   and no deceit was found in his mouth."

When they hurled their insults at him, he did not retaliate; when
he suffered, he made no threats. Instead, he entrusted himself to
him who judges justly. (1 Peter 2:21–23)

This is all very beautiful and very true. But this is only the beginning.
Peter goes much farther than this and soon parts company with his
Unitarian friends.

2. Our Sacrifice and Substitute

He goes on to tell us of Christ as our Sacrifice and Substitute on the cross.
"He himself bore our sins in his body on the tree, so that we might die to
sins and live for righteousness" (2:24). Here there is no mistake about the
substitutionary character of the Savior's sufferings. He bore our sins on the
tree. Thank God, He left them there, and so died to them that we with Him
are also dead to sin and alive unto righteousness.

3. Our Redeemer

He makes all this plainer in another passage in the first chapter, where he
describes the suffering One as our Redeemer.

> For you know that it was not with perishable things such as silver
> or gold that you were redeemed from the empty way of life
> handed down to you from your forefathers, but with the precious
> blood of Christ, a lamb without blemish or defect. He was
> chosen before the creation of the world, but was revealed in these
> last times for your sake. Through him you believe in God, who
> raised him from the dead and glorified him, and so your faith
> and hope are in God. (1:18–21)

We hear some speak with scorn of the theology of the shambles, and that
it degrades the Lord Jesus to represent Him under the gross imagery of
sacrificial death. But here Peter uses no roundabout phrases, but tells us
straight and plainly that Jesus suffered for us as a lamb on the altar of
sacrifice. We see the precious blood. We see the dying Lamb. We see the ransom paid for the guilty, and we hear again, "the sweetest note in seraph
song" and "sweetest word on mortal tongue"—*redeemed.* Not only so, but
he tells us that redemption is God's most ancient thought, and that Christ
was foreordained before the foundation of the world to suffer and die for the
sins of men, so that the cross is really the center of God's plan, and the final

cause of the whole work of creation. It is not merely an afterthought or a remedy suddenly conceived to meet an emergency, but Christ is "the Lamb that was slain from the creation of the world" (Revelation 13:8), and His redeeming work will forever be the supreme glory of the universe.

"You were redeemed," Peter says, "from the empty way of life handed down to you from your forefathers" (1 Peter 1:18). So that redemption is much more than deliverance from a future hell. It is deliverance from this present evil world, deliverance from our life of sin and folly, deliverance from the spirit and maxims of the world, deliverance from the traditions we have inherited from our fathers. Beloved, have we been redeemed from these things? And have we claimed our freedom?

4. Our Atonement

Christ as our atonement is still more definitely presented in First Peter 3:18, "For Christ died for sins once for all, the righteous for the unrighteous, to bring you to God." This passage is an excellent statement of the doctrine of the atonement. It asserts the once-for-all-ness of that great transaction, the finished work of Christ as a complete and eternal settlement of the question of sin. This passage has special reference to the relation of Christ's sufferings to the justice and law of God. "For Christ died for sins once for all, the righteous for the unrighteous, to bring you to God" (3:18). There were questions on God's side that must be answered, and problems that must be solved, arising out of His inflexible justice and demanding a settlement of the debt of sin. Had God simply blotted out the record of man's sin without an adequate satisfaction, the majesty of His law and His righteousness would have been compromised. His word would have been set at nought and His authority annulled throughout the universe. It was necessary that He should be a just God as well as a Savior. The debt could not be canceled. It must be paid and receipted in full. And this is just what the atonement of Christ has provided, putting the believer in the same position as if he had never sinned, and not only forgiving his fault, but judging him and pronouncing him righteous through the righteousness of Christ.

Then on the side of the sinner there were difficulties to be adjusted before He could bring us to God. The distrust and dread of the guilty soul must be removed and a spirit of confidence awakened. We must be reconciled to God. And, therefore, "God was reconciling the world to himself in Christ, not counting men's sins against them" (2 Corinthians 5:19). By the exhibition of the Father's love and the place of salvation into which He brings us through His cross, the sinner is brought nigh to God by the blood of Christ, and thus atonement, that is literally at-one-ment, is accomplished, and we are brought to God in confidence and love.

5. Our Healing

Christ's sufferings have accomplished our healing, "by his [stripes, KJV] you have been healed" (1 Peter 2:24). Our body as well as our soul is included in this great redemption. This is one of our redemption rights. Let us not suffer it to be lost by our default. Literally this means, "by His stripes." His whole body was one dreadful laceration, and in that deadly stripes all our physical liabilities on account of sin were met. Well may it fill us with shame to think what our redemption cost, and with jealous love to make sure that such a costly boon shall not be lost.

6. The Pattern and Price

Christ's death is the pattern of our death as well as the price of our life. "Therefore, since Christ suffered in his body, arm yourselves also with the same attitude, because he who has suffered in his body is done with sin" (4:1). That is to say, as Christ died to sin, so let us die with Him and thus arm ourselves against sin by entering into the fact of His death and resurrection. While in one sense "He died for us that we might live," in another sense it is even more true that "He died for us that we might *die*."

The deepest experience of the Apostle Paul was this: "I have been crucified with Christ and I no longer live, but Christ lives in me" (Galatians 2:20).

There is an absurd story told of an official on one of the Irish railroads whose superior had just died, and who, in sending by wire the announcement of his master's death, did not feel at liberty to send it in his own name, but used the usual form signed by the principal, and running like this: "I regret to have to inform you that I died this morning at ten o'clock of pneumonia, W.J. Brown, Mgr., per J. Jones." There is a real truth behind this Irish bulletin. The greatest crisis in our spiritual life is when we are able to say with the apostle, "I died today, nevertheless I live, yet not I, but Christ lives in me." That is the only way to get victory over sin. So long as we identify ourselves with our past self we are under the power of our old life. It is when we bury it and take the position that we are no longer the person that sinned, but that we have died with Christ and risen again in Him, and are now living His life, we have power over sin, and the wretched man that we dragged about with us is consigned to an eternal grave, and the new life springs into liberty and power.

Such then is Peter's view of the sufferings of Christ, and the vision from which he once recoiled with intense antagonism is now to him so blessed that he speaks of it as one "even angels long to look into" (1 Peter 1:12), and he condenses into a single phrase his intense appreciation of the value and the glory of the cross when he tells us not only of the precious Christ, but "the precious blood of Christ" (1:19).

CHRIST'S RESURRECTION

He next bears testimony to the power of His resurrection.

1. The Source of Life

It is the source of our life. He "has given us new birth into a living hope through the resurrection of Jesus Christ from the dead" (1:3). Our regeneration comes to us through the fellowship of His resurrection. We are born again through the fellowship of His resurrection life. We are born again through that life.

2. The Ground of Our Faith and Hope

Christ's resurrection is the ground of our faith and hope. "Through him you believe in God, who raised him from the dead and glorified him, and so your faith and hope are in God" (1:21). Christ's resurrection is the foundation of our faith. For "if Christ has not been raised, our preaching is useless and so is your faith. . . . you are still in your sins" (1 Corinthians 15:14, 17). He went into the prison of the grave a debtor for your sins. Had He not come out, it would mean that the debt is still unpaid. But when we see Him rise in glory and ascend to the Father's right hand, we know that the ransom has been accepted, the debt is paid and our sins are gone. Therefore, He "was delivered over to death for our sins and was raised to life for our justification" (Romans 4:25).

His resurrection is also the foundation of our hope. "And if Christ has not been raised, . . . Then those also who have fallen asleep in Christ are lost" (1 Corinthians 15:17–18). The resurrection of Christ is the pledge of our resurrection and our future glory. Therefore our hope as well as faith rests upon His open grave.

3. Set Forth in Baptism

The resurrection of Christ is set forth in Christian baptism. "this water symbolizes baptism that now saves you also—not the removal of dirt from the body but the pledge of a good conscience toward God. It saves you by the resurrection of Jesus Christ" (1 Peter 3:21). That is to say, baptism does not signify the putting away of our uncleanness by washing, but by death and resurrection. We are so vile that no water can wash away the stain. The only thing to do with us is to bury us and raise up a new life through Christ's resurrection. This is implied in the figure of baptism. "We were therefore buried with him through baptism into death in order that, just as Christ was raised from the dead through the glory of the Father, we too may live a new life" (Romans 6:4).

Now Peter tells us here that the ark and the deluge were also typical of the same spiritual truth and experience. The expression is used in the 20th verse that "only a few people, eight in all, were saved through water" (1 Peter 3:20). It is not *from* water they were saved, but *through* water. The deluge saved Noah and his family from the sin that was engulfing the world; and through the ark his family was carried as by a seeming death and resurrection into the new world where the race began again its career. So in baptism we pass through a seeming death and resurrection with Christ into a new life. The resurrection, therefore, is the brightest and most uplifting object of the believer's faith. While it is true that we die with Christ once, it is more gloriously true that we live with Him forevermore. Have we entered into the fellowship of His sufferings and the power of His resurrection?

THE POSTHUMOUS MINISTRY OF CHRIST

This is His ministry in the interval between His death and resurrection. This is a part of His work of which Peter is almost the exclusive witness. It is true that the Apostle Paul alludes to it when he speaks of Him who "also descended to the lower, earthly regions" (Ephesians 4:9). Peter, however, tells us definitely that, during the interval after His death, He was quickened in the spirit, and in this state "he went and preached to the spirits in prison who disobeyed . . . in the days of Noah" (1 Peter 3:19–20).

There is little room to question the literal reference of this passage to the disembodied spirits of those who had lived in the days of Noah, and who were now in prison in the realm of the dead, the region called Hades in the Scriptures. That Christ visited this region is certain, and that He gave some message there is also plain. That it was a message of salvation to these imprisoned spirits there is no reason to believe, and there is no hint of it anywhere in the Scriptures. The word translated "preached" here is not the word usually employed for the preaching of the gospel, but it literally means to herald, to give a proclamation. It is not difficult for us to surmise what He might have proclaimed in the realms of the dead. These souls had heard the gospel for 120 years in the days of Noah and rejected it with scorn while God's Spirit strove with men. Now they are informed by the authority of the Son of God that the message which they rejected and ridiculed is true, and has been at last fulfilled, and the testimony of Noah is vindicated. At the same time how natural it would be for Him to proclaim to the other spirits in Hades that had died in faith and waited for His coming, that at last the great redemption was complete, that sin was canceled, that death was conquered and that He was about to open their prison doors and lead their captivity captive and take them up with Him to heaven, to which He was about to ascend and open its portals henceforth to all believers. When He did ascend to heaven, we know He took with Him these captive spirits; and since that time the souls of believers, like Stephen, no longer pass into Hades to wait for their reward, but pass immediately into glory and are with Jesus Christ Himself in heaven, awaiting the resurrection of their bodies and their full inheritance and reward at His second coming.

THE EXALTATION AND GLORIOUS SECOND COMING OF JESUS CHRIST

1. His Ascension and Exaltation

"Who has gone into heaven and is at God's right hand—with angels, authorities and powers in submission to him" (3:22). This is the picture of His present high priestly and kingly work. There He sits in the place of supreme authority and power; Head over all things for His body, the Church, every angel at His bidding, every authority and law in the universe subject to His command or suspension, and every power available for the help of His redeemed people.

2. His Coming Again in Glory

It is only necessary to quote the apostle's repeated references to this blessed hope. In First Peter 1:7, He tells us that our trial "may result in praise, glory and honor when Jesus Christ is revealed." In chapter 4:13, we are told that "you may be overjoyed when his glory is revealed"; and in First Peter 5:4, the faithful minister of Christ is reminded that "when the Chief Shepherd appears, you will receive the crown of glory that will never fade away." Thus we see that the blessed hope of the Lord's return was very clear to Peter's mind, and very dear to his affection and his hope.

HIS RELATION TO THE CHURCH AS THE CHIEF CORNERSTONE

"As you come to him, the living Stone—rejected by men but chosen by God and precious to him . . ./ 'See, I lay a stone in Zion,/ a chosen and precious cornerstone,/ and the one who trusts in him/ will never be put to shame" (2:4, 6).

It is recorded as a Jewish legend that when the temple of Solomon was being reared with noiseless hands, each prepared stone and timber being simply adjusted to its place, one stone of singular form was laid aside as unsuited to any place that they had found for it. After a while it became covered up with refuse and was known as the stone which the builders rejected. But later a niche was found on the principal corner that no stone would fit, and then they looked at this rejected stone and found it was the chief cornerstone—one designed to fill this place and connect together the two walls—thus make the building one. And so it came to be a proverb among the Jews that the stone which the builders rejected is made the head of the corner. Our Lord applied the proverb to Himself. And well He might.

For it is in Him that all the parts of the building are united and compacted and grow together into an holy temple in the Lord. It is as we are united to Him that we are attached to each other, and all Christian unity depends upon oneness with the Lord. The nearer we grow to the Master's heart, the closer will we stand heart to heart in unison with each other. The secret of Christian union is not platforms, creeds, or even cooperative work, but it is one life, one heart, one spirit, in the fellowship and love of Jesus Christ.

CHRIST'S RELATION TO THE INDIVIDUAL BELIEVER

"To you who believe, this stone is precious" (2:7). Literally this means as in the revised version, "Unto you which believe he is the preciousness." He is called in the previous passage the precious stone of God's election. Now His preciousness passes over to you who believe. His merits are imparted to you, and His rights and glories become yours also. And thus "you also, like living stones" (2:5) are built up into Him and become as precious as He. Just as when the iron touches the magnet it becomes partaker of its magnetism and in turn a magnet, too, so the soul that is united to Christ partakes with Him of His divine purity and power, and is no longer earthly and common, but precious and divine. Peter is undoubtedly referring to the interview between him and his Master when he was first called. "You are Simon son of John" (John 1:42) the Lord had said. That is, you are but a piece of earthly clay. But "You will be called Cephas (which, when translated, is Peter [a stone, KJV] (John 1:42)." That is, "your nature shall be transformed by contact with Me, until you shall become part of the living Rock," which the word Peter signifies. And so we find in the vision of the New Jerusalem that Peter and the apostles of the Lamb are there as precious stones laid first on the Cornerstone, Jesus Christ, and reflecting all His transcendent glory. This, then, is the meaning of the preciousness of Christ. It is not only that He is dear to us, for that is ineffably true, but rather that we are dear to God even as He—that we share His preciousness, shine in His beauty, stand in His merits, and will be partakers of His glory.

> All that He has shall be mine,
>   All that He is I shall be;
> Robed in His glory divine,
>   I shall be even as He.

CHRIST'S RELATION TO THE UNBELIEVER

"A stone that causes men to stumble—a rock that makes them fall" (1 Peter 2:8). If you reject this precious Savior, if you miss this supreme opportunity, if you pervert the grace of God and make it only an occasion for your idle criticism, Christ will become to you as great a curse as He might have been a blessing. "Everyone who falls on that stone will be broken to pieces," but, oh, there is something immeasurably worse, "but he on whom it falls will be crushed" (Luke 20:18).

CHAPTER 3

OUR HIGH CALLING IN CHRIST

I urge you, as aliens and strangers. (1 Peter 2:11)

Peter has told us about Christ. Now, what has he to tell us about ourselves? His first epistle contains a number of significant titles and attributes of the believer.

1. Strangers

"Peter, an apostle of Jesus Christ, To God's elect, strangers in the world" (1 Peter 1:1). This applies primarily to the Jews, as Peter was especially the apostle of the dispersion. How truly they may be called "strangers in the world, scattered . . ." a land without a people, a people without a land!

> Tribes of the wandering foot and weary breast,
> Where shall you fly away and be at rest?
> The wood dove hath her nest, the fox his cave,
> Mankind his country, Israel but the grave.

But the term also applies to the Christian of Gentile as well as of Jewish blood. This is not our home. We are strangers here, or should be.

2. Elect

"Who have been chosen according to the foreknowledge of God the Father, through the sanctifying work of the Spirit, for obedience to Jesus Christ and sprinkling by his blood" (1:2). Though strangers and aliens, for whom the world has no more place than for their Master, they are of great value to God, and they have been chosen and selected out of the great mass of the human family for the work of grace and the destiny of glory. But their election is not arbitrary and apart from their personal character and conduct. No man can plant his feet in dogmatic willfulness on the decrees of God and say, "If I am elected, I will be saved, whatever I do," for the Lord Jesus has given us the first test of our election in these simple words, "All that the Father gives me will come to me" (John 6:37). If we have not come to Christ, it is as idle to talk about our election, as for a man to expect a civic election until he has first become a candidate. Then the Apostle Peter has told us here that our election is through sanctification and to obedience. If, therefore, we are not receiving the sanctifying grace of the Holy Spirit and walking in obedience to Christ, we have no right to claim our election. The last phrase, "sprinkling by his blood," (1 Peter 1:2) has a special application to the deeper work of our sanctification. The shed blood was the special symbol of Christ's atonement for our guilt. The sprinkled blood, applied in every case of fresh defilement, stands for the cleansing efficacy of that precious blood. God has called us, therefore, not to an absolute destiny so much as to a high and holy character, and we are to make our calling and election sure by claiming all the privileges of grace and giving all diligence to walk in all the will of God.

3. Born Again

Begotten, born again, newborn babes (1:3, 23; 2:2). This is translated literally, "regenerated." It refers, of course, to the work of the Holy Spirit, through which we become the children of God and partakers of the new life, and without which our Lord has told us that we shall neither see nor enter into the kingdom of God. But in the third of these passages is a special and most beautiful sense intended by the phrase, "Like newborn babies, crave pure spiritual milk, so that by it you may grow up in your salvation" (2:2). The idea is not that at a certain stage of our experience we are to be newborn babes, but that this is to characterize our whole Christian life, and that the ideal spirit of the child of God is the simplicity, sincerity, docility and sweetness of the little child. We are not to be childish, but we are to be childlike. The ordinary conception of Christian life looks back to the halcyon days when we first believed as a springtime that will never come again. We speak and sing of

> The sweet comfort and peace
> Of a soul in its earliest love.

But our Lord severely rebukes the Ephesian church because it had left its first love. And He means surely to imply that we should never lose the tenderness of the newborn babe. This will keep us surely, as the apostle so well expresses it, from "all malice and all deceit, hypocrisy, envy, and slander" (2:1).

4. Obedient Children

"As obedient children, do not conform to the evil desires you had when you lived in ignorance. But just as he who called you is holy, so be holy in all you do; for it is written: 'Be holy, because I am holy' " (1:14–16). Literally this verse means, "As the children of obedience." that is, it is so natural to them to obey that they are, as it were, born of the spirit of obedience. The following verse suggests also the idea of imitating the Father. "But just as he who called you is holy, so be holy" (1:15). It is the same thought expressed by the Apostle Paul in Ephesians 5:1 R.V., "Be ye therefore imitators of God as dear children." Obedience should be instinctive with us as God's children. This is also suggested in the next term attributed to believers.

5. Servants

"As servants of God" (1 Peter 2:16). Literally this is "as the slaves of God." Our ideas of service were unknown in classical times. A servant was a slave, his master's property, and belonged to him absolutely for purposes of pleasure, gain or even crime. The apostle did not announce a crusade against slavery, though it was wrong in a hundredfold more aggravated sense than modern slavery ever was. But he told the slaves to be so true to their masters, and so blameless in their lives, that with well doing they should put to silence the ignorance of foolish men. Christianity does not call us to great socialistic movements against the wrongs of society, but rather to purify and elevate the individual influence of Christians, so abolishing as it has done, the wrongs of woman and the cruelties of slavery. But from the human relation of the slave the apostle rises to the conception so dear to all New Testament writers, of God's ownership of us and our absolute slavery to His authority and will. The term despot is applied to God in this epistle, conveying the idea of the right of absolute proprietorship and control, and this the disciple loves to acknowledge and accept in implicit surrender and obedience.

6. A Series of Figures

The apostle now begins a series of figures with reference to believers, founded upon the types of the Old Testament and the calling of Israel as a people. The first of these is *living stones*. "You also, like living stones, are being built into a spiritual house" (2:5). This is an allusion to the Hebrew temple, and is connected with what he has already said about Christ, the Cornerstone. We are built upon Him and so attached to Him that we become partakers of His nature and His life. Just as you have seen a powerful magnet or loadstone attracting and holding to itself a great number of smaller pieces of metal so that they seem to be part of its substance and are held by an invisible and irresistible bond, so we are attracted and attached to

Christ and built up in Him as a spiritual temple.

7. A Spiritual House

"You . . . are being built into a spiritual house" (2:5). This carries forward the figure from the individual stones to the entire temple, and at once brings before our minds the splendid figure of the temple and tabernacle service as a type of our spiritual life. Each of us should be a miniature of that sacred temple and our whole life a constant offering up of spiritual sacrifices, acceptable to God through Jesus Christ. For God has said to us, "for a little while I have been a sanctuary for them" (Ezekiel 11:16); and we may so "[dwell] in the shelter of the Most High" (Psalm 91:1), and "rest in the shadow of the Almighty" (91:1), and have "confidence to enter the Most Holy Place by the blood of Jesus" (Hebrews 10:19), that every moment of our experience shall be a rehearsal of the sacred service of that ancient tabernacle. It is a delightful spiritual exercise to come in the secret fellowship of the soul, first to the altar of burnt offering, where we lay our guilt and sin upon the Lamb of God, and know that we are accepted through His precious blood as a sacrifice and a sweet smelling savor. Then we may come to the cleansing laver, where first we see our sins in its mirrored bosom, and then wash them away in its flowing waters. Now we are prepared to enter into the holy place through the sacred door which the priests might enter, and claim the privilege of Christian priesthood. This leads us to the next of these significant figures.

8. A Holy Priesthood

"You . . . are . . . to be a holy priesthood" (1 Peter 2:5). For the priesthood is not now confined to any exclusive class as in the Aaronic line, but we are all called to be priests unto God. And yet that does not mean that all believers really enjoy the privilege of priesthood, although they are entitled to it, for we must first qualify for this high and holy ministry. We are a holy priesthood, and he alone who has clean hands and a pure heart can ascend into the hill of God and stand in the holy place (Psalm 24:3). Therefore we must wash in the laver and enter in by the door which is Jesus Christ Himself in the fullness of His life. For He has said, "I have come that they may have life, and have it to the full" (John 10:10). The "full" life is the holy priesthood of which we have just spoken, and the secret place of the Most High where we may dwell as His hidden ones. There stands the golden lampstand with its perfect and supernatural light. For there is an inner light for the consecrated believer which the world cannot comprehend, but which speaks to the finer senses of the quickened spirit and makes divine truth a vivid reality and Christ more real "than any outward object seen."

Next we come to the table of the bread of the Presence, a type of Christ our living bread, and find in Him the supply of all our need and the sustenance of all our life. A little farther on stands the golden altar of incense with the censer with burning coals and fragrant frankincense, and the whole chamber of this inner sanctuary is filled with the sweet odors of divine communion, "the peace of God, which transcends all understanding" (Philippians 4:7), and the very breath of heaven. Yes, and even farther in we may enter now, through the torn veil into the Most Holy Place, and dwell in the innermost presence of God where the Shekinah shines and the overshadowing wings of the cherubim remind us of our coming glory into which, indeed, in foretaste we may already enter. Thus we are a holy priesthood, and in the fellowship of the Spirit offer up spiritual sacrifices acceptable to God by Jesus Christ.

9. A Chosen People

"You are a chosen people, a royal priesthood, a holy nation, a people belonging to God" (1 Peter 2:9). Now just as the previous phrases were all connected with the tabernacle and temple, so this series is similarly connected with the calling of Israel as a people. They were an elect race, a holy nation, a kingdom of priests, and a people for His possession. Had they fulfilled their high destiny, they would have become to the world what the 24 elders and the four living creatures are to the heavenly temple. They would have represented God to men and become the custodians of His sacred oracles and the leaders of His worship and His work among the nations. But Israel failed to understand and fulfill her high calling. Instead of being a peculiar people, she sought to be like the nations. Instead of recognizing God as her King, and being a theocratic kingdom as He had intended, she said, "Appoint a king to lead us, such as all the other nations have" (1 Samuel 8:5), and soon her kings and people were sunk in all the gross idolatries of the nations around them. No sooner had the kingdom reached its zenith in the glory of Solomon than he introduced not only the luxuries but the abominable idolatries of Egypt and the world. And God had to rend the kingdom and send its people into captivity and even give over the sovereignty of the world to the Gentile nations, until Israel should learn that her only place must ever be that of a kingdom of priests and of a peculiar people. To that high destiny she is once more to come in the glorious day of her restoration under Christ her King. But now having lost her national calling for the time, God has called His Church to take her place, and to be instead His chosen people, His holy nation, His royal priesthood, His peculiar people. Let us not forget that we can only enjoy this high destiny in separation from the world; and that when we become like the present evil age, we lose our separation and our glory, and the Lord will have to reject us too. This indeed is the sad picture of the last stage of Christianity as set forth in the Laodicean church just before the coming of the Lord. But while the Church as a body and a visible institution may thus be rejected by her coming Lord, the true Bride of the Lamb, the little flock of His hidden ones shall be kept true and pure as a people for His possession. Let us remember that this is our calling, to belong to Him and to Him alone, to represent Him to the world and to wait for our kingdom and glory when we also shall be glorified at His coming.

10. Aliens and Strangers

"I urge you, as aliens and strangers in the world" (1 Peter 2:11). The apostle began with one of these titles. It is fitting that he should return to it again at the close of this series of sacred names and titles for the people of God. Literally these terms may be translated sojourners and pilgrims. The first expresses the idea that we have no home here; the second, that we have a home beyond, that we are pressing forward to it and that we are having it ever in view. One may be a stranger without being a pilgrim. A stranger is a tramp. The pilgrim is a traveler. The tramp is homeless. The traveler is going home. Both should be true of the child of God. We should be weaned from the world as a resting place or a goal of final hope and expectation. We are in it but not of it. We have our earthly duties, occupations and relationships, but it is only a stage on our journey home. The true heart will often be lonesome for the home beyond.

A poor Irish laborer who had spent 40 years of his life amid the brick and mortar of the great city, went out to the country for a few days to work at a special job. One morning as he stood in the field he heard a sudden whir of wings and saw a little speck shooting up into the air, and immediately there came a burst of music that filled his eyes with tears, and sent him to sit down on one of the rough building stones until the flood of memories that song awakened had surged through his simple heart. An American who had never noticed the song of the lark asked him what was the matter. "Oh," said the poor Irishman, "that bird made me think of the old country and the days long gone by." Poor fellow, he had not heard the lark since his childhood, and it made him feel that he was a stranger in a strange land. Beloved, do you know the home longing? And best of all, are you going home? Are you not only a stranger, but a pilgrim too?

They say the Swiss soldiers, when they sometimes hear the old horn that calls the sheep and cattle home at night in the Alpine valleys, throw down their arms and cannot be restrained from starting home. Is the heavenly country drawing you? Can you say like the little fellow whose kite was out of sight and some one asked him how he knew it was there, "I feel it pull"? Is your life projected on the heavenly scale? Are your friendships, your ambitions, your occupations, your money, your studies and your life plans invested where moth and rust cannot come, nor thieves break through and steal?

> I am waiting for the coming of the Bridegroom in the air,
> I am longing for the gathering of the ransomed over there;
> I am putting on the garments which the heavenly Bride shall
>   wear,
>   For the glad homecoming draweth nigh.
>
> I am letting go the pleasures and the treasures worldings prize,
> I am laying up my treasures and ambitions in the skies;
> I am setting my affections where there are no broken ties;
>   For the glad homecoming draweth nigh.

CHAPTER 4

SOCIAL AND CIVIC DUTIES OF THE CHRISTIAN LIFE

Submit yourselves for the Lord's sake to every authority instituted among men: whether to the king, as the supreme authority, or to governors, who are sent by him to punish those who do wrong and to commend those who do right. . . . Show proper respect to everyone: Love the brotherhood of believers, fear God, honor the king. (1 Peter 2:13–14, 17)

T he apostle here calls our attention to the duties of the Christian in all the various relationships of life.

1. As Human Beings

"Show proper respect to everyone" (1 Peter 2:17). Peter had a great deal of human nature in him, and human nature is a very good thing to have if we have the divine nature, too. "Simon son of Jonah" (Matthew 16:17), as the Lord often called him, was a real man and had every cord of human feeling and sympathy vibrant. It cost him a great deal to be so human; but when a human heart is divinely sanctified, it is a great storehouse of power. So Peter looks at all men as men. He sweeps the larger circle of the race, and reminds us that in every human being there is something of infinite value, something that God appreciates, something that brought Christ all the way from heaven to die, and something that we can find in every soul and make it a point of contact to better things.

It was this that Jesus sought and found when He reached the woman at the well through her heart, and when in the man in the sycamore tree He saw something worth saving and transforming into heavenly gold. God help us to see the value of a human soul, and to be able to touch it. It was Lord Shaftsbury who once slapped on the shoulder a poor drunken fellow just getting over a terrible temptation and said, "John, by the grace of God, we'll make a man out of you yet," and that touch of human hand was never forgotten. The poor drunkard lived to be a man of God and a blessing to his fellowmen. Over in Indiana there was a woman who had been the terror of her town, and even in the penitentiary she had to be confined and bound with chains. Nobody had ever been able to approach her. One day a quiet Quaker called at the prison and asked to speak to her; and as the manacled criminal was brought in with scowling and cursing lips, she simply stepped up to her, and saying with unobtrusive kindness the two little words "My sister," she kissed her on both cheeks. The woman staggered as if struck. She tried for a moment to resume her old violent manner, and then burst into tears, saying that it was her first pure kiss since her mother died, and from that hour she was a changed woman. God help us to "honor all men," and by His grace to find the angel in the roughest block of marble.

2. As Citizens

"Submit yourselves for the Lord's sake to every authority instituted among men: whether to the king, as the supreme authority, or to governors" etc. (1 Peter 2:13–14). Peter had his lesson on the subject of civil government that day in Capernaum when the natural Simon rose in irritation against the tax collector, and the Lord so graciously supplied the money and shared the burden with Peter as he uttered that beautiful phrase, "For my tax and yours" (Matthew 17:27). No true Christian can be an anarchist. While there is an extreme of spread-eagle patriotism, there is also a middle ground of Christian loyalty which recognizes the powers that be as ordained of God; and even when they are not altogether as they should be, submits and supports "for the Lord's sake." Especially in a country like the United States, and to a great extent even under limited monarchies, is the individual Christian responsible for his part in good government; for if the people are the kings and their elective voice determines the quality of the government, surely no sincere Christian can be indifferent or negligent concerning his civic duties.

3. As Members of Society

Finally, all of you, live in harmony with one another; be sympathetic, love as brothers, be compassionate and humble. Do not repay evil with evil or insult with insult, but with blessing, because to this you were called so that you may inherit a blessing. For,

"Whoever would love life
  and see good days
must keep his tongue from evil

and his lips from deceitful speech.
He must turn from evil and do good;
   he must seek peace and pursue it." (1 Peter 3:8–11)

Here we have a fine picture of the good manners of the child of God. There is nothing among the things of secondary importance more attractive than social grace, refinement of manners and the spirit of deportment of a true lady or gentleman. The Christian should always be a gentleman or a lady. The spirit of Christ will lift the commonest life to a higher plane of culture, and you can tell immediately by the dress and the deportment of the new convert that he has come into the society of higher beings. The lack of this is very sad and very hurtful to the cause of Christ. Fénelon was so much of a gentleman that one of the courtly infidels of England, upon leaving his house, said that if he had stayed much longer, he would have been compelled by the charm of the French divine to become a Christian. On the other hand, by our brusqueness how much we dishonor our Master, and repel hearts that would have sought Him!

The Spirit of Christ will invariably show itself on the railroad train, in the church aisle, in the little courtesies of the home, in a thousand minute touches which together constitute a great part of the experience of everyday life. These things are not matters of temperament or education. They can be cultivated until they become the habit of our life. There is a little tract entitled *The Girl for Whom Nobody Cared.* She was good in her way and had no serious faults of character or conduct, but rather prided herself on her independence, met her friends with a careless nod, and never wasted words in social amenities and what she was pleased to consider empty forms. The result was that in due time she became thoroughly disliked, and people avoided her as much as she had avoided them. Of course, it became extremely embarrassing to her when she really discovered it, and she had a good cry and an earnest conference with her sensible aunt. The result was that she took some good advice and resolved from that time to study her manners as well as her intentions, and deliberately to plan to say or do some courteous thing to everybody she met. The first person was a garrulous neighbor of whom she was always particularly tired. But this morning she set to work on her with her new lesson. "How is Jimmie?" she asked. And the neighbor was delighted to tell her how Jimmie had just got over the measles and a dozen little tiresome things that made that mother's face glow with pleasure to find a willing listener, and the effect was contagious. The young lady herself became strangely interested in the pleasure she had so easily given to the other. And so the first lesson was a complete success. A little farther on she met Sissy, the daughter of the washerwoman, whom she used to pass with a very curt nod as quite beneath her. But now there was a gracious smile, a moment's pause, and a kind word of thanks to Sissy for having brought the laundry so promptly the day before, and greatly accommodated her as she had a social engagement for which she needed her clean dress. Before long she had exhausted all subjects except the weather, but even a kindly remark about the weather, especially in good weather, is more cheerful than a silent nod; and so when she returned home her face was shining and her day had been a great success. It was not long before the girl that nobody liked was the girl that everybody liked, and she had found inexpensive kindness more precious than gold.

A good deal of this has to do with faults of the tongue, and so Peter is as decided as James in reminding us that if we would have good health, long life and God's blessing, we must keep our tongue from evil and our lips from speaking guile. This, too, can be studied if we habitually remember the Psalmist's prayer, "Set a guard over my mouth, O LORD;/ keep watch over the door of my lips" (Psalm 141:3). In this way many of the weakest and most foolish of God's children have learned to be so guarded that their very silence speaks for Christ and a life of victory as no words could. Let us remember that we are called to dispense blessing. This is our occupation to scatter sunshine and make others glad.

An old Quaker was once visited by a garrulous neighbor who complained that he had the worst servants in the world, and everybody seemed to conspire to make him miserable. "My dear friend," said the Quaker, "let me advise you to oil yourself a little." "What do you mean?" said the rather irritated old gentleman. "Well," said the Quaker, "I had a door in my house some time ago that was always creaking on its hinges, and I found that everybody avoided it; and although it was the nearest way to most of the rooms yet they went round some other way. So I just got some oil, and after a few applications it opened and shut without a creak, and now everybody just goes to that door and uses the old passage. Just oil yourself a little with the oil of kindness. Occasionally praise your servants for something they do well. Encourage your children more than you scold them, and you will be surprised to find that a little sunshine will wear out a lot of fog, and a little molasses is better than a great deal of vinegar." Be courteous.

4. As Servants

"Slaves, submit yourselves to your masters with all respect, not only to those who are good and considerate, but also to those who are harsh" (1 Peter 2:18). We have already seen that the condition of a Roman slave was not only much worse than that of a modern servant, but really very much worse than anything we know in connection with modern slavery. And yet to these selfish, brutal, cruel masters and mistresses, the Christian slave was to be obedient, and by his conduct seek to win them to higher things. If they were in error, as servants sometimes are, and were buffeted for it, they were to take it patiently. And there is no higher quality in man or woman than to be able to make an apology with humility and yet with dignity. But if they were innocent, how much more might they endure their wrong and wait for God's vindication.

In the present day almost every position in life involves the idea of service, and more or less of subjection to a higher authority. Let us render this for Christ's sake, even when it is not due for the sake of the person immediately concerned. How it exalts our menial toil to realize that we are working for Him, and that some day He will thank us and reward us before the universe! In such a service nothing is menial or degrading. The motive glorifies the deed. There is no smaller man in the world than he who is ashamed of manual labor or honorable employment. In a book of *The Life of Washington* it is said that riding by among his encampments in civilian dress, he found a petty officer ordering a small squad of men to change the position of a heavy gun which seemed beyond their strength, while he was coolly looking on, giving orders, but not touching the heavy burden himself. The general, unrecognized by the officer or men, sprang from his horse, and putting his shoulder to the wheel soon helped them to lift the heavy load and place the gun in position. Then he turned to the petty officer and asked him why he wasn't helping. "Why," said he, "I'm a corporal." "Then, Mr. Corporal," said he, "the next time you have a load too heavy for your men and want assistance just send for the commanding officer to come and help you. I bid you good morning," and the General withdrew, leaving the Corporal discomfited and the men infinitely amused. Let us take up our burdens with new heart and bear them for Him, who, like us, was a Man of sorrow and toil, and even in heaven is not thinking of His own ease or self-indulgence, but as our girded Priest ever living to make intercession for us.

5. As Wives and Husbands

> Wives, in the same way be submissive to your husbands so that, if any of them do not believe the word, they may be won over without words by the behavior of their wives, when they see the purity and reverence of your lives. Your beauty should not come from outward adornment, . . . Instead, it should be that of your inner self, the unfading beauty of a gentle and quiet spirit, which is of great worth in God's sight. (3:1–4)

If the position of a servant was extremely trying in ancient Rome, much more difficult and confused was the position of a wife, and the state of society with regard to marriage. Woman was by universal consent regarded as the inferior of man, and the wife of a heathen was subject to much humiliation and wrong. But the apostle tells the Christian wives not to desert their unworthy husbands, but so to live as to win them for God. Many a wife has done this. The Scriptures clearly prohibit the marriage of Christian women to ungodly men, yet it often happens that both are unsaved at the time of marriage; and, when the wife becomes a follower of Christ, under these circumstances there are the strongest reasons for expecting the grace of God to interpose for the salvation of her husband. And even if she has made the mistake of marrying against the Word of God, all the more should she repair her wrong by endeavoring to bring her husband to Christ.

The secret of woman's supremest and sweetest attraction is here in a most beautiful phrase. Her ornament is not to be outward fashion and display, but a meek and quiet spirit, the beauty of the hidden man of the heart, the loveliness of character, gentleness and love. This is woman's kingdom, and there is no doubt that many a man would be a better man if he had a different wife. Dear sisters, recognize your calling and rise to your high scepter and noble ministry. While marriage is not the lot of every woman, yet if God gives to woman a true and happy marriage, there is no higher vocation, there is no sweeter or nobler task than to live to be the blessing and crown of another life of which hers is the inspiration and the benediction.

"My wife had been an open book to me," said an infidel who had read all other books in vain, and who yielded his heart to Christ because the beautiful life that was linked with his compelled his confidence and wooed his heart.

And the husband, too, has his reciprocal responsibilities. "Husbands, in the same way be considerate as you live with your wives, and treat them with respect as the weaker partner and as heirs with you of the gracious gift of life, so that nothing will hinder your prayers" (3:7). The phrase "according to knowledge" (KJV) seems to require of the husband an intelligent understanding of the partner of his life, a thoughtful love that recognizes her disabilities and difficulties as the weaker vessel, and finds his highest honor in honoring her. The tendency of modern social life is disintegrating the home. The husband finds his substitute in his club, and the wife follows with her receptions and the program of social calls, and, of course, it is his fault as much as hers. A wise wife uttered a well-merited reproof of this state of things one day when she asked her husband to permit her to make an appointment for some evening to meet a mutual friend. But every evening was occupied by him with some society. On Thursday night it was the Odd Fellows' Society, on Friday night it was the Foresters' Society, on Saturday night it was the Masonic Society, and on Sunday night it was the Church Society. At last his wife gave him a keen look and said, "My dear, I think in the multitude of your societies you have forgotten one." "What one is that?" he asked. "Why," said she, "it is your wife's society."

But the real secret of a true Christian home life is given us by the apostle's reference to united prayer. Walk together, he says, "as heirs with you of the gracious gift of life, so that nothing will hinder your prayers" (3:7). This is the spark of celestial fire that will keep the altar of home from growing cold and love from dying out in the ashes of bitterness. How many of you fathers and husbands are keeping up the family altar? How many of you are praying every day with your wife? Is not this the telltale secret of all your troubles? Let us go back to Bethel and dwell there, and God will love and bless the dwellings of Jacob as well as the tabernacles of Zion.

Dr. Norman McLeod tells of a father that burst into his study one day with the bitter cry that his daughter had died that morning; and, added the father, "I hope she has gone to be with Christ, but if she has, she has gone to tell that never in all her life did she hear a prayer in her father's house."

6. As Christian Brethren

"Love as brothers" (3:8). "Offer hospitality to one another" (4:9). "Clothe yourselves with humility toward one another" (5:5). "Each one should use whatever gift he has received to serve others, faithfully administering God's grace in its various forms" (4:10). These are some of the social obligations of the disciples of Christ. Space will not allow us to enlarge upon them now, but the keynote of all is the same that has rung through all other relationships, *"For the Lord's Sake."* This will make you a faithful servant to the worst of masters, a loving wife to the man that you could not love for his own sake, a genial and courteous friend, that you may the better represent your Lord and attract others to Him, a subject and a citizen for Christ, and a Christian worker adjusted to your brethren, fitted into your place, and so "whatever you do, whether in word or deed, do it all in the name of the Lord Jesus" (Colossians 3:17). Lord, shed this supernal light on every common thing till it shall shine in the light of God like the glory which the sun reflects from the meanest bit of broken glass.

> So let your works and actions shine
> To show the doctrine all divine.

CHAPTER 5

SANCTIFICATION

Be holy, because I am holy. (1 Peter 1:16)

Grow in the grace and knowledge of our Lord and Savior Jesus Christ. (2 Peter 3:18)

W e have already seen what Peter has to say to us about regeneration and the Christian life and calling. Let us now listen to his testimony concerning sanctification and the deeper experiences of our Christian life and growth.

REGENERATION AND SANCTIFICATION

1. Life More Abundant

Regeneration brings us life, but sanctification brings us "life more abundantly."

2. Life Out of Death

Regeneration brings us life, but sanctification brings us life that comes out of death; the death-born life which has entered into the crucifixion of Christ and the power of His resurrection.

3. Brings Christ into Us

Regeneration brings us into Christ, sanctification brings Christ into us. "Remain in me, and I will remain in you" (John 15:4), implies a twofold relation. "In Him" is to be saved; "In you" is to be sanctified. It is the indwelling life of the Lord Jesus in personal union and manifestation to the soul.

4. Temples for the Holy Spirit

Regeneration makes us the subjects of the Holy Spirit's working, but sanctification makes us temples of the Holy Spirit's indwelling. In regeneration the Spirit is working upon us as the builder of the house; in sanctification He has become the resident of the dwelling and enters to abide as our guest, or, rather, as our host, while we dwell with Him in the fellowship of the Spirit.

5. Faith in the Indwelling Counselor

Regeneration comes to us through repentance and faith in Jesus Christ as our Savior; sanctification comes to us through full surrender and faith in the incoming and indwelling of the Counselor. It is as we yield ourselves to God and give Him the right of way, without a single reservation, that He accepts the offering and makes us His abode.

Now this twofold experience runs through all the personal and public types of the Bible. We see in Jacob the revelation of God at Bethel, through which he became the servant of Jehovah, and then the deeper experience at Peniel, through which he became the prince of God. We see it in Moses, in his first choice of God in Egypt, and then his deeper experience in Midian. We see it in Job and Isaiah; we see it in Simon Peter and the other disciples with their new experience after Pentecost; and Paul seems to give us this chapter in his own experience in the seventh chapter of Romans, through which he passed into the victory of the eighth. We see it very definitely in the passage of the Red Sea and the exodus of Israel, which represents our salvation; and then the crossing of the Jordan and the entrance into Canaan, which represents our sanctification. We see it in the Passover, which marked the first year of Israel's history, the setting out under the blood, even as we step out from the cross of Calvary; and then the equally marked beginning of the second year when the tabernacle was dedicated and anointed, and the cloud came down and entered in as the Shekinah presence of Jehovah in the holy of holies, the latter representing the incoming and indwelling of the Holy Spirit in the consecrated soul. But time and space forbid enlargement. Have you also entered into the "twofold life"?

SANCTIFICATION—ITS PRINCIPLES AND PROCESS

1. An Obligation

Sanctification is an obligation. God commands us to be holy. We are called to be holy. He will not excuse anybody from holiness. We have no right to call ourselves His children if we continue to live in sin. "Shall we go on sinning so that grace may increase" (Romans 6:1)? God forbid. God forbids you to continue in sin. There are no two classes of Christians between which you may choose; there are no options here. Every child of God is called to be holy.

2. The Pattern and Source of Sanctification

"Be holy; because I am holy" (1 Peter 1:16). God is our standard, and as His children we must be like Him. No lower standard will pass. We must not aim to be as good as some people; we must not excuse ourselves because we are no worse than others. It is God who is our pattern. "Be perfect, therefore, as your heavenly Father is perfect" (Matthew 5:48).

But He is not only the pattern, but the source. His holiness is the guarantee of ours. He commands because He gives what He commands. Out of His fullness we receive and shine in His reflected light, even as the planets that shine in the light of the great day star.

3. The Secret of Holiness

The secret of holiness is death and resurrection. Peter gives it to us very profoundly when he says: "Therefore, since Christ suffered in his body, arm yourselves also with the same attitude, because he who has suffered in his body is done with sin" (1 Peter 4:1). This thought, this great principle and truth that Christ died, will become a powerful weapon and victorious armor in our experience as we enter into it in fellowship with Him. Sanctification is not the improvement of our natural character, not even the cleansing of our spirit. It is to discover that we are wholly lost and utterly helpless, and to yield ourselves over to Him, to die to self as well as sin, to our natural goodness as well as natural sinfulness, and then receive a new life altogether from Him. Indeed, we are to receive Christ Himself, the risen one, as our new life, and then be as though we had been born out of heaven, and were not the same spirit that formerly lived in sin. Oh, what an inspiration this gives to the new life—to be wholly free by death from the entangling weight of our old habits, memories and the discouraging sense of our past, and to spring, death-born, into a life of holiness and victory. It is our privilege.

4. The Gift of Grace

Sanctification is the gift of God's grace. The second epistle of Peter supplements the teaching of the first. There we are taught that "His divine power has given us everything we need for life and godliness through our knowledge of him who called us by his own glory and goodness" (2 Peter 1:3). He has given unto us this higher life. It is not an attainment, but a bestowal. God has provided the robes of the sanctified, and we simply put them on, and claim His efficiency and His complete provision for every spiritual condition and need. It is now awaiting you, beloved reader, if you will simply recognize your need of it, your helplessness to work it out yourself, and in full surrender accept Him for all that you can never be alone. "Clothe yourselves with the Lord Jesus Christ" (Romans 13:14), and put Him on now!

5. Participating in the Divine Nature

Sanctification comes to us through our being made able to "participate in the divine nature" (2 Peter 1:4). God is our sanctification. The very nature of God passes into us. It is a divine holiness. Sanctification is not a degree of progress on the old plane, but it puts us entirely upon a new plane, and we pass out of the human into the divine, and henceforth it is not the best that man can be and do, but the best that God can be and do. Therefore, it becomes natural for us to be holy, just as once it was natural for us to be sinful. We act according to the divine nature in us, and our choices, desires and ministries are spontaneous and free, and obedience is just a luxury instead of a duty.

6. Comes through Knowing and Believing

Sanctification comes to us through knowing God and believing His word of promise. This is very finely brought out by the apostle in the opening verses of his second epistle. "Through these," he says, "he has given us his very great and precious promises, so that through them you may participate in the divine nature" (1:4). It is through claiming the promises that we receive the Holy Spirit and the divine nature. We take His Word and present it as a check on the Bank of Grace, and He turns it into the currency of spiritual blessing and actual grace. So again Peter says, "His divine power has given us everything we need for life and godliness through our knowledge of him who called us by his own glory and goodness" (1:3). Notice it is not "*to* glory and goodness," but "*by* his glory and goodness." That is to say, His glory and goodness, His divine excellency, revealed to us by the Spirit, calls us to the same high and holy character; and as we know Him, we become like Him.

The power by which we appropriate these precious promises and make the gifts of God's grace personal and real is faith. But even this faith is not a struggling effort of our weak will, but the apostle tells us we "have received a faith as precious as ours" (1:1). The faith is given, and so from first to last it is all grace. God reaches out to us in the fullness of His love and power, and then He puts into our paralyzed hand the energy to reach out and grasp the blessing and make it ours.

7. A Definite Moment of Time

Once more the apostle's language implies that we enter into this experience of sanctification at a definite moment of time. It is not something into which we gradually drift, but it is a crisis point up to which we come and at which we settle something forever. This is implied in the peculiar Greek tense known to scholars as the aorist tense, used in this passage, "having escaped the corruption that is in the world through lust" (1:4, KJV).

We have no tense in the English grammar corresponding to this. It denotes an act accomplished at a given moment in the past, and quite finished. Therefore, at a given moment we have escaped the corruption that is in the world through evil desire; we were delivered from the world and the flesh by becoming "participat[ors] in the divine nature" (1:4) and receiving "everything we need for life and godliness" (1:3). We do not drag through a dreary and endless circle of vain attempts; but we come up to Jordan, we enter in, we pass over, and we sing henceforth, "I am over in the promised land." Beloved, this is the gospel of holiness according to Peter. Surely, it is good news; it is all divine; it is all freely given; it is all for you. Have you received it? Will you receive it?

SANCTIFICATION AND GROWTH IN GRACE

Now we are ready to grow, and, therefore, it is in the second epistle that the writer advances to these higher experiences and bids us to go on to perfection. Had we attempted to grow before, it would have been distortion. We must have a true life complete in all its parts before we can safely develop it. There must be a good foundation and every wall connected before we can rear the superstructure with safety. Now then, the foundation is laid, and so the apostle adds, "[And beside, KJV] this, make every effort to add to your faith" (1:5). Dean Alford has translated this, "Because of this thing"; not "beside," but "because." Just because you are sanctified, therefore, grow. Because you have resources, such a glorious guarantee, and divine supplies, therefore, go forward and make the most of them. But notice even in our growth that the same principle of grace must be recognized all the way through. We are not to grow in character and virtue and strength, but we are to grow in grace. That means we are to grow in the habit of receiving, of being more and more helpless and dependent every moment to the end of life; it is to be all grace to the finish, and the more we grow, the more will it be true, "He must become greater; I must become less" (John 3:30).

This is also finely expressed in the phrase, "Add to your faith" (2 Peter 1:5). You are not to add to yourself, but to your faith. And what of faith? It is just the power to receive from God something which you yourself cannot do or have independently. Faith is just a hand to take His grace. Therefore, the way to grow is just to take from Him in each new emergency the supply needed for that occasion. Do we want more love? When we come up to some hard place where we are wronged, we are not to struggle to work up love in ourselves. We are not to be discouraged because we do not find the love there. We are not to pump at our dry well until we get worn out and discouraged. But we are to do as you would do with such a well; pour a little water in, and then it will flow freely out. Go to God and take the love from Him. Tell Him you are unloving and helpless, and ask Him to put the heart of Christ into your cold heart, and thus add to your faith His love. And so, if you need courage or patience or joy, no matter what, just draw upon your bank account. Use the faith that He has given to claim the exceeding great and precious promises, and you will get tired of asking before He gets tired of giving.

1. Add Goodness

And now the apostle gives us a very fine and symmetrical portrait of the graces and features in which we are to grow. First he says, "Add to your faith goodness" (1:5). This does not mean moral purity, for all this has already been settled in your sanctification; but the word "goodness" (virtue, KJV) is derived from a old Latin root, which means manhood, courage, virility. It is spiritual forcefulness. God does not want us good and amiable weaklings, but men and women that accomplish things; lives that tell for God and the race. He will give us His strength and make us good soldiers of Jesus Christ, "strong in the Lord and in his mighty power" (Ephesians 6:10).

2. Add Knowledge

Next is knowledge. Blind courage is often wild and dangerous. Power without intelligence and judgment is distortion. He wants us not only to have the "spirit of power," but also the spirit of "a sound mind" (2 Timothy 1:7, KJV). He will give us His wisdom and knowledge, for "if any of you lacks wisdom, he should ask God . . . and it will be given to him" (James 1:5). How wise Christ was! How beautifully we find Him always in order, on time, with a ready answer for His enemies and a right message for needy souls—a pattern of divine wisdom. And so, by faith we may take His Spirit to rest upon us, as "the Spirit of wisdom and of understanding,/ the Spirit of counsel and of power,/ the Spirit of knowledge and of the fear of the LORD" (Isaiah 11:2), that shall make us "delight in the fear of the LORD" (11:3).

3. Add Self-control

Next is self-control, the power of poise, the balanced character, the reserve force that can hold your tongue, and wait in the silence that so often speaks more vitally than words. He will give it through your faith and through His grace, if you are willing to be taught to be silent unto God and let Him mold you.

4. Add Perseverance

Next is perseverance or patience. That is the power to suffer not only that which comes to you from the hand of God, but that, so much harder, which comes to you from the hand of man. This is the fusing process that burns all the ingredients into one living mass of spiritual strength. No character is permanent, no quantity is fixed, until it has been proved in the furnace of affliction. But patience is His gift. The savage can meet suffering with stoical indifference, but only the heart of Christ can stand in the judgment hall or the garden of Gethsemane and suffer long and yet be kind. You will come up to your trials and fail at first, but you will find the unfailing One at your side; and if you will lean hard on Him, He will give you His victory. And through each new trial you will add to your faith perseverance, until perseverance has her perfect work, and you will stand "mature and complete, not lacking anything" (James 1:4).

5. Add Godliness

Next comes godliness. This is the quality of the Spirit which crowns the character. This is the upper chamber, the observatory, where we look up and out upon the heavens, where we meet and know God, where we commune with Him and worship Him and do all things unto His glory. It is this which gives spirituality and devoutness to the character, and makes saints like Rutherford, McCheyne, Fénelon, and the souls whose very names crush our hearts with sacred veneration. Into this we may grow by faith, for piety is one of the gifts of God; and we can have as much as we can claim and wear as a divine habiliment.

6. Add Kindness and Love

But there is danger even on spiritual lines. We may become extreme and selfish. The cloister and the cell are not the finishing rooms for holy character, but the slums of sin, the wastes of heathenism, and the dark places of human suffering. It is here we reach the largest circumference of spiritual growth. There is a circle, a vertical circle, that rises heavenward and takes in God and all the heights of devotion and communion. But there is another circle, a lateral circle, that takes in all the length and breadth of loving sympathy and service. And so he adds two more features to this divine portrait: "brotherly kindness" and "love." The first relates to our brethren, the love we owe to the household of faith. The second relates to the great world beyond, the unsaved, the unhappy, the sick, the poor, the lost, our enemies, the people that we cannot love naturally, but whom God has placed in our pathway to teach us that great and heavenly grace Peter here calls love.

Such is the fullness of the stature of a perfect man in Christ; the ideal up to which God would have us grow under the molding hand of His grace. Such are the seven colors of this sacred prism—seven, yet one; the white light of faith and grace separated into the sevenfold graces of goodness, knowledge, self-control, perseverance, godliness, brotherly kindness and love.

There is a fine shade of expression in the beautiful Greek in connection with the word "add." Literally, it means "chorus." It is a technical word, describing the business of the choir leader who harmonized the music at some great concert in all the parts, voices and instruments, until they blended in one magnificent harmony; many, yet one. And so we are to chorus into our Christian life all the graces of the Spirit until they will blend in symmetrical proportion, and nothing will be exaggerated, but all will be in harmony, and the effect of the whole will be that our lives will become a sublime chorus of praise, a doxology to the glory of Him of whom and by whom and for whom are all things.

Once more, we are to give all diligence to this. The Greek word again is forceful. It reminds one of the finger post which they used to place on the amphitheater in the Grecian games at the homestretch, containing one Greek word, meaning, literally, "make speed." They did not place this at the beginning of the course, but near the end, just at the place where the prize was to be lost or won. There the racers were summoned to the last strenuous endeavor. And so it is after we are sanctified, and have learned the fullness of Jesus, that God is calling us from on high to the utmost vigilance and diligence, and to make speed, that we "run in such a way as to get the prize" (1 Corinthians 9:24).

In conclusion, the apostle gives us several strenuous reasons why we should thus make speed.

1. Saved from Spiritual Nearsightedness

This will save us from spiritual nearsightedness. "But if anyone does not have them, he is nearsighted and blind" (2 Peter 1:9). The reason some people never get a vision of God or deeply realize spiritual things is because they live on too low a plane.

2. Keep from Living Too Near the Edge

It will keep one from living too near the edge. "And has forgotten that he has been cleansed from his past sins" (1:9). Some people seem to like to live on the edge of the pit and the wonder is that they do not slip back again. God bids you press on from the borderland of danger into all the strength and breadth of the land of promise. If you do not, you will find yourself back even in your old sins.

3. Keep from Stumbling

"For if you do these things, you will never fall" (1:10); literally, "stumble." Would you be kept from stumbling? Then press on. It is easier to be holy than to be half sanctified, just as it is easier for the car to run on both tracks than to run with one wheel on the paving stones.

4. Make Life Full

This will make your life fruitful and active, "For if you possess these qualities in increasing measure, they will keep you from being ineffective and unproductive" (1:8); literally, "idle or unfruitful." How little some Christians accomplish for God! How wasteful of time and opportunity their precious lives! It is because they live too low. Get filled with the Spirit, and you will neither be idle nor unfruitful.

5. The Crowning Reason

"And you will receive a rich welcome into the eternal kingdom of our Lord and Savior Jesus Christ" (1:11). This is the crowning reason for a life of devotion. There is a glorious prize and there is a solemn possibility of missing it. I have seen three different persons land from a great ocean steamer. One landed as a criminal, a prisoner bound with chains, and led away to the Tombs and the dark future of punishment. And so some will reach yonder destination. A second stepped down from the deck on the gangplank, a stranger in a strange land. He was not in danger of arrest, but there were no familiar faces to greet him, and he almost wished he were back in his own country. And some will reach the eternal port in this way, saved as by fire, but no soul to meet them at heaven's gate, strangers even in the home above. God save you from such a homecoming. But I have seen another figure on that deck, his face glowing with pleasure, his eyes sparkling with tears of joy, his hat and handkerchief waving in response to thousands on the shore who were welcoming him home. And as he landed amid the cheers of the musical bands and the shouts of 10,000 voices, they carried him on their shoulders to receive ovations of honor and the highest rewards that his nation could bestow. He was a public servant and had done his duty and had finished his course with joy. He was coming home to his reward. There will be such abundant entrance through yonder heavenly gates. Will they be for you? Will they be for me? We are making our history now. God help us to write it in enduring letters that shall shine in that glorious day.

The same word translated "chorus," in verse five, is used again in verse eleven, and translated "ministered"; literally, "an entrance shall be chorused unto you abundantly." The things you did and suffered for God, the graces of your Christian life which you put on in the earthly struggle, the souls you led to the Savior—all these shall meet you there, and like celestial attendants accompany your triumphal march and sing your coronation hymn as they bid you welcome to your great reward. Oh, with such an inspiring hope, let us give all diligence to receive all the possibilities of grace and obtain all the rewards of glory!

CHAPTER 6

MINISTERS OF CHRIST

Be shepherds of God's flock that is under your care, serving as over-seers—not because you must, but because you are willing, as God wants you to be; not greedy for money, but eager to serve; not lording it over those entrusted to you, but being examples to the flock. And when the Chief Shepherd appears, you will receive the crown of glory that will never fade away. (1 Peter 5:2–4)

One cannot help seeing the personality of the man back of all his letter. All through there looms up the figure of "Simon son of John" (John 21:15), as we see him so vividly in the portraits of the gospels. And no one can read these last words of his without hearing like an undertone the last words of his own Master to Simon on the shores of the Galilean sea as by sweet, delicate indirection He just barely recalled Peter's threefold denial. Though He did not directly mention it, He just recalled enough to remind him that it was forgotten and forgiven, and then prompted him to higher service than he had ever been trusted with before, and gave him the threefold commission as a kind of salve for the threefold wound of his guilty heart: "Feed my lambs" (21:15); "Take care of my sheep" (21:16); "Feed my sheep" (21:17). This is the literal force of the words given in John's gospel. And Peter carries it out here with such tender, sacred sweetness. "Tend the flock of God that is among you, exercising the oversight thereof . . . according to God" (as the Revised Version translates it). That is just how God cares for us, just how the great Shepherd cares for you and me. "And when the Chief Shepherd appears, you will receive the crown of glory, that will never fade away" (1 Peter 5:4).

There are three distinct lines of thought unfolded here.

THE SOURCES OF THE CHRISTIAN MINISTRY

"If anyone speaks, he should do it as one speaking the very words of God.

If anyone serves, he should do it with the strength God provides" (1 Peter 4:11). There is the source of our ministry. It is all of God. There are two points very clearly brought out here; first, the matter of it, and secondly, the manner of it. It is an oracle of God. It is not your own opinion you are to give, not your own ideas, not your own knowledge, culture or wisdom; but you just stand as an oracle to give the message that came from heaven and that you cannot change or modify, but your sole business is to repeat it, to give to men what God has given to you—the oracle of God, the authority of God, the very message of God Himself.

It is said that David Hume used to go to hear John Brown, a devoted Scotch preacher. David Hume was an infidel of the boldest type. They asked him why he went to hear Brown. "It is a real pleasure to me," he said, "for the man believes what he says, and it is a perfect luxury to listen to a man who preaches what he believes." Someone took David Hume to hear one of the most popular preachers of the time, and when asked afterwards whether he liked it, replied, "That man preached as if he did not believe a word of it." He went to hear Brown on the same afternoon, and came away saying, "That man preaches as though he got the sentence straight from heaven, and then waited, as if Jesus was standing at his elbow, and said, 'Lord, what will I say next?' " That was the testimony of an infidel to a man that preached as the oracle of God, the voice of God, the messenger of the divine revelation. Oh, in these days when every sort of substitute is being sought for the Word of God, give us the ministry of the Word!

"Is this God's Book?" asked a little child of his mother. "Yes, dear." "Had we not better send it back to God, if it is God's Book, because we never use it?" And that might be said of a good many today.

It is very sad that so many modern preachers should waste their own and their hearers' time exploring heaven and earth for some new and original idea, when God's Word is a great mine of yet unexplored wealth and priceless treasure. God will always honor the ministry that honors His holy Word. "Preach the Word" (2 Timothy 4:2).

The manner of the message is: "If anyone serves, he should do it with the strength God provides" (1 Peter 4:11). Not only are we to give God's Word, but with God's ability, with the enduement of the Holy Spirit. We are to give it with the consciousness of our inability, and we are to seek each new message from Him, and then seek the power to speak it. How Paul constantly cried out for "utterance" to be given to him; not merely the truth—he taught the truth, he knew his message—but each time he wanted the fire of God to infuse it, the Holy Spirit to somehow put life into it. We may give the same message, and it will be powerless if it is not in that ability that God gives. We need the flash of power every time, and especially when we are speaking the word that is to be the creating word to bring a soul from death to life. Oh, how we need to be steeped in the very life and heart of God! God help you to help your pastor with the ministry of believing prayer, that he may go, like John Brown, with Jesus Christ at his elbow and the power of the Holy Spirit in his heart.

It is said that a church once began to complain about its minister who had lost his power, and when they came to him, he said, "Yes, and the reason is I have lost my prayer book." "Why," they said, "we thought you were a dissenting clergyman." "Yes," he said, "but my people are my prayer book; and they have stopped praying for me, and I have, therefore, lost my prayer book." God give you the ministry of prayer. You will get back just what you ask for, all the blessing you give your pastor. You will wonder how he will meet your difficulties, answer your need and speak every word you are waiting for, and just because you prayed for him. And so may our ministry be strengthened by the ministry of prayer, and we speak "with the strength God provides" (4:11).

THE SPIRIT OF THE MINISTRY

1. A Humble Spirit

It is a humble spirit. If Peter had wanted to tell the Church that he was going to be the Pope, what a splendid chance he had here! Why, Peter, you lost your opportunity; you could have let all the ages know that you were the first Pope, and that every man who came after you was going to be the lord of the whole Church of God. How could you miss your opportunity? Why, you only told the people that you were but an elder—"I appeal as a fellow elder" (5:1), and he adds, "If I want any higher honor, I was 'a witness of Christ's sufferings' (5:1)." Perhaps he stole away that afternoon after they hung Him on the cross. Perhaps he was ashamed to be seen; but when it was all past and Jesus was hanging there, Peter came around when no one saw him, and for six long hours saw Christ dying. That was his honor—a "witness of Christ's sufferings." But he says he is a common elder, an ordinary minister of Jesus Christ the same as they. One is so struck with the simplicity of the early Church, as Peter suggests it here, and this is the design of the great Head of the Church, to keep it simple, and to honor us according as we honor Him, and bow our heads in the dust at His blessed feet. God give us humility! I think it is the prayer we covet most, that God will keep our spirit lowly and broken. "Those who honor me I will honor" (1 Samuel 2:30).

2. Deep Sympathy

Deep sympathy with the suffering Savior; "witness of the sufferings of Christ." He was bathed in the tender sense of what it cost to redeem us, the

Church of God. It was purchased with His own blood, the blood of Calvary, and this should be the inspiration of all our ministry.

3. A Spirit of Inspiration

Along with that, there is the spirit of inspiration, hope, our glorious reward, and also the privilege of being "one who also will share in the glory to be revealed" (1 Peter 5:1). It is no common ministry, but a high ambassadorship, an honor before which all earthly honors are naught and not worthy to be compared. We are to be glorified with Him and bear away the crown of glory that shall never fade.

4. The Shepherd Spirit

The shepherd spirit is intent on feeding the flock of God, tending the flock of God. If you have ever seen a shepherd in the Scottish Highlands or in some Eastern country, you will know something of what this means— the picture of the veteran shepherd dying with his boys around him, while the wolves are howling over in the plain and mountain and valley. And he calls them to his side as he breathes his last—how sweetly the picture has been given to us—and they bend down to hear his last words while he breathes them out: "Boys, be good to the sheep." That was the shepherd's last thought. He knew them all by name; he had rescued them many a time. They were personally dear to him; he had risked his life for them. It is the shepherd spirit that loves and follows and personally tends the sheep. Literally it reads, "Tend the little flock." It is not a great popular church, but a little flock. Look out for the hidden ones, the poor ones, those that belong to Him and will stand with the Lamb on Mount Zion. Jesus expresses to Peter the tenderness He would have the elders show to the little flock. "Simon son of John, do you truly love me more than these?" And Peter answers, "Yes, Lord . . . you know that I love you" (John 21:15). But the Lord would not have it at first. He spoke to him again, using the common word of love; and Peter was hurt. "Yes, Lord, you know that I love you" (21:16). And then Jesus takes him at his own word, and says, "Do you love me?" "Lord, you know all things; you know that I love you" (21:17). And the Master tells him that He is going to test him, so He says, "Feed my sheep" (21:17). Go and help the people that are all broken up, and are hard to get along with, and are always getting lost and forgetting what they learn and are going astray. I love them best of all, Simon, and if you love Me dearly, that is the ministry that can only be done by a heart that has been right up to My heart.

5. Disinterested in Other Pursuits

It should be disinterested in other pursuits: "Not greedy for money, but eager to serve" (1 Peter 5:2). Rotherham's translation is, "not for shameful gain, but of eager mind." That is, a mind impelled by such intense desire for usefulness and such a genuine love for souls that it needs no other incentive for any sacrifice or service. The spirit of gain has so penetrated everything in our age that even the ministry is not free from the danger of mercenary and selfish ambition. The most sacred callings are approached by the men who think that everything has its price. One of our distinguished bishops once stated in a public address in Philadelphia that he was visited in his library by a gentleman from the West who introduced himself as the representative of a politician, and then added, "Now, Bishop, one of your preachers is giving one of my friends a great deal of trouble by attacking his moral character. We want you to stop him, and I am authorized to say that my friend will make it worth your while." The good Bishop quietly walked to the door, opened it and stood there holding it, while the visitor seemed unable to take in his meaning. "Does it not occur to you," said the Bishop, "that this interview is ended?" And yet, there are less glaring ways in which even the pulpit can be subsidized and its voice at least modified, if not silenced, for fear of offending wealthy and fashionable ears with too plain a message against popular forms of sin. If a man wants to be rich or successful, let him go into some other calling; but whatever else he does, let him not prostitute the ministry of Christ for sordid gain.

6. A Holy Example

A consistent life and a holy example are the most potent factors in every ministry. The shepherd never drives, but always leads his flock, and the Chief Shepherd Himself says, "When he has brought out all his own, he goes on ahead of them" (John 10:4). The true minister will always live first what he preaches. The most spiritual messages will be neutralized without a holy life. Piety gives power to the simplest messages and to the life behind our words in ways most eloquent. "Being examples to the flock" (1 Peter 5:3).

A native convert among the Indians of North America once said to an inquiring visitor, "Your white men used to come and tell us about Christianity, about the Great Spirit of the heavens, and His Son Jesus Christ; but we looked at the white men, and they drank worse than us Indians, and they cheated us worse than we knew how, and we did not believe their doctrine. But one day Henry Ranch came among us, and after telling us about the great Spirit and His Son Jesus Christ who came to die for sinful men, he laid down among us with my bow and tomahawk beside him, but without a fear, and he slept like a little child, knowing that I could kill him and no one would ever know it. He awoke and lived among us like ourselves, sharing our hardships and doing everything good; and we saw as we looked at him that his doctrine was true, and that is why we are Christian Indians."

Mr. Spurgeon once told in a sermon how he had been tormented with doubts about the Bible, and at the close of the sermon a wise old deacon said to him, "Pastor, never tell us about your doubts again; it disturbs the weak and doubting. If they think that you are unsettled, they will be unsettled much more. They look not so much to what you say as to what you are." And Mr. Spurgeon told his students never to throw the shadow of their weakness on the flock, but to stand before them in the strength of faith and holiness, and lead them as well as teach them.

THE REWARD OF THE FAITHFUL MINISTER

"When the Chief Shepherd appears, you will receive the crown of glory that will never fade away" (5:4); literally, "you will bear away the crown of glory." There is no investment like a good life. There is no reward so enduring as that which comes from the souls that we lift up and save, for the reward will last as long as the soul which is its enduring monument. The mother who launches on the ocean of life a noble son and sees him take his place among the best of men, successful, honored, useful, blessed and a blessing, has a reward that "will never fade away." That life is her lasting imperishable recompense. The teacher who trains some splendid intellect for great achievement, and sees his favorite pupil become the leading statesman, philosopher, poet or teacher of his time, has a "crown . . . that will never fade away," for that enduring life and its wide and lasting influence is his recompense.

Thomas Arnold, the great teacher of England, lived in his distinguished pupils, many of whom became the most illustrious names of English literature and history. The soul-winner that leads someone to Christ, and then that soul in turn becomes the instrument in the conversion of a thousand more, has "a crown of glory that will never fade away," for as long as those souls last, he will be identified with that service. The millions who are yet to come from the land of Sinim will be the crown of the humble Sunday school teacher in an English village who brought Robert Morrison, China's pioneer missionary, to Jesus Christ. The glory of regenerated Africa will be the crown of the man that led the weaver of Blantyre to become the missionary David Livingstone.

Occasionally here we find the fruits of our prayers and tears, and we greatly wonder at the train of blessing that has come out of some loving ministry for Christ. But oh, what will it be when we meet the accumulation of it all yonder, and when it in turn has all eternity in which to multiply!

A modern writer has calculated how much money would have accumulated from a single penny invested at compound interest at the birth of Jesus Christ, and it has been discovered by a simple calculation that it would take a row of 57 figures to count the interminable millions, and the pile of gold that it would make would be bigger than a world—nay, bigger than 5,000 worlds! That is the investment of one penny if you give it time enough to grow. Then tell me what the investment of a soul will grow to through the countless ages of eternity! Oh, for a holy ambition to put our lives into such service, not for the reward, but for the love of Him who gave Himself for us, and who will not forget to add the glorious recompense when the great work is done.

CHAPTER 7

THE COMING OF THE DAY OF GOD

You ought to live holy and godly lives as you look forward to the day of God and speed its coming. (2 Peter 3:11–12)

We have the Apostle Peter's testimony to the preciousness of Christ, the blessedness of trial, the calling and life of the believer, the spirit and reward of true ministry, and now it remains to hear what he has to tell us about the coming of the Lord. His first epistle repeatedly refers to this blessed hope as a matter of course, but his second letter might almost be called a special treatise on the Lord's coming, and a manual of warning and teaching peculiarly for the last days.

His testimony is the more impressive from the fact that he tells us in the beginning of his second letter that the Lord has shown him that he is not to live to see the advent, but is shortly to put off his earthly tabernacle. He speaks of it, therefore, under no bias of eager personal enthusiasm, but in the most calm and disinterested spirit, and gives them the message of the Lord as one who is to stand face to face to give his own account to God. This leaves no doubt, whatever, that Peter in no degree confounded the coming of the Lord with the experience of death. His going to be with Christ was a very different matter from the coming of Christ for His own. It would seem that up to a certain period, at least, even Paul had almost expected personally to live to meet the Lord in the air, and even John writes in the first person in expressing the blessed hope of seeing Him when He should appear. But Peter has no such expectation. Therefore, his message is an entirely disinterested one, and is one of the Lord's last words to us, the people of the last days. Let us gather up these solemn and impressive teachings about the theme of all others most momentous in these crisis times.

GENERAL REFERENCES TO THE LORD'S APPEARING IN FIRST PETER

Peter speaks of the Lord's appearing as the goal of hope for the tried and troubled ones, and he cheers them by the assurance that the trial of their faith shall "result in praise, glory and honor when Jesus Christ is revealed" (1 Peter 1:7). Again, he speaks of the salvation that is to be given to us when Jesus Christ is revealed (1:5). It is only when Christ shall come that we shall fully know the length and breadth, the height and depth of the great salvation. It is hidden now; then it will be revealed. Later in the chapter he tells us of the "grace to be given you when Jesus Christ is revealed" (1:13). This is the same thought as expressed in the last citation. In the fourth chapter and the 13th verse he assures the martyrs of Rome, who were about to be made blazing lamps, by Nero's cruel order, to light the streets of Rome, that when their Master's "glory is revealed," they will be "overjoyed." In chapter 5 he holds out to the faithful minister the coming of the Lord as the time of his great reward, for he says, "when the Chief Shepherd appears, you will receive the crown of glory that will never fade away" (5:4). Back in chapter 4 he addresses to the whole flock of Christ this serious admonition: "The end of all things is near. Therefore be clear minded and self-controlled so that you can pray" (4:7).

Thus we see that the coming of Christ was a sort of undertone in all his messages and is constantly assumed as the ground of warning and comfort, of faith and hope, of holy living and faithful service—this, the one supreme incentive and inspiration of everyday life, "until the Lord's coming" (James 5:7).

THE TRANSFIGURATION: A FORESHADOWING OF THE PAROUSIA

Passing now to the second epistle, with its more explicit teaching on this subject, he first tells them that the transfiguration of the Lord was a rehearsal and foreshadowing of the greater event of the Lord's Parousia. He uses this very term, which has come to be almost the technical term for the coming of Jesus for His saints, when he says,

> We did not follow cleverly invented stories when we told you about the power and coming of our Lord Jesus Christ, but we were eyewitnesses of his majesty. For he received honor and glory from God the Father when the voice came to him from the Majestic Glory, saying, "This is my Son, whom I love; with him I am well pleased." We ourselves heard this voice that came from heaven when we were with him on the sacred mountain. (2 Peter 1:16–18)

This word, parousia, describes the first stage of the Lord's coming. Literally it means "presence," and it denotes, not the sudden and glorious epiphany in the clouds, but the gentle and secret appearing of the Bridegroom for His Bride—the presence which is already drawing near, and which, ere long, will be fully manifested to His waiting ones as they are caught away when He comes as suddenly "as a thief" to gather His treasures from the earth.

Now the transfiguration was a rehearsal, we have said, of all this. First, it manifested the Lord Himself in His glory, as He shall come in that day. Next, it brought the risen dead, in the person of Moses, to represent the great multitude who sleep in Jesus who shall be brought forth in resurrection glory at His coming. And further, it revealed the presence of the translated ones, who, without death, shall be caught up to meet Him, represented on the Mount by Elijah. All the parties are there, and the steps that lead to it are beautifully significant of the coming parousia. First, the little company, Peter and James and John, are detached and drawn a little closer to the Master. Then they rise with Him a little higher through the darkness of the night as they slowly ascend the heights of Hermon; and then, quietly, imperceptibly, while they almost slept, the glory has descended, and the transfiguration is there. So He is calling apart His little flock today; so He is taking them nearer and higher in the darkening shadows of these last times; and so, some night or morn, suddenly they will find that He has come and that they are with Him in glory. Oh, that we may understand and be ever ready for that happy consummation!

THE WORD OF PROPHECY: BETTER THAN THE TRANSFIGURATION

Next he tells them that, "we have the word of the prophets made more certain, and you will do well to pay attention to it, as to a light shining in a dark place, until the day dawns and the morning star rises in your hearts" (2 Peter 1:19) That is, we have something better even than the Transfiguration scene which only the three disciples saw. We have the whole Word of God, which is a Word of Prophecy, its one burden being the coming of the Lord, and which is more sure than any vision or personal revelation that we could have. From Genesis to Revelation this Word continually unfolds the blessed hope. Even in Eden it was foreshadowed by the cherubim, the tree of life and the lordship of man over nature. In antediluvian times Enoch was sent with this word of prophecy to proclaim to his age that "He came with myriads of holy ones" (Deuteronomy 33:2). Abraham saw this day afar and understood his covenant as reaching on to millennial times, for the land was given to him for an everlasting possession. Jacob foresaw the coming of Shiloh and the going of the nations to Him. Joseph died giving commandment concerning his bones, because he wanted to have a part in the better resurrection. David sang of it in his triumphant songs. All the prophets from Isaiah to Malachi are crowded with this message. Daniel gives us the whole panorama of history, with this one supreme outlook; and John takes up the thread where Daniel left it, in his grander Apocalypse, and finishes the scroll of prophecy with the repeated echo, "Yes, I am coming soon" (Revelation 22:20). Teachings of Jesus and His apostles continually repeat the message, and the whole Bible is a "word of the prophets made more certain" (2 Peter 1:19), from beginning to end, concerning the coming of the Lord. Let us so study it, understand it, and use it, for "Blessed is the one who reads the words of this prophecy, and blessed are those who hear it and take to heart what is written in it, because the time is near" (Revelation 1:3).

THE LORD'S COMING: AN OBJECT LESSON

Next, the Apostle Peter gives us an object lesson of the Lord's coming from the Fall and the days of Noah and Lot. There are two passages:

> For if God did not spare angels when they sinned, but sent them to hell, putting them into gloomy dungeons to be held for judgment; if he did not spare the ancient world when he brought the flood on its ungodly people, but protected Noah, a preacher of righteousness, and seven others; if he condemned the cities of Sodom and Gomorrah by burning them to ashes, and made them an example of what is going to happen to the ungodly; and if he rescued Lot, a righteous man, who was distressed by the filthy lives of lawless men (for that righteous man, living among them day after day, was tormented in his righteous soul by the lawless deeds he saw and heard)—if this is so, then the Lord knows how to rescue godly men from trials and to hold the unrighteous for the day of judgment, while continuing their punishment. (2 Peter 2:4–9)

> But they deliberately forget that long ago by God's word the heavens existed and the earth was formed out of water and by water. By these waters also the world of that time was deluged and destroyed. By the same word the present heavens and earth are reserved for fire, being kept for the day of judgment and destruction of ungodly men. (3:5–7)

These passages combine to teach us:

1.   That a great catastrophe has more than once already overtaken this sinful world, and give us evidence that such a catastrophe may yet await

ungodly men. The very strata of the globe tells the story of the Flood; and the Dead Sea, as it rolls its sluggish waves over the ruins of Gomorrah, is one of the gates of hell, and both proclaim the coming of a day of judgment.

2. The elements were ready for the Flood. The waters were there, awaiting God's hand; and so the element of fire is stored up now, and needs only the touch of His hand to involve the terrestrial system in final conflagration.

3. The wickedness of man, ripened as the judgment drew near; and so it is ripening again for the last cataclysm. "Just as it was in the days of Noah, so also will it be in the days of the Son of Man" (Luke 17:26). As it was in the days of Lot, so shall it be once more. The crimes of violence and blood, the defilements of lust and unnatural crime, these are the increasing signs of our age, and these were the provocations of God's former judgment. The very shadows of our time are tinged with rays of light, for they betoken the coming day.

4. The longsuffering God waited in the days of Noah and gave the race 120 years of warning and mercy. So today, as Peter says, "The Lord is not slow in keeping his promise . . . He is patient with you, not wanting anyone to perish, but everyone to come to repentance" (2 Peter 3:9). This is the reason that His coming waits.

5. The catastrophe came at last, sudden, swift, irretrievable; and so it will be then. It was too late to enter that ark when the flood came, and so, "While people are saying, 'Peace and safety,' destruction will come on them suddenly, as labor pains on a pregnant woman, and they will not escape" (1 Thessalonians 5:3).

6. A remnant was saved. "Noah, a preacher of righteousness, and seven others" (2 Peter 2:5), Peter says, were saved, and "[God] rescued Lot, a righteous man, who was distressed by the filthy lives of the lawless men" (2:7). And so once more shall it be true: "the Lord knows how to rescue godly men from trials and to hold the unrighteous for the day of judgment" (2:9). The little flock shall be saved. They shall be caught away before the tempest breaks. That is a thrilling word in the Master's announcement of His coming. "At that time they will see the Son of Man coming in a cloud with power and great glory" (Luke 21:27). But remember, beloved, that the emphatic word is *they*. It is not for you. God grant that you may never see this awful sight, for "all the nations of the earth will mourn" (Matthew 24:30). You should be nearer to His side that day. Your word is: "Be always on the watch, and pray that you may be able to escape all that is about to happen, and that you may be able to stand before the Son of Man" (Luke 21:36). You are to escape these things. They are to see them, but you shall be above them all.

THE FINAL CATASTROPHE

1. It will be sudden. "The day of the Lord will come like a thief" (2 Peter 3:10).

2. It will be awful. "The heavens will disappear with a roar; the elements will be destroyed by fire, and the earth and everything in it will laid bare" (3:10). The word here translated "destroyed" means "dissolved." The thought is not that the elements shall be destroyed, but they will be melted, dissolved and then re-formed.

3. It will be by fire as once it was by flood.

4. It will be followed by "a new heaven and a new earth, the home of righteousness" (3:13). This is the *Palingenesis*, the beginning again, the new creation. "He must remain in heaven until the time comes for God to restore everything, as he promised long ago through his holy prophets," as Peter said once before, in Acts 3:21.

A RESPONSE TO SCOFFERS AND SKEPTICS

The apostle tells us that in the last days, this old prophetic Word will be rejected. The cultured science and philosophy of these times will not believe anything so absurd. Certain schools of science have been telling us that nature is uniform and invariable, and that there is no room for a crisis, for the principle of evolution has been established. One thing just grows out of another, "everything goes on as it has since the beginning of creation" (2 Peter 3:4). This is a fine statement of evolution, and Peter's prophecy has already been fulfilled in the teaching of these doctrines in our day. That is just what men are saying. But Peter answers them from the simple fact that nature is not invariable, that once already the waters have overwhelmed the land in the deluge, and that once again the pent-up fires of the earth's own core or the elements of combustion that fill the universe, will overwhelm the earth and heavens. Science furnishes her own answer. We know that it is one of the late discoveries of scientific philosophy that motion is convertible into heat. The coming of a meteor to our atmosphere sets the meteor immediately on fire. Were one of yonder worlds to strike the atmosphere of this globe, long before it reached the solid earth, the air would be a blaze of destruction. Yes, they tell us truly that were the earth's own motion to be arrested for an instant, that instant would set the whole earth on fire by the sudden shock of her swift movement of a million miles a day. Nay, from yonder heavens science has furnished the testimony of just such conflagration and dissolutions in the realms of space.

Years ago, in the constellation Perseus, there blazed into prominence a star of the first magnitude and shone for many nights brighter than any other star in the heavens, and then it faded away, and it was pursued by the astronomers into invisibility. Several times since just such startling things have happened in yonder sky. In the constellations Auriga and Bootes, two such remarkable stars suddenly blazed before the eye of the telescope and then disappeared, and later one of them was rediscovered in an entirely different form floating on the sky as a planetary nebula. What did these things mean? Probably a great sun, perhaps with his attendant planets, burned out in some awful conflagration, and then re-formed on a new plane, even as the earth and the heavens will be dissolved and then made new. Someday, from yonder stars, they shall behold just such a spectacle. This earth will blaze into awful brightness, and then will fade away. New scenes will afterwards arise, perhaps not only on this planet, but also on the larger system of worlds of which it is to be in the coming ages, perhaps, the center.

THE PRINCIPLE OF TIME IN CONNECTION WITH THE COMING OF THE LORD

The apostle lays down a great principle with regard to our calculations of dates and chronologies. "Dear friends," he says, "With the Lord a day is like a thousand years, and a thousand years are like a day" (3:8). That is, we cannot fix the date of the Lord's coming by our chronometers or chronologies. It is fixed rather by spiritual conditions. One of our days may hasten it a thousand years, and one of our decades may mean little or nothing to bring it near. For 1,000 years the church slept, and the coming of the Lord did not move forward perceptibly. In these last times it is being intensely hastened. God says, "I will shorten the days"; and we may help to shorten them.

THE PRACTICAL PREPARATION FOR THE LORD'S COMING

Finally, this leads us to practical preparation for the Lord's coming which devolves upon us in view of these considerations. How may we hasten it?

1. It should be with us a matter of earnest longing and personal hope. "Looking for," means longing for and expecting. Do we "love his appearing"? Are we longing for the Bridegroom?

2. We can hasten it by preparing the world for His advent. "Hasting unto," literally means "look forward to the day of God and speed its coming" (3:12). We can do this by sending forth the gospel as a witness, for when this shall have been accomplished in all the world, then shall the end come.

3. By personal purity and spiritual holiness we can be ready for His coming. "What kind of people ought you to be?" (3:11.) "Since you are looking forward to this, make every effort to be found spotless, blameless and at peace with him" (3:14). This is the personal preparation that He claims from each one of us. It calls for the utmost diligence and vigilance. The language is very suggestive: "make every effort to be found spotless, blameless

and at peace with him" (3:14). Do not wait until the signal comes to get ready. Be ready. Be found of Him, not flurried and alarmed, but calm, waiting, ready and longing for His call.

4. "Bear in mind that our Lord's patience means salvation" (3:15) That is, remember it means salvation to some that you love and that He loves, and some that He wants to have in that happy company. He is giving you another chance to bring them in. Let it be your loving and intense concern that none will be left out; but that through the long eternity to come, their heaven will make your heaven complete.

5. Finally, the beautiful phrase, "until the day dawns and the morning star rises in your hearts" (2 Peter 1:19), suggests the inner revelation of Jesus Christ to His waiting Bride through the Holy Spirit, as the deepest and dearest of all preparations for His coming. The morning star before the day dawns. It means that inner whisper of the Master's own voice, that secret presence of His Spirit in the soul which will give intimation and intuition of His coming even before the world shall see him. It is "Christ is in you the hope of glory" (Colossians 1:27). O beloved, claim it, cherish it, and hearken to the whispered message, speaking tenderly, solemnly in these last days to those that are close enough to His heart to hear Him.

" 'Yes, I am coming soon.' Amen. Come, Lord Jesus" (Revelation 22:20).

FIRST, SECOND AND THIRD JOHN

CHAPTER 1

THE LIFE

The life appeared; we have seen it and testify to it, and we proclaim to you the eternal life, which was with the Father and has appeared to us. (1 John 1:2)

He is the true God and eternal life. (5:20)

Could we compress into a single word all the voices of nature and redemption on Easter morning, that one word which would come throbbing from the full pulses of the spring, the flowers, the bursting buds, the songs of birds, the open grave of the risen Lord and the overflowing hearts and thankful praises of rejoicing saints would be—LIFE.

And this one significant word is the keynote of the profoundest books in the New Testament, the Gospel and the Epistles of John. The others tell us of the truth and character and righteousness, but these tell us of life. The others tell us what to do and be, but these tell us the secret of what we may become and how we may accomplish the things set before us. The mystery of nature is life. The one thing short of which all man's wisdom and resources reach is life. Science can give us the principles of things and can even construct the forces of nature, but only God can give this strange and subtle thrill which sets all in spontaneous motion and gives it life.

The Sermon on the Mount tells us what an ideal life should be, but the Gospel of John tells us how that ideal may become a reality. It starts with the mysterious secret of the new birth where life begins, and it leads up to the highest developments of the sanctified and glorified life in the age to come. The Epistles of John still more fully unfold the source, the evolution and the outflow of divine life. Let us follow it through five successive stages.

CHRIST IS THE ETERNAL LIFE

Before a planet rolled, an insect buzzed or an angel sang, Christ was Himself the eternal life. Our text has in the original a stronger emphasis than the Revised Version expresses, and it reads literally thus: "We show unto you that life, the eternal, which was with the Father and was manifested unto us" (1 John 1:2). And so our second text more fully expresses the same thought, "He is the true God, and the life eternal" (5:20). Jesus is the life and from Him all life has come. The life of nature is the outflow of His creating power. The life of mind and thought and intellect is but a radiation from His infinite mind. The power that moves the universe from the mightiest sphere to the minutest spray is His personal life, for "in him all things hold together" (Colossians 1:17), and "In him we live and move and have our being" (Acts 17:28). The tint of the Easter lily, the fragrance of the hyacinth, the teeming life of the vegetable world all come from Him. The birth of every newborn soul is begotten of His life. The Church of every age and clime is the new creation of His life and power. The life of every saint is sustained every moment by the life of His living Head. It is so good therefore, to know that His life is life eternal, and that in Him there is a fountain of life that never can run dry, a sufficiency that never can fail. The word "eternal" here does not merely convey the idea of existence that has neither beginning nor ending, but it lifts us into a higher sphere of life. It is a kind of life that belongs to a loftier plane than the things that are seen and temporal. It is a life that is as infinite in its scope as it is enduring in its length; a great unfathomable ocean of infinite fullness and glorious all-sufficiency. Let us adore the Prince of Life, the Living One, the glorious Son of God who stands before us in His radiant and eternal life, proclaiming, "I am the Living One; I was dead, and behold I am alive for ever and ever!" (Revelation 1:18).

THE LIFE MANIFESTED

"The life appeared" (1 John 1:2). This includes the whole story of the incarnation and earthly life of the Lord Jesus. This also covers the meaning of the phrase so often used by John in his gospel and epistle, "The Word of life" (1:1). Here it is in the original, "The Word of the life." Just as a word is the expression of a human thought, so He is to us the expression of God's thought and will, the manifestation to us of what was already there, but unrevealed. Instead of giving us merely a written word, He sends to us a living Person to exhibit in the actual details of His earthly life the character of God and His purposes of love to the human race. The story is a familiar one of the missionary who had failed to bring conviction to the natives of the Congo by years of preaching. At last he stopped in the midst of a course of lessons on the Sermon on the Mount and announced to the Africans that he was going to live this chapter himself among them. Before the day was over they gave him ample opportunities of doing so by claiming all his worldly goods; and he, unresistingly, gave "to the one who asks you, and do not turn away from the one who wants to borrow from you" (Matthew 5:42). At nightfall the missionary's wife was in dismay, for her home was stripped and starvation stared them in the face. But that was only the first act in the drama. Before the night was over the natives began to reflect upon the strange example they had witnessed. This man, they said, is not like the traders. He does not ask us for things, but he gives us all he has. He must be God's man, and we had better be careful how we treat him. And so the following day witnessed the scene of yesterday reversed and everything brought back with compound interest. This was the second act. The third act was a great revival, the conversion of a thousand souls, and the organization of the largest church on the Congo. "The life appeared" (1 John 1:2), and they saw it, and it was an object lesson more mighty than any words. So Christ has manifested in His life the message of the Father and the meaning of the gospel. His earthly life was a complete pattern of all that God expects a true human life to be. For the first time in the history of the race the Father beheld a man of whom He could say, "With him I am well pleased" (Matthew 3:17). Christ's human life covered every side of our experience touching the physical and the spiritual and every earthly relationship that we are called to sustain. The life was manifested in every tint and shade and in every minute detail of a typical human experience, so that there is no situation which can arise to which we may not apply the simple watchword, "What would Jesus do?" In our zeal for the great doctrines connected with His death, let us never depreciate the value of His life and the importance of His perfect example, both as a revelation of God and as an ideal for humanity.

THE LIFE CRUCIFIED

While we must not undervalue the life of Christ, we cannot overestimate the significance of His death. There is a school of teachers who say much about Christian Socialism and the application of Christ's example to the practical details of all our social and secular questions. But these men stop short of Calvary and leave out of view that great event which is the key to all Scripture and all Christian hope and experience. And so we very soon come, even in this deeply spiritual epistle, to that expression which bids us pause with a hush of holy awe and tenderness—the blood. John has hardly got started in his letter before two deep crimson shades cover all the page, the one the dark stain of sin, the other the precious blood of Christ. "The blood of Jesus, his Son, purifies us from all sin" (1 John 1:7). This is the great fact back of Easter and the resurrection: the cross of Calvary, the death of Jesus Christ, the life so divine, so human, so beautiful, laid down in sacrifice and self-surrender—not only as an example of submission and resignation, teaching us how to die, but a ransom for the guilty and a satisfaction to the righteousness of God for the sins of men. With all his deep insight into the spirit and life of Jesus, John, above all the disciples, recognized the sacrificial meaning of His blood. "Look, the Lamb of God" (John 1:36), seems to ring out as the undertone of all his beautiful gospel. "The blood of Jesus" (1 John 1:7), is the background of his epistle. "To him who loves us and has freed us from our sins by his blood" (Revelation 1:5), is the keynote of the oft-repeated redemption song of his sublime Apocalypse. The blood of Jesus Christ just means His life, with all its infinite value given as a substitute and ransom for our forfeited life.

Now it is not enough for us to appreciate in a sentimental way the sufferings of our Lord and weep in sympathy over His shame and agony—all this we may do over some pathetic story of human sorrows; all this we may do under the spell of moving eloquence, and yet know nothing of the power of Christ's blood. The death of Christ stands for a great and potential fact, and it is of no value to us until faith enters into partnership with Him in that fact, and knows by personal appropriation "the fellowship of sharing in his sufferings" (Philippians 3:10). The death of Christ simply means for me that when He died I died; and in God's view I am now as if I had been executed for my own sin and am now recognized as another person who has risen with Christ and is justified from his former sins because he has been executed for them, "Because anyone who has died has been freed from sin" (Romans 6:7). Not only so, it is the secret of my sanctification, for in that cross of Calvary, I, the sinful self, was put to death; and when I lay myself over with Him upon that cross, and reckon myself dead, Christ's risen life passes into me, and it is no longer my struggling, my goodness or my badness, but my Lord who lives in me, and through whom, while I abide in Him, I am counted even as He and enabled to walk even as He walked.

Beloved, have you entered into the death of Christ and counted it yours, and through it are you now alive unto Him in "the power of his resurrection" (Philippians 3:10)?

THE LIFE RISEN

It is just as wrong to stop at the cross as it is to stop before coming to the cross. It is just as wrong to have merely a dead Christ as to eliminate the death of Christ from our theology. Christ's death is only the background for His resurrection. The life that was laid down was taken up again and now He stands before us saying, "I was dead, and behold I am alive for ever and ever!" (Revelation 1:18). It is not the cross with the Savior hanging on it, but it is the cross on which He hung, but where He hangs no longer—the grave in which He lay, but open now, and the very gateway of life immortal. And so this passage is full of suggestions of the risen Lord. That which our hands have touched of the Word of life brings back to us immediately the memory of the morning when He stood among them and said, "Look at my hands and my feet. It is I myself! Touch me and see; a ghost does not have flesh and bones, as you see I have" (Luke 24:39). There is something infinitely touching in language like this from the pen of John, for he had leaned upon the Master's breast, and doubtless he had proved the reality of his Master's resurrection and claimed once more the familiar place and touch of love.

And this leads us to notice that this expression, the blood of Christ, has a higher and a deeper meaning in connection with the resurrection, for the blood is the life, and it is the life of Jesus Christ, His risen life as well as His atoning death which cleanses us from all sin. We are "saved through his life" (Romans 5:10), quite as truly as by His death. In one of the ancient types of Exodus (24:8–18) we read of an occasion when Moses having sacrificed certain bullocks at the foot of the mount and shed their blood upon the altar, took part of the blood in basins and sprinkled it upon the people. Then Moses, Joshua and the elders went up into the mount where they met with God and were accepted because of the blood. This second action of the blood seems to denote the resurrection life of Christ, the life taken back again after it had been once laid down. And so on Easter morning we celebrate the victory of our risen Lord and hail Him as the Prince of Life and the Living One, living now as the Conqueror of death, as the possessor of a new life, and as the Source and Head of that new life for all who are united to Him in His death and resurrection.

THE LIFE INDWELLING

For this life is not for Himself, but for us, and having risen from the dead He now comes to relive His life in us. This is the secret of sanctification as it is unfolded in the first epistle of John, and it is the solution of every puzzling problem in connection with that epistle. Perhaps no portion of the New Testament has so many seeming contradictions on the subject of holiness as the first epistle of John. For example, we are told in the first chapter, "If we claim to be without sin, we deceive ourselves and the truth is not in us" (1 John 1:8), and again, "If we claim we have not sinned, we make him out to be a liar and his word has no place in our lives" (1:10). And yet a little later we are told with equal emphasis that "No one who is born of God will continue to sin, because God's seed remains in him; he cannot go on sinning, because he has been born of God" (3:9). Now how can these be reconciled? It is all very simple. First it is true that we—that is, the human we—have sin and have sinned. There is no good in us, and we have renounced ourselves as worthless and helpless; but on the other hand, we have taken Him to be our life and His life is a sinless one. The seed that He plants in us, as spotless as that beautiful bulb and blossom which you plant in the unclean soil, but which grows up as pure as an angel's wing unstained by the soil around it belongs to another element and is in its own nature essentially and inherently pure.

The key to this whole mystery is supplied by two verses in this epistle. "No one who lives in him keeps on sinning" (3:6). Here is the secret of holiness—it is not our holiness but Him. There is no account made here of our perfection, but it is only as we cling to Him and draw our life each moment from Him that we are kept from sin. It is the indwelling life.

Again, "We know that anyone born of God does not continue to sin; the one who was born of God keeps him safe, and the evil one cannot harm him" (5:18). Here again the same truth is expressed in a different way. The only begotten Son of God, dwelling in us, keeps us from the power of sin and the assaults of Satan; and although the devil often strikes, yet we are like the little insect with the pane of glass between it and the bird of prey, "and the evil one cannot harm him" (5:18).

There is one more passage which belongs to this connection. "He who has the Son has life; he who does not have the Son of God does not have life" (5:12). Here it is our union with the person of the Lord Jesus that constitutes the source of our spiritual life. The secret therefore which Paul had found, "Christ in you, the hope of glory" (Colossians 1:27), is the secret also of the disciple who leaned yet closer on the Master's breast. God grant that it may be the secret of our life, too, and that we may know in all of His fullness the life eternal, the life manifested, and the life crucified, the resurrection life, and the life indwelling, through Jesus Christ our Lord, to whom be glory forever and ever. Amen.

CHAPTER 2

THE WALK

Whoever claims to live in him must walk as Jesus did. (1 John 2:6)

The life naturally leads to the walk. The term describes the course of life, the conduct, the practical side of our Christian life. The reference to the walk of our Lord Jesus Christ recalls His character and life. The character of Jesus stands out as the divinest monument of the Bible and the gospels.

Even men who do not believe in Him as we do have been compelled to acknowledge the grandeur and loftiness of His incomparable life. Here are some of the testimonies that the world's illustrious thinkers have borne to Jesus of Nazareth. Renan says, "The Christ of the Gospels is the most beautiful Incarnation of God. His beauty is eternal; His reign shall never end." Goethe says, "There shines from the Gospels a sublimity through the person of Christ which only the divine could manifest." Rosseau writes, "Was He no more than man? What sweetness! What purity in His ways! What tender grace in His teaching! What loftiness in His maxims! What wisdom in His words! What delicacy in His touch! What an empire in the heart of His followers! Where is the man, where is the sage that could suffer and die without weakness or display? So grand, so inimitable is His character that the inventors of such a story would be more wonderful than the character which they portrayed." Carlyle says, "Jesus Christ is the divinest symbol. Higher than this human thought can never go." Napoleon said, "I am a man, I understand men. These were all men. Jesus Christ was more than man. Our empire is built on force, His on love, and it will last when ours has passed away."

But if Jesus Christ thus appears at a distance to the minds that can only admire Him, how much more must He be to those who know Him as a personal Friend and who see Him in the light of love, for

The love of Jesus, what it is,
None but His loved ones know.

The character and life of Christ have a completeness of detail which no other Bible biography possesses. The story has been written out by many witnesses, and the portrait is reproduced in all its lineaments and features. He has traversed every stage of life from the cradle to the grave, and represented humanity in every condition and circumstance of temptation, trial and need, so that His example is equally suited to childhood, youth or manhood, to the humble and the poor, in life's lowliest path, or to the sovereign that sways the widest scepter, for He is at once the lowly Nazarene and the Lord of lords. He has felt the throb of every human affection. He has felt the pang of every human sorrow. He is the Son of man in the largest, broadest sense. Nay, His humanity is so complete that He represents the softer traits of womanhood as well as the virility and strength of manhood, and even the simplicity of a little child, so that there is no place in the experiences of life where we may not look back at this pattern life for light and help as we bring it into touch with our need and ask, "What would Jesus do?"

God has set forth the life of Christ as our example and commanded us to imitate and reproduce Him in our lives. This is not an ideal picture to study as we would some paragon of art. It is a life to be lived and it is adapted to all the needs of our present existence. It is a plain life for a common people to copy, a type of humanity that we can take with us into the kitchen and the family room, into the workshop and the place of business, into the field where the farmer toils, and the orchard where the gardener prunes, and the place where the tempter assails, and even the lot where want and poverty press us with their burdens and their cares. This Christ is the Christ of every man who will receive Him as a Savior and follow Him as an example and a master. "I have set you an example," He says, "that you should do as I have done for you" (John 13:15). He expects us to be like Him. Are you copying Him and being made conformable unto His image? There is but one pattern. For ages God "looked for a man . . . but I found none" (Ezekiel 22:30). At last God produced in humanity a perfect type. Since then God has been occupied in making other men according to this pattern. He is the one original.

When Judson came to America the religious papers were comparing him to Paul and the early apostles. Judson wrote expressing his grief and displeasure and saying, "I do not want to be like them. There is but one to copy, Jesus Himself. I want to plant my feet in His footprints and measure their shortcomings by His and His alone. He is the only copy. I want to be like Him." So let us seek to walk even as He walked.

The secret of a Christlike life lies partly in the deep longing for it. We grow like the ideals that we admire. We reach unconsciously at last the things we aspire to. Ask God to give you a high conception of the character of Christ and an intense desire to be like Him and you will never rest until you reach your ideal. Let us look at this ideal.

THE MOTIVE OF HIS LIFE

The key to any character is to be found in its supreme motive, the great end which it is pursuing, the object for which it is living. You cannot understand conduct by merely looking at facts. You want to grasp the intent that lies back of these facts and incidents, and the supreme reason that controls these actions. When a great crime has been committed, the object of the detective is to establish a reason for it, then everything else can be made plain. The great object for which we are living will determine everything else, and explain many things which otherwise might seem inexplicable. When the ploughman starts out to make a straight furrow he needs two stakes. The nearer stake is not enough. He must keep in line with the farther one, the stake at the remotest end of the ridge, and as he keeps the two in line his course is straight. It is the final goal which determines our immediate actions, and if that is high enough, and strong enough, it will attract us like a heavenly magnet from all lesser and lower things, and hold us irresistibly to our heavenly pathway. The supreme motive of Christ's life was devotion to the will and glory of God. "Didn't you know I had to be in my Father's house?" (Luke 2:49). This was the deep conviction even upon the heart of the child. " 'My food,' said Jesus, 'is to do the will of him who sent me and to finish his work' " (John 4:34). "By myself I can do nothing; I judge only as I hear, and my judgment is just, for I seek not to please myself but him who sent me" (5:30). "For I have come down from heaven not to do my will but to do the will of him who sent me" (6:38). This was the purpose of His fully matured life. "I have brought you glory on earth by completing the work you gave me to do" (17:4). This was His joyful cry as He finished His course and handed back His commission to the Father who sent Him. Is this the supreme object of our life, and are we pressing on to it through good report and evil report, caring only for one thing, to please our Master, and have His approval at the last?

THE PRINCIPLE OF HIS LIFE

Every life can be summed up in some controlling principle. With some it is selfishness in the various forms of avarice, ambition or pleasure. With others it is devotion to some favorite pursuit of art or literature or invention and discovery. With Jesus Christ the one principle of His life was love, and the law that He has left for us is the same simple and comprehensive law of love, including every form of duty in the one new commandment, "Love each other as I have loved you" (John 15:12). This is not the Old Testament law of love with self in the center, "love your neighbor as yourself" (Matthew 19:19). But this is a new commandment with Christ in the center, "Love each other as I have loved you" (John 15:12). Love for His Father, love for His own, love for the sinful, love for His enemies, this covered the whole life of Jesus Christ, and this will comprehend the length and breadth of the life of His followers. This will simplify every question, solve every problem, and sweeten every duty into a delight. It will make our life, as His was, an embodiment of that beautiful ideal which the Holy Spirit has left us in the 13th chapter of First Corinthians:

> Love is patient, love is kind. It does not envy, it does not boast, it is not proud. It is not rude, it is not self-seeking, it is not easily angered, it keeps no record of wrongs. Love does not delight in evil but rejoices with the truth. It always protects, always trusts, always hopes, always perseveres.
> Love never fails. (13:4–8)

THE RULE AND STANDARD OF HIS LIFE

Every life must have a standard by which it is regulated, and so Christ's life was molded by the Holy Scriptures. "This is what I told you while I was still with you: Everything must be fulfilled that is written about me in the Law of Moses, the Prophets and the Psalms" (Luke 24:44). It was necessary that Christ's life should fulfill the Scriptures, and He could not die upon the cross until He had first lived out every word that had been written concerning Him. It is just as necessary that our lives should fulfill the Scriptures, and we have no right to let a single promise or command in this holy Book be a dead letter so far as we are concerned. God wants us while we live to prove in our own experience all things that have been written in this Book, and to bind the Bible in a new and living edition in the flesh and blood of our own lives.

THE SOURCE OF HIS LIFE

Where did He derive the strength for this supernatural and perfect example? Was it through His own inherent and essential deity? Or did He suspend during the days of His humiliation His own self-contained rights and powers, and live among us simply as a man, dependent for His support upon the same sources of strength that we enjoy? It would seem so. Listen to His own confession:

> I tell you the truth, the Son can do nothing by himself; he can do only what he sees his Father doing . . . By myself I can do nothing; I judge only as I hear . . . Just as the living Father sent me

and I live because of the Father, so the one who feeds on me will live because of me. (John 5:19, 30; 6:57)

This seems to make it very plain that our Lord derived His daily strength from the same source as we may receive ours, by communion with God, by a life of dependence, faith and prayer, and by receiving and being ever filled with the presence and power of the Holy Spirit. Would we therefore walk even as He walked, let us receive the Holy Spirit as He did at His baptism. Let us constantly depend upon Him, and be filled with His presence. Let us live a life of unceasing prayer. Let us draw our strength each moment from Him as He did from the Father. Let our life for both soul and body be sustained by the inbreathing of His, so that it shall be true of us "For in him we live and move and have our being" (Acts 17:28). This was the Master's life and this may be ours. What an inspiration it is for us to know that He humbled Himself to the same place of dependence to which we stand, and that He will exalt us through His grave to the same victories which He won.

THE ACTIVITIES OF HIS LIFE

The life of Jesus Christ was a positive one. It was not all absorbed in self-contemplation and self-culture, but it went out in thoughtful benevolence to the world around Him. His brief biography as given by Peter is one of practical and holy activity. "He went around doing good" (Acts 10:38). In His short life of three and a half years He traveled on foot over every portion of Galilee, Samaria and Judea, incessantly preaching, teaching and working with arduous toil. He was constantly thronged by the multitudes so that Mark tells us "they did not even have a chance to eat" (Mark 6:31). Once at the close of a busy day He was so weary that He fell asleep on the little ship amid the raging storm. Leaving His busy toil for a season of rest, still the multitudes pressed upon Him, and He could not be silent. After a Sabbath of incessant labor at Capernaum, we find Him next morning rising a great while before day that He might steal from His slumbers the time to pray. His life was one of ceaseless service, and even still on His ascension throne He is continually employed in ministries of active love. So He has said to us that we must copy Him. No consecrated Christian can be an idler or a drone. "As the Father has sent me, I am sending you" (John 20:21). We are here as missionaries, every one of us with a commission and a trust just as definite as the men we send to heathen lands. Let us find our work, and, like Him, "Whatever your hand finds to do, do it with all your might" (Ecclesiastes 9:10).

SEPARATION

The true measure of a man's worth is not always the number of his friends, but sometimes the number of his foes. Every man who lives in advance of his age is sure to be misunderstood and opposed, and often persecuted and sacrificed. The Lord Himself has said, "Woe to you when all men speak well of you,/ for that is how their fathers treated the false prophets" (Luke 6:26). Like Him, therefore, we must expect often to be unpopular, often to stand alone, even to be maligned, perhaps, to be utterly and falsely assailed and driven "outside the camp" even of the religious world. Two things, however, let us not forget. First let us not be afraid to be unpopular, and secondly let us never be soured or embittered by it, but stand sweetly, triumphantly in the confidence of right, and our Master's approval.

THE SUFFERING LIFE

No character is mature, no life has reached its coronation, until it has passed through fire. And so the supreme test of Christ's example was suffering, and in all His sufferings He has, as the Apostle Peter expressed, left "you an example, that you should follow in his steps" (1 Peter 2:21). He suffered from the temptations of Satan for "we have one who has been tempted in every way, just as we are—yet was without sin" (Hebrews 4:15). In this He has called us to follow Him in suffering and victory, for "because he himself suffered when he was tempted, he is able to help those who are being tempted" (2:18). He suffered from the wrongs of men, and in this He has left us an example of patience, gentleness and forgiveness, for "when they hurled their insults at him, he did not retaliate; when he suffered, he made no threats. Instead, he entrusted himself to him who judges justly" (1 Peter 2:23). Never was He more glorious than in the hour of shame. Never was He more unselfish than in the moment when His own sorrows were crushing His heart. Never was He more victorious than when He bowed His head on the bitter cross and died for sinful men. He is the crowned sufferer of humanity, and He calls us to suffer with Him in sweetness, submission and triumphant faith and love.

THE FINER TOUCHES OF HOLY CHARACTER

The perfection of character is to be found in the finer touches of temper and quality which easily escape the careless observer. It is in these that the character of Christ stands inimitably supreme. One of the finest portraits of His Spirit is given by Paul in the second chapter of Philippians as he tells us of Christ's humility—He might have grasped at His divine rights, but voluntarily surrendered them, emptied Himself and gladly stooped to the lowest place (2:5–8). His unselfishness in dealing with the weak and the selfish is finely expressed in Romans 15:3: "For even Christ did not please himself but, as it is written, 'The insults of those who insult you have fallen on me.'" His gentleness and lowliness are finely expressed in His own words, "learn from me, for I am gentle and humble in heart" (Matthew 11:29). The highest element of character is self-sacrifice, and here the Master stands forever in the front of all sacrifice and heroism. "If anyone would come after me, he must deny himself and take up his cross and follow me" (16:24). "Whoever wants to be first must be slave of all. For even the Son of Man did not come to be served, but to serve, and to give his life as a ransom for many" (Mark 10:44–45). Here we are taught what it means to walk even as He walked. It is the surrendered life. It is the life of self-sacrifice. So the apostle has finely expressed it in Ephesians 5:2, "Live a life of love, just as Christ loved us and gave himself up for us as a fragrant offering and sacrifice to God." This is love, self-sacrifice, and this is to God as sweet as the fragrance of the gardens of Paradise. There was something in the Spirit of Jesus, and there ought to be something in every consecrated life, which can be expressed only by the term sweetness. It is with reference to this that the apostle says, "For we are to God the aroma of Christ among those who are being saved and those who are perishing" (2 Corinthians 2:15). God give to us this heavenly sweetness that breathes from the heart of our indwelling Savior.

The refinement of Jesus Christ is one of the most striking traits of His lovely character. Untrained in the schools of human culture, He was, notwithstanding, as every Christian ought to be, a perfect gentleman. His thoughtful consideration of others is often manifested in the incidental circumstances of His life. For example, when Simon Peter was distressed about the tribute money at Capernaum, and hesitating to speak to the Master about it, the Lord "prevented him" (Matthew 17:25, KJV); i.e., anticipated his very thought, and sent him down to the lake to catch the fish with the coin in his mouth. Then He added with fine tact, "Take it and give it to them for my tax and yours" (17:7), assuming the responsibility of the debt first for Himself to save Peter's sensitiveness. Still finer was His high courtesy toward the poor sinning woman whom the Pharisees had dragged before Him. Stooping down He evaded her glance lest she would be humiliated before them. And as though He heard them not, He finally thrust a dart of holy sarcasm into their consciences which sent them swiftly like hounds from His presence. Only when they were gone did He look up in that trembling woman's face, and gently say: "Neither do I condemn you . . . go now and leave your life of sin" (John 8:11). So let us reflect the gentleness and courtesy of Christ, and not only by our lives but by our "manner of love" commend our Christianity and adorn the doctrine of God our Savior in all things.

There is one thing more in the spirit of the Master, which He would have us copy, and that is the spirit of gladness. While the Lord Jesus was never hilarious or unrestrained in the expression of His joy, yet He was uniformly cheerful, bright and glad, and the heart in which He dwells should likewise be expressed in the shining face, the springing step and the life of overflowing gladness. There is nothing more needed in a sad and sinful world than joyous Christians. There was nothing more touching in the Master's life than the fact that when His own heart was ready to break with the anticipation of the garden and the cross, He was saying to them, "Peace I leave with you; my peace I give you. I do not give to you as the world gives. Do not let your hearts be troubled and do not be afraid" (John 14:27). God help us to copy the gladness of Jesus, never to droop our colors in the dust, never to hang our harps upon the willows, never to lose our heavenly blessing or fail to "rejoice evermore."

THE POWER OF HIS LIFE

But we must hasten to notice finally some of the positive elements of forcefulness and power in the life of Jesus. It is possible to be sweet and good and yet to be weak and unwise. This was not the character of Jesus. Never was gentleness more childlike, never was manhood more mighty and majestic. In every element of His character, in every action of His life, we see the strongest virility and we recognize continually that the Son of man was indeed a man in every sense of the word.

Intellectually His mind was clear and masterful. There is nothing finer in the story of His life than the calm, victorious way in which He answered and drove from His presence the keen-witted lawyers and scribes who hounded Him with their questions, and who were successfully humiliated and silenced before the jeering crowd until they were glad to escape from His presence. After that no man dared ask Him any more questions. So majestic and impressive was His eloquence that the officers which were sent to arrest Him forgot all about their commission as they stood listening to His wonderful words, and went back to their angry masters to exclaim: "No one ever spoke the way this man does" (7:46). There was about Him a dignity which sometimes rose to such a height that we read on one occasion as He set His face steadfastly to go Jerusalem, "the disciples were astonished, while those who followed were afraid" (Mark 10:32). In the darkest hour of His agony He reached such a height of holy dignity that even Pilate gazed with admiration, and pointing to Him even amid all the symbols of shame and suffering, he cried: "Here is the man!" (John 19:5). Even in His death He was a conqueror, and in His resurrection and ascension He arose sublime above all the powers of death and hell.

In conclusion, how shall we walk like Him?

1. We must receive Him to walk in us for He has said "I will live with them and walk among them" (2 Corinthians 6:16).

2. We must study His life until the story is burned into our consciousness

and impressed upon our heart.

3. We must constantly look upon the picture and apply it to every detail of our own conduct and so "we, who with unveiled faces all reflect the Lord's glory, are being transformed into his likeness with ever-increasing glory, which comes from the Lord, who is the Spirit" (3:18).

4. Do not be discouraged when you meet with failure in yourself. Do not be afraid to look in the glass and see your own defects in contrast with His blameless life. It will incite you to higher things. Self-judgment is the very secret of progress and higher attainment.

5. Finally, let us ask the Holy Spirit, whose work it is to make Jesus real to us, to unveil the vision and imprint the copy upon our hearts and lives, and so shall we be "transformed into his likeness with ever-increasing glory, which comes from the Lord, who is the Spirit" (3:18).

CHAPTER 3

THE FATHER

I write to you, dear children,
because you have known the Father. (1 John 2:13)

How great is the love the Father has lavished on us, that we should
be called children of God! (3:1)

The Fatherhood of God is one of the most misused and abused religious phrases of current literature. The Bible recognizes no divine paternity apart from our relation to Jesus Christ. Indeed, the doctrine of God's Fatherhood of individual saints was even unknown to the Old Testament writers and saints. God was recognized as the Father of Israel as a nation, but no individual Hebrew ever dared to appropriate the name to himself. It is the special revelation of the Lord Jesus Christ. "No one knows the Father except the Son and those to whom the Son chooses to reveal him" (Matthew 11:27). It is He who has taught us to say "Our Father in heaven" (6:9). No wonder, therefore, that it was received by His first disciples as a truth of the highest importance and regarded by them with wondering veneration. "Behold," exclaims even the beloved disciple who had grown familiar with the love of God. "How great is the love the Father has lavished on us, that we should be called children of God!" (1 John 3:1). The exclamation in the original is in an unusual form and expressive of the strongest emphasis and the most profound admiration. No wonder that the Greenland chief, when he first heard it exclaimed, said, "It is too great, rather let me kiss His feet." Let us look at this wonderful love.

WHAT THE DIVINE FATHERHOOD MEANS

1. Not Our Father by Creation
God is not our Father by creation. He is our Creator, and the Creator of

all things. But this is not Fatherhood. Speaking of the sparrows the Lord Jesus says, "your heavenly Father feeds them" (Matthew 6:26). But He is not their heavenly Father. Human beings by nature are not the children of God, but our Lord very plainly tells them that they are the children of the devil. "You belong to your father, the devil" (John 8:44). Men do not like this and so they try to change their pedigree in the church registers. But their names will not be found in the family record of the skies. The only children that God will ever recognize are those that have been born of the Holy Spirit through Jesus Christ.

2. Not Children by Adoption

We are not the children of God by a special act of adoption. Earthly families are sometimes increased by the addition of the foundling child or the drawing up of legal papers by which a fatherless orphan is added by adoption to the family circle. This may be all very well as a theological discussion and diversion, but it never can satisfy a heaven-born soul. Nay, it is said with beautiful force in our second text not only that we are "called the sons of God," but in the revised version it is added "and we are."

3. Children through the New Birth

We are the sons of God by the new birth. We have been begotten of the Father and quickened by the Holy Spirit into a divine life which makes us partakers of the very nature of God Himself. We have all heard of the little fellow who lost heart in his home and became reckless in his life because he had listened to the street boys who had told him he was only a little foundling. When at last his mother learned the secret of his waywardness, and took him in her arms and reassured him, he looked up through his streaming tears and asked her again and again, "Am I really your very own boy? Did you born me?" It was a child's expression, but back of it was an instinct as deep and high as our eternal hope. Thank God that hope is not disappointed, for "to all who received him, to those who believed in his name, he gave the right to become children of God. . . . born not of natural descent, nor of human decision or a husband's will, but born of God" (John 1:12–13).

4. Children through Union with Jesus Christ

We are the sons of God through union with Jesus Christ. We are not only born into the family, but we are married into the family. We are not only children of second birth and a lower grade, but we are the firstborn sons of God even as He, our elder Brother. In Oriental countries, and indeed in all the older social conditions of the world, the eldest son usually inherits a larger fortune and a higher dignity than his brothers, but by our union with

Christ we all rise to the place of the elder Brother and the firstborn ones. It was this that He meant when He taught us to say, "Our Father in heaven" (Matthew 6:9), for the "our" consists of Christ Himself and His brethren. It was this that He meant when He hastened to say just after His resurrection, "I am returning to my Father and your Father, to my God and your God" (John 20:17). This is the meaning of that precious assurance, "Because you are sons, God sent the Spirit of his Son into our hearts, the Spirit who calls out, '*Abba*, Father' " (Galatians 4:6).

Not only have we the legal status of sons, but we have the very heart and spirit of the Son of God Himself, feeling toward the Father the very same sentiments of confidence and love that He felt, and entering in actual experience into the very spirit of His own Sonship. This is the scriptural doctrine of the Fatherhood of God. The divine family circle is not a mongrel crowd of promiscuous souls singing the heathen song:

> Father of all in every age,
>   In every clime adored,
> By saint, by savage, or by sage
>   Jehovah, Jove, or Lord.

Nay, it is a select and beautiful company of redeemed and called-out ones all bearing the likeness of the one blessed Head, and deriving their heavenly life from the very heart of Jesus Christ Himself. These are the children of God, and these He is not ashamed to call His brethren.

5. Children by the Seal of the Holy Spirit

We are the children of God by the witness and seal of the Holy Spirit. "The Spirit himself testifies with our spirit that we are God's children" (Romans 8:16). He does this by imparting to us the divine consciousness of our union with Christ and the filial spirit which instinctively cries "Abba, Father." He does not bear witness to our spirit as one person would to another, but conjointly with our spirit by coming into it and breathing into us the feelings and sentiments of a loving, trusting, happy child. He gives us a filial heart. He makes us to feel at home in our Father's presence. He enables us to draw near with a true heart in full assurance of faith. He sheds abroad the love of God in our hearts, and He gives to us the simplicity, freedom and holy affection of little children, so that we know we are the sons of God; and it is natural for us to love and trust our heavenly Father even as it was for the Lord Jesus Himself. Such then is the meaning of sonship.

ITS PRIVILEGES AND BLESSINGS

1. Brings the Divine Nature

It brings us the divine nature. It puts into us a new and higher life. This makes all our experience delightfully spontaneous and easy. We do not have to act against our nature, but according to our nature. There is something within us to walk in our Father's will and love to please and obey Him.

2. A Privilege of Sonship

The peculiar love of the Father is one of the privileges of sonship. God has a love for the world which is very strong, but it is the love of compassion. It was strong enough to induce him to send His only begotten Son to die for sinful men, but it is a very different love that He has for His children. This is the love of complacency. It is of this that it is written: "Having loved his own who were in the world, he now showed them the full extent of his love" (John 13:1). This is a love that is based on something in His own heart. The instinct of fatherhood and motherhood in us loves our children not because they are beautiful, dutiful or good, but because they are ours. We are bound to them. We cannot cease to be part of their life, and they cannot cease to belong to us. Our hearts follow them in their sufferings and even in their sins. Their degradation is our dishonor. Their honor is our delight. Their pleasure is to us a double pleasure. So the Father loves His children. The measure of His love to us is His love to Christ. As He delights in the eternal Son so He delights in all His sons and daughters. Our Savior's parting prayer was infinitely tender and sacred in that last utterance in which He gives away to His beloved disciples the very love the Father had to him, "that the love you have for me may be in them and that I myself may be in them" (John 17:26). Dear child of God, do you believe this? Do you realize it? Will you let it comfort you, consecrate you, and make it impossible for you henceforth either to doubt or grieve your Father's love?

3. Intimacy, Access and Fellowship

Another privilege is that of intimacy, access and fellowship. The child has the freedom of the house. In the old wartime when no one else could get the President's ear there was one that could always get inside. Many a message did he carry unofficially to the Chief Magistrate of the country, and many a troubled heart obtained a hearing through that irregular boy. No official sentries and no door fastenings stood between him and his father's arms. And so we have access to the Father. We may draw near. We may abide in the secret place of the Most High and dwell under the shadow of the Almighty. We may have boldness to enter into the holiest by the blood of

Jesus. There is no moment when His ear is not open to our cry. There is no situation where we may not claim His presence. And even when our lips cease to pray, and our communion no longer expresses itself in articulate language, there is a silent fellowship of the filial heart upon the Father's breast, which is deeper and sweeter than even the words of prayer, where we may abide continually in the communion of the Holy Spirit.

4. Protection and Provision

Then there is the protection and provision of the Father's house. We are entitled as children to sit at the King's table and to enjoy His almighty care. "If you, then, though you are evil, know how to give good gifts to your children, how much more will your Father in heaven give good gifts to those who ask him!" (Matthew 7:11). And in the higher realm of spiritual blessings, "how much more will your Father in heaven give the Holy Spirit to those who ask him!" (Luke 11:13). To His own beloved children He says: " 'My son,' the father said, 'you are always with me, and everything I have is yours' " (15:31).

Have you ever come to some hard place in life and sat down and thought, If my father were only here, my earthly father, who was always so kind and helpful, and if he had the power to help me in this hour of need, there is nothing that he would not do for my relief? But God is my Father more truly than he. He loves me better and His power is unlimited, His resources are unbounded. Will He not, therefore, do for me all that my earthly father would if he were here? And your heart has become encouraged. Your faith has grown bolder and you have been able to take from God the supply of all your need according to His riches in glory by Christ Jesus. Why should it not be ever thus? Has He not said to us in the very earliest teachings of the Son of man, "Your heavenly Father knows that you need them. But seek first his kingdom and his righteousness and all these things will be given to you as well" (Matthew 6:32–33).

5. Training, Discipline and Education

The training of a child and the discipline and education of the family— this is one of the privileges of the sons of God. There comes a time in the life of the child when soft indulgence must give place to sterner discipline, and when the little one must learn the difference between right and wrong, self-will and obedience, indolence and duty. Sometimes the father's heart has to be sorely pained by the penalty that hurts him much more than it does his child. But he loves too wisely to neglect the training of his child, and some day that child will bless his memory for a father's firm and faithful love. So God, our Father, sends us to the school of discipline, of suffering, of life's severe experience, of the Holy Spirit's faithful training. Therefore in the

12th chapter of Hebrews we have seen that the word "chastening" literally means child training, and it is introduced as the highest proof of the Father's love, and although not now joyous, but often grievous, nevertheless afterward it yields the peaceful fruit of righteousness unto them that are exercised thereby. Let us trust our Father's faithful love even here, and when we cannot understand His hand let us always lie close to His heart and be like the child whom his father was about to strike with the rod of chastening, when with one bound the little fellow sprang into his father's arms where the rod could no longer reach him.

6. The Inheritance of Glory

The inheritance of glory is the right and privilege of every child. "Now if we are children, then we are heirs—heirs of God and co-heirs with Christ" (Romans 8:17). And therefore the children of God, like their elder Brother, are often hidden in the present world, and it is true as the apostle says, "The reason the world does not know us is that it did not know him. Dear friends, now we are children of God, and what we will be has not yet been made known. But we know that when he appears, we shall be like him, for we shall see him as he is" (1 John 3:1–2).

There is a day spoken of in the eighth chapter of Romans as the day of the manifestation of the sons of God. It is the day when they will emerge from their obscurity, and when the King's children who have been in disguise, going to school in the lowly places of trial and suffering, will come forth into the light and appear in all the glory of their royal robes and everlasting crowns. Then it will little matter what the world thought of us once, and how the heart ached and waited through the dark and trying hour. It will be forgotten in "an eternal glory that far outweighs them all" (2 Corinthians 4:17).

And so as we enter into the full realization of all that our sonship means, duty and trial will become easy and light, and the song of hope will be heard above the sorrowful echoes of the vale of tears. Then it will be so easy to let the world go by and even to surrender our rights and often suffer our wrongs because of the joy set before us.

Just after the close of the Civil War, the army that had marched in triumph through Georgia under General Sherman was to be reviewed in one of our great cities and march in triumphal parade. The night before the parade General Sherman called General Howard to him and said: "You know, General, you were the head of one of the divisions that marched with me through Georgia, and you ought rightfully ride at the head of your division in the parade tomorrow. But I find that through political influence a plan is being pressed to have the general who preceded you in the command represent the division, and as political pulls are sometimes stronger than personal rights, I hardly know how to meet the case." Very naturally General Howard replied, "I think I am entitled to represent my division, as it was I who led them to victory." "Yes," said General Sherman, "you are, but I believe you are a Christian, are you not? And I was wondering if Christian considerations might not lead you to make an exception and even to yield your rights for the sake of peace." "Oh," said good General Howard, "if it is a matter of Christian consideration, of course I yield, and he can have the place." "All right," said General Sherman, "I will so arrange, and will you please report to me tomorrow morning at nine o'clock and you shall ride with me at the head of the army."

Beloved, that is the way that the Father some day will make up for our disappointments and wrongs. Let us trust His everlasting love. Let us love Him as our Father. Let us be followers of God as dear children. Let us obey implicitly His commandments "so that we might always prosper and be kept alive" (Deuteronomy 6:24). And let us go forth into good report or evil report, unmoved because He is ever whispering to us through the darkness or through the light, "I have loved you with an everlasting love" (Jeremiah 31:3). " 'My son,' the father said, 'you are always with me, and everything I have is yours' " (Luke 15:31).

CHAPTER 4

THE ANOINTING

As for you, the anointing you received from him remains in you, and you do not need anyone to teach you. But as his anointing teaches you about all things and as that anointing is real, not counterfeit— just as it has taught you, remain in him. (1 John 2:27)

After the revelation of the Son and the Father, the person and work of the Holy Spirit naturally follows. This is presented under the significant symbols of the anointing.

THE ANOINTING OF JACOB

The first reference in the rite of anointing is in connection with the vision of Jacob in the 28th chapter of Genesis, where God first appeared to the lonely wayfarer in Bethel's cave as he slept on his stony pillow, and revealed to him the mystic ladder that reached from earth to heaven. When he woke from his wondrous sleep he realized that he had met with God; and his first act was to anoint the stone on which he had rested his head as a sacred shrine and enter into his first covenant with God. This anointing was a sign of dedication. He was setting apart his first sanctuary to God. It was a very imperfect consecration, full of doubts and fears. It was the first touch of the Holy Spirit in the awakening of the new life. And so it stands for the work of the Holy Spirit in calling the soul to God in the experience of conversion. There was the recognition of God and the consecration of service to Him. But there was the accompaniment of much bondage and unbelief. "Surely the LORD is in this place, and I was not aware of it." But he adds with all the force of the old natural heart, "How awesome is this place!" (Genesis 28:16–17). And then his consecration of the 10th to God is only Old Testament consecration, for the New Testament teaches us to give not a part, but the whole. But even this he accompanied with a doubtful if, "If God will be with me . . . then the LORD will be my God" (28:20–21).

355

So the anointing first comes to us revealing God to the soul and calling us to yield ourselves to Him as our covenant God. But the heart still has its "ifs" and its "buts" and has much to learn before it is ready for the full anointing and indwelling of the Holy Spirit.

THE ANOINTING OF THE TABERNACLE

"Take the anointing oil and anoint the tabernacle and everything in it; consecrate it and all its furnishings, and it will be holy. . . . Then the cloud covered the Tent of Meeting, and the glory of the LORD filled the tabernacle" (Exodus 40:9, 34). We are now coming to the deeper meaning of this blessed anointing. The tabernacle here represents the consecration of our body and life to the Lord, and the anointing denotes the baptism and filling of the Holy Spirit.

This incident marked the beginning of the second year of the history of Israel. During the first year the Holy Spirit had been present with them through the cloud as it marched before and followed behind, or sometimes covered the brow of Mount Sinai. Now, however, after the tabernacle was anointed the cloud came down and entered into the sanctuary and took its permanent residence within the Holy of Holies as the Shekinah that hovered between the cherubim. God was now residing in the midst of Israel. So we come to the second year of our spiritual record, and the Presence that has led us to Christ and guided us from a distance, now becomes resident in our inmost being, and the promise is fulfilled, "I will walk among you and be your God" (Leviticus 26:12). Our body becomes the temple of the Holy Spirit and the anointing abides in us.

All this was preceded by a series of acts of obedience and consecration. The preceding chapter tells in full detail of the successive steps that Moses took in finishing and setting apart the various sections of the tabernacle and its furniture. Again and again we read the phrase, "Moses did everything just as the LORD commanded him" (Exodus 40:16), until at last it is added,

> The Israelites had done all the work just as the LORD had commanded Moses. Moses inspected the work and saw that they had done it just as the LORD had commanded. (39:42–43)

> So Moses finished the work. (40:33)

Then it was that the cloud descended and the Spirit came. So we will find that there are steps of obedience and consecration to be taken, the heart and the life surrendered to God in every detail as the Lord has bidden, and when we have yielded our members and all our being completely, then the Holy

Spirit comes down, and comes in and makes the surrendered heart His dwelling place and His peculiar possession.

THE ANOINTING OF THE PRIESTHOOD

The next anointing of which we read is the anointing of the priesthood represented by Aaron and his sons. "He poured some of the anointing oil on Aaron's head and anointed him to consecrate him. . . . Then Moses took some of the anointing oil and some of the blood from the altar and sprinkled them on Aaron and his garments and on his sons and their garments. So he consecrated Aaron and his garments and his sons and their garments" (Leviticus 8:12, 30).

Here the figure advances from the anointing of a building to the anointing of living persons, and still more perfectly represents the pouring of the Holy Spirit upon the consecrated believer.

For we are all recognized as a holy priesthood. Aaron represented the Great High Priest and his sons represent believers as the priests of God. Their anointing in conjunction with Him teaches us that we are baptized with the Holy Spirit in union with the Lord Jesus Christ. We share His priesthood and His anointing. Therefore the name Christ is given to Him, meaning the Anointed One, and the name Christian applied to us means anointed ones. The true Christian is one that has received the anointing of the Holy Spirit and is thus a *Christ one.*

In the 30th chapter of Exodus we have a very full account of the preparation of this anointing oil and its application. There were certain ingredients in it which were known, and certain which were unknown. Even so the person of Christ, the Anointed One, is not only human, and thus familiar to us in His human nature, but there is also the deep mystery of His deity. The anointing oil was to be separated from all other preparations as a holy anointing oil, and under the most solemn penalties all counterfeits or imitations were prohibited. "Whoever makes perfume like it and whoever puts it on anyone other than a priest must be cut off from his people" (Exodus 30:33). It was carefully guarded from desecration by not being applied to any improper object. "Do not pour it on men's bodies and do not make any oil with the same formula," was the sacred restriction and prescription (30:32). And so the Holy Spirit is given only to the separated and consecrated life. He cannot be received by the carnal heart. He will dwell only with the holy. Nor may we imitate Him or counterfeit His blessed influences. Man's modern imitations of divine things He will not acknowledge. The operatic music, the eloquence born of mere emotion, the worship inspired by earthly feeling, the fervor that is wrought up by our feelings, the revival that is the product of human sensation and excitement—all these things are but human counterfeits and strange fire. But in contrast with them, there is a divine anointing, a sacred fire, a heavenly inspiration, a touch of the super-natural and divine that God will give to the holy heart and the consecrated life. Through this anointing we may draw near in our heavenly priesthood and know the living power of God as truly as when His presence shone in the Shekinah flame and the pillar of fire. Have we received this divine anointing? And has it brought us near to God in fellowship and ministry, making us the priests of God and ministers of the heavenly sanctuary?

This ancient anointing was for service, and so all true ministry must begin with the baptism of the Holy Spirit. Without that baptism even Jesus would not presume to preach the message of His Father, and without it our minis-try is a presumption and a failure. Only through the Spirit's power can we perform any service which will be effectual to man or acceptable to God. "If anyone speaks, he should do it as one speaking the very words of God. If anyone serves, he should do it with the strength God provides, so that in all things God may be praised through Jesus Christ. To him be the glory and the power for ever and ever. Amen" (1 Peter 4:11).

THE ANOINTING OF THE LEPER

In Leviticus 14:15–18 we find a new link in this chain of blessing. It is the lowest link attaching all the gifts and graces of the Holy Spirit to the lowest and vilest sinner. The leper represents the full effects of the curse both upon the body and the spirit of the sinner, and his condition is one of utter help-lessness and ruin. In this condition he is brought to the priest, and the first steps in his salvation and restoration are connected with the atoning blood. The sacrifice of the two birds represents the death and resurrection of the Lord Jesus. The sprinkled blood upon the right ear, the right thumb, and the right foot tell of the quickening life of the Lord Jesus. Then comes the anointing oil mingled with the blood, representing the power of the Holy Spirit applied in turn to the different members of our being, until at last when the right ear, the right thumb, and the right toe have been successively anointed, the rest of the oil, representing the fullness of the Spirit, is poured upon the head, and the whole being bathed in the Spirit's power. Here we see the fullness of the Spirit placed within reach of the vilest sinner, until step by step he rises from the depths of misery to the heights of grace and glory, and where sin abounded grace does much more abound. This is an ut-termost salvation. It saves from the uttermost to the uttermost. It is the only salvation large enough and full enough for lost humanity. Is there a poor leprous life reading these lines? Beloved, this anointing is for you, and if you will receive it the measure of your fall will become the measure of your res-toration and your hope, "So that, just as sin reigned in death, so also grace might reign through righteousness to bring eternal life through Jesus Christ our Lord" (Romans 5:21).

THE ANOINTING OF THE SICK

During the ministry of our Lord we are told that He sent forth His disciples not only to preach the gospel, but also to heal the sick. And in closing the New Testament canon we find the Apostle James, who was the head of the apostolic council at Jerusalem and especially fitted to represent the ecclesiastical action of the New Testament Church, committing to the Church of the present dispensation the permanent ordinance of anointing for healing. "Is any one of you sick? He should call the elders of the church to pray over him and anoint him with oil in the name of the Lord. And the prayer offered in faith will make the sick person well; the Lord will raise him up. If he has sinned, he will be forgiven" (James 5:14–15).

This was the divine prescription for sickness among the children of God in the early Church, and it only fell into disuse when the spirit of faith disappeared through the entrance of worldliness and unbelief. The anointing here is evidently a religious and not a medical application. It is administered by an elder and in the name of the Lord, and it is not the anointing, but the prayer of faith that saves the sick, and the Lord that raises him up. Nothing but the most strained and specious and plausible reasoning can turn aside the plain meaning of the passage, and construe it as a medical prescription. To attempt this is to handle the Word of God deceitfully and find an excuse for our unbelief and failure. In the present day God has too frequently fulfilled this promise to make it possible to deceive any longer the candid inquirer. But let it not be forgotten that divine healing, real and blessed as it is, is not a matter of mere rite or ceremony, or even intellectual faith, but the work of the Holy Spirit and connected with the divine anointing. It is nothing less than the life of Christ in our body, the very quickening of the divine Spirit in our mortal frame. We cannot come to Christ as they did in the days of His flesh, as a visible and material presence. We can only approach Him through the Holy Spirit and know Him as the Spirit reveals Him. Therefore a spiritual preparation is indispensable to receiving Him as our Healer. There is a double anointing. First the heart becomes the temple of the Holy Spirit, and then it becomes also true: "Don't you know that you yourselves are God's temple and that God's Spirit lives in you?" (1 Corinthians 3:16). Beloved, have we received the physical anointing of the divine Spirit? This will not only bring us healing from disease, but a higher type of physical life even in health. It unites us with the risen Lord and lifts every function and force into blessed fellowship with His risen life and power.

Such are some of the scriptural illustrations of the divine anointing. Turning from all figures of speech, which might be largely increased, it means simply this: that the third person of the Godhead who dwelt in the Lord Jesus during His earthly ministry, comes to dwell in us when we yield ourselves fully to His possession and control. He brings to the heart the revelation and realization of our union with the Lord Jesus. He quickens us with His life, comforts us with His love, and illuminates us with the vision of His person and the light of His truth. He makes the Word of God a living reality to our spiritual consciousness. He becomes to us the Spirit of peace, joy and rest. He teaches us to pray and inspires our communion with God. He gives us our messages and clothes them with power. He becomes to us the Spirit of purity and holiness. He fills the heart with love, and the life with sweetness and beneficence. Even our very body He quickens with divine strength, lifts us above the power of disease, and makes us partakers of the risen life of our glorified Lord. He is our Guide and guards us from seducing spirits and from dangers seen and unseen, and the promise becomes true, "As for you, the anointing you received from him remains in you, and you do not need anyone to teach you" (1 John 2:27).

Beloved, are we thus abiding and does the anointing so abide? Or have the channels become obstructed, and is the divine life interrupted by some hidden cause? Let us watch and pray. Let us search and try our ways to turn again unto the Lord. And if our communion is interrupted, our peace is broken, our power is gone, our spiritual life waning and unsatisfactory, we may find, we surely shall find the cause if we will dare to be true.

Someone relates the fact that when the water supply in a certain public institution failed and an examination of the premises was made, it was found that the water was all right in the reservoir and the main supply pipe, but that at the point where it connected with the house a great toad had gotten into the pipe that was so big that he had completely blocked the channel. Is it not sometimes true that some of the devil's brood have got into the channels of faith, obedience, and of communion, and while the living water is still flowing as freely as ever around us it cannot enter our heart or satisfy our being because the channels are clogged by worldliness or sin? Therefore with peculiar fitness in this chapter has the apostle warned us against the world and all its unholy lusts as the enemy of God and the great obstruction to the spiritual life of the believer. "Do not love the world or anything in the world. If anyone loves the world, the love of the Father is not in him" (2:15). May His wisdom make us watchful and wise. "And now, dear children, continue in him, so that when he appears we may be confident and unashamed before him at his coming" (2:28).

CHAPTER 5

THE LOVE OF GOD

Whoever does not love does not know God, because God is love.
(1 John 4:8)

It was peculiarly appropriate that it should be given to John, the beloved disciple, to unfold the Father's love. It was in keeping with the principle which he himself has announced in this chapter, that as it takes sin to know sin, so it requires love to understand love. "Whoever does not love does not know God." John was the disciple of love and therefore the revealer of love. In this passage he has given to us the seven great principles of divine love.

GOD IS LOVE

God is not justice. God is not wisdom. God is not power. God has all these attributes but none of them is great enough to constitute His essence. But love is His very nature and in love all other attributes find their completeness. Just as in the process of color printing all the cardinal colors when combined produce a perfect white; so when all the attributes of God meet they form the immaculate purity of divine love. Wisdom without love would be harsh. Justice without love would be severe. Power without love would be terrible. But love modifies, directs and softens every one of them, and blends them into the beautiful harmony of the divine character.

We should, therefore, always recognize the love of God as His supreme purpose in everything He does. He always loves, and He loves all as much as it is possible under the circumstances for them to receive. And when His love cannot avail, even then His heart is full of sorrow and compassion and He gives them at least the love of pity if not of approval. This is made very plain and very pathetic in our Savior's bitter tears over Jerusalem when they would not let Him save them; at least He would let them know that He loved them still. Perhaps it will be true in the last great day that the final remembrance which lost men will have of the Father's face and the Savior's heart will be a look of infinite tenderness, and perhaps once more a flood of tears.

We should look at everything that comes to us in the light of love, and believe that God means it for good. This may not appear at first. Again as in the process of color printing, the first impression may be crimson and the dark tints may follow, one upon the other, but when the last color has been put on, it will always result in the spotless white. So if God's providence has seemed so far to be strange and painful, wait a little longer. The process is not finished. Trust Him through every testing; and when His work is finished, you, too, like Jacob, will be compelled to say, "who has delivered me from all harm" (Genesis 48:16), or like Paul, "And we know that in all things God works for the good of those who love him" (Romans 8:28).

CHRIST IS THE MANIFESTATION OF GOD'S LOVE

Had it been left for us to read the revelation of God upon the face of the earth and sky we could certainly have discerned two mighty words in letters of light and fire: "God is." But there the sentence would have paused and the universe waited for the next great word. The sunshine could have painted goodness there. The blossoms of the spring might have added richer tints to the same word. The joyous festival, the laughter and the song of youth—all these might have emphasized the same gracious inscription. But as we look and wait, lo, there comes the angry lightning, the wild tempest, the sinking vessel, the raging conflagration, the funeral procession, the deep, dark, lonely grave. Then the writing is blotted out, and instead we read, God is power, God is justice, God is mystery; and the heart falls back in helplessness and perplexity and cries, "Oh, that I knew where I might find him"; "Show us the Father and that will be enough for us" (John 14:8). But now another hand takes up the pencil and the brush and writes across the sky, the earth, the guilty conscience, the broken law, the gloomy grave, the very judgment seat: "God is love."

So long as man is innocent, so long as the fact of sin does not intrude, nature reveals nothing but beneficence. But when we come up against the fact of disobedience to law and personal wrong on the part of the sinner, all this is changed. Nature has nothing but retribution and pain for the transgressor. It is just here that love comes in with its glorious triumph and finds a way by which even sin can be forgiven and sinners loved and saved by a holy God. The very scene where divine love most sublimely triumphs is the fall and the ruin of the human race, and the dark cloud of man's condemnation becomes the background on which Calvary and redemption have written in eternal luster, "God is Love." Just as the gulf stream flows northward through the cold Atlantic, warming its waves into tropical mildness until at last it embraces in its current the icebergs of the pole and melts them in its embrace; so God's love was poured through the dark waters of time and met man's guilt in the embrace of its mighty sacrifice and melted it away. And so John adds,

> This is how God showed his love among us: He sent his one and only Son into the world that we might live through him. This is love: not that we loved God, but that he loved us and sent his Son as an atoning sacrifice for our sins. . . . And we have seen and testify that the Father has sent his Son to be the Savior of the world. (1 John 4:9–10, 14)

LOVE BEGETS LOVE

It is the love of God to us that calls forth our love to God. "We love because he first loved us" (4:19). Here is the divine order of Christian morals and Christian holiness. Here is the essential distinction between law and grace. Here is the key to all true spiritual motives. We never can work up our love to God by trying or fearing. Only when we fully believe in His love to us will our love flow forth spontaneously in return. Therefore, redemption meets man with unconditional mercy, forgives him without his deserving it, and finds that as the fruit of forgiveness a new life and a responsive love flow from the ransomed soul and make every service and sacrifice a delight.

The proud English queen tried in vain to break the spirit of her would-be assassin by threatening her with punishment, or even by asking her what she would do if she received a pardon. "Madam," said the haughty French maiden who sought her life, "Grace with conditions is no grace at all." "Then," said the queen, "I forgive you without conditions." And the girl fell at her feet and cried out with tears of gratitude, "Then I am your servant forever." But the unsought, unmerited love of God in Christ breaks down the sinner's heart. Well may he say as the Cornish miner is made to say in the old ballad:

> There's a word that burns in my heart like a fire,
>   And will not let me be.
> Jesus, the Son of God, who loved
>   And gave Himself for me.

LOVE IS THE ORGAN BY WHICH WE KNOW LOVE

"Whoever does not love does not know God, because God is love. . . . No one has ever seen God; but if we love one another, God lives in us and his love is made complete in us" (4:8, 12). Our love is the alphabet by which we understand God's love. Hearts, therefore, that know little of love know but little of God. Therefore God has given us every human tie of love and affection as an organ of divine knowledge that through these we might rise to the comprehension of His greater love. I have known two hearts to receive the baptism of the Holy Spirit in the moment after they met after a long separation, and both bowed together at the throne of grace. As those two brothers mingled their tears and wept on each other's necks, the blessing for which their frigid hearts had been breaking for many years found right of way through the open channels of love, and poured in until the love of man overflowed into the mighty billows of the love of God.

On the other hand I have known a soul so ignorant of human love that she could not comprehend at first what I meant when I told her of the love of God. She had been poor, neglected, abused and wronged so long that her hand was against every man and every man's hand was against her. I found her in the outskirts of the city, one of our neglected poor, and tried to lead her to the knowledge of Jesus. But she looked up in my face and said "I do not understand you. Nobody ever loved me and I do not even know what love means." I went home that night to my proud, wealthy church and I told them I wanted them to make a poor sister understand the meaning of love. And so they began one by one to visit her, to give her little tokens of their interest and regard; until at last one day, months later, as I sat in her humble room, she looked up in my face and said with much feeling, "Now I think I understand what love means, and can accept the love of God." Beloved, has God given to you earthly friends, earthly ties, earthly affections? They are steppingstones to Him. Have you ever felt a throb of pure heart love? That is just a taste of what it is to lie forever on His bosom and drink in His everlasting love. Do not rest in the human love as an end, but receive it and rise from it to the love of your Heavenly Friend. And as you receive His love you will better understand it, until at last your heart shall grow into all the depths and heights of heavenly love.

FAITH IS THE MEANS BY WHICH GOD'S LOVE IS REVEALED

So we read again, "And so we know and rely on the love God has for us" (4:16). We know the love of God by believing it. But we cannot know it until we believe that it is for us. I remember visiting a sick man once in a yellow fever hospital. He was not prepared to meet the Lord and he told me he did not know how to become a Christian. I explained to him the gospel and the way of faith. But he told me that he believed in the gospel and always had believed it. I suggested that we take a verse as a specimen to see if he believed it. I took that verse in this epistle, "the blood of Jesus, his Son, cleanseth us from all sin" (1:7, author's paraphrase). I asked him if he believed it. Of course he did. "What do you believe?" "Why," he said, "I believe the blood of Jesus Christ can cleanse us from all sin." I told him that was not the verse and to read it correctly because the verse says "cleanseth us." Then he tried again. "Well," he said, "I believe that the blood of Jesus Christ cleanseth all Christians from all sin." Still I held him to the words of the text, and insisted that it meant "us." "That is," I said, "you and me. Now, do you believe that the blood of Jesus Christ cleanseth you and me from all sin?" Then he saw that he did not believe the Bible as true for him, and before we parted he put the "us" in it and the "me" in it, and the light of faith and joy came into his heart so that which he believed first he came to know experientially as a fact, in his own personal consciousness. Then he could say in the words of the text, "And so we know and rely on the love God has for us" (4:16). Do not, therefore, wait to feel the love of God, but believe it on the testimony of His Word. Take it as for yourself. Tell Him so. Rise to the place of confidence, to the place of the disciple whom Jesus loves, and God will place you where you dare to put yourself and make real to you every promise that you reckon true.

LOVE LEADS TO CONFIDENCE

Just as in the beginning faith leads to love, so in the end love leads to higher faith, and brings to us the perfect confidence which this passage so beautifully describes, "In this way, love is made complete among us so that we will have confidence on the day of judgment, because in this world we are like him. There is no fear in love. But perfect love drives out fear, because fear has to do with punishment. The one who fears is not made perfect in love" (4:17–18). There is a kind of faith that fights its way to the throne and claims its rights by a logical process. But there is a kind of faith that wins its way to the heart of God and takes its rights as a matter of course, because it knows that He is far more willing to give than we can be to receive. Therefore the prayer of love is the quickest to reach the ear of God, and the confidence and boldness of faith are only born of perfect love. There is a confidence that comes from holding fast to His Word. But there is a confidence that grows out of 10,000 cords of memory and blessing. Promises fulfilled, prayers answered, deliverance given, mercies as countless as the sand, weave themselves at length into a cable of a thousand strands that never can be broken. Or, like the great banyan tree of India, which first starts with a single root and trunk, but after a while sends down a hundred smaller trunks from the branches to take fresh root in the soil until its spreading arms are upheld by innumerable props that grow out of its very life. So the life that has been spent in the intimate fellowship of God becomes so interlinked with Him by every memory and experience of blessing that all the power of earth and hell cannot separate it from His love or make it ever doubt His perfect faithfulness. This is the perfect love that casts out fear and it is our privilege to abide in this love and rest under the shadow of His wings.

THE LOVE OF GOD LEADS TO THE LOVE OF ONE ANOTHER

It cannot be confined within the limits of even religious selfishness, but it overflows in beneficence to our brethren and all mankind. Therefore the apostle reaches the great conclusion "If anyone says, 'I love God,' yet hates his brother, he is a liar. For anyone who does not love his brother, whom he has seen, cannot love God, whom he has not seen. And he has given us this command: Whoever loves God must also love his brother" (4:20–21). Divine love is therefore practical and leads to every Christian duty, sacrifice and service for our brethren and for a suffering and sinning world. God has made us His representatives and His channels to reach humanity, and without us He cannot bring to them the blessings of the gospel. It is not His fault that men and women are dying in sin, but it is ours. He has "so loved the world that he gave his one and only Son, that whoever believes in him shall not perish but have eternal life" (John 3:16). But we have failed to supply the missing link between His love and their need, and we have hoarded to ourselves the grace that was meant for all and sufficient for all.

"How can you say your Father loves you?" a skeptic harshly asked of a little boy who had just testified in a mission to the goodness of God in saving him, though he was clothed in rags and looked half starved. "If He loves you," said the critic, "why doesn't He tell somebody to send you clothes and feed your hunger and supply your need?" The little fellow looked at himself for a moment and colored with mortification. But in a moment he was himself again and looking up manfully, he said "My Father does love, and perhaps He does tell somebody to help me, but somebody forgets." Was there ever a more truthful or touching reproof and appeal! Ah, beloved, if we loved we would not forget. This is just the essence of love that it remembers, and its sweetest tokens are the little acts of thoughtfulness that show that it was not indifferent or forgetful of the comfort and happiness of the object beloved. And so if we truly love as He loves, we will remember, we will sacrifice, we will send or go or give to save a dying world.

CHAPTER 6

THE CONFIDENCE

This is the confidence we have in approaching God. (1 John 5:14)

T he universe is held together by the one great law of gravitation. Society is held together by the one great law of confidence—in the family, the commercial world and the larger circle of tribes and nations. The spiritual world is held together by the law of faith which binds man to God, and adjusts him to his fellow man, even as the law of gravitation binds the solar system and the larger universe.

The Apostle John, whose great heart and divine intuition reached to the essential principles of things rather than mere outward forms, having unfolded already the great principles of life and love in this epistle, now leads us to the law of faith and the principle of confidence, which underlies all spiritual life and experience. Again and again we find in this epistle the expression "we know," and in the closing chapter it rises to the highest and most comprehensive range of spiritual truth and experience.

WE KNOW WE HAVE ETERNAL LIFE

"I write these things to you who believe in the name of the Son of God so that you may know that you have eternal life" (5:13). No truth has become more pronounced and more practical and powerful for good in the Christian teaching of our day than this: that it is the privilege of every child of God to possess not only a hope of heaven, but a full assurance of his acceptance in Christ. Two blessed facts enter into this assurance. First, we have eternal life, and second, we *know* we have it. Nothing less than this can satisfy an earnest soul. The more valuable an object is, the more necessary it is that our title to it should be sure. You are willing to purchase a bill of goods for 50 cents without a title of deed, but you would not purchase a house and lot at 10,000 dollars without a title guarantee. The foundation of this assurance is very clearly stated in this passage. It is not our personal consciousness, our happy feelings, our new experience or our better life; but it is a record that God has given and that God requires us to believe.

> And this is the testimony: God has given us eternal life, and this life is in his Son. He who has the Son has life; he who does not have the Son of God does not have life.
> I write these things to you who believe in the name of the Son of God so that you may know that you have eternal life. (5:11–13)

The record is very simple and easy to be believed. It is not that we may have eternal life, but that God has already given it and laid it at the feet of every man who will receive it. The gift has been bestowed, the proffer has gone forth. God is committed to us, and we have only to endorse the Word that He has given, put our name in the promise and claim the salvation as our own. Not only may we do this, but we are commanded to do it and very solemnly told that "Anyone who does not believe God has made him out to be a liar, because he has not believed the testimony God has given about his Son" (5:10). In His great love God has adjusted the offer of the gospel to our intelligent nature. He has given us an understanding, a will and a reasoning mind, and He meets our intelligence with a simple business proposition offering to us the free gift of eternal life on the simple condition that we accept it and begin to count it our own. Then He reckons it to us according to our reckoning by faith. He puts us in the place we put ourselves, and the gift is ours for the taking. A man, therefore, may have eternal life just as simply and certainly as a citizen of the United States could have become the owner of a free grant of land in the great West by putting in his claim according to the offer of the government and settling upon the land as his own. As we read these lines, if the question is still unsettled, we may decide it now and receive the precious gift of eternal life through Jesus Christ our Lord.

But it is not all a matter of intellectual faith or decision of the will to believe. The moment we commit ourselves to God's Word and count it true for us, God Himself, by the Holy Spirit, imparts to the soul a distinct sense of its acceptance and a conscious assurance of His peace and love. This is what is meant by the statement, "Anyone who believes in the Son of God has this testimony in his heart" (5:10). In the very act of believing there comes to the soul a rest, a satisfaction and a confidence born of the Holy Spirit and attesting to the great fact which our faith has already claimed. There are two seals. First we must affix our seal to the simple document. "The man who has accepted it has certified that God is truthful" (John 3:33). That is the seal of our faith. But now comes the second seal of the Holy Spirit's touch. "Having believed, you were marked in him with a seal, the promised Holy Spirit, who is a deposit guaranteeing our inheritance until the redemption of those who are God's possession" (Ephesians 1:13–14). Thus we may know that we have eternal life. Beloved, have we this confidence?

WE HAVE WHAT WE ASK OF HIM

Having settled the question of our salvation by faith we now go on to apply the same principle of faith to our whole Christian life, and we receive the answers to our prayers by the very same principle which enables us to take the first step. Indeed, a right faith at the start will be of infinite help to us all the way through, and a halting confidence for our salvation will make us halting Christians to the end of the chapter. The first thing required of us when we pray is that we ask according to His will. "This is the confidence we have in approaching God: that if we ask anything according to his will, he hears us" (1 John 5:14). We should spend more time in determining what to pray for than in pleading for it afterwards. His will is revealed in His Word, and every promised blessing within the covers of the Bible is a proper thing to ask and believe for. His will is very large and generous and covers all our needs of spirit, soul and body.

Then, having asked according to His will, we are next to believe that we have the petitions that we desired of Him. This is according to the command of our Lord during His earthly ministry. "Therefore I tell you, whatever you ask for in prayer, believe that you have received it, and it will be yours" (Mark 11:24). We may not have the actual thing for which we have prayed in tangible and visible possession, but we have the petition. His consent has been given. The request has been honored. The decree has been passed. The blessing is on the way and the delivery will come in God's due time. We can afford to wait. We can afford to suffer. We can afford to be tested. We have His Word and we count the things that are not as though they were. This gives to prayer a definiteness and a force which are most satisfying. Without this our prayers are mere ventures, like the soap bubbles which a child may blow into air and they float away and disappear, and he never expects to see more than one in a score again. True prayer, like the echo, should come back to us, first in the shout of praise and then in the glad song of deliverance. This is the prayer that can help others and can call into action all the forces of omnipotence for the work of Christ and the salvation of men. This was the way Christ prayed. "Father, I thank you that you have heard me. I knew that you always hear me" (John 11:41–42). And this is the way that Christ has bidden us to pray, for He has said, "If you remain in me and my words remain in you, ask whatever you wish, and it will be given you" (15:7).

WE KNOW THAT HE SANCTIFIES AND KEEPS US

"We know that anyone born of God does not continue to sin; the one who was born of God keeps him safe, and the evil one cannot harm him" (1 John 5:18). Most of our spiritual failures arise from discouragement. We go out expecting to fail, and of course we fail. If we would but know that there is One within who is mightier than our weakness and stronger than all the strength of our foes, and that He is keeping us and will keep us, we should not fear and would not fall. It is confidence that keeps the soul.

This confidence, however, must be founded upon a right understanding of God's way of sanctification. First we must learn to distinguish between our new self and our old self. We must count the old life as wholly renounced and refuse any more to fear or obey it. We must recognize ourselves as having a new life, born of God. We are as free from sin as the rose is free from the soil or the sand that touches it, but cannot defile it; as the seafowl is free from the defiling stain of the miry waters in which it plunges; as the Son of God was free from the pollution of the world through which He passed with His immaculate holiness. Then we must learn that sin consists not in the temptation of the evil one or in the various moods and feelings which he may throw over our minds and hearts, but in the deliberate attitude of our will. The evil thoughts which Satan hurls upon us like fiery darts, are not our sins but his, unless we accept them and endorse them. We can throw them off as the rose washes off the dust of highway, as the seafowl sheds the brine from its burnished wing, as the ship throws off the waves that threaten to submerge it. We can say to the tempter that these thoughts are yours, not mine. I refuse them. I am not defiled. I will not sin and I will not fear. God accepts our will as our real action and counts us victorious according to the fixed purpose of our hearts. Then we must also understand that sanctification is not our holiness, our self-perfection, our goodness, but, as so well expressed here, the keeping of the Lord Jesus Christ. It is in Him we stand, in Him we overcome, in Him we are perfect. So He that was born of God keeps us and that wicked one cannot touch us. To know this is to be armed with omnipotence and clothed with victory. Beloved, is this the confidence that you have in Him?

WE KNOW HIM

This is the best of all. Our confidence is not merely in His Word, His answers to our prayers, His help in our conflicts, but in His own character and love as He has revealed Himself to us and taught us as the sum of all knowledge to know Him. And so the sublimest height of this whole epistle is reached at last. "We know also that the Son of God has come and has given us understanding, so that we may know him who is true. And we are in him who is true—even in his Son Jesus Christ. He is the true God and eternal life" (5:20). Higher than all blessings received, deeper than all truth revealed, back of all that He has said and all that He has done, is what He is Himself and what He is to us. But, before all this can become a fact and an experience, there must come to us a divine revelation and a divine understanding. And so the apostle tells us that He "has given us understanding, so that we may know him" (5:20). This is something the natural heart cannot know itself. This is something that genius and learning cannot find. This is something that eloquence cannot make plain. This is something that must come to us through the direct vision of the Holy Spirit, giving us a new conception, a divine intuition, a personal revelation of the Lord Jesus Christ in our very hearts.

Therefore, it comes to pass that many of the most gifted minds of earth are dark and blind with respect to the knowledge of God. To them He is but a name, a possible force, a remote and unreal fact. By all their searching they cannot find out God. Talk to them about the delights of His presence and it is all to them as an unmeaning sound. " 'No eye has seen,/ no ear has heard,/ no mind has conceived/ what God has prepared for those who love him'—/ but God has revealed it to us by his Spirit" (1 Corinthians 2:9–10). There is nothing more sad than the helplessness of the human heart to reach the conception of God and to realize the presence of Christ. It is one of the most precious gifts of divine love. It is as new a sense in the soul as the instinct of a bird. And so on the other hand, there are souls that are illiterate and unrefined, but their whole being is alive with the spiritual sense. Christ is more real to them than any material thing. His presence is a fountain of perpetual joy. They live in a world of ever changing, ever fresh delight and their happy heart is a heaven below. God has given them an understanding that they may know Him that is true, and they are in Him that is true, even in His Son, Jesus Christ.

Then there comes with this the deep delightful assurance that the soul has found at last the true, the real, the eternal. Everything else has disappointed us. Everything else has failed us. Everything else has proved transitory or false. But this is true. This satisfies the heart. This meets every intuition and longing of our nature. This fills the fullness of our being, and the transported heart sinks into infinite rest and sings with holy gladness,

> Here rest, my long divided heart,
> Fixed on this blissful center, rest.

Somehow we know that this will never fail us, this will never change, this will never pass away. This will grow deeper, sweeter, stronger, through all time and all eternity. This is truth. This is God. This is everlasting rest. Oh, the satisfaction that it brings to the poor tempest-tossed heart after it has been buffeted by the billow of skepticism, by the storms of doubt, by the assaults of Satan and sin, by the disappointments of life, by the sorrows, sickness and heartbreaks of this vale of tears. It has got home at last and it understands the sublime strains of the ancient song that first echoed on the plains of Paran, "Lord, you have been our dwelling place/ throughout all generations" (Psalm 90:1). Beloved, have you found Him that is true? Have you come to know Him? Have you received the revelation of His face, of His presence, of His love? Have you entered into His rest?

Perhaps as you read these lines your heart is chilled with a sense of loneliness and disappointment. Perhaps the very joy these words describe only makes you the more conscious of your strangeness to it all. Perhaps the very happiness of the hearts around you only depresses you with a deeper discouragement because it is all a blank to you. Listen! He is waiting to make this vision real to your heart. He is ready to give you this revelation of Himself. You have tried to think it out. Your religion has been too much in your head, your hands, your feet, what you are pleased to call your practical nature. There is something else in the human soul that needs to be educated and fed. It is the heart. It is the spiritual sense. It is that which feels and knows and loves. It was made for God, and God alone can awaken it and satisfy it. Ask Him to do so. Fall at His feet in helplessness, and yet in confidence say to Him, "Now show me your glory" (Exodus 33:18). Upon you will open the vision of God, and to you will come the joyful testimony:

> Thou hast bid me gaze upon Thee,
>   And Thy beauty fills my soul,
> For by Thy transforming power,
>   Thou hast made me whole.

> Simply trusting Thee, Lord Jesus,
>   I behold Thee as Thou art,
> And Thy love so pure and changeless,
>   Satisfies my heart.

> Ever lift Thy face upon me,
>   As I live and work for Thee;
> Resting 'neath Thy smile, Lord Jesus,
>   Earth's dark shadows flee.

> Brightness of my Father's glory,
>   Sunshine of my Father's face,
> Keep me ever trusting, resting,
>   Fill me with Thy grace.

CHAPTER 7

THE CONFLICT

You, dear children, are from God and have overcome them, because the one who is in you is greater than the one who is in the world. (1 John 4:4)

The picture which John has given us of divine life and love, has been so full of brightness that we have scarcely seen the shadows. The testimony with which he began his letter, that "God is light; in him there is no darkness at all" (1:5), has given the keynote to the whole epistle. Yet back of the light and the love, there ever follows the shadow of evil. The very brightness of the light makes the shadow deeper and darker; and our study of His blessed message would not be complete unless we looked for a time at the shadow side, and then at the light which illumines it and is able to turn "blackness into dawn" (Amos 5:8). Or, to change the figure, back of all the notes of victory which ring through this epistle, there is the noise of battle and the form of the conflict and the foe. Just as surely as the apostle sees the vision of his Almighty and all-victorious Lord, does he also behold the dark form of the wicked one and the legions of his hostile forces—our spiritual foes.

Six different adversaries are set forth in the first epistle of John.

THE DEVIL

The devil is himself described as "the evil one." "We know that anyone born of God does not continue to sin; the one who was born of God keeps him safe, and the evil one cannot harm him. We know that we are children of God, and that the whole world is under the control of the evil one" (1 John 5:18–19). Certainly John had no skepticism about the existence and power of the devil, and no one who knows God will ever doubt the reality of Satan. It is the men who have never had their eyes opened to behold the Father, who are still blind to the reality of the wicked one. The light reveals the shadow. Infernal wickedness always follows supernatural power and love. The period of Christ's earthly ministry was coincident with the outbreak of satanic evil, and the revelation of God in a human life always brings the experience of deep and fiery temptations. It is in the heavenly places that the spirits of wickedness fight their most desperate battles against the saints of God.

John's language here points out the devil in the most emphatic manner as the very personification of all that is evil. "The evil one" indicates a personality about whose identity there can be no mistake. There he stands, patent to all eyes—the embodiment of evil, the one who has no double, the prince of darkness, preeminence above all other things as the paragon of wickedness and the enemy of God and man. This world is still his throne, and the most helpless of his subjects and victims are those who least understand their master and are so deceived that they even doubt his existence. He has blindfolded them with delusion, and bound them with the silken fetters of self-confidence and deceit; and as the Word of God describes it, he "has taken them captive to do his will" (2 Timothy 2:26).

FALSE SPIRITS

Satan has many emissaries and agents whom he sends forth to carry out his behests in the hearts and lives of men. Therefore, the apostle warns his readers, "Dear friends, do not believe every spirit, but test the spirits to see whether they are from God, because many false prophets have gone out into the world" (1 John 4:1). There are supernatural beings inhabiting the realms of evil, and permitted to have access to the hearts and minds of men. The origin of these beings, we do not know. A distinguished writer, who has become familiar with the subject of demonology by much contact with it, has suggested that they may be the spirits of a former human race before the fall of Adam. Of their existence there is no question. The hearts of men were filled with them in the days of Christ, and their casting out was one of His chief ministries.

There are two ways in which these evil spirits control men, directly and indirectly. Sometimes they take possession of men—dominate their will, driving them to insanity and self-destruction. This is actual demon possession in spite of the consent of the victim, and is one of the most distressing calamities that can come to a human soul. Then there is the indirect influence, which they seek to gain over the wills and hearts of men—deceiving, alluring, infatuating human hearts with their subtle wiles and leading them into sin. This form of spiritual influence is universal. It controls much of the literature of our age, much of the art and culture, nearly all of our popular amusements, and much of our philosophical teaching. These bright and seductive intelligences paint the vision of error and the fascination of pleasure in such attractive colors that multitudes of human souls are beguiled like the mother of our race, and are following the course of this world, "the ruler of the kingdom of the air, the spirit who is now at work in those who are disobedient" (Ephesians 2:2).

The most portentous form of spiritual peril is in connection with the system known as Spiritualism. There is no doubt of the reality of these manifestations of their power, but they are certainly evil and of the devil. Many are drawn lightly and thoughtlessly by idle curiosity into the mysteries of Spiritualism, only to find that their souls have been scorched by its fearful sorceries, and only by the narrowest escape have they ever got back from the very brink of the lake of fire. Do not play with it even in its most simple and insinuating forms, as it comes to you, perhaps, as a parlor amusement in the form of table rapping, or through the ministrations of some clairvoyant medium or in the more dangerous circle of the spiritual seance. It is sorcery. It is devil worship and it is soul destroying. So also it comes in many forms of religious fanaticism through teachers, miracle workers, divine healers, so-called, and inward visions and revelations which are presented as the voice of God, and appeal to spiritual pride as a higher revelation and an evidence of deeper light. The simple test of all these things is the Word of God, and the practical test of righteousness and holiness. Let us be prepared for false spirits and let us not fear to try them, for if God is giving us any message or revelation, He will always give us ample time to be quite sure that it is God.

FALSE PROPHETS AND ANTICHRIST

Besides the spirits of evil that come unseen, there are human spirits and prophets, who are also the emissaries and agents of the wicked one. The apostle speaks of many antichrists, and particularly of some of whom he gives us the touchstone by which they may be tested.

> Dear children, this is the last hour; and as you have heard that the antichrist is coming, even now many antichrists have come. (2:18)

> Because many false prophets have gone out into the world. . . . Every spirit that acknowledges that Jesus Christ has come in the flesh is from God, but every spirit that does not acknowledge Jesus is not from God. This is the spirit of the antichrist, which you have heard is coming and even now is already in the world. (4:1–3)

The description here given fits so exactly the latest form of false religion, that one is almost forced to apply it. The very cornerstone of Christian

Science, so-called, is the point raised by John in this passage; namely, has Jesus Christ come in the flesh? Was the incarnation real? Did Christ have an actual human body? Is there such a thing as matter and a material body at all? All this Christian Science denies, and, of course, denies that Jesus Christ has come in the flesh, thus constituting itself, by its own direct testimony, to be at least one of the antichrists of the last times. Indeed, it is a wonder how the intelligent American mind can be deceived by teachings so absurd, and so contradictory even to common sense, to say nothing of Scripture. And, indeed, it is not new. It is but a rehash of the old Sabellian heresy of apostolic times, and idealism taught in England in the 17th century by David Hume and Bishop Berkely. At the time of Hume's death, his foolish philosophy was labeled by the inscription on his tombstone:

> Within this circular idea,
>   Vulgarly called a tomb,
> Impressions and ideas rest
>   Which constituted Hume.

Berkeley had a still more serious setting down by a plain woman in his congregation, who one day found him lying in a ditch and begging to be helped out. Looking down upon her pastor with a smile of mischievous triumph, she cried, "So, Doctor, you've got into a real ditch at last." "Oh, no, madam," said the doctor, as he tried to spit out the mud and keep himself afloat, still manfully sticking up for his principles, "I-I-I've got a painful idea that I've fallen into a ditch." This, alas, is but one of the fanaticisms abroad today, seeking to counterfeit the truth and mislead the simple. May the Holy Spirit give us that blessing so finely described in Philippians, "That your love may abound more and more in knowledge and depth of insight, so that you may be able to discern what is best and may be pure and blameless until the day of Christ" (Philippians 1:9–10).

FALSE BRETHREN

Not only are we opposed by false teachers, but by unworthy fellow workers and brethren, who often prove untrue. "They went out from us, but they did not really belong to us. For if they had belonged to us, they would have remained with us; but their going showed that none of them belonged to us" (1 John 2:19). It would be harsh and serious for us to say that all who turned aside from the fellowship of the truth and the cause for which we are standing are false to God. And yet it is one of the trials of Christian work, that we often have to bear the painful severance of the bonds of fellow service that have held us in fellowship with former workers, and we have often to see the most sacred interests betrayed by those that should have been most true. This should not distress us, but rather make us glad and thankful that we learned before it was too late that they were not of us. Better they should withdraw if they were not true, than to continue in a false position and do more harm from within than they can do without. No work can be injured from the outside if it is right and true within the heart and in all the constituent elements that form its inmost center.

THE WORLD

"This present evil world" (Galatians 1:4, KJV) is the next great adversary.

> Do not love the world or anything in the world, If anyone loves the world, the love of the Father is not in him. For every-thing in the world—the cravings of sinful man, the lust of his eyes and the boasting of what he has and does comes not from the Father but from the world. The world and its desires pass away but the man who does the will of God lives forever. (1 John 2:15–17)

Here the apostle presents the world as a great trinity, or rather, antitrinity of evil as the counterfeit and rival of God. The three persons in this trinity are the lust of the flesh, representing the grosser forms of worldliness and animal indulgence; the lust of the eyes, representing the more refined and aesthetic tastes which find their gratification in earthly things; and the pride of life, expressing the loftier ambitions of the human mind for preeminence and power in the world of fashion, of commercial competition, of political prominence, of intellectual greatness, or even of ecclesiastical honor and influence. For every one of these varied forms of human desire the devil has a proffered prize.

But it is not the world that hurts us, but love of the world, or rather, the lust of the world. It is the thing in us that wants the world that does all the harm. It is the spark within the soul which kindles the conflagration. An angel might pass through all the beauty, brilliancy and wealth of our world, and not feel one heart throb of attraction, because he had just left the dazzling glories of heaven, and was immediately to return. It is the earth hunger within us that makes us want the earth, and if this in any measure possesses us, it excludes the love of the Father and makes the smallest earthly thing an idol and a curse. The humble housewife setting her heart upon the paltry savings of a few hundred dollars, and the miserly farmer, laying up in a long life of saving his paltry treasure of a few thousands, yes, the very minister of the gospel building up a church for his own ambition, very much as the merchant is building up a business—these people may be just as worldly as the millionaire pursuing his larger prize, or the social queen seeking the worship of her more brilliant court of splendid admirers. It is very solemn that the last message of John, in this epistle is this: "Dear children, keep yourselves from idols" (5:21). The idol is anything in our heart or life which takes the place of God. And this is just what the world does in the heart where it becomes the ruling motive, and thus the mammon of unrighteousness. Well may we heed the warning, and ask the Father's love to counteract the danger, "Do not love the world or anything in the world" (2:15).

THE POWER OF SIN

The last and most terrible of all our foes is that subtle power which Satan injects into the soul, and which perverts every good and holy thing from a divine to a selfish and a wrong direction. It is sin. And so we read, "If we claim to be without sin, we deceive ourselves and the truth is not in us. . . . If we claim we have not sinned, we make him out to be a liar and his word has no place in our lives" (1:8, 10).

The reality and malignity of sin are only fully appreciated by the soul that has learned the secret of deliverance from sin. It is only holiness that can rightly measure sin, and it is only the heart that has learned to know God, that fully knows the exceeding evil and bitterness of sin. Some forms of modern philosophy and religious teaching lightly ignore it, as they do a personal God; but it is only the deeper evidence of the power of sin in blinding the minds of them that believe not. It is those who are dead that know not even that they are dead. It is the poison of sin in the human soul that gives the world its power to allure, and the devil his vantage ground to assail. Passing through an infected land with disease lurking in the air, if there is a scratch upon the skin, the poison is apt to be absorbed and the blood infected. But if the skin is whole the traveler passes unscathed. Sin has left its deep wound in the human soul, and everything becomes defiled by its subtle and malignant power. It is the worst of all our foes, but thank God it is the one evil with which divine grace and power have grappled first, and grappled victoriously. For the victory which this blessed epistle reveals, is the victory over sin as well as Satan, and the world; and we go into the battle from the very beginning with the blessed assurance, "The blood of Jesus, his Son, purifies us from all sin" (1:7).

CHAPTER 8

THE VICTORY

You . . . have overcome them, because the one who is in you is greater than the one who is in the world. (1 John 4:4)

W̲e enter this conflict with the prestige of victory. We meet the enemy as a conquered foe. This is the high standpoint of faith. This is the only ground where the child of God should meet temptation. You have overcome them!

The elements and resources of our victory are unfolded with as much fullness as the resources of the foes.

THE BATTLE IS THE LORD'S

"The reason the Son of God appeared was to destroy the devil's work" (3:8). The battle is not ours but God's. Christ is the leader in the conflict. From the beginning it has ever been so. When the battle first began in Eden it was the seed of the woman that was to bruise the head of the serpent. And, ever since, God has recognized the great conflict between good and evil as a personal issue between the Prince of Darkness and the Son of God. When He came to earth as the captain of our salvation, He met the adversary in single combat and overthrew him once for all. And now He still comes to lead us in triumph and overcome for us and in us. Let us enter every conflict with the confidence that the Lord is fighting for us, and that we are simply following His banner and fighting His battle.

THE BLOOD OF CHRIST

The next element of victory and weapon of warfare is the blood of Christ. "The blood of Jesus, his Son, purifies us from all sin" (1:7). "They overcame him/ by the blood of the Lamb/ and by the word of their testimony" (Revelation 12:11), must ever be the battle cry in the conflict between good and evil. Not by ethical principles, social culture and moral example, do we

379

overcome the forces of evil. The crimson banner of Calvary must lead the conflict and claim the victory. The great fact of sin must be recognized and met by atonement and sacrifice. The death of Christ must be reproduced in the death of the believer to self and sin. The old life of nature is not capable of reaching the divine ideal. It must die and be superseded by a heaven-born life, by the nature of God Himself, implanted in the soul through the resurrection life of Christ within. And so the blood of Christ which signifies and sets forth the idea of sacrifice and crucifixion, signally sets forth the idea of the new life imparted to us from the very life of our risen Lord. The blood is evermore the life, the life shed for us, the life breathed in us. And, as we enter into the deep, full meaning of the cross, sin loses its power, and Satan can no more reach us than he can reach the risen, ascended Lord Himself.

THE WORD OF GOD

God's Word is the weapon of our warfare. "I write to you, young men,/ because you are strong,/ and the word of God lives in you,/ and you have overcome the evil one" (1 John 2:14). It is through the Word of God that the power of the blood is applied to our soul. Believing the gospel we enter into the enjoyments of its blessings and come under the power of divine grace. It is the Word of God upon which faith rests its claims and from which it draws its comfort and inspiration to purify the heart and transform the life. It is the Word of God that detects the subtleties and snares of the devil's temptations, exposes the false spirits that have gone forth into the world, and enables us to overcome all the wiles of the wicked one. "Then you will know the truth, and the truth will set you free" (John 8:32).

It was by this weapon that Christ overcame in His threefold conflict with the enemy in the wilderness. And it is by it we are established in the truth and the Word of God abides in us, that we will overcome the wicked one and be strong in the grace that is in Christ Jesus. As for him, the Psalmist could say, "By the word of your lips/ I have kept myself/ from the ways of the violent" (Psalm 17:4). Beloved, are you armed with the Word of God? Is it for you the supreme test of truth and error, of right and wrong, the manna of your soul, the guide of your life and the sword of the Spirit, before which Satan cannot stand?

THE ANOINTING OF THE SPIRIT

This is our safeguard against the adversary. "I am writing these things to you about those who are trying to lead you astray. As for you, the anointing you received from him remains in you, . . . and as that anointing is real, not counterfeit—just as it has taught you, remain in him" (1 John 2:26–27). It was the Holy Spirit that led Christ into the wilderness to be tempted of the devil and it is He that still guides and guards us in our spiritual conflicts.

"For he will come like a pent-up flood/ that the breath of the LORD drives along" (Isaiah 59:19). The true antagonist of the spirit of evil is the spirit of good. As the devil is the counterfeit of the Holy Spirit, so the Holy Spirit is the conqueror of the devil. Good reason has the devil to dread his divine Victor, and well may we take refuge under the guardian wing of the blessed Comforter, if we would be safe from the dragon's power. Just as the burnished covering on the plumage of the seafowl preserves it unstained as it plunges into the brine, so the anointing of the Holy Spirit protects us from the defiling touch of the serpent and carries us unspotted through all the pollution of a sinful world. Hence we are never safe until we receive the seal and anointing of the Holy Spirit. Do not go forth into the conflict without it. Having received the Lord Jesus as your Savior, accept the Holy Spirit as your Keeper, Comforter and Guide, and learn to put Him between you and everything you meet. So shall He prove "a wall of fire around it . . . and I will be its glory within" (Zechariah 2:5). And sheltered beneath His feathers we shall ever sing:

> I am safe from all danger
> While under His wings.

THE DIVINE INDWELLING

"The one who is in you is greater than the one who is in the world" (1 John 4:4). The interior life is what is meant by this. To most Christians their religion is external. It is a matter of their convictions, their creed, their intellect. It consists in what they believe and know. It is theology, doctrine and religious discussion. Or perhaps it is ceremony, churchgoing, rites, religious worship, singing, praying and performing acts of religious service, so-called. Or it may be more than this. It may have to deal chiefly with their conduct, their practical life from day to day, the things they do and say, or do not do or say; their acts of benevolence, their Christian work, service, so-called, for others, preaching, teaching, seeking to help and save. All this is good and has its place. But all this is external. The true secret of divine religion is this: "For this is what the high and lofty One says—/ he who lives forever, whose name is holy:/ 'I live in a high and holy place,/ but also with him who is contrite and lowly in spirit/ to revive the spirit of the lowly/ and to revive the heart of the contrite' " (Isaiah 57:15). This is the home that God is seeking. "God is spirit, and his worshipers must worship in spirit and in truth" (John 4:24); that is, in the depths of the human spirit, "for they are the kind of worshipers the Father seeks" (4:23).

God is longing only to find a welcome and a home in human hearts. He is standing at the door and knocking, and ever crying, "If anyone hears my voice and opens the door, I will come in and eat with him, and he with me"

(Revelation 3:20). "If anyone loves me," the Lord Jesus has told us, "My Father will love him, and we will come to him and make our home with him" (John 14:23). It is when God thus comes to dwell within and undertakes to work out our life from the interior, that He is able "to do immeasurably more than all we ask or imagine, according to his power that is at work within us" (Ephesians 3:20).

The great question therefore, is, where do we meet God? Where does He reside? Is He for us a God in heaven or the God in the heart? Is the throne of His omnipotence within the secret place of our being? Then, indeed, it is true, "the one who is in you is greater than the one who is in the world" (1 John 4:4). Enthroned in the depths of our being, God and our heart are in such perfect alliance that nothing can come between them. He is instead of every evil thing, every unholy presence, every threatening danger, nearer to us than our own very consciousness, a very present help in time of trouble. Have you learned the secret of the interior life? Have you become the temple of the Holy Spirit? Is God more real to you than the facts of your own consciousness and the operations of your own soul?

FAITH IS THE VICTORY

"For everyone born of God overcomes the world. This is the victory that has overcome the world, even our faith. Who is it that overcomes the world? Only he who believes that Jesus is the Son of God" (5:4–5). It is through faith that we become united to the Son of God, that we become the subjects of the cleansing blood, that the truth becomes effectual in our lives and the Word of God abides in us, that the anointing is received, and the indwelling presence of the Holy Spirit is constantly and joyously realized. Faith is the spiritual sense which brings us into contact with the unseen and the divine. It is a sort of sixth sense opening to us a new world of external realities which others cannot see or know. Just as a man who has never had the sense of smell is ignorant of a whole world of sweetness, so a soul without faith can never come in contact with the divine realities of the world to come, and bring them to bear as a personal matter upon our life and conduct. Therefore faith unites us with divine omnipotence, and it is true, "Everything is possible for him who believes" (Mark 9:23), as much as it is true that "All things are possible with God" (10:27). Therefore faith is represented by a military figure as the "shield of faith, with which you can extinguish all the flaming arrows of the evil one" (Ephesians 6:16). The shield covers the soldier so that the darts do not reach him. So faith hides behind the person of Christ, and all the blows fall upon Him.

There are two kinds of shields constantly referred to in the figurative language of the Bible. There is the buckler as well as the shield. The buckler is a shield which is so attached to the arm that it cannot be lost. It is fastened to the soldier. Through the thickest of the conflict he finds it still there even should his fingers cease to grasp it. So there are two kinds of faith. There is our faith, which we may easily lose, and there is the faith of God, which holds and keeps us. This is one of the deepest secrets of the Christian life, that Christ within us becomes the power of an overwhelming faith. There is nothing more wonderful than that spirit of trust, which, through the darkness and the light, clings and fears not, but knows by an unspeakable instinct that He will not fail us, that He loves and leads and keeps, and will carry us through. Sometimes the thought comes to us, what if we should lose this trust; what if our confidence should fail? What if in some dark and dreadful hour we should be stricken with panic and sink in despair, and lose our confidence? This would be dark and terrible indeed! Perhaps we have come to such an hour. I once came to such an hour, and in the darkness of that dreadful moment, when Satan seemed to have destroyed by one fell blow, all my faith, I became afraid even to pray, and sinking in desolation I could only cry, "What shall I do? I cannot even trust!" It was then that for the first time I learned the faith of God. For, as I sank in the depths of my desolation and helplessness, there stole over my heart such a strange, new sweetness, such a sense of God's love, God's arms, God's overshadowing presence, and a trust that could not die, that I looked up and loved, and leaned, and rested with a simplicity at which I could only wonder and weep and say, "How blessed! How safe! How good God is! How wonderful His love, His trust, His presence!" And so, beloved, we must lose our faith to find His, and when we find it, we have something that Satan cannot steal, and that the world can neither give nor take away.

Therefore, these trials "have come so that your faith—of greater worth than gold, which perishes even though refined by fire—may be proved genuine" (1 Peter 1:7). Therefore it was of Peter's faith that Jesus said: "I have prayed for you, Simon, that your faith may not fail" (Luke 22:32). Therefore, we are exhorted in view of the devil's rage and hate, to stand "firm in the faith, because you know that your brothers throughout the world are undergoing the same kind of sufferings" (1 Peter 5:9). Therefore, again, we have the admonition:

> So do not throw away your confidence; it will be richly rewarded. . . .
>
> > "But my righteous one will live by faith.
> > And if he shrinks back,
> > I will not be pleased with him."

But we are not of those who shrink back and are destroyed, but of those who believe and are saved. (Hebrews 10:35, 38–39)

Lord, give us such a faith as this,
  And then whate'er may come,
We'll taste even here the hallowed bliss,
  Of our eternal home.

CHAPTER 9

THE MINISTRY OF LETTER WRITING

The elder,
To the chosen lady and her children, whom I love in the truth.
(2 John 1)

The letters we write are a mirror at once of the character of the writer and the person addressed. We can usually form a fair picture of both lives from a confidential correspondence between two human friends. The best biographies in literature are largely made up of personal letters. And so the New Testament consists, to a great extent, of personal correspondence. The epistles were all written to churches or individuals, and had a direct and local coloring as well as a general application. Many of them, however, were written to single persons. Happy for us if all our letters were as wisely and nobly conceived, and as finely expressed. These two letters of the Apostle John form a necessary supplement to his first epistle and bring home to our hearts some additional messages in the less conventional form and the more direct and personal channel of his private correspondence. The first of these letters is addressed to an honored sister in the primitive church, the mother of a family and the intimate friend or relative of some Christian lady with whom John was at the time residing.

THE FIRST LETTER

1. The Lesson of Humility

The first lesson we learn from this letter, and indeed from both, is the lesson of humility. John might have called himself an apostle, or the last of the apostles, as he probably was at this time, and certainly the dearest to Christ of all the twelve. But he says nothing of all this, but modestly speaks of himself as one of the very humblest officers in the Church of Christ, just an elder. Surely, this is in fine contrast with the self-importance and lofty

pretensions of ecclesiasticism through every age. When we find men announcing themselves by a long array of titles, and even in some cases with
glaring fanaticism claiming to be the very apostles of the Lord to speak with
the authority of divine inspiration, we may well lower our estimate in in-
verse proportion to their self-exaggeration. These claims belong to the school
of Simon Magus and Lucifer, rather than to the meek and lowly Jesus.
Modesty will always be found to be the badge of merit, both in the literary
in the spiritual world.

2. The Lesson of Friendship

The next lesson we learn is a Christian friendship. John addresses this
sister in terms of the tenderest regard, and yet as a regard sacredly guarded.
"Whom I love in the truth . . . because of the truth, which lives in us and
will be with us forever" (1–2). This is a love that is founded on spiritual
bonds, and will be as lasting as the truth itself, which is eternal.

3. The Example of a Christian Family

We have an example of a Christian family, for this sister had children and
John especially refers to them that they were walking in the truth. And so it
is the privilege of the child of God to claim the same salvation for his family
as for himself. "Believe in the Lord Jesus, and you will be saved—you and
your household" (Acts 16:31). And yet not all her children were saved, for
the expression here is, "It has given me great joy to find some of your
children walking in the truth" (2 John 4); that is, I found many of your
children; but there were still some lost lambs even in this fold, that no
doubt, a mother's faith and an apostle's faith were gently and patiently
bringing in.

4. An Example of Christian Life

Next there is an example of a true Christian life. Two things especially
enter into it, practical obedience and holy aspiration. Christian life is first of
all obedience to God. For "this is love: that we walk in obedience to his
commands. As you have heard from the beginning, his command is that you
walk in love" (6). But it is not all plod. There is a lofty plane of noble ambition and a great reward to win. And so he adds: "Watch out that you do not
lose what you have worked for, but that you may be rewarded fully" (8).
There is a prize to be obtained and a constant vigilance and courage are essential to the victory, and the final recompense.

5. Our Attitude toward Error and Evil

We are specially taught here our attitude toward error and evil. The Antichrist is described in almost the same terms as we noted in the first epistle,

and all who bring false doctrine are to be avoided and renounced so distinctly that we can have no complicity with their errors nor responsibility for their evil courses. This is a most emphatic and needed prohibition. "If anyone comes to you and does not bring this teaching, do not take him into your house or welcome him. Anyone who welcomes him shares in his wicked work" (10–11). We cannot be partners in error. We cannot cooperate with those with whom we are not of one accord. It is not enough merely to love the Lord, but we must hate evil. We cannot say God bless you to every person with whom we talk or pray. We are to lay hold suddenly on no man nor are we to be partakers of other men's sins. But we must always take such a stand in gentleness and love.

THE SECOND LETTER

The second letter was addressed to the well-known disciple of whom we read elsewhere in the New Testament, that he was the companion of Paul, and the host of the Church of God. He was probably a man of sufficient means to be at least independent, and to be able to do much to help the brethren. It is needless to dwell on the many beautiful points in this letter which are identical with the previous one. There is the same spirit of personal love, Christian fellowship and beautiful modesty. But there are five distinctive and important points.

1. The Apostle's Views

We have the apostle's views upon divine healing and temporal blessing in answer to prayer very fully brought out in the second verse. Literally translated it is, "Beloved, I pray above all things that thou mayest prosper and be in health, even as thy soul prospereth" (3 John 2). This is very strong language and yet very safe. He does not put divine healing and outward blessing above spiritual things, but he makes them conditional upon our spiritual state. He prays for his friend that he may prosper and be in health just as much as his soul prospers. The word prosper, here, denotes more than mere sanctity and soundness. It expresses rather a condition of spiritual fullness, and rich and abundant blessing, and it implies that we cannot expect the Lord's blessing upon our bodies and our business, if we cherish in our hearts those spiritual conditions which bring divine chastening and produce misery and pain. When the heart is overflowing with the love of Christ and the power of the Holy Spirit, then the blessing will reach every fiber and extremity of our mortal frame, and the providence of God will cover our temporal interest, protecting and providing for all our conditions and needs. Let us not, therefore, hesitate in the face of this bold announcement to come to our heavenly Father as freely for our temporal needs as for our spiritual conditions, for, He "is able to do immeasurably more than all we ask or imagine, according to his power that is at work within us" (Ephesians 3:20). The inworking will always bring the outworking.

2. A Testimony to a Faithful Life

We have a fine testimony to a faithful life. "Dear friend, you are faithful in what you are doing for the brothers, even though they are strangers to you" (3 John 5). It is not a brilliant life, but it is a faithful one. He is true to every obligation, trust and relationship. He is a faithful servant to his Master. This is not only true of his Christian relationships, but in his dealings with strangers and the world outside. What a world this would become if this were always true of every disciple of Christ. Here is a pattern for you businessmen. You may never be great, brilliant, nor marvelously useful, but you can be faithful. We know that in the great day when the rewards shall be given, the commendation will be not for our services or our talents, but "Well done, good and faithful servant! . . . Come and share your master's happiness!" (Matthew 25:21).

3. The Picture of a Missionary Home

We have the picture of a missionary at home.

> They have told the church about your love. You will do well to send them on their way in a manner worthy of God. It was for the sake of the Name that they went out, receiving no help from the pagans. We ought therefore to show hospitality to such men so that we may work together for the truth. (3 John 6–8)

Here we have a fine example of a Christian layman, who cannot himself go forth to preach the gospel to the lost, living and working to send others, and like good old Gaius bring them forward on their journey after a godly manner. Perhaps Gaius did it by his hospitality, and his personal gifts as they visited him on their way. We can do it through the organized missionary movements of our time, as well as the individual opportunities afforded us in the providence of God. It was stated by one of our most successful missionary workers, that many hundreds of the missionaries of the Presbyterian and American Boards, now in the field, were supported either by individual congregations or single persons at home. It was added that the number of churches and individuals, who might easily assume the support of a missionary, might be extended to the thousands and tens of thousands, and thus the number of missionaries on the field multiplied many times over.

At a session of the Ecumenical Council, it was stated by the president and others in the great meeting of laymen, that if the businessmen of this country would supply the means, the number of missionaries sent forth to the foreign fields could easily be doubled, or even still more largely multiplied within a very short time, as there were thousands of earnest young lives ready to go out, but were depressed and discouraged by the constant cry of retrenchment, and the lack of financial resources on the part of the missionary societies. Let us pray, let us plead, let us labor until the Church of Jesus Christ awakens to realize the responsibility of those in the homeland, whom God has raised up in order that we may be trustees of His bounty and His grace to our perishing fellow men.

4. The Picture of a True Foreign Missionary

We have a picture of the true foreign missionary. "It was for the sake of the Name that they went out, receiving no help from the pagans. We ought therefore to show hospitality to such men so that we may work together for the truth" (7–8). Here is the true missionary motive: for His name's sake. Nothing less than love to Christ, and a sense of His supreme call, can ever sustain a successful missionary life. "Receiving no help from the pagans." This is the spirit of true missionary self-sacrifice. The most difficult task of the missionary is to convince the national that he is disinterested. They cannot really believe that anybody can love them well enough to leave home and country, and every prospect of earthly gain and pleasure, simply for the purpose of teaching and helping them; and when at last they become convinced of the sincerity and unselfishness of the messenger, they accept the message, and they become themselves the most beautiful examples of self-sacrifice and devotion.

In China, to which today, the eyes of the world are turned with the deepest concern, almost every national believes that our missionaries have some ulterior motive, and are seeking to make something out of them. This is the real secret of the anti-foreign prejudice, and the wild stories that are everywhere circulated about our missionaries, digging out the eyes of the babies to make medicine, and discovering gold by a process of second sight behind every rock and river bed. The answer to all this must be an unselfish life, and a spirit of devotion—such as is exhibited today in that dark land—which is ready to give all, even life itself, for the sake of the people that do not even appreciate their love. It is very sad, when missionaries use their opportunities to promote their selfish interest and aggrandizement, and it seems most unfortunate when they allow themselves to be tempted to go into the service of the wealthy natives for the sake of large emoluments. Nothing can repay the loss of influence sustained by a surrender of independence and the suspicion of any sordid or selfish motive. But the self-sacrifice of the missionary should not be confined to him but shared by the missionary at home who stands behind him, and by self-sacrifice in living and giving, carries out the apostle's exhortation, "We ought therefore to show hospitality to such men so that we may work together for the truth" (8).

5. The Picture of a Backsliding Church

We have one more picture in this letter; namely, a backsliding church. Already the spirit of declension, that afterwards culminated in the great apostasy, had entered the primitive churches. Paul tells us that, "At my first defense, no one came to my support, but everyone deserted me" (2 Timothy 4:16). They had turned away from him, and now John makes the still more painful confession, "I wrote to the church: But Diotrephes, who loves to be first, will have nothing to do with us. So if I come, I will call attention to what he is doing, gossiping maliciously about us. Not satisfied with that, he refuses to welcome the brothers. He also stops those who want to do so and puts them out of the church" (3 John 9–10).

It was out of this spirit of ecclesiastical ambition and pride, contending for preeminence and earthly honor, that the Romanish apostasy first arose; and the same cause is destroying the purity and separation of many in the Church today. We must not blame the pulpit for it all, although it takes its most hideous form in ministerial pretensions, high sounding titles and selfishness and luxury on the part of the preachers of the gospel. The spirit of the pew will soon be reproduced in the pulpit. And why should there be a severer standard for one than for the other. If the church warden, the official steward, the wealthy trustee and the fashionable parishioner insist upon going to the opera and taking part in the dance and the card party, do not be surprised if the General Conference shall itself someday begin to talk about modifying the Book of Discipline, and make it easier for the people to live up to the advanced spirit of our cultured age. It is said that a minister who had grown tired of preaching against all these things, at last thought he would give his people an object lesson in worldliness, and so he announced one day, that the prayer meeting would be omitted that week, as the pastor and his family had a prior engagement at the opera. The following week he begged to be excused from board meeting of the trustees, as his wife and he had to entertain a card party. Before the third announcement could be made, however, the church board had been called, and that preacher tried and deposed from the ministry for conduct unbecoming a preacher of the gospel. It was in vain that he pleaded that he was only doing what his people did. They could not see the rightness of it when presented in such a striking object lesson. But his logic was sound, and the lesson, if ineffectual, was at least consistent. The spirit of selfishness and worldliness, which is sapping the vitals of modern Christianity, is but the outgrowth of a lower standard of Christian living, and the demand of the people for a liberty which would shock and disgust them, if they saw it carried out to its legitimate fruit on the part of those to whom they look up as examples of true Christianity. It is very solemn to find that even as early as the days of John, the doors of the Church were shut against true spiritual testimony. Let us not be surprised if we often find that we must stand alone. But it is blessed to be in the minority with John the Beloved, Paul the Apostle, and Jesus the ascended Lord.

JUDE

CHAPTER 1

THE EPISTLE OF JUDE

This little epistle of 22 verses and less than 700 words is replete with the most solemn warnings and the loftiest spiritual lessons, conveyed with a vigor and vividness worthy of comparison with some of the finest visions of the old prophets, such as Jeremiah, Hosea and Zephaniah,

Its author is Jude who described himself here as "Jude, a servant of Jesus Christ and a brother of James" (Jude 1). The James to whom he refers as his brother is the author of the epistle of James, and was one of the three most prominent apostles and associated with Peter and John in many of the important scenes in the life of our Lord. James was the presiding officer in the church at Jerusalem, and represented in a special way the Hebrew element in the early Christian Church. He was also the presiding officer of the council at Jerusalem described in the 15th chapter of Acts. He and Jude both were literal brothers of the Lord Jesus, afterwards born of the same mother. But their earthly relationship was completely dropped and forgotten in the higher bond of the heavenly Master and the earthly disciple.

The epistle is addressed "To those who have been called, who are loved by God the Father and kept by Jesus Christ" (1). If this language is too strong to apply to all Christians literally, it is well to remember that the Lord assumes that all the disciples of Christ are living up to their true standard. He speaks of them all, therefore, as "loved," "kept" and "called," because all ought to be conformed to this divine standard.

To be truly sanctified is not merely to be chosen and set apart as the people of God, but to be self-surrendered and wholly dedicated to Christ, and then really filled with the Holy Spirit, cleansed from sin, and conformed to the character of Jesus Christ.

But even after this experience we still need to be "kept." No blessing takes us out of the sphere of temptation, and the Christian's attitude is one of abiding and being "kept by Jesus Christ."

The expression "called" has reference, we believe, not so much to a spiritual experience, as to the divine purpose in each life, and the special ministry and service which God has for each of His children, to which we are called as the servants of Christ and for which we are specially enabled by the enduement of the Holy Spirit.

Then follows the writer's salutation: "Mercy, peace and love be yours in abundance" (2). "Mercy" is the divine fountain of all our blessings. "Peace" is the stream that flows from that fountain. "Love" is the expression of divine fellowship toward all His redeemed children.

After this introduction the epistle naturally divides itself into the following sections:

1. Certain reference to salvation and the gospel of the Lord Jesus Christ (3).

2. Warnings against false brethren who had crept in among them and were exercising a baneful influence in the Church of God (4–13).

3. A remarkable announcement of the Lord's second coming, quoted from Enoch (14–16), coupled with warnings (17–19).

4. A beautiful exhortation to the true followers of the Lord Jesus Christ (20–21).

5. Counsels about Christian service and soul-winning (22–23).

6. A glorious doxology (24–25).

SALVATION AND THE GOSPEL

"Dear friends, although I was very eager to write to you about the salvation we share, I felt I had to write and urge you to contend for the faith that was once for all entrusted to the saints" (3).

In this remarkable passage two phrases of striking significance are used. First, he speaks of the "salvation we share." By that he means the salvation which belongs alike to Jew and Gentile and is offered to every sinner on equal terms. Its watchword is, "Whoever wishes, let him take the free gift of the water of life" (Revelation 22:17). Next, he uses the still more striking expression, "the faith that was once for all entrusted to the saints" (3). This is the meaning of the Greek word translated "once." The writer's idea is that God's word of salvation has been proclaimed once as his final word, and as the one gospel that He ever will offer to lost men. It is here described not so much as a system of truth, but rather as a faith, something to be believed. The gospel is not a theory but a faith. There is nothing in the gospel of the nature of theory, philosophy and speculation. Every word is given for faith to claim, and for love to obey. And so it is called "the faith" rather than "the creed." Beloved, have we added our faith to this Word of God, and are we standing first *upon* and then standing *for* this faith, "the faith that was once for all entrusted to the saints"?

Jude reminds them that they must "contend" for this faith. The enemy will try to destroy it, either by discrediting the Word of God, or by keeping us from fully believing it. The apostle, therefore, means that "the faith that was once for all entrusted to the saints" should be preserved in its integrity. There is no new Bible for modern times, and there is no part of the Old Bible that is obsolete. Are we believing, and living every bit of it and proving in our lives that Jesus Christ and His Word are "the same yesterday and today and forever" (Hebrews 13:8)?

WARNINGS AGAINST FALSE BROTHERS

Jude now proceeds to expose certain false brethren, whose pernicious influence is already defiling and subverting the Church. Peter had warned his readers that in the last days such mockers should come, and perhaps Jude is referring to Peter when he says, "But, dear friends, remember what the apostles of our Lord Jesus Christ foretold. They said to you, 'In the last times there will be scoffers who will follow their own ungodly desires' " (17–18). The book of Jude was evidently written after Peter, and the things which that apostle had intimated, had already come. Briefly summed up, the false teachers against whom he directs the larger portion of his epistle, were as follows:

1. Certain men had crept in unawares, and, through their personal and pernicious influence, error and sin were being communicated and circulated. The false seed consists not merely in false doctrine, but in living embodiments of it. It is error in an ungodly and wicked man which is Satan's choicest instrument of attack upon Christianity, and the adversary is always trying to sow these tares in the Lord's husbandry.

2. The particular character of their false teaching was to "change the grace of our God into a license for immorality" (4). They abused the doctrine of divine grace by proclaiming liberty to sin because of Christ's salvation. They especially encouraged and practiced the sin of moral uncleanness. Jude speaks of them again in the eighth verse as "dreamers" who "pollute their own bodies"; and in the 16th verse as "they follow their own evil desires." In the 10th verse he uses still more realistic language in describing their coarse and brutal depravity: "what things they do understand by instinct, like unreasoning animals—these are the very things that destroy them."

3. The result of their teaching and their lives is to "deny Jesus Christ our only Sovereign and Lord" (4). Elsewhere in the Scriptures we are reminded that men may confess Christ by their lips, but by their works deny Him.

4. These wicked men were also intolerant of all spiritual authority, self-willed and scornful of the restraints and the warnings of those that were over them in the Lord. They "reject authority and slander celestial beings" (8). Already, in the time of Paul, such men had risen, setting at naught his apostolic authority, ridiculing his peculiarities and infirmities, and claiming for

themselves the highest spiritual authority as equally inspired and authorized to teach and command.

These false teachers were schismatics and tried to break up the peace and harmony of the Church. "These are the men who divide you, who follow mere natural instincts and do not have the Spirit" (19). They claimed a higher sanctity and larger liberty and a loftier experience.

5. But Jude declares they "follow mere natural instincts and do not have the Spirit" (19). Now this is an unfortunate translation. The word translated "natural instincts" literally means "psychical." That is the favorite word of our modern new theologists. They claim to be psychical. They mean some higher, finer quality of ethical and spiritual life. But Jude says they did not have the Holy Spirit, but merely a human spirit. They were what might be called "soulish people." We find this type among Christian Scientists, Spiritualists and Theosophists. It is a Satanic imitation and counterfeit of the Holy Spirit. It is the devil's spirituality and not the Lord's.

6. Jude next proceeds to emphasize his warnings against these teachers by a threefold reference to God's judgments in the past, against those guilty of such errors and crimes.

> Though you already know all this, I want to remind you that the Lord delivered his people out of Egypt, but later destroyed those who did not believe. And the angels who did not keep their positions of authority but abandoned their own home—these he has kept in darkness bound with everlasting chains for judgment on the great Day. In a similar way Sodom and Gomorrah and the surrounding towns gave themselves up to sexual immorality and perversion. They serve as an example of those who suffer the punishment of eternal fire. (5–7)

First, he reminds them of God's judgments upon His own people Israel even after He saved them from the land of Egypt, when they fell into sin in the wilderness as they did on several occasions through the weakness of Aaron and the wickedness of Balaam.

Secondly, he recalls the doom of those "angels who did not keep their positions of authority," but fell into sin. The nature of their sin has been the subject of much controversy, some even alleging that they were guilty of impure and literal connection with human beings; and that it was through such vile intercourse between demons and the daughters of men in the days of Noah that the giants of that age were born, and the earth was filled with violence and sin. There is no need, however, that we should go beyond the simple statement of Jude and other Scriptures. We may simply apply this to the fall of those beings who once were holy angels, but now are demons, doomed in everlasting judgment.

Thirdly, he tells them of the destruction of Sodom and Gomorrah and the special reason for that fearful retribution; namely, the defiling of their own bodies both in natural and unnatural sins of the flesh.

7. Next, Jude gives us three types of these wicked men in the 11th verse: "Woe to them! They have taken the way of Cain; they have rushed for profit into Balaam's error; they have been destroyed in Korah's rebellion."

The first of these types is Cain, who represents the unbelieving man, the man who rejects the blood, and who presumes to approach God in his own righteousness. This is the type that is growing so common today, the men who reject the cross, dishonor the blood and go about to establish their own righteousness.

Balaam is the second type. Balaam represents the world, especially the attempt on the part of the followers of God to compromise with the world. This, too, alas, is the almost universal type of the worldly church of today.

The third type is Korah who rose up in rebellion against the authority of Moses and claimed for himself and his brethren an equal right to receive and proclaim the will of God. This is our blatant new theology, claiming that the gifted intellects of our time are just as true prophets of God as Isaiah, Paul and John.

8. Finally, Jude reaches his climax in a series of magnificent and awful metaphors, whose fiery eloquence it would be difficult to translate into ordinary speech.

> These men are blemishes at your love feasts, eating with you without the slightest qualm—shepherds who feed only themselves. They are clouds without rain, blown along by the wind; autumn trees, without fruit and uprooted—twice dead. They are wild waves of the sea, foaming up their shame; wandering stars, for whom blackest darkness has been reserved forever. (12–13)

Briefly summed up, these lurid sentences imply that these wicked men, with cool and insolent assurance, were making themselves perfectly at home in the love feasts of the Church, and presuming to make these sacred feasts occasions for their own gluttony and indulgence. The apostle compares them to empty clouds at the sport of every wind; showy trees whose luxuriant foliage bears no fruit; rolling waves of the sea frothing with the foam of their own wickedness; falling meteors which blaze out for a moment in the sky of night and then disappear in the darkness forever. God save us from any partnership with such awful examples of ungodliness, wickedness and presumption. But let us not forget that the picture belongs to the last days, and that the last days are upon us.

AN ANNOUNCEMENT OF THE SECOND COMING

"Enoch, the seventh from Adam, prophesied about these men: 'See, the Lord is coming with thousands upon thousands of his holy ones to judge everyone, and to convict all the ungodly of all the ungodly acts they have done in the ungodly way, and of all the harsh words ungodly sinners have spoken against him' " (14–15).

In an old apocryphal book called the book of Enoch, we have this prophecy almost word for word. Whether the book of Enoch has any real authority or not, no doubt the prophecy was really given and divinely revealed to Jude. He notes particularly the fact that Enoch was the seventh from Adam, as though it had some typical significance. Did it mean that in Enoch the race reached its perfect development, seven being the number of perfection? Certainly Enoch's prophecy is one of the most complete and striking revelations of the Lord's coming to be found in the holy Scriptures. And as certainly Enoch himself was made a glorious sample of the translation of the saints before the coming of the Lord.

1. He announces the Lord's coming with His saints. That is not His parousia to take away His waiting bride, but His glorious epiphany when He will come back with His saints, and judge the wicked world, and set up His millennial throne.

2. He announces the judgment which the Lord is to execute upon the ungodly. There are some striking expressions here. Not only is He to judge the wicked, but He is to convince and convict them of their wickedness, so that there shall be no answering back in that day, but every conscience shall admit its guilt, "so that every mouth may be silenced and the whole world held accountable to God" (Romans 3:19). This judgment is not for the saints, but for the wicked world. Thank God, we are saved from that by our glorious Substitute, who bore our judgment on the cross of Calvary. The coming of the Lord is here recognized in its relationship to the wicked. The saints are seen only as assessors with the Judge, and sharers in His glory and His dignity.

AN EXHORTATION TO TRUE FOLLOWERS

But now Jude turns from this painful picture of wickedness and addresses to the saints one of the sweetest and loftiest messages in all this volume of inspiration. "But you, dear friends, build yourselves up in your most holy faith and pray in the Holy Spirit. Keep yourselves in God's love as you wait for the mercy of our Lord Jesus Christ to bring you to eternal life" (Jude 20–21).

1. He bids them build themselves up in their most holy faith. The same word "faith" which we notice in the beginning of the epistle is fundamental

in Christian life and character as here portrayed. It is a process of building, but faith is the foundation of all. It is the same thought which Peter expresses in his second epistle: "For this very reason, make every effort to add to your faith goodness; and to goodness, knowledge; and to knowledge, self-control; and to self-control, perseverance; and to perseverance, godliness; and to godliness, brotherly kindness; and to brotherly kindness, love" (2 Peter 1:5–7). Christian life grows, not by adding one grace to another in our human character building, but by taking every grace directly from Jesus Christ Himself, and making each addition to the building an act of simple faith. We become complete in holiness simply by appropriating the life of Jesus, moment by moment, until He has become incarnate in all our actions and relationships.

2. Praying in the Holy Spirit (Jude 20) is the process by which our life is built up. It is a continual communion in the Spirit, a breathing out of self, a breathing in of Christ; and just as the human body grows by the exhaling of our exhausted breath and the inhaling of fresh life moment by moment, so the secret process of the soul's growth is a ceaseless fellowship with God in the Holy Spirit. Each moment brings some new need, and that need is transformed into a prayer, and that prayer into a grace, and that grace into an added element in our Christian character and life. There is not a moment in our conscious existence that we may not be thus occupied in communion, and there is not a thing that comes to us that should not be made an occasion for this unceasing habit of prayer.

3. "Keep yourselves in God's love" (21). Here we have the element in which we grow. It is a glorious tropical climate of divine love. It is ever warmed by the sunshine of His heart and illumined by the radiance of His smile. It does not mean our love to God, but it means our constant consciousness and recognition of His love to us. It is the same thought which the Lord Jesus expressed: "As the Father has loved me, so have I loved you. Now remain in my love. If you obey my commands, you will remain in my love, just as I have obeyed my Father's commands and remain in his love" (John 15:9–10).

4. The last step in this beautiful ascent is hope. "As you wait for the mercy of our Lord Jesus Christ to bring you to eternal life" (Jude 21). That means looking for the coming of our Lord and for the glory that is to be brought unto us at His appearing. It is the uplook of a spirit that is ever gazing sunward, heavenward. How beautifully Dr. Bonar has expressed it:

> My hopes are passing onward, upward,
>   And with my hopes my heart has gone;
> My eyes are turning skyward,—sunward,
>   Where glory brightens 'round yon throne.

CHRISTIAN SERVICE AND SOUL-WINNING

For a moment Jude turns his thought toward the sinner, and he gives two very practical directions for service and soul-winning. "Be merciful to those who doubt; snatch others from the fire and save them; to others show mercy, mixed with fear—hating even the clothing stained by corrupted flesh" (Jude 22–23).

First, we are to save people by compassion. We must love souls if we would win them. And surely, if we realize their danger and their need, we shall understand the compassion of which the apostle speaks. We are to have great tenderness, gentleness and love, or we shall be little used in bringing men to God.

But there are others with whom we must take a different course, and sometimes the sternest measure is the kindest. It is said that Dwight Moody was once talking with an inquirer who tried him with his indifference. Mr. Moody broke away from him, saying, "I guess God can get along without you, if you can get along without Him." And for the remaining meeting Mr. Moody paid no attention to the man. First, the man's pride was wounded, but soon his conscience was aroused; and before the meeting was over, he himself came imploring the prayers of the evangelist. Sometimes we must use messages as severe as Jude's strong language expresses, "Snatch others from the fire and save them; . . . hating even the clothing stained by corrupted flesh" (23) and, making no compromise with sin or cowardice, press the soul right through to the most real and complete confession and renunciation of all sin as the only condition of the mercy and peace of God.

A DOXOLOGY

Finally, Jude closes with this beautiful doxology: "To him who is able to keep you from falling and to present you before his glorious presence without fault and with great joy—to the only God our Savior be glory, majesty, power and authority, through Jesus Christ our Lord, before all ages, now and forevermore! Amen" (24–25).

1. He speaks of "him that is able to keep you from falling." This is an inadequate translation. Literally it means from "stumbling." He is not only able to keep us from the great falls, but from the slightest missteps. Oh, let us claim this great and wonderful grace.

2. He is "able . . . to present you before his glorious presence without fault and with great joy" (24). This is His purpose. For this end He is taking us through all processes of His grace and all the discipline of His love. Some day we shall understand and thank Him for it all. Some day we will shine forth in the kingdom of our Father even as He, "without fault" or "without blemish," which the original word literally means.

3. He is here described as "the only God our Savior." This is a glorious name, and it is given to Jesus, the Son of man, our blessed Savior. Let us adore His glorious majesty as well as love His wondrous grace.

4. To Him "be glory, majesty, power and authority, through Jesus Christ our Lord, before all ages, now and forevermore! Amen" (25).

REVELATION

PUBLISHER'S FOREWORD

For years Albert B. Simpson's *Christ in the Bible* volume covering *Revelation* has been unavailable. Even when the other books were in print, *Revelation* was not.

As you read this final volume in the series you may understand why it was not kept current. It was not simply that Simpson's view of a partial rapture ran counter to the prevailing evangelical opinion in the first half of the century. But much of Simpson's interpretation of the book was tied to increasingly obscure 19th century events unrelated to the return of Jesus Christ. It is important to realize that the views and positions expressed in this book do not necessarily constitute the views and doctrinal positions of Christian Publications or its parent denomination, The Christian and Missionary Alliance.

So why publish Simpson's *Revelation* now?

First, *Revelation* is needed to round out what many recognize as a still-significant commentary on the whole Bible. To stop one book short of the end leaves the work incomplete.

Second, Simpson readers are curious concerning his eschatological views. They are here—in detail.

Third, times have changed. Regarding the rapture, many evangelicals have returned to the historic post-tribulation view. (Simpson expected only a few believers—the "firstfruits"—to be raptured prior to the tribulation; most believers would go into that awful period.) And today's Bible students are less persuaded than those of a generation or two ago that the *Revelation* is transparently clear in detailing the future. Simpson offers another viewpoint.

Fourth—and most important—present-day readers need exposure to the warm, evangelical heart of this mighty crusader. Simpson was unashamedly in love with Jesus Christ, and he longed for His return. Simpson was concerned for a lost world of people, and he worked night and day for their evangelization. He was persuaded that world evangelization *must* precede the end-time events portrayed in *Revelation.* All of that comes through forcefully in this final commentary in Simpson's long series.

Read *Revelation* not for enlightenment concerning all of the details in the Bible's last book. Rather, read it devotionally. May you share Simpson's love for Jesus Christ and the world He died to save. May you anticipate as eagerly as he did our Lord's glorious return.

CHAPTER 1

HEAVEN OPENED

Blessed is the one who reads the words of this prophecy, and blessed are those who hear it and take to heart what is written in it. (Revelation 1:3)

Such is God's special benediction on the work in which we are about to be engaged, the study of the Apocalypse. May we hear its revelations aright; may we hear its wondrous words with quickened spiritual ears, and may we keep its warnings and commandments with holy vigilance and humble obedience; so that we will inherit this blessing in all its fullness and find this last volume of inspiration, not a scroll of vague unintelligible mystery, but a manual of spiritual and practical helpfulness, "useful for teaching, rebuking, correcting and training in righteousness" (2 Timothy 3:16).

The title of the book is deeply significant. The Apocalypse literally means, the unveiling of something covered, the unveiling of something hidden. It suggests that back of the blue firmament there is a world above which spiritual eyes may see. Beyond the narrow horizon of human sight there is a future world of living, solemn realities profoundly affecting and concerning our present life. This book lifts the mysterious veil and opens to our view those two infinities, God and eternity. Let us approach the vision with deep solemnity, with chastened spirit and humble dependence upon Him who must give the sight as well as the light.

It is commonly accepted that the book of Revelation is too mysterious for the ordinary mind to understand, and that it is scarcely practical or profitable for the study of the unskilled and unscholarly. On the contrary it is here presented to us as God's message to all His people, with a special blessing pronounced on those who read, hear and keep it. Like the whole precious Bible it is the book of the common people, and if we read it aright the Holy Spirit will make it plain to the humblest capacity and the simplest mind. Indeed a special and emphatic blessing is pronounced upon this more than any other message of the Scriptures, and if we look carefully at the character and purpose of the Apocalypse we shall perhaps be able to understand why God has promised to thus bless it.

GOD'S LAST WORD

It is God's last word to His people in the present dispensation. Sixty-six times has He spoken from heaven through His inspired messengers. This is the last message till He Himself shall come and close the dispensation. Islam claims that it has a later message. Science and philosophy lightly talk about the new light of culture and the inspiration which exalted genius gives to certain men; but all their light is as the flashing of a meteor or the firefly of the summer night. This is the final message of heaven to man, and he that dares to add another sentence to the word of inspiration will inherit the fearful curses pronounced in this awful volume. With what intense interest, with what prompt obedience, should we wait to hear God's final word as He speaks to us once more by His Son!

SPECIALLY FOR OUR TIMES

This word is God's special message to the last times. It was not written for the apostolic age, for that had passed. It was not written for the Jew, for Jerusalem had fallen. It was given to the Church and was intended for the Church to the end of the Christian age. It is especially addressed to seven churches of Asia which represent the whole body of the Church to the end. It is therefore our manual of divine instruction and commission and claims our special attention and careful obedience.

It is intimated in the very terms in which it is given that the times for which it was intended were to begin immediately and were to be most critical and momentous. It starts out with the significant statement, "The time is near" (Revelation 1:3). Literally this means the *crisis time* is at hand. It is that Greek word so specially used in the New Testament to indicate the time of peculiar privilege, opportunity and crisis. It is the same expression used when the apostle bids us "redeem the time," buy up the opportunity, make the most of the crisis. It is therefore a message written for momentous times and calling for the most careful attention and the most significant action. Well may we give heed to such a message.

CHRIST'S OWN REVELATION

More especially than any other message, it is Christ's message. It was not given through an angel merely, although angelic ministry was used in connection with it, but Jesus Christ Himself came down personally, 60 years after His ascension, to the Isle of Patmos, making a second visit to earth—after He had been more than half a century in heaven—telling with His own living voice to John the words of the Apocalypse, and was speaking in His own person to the churches for whom the message was primarily intended. It is therefore our own Master's personal message to us, the people of these last times. And we can see that face which is "like the sun shining in all its brilliance" (1:16), and hear that voice which is "like the sound of rushing waters" (1:15), as He calls to each of us: "I know your deeds" (3:8). "He who has an ear, let him hear what the Spirit says to the churches" (3:13).

AN UNSEALED VISION

The message which Daniel gave was sealed and the prophet was specially told that it was for later times and would not be understood until the end drew near. But a very different command is given to John, "Do not seal up the words of the prophecy of this book, because the time is near" (22:10). And again, "The revelation of Jesus Christ, which God gave him to show his servants what must soon take place" (1:1). This is translated literally: "Things which in swift, successive haste come to pass." The events were to begin immediately. The message of the Apocalypse is a present truth. The Church needs it. The world should know it. The action is suited to the word. The vision becomes a swift reality. The panorama is already moving on to its final consummation: "Write down the revelation/ and make it plain on tablets/ so that a herald may run with it" (Habakkuk 2:2). It means action, preparation and cooperation with God, and it is fitted to inspire and encourage in the trials and tests that we are called to meet, and to prove as practical as it is sublime.

GOD'S PICTURE OF THE ASCENDED CHRIST

This book gives a view of the Lord Jesus Christ as He is now in the heavenly world and on the throne. In the other books of the Bible, except the epistles, we see Him either coming or already present in the world; but here we behold Him in His glory as our Prophet, Priest and King, administering the government of the age, representing His people at God's right hand and preparing for His coming. Would we see Jesus as God's enthroned Lamb? Would we see Him in His almightiness and gentleness? Would we see Him as our Great High Priest presenting the incense of our prayers before the Father? Would we see Him in His victorious power silencing our accusers and pleading our cause? Would we see Him making all His enemies His footstool and coming in His glory soon to reign? Let us read this prophecy and hear the words that are written in it, and in its sublime visions behold the Lamb of God, to whom it is specially dedicated in the opening paragraph, "To him who loves us and has freed us from our sins by his blood, and has made us to be a kingdom and priests to serve his God and Father—to him be glory and power for ever and ever! Amen" (Revelation 1:5–6).

GOD'S THOUGHT FOR HIS CHURCH

It contains God's highest, latest and largest thought for the Church. It is specially addressed to the Church. It reveals Christ's attitude to the Church, and it unfolds the Church's attitude to Christ and her innermost condition in the light of His searching eye. In this symbolic book the Lord appears standing in the midst of the seven golden lamps and holding the seven stars in His right hand. He is intensely real to His Church and intensely interested in all that concerns her. He is watching her spirit and weighing her character every moment. He knows her works and deals with her in faithful discipline and stern and awful warning, as well as in loving and gracious promise and reward. There is no book more fitted to arouse a slumbering Church, to search and separate a worldly Church, to comfort His suffering Church, and to awaken the ministry of the Church to a more profound sense of responsibility to God, than these seven letters of the ascended Lord to the seven churches of Asia, and through them to the Church of every century.

As we shall see, these letters present a panorama of the whole Church from the apostolic age to the end of time. They show her in all her various developments of busy activity, of spiritual declension, of martyr suffering, of terrible apostasy, of reformation and revival, and finally of the lukewarmness of our Laodicean times, when the Lord is standing knocking outside the door of His own Church and just about to come in judgment and glory. If we would understand the history and the state of the Church of Christ and know how to be true to God amid all the alarming conditions of these last times, let us study this book and give heed to its faithful warnings.

GOD'S THOUGHT FOR THE WORLD

This book gives to us God's thought about the world we live in, as well as the Church; for after the vision of the churches we have the seals and the trumpets, the thunders and the vials and the seven-headed beast embodying in symbol the governments of earth and the Satanic power behind them. Man looks upon earth's kings with something of splendor and luster. To God's mind they are wild beasts ravening and devouring.

In varied symbolism their power, their wickedness, their Satanic origin and their awful doom are here portrayed. And their end is the winepress of the wrath of God and the battle of Armageddon, the judgment of the nations and the new kingdom of peace and righteousness with Christ alone as Lord.

If we would understand our age, if we would comprehend the mingled events of providence, if we would know the utter corruption of human politics, and the necessity of being separated from the world, and living as "aliens and strangers on earth" (Hebrews 11:13), "longing for a better country—a heavenly one" (11:16), let us read this book, let us hear the things that are written in it, and let us walk on earth with our heads and hearts in heaven.

GOD'S PROGRAM FOR THE FUTURE

This book contains God's plan for earth's future. Men are talking about the future of the country. They are writing their stocks and bonds for the 20th century. They are dreaming of the marvelous things that the new gospel of science is to bring. They have their utopian schemes, republicanism and liberty, but God's plan for the future is very different. It is like Zechariah's wondrous day: "A unique day, without daytime or nighttime—a day known to the LORD. When evening comes, there will be light" (Zechariah 14:7). Through clouds and darkness one purpose moves through all the ages; namely, the coming of the Lord Jesus Christ, earth's promised King.

This is the key of history. This is the solution of every mystery. This is the goal of providence. This is the great consummation to which the Apocalypse and the ages move. "I saw heaven standing open and there before me was a white horse, whose rider is called Faithful and True" (Revelation 19:11). "On his robe and on his thigh he has this name written:/ KING OF KINGS AND LORD OF LORDS" (19:16). "Look, he is coming with the clouds,/ and every eye will see him" (1:7). "Amen. Come, Lord Jesus" (22:20).

PRACTICAL VALUE

This book is not visionary though it is the grandest of visions, but it is intensely practical.

1. Tells of Salvation

It tells us of salvation. There is no new gospel here of second probation, or bloodless theology; but sin is as crimson as God can stamp it, and the blood of Jesus Christ is as real as the stain of sin, and the echo of every chorus is, "Salvation belongs to our God,/ who sits on the throne,/ and to the Lamb" (7:10).

2. Tells of Deeper Life

It tells us of a deeper spiritual life. It warns us against the loss of our first love. It rouses us from the curse of lukewarmness. It points us to the souls that are to enter in as the firstfruits and the wedding guests, and "no lie was found in their mouths; they are blameless" (14:5). "They follow the Lamb wherever he goes" (14:4). It connects the most holy watchfulness with the hope of His coming and it tells us how the spotless robe can be obtained.

"His bride has made herself ready./ Fine linen, bright and clean,/ was given her to wear./ (Fine linen stands for the righteous acts of the saints.)" (19:7–8).

3. Calls to Highest Service

It calls to highest service. Its promises are "to him who overcomes" (2:7). It sets before us "an open door" (3:8) and its rewards are for those that hold fast to His truth and hold forth His name. The rewards of His coming are according to our works. We behold among its living scenes the figure of an "angel flying in midair, and he had the eternal gospel to proclaim to those who live on the earth—to every nation, tribe, language and people" (14:6); and we see in this the symbol of the great missionary movement in our times and the call to worldwide evangelization.

4. A Message of Comfort and Hope

It is a message of comfort and hope to the suffering and the sorrowing. It offers to the martyr a crown of life. It offers to the overcomer a sevenfold promise. It tells the mourner of a time when all tears will be wiped away. It points the wanderer and the exile to a land where there will be no more sea. The poor are reminded that some day they will hunger no more, neither thirst any more; but their home will be a city of gold with palaces surpassing the glory of the sun. The sick learn that soon there will be no more pain, sorrow, crying, death. And the souls that are sick of sin and the horrid spectacle of the "open city" and the prostitution of virtue and innocence rejoice to know that in that city "nothing impure will ever enter it, nor will anyone who does what is shameful or deceitful" (21:27). All will be right at last. God's remedy will be mightier than man's ruin. "Where sin increased, grace increased all the more" (Romans 5:20), and earth and heaven and all the far-off universe will yet unite around the throne to echo the universal chorus: "Praise and glory/ and wisdom and thanks and honor/ and power and strength/ be to our God for ever and ever./ Amen" (Revelation 7:12).

But there is no evasion of the darker facts of sin and hell. Over against the vision of glory there is the awful judgment and the eternal abyss; and the last word of the Apocalypse, like the vision of Christ weeping over Jerusalem, is an intense and loving appeal from One whose judgment is as inexorable as His mercy is infinite, and who cannot save unless we believe and obey Him. "The Spirit and the bride say, 'Come!' And let him who hears say, 'Come!' Whoever is thirsty, let him come; and whoever wishes, let him take the free gift of the water of life" (22:17).

CHAPTER 2

CHRIST IN THE APOCALYPSE

To him who loves us and has freed us from our sins by his blood,
and has made us to be a kingdom and priests to serve his God and
Father—to him be glory and power for ever and ever! Amen.
(Revelation 1:5–6)

The testimony of Jesus is the spirit of prophecy, so Christ is the theme as well as the Author of the book of Revelation. It gives us the picture of our enthroned Redeemer as John beheld Him in the heavens 60 years after His ascension. It is therefore the picture of Christ as He is today, and possesses a present and profound interest for every Christian heart. Let us gather up the scattered rays and focus them into a living picture of our glorious Redeemer.

JESUS AS DIVINE
We behold our blessed Redeemer all through this apocalyptic vision in the glory of the Son of God. "His face was like the sun shining in all its brilliance" (Revelation 1:16). "His voice was like the sound of rushing waters" (1:15). From His face the earth and heaven flee away. He sits upon the judgment throne and the kings of the earth call upon the rocks and the mountains to hide them from the wrath of the Lamb. He is in the midst of the throne of deity and all the universe worships Him jointly with the Father ascribing "to him who sits on the throne and to the Lamb/ be praise and honor and glory and power" (5:13). He is the King of kings and Lord of lords, the divine and eternal Word of God.

JESUS AS HUMAN
But nonetheless do we see Him as the Son of man. It is the same Jesus who lived and loved, suffered and died on earth. He uses the same old phrase in speaking to John the beloved that He used once on the Sea of Galilee to calm the disciples' fears. When John fell at His feet as dead He

415

gently lifted him by the hand and said in the old sweet phrase, "Do not be afraid. I am the First and the Last. I am the Living One; I was dead, and behold I am alive" (1:17–18). Amid all the glories of heaven, could you look through the open door which John saw, you would behold a Man in the midst of the throne and in control of all the governments of the universe and all the destinies of men.

JESUS AS CRUCIFIED

There is no compromise about the theology of the Apocalypse. There is no attempt to evade the literal meaning of the cross and the atonement. The central figure of the heavenly court is "a Lamb, looking as if it had been slain" (5:6). The marks of Calvary are worn without disguise or shame. They are the very glory of our exalted Lord. It is not as the Lion of the tribe of Judah so much as the Lamb, with the memorials of suffering, that He has power to loose the seals and open the book of destiny and set in operation all the procession of events that lead to the coming glory. The opening tribute of the beloved apostle is "To him who loves us and has freed us from our sins by his blood" (1:5). The description of the ransomed and the glorified is this: "They have washed their robes and made them white in the blood of the Lamb. Therefore, 'they are before the throne of God' " (7:14–15). The chorus of the heavenly hosts is this, "Worthy is the Lamb, who was slain,/ to receive power and wealth and wisdom and strength/ and honor and glory and praise!" (5:12). "You are worthy to take the scroll/ and to open its seals,/ because you were slain,/ and with your blood you purchased men for God/ from every tribe and language and people and nation" (5:9).

In one of the closing passages of this sublime book, the lower criticism tried for ages to eliminate the language of the cross and introduce a text which might support their foundation for human salvation. In Revelation 22:14, the former reading, "Blessed are they that do His commandments that they might have right to the tree of life and enter through the gates into the city," has been happily restored to the original text, "Blessed are those who wash their robes, that they may have the right to the tree of life and may go through the gates into the city." This book opens no other door, reveals no other right of way, and speaks no other message of salvation than the blood of the Lamb.

JESUS AS THE RISEN AND THE LIVING ONE

The very second name given to our blessed Lord in the Apocalypse is the "firstborn from the dead" (1:5). He comes to us in this vision not in the nature of the first but the second Adam; not as the Christ of Judea and Galilee now, but as the Christ of the open grave, the 40 days and the heavenly glory. He comes as the great Author and Leader of a new race, men that have passed through death with Him and entered into the resurrection life. This is not the book of the old creation, but of the new. The only pathway to it is the rent veil of the flesh, and the only passport is to "know Christ and the power of his resurrection and the fellowship of sharing in his sufferings, becoming like him in his death" (Philippians 3:10). The inheritance revealed in this Apocalypse is for those who, like their Leader, have been begotten from the dead and entered upon a resurrection life, dead to self and sin through the power of the Savior's cross and blood.

JESUS AS OUR GREAT PROPHET

The very first name by which He stands revealed in the Apocalypse is "Jesus Christ, who is the faithful witness" (Revelation 1:5). We find this again quoted in His address to the church of Laodicea, the last of His messages to the churches, written to an age when men are questioning the authority of the Scriptures and the messages of Christ. He stands revealed as the Truth as well as the Life—God's supreme, authoritative and final Messenger of His will to man. He is our great Teacher, the Light of the world, the Author and Finisher of our faith, and once more in this book God "has spoken to us by his Son" (Hebrews 1:2). Let us "pay more careful attention, therefore, to what we have heard, so that we do not drift away" (2:1).

JESUS AS OUR GREAT HIGH PRIEST

The Apocalypse reveals our blessed Lord in the very array and form of the Jewish priesthood. He stands before us in the opening vision on the Isle of Patmos arrayed in the priestly garment and wearing the girdle of priestly service. And later on in the apocalyptic vision we behold Him in the eighth chapter as the mighty Angel who stood over the altar having the golden censer and much incense that He should add it unto the prayers of all the saints upon the golden altar which was before the throne. It is He who represents us at the Father's side. It is He who takes our prayers, mingles with them the incense of His merits and His influence and secures their efficacy and their answer, and fills the censer with fire from the altar and then pours it back again upon the earth in the mighty results that come from believing prayer in Jesus' name. "Since we have a great high priest who has gone through the heavens, Jesus the Son of God, let us hold firmly to the faith we profess," (4:14) and "let us then approach the throne of grace with confidence, so that we may receive mercy and find grace to help us in our time of need" (4:16).

JESUS AS THE LORD OF PROVIDENCE

We behold Him not only as the Priest but as a King. First He is our mediatorial King. He sits at the right hand of God administering the government of the world and exercising that authority and dominion by the right of His accomplished redemption. Therefore it is He who looses the seals and opens the book of destiny. It is He who orders and arranges the events of providence. It is He who plans the life of every believer. "God exalted him to his own right hand as Prince and Savior" (Acts 5:31). He is the Lord of all and our Lord, Head over all things for His body, the Church, and sitting on His throne and from henceforth expecting until all His enemies are made His footstool. Nothing happens without His permission. Nothing is to Him a surprise or an insuperable obstacle. He is turning and overturning and preparing His kingdom amid all the vicissitudes and convulsions which distract the ages and often perplex the hearts of the saints. Christ is on the throne and we may trust His wisdom, power and love.

JESUS AS THE KING OF THE NATIONS

He is specially referred to in this book as the Prince of the kings of the earth (Revelation 1:5). He wears upon His vesture and upon His thigh the name "KING OF KINGS AND LORD OF LORDS" (19:16). He is earth's true sovereign. Not only is He now ruling over the domain of providence but He is yet to rule over the earth, in view of all the nations and with the submission of every throne and tribe and tongue. He is earth's coming King and earth never will be at rest until He reigns supreme and universal Lord of lords.

JESUS AS THE KING OF ISRAEL

He is here revealed as the Lion of the tribe of Judah, the One who has the right to wear upon His escutcheon the arms of David and Judah. He is the Root and Offspring of David. Thus He is at once his Progenitor and Heir. David but represented Him upon Israel's throne, and He is yet to sit there as David's natural Heir. He "holds the key of David. What he opens, no one can shut, and what he shuts no one can open" (3:7). Very clearly does Israel's future destiny shine out through the lurid clouds of the Apocalypse and the coming age for which her children wait when her King again will sit on Mount Zion, on David's throne.

JESUS AS THE KING OF THE SAINTS AND THE HEAD OF THE CHURCH

Very specially is this aspect of His enthroned life emphasized in the Apocalypse. He reveals Himself as the One who walks amid the seven golden lampstands which are the seven churches. He claims the supreme authority and control over His Church. Very searching is the light of His omniscience and omnipresence; very high is the standard of holiness, faithfulness and watchfulness which He claims from her; very solemn are the warnings and rebukes which He addresses to the unfaithful, the lukewarm and the lifeless. "I know your deeds" (3:15), He is saying over and over again. He is quick to perceive the declension of the life of Ephesus and to warn her of her impending judgment. His searching glance instantly detects the depths of Satan in Thyatira. He cannot be deceived by Laodicea's riches and pretensions. He knows that her heart is lukewarm and He is ready to spew her out of His mouth because she is neither cold nor hot. He is as quick to appreciate the faithfulness of Smyrna and Philadelphia and the "few people in Sardis who have not soiled their clothes" (3:4).

Oh, how heart-searching His flaming eye and His consuming Word! He is walking among the churches. He is sitting in every audience and listening to the preacher, and He is passing through every prayer meeting and feeling its pulse; He is present at every business council and general assembly and judging of the faithfulness or worldliness of His people. He will accept but gold tried in the fire, and when His people meet Him their works shall be tried with fire, and only that which is divine and God-touched can pass the solemn scrutiny of the judgment seat of Christ. Let us deeply realize the solemn significance of Christ's presence and sovereignty over His Church and His own people.

JESUS AS OUR COMING LORD

It is needless to say that this is the one burden of all the book, the one outlook of all its visions, the one solution of all its mysteries, the key of history, the goal of the ages, the blessed hope of the Church and the saint. "Look, he is coming with the clouds" (1:7), is its opening message. "Yes, I am coming soon" (22:20), is its parting word. Maranatha might well be its motto, "Even so" (22:20, KJV), the amen of His people's response.

JESUS AS THE LIGHT AND GLORY OF HEAVEN

Many a beautiful vision is given in the Apocalypse of the heavenly city, both as it is today and as it will be when all tears are wiped away and all the ransomed will have been gathered home. But amid all the visions and all the ages, the central thought is ever this, "For the Lamb at the center of the throne will be their shepherd;/ he will lead them to springs of living water" (7:17). "They will not need the light of a lamp or the light of the sun, for the Lord God will give them light" (22:5). To be with Jesus, to be like Jesus—this is heaven.

JESUS AS THE LOVER OF HIS PEOPLE

"To him who loves us" (1:5) is its opening ascription. This glorious Christ, this Lord of heaven and Lord of earth, this Christ is our beloved Lord and everlasting Friend, "Having loved his own who were in the world, he now showed them the full extent of his love" (John 13:1). Amid all the glories of heaven His heart is ever upon us and His love to us can never grow old; and as sometimes amid the royal pageant a little child will leap from the arms of its nurse to the bosom of the queen, before whose majesty all others bow, so amid all the grandeur of His throne, John can still lean upon His breast and you and I can look up into His face and sing

> Jesus, Lover of my soul,
> Let me to Thy bosom fly.

JESUS AS THE LOVER OF SINNERS AND SAVIOR OF THE LOST

The last picture of Jesus Christ in the Apocalypse is one of tender compassion and infinite mercy to the unsaved. Bending from His throne above, before the hour of judgment strikes and the awful realities of this vision begin to be fulfilled, He cries in the one last invitation which seems to condense into deeper and tenderer meaning all that He ever said before. "Let him who hears say, 'Come!' Whoever is thirsty, let him come" (Revelation 22:17). And as if He would make it easier still, "whoever wishes, let him take the free gift of the water of life" (22:17).

CHAPTER 3

THE VISION OF THE CHURCHES

He who has an ear, let him hear what the Spirit says to the churches.
(Revelation 2:7)

There is something very touching and solemn about the personal aspect of the Lord's last messages to the churches. It is very much the same as if your pastor should arise in the pulpit some Sunday morning and say, "I have a letter from the Lord Jesus, which He sent an Angel to deliver to me during the night, addressed particularly to this congregation, and which He has commissioned me to read to you as His personal and final message."

Such a message would produce a profound impression and thrill every hearer with a deep concern and holy earnestness.

Each of these epistles is really a letter from the Lord Jesus to a particular church, and the fact that they were addressed to the seven churches of Asia does not make them the less personal and appropriate for us, for the very fact of the number seven being used shows that it is symbolic and designed to represent every church in the whole body of Christ to the end of the age.

The order in which these churches are named represents an exact geographical line, so that a messenger starting out with seven letters to deliver would naturally begin at Ephesus, then go to Smyrna, and thence in turn to Pergamum, Thyatira, Sardis, Philadelphia and end at Laodicea. They were selected from the great body of the churches at the time, to represent every particular congregation and the whole Church of Jesus Christ throughout the Christian age.

We have already seen that the Apocalypse begins with the vision of the Lord Jesus Christ Himself in His ascended glory as our Prophet, Priest and King. It next proceeds to the vision of the churches and then passes on to the providential dealings of God with the world, as Christ cannot deal with the world in judgment till He has first dealt with His Church. He is Head over all things in the realm of nature and providence; but He is the Head of the Church which is His body, and He governs the world with sole reference to His own people. Therefore the vision of the Church must precede the vision of the world. In this vision we have

SEVEN TYPES OF CHURCH LIFE AND CHARACTER

These seven churches represent different classes of ecclesiastical assemblies and Christian congregations. Each picture is unique and strongly marked, and we shall have no difficulty in finding its counterpart among the churches of today.

1. An Active and Orthodox Church

We have in Ephesus the picture of an active and orthodox church. But it is a church whose love and spiritual life are already on the decline and which is more marked by outward organization, religious activity, Christian work and great zeal for denominational truth than for simple fervor and deep spirituality. "I know your deeds" (Revelation 2:2), He says to Ephesus, for she is chiefly characterized by works: "your hard work" (2:2), and that is more than works, it is hard works; "and your perseverance" (2:2), it is continued work.

There are manifold agencies of Christian usefulness in this church. It has every kind of society, from a sewing society and an entertainment committee up to a foreign mission board. It is like a hive of ceaseless industry and busy work. Then it is thoroughly loyal to the denomination and the truth. It has no use for heresies or lax views of doctrine. The ring of the pulpit is true to the old theology and specially true to the denominational standards, for He says, "I know that you cannot tolerate wicked men, that you have tested those who claim to be apostles but are not, and have found them false" (2:2).

All this is well, but, alas, there is a worm at the core! There is a skeleton in the heart of this church. But there is even more. "Yet I hold this against you: You have forsaken your first love" (2:4). This does not merely mean the fervor of the early experience of Christian enthusiasm. This may change to a soberer but not less spiritual tone; He means supreme love to Christ, the love that puts Him first; for this Christ will take no substitute or excuse. This is one of the most serious dangers of our time, to substitute orthodoxy and activity for spiritual life, and it will most surely lead, as at Ephesus, to decay and final extinction.

2. A Blameless Church

The next picture is very different. It is a blameless church. The Lord has nothing but praise for Smyrna. The very name means myrrh, sweetness, fragrance. This is the suffering church, persecuted for its fidelity to Christ. It is unpopular, severely tried in the furnace of affliction; but the pressure which brings out the myrrh and the suffering becomes the means of deeper sanctity and holy sweetness. How often we find some little flock that has been sorely tried and forced to maintain itself in the face of constant difficulty, opposition and even persecution, held by its very sufferings closer to the Lord.

3. A Worldly Church

The next picture is the opposite. It is a worldly church. Prosperity has come in the place of trial. It dwells where Satan has his seat, and Satan's seat is the throne of the world. It has influence, wealth, fashion, culture and every earthly advantage on its side; and the result is compromise, fellowship with the unfruitful works of darkness, the banquet, the festival, worldly and forbidden pleasure, licentiousness, the doctrines of the Nicolaitans which allow looseness of life along with a high profession, and the more dangerous doctrine of Balaam, which, failing to destroy the people by open attack, seduced them into unholy alliances with the people of the world. And so we find this church at the theater, at the dance, and celebrating the mixed marriages of its daughters with the men of the world, and aping the attractions of social entertainment and even of the very stage itself to draw the crowd to its door. Of course it is popular. Of course it draws. Of course wealth and culture and fashion throng its aisles and pews, but Christ says, "Repent therefore! Otherwise, I will soon come to you and will fight against them with the sword of my mouth" (2:16).

4. A Corrupt Church

The next picture is the corrupt church. It is Thyatira. It is also full of works: "I know your deeds, your love and faith, your service and perseverance, and that you are now doing more than you did at first" (2:19). The farther its heart gets from God the busier its hands become in the activities of ritualism. But at the heart the leaven of corruption has long been working, and its leading type is "that woman Jezebel" (2:20), the old sorceress of Sidonia who teaches its people to commit fornication and to sacrifice unto idols. In its secret councils are found "Satan's so-called deep secrets" (2:25).

This verse reveals a whole world of subtle sophistry and unholy spiritualism. It is that false mysticism that calls good evil and evil good; which cloaks wickedness under the guise of spiritual leading; which commits sin in the very name of the Holy Spirit, and which claims indulgences for the grossest violations of right by simply performing some religious penance or paying some high price for a mass or indulgence. It is not hard to find this type in the story of Roman Catholicism, Ritualism and Spiritualism.

5. Utter Spiritual Death

We now reach an advanced type of this downward grade. It is the church of Sardis which represents utter spiritual death. It is a dead church. It still has a great name to live, but it is dead. There is no conscience that you can appeal to. There is no sense of fear or shame. It has sunk into carelessness and formalism and is like the poetic picture of the ship at sea, frozen stiff on the Arctic Ocean with a dead man standing at the helm and a dead man on the bridge and a dead man at every post while the ship drifts on as usual on her course. So many a church is moving through the age with a dead man in the pulpit, and dead men in the pews and dead men in the committee rooms, living by a kind of momentum given to it long ago when in a state of life and fulfilling like an automaton the law of habit without the power of a true spiritual life.

6. The Revival Church

But now there is a sudden and delightful change. The church of Philadelphia is the revival church. Here all is different. There is life and loyalty to Christ. It is a feeble church: "You have little strength" (3:8). But it is true to His Word, His Name, His work. We have seen such churches that seem to be strong in proportion to their natural weakness and blessed just because they have nothing to depend upon but God.

7. The Lukewarm Church

But once again the picture changes and the church of Laodicea represents the lukewarm church. Here all is moderatism, respectability and ease. It is self-satisfied, delightfully estimable, and free from all extravagances and extremes. Thoroughly adjusted to the spirit of the age; but to Christ it is simply offensive and intolerable, and He is about to reject it as a nauseous and disgusting drug, and rescue from its midst the few faithful ones that are willing to be true.

Such are the seven types of the Church life to be found in every age, and found in the more objectionable forms more frequently today than ever before.

SEVEN PROPHETIC ERAS

These seven churches of Asia represent not only the various phases of Church life but successive epochs of Christianity. The progression is so true to life that we cannot doubt that the Lord was giving a designed forecast of the conditions of His Church from that period to the end of the age. A glance at the inspired picture and the corresponding chapter of Church history can leave no doubt in any candid mind of the striking and complete resemblance.

1. The Apostolic Age

The church in Ephesus represented the condition of things in the Apostolic Age. Then the Church was in the meridian of her prosperity, full of activity and zealous for the truth. But already we find traces in the apostolic writings indicating that her spirit was beginning to decline. Paul was compelled to declare in his second epistle to Timothy that all who were in Asia had turned away from him; and even John complained in one of the latest epistles that he had written to the Church that Diotrephes who loved the preeminence had refused to receive him. The old apostles had become obsolete in the more cultivated and progressive age of prosperity, and the Church had already left her first love.

2. The Age of Persecution

This was followed by the age of persecution, represented by the church of Smyrna. The 10 days of persecution which the apostle speaks of may perhaps refer to the 10 great persecutions of the first three centuries. Certainly we know that this was the second chapter of Christian history, and it was a very terrible one. But in the furnace of affliction the Church became separated from the world, purified and deepened in her spiritual life and power.

3. The Age of Pergamum

Then came the next transition, the Age of Pergamum, the age of prosperity and worldly power and influence on the part of Christ's people. Constantine, the great emperor of Rome, became a Christian on the eve of his most signal victory and, immediately after his accession to the throne, Christianity was proclaimed the religion of the state and of the world and the first great Christian emperor summoned the followers of the once despised Christ to gather together at Nice for the first great Council of the age. It was a strange sight to see men come together from dens and caves of the earth—many of them doubtless scarred and partly dismembered, bearing the marks of hideous suffering. It was a strange sight for them to see the symbol of the cross and the banner of the empire side by side, and the mighty ruler of the world standing up as the presiding officer of the great Council, and leading that vast multitude to the feet of Jesus Christ in reverent worship.

Immediately the great heathen temples were transformed into Christian sanctuaries. Priests, presbyters and bishops were elevated to be princes and councilors of state, and it became true that the Church dwelt where Satan's seat was, the imperial throne. Then came the state banquets, the eating of things sacrificed to idols, the mixture of the people of God with the world, and the baneful effects that Balaam brought of old in the corruption of Israel. The Church fell through her very prosperity, and leaning on the arm of flesh forgot the simplicity and singleness of her consecration to God.

4. The Apostate Age

It was not long before the more fearful condition of Thyatira followed that of Pergamum. Close upon the heels of the world always comes the devil, and the depths of Satan followed quickly the worldliness of Pergamum. This is the picture of the rise of the Papacy with its manifold superstitions and deep corruptions. "That woman Jezebel" (2:20), who stands out from the picture of Thyatira as the central figure, is the appropriate type of the Apostate Church, the harlot of revelation, the corruptor of the ages.

5. The Middle Ages

In due time this is followed by the condition of Sardis, the dead church, the darkness and settled apostasy of the Middle Ages. This is the picture of Sardis and this was the state of the Church of Rome and most of the churches of Christendom for well nigh a thousand years. There were a few exceptions: "a few people in Sardis" (3:4); such men as Wycliffe, Huss, Cranmer and Luther who had not "soiled their clothes" (3:4), but who were living in protest against the evils of their time.

6. A Bright and Glorious Age

Suddenly we come to a bright and glorious age. It is the church of Philadelphia and it corresponds to the Church of the Reformation. The features of this church are very distinct. The very name suggests brotherly love. It is not a strong church. "You have little strength" (3:8). It is always in the minority with God. It is particularly noted for its devotion to the Word of God. "You have kept my word" (3:8). This was the banner and the armor of the Reformation Church. It emancipated the Bible and made that Bible the terror of the Apostate Church.

It is next marked by its devotion to the name of Jesus. The person of Christ is exalted. It is not so much a denomination, a church, as the Christ to whom all the life of the Church should ever crystallize and who should stand like Saul, head and shoulders above every organization, every leader, every man. It is marked also by an open door, a faithful service and a glorious work for God.

Now at this point it is well to observe that while these different churches represent special eras of history yet they run on through the next era to the end of the chapter like seven rivers running into one great central stream, each distinct and yet all flowing on together to the end. This is the conception of the panorama of the Apocalypse. Therefore, the church of Philadelphia does not end where Laodicea begins but runs on through the period to the close.

It is remarkable that this church is characterized by one other feature; namely, it is a pre-millennial church. It expects the Lord's coming. It is holding fast its testimony and trust, that no man take its crown, while the Master whispers, "Yes, I am coming soon," (22:20) and promises that this church will be kept from the hour of tribulation which is to come upon the face of the whole earth. Therefore it reaches on to the coming of the Lord Jesus Christ and gathers into it the Bride of the Lamb, educating her and preparing her for His glorious appearing. But before the end another development of the organized church appears upon the stage.

7. The Modern Church

The church of the Laodiceans represents the apostasy of Protestantism and the liberal movement which is starting out in these last days from a true center but is developing and is yet to develop toward the end the worst features of the false church movements of the past. It is the blending of the spirit of Ephesus with the worldliness of Pergamum, the corruptions of Thyatira and the deadness of Sardis.

The first striking feature of this modern church is that it is no longer recognized by Christ as His Church but as "the Church of the Laodiceans." It belongs to them. They have made it after their pattern and for their pleasure. The Lord will have none of it, but stands outside its door calling for those who will yet escape to receive Him and be ready for His coming. This is the second sad characteristic of it—that Christ is outside. He is represented as standing and knocking, and it is not usual for one to knock inside the door. This is a Christian church, but is so full of itself and the world that it has no room for the Lord within. We cannot call this an ideal picture when we remember the statements made by many of the leading teachers of modern Christianity to the effect that it is not necessary to believe in the blood of Christ or the divinity of the Savior to be a true Christian.

Another characteristic of this church is its wealth, its prosperity, its popularity, and its utter self-complacency. The very name Laodicea means to "please the people," and it certainly is quite pleased with itself, for its language is: "I am rich; I have acquired wealth and do not need a thing" (3:17).

But its most marked feature is its utter indifference. It is too respectable to go to any religious extreme. A "hallelujah" is not heard within its courts and any undue earnestness and intensity of feeling is regarded as bad form, fanaticism or sensationalism. It is gauged exactly to suit the people. It apes the attractions of the theaters and yet takes good care to close its services in time to let its members go to the opera if they want to after the prayer meeting. It has studied out well the old maxim, "Be not righteous overmuch." It takes good care to keep religion in its place on Sunday mornings and not allow it to infringe upon the week's business, society or pleasure. It is a thoroughly comfortable, easygoing, selfish and fashionable religious club, and the Lord has become so sick of it that He is about to spit it out of His mouth as a loathsome and offensive nuisance. It has at last reached the stage where He refuses to recognize it as His Church at all. He has gone to live with the little flock at Philadelphia, and He has said to proud Laodicea as she pursues her self-complacent way without Him: "Look, your house is left to you desolate."

A CHURCH WITHIN THE CHURCH

All through these letters we behold a third picture. It is a little minority in each of these corrupt churches to whom the Lord speaks His words of gracious promise and approval. There are some of them in Pergamum. There are some of them in Thyatira. There are some even in Sardis who have not defiled their garments, and He is trying to gather some of them even out of Laodicea; and, while He does not expect the Church to reform, He is rescuing the individual believers who are willing to hear His voice and meet His claims. Two things characterize these:

1. Know God's Voice

They are described as, "He who has an ear, let him hear what the Spirit says to the churches" (2:29). They are the men and women that know the voice of God and are hearkening to His voice and meeting His call.

2. Overcomers

They are described as, "Him who overcomes" (2:26). The word in the Greek is more significant still. *The conqueror* would be a more expressive translation. They are men and women who have gone in for victory in an Apostate Age over both the sufferings and seductions that surround them. And whatever others do, as for them they will be true and win the victor's crown.

Now it is most remarkable and solemn that in these epistles, and especially in the last one, the Lord seems to have abandoned the hope of saving the Church as a whole and is seeking now to save the individual. The whole body has become hopelessly corrupt and the remnant alone are to be saved. This was the case in the closing days of the Old Testament when God had to turn from Israel and Judah to Daniel, Ezekiel, Nehemiah and the faithful ones and twos of that last time. So it will be in the end of the age. We do not say that that hour has yet come in the history of the Church, but it is coming and we may well prepare for it. Sometimes it seems very near. The last days are to show how much God can accomplish by consecrated individuals who will utterly believe in Him and wholly obey Him. We will never see a single perfect church on earth till the Lord comes. The Church is but a scaffolding on which He is building the unseen temple which is yet to rise with the jeweled walls and pearly gates of the new Jerusalem. Each of us may be a stone; and the Lord is calling us one by one to hear His voice, to open the door to receive Him, to overcome and sit with Him on His throne.

THE RELATION AND THE REVELATION OF THE LORD JESUS TO THE CHURCHES

Christ's attitude toward these various forms of church life is very distinctly revealed and very solemnly significant.

1. Holds Their Ministers

He holds their ministers in His hands controlling, protecting, directing. Oh, faithful minister of Christ, He holds you by the hand. What have you to fear? Oh, brother, He holds your brother's hand. Be careful how you wrong him by a word or act of wrong.

2. Walks in the Midst

He walks in the midst of the churches. He is always present continually in the midst of His people. He listens to every sermon; He looks at every entertainment. He is in touch with all our busy lives.

3. Searches and Inspects

He searches and inspects His churches with eyes like a flame of fire. He is looking at us through and through, and He is ever saying: "I know your deeds"; for He judges. How heart-thrilling are the words in which He speaks of His discipline toward His unfaithful people. "Repent," He cries to Ephesus, or "I will come to you and remove your lampstand from its place" (2:5). "Repent," He cries to Pergamum, or "I will soon come to you and will fight against [you] with the sword of my mouth" (2:16). "Repent," He cries to Thyatira, or "I will cast her on a bed of suffering, and I will make those who commit adultery with her suffer intensely, unless they repent of their ways. I will strike her children dead" (2:22–23). "Repent," He cries to Sardis, or "I will come like a thief, and you will not know at what time I will come to you" (3:3). And to Laodicea he cries "Those whom I love I rebuke and discipline. So be earnest, and repent" (3:19). "Repent or I will spit you out of my mouth" (see 3:16).

This is no weak and effeminate Christ. This is no sentimental and indulgent Being against whom we can sin with impunity, but this is the stern heart-searching and mighty God who will render unto everyone according to his works.

We must also notice the names and titles under which He reveals Himself to these churches. They correspond exactly with the state of the church. To

Ephesus, He is the One who holds the seven stars in His right hand and walks in the midst of the seven golden lampstands (2:1). To suffering and martyred Smyrna, He is the One "who died and came to life again" (2:8), and for whom death has no terrors. To compromising Pergamum who needed the separating sword, He is the One that has the sharp sword (2:12). To Thyatira with her subtle deceitfulness, He is the One whose eyes are a flame of fire and whose glance no imposture can deceive (2:18). To dead Sardis, He is the One that has the seven spirits of life (3:1), able to give life even to her. To Philadelphia, He is the One with the key of David (3:7) about to open the door of return to Israel and to establish His kingdom on earth. And to Laodicea, the last of the seven, He is the "Amen," (3:14) God's last word.

But in contrast with this it is blessed to observe that He not only comes to judge, but to reward. How blessed the promises that He gives in these letters to the conquering ones! How rich and heavenly the exquisite symbolism by which our hearts are tempted to turn from earth's delusions and win the crown He brings! "To him who overcomes," He says, "I will give the right to eat from the tree of life, which is in the paradise of God." (2:7). "Be faithful, even to the point of death," He cries to Smyrna, "and I will give you the crown of life" (2:10). Let go the forbidden bread, and the forbidden love of earth and sin, He says to Pergamum, and I will give you "the hidden manna" (2:17) of heaven, and the white stone of the palace of the King, My card, with My own new name of love written on it for you alone to understand. Let go the false and fascinating promise which the devil holds out to Thyatira—false power, false light—and I will give you, at My coming, power over the nations, and the true light of the morning star and the eternal glory. And to the faithful ones in Sardis where all was so corrupt and dead, He offers the white robe and the public acclamation of their names before the Father and the holy angels. To little Philadelphia almost the richest promises of all are held out; namely, that her enemies will be brought to worship at her feet and to know that He has loved her, and that she will be saved from the hour of tribulation which is coming upon the whole earth, that she will receive the crown that He is to bring and will become a pillar in the temple of God with the name of God and Christ and the New Jerusalem upon her brow. But to Laodicea, the most faithless, He offers the most tender and magnificent promises of all. It would seem as if her very unworthiness drew out His tenderest compassion and challenged the most magnificent inducements which He could offer her to turn away from her folly and her sin. Instead of denouncing, condemning and commanding, He falls upon His knees at her very door, He knocks at her closed gates, He beseeches her to let Him in. He cries with locks wet with the dew of the morning: "Here I am! I stand at the door and knock. If anyone hears my voice and opens the door, I will come in and eat with him, and he with me" (3:20). And then He crowns it all with that grandest of all His promises. Just about to come in all His glory and rear His millennial throne over the great world, He cries: "To him who overcomes, I will give the right to sit with me on my throne, just as I overcame and sat down with my Father on his throne" (3:21). Oh, matchless condescension! Oh, marvelous and glorious grace! How will we escape if we neglect or despise that pleading tenderness, that precious promise?

CHAPTER 4

THE THRONE, THE LAMB, AND THE SEALS

After this I looked, and there before me was a door standing open in heaven. And the voice I had first heard speaking to me like a trumpet said, "Come up here, and I will show you what must take place after this." (Revelation 4:1)

W e have seen the vision of the Lord Jesus Christ and the Church of Christ. We are now to behold the vision of the world up to the coming of the Lord Jesus Christ and the plan of God with respect to it as set forth in the seven seals. Before, however, the seals are opened and the plan of God's providence is unfolded we have a vision of the throne in heaven and the enthroned Lamb who is to administer the execution of the divine plan and the opening of the seven seals.

There has been much discussion about the place of this section in the panorama of the future. There are some who believe that, from the fourth chapter on, the revelator is referring exclusively to things yet future and to events which are to come to pass after the Parousia. Those who hold this view apply the words in the first verse of the fourth chapter, "Come up here," to the translation of the Bride, and regard them as the call to the prepared ones who will be found waiting for the return of the Lord to ascend to the throne through the door which John saw opened in heaven.

This is very much strained and most unnatural in every way. The call to come hither was not a call to the glorified, but it was a special call to the seer to behold things which he was to see in vision, and when he did ascend it was not a literal translation, but immediately he adds, "I was in the Spirit" (Revelation 4:2). It was a spiritual vision of the heavenly world.

To make it still more certain that this chapter does not refer to events after the coming of the Lord, the four living creatures in their adoration refer to God as "who was, and is, and is to come" (4:8). This expression so frequently repeated in the Apocalypse seems to look directly forward to the Advent, and its being repeated by the glorious beings who worship around the throne clearly intimates that the time of the coming has not yet occurred. This is the more marked when we consider the fact that in the 11th chapter, where they again worship God and the Lamb, they change this expression and leave out the clause, "who is to come."

This does not appear in the authorized version, but in the revised version of Revelation 11:17, which contains the true and accepted reading, it is, "We give Thee thanks O Lord God Almighty, which art and wast because Thou hast taken to Thee Thy great power and hast reigned."

It is certain, therefore, that the Lord's coming occurs somewhere between the fourth and the eleventh chapter, but had not occurred when these beings uttered their adoring ascription in the fourth chapter. There seems no doubt that this chapter simply describes the throne of God as John beheld it in heaven at the commencement of the great series of events which immediately followed Christ's ascension and led on through the Christian age to the consummation in the Lord's coming. It is the scenery, as it were, of the mediatorial government and plan of God. It marks the beginning of the Christian age and leads up to all the events symbolized by the seven seals.

And so we behold the Father seated upon His throne in all His eternal glory, with the adoring hosts of the heavenly sanctuary and the glorious worship of the celestial world, while the Son under the image of the Lamb slain, ascends and takes His place by His side on the throne and begins to open the seals and solve the mystery of the ages as the great Redeemer and mediatorial King.

Let us look briefly at the Throne, the Lamb and the seals.

THE THRONE

The throne is the throne of God in heaven. It is the seat of sovereignty. It is the symbol of supremacy and government. The surroundings are majestic and glorious, but He who sits upon the throne is indescribable, and there is no attempt to paint a picture of His person or His ineffable face save that He was like a jasper and carnelian stone (4:3)—the jasper, the most brilliant gold, and the sardine, the most vivid crimson or scarlet. They were the royal colors and emblematic of splendor and glory.

The surroundings of the throne were all in keeping with the majestic vision. There was a rainbow round about the throne like unto an emerald. This was the symbol of a covenant God, and told the glorious story that judgment was past, and that God was now dealing with men on principles of mercy. The rainbow was all around the throne. It was not the half circle of our incomplete firmament but the completed sphere of God's perfect plan and finished redemption.

The emerald color marks the tint of earth and suggests that the purpose that is to be wrought out from the throne in connection with the vision has reference to the green earth where man dwells and where Jesus died.

The sea of glass that stood before the throne tells of the deep, calm purpose of God, the power that moves unruffled and resistless through all the ages working out His sovereign will.

The seven lamps before the throne were symbols of the sevenfold power of the Holy Spirit, and show that the purpose that was to be wrought out was not connected merely with the natural government of the world, but was to be a spiritual plan under the direct agency and through the infinite resources of the Holy Spirit.

Still more marked were the living forms around the throne. Seated upon thrones were 24 elders. These correspond to the 24 courses of the Jewish priesthood, and they seem to denote an order of heavenly worshipers, priests of the heavenly sanctuary. Many have supposed that they were representatives of the redeemed standing for the 12 tribes of Israel and the 12 apostles of the Lamb. But this is improbable. The argument for their human character is usually the language of the song they sing in the ninth verse of the fifth chapter: "With your blood you purchased men [us, KJV] for God/ from every tribe and language and people and nation." The true reading, however, nullifies the force of this argument by taking the word "us" quite out of the passage and making the redemption apply to others. If this chapter describes a period anterior to Christ's coming, as we have already assumed, and as seems certain from the heavenly ascription, "Who was, and is, and is to come" (4:8), then it is out of place to regard these beings as redeemed men, for the redeemed have not yet attained their place of glory before the throne, but are waiting until Jesus comes and the number of the elect shall be completed when all together will be crowned and glorified.

Still nearer to the throne were four living creatures corresponding to the symbolic beings that we find all through the Bible from the gate of Eden and the tabernacle in the wilderness down to the visions of Isaiah and John. In any case they are heavenly beings and not human beings, and they seem to be part of the sanctuary above and its glorious worship.

THE LAMB

Soon the center of interest in the throne becomes personified in a single figure—the Lamb. The inspired apostle beholds a strange spectacle of suspense in the heavenly court. He that sat upon the throne was holding in His right hand a book or scroll, written over in every part, both within and without, yet sealed with seven seals; a scroll which no one could read and no one could fulfill. It seems to represent God's plan of destiny for man, and there was no one able to work it out. The universe was at a deadlock.

As John beheld this strange perplexity and suspense he began to weep, until suddenly one of the elders addressed him and bade him dry his tears, for One had appeared who was to open the book and loose the seals. He described Him as the Lion of the tribe of Judah, the Root of David. And as John turned to behold Him, suddenly there stood before him and in the midst of the heavenly scene, not a lion in its majesty, but, as the Greek finely expresses it, "a Lamb, looking as if it had been slain," (5:6) with the marks of blood upon it. And yet the Lamb had the glory of infinite wisdom and power back of all its gentleness and lowliness. This is expressed by seven horns of power and seven eyes of wisdom, which told the story of infinite resources and the sevenfold light and power of the Holy Spirit which are under the direction and control of this enthroned Lamb.

It was a scene of unspeakable dramatic power and interest. It is said that once in the Roman Coliseum a crowd was waiting, as there stood a martyr in the midst of the arena, for a roaring Numidian lion to burst from its cage and devour the holy saint. Suddenly, as a little piece of play for the amusement of a Roman crowd, the keeper led forth from the stable under the galleries not a lion but a lamb, which stepped up and licked the hand of the martyr, while the crowd thundered out its surprise and applause.

More majestic infinitely is this heavenly scene as He who has all power and glory, instead of ostentatiously displaying His greatness, presents Himself in all the simplicity and humiliation of the cross and its shame, and undertakes to solve the problems of destiny and wield the scepter of the universe, not as the Lion, but as the Lamb.

Immediately He becomes the center of attention, and there bursts forth, from all the choirs of heaven and all the myriads of earth and sea, the sublimest chorus of adoration ever heard in earth or heaven. First, the living creatures and the elders fall down before the throne and sing a new song composed especially for that grand occasion, saying, "You are worthy to take the scroll/ and to open its seals,/ because you were slain,/ and with your blood you purchased men for God/ from every tribe and language and people and nation./ You have made them to be a kingdom and priests to serve our God,/ and they will reign on the earth" (5:9).

Then as the song reaches the outer circle of angels, 10,000 times 10,000, and myriads whose numbers could not be told take up the chorus and they sing, "Worthy is the Lamb, who was slain,/ to receive power and wealth and wisdom and strength/ and honor and glory and praise!" (5:12). And as the echoes of their song go ringing out and resounding back from the courts of heaven and the realms of immensity, still farther out there comes another chorus from "every creature in heaven" (5:13), and there seemed to be other creatures there, and "on earth and under the earth and on the sea" (5:13). Every created voice seemed to join in the anthem, "To him who sits on the throne and to the Lamb/ be praise and honor and glory and power,/ for ever and ever!" (5:13).

The mighty song has rolled through space and echoed along the galleries of heaven, and as the echo comes back the four living creatures answer with their mighty response, "Amen" (5:14), and deeper and higher than all speech or song the 24 elders fall down in prostrate silence and worship Him who lives forever and forever.

THE SEALS

But next the interest moves on even from the blessed Lamb Himself to the great task He has undertaken. He takes the book out of the Father's hands, and as He looses the seals one by one and unfolds the scroll, lo, a series of events begins to take place on earth and a procession of mighty providences moves down through the ages to the end. These are the successive events that are to follow each other up to the coming of the Lord. They are described in the sixth and seventh chapters of Revelation.

As each of the first four seals is opened in succession there is a strange and mighty voice going up from one of the living creatures, the single word, "Come!" (6:3). Not "Come and see," as the authorized version, but "Come." It is the keynote of all the history of this book. It is the deep undertone of all the thought and teaching of the Apocalypse. It is the meaning of the seals expressed in one unutterable word, "Come."

What is the specific meaning of each seal? The first four present a general resemblance to each other. In the first we behold a white horse, and he that sat upon it was armed with "a bow, and he was given a crown, and he rode out as a conqueror bent on conquest" (6:2). The second shows a red horse and he that sat upon it crimsons the earth with carnage and war (6:4). The third presents a black horse, and behind it follow famine and destruction (6:5). The fourth is a livid horse, and he that sat upon it was Death, and Hell came hard behind (6:8). These four horses and their riders represent successively the destructive forces of the early centuries, the conquering power of Rome, the carnage of the revolutions that followed, the horrors of famine that came with the inroads of the Barbarians, terrors of the Middle Ages and the crowning holocaust of death which filled up and finished the picture.

As the fifth seal is opened the cry of the living creature ceases, but instead there comes a deep moan from the souls of the martyrs under the altar. They echo the same old cry, but more plaintively for their voice is, "How long, Sovereign Lord, holy and true, until you judge the inhabitants of the earth and avenge our blood?" (6:10). It is the vision of persecution and suffering for Jesus' sake. It is the story of the Roman martyrs and the Papal martyrs. It is the picture of the suffering Church under the ban of a cruel world and it leads on far through the age.

Next comes the sixth seal, and lo, as it breaks and the scroll unfolds, there is a sudden catastrophe. It seems for a moment as if the end had already come. There is a great earthquake. The sun is black and the moon is blood. The stars of heaven fall and the heavens roll up like a scroll, while mountains and islands are shaken and the kingdoms and peoples of earth are filled with terror, and cry to the rocks and mountains to fall on them and hide them from "the face of him who sits on the throne and from the wrath of the Lamb! For the great day of their wrath has come, and who can stand?" (6:16–17).

Yes, it would seem that this is at last the end. But no, not quite. Just on the eve of the catastrophe it is suspended for a little while, and four mighty angels who hold the cyclone of judgment that is about to strike the earth, are commanded to hold back a little longer until two necessary things are done.

First is the sealing of Israel's tribes, an elect number out of each. The Jew is to pass through the tribulation time, and God has already told us in Zechariah and Daniel that a certain number of His chosen people are to be preserved through the fire of that awful day. These are now sealed. Some mark is put upon them by which their lives shall be inviolate during the terrible times that are to come.

But what is the next great scene? What means this mighty throng that suddenly has appeared before the throne and the Lamb?

> After this I looked and there before me was a great multitude that no one could count, from every nation, tribe, people and language, standing before the throne and in front of the Lamb. They were wearing white robes and were holding palm branches in their hands. And they cried out in a loud voice:
>
> "Salvation belongs to our God,
> who sits on the throne,
> and to the Lamb." (7:9–10)

John asks in wonder, and is told that these are redeemed men, not Jews, but men of every nation, that have come up out of the great tribulation that is already beginning, and are now before the throne and the Lamb.

This is the rapture of the saints. This is the translation of the waiting Bride. This is the blessed hope for which we are told to watch and wait and stand prepared. God grant that we may understand it, be ever ready for it and at last be found in that happy company.

CHAPTER 5

THE TRUMPETS AND THE TRIBULATION

*The seventh angel sounded his trumpet, and there were loud voices
in heaven, which said:*

> *"The kingdom of the world has become the kingdom of our
> Lord and of his Christ,
> and he will reign for ever and ever." (Revelation 11:15)*

The opening of the seventh seal leads to a new series of developments in which seven angels appear upon the scene with seven trumpets, and as they successively sound them, judgment after judgment rolls over the earth, until at length the seventh angel sounds his trumpet and the heavenly voices proclaim the mystery finished, the crisis over, the tribulation ended and the kingdoms of the world transformed into the kingdom of our Lord and of His Christ. It is quite certain from the close of the series that it leads right up to the millennial appearing and reign of our Lord. Therefore the series must represent the tribulation time and the judgments which it is to bring upon the earth. This is still more evident when we bear in mind the interpretation already given to the section immediately preceding, which we have seen represents the first coming of our Lord and the translation of the saints just prior to the opening of the seventh seal. That, as we have seen, gives us the vision of the sealing of the tribes of Israel on earth and the translation of the saints of heaven.

Of course, it must be conceded that much of the prophetic description of this whole period must necessarily be more or less obscure. The exact nature of these terrific events cannot be comprehended until their fulfillment. At the same time the general features of this period can be plainly discerned, and these four chapters, Revelation 8 to 11, give us a general view of the various judgments that are to roll over the earth during these terrible times.

THE AWFUL SILENCE

It will be noticed that this whole series of judgments is preceded by an impressive hush of awful silence that fell upon the heavenly world for half an hour. This was perhaps the hush before the storm. It was also perhaps one of God's mighty pauses, marking the close of one great period and the beginning of another. God punctuated the dispensation with a mighty period, and heaven stopped to take its breath before the beginning of the next chapter of the prophetic scroll.

THE SOLEMN PRAYER OFFERING

Next comes the solemn offering up of the prayers of all the saints by the mighty Angel who seems to represent the Lord Jesus Christ, the heavenly High Priest. It would seem as if these prayers had been long accumulating, and now, at last, were solemnly summed up and formally presented before God for His answer. It was a mighty holocaust of prayer. The cries of the martyrs under the altar, the tears and sighs and breathings of the saints that had been treasured up in vials before the throne are now taken by Christ Himself, and formally presented before His Father, while He claims that the answer long deferred will now at length come and this world will be taken out of the hands of the wicked, and given over to Christ and His saints.

As these prayers are formally presented to God they are next poured back upon the earth mingled with coals of fire from the sacred altar; and as they fall upon the earth, there are voices, thunderings, lightnings, and an earthquake, and the seven angels bearing their seven trumpets prepare themselves to sound their notes of solemn warnings of judgment.

How beautiful and encouraging the picture here given of the power of prayer! Long may our supplications wait before they seem to be fulfilled, but God has not forgotten them. Every breath of true intercession will yet reach the Father's ear. Indeed, perhaps the hush of silence that fell upon the heavens was in order that nothing might interrupt the hearing of these prayers. How comforting to know that, notwithstanding the imperfections of our petitions, our great High Priest presents them mingled with His perfect incense and makes them acceptable even amid the purity of heaven!

But still more striking and impressive is the picture of the return of these prayers to earth again as they come back from the heavenly altar, and become the mighty and moving forces that set in operation the whole procession of angelic ministries, and earthly providences that is to usher in the reign of Christ.

HAIL, FIRE AND BLOOD

Next we behold a series of natural judgments upon the physical realm represented by a storm of hail and fire mingled with blood, suddenly cast upon

the earth, by means of which the trees and grass are burned up and the earth
is scorched and withered. This follows the sounding of the first trumpet and
marks the beginning of the tribulation judgments.

THE NATIONAL JUDGMENTS

The second angel sounds, and we next behold a series of national judgments. A great mountain burning with fire is cast into the sea and part of
the sea becomes blood and many of its living creatures perish and multitudes
of the ships that crowd its waters are destroyed. A mountain always represents a great nation, and this undoubtedly describes some tremendous political convulsion, which covers the earth, and especially the sea, with blood
and desolation.

THE ECCLESIASTICAL JUDGMENTS

The third angel sounds his trumpet and there comes a series of ecclesiastical judgments. A great star falls from heaven burning like a lamp, named
"Wormwood" (8:10), and as it falls upon the rivers and fountains of waters
they become bitter, and multitudes die from their poisonous draughts. The
star represents an ecclesiastical leader and power. Some false teacher, some
mighty leader of religious excitement or fanaticism, or, perhaps some of the
existing systems of error, is permitted to scourge the earth with delusion,
perhaps with persecution as in the awful days when Islam offered to many
the Koran or the sword.

THE DARKNESS

The fourth angel sounds his trumpet and now the sun is smitten, and the
moon and the stars, so that a third of their light is obscured, and men walk
in darkness and confusion. This may represent an intellectual and social
scourge and the obscuring of the human mind, the possession of the intellect
and reason of man by some fearful delusion, some form of mania or mad-
ness or some terrible error that leads men into every excess and crime. We
have seen such things before and how much more terrible they can become
in earth's last times when the holy are withdrawn from the earth and the
devil is supreme, one can scarcely imagine now.

These first four warnings and judgments are but the precursors of still
more terrible plagues that are soon to follow; and so, before the next angel
sounds, a voice is heard announcing in the heavens, "Woe! Woe! Woe to the
inhabitants of the earth, because of the trumpet blasts about to be sounded
by the other three angels!" (8:13).

THE FALLEN STAR

The fifth angel now sounds his trumpet, and, lo, a star falls from heaven, representing another spiritual force. This time it would seem to be one of the fallen angels, one of the spiritual rulers of the dark underworld. Immediately he is given the key of the bottomless pit, and there pours forth from the depths of hell a smoke so dense that sun and air are darkened. Out of the smoke there sweeps over the earth a brood of locusts like scorpions whose power is exercised, not over the grass or trees, but upon the bodies of men who have not the seal of God in their foreheads. They have not the power to kill but only to torment, and their torture is so terrible that "during those days men will seek death, but will not find it; they will long to die, but death will elude them" (9:6).

A description is given of these terrible tormentors which will be like horses with crowns on their heads and faces like men, with hair like women and teeth like lions. They are winged creatures and the sound of their wings is as the sound of horses and chariots running to battle. They have stings in their tails and they have a king over them who is the angel of the bottomless pit, and whose name is Abaddon and Apollyon (9:7–11).

How this brood of hell can be identified as any body of men who have ever yet scourged this earth, whether Saracen or Turk, we cannot imagine. To us they seem to represent some diabolical swarm of tormentors and destroyers from the very depths of hell, such as can only be understood when the prophetic vision is literally fulfilled.

We know already that the germs of disease are living things. Science has described the minute creatures that grow up in the human form until they have consumed and destroyed it with malignant sickness; and we know from the Scriptures that these sources of disease are not merely earthly, but they are devilish, too, for Satan is the author of disease and these myrmidons are but his servants. If, in this age, he is able so to torture the human form with sickness how much more may this become the case when all the restraints of this dispensation of grace will be removed, and the floods of hell will be let loose in the last days upon the devoted earth.

THE ANGELS OF JUDGMENT

The sixth angel next sounds his trumpet, and four great angels of judgment are loosed from the river Euphrates, and an army of 200 million marches forth to inflict upon men the last of the tribulation judgments. This army is too vast to be identified with any chapter of past history and it is too devilish to be compared with Turkish Pashas and modern potentates. These soldiers strike men with infernal fire and brimstone, and this judgment is the letting loose of all the power of hell on an impenitent world; for, notwithstanding all these judgments, earth's inhabitants still did not repent "of their murders, their magic arts, their sexual immorality or their thefts" (9:21).

THE TWO WITNESSES

The series of tribulation judgments is arrested at this point for a little while and we next behold the future of this dark and dreadful time with peculiar interest. It is the witnessing for God of the few faithful ones who still represent on earth the cause of truth and righteousness. The 10th and 11th chapters of Revelation give us an account of the two witnesses. Who these witnesses are has been one of the puzzling questions and exegetical battles of the century. Even so wise and great an interpreter as Dean Alford is not ashamed to confess his inability to explain who they are. It seems enough for us to know that they are witnesses for Christ, and that in these dark times there will be those on earth who will not be afraid to speak for God and sacrifice life itself in their fidelity to the truth.

These witnesses will be clothed with mighty power. They will be endowed with all the gifts of the Spirit, and the seal of God will be upon their heads and hands in all the signs of wonders of the apostolic ministry. They may be two individuals, perhaps Enoch and Elijah, coming back again to earth. Perhaps John himself may be one of them, for it is intimated in the 11th verse of the 10th chapter that he will prophesy again before many people, and nations, and tongues and kings. Or, it may be that they represent two churches or two companies of believers, one of the Jewish people sealed and saved and true to Christ during the tribulation times; the other, the remnant of the Gentile church, the tribulation saints who had not been caught up at the rapture, in the seventh chapter, but who have come to Christ or come nearer to Him during these trying times. At least we know that there will be witnesses, and they will be true. The power of God will rest upon their testimony; and at last their lives will be laid down as the seal of that testimony, and a wicked world will greatly rejoice because at last their power is destroyed and there is no voice left to rebuke them for their sins.

But suddenly, these martyred witnesses are raised from the dead and they stand upon their feet before their persecutors, and a great voice from heaven calls them, "Come up here" (11:12), and they ascend to heaven in a cloud in the sight of all their enemies. This is followed by fearful convulsions, a great earthquake in which the city falls and multitudes are destroyed, and men in terror, and perhaps repentance, fall upon their faces and give glory to the God of heaven.

This resurrection of the witnesses seems to represent the taking up of the tribulation saints to the Lord in the air to join the translated ones who had already been caught up.

And this resurrection scene closes the events of the tribulation and is immediately followed by the final catastrophe and the appearing of the Lord in the glory of His reign.

THE JEWISH PEOPLE

The tribulation time will be a time of special interest and severe trial to the Jewish people, therefore they appear very prominently in these chapters. We see the apostle commanded to take a measuring rod and measure the temple of God and the altar and them that worship therein; but the court which is outside the temple he is commanded to leave out and not measure, for it is given to the Gentiles, and they will tread under foot the holy city for 42 months. Here we see a very clear representation of the down-treading of Jerusalem and the afflictions of God's chosen people, but, at the same time, of the security of those that are within the temple and under the protection of His covenant and seal.

According to other Scriptures, it seems certain that Israel will be one of God's chief witnesses during these days of trial. "This third I will bring," He says in Zechariah, "into the fire;/ I will refine them like silver/ and test them like gold" (Zechariah 13:9). And again in Daniel we are reminded that there shall "be a time of distress such as has not happened from the beginning of nations until then. But at that time your people—everyone whose name is found written in the book—will be delivered" (Daniel 12:1).

THE COMING OF THE LORD

At length the seventh trumpet sounds the signal of the coming of the Lord. The mystery is finished, the crisis is passed, the Lord is here! The result is described not so much by a dramatic scene representing the events themselves as by a shout that rings throughout the heavens: "The kingdom of the world has become the kingdom of our Lord and of his Christ,/ and he will reign for ever and ever" (Revelation 11:15).

Exactly what is meant by this event is made more clear in the ascription of worship,

> We give thanks to you, Lord God Almighty,
>   the One who is and who was,
> because you have taken your great power
>   and have begun to reign.
> The nations were angry;
>   and your wrath has come.
> The time has come for judging the dead,
>   and for rewarding your servants the prophets
> and your saints and those who reverence your name,
>   both small and great—
> and for destroying those who destroy the earth.
>   (11:17–18)

We learn from this that:

a. The Lord has already come because the phrase "who is to come" is omitted from the 17th verse in the correct reading. It would be out of place because He has come.

b. The reign of Christ on earth has begun. "Because you have taken your great power/ and have begun to reign" (11:17).

c. This is not a time of gradual conversion among the nations but a sudden shock by which they have been surprised and broken; for we read, "The nations were angry;/ and your wrath has come" (11:18). It is the prophecy of the second Psalm, the breaking of the nations. "You will rule them with an iron scepter;/ you will dash them to pieces like pottery" (Psalm 2:8).

d. This is the time of the resurrection of the dead, as we are distinctly told that, "The time has come for judging the dead" (Revelation 11:18).

e. This is the time when the saints of God are to be rewarded, "For rewarding your servants the prophets/ and your saints and those who reverence your name,/ both small and great" (11:18). We know the time of reward for the saints and servants of God is at the coming of the Lord Jesus to reign upon the earth.

It is very comforting to note that these rewards are not wholly for the prophets and distinguished servants of God, but for "those who reverence your name,/ both small and great" (11:18). Most of us, therefore, if we are but faithful, will have a part in that blessed hope and glorious recompense.

f. It is the time when earth's oppressors, destroyers and false rulers will be set aside, for it is added, "for destroying those who destroy the earth" (11:18). It is quite certain, therefore, that it means the final crisis, the end of the age, the judgment of the nations, and the setting up of Christ's millennial throne.

CHAPTER 6

THE MOTHER CHURCH AND THE MANCHILD

A great and wondrous sign appeared in heaven: a woman clothed with the sun, with the moon under her feet and a crown of twelve stars on her head. She was pregnant and cried out in pain as she was about to give birth. (Revelation 12:1–2)

The prophetic cycle was completed with our last subject. The panorama led up to the climax, the very coming of the Lord Jesus, and so far as the sequence is concerned, the Apocalypse might have closed at that point, and we should have had a complete vision of the age in its general outline up to the point where the story is resumed in the 19th chapter of Revelation, and carried on through the millennium and the new heavens and earth in the last three chapters.

But the survey has been a hurried one and now the vision pauses for a little and goes back over the period that has been swiftly traversed, and draws a number of special pictures of scenes and incidents which had been rapidly passed over. To illustrate it perfectly, it is like the insertion of a number of vignette pictures around a great central picture—the central picture representing the principal scene and the others a number of minute details.

The chapters which follow, from the 12th to the 18th inclusive, give us a number of special pictures of important characters and scenes throughout the Christian age. Chief among these is the Church of Christ and her counterfeits, especially the systems of worldly power and ecclesiastical corruption that have risen up during the age and been channels and special instrumentalities for the corruption or destruction of the true Church of Christ.

These systems of evil are described by a number of striking figures; such as "the seven-headed beast," the other beast with "two horns like a lamb" (13:11), "Babylon" (14:8), "the woman sitting on a scarlet beast" (17:3), and the special judgments and plagues by which this system of iniquity is at last to be scorched and destroyed.

THE MOTHER CHURCH

In this beautiful picture the whole body of God's people in every age is set forth. This woman represents the great invisible Church of God from the first believer down to the latest age. The figure of the woman leads on later to the figure of the Bride.

This woman is clothed with the sun, the imagery representing her as illumined by the light of God, the Holy Scriptures, the Holy Spirit, the light and beauty of holiness. All the sources of her light are heavenly and she shines in the reflected light of God Himself. This is but an adaption of an Old Testament figure. This is but the response of the Church to the summons of Isaiah: "Arise, shine for your light has come,/ and the glory of the LORD rises upon you" (60:1).

Again, the moon is under her feet. The moon represents the lesser light of earth and night. She has been lifted above the need of earthly light. She had put her feet upon the pride of intellect, the wisdom of man, the self-sufficiency and self-consciousness of earthly culture and human agencies or virtues. Like the tabernacle of old, which had no windows but received its light from the sevenfold lamp, so her light is all divine and her glory the reflection of her God.

Again, she is crowned with 12 stars. These stars represent, as we are taught in the previous chapters, the men and women who have adorned the pages of her history and reflected the light of holy character and heavenly power.

THE DRAGON

Over against this beautiful figure of the woman stands the impious form of the seven-headed Dragon. He is introduced to us in this message by many reputations and many names. There is no doubt about his identity. He is called "the Devil," and "Satan," "that ancient serpent . . . who leads the whole world astray" (Revelation 12:9). It is the great ruler of the underworld and the head of the principalities and powers of the kingdom of darkness.

Of his greatness there can be no doubt. He apes the sovereignty and authority of God Himself. He has seven heads corresponding to the earthly powers which represent him. He has 10 horns, the instruments and agencies by which he strikes and pushes his assaults and advances. The numbers seven and 10 are symbolic of perfection and they represent the completeness of his resources and equipment. He is not almighty or infinite; but he is only less than God.

He has seven crowns upon his seven heads and he claims universal empire and even presumes to defy the very throne of heaven itself. It is added that his tail drew the third part of the stars of heaven and did cast them to the earth. Surely this describes the fall of the angels who were swept from their high estate to follow in the track of this mighty rebel and to share his everlasting doom.

Of his wickedness there can also be no doubt. He stands before us in this picture ready to destroy and devour. He refuses to be expelled from the holy presence of heaven. He is the great adversary, who deceives the whole world; and the same subtle serpent who represents all the depths of malignity and treachery. It is the great enemy of God and man—Satan, whose existence and reality no one can doubt who has ever rebelled against his authority and refused to obey his wicked will.

THE MANCHILD

There now appears upon the scene a figure that engrosses much of the interest of the whole scene. It is the Firstborn of this glorious woman, her illustrious Seed. He is here described by a peculiar Greek word which literally means a "male son." It is not an ordinary son nor an ordinary man but it is a man representing in a peculiar sense the qualities of manhood and in some sense a representative man, the Man of men. Does it not at once recall the expression which our blessed Lord so often used about Himself, the Son of man, the representative Man, the One who crystallized and summed up in Himself the race? We know there have been many theories about this Manchild, and perhaps the most plausible is that which applies the figure to a special company of holy men and women who are to be separated unto God in the last days and specially called to be the Bride, the firstfruits, the called-out ones, who will be the first to go up to meet the Lord in the air.

The first impression which this interpretation gives to the average mind is one of strain and repulsion. It is not easy to think of the great plan of God and the stupendous prophecies of Himself, for whose fulfillment the ages have waited, being monopolized by a little company of self-constituted elect ones in the very last days of the Christian age. God's plan is too large and His thought too great for this. The interpretation is unworthy of the character of the description. Surely no one else than Jesus Christ Himself, the Son of God and the Son of man, is worthy of all that is predicted of this wondrous Child. Let us assume this application first and not take a less one, so long as it satisfies the description and prediction of this chapter.

How perfectly the first description applies to Him! He is to rule all nations with a rod of iron. This is the very promise of the second Psalm which is strictly Messianic. "You will rule them with an iron scepter;/ you will dash them to pieces like pottery" (Psalm 2:9).

Next, He is born of the Church of God, the first great issue of the glorious Woman. At first it may seem a little strained to represent Jesus Christ as at once born of the Church and yet the Husband of the Church. But there is a very real sense in which Christ was the outcome and issue of the Old Testament Church. He is distinctly called the "Seed of the woman," and He was born of the faith, love and hope of the whole body of the Old Testament saints. It is no more strained to apply this to Christ than to speak of Him as at once "The Root and the Offspring of David" (Revelation 22:16). It is a very true and beautiful figure to think of the Old Testament Church as receiving from God the conception of the coming Redeemer, cherishing, nurturing, maturing the thought, the hope, the promise of the coming Savior until at last it ripened into fullness and was born into the Incarnate One. In a very real sense the Lord Jesus Christ was given to the faith of the mother that bore Him, and the little flock that waited for redemption in Jerusalem.

Then, again, the "rest of her offspring" (12:17) are spoken of later in the passage and we know that these mean the brethren of the Lord Jesus, the other members and children of the mother Church who will be added in due time down to the end of the age. The figure becomes symmetrical and complete when we think of Him as the Elder Brother and these as the "rest of her offspring."

Still further notice that the Dragon was waiting to devour this Child as soon as He should be born. How literally this was fulfilled in the cruel purpose of Herod as He waited for the life of Jesus at Bethlehem, and, when he failed to find Him, massacred all the little ones in Bethlehem in the hope of destroying Christ also.

Notice again that the Manchild is caught up to God and His throne. This is applied by our friends, who hold the view above referred to, to the translation of this little company of saints just before the Lord's coming. But the translation of the saints will not take them up to the throne of God. It will only take them into the air where Christ will meet them. But Christ was literally caught up to God and to His throne and ever since has been sitting there at the right hand of God.

Notice again how perfectly the account of the war in heaven, which we will refer to later, agrees with the facts that immediately followed Christ's ascension. That glorious ascension settled all claims against the believer, silenced the adversary and accuser, and led to his expulsion from heaven to the lower earth where he has ever since been seeking to destroy the Woman and her seed.

THE CONFLICT

The conflict begins on earth with the attempt of the Dragon to destroy the Manchild. This may well represent Satan's attack upon the Lord Jesus Christ personally from His cradle to His cross.

It next appears in the heavens after Christ's ascension when the Dragon and his angels are cast out by Michael and his angels, and a loud voice is heard proclaiming: "Now have come the salvation and the power and the kingdom of our God,/ and the authority of his Christ./ For the accuser of our brothers,/ who accuses them before our God day and night,/ has been hurled down" (12:10).

This picture is very real and in perfect harmony with Christ's ascension as given in other parts of the New Testament. Up to the time of Christ's ascension Satan had access to heaven as the accuser of the brethren. Their debt was still recorded against them, the redemption price had not been paid and Satan had grounds for his assaults. But when Christ ascended and presented the ransom and claimed the discharge of all the liabilities of His people on account of His finished work, then Satan was silenced, his case was gone, there was nothing more that he could say against the brethren and so he was dismissed from the heavenly court; and when he refused to leave, the heavenly armies were turned upon him and he and his followers were hurled from the skies and cast out into the earth. Since that day no voice has dared to speak a word of accusation against any believer in the Lord Jesus Christ. We are without fault before the throne and our glorious commendation is this, "Who is he that condemns? Christ Jesus, who died—more than that, who was raised to life—is at the right hand of God and is also interceding for us" (Romans 8:34). This passage is almost a parallel passage to the present chapter, and presents exactly the same view of the effect of Christ's ascension in the vindication of His people.

The scene of the conflict now shifts to the earth, and it is turned against the Woman, the Church. The Dragon persecutes the Woman and she flees into the wilderness from the face of the serpent. He pursues her and casts out of his mouth a flood of waters that he might sweep her away. This represents the floods of barbarous nations always represented by the troubled waters of the sea, who came up against civilization and Christianity in the fourth and fifth centuries, and for a time threatened to sweep away from earth the last vestige of true religion. The wild myriads that swept down upon the plains of Italy, and the Muslim hordes that rolled across the plains of Asia obliterating churches, Christian institutions and every vestige of the religion of Jesus Christ, may well be represented by those floods of waters that the Dragon poured out against the Woman.

But we are told that the earth helped the Woman. This represents some national and political agency employed by God to counteract these wild invasions. While the waters represent the disorganized people, the earth represents the stable nations. God used these nations as a bulwark against the incursions of wild fanaticism.

As a single example we have but to recall the crisis hour in Europe when the Muslims had swept across from Africa and the armies of Europe and Asia met on the plains of France and the victory of Charles Martel practically saved Christianity from extinction. The earth helped the Woman. The organized Christian nations were God's bulwark against the wild waves of Satan's rage and earth's convulsions.

Then we are told the Dragon, unable to destroy the Woman, went forth to make war with the remnant of her seed which keep the commandments of God and have the testimonies of Jesus Christ. The remnant of her seed are individual Christians who stand true to God amid the hate of Satan and the oppositions of the world. The scene of the battle now is this earth, and as the heavens behold this battlefield a great cry goes up: "Woe to the earth and the sea,/ because the devil has gone down to you!/ He is filled with fury,/ because he knows that his time is short" (Revelation 12:12). This is the battle that is raging today and every man and woman that stands true to the commandments of God and the testimony of Jesus Christ will feel its terrible force.

The weapons of our warfare in this terrible conflict are shown in the 11th verse: "They overcame him/ by the blood of the Lamb/ and by the word of their testimony;/ they did not love their lives so much/ as to shrink from death" (12:11). There are three weapons in this warfare. The first is the atoning blood of Jesus Christ, which we can never compromise or dishonor if we would expect victory in the crisis of these last days.

The second is the Word of God, believed and witnessed to—the Word as a personal experience and the testimony of one that has proved it and knows it to be true.

The third weapon is the spirit of self-sacrifice. This is but another name for love. It is the fire of heroism, the ardor that consumes the life of self and makes the heart a living sacrifice for the cause to which it is devoted. It is this that gives victory in earthly conflicts. It is the hero who wins, the man who stakes all upon his venture and flings himself headlong into the depths of danger and the jaws of destruction. And in the battle of the Lord nothing can conquer but heroic self-sacrifice, Christlike love—the love that, if it were the call today, could die for Christ, the love which not being called to die can live for Christ and put our life into the cause He has put into our hands. It is the holy man, the holy woman, the holy heart poured out for our trust and our testimony. It is earnestness. It is sacrifice. This is the secret that explains every glorious and glorified life. Back of the story of achievement and success there is an altar fire where a heart has been consumed and gone up as an odor of sweet-smelling savor to God and for mankind.

It is the old story of the Scottish girl who had been so strangely changed from a selfish belle of society, the butterfly of fashion, the queen of her little circle of folly, admired and worshiped by her votaries and living only for herself, suddenly transformed into an angel of love and a messenger of blessing, forgetting herself and living for others, bearing upon her face the light that never shone on earthly skies. No wonder people wondered and the old women said she had given her heart to some noble missionary, and this was the secret of the change. They were doubly sure because she wore upon her breast a little locket whose secret no one had ever seen. At last her devoted life burned itself out, and the hectic flush told of the sacrifice that should soon be finished. Before she died she called her bosom friend to her side and handing her the sacred locket she charged her to keep it sealed until she closed her eyes in death and laid her dust to rest, and then, she said, "Go alone to your room, open it upon your knees and may it mean as much to you as it has meant to me." The tender charge was faithfully fulfilled, the last offices of affection and sorrow were finished, and home from the city of the dead that lone and broken-hearted one came to her little room, and after a flood of tears had subsided she threw herself upon her knees and opened the sacred jewel.

There was no face within that golden frame; there was no human name; but printed in golden letters on a little band of satin were the words, "Whom having not seen we love."

That was all and—that was everything. That was the hero that had won her heart. That was the glorious attraction that had lifted her from selfishness to loving sacrifice, from a fluttering summer flower to an angel of love and a saint in glory. God gives to us all, if we will dare to have it, the heavenly talisman, the passion sign of the cross, the love of Christ. May it be true of us, "They overcame him/ by the blood of the Lamb/ and by the word of their testimony;/ they did not love their lives so much/ as to shrink from death" (12:11).

CHAPTER 7

THE TWO BEASTS

And I saw a beast coming out of the sea. He had ten horns and seven heads, with ten crowns on his horns, and on each head a blasphemous name. (Revelation 13:1)

Then I saw another beast, coming out of the earth. He had two horns like a lamb, but he spoke like a dragon. (13:11)

We have seen the true Church of God, His representative on earth. We are now to see the counterfeit, the devil's representative on earth. In the vision of the Apocalypse it takes the form of many symbols. Later on it appears as Babylon, and again as a vile woman sitting on a wild beast, the antithesis of the holy Woman in chapter 12. In this chapter it is presented to us under the image of two beasts.

In order to get at once to the heart of the subject we will premise that these two Beasts represent respectively the secular and ecclesiastical powers by which the devil has sought to destroy the Church of Christ and build up his own kingdom on earth. Let us immediately turn our attention to these two powers.

The first is described as a wild beast rising up out of the sea having seven heads and 10 horns. He is further described as a composite creature, part leopard, part lion, part bear. The imagery at once recalls the vision of Daniel in which he saw the four great empires of the world respectively under the image of a lion, a bear, a leopard and a monster that seemed composed of the attributes of all other fearful creatures. The difference between this vision and Daniel's is that here they have seven heads, while in Daniel there were but four. We infer, therefore, that while this describes substantially the same world-power, yet it looks farther back in the history of the world to the very beginning of this world-power, and on the other hand looks farther down to its last development. We will inquire immediately what these seven heads mean. It is sufficient at present to identify the picture generally with Daniel's vision of the great empires of the world.

As the scene unfolds, numerous particulars are added. It is a blasphemous power. It is a universal dominion. One of its heads is wounded to death and then soon after is succeeded by another and thus the wound is healed. It makes war with the saints and overcomes them and its dominion continues through 42 months, or 1,260 prophetic days, that is, years. Let us look at these points in detail, meanwhile premising again that this wild beast represents the universal empires of the world from the beginning to the end, the successive heads of the worldwide authority and power through which Satan has ruled the earth and sought to destroy the cause of God.

THE POLITICAL WILD BEAST

This beast rises out of the sea. Now the sea always represents the great masses of earth's peoples and tongues, the hordes and myriads of teeming tribes not yet organized as nations. Later, in the 11th verse, we see another beast coming up, not out of the sea, but out of the earth, which represents the organized political powers of the earth. But out of the primitive and disorganized masses of the world's population there grew up seven forms of worldwide dominion, crystallized around certain cities and certain human leaders.

SEVEN HEADS

It had seven heads which we believe represent the seven successive forms of worldwide dominion. The first of these was the Egyptian power which for ages was the great oppressor of the people of God and the devil's chosen instrumentality for opposing and defying Jehovah. Egypt was Satan's ancient throne and it was against the gods of Egypt that Jehovah took vengeance when He sent the Egyptian plagues by the hand of Moses.

Assyria was the second. Around the center of mighty Nineveh, it stretched out its scepter to the confines of the world, again and again invading Palestine, finally destroying Samaria, taking the 10 tribes captive and blotting out the kingdom of Israel from the page of history.

The third of these seven heads was, of course, Babylon. And now our course becomes very plain, for Daniel has given us all the others but one, and not only revealed the image, but its interpretation.

The fourth was Medo-Persia, the power that conquered Babylon and expanded its empire over a still wider realm.

The fifth was Greece, or Macedonia, the mighty empire of Alexander, that subdued and succeeded Persia and stretched out its borders still farther over the mighty East.

The sixth was colossal Rome, mightier than them all. But who is the seventh?

The solution is in Revelation 17:10: "They are also seven kings. Five have fallen." These five are Egypt, Assyria, Babylon, Persia and Greece. These all were fallen when John wrote the Apocalypse. "One is." That was old Rome which was then existing. "The other has not yet come." That was the seventh. Then we are told in the 11th verse the devil himself was to come in person and be the eighth head and last.

Now this seventh head was the one that succeeded old Rome. What earthly power took the place of the empire of the Caesars? It is not hard to answer. The story of the Middle Ages tells us that mightiest sovereignty of the world for a thousand years was the Papacy, not now considered as a church, but as a civil power, an organized dominion with a triple crown on its head, an army, and a right to use all the other armies of the world to carry out its behests. This is the seventh head of the beast, and the eighth is the devil incarnate, who will wind up the series.

THE TEN HORNS

What are these? We have already learned from Daniel and his two visions of the 10 toes and the 10 horns, that they represent the smaller kingdoms and political systems that were to come upon the stage after the fall of Rome. It is a fact that after the empire of the Caesars fell it was succeeded by a lot of broken states which have continued to divide what remains of the old Roman empire up to the present day. Now, in the 17th chapter of Revelation, John tells us that these "ten horns you saw are ten kings who have not yet received a kingdom, but who for one hour will receive authority as kings along with the beast. They have one purpose and will give their power and authority to the beast" (17:12). There we see these 10 powers existing and working coordinately with the Papal power, assisting it and maintaining its cause. We will be led more fully into this view of the subject when we come to the 17th chapter. Meanwhile the light it sheds upon these horns is sufficient to identify and explain them. If we look at the map of Europe today [originally published in 1905], we will find that there are just 10 powers, counting those states as one which belong to the same family and race. They are Russia, Turkey, Scandinavia, including Sweden and Norway, the Netherlands including Belgium and Holland which have always been associated, Spain and Portugal which are also practically one, France, Germany, Austria or Austro-Hungary, Italy and Great Britain with her colonies and children. Ten in all.

THE WOUNDED HEAD AND ITS HEALING

One of the heads was wounded to death. This vividly describes the fall of Imperial Rome by the successive onslaughts of the barbarians until at last, when the city fell, it seemed for a time as if all organized government had ceased from the earth. The wild beast seemed to be at last extinct, with the destruction of this mighty head. But gradually another power arose in its place. It was the sovereignty of the Popes. The disturbed condition of Italy demanded that someone come to the front to restore order and government, and it was then that the Pope established his temporal authority, annexed three of the states of Italy to his kingdom by right of which he wears a triple crown to this day, and brought back the ruined capital of the Caesars to a glory and an eminence even greater than during the most prosperous age of the Empire itself. Down through the Middle Ages, for more than a thousand years, Rome continued to be the capital of the world, and from its proud throne dictated not only the policies of the States of the Church but of all other earthly kingdoms. Nothing is more vivid than the description which an infidel historian has given of the strange resuscitation of this fallen head.

The following extract from a Roman Catholic secular historian will illustrate this.

> The rise of the temporal power of the Popes presents to the mind one of the most extraordinary phenomena which the annals of the human race offer to our wonder and admiration. By a singular combination of concurring circumstances a new power and a new dominion grew up silently and steadily on the ruins of that Roman Empire which had extended its sway over, or made itself respected, by nearly all nations, peoples, and races that lived in the period of its strength and glory, and that new power of lowly origin struck a deeper root and exercised a wider authority than the empire whose gigantic ruins it saw shattered into fragments and moldering in the dust. In Rome itself the power of the successor of Peter grew side by side with, and under the protecting shadow of that of the emperor and such was the increasing influence of the popes that the majesty of the supreme Pontiff was likely ere long to condemn the splendor of the purple.
>
> The removal by Constantine of the seat of the empire from the West to the East, from the mystic banks of the Tiber to the beautiful shores of the Bosphorus, laid the broad foundation for a sovereignty which in reality commences from that momentous age. Practically almost from that day Rome was gradually abandoned by the inheritors of her renown and its people deserted by emperors and an easy prey to the ravages of the barbarians whom they had no longer the courage to resist, beheld in the Bishop of Rome their guardian, their protector, their father. Year by year the temporal power of the popes grew into shape and hardened into strength without violence, without bloodshed, without ef-

fort by the force of overwhelming circumstances fashioned as if visibly by the hand of God.

This could scarcely have been more exact if the author had been writing with the 13th chapter of Revelation open before him.

A WORLDWIDE POWER

This was to be a worldwide power. The dominion of the Papacy was worldwide. The official seal of the Papal government is a woman holding in her hand a cup with the inscription on the seal, "She sits supreme above the world." It needs only a very little knowledge of medieval history to understand that the Popes of Rome not only conferred the crowns upon the heads of the kings of France, Germany and sometimes England, but took them away when they pleased and compelled the wearers to hold them always subject to Rome's dictation.

A BLASPHEMOUS POWER

It was a blasphemous power. "On each head a blasphemous name" (13:1). The beast was given a mouth to utter proud words and blasphemies. The blasphemies were of the nature of great assumptions. A simple list of some of the titles claimed by the Pope is a sufficient interpretation of this prophecy. One of his usual titles is, "Our Lord God, the Pope," and the following quotations from Romish authorities themselves will more than verify the application of this prophecy to this system of presumptuous pride.

The blasphemous character of the Papacy is evident from the following titles ascribed to the Pope by a leading Roman Catholic writer, Monsignor Capel: Prince of Bishops, Vicar of Christ, Sovereign Pontiff, Apostolic Lord and Father of Fathers, Infallible Pope, Most Divine of all Heads, Moses in Authority, High Priest, Supreme Bishop, Head of all the Holy Churches, Ruler of the House of the Lord.

Another Roman Catholic writer ascribes to him the following powers:

> The Pope is of such dignity and highness that he is not simply a man, but as it were, God, and the representative of God, hence the Pope is crowned with a triple crown as the king of heaven, of earth and of hell. He is above angels and is their superior, so that if it were possible that angels could err from the faith or entertain sentiments contrary to authority, they could be judged and excommunicated by the Pope.
>
> He is of such dignity and power that he occupies one and the same tribunal with Christ, so that whatsoever the Pope does seems to proceed from the mouth of God. The Pope is, as it

were, God on earth, to whom the government of the earth and heavenly kingdom is entrusted.

The following is from various Papal bulls. The bull of Sixtus V says:

> The authority given to St. Peter and his successors excels all the power of earthly kings and princes, and if it find any of them resisting God's ordinance it takes more severe vengeance on them, casting them down from their throne, however powerful they may be, and tumbling them down to the lowest abyss of the earth as the ministers of Lucifer.

Pope Innocent III says, "The Pope holds the place of the true God."
Pope Nicholas I says, "The Emperor Constantine conferred the name of God on the Pope, who, therefore, being God, cannot be judged by man."
The canon law of the Church of Rome designates the Pope "Our Lord God, the Pope."
Another of the Popes quoted by Fox in his acts and monuments declares,

> I am all in all, and above all, so that God Himself and I, His vicar, have both one consistory, and I am able to do almost all that God can do. In all things that I list, my will is to stand for reason for I am able by law to dispense above the law and of wrong to make justice in correcting laws and changing them. Wherefore, if those things I do be said not to be done of man but of God, what can ye make of me but God? Again, if the prelates of the Church be called and counted of Constantine for God's, I, then, being above all prelates, seem by this reason to be above all gods. Wherefore no marvel if it be in my power to change times and times, to alter and abrogate laws, to dispense with all things, yea, with the precepts of Christ.

Cardinal Manning endorses the following declaration: "We declare absolution and penance to be necessary to salvation for every human creature to be subject to the Roman pontiff."
The following references to the indulgences sold by Tetzell will show the blasphemous character of this extraordinary institution. Tetzell was one of the vilest of men and yet he was selected to carry these indulgences to all that would buy of them. He declared that the red cross which accompanied him had as great efficacy as the cross of Christ, that there was no sin so great that he could not remove it. Indulgences saved not the living alone but they also saved the dead. The very moment the money chinks against the bottom

of the chest the soul escapes from purgatory and flies free to heaven.

Among the abominations of the system was a regular scale of price: polygamy cost six ducats: sacrilege and perjury nine; murder eight.

The final climax was the mad and fatal folly which 30 years ago dared to claim infallibility and lifted itself so high that it fell from its citadel of supremacy to rise no more, at least to political preeminence.

Many of us can remember a time during our own lives when the Pope was a king in the Vatican and took part in conferences of European sovereigns and always claimed and received the right to occupy the chief place of honor and respect in diplomatic banquets and conferences. But the world has just witnessed the extraordinary spectacle of the refusal of the great powers of Europe to even allow him to be represented at the Peace Conference to be held at the Hague during the present year.

It is not necessary to suppose that blasphemy is always marked by open hostility to God. It is just as great a blasphemy to usurp the place of God or call ourselves His representatives, and we know that the vital principle of the Papacy is that the Holy Father is the Vicar of Christ, and the supreme authority on earth for law, right and human conscience. Several of the Popes have even officially declared that no man can convict the Pope of wrong even if it be open immorality. It ceases to be wrong if he chooses to call it right.

A PERSECUTING POWER

It was to be a persecuting power, to make war with the saints and afflict them. Was there ever any earthly power that so fulfilled this terrible picture? Imperial Rome was cruel, but it was reserved for Papal Rome to outdo all her cruelties by her fiendish outrages. The number of her martyrs has been estimated in the millions.

The massacre of St. Bartholomew wiped out the Protestants of France in a single night to the number of at least 50,000, and when the news reached Rome, a solemn Te Deum was celebrated and a medal was issued by the Pope in commemoration of this joyful event.

Spain sent the Duke of Alva to the Netherlands to stamp out the Protestant heresy. And during all the years of that terrible war, women and little children were murdered, outraged and exterminated, whole cities at a time often, with a fiendish barbarity unequalled in the annals of pagan war.

The story of the Spanish Inquisition is the most hideous chapter of the Middle Ages. Men were set apart for the one purpose of inventing the most ingenious tortures for the human body and mind, and while martyrs were literally being clawed to pieces with red hot flesh hooks, or torn limb from limb on wheels, a lot of robed priests were standing by denouncing upon them the curses of heaven and telling them that they were going down to hell and everlasting torment. Papal decrees regularly announced the names of men that had exterminated the greatest number of heretics, and they were held up for emulation to the Catholic world. Today, Spain is drinking in her turn the dregs of that cup which so long she held to the lips of the saints of God.

THE LENGTH OF TRIUMPH

This destructive, blasphemous and devilish power was to triumph for 1,260 years. Here we come to the great subject of prophetic chronology upon which we have not time to enter fully in this brief space. It will suffice to say that the rise of the papacy was gradual and its fall will also be gradual. In measuring its duration we must reckon therefore from the different dates which mark the standing points of the system and we must carry the measuring line forward to the corresponding dates which mark the epochs of its downfall. There were several marked periods in connection with the rise of the Papacy. Measuring from one of the most important of these, the decree of Phocas establishing the supremacy of the Pope, 1,260 years brings us to the year 1870, when the death blow was finally struck at the temporal power of the Papacy. Through a most marvelous series of providences the Pope was led first to claim his infallibility before the world and then before the echoes of that blasphemous announcement had ceased it was answered by war between France and Germany, which crushed the power of France and rendered it impossible for her to further sustain the Papacy, whereupon Victor Emanuel and Garibaldi raised the standard of Italian liberty and in a few days the throne of the Pope had fallen and Rome became the capital of united Italy. Thus precisely within the prophetic limit one phase of this system of blasphemy, persecution and oppression finished its career and met its judgment.

THE SPIRITUAL BEAST

We now come to another image of evil power, to the second beast. This beast unlike the other, rises out of the earth and not out of the sea. It comes from the midst of the organized political powers of the earth. Its principal is at first entirely different from the other. It is not a wild beast but looks like a gentle lamb and it is only when it speaks that its voice is like a dragon. It bears a very intimate relation to the beast that has just preceded and is really an ally to its power. It is a wonder-working power claiming to work great miracles and to make fire come down out of heaven. It is especially a deceiving power. It is also a despotic power claiming the right to control men's consciences and to compel them to worship its head and obey its authority under the penalty of the severest civil and social disabilities and punishments, boycotting even the ordinary avenues of trade when men refuse to be dominated by its despotic will.

Finally its very name is hinted at by the symbolical number 666. Let us look in detail at these particulars. First, however, let us premise again that this second beast represents not a political but an ecclesiastical power in very close alliance with the political power already described. What can so well fulfill all these specifications as the system of Papacy, not now as a state and sovereignty, but as a great false church. Let us now notice some particulars of this picture.

1. It arises out of the earth from the organized political states of the world.

2. It has the appearance of a lamb, is most plausible and insidious in its bearing and claims.

3. But it speaks as a dragon. Its voice is harsh, cruel, proud and blasphemous. It issues its Bulls and Interdicts, its maledictions and curses and has shown a fiendish cruelty in its dealing with mankind.

4. It is allied to the first beast, the Papal sovereignty, helping it and helped by it. It used through the Middle Ages its authority over the consciences of men to hold them in subjection to the basest bondage.

5. It claims the power of working miracles, and its largest stock in trade is relics, images, bones and records of false miracles through the power of the prayers of countless saints.

6. It is a deceiving power. Its miracles are false. Its claims are contradicted by the facts. It is built upon duplicity, hypocrisy and Jesuitism and it is essentially a system of deepest subtlety and Satanic guile.

7. It had power to give life to the image of the beast; that is to say it revived and restored the old Roman power that had been dying out, and aimed in the eighth century to reestablish the whole Roman Empire under Charlemagne, and literally fulfilled the prophecy of the 15th verse.

8. It compelled the obedience of men to its authority even in civil and social as well as spiritual matters. We know what a Papal interdict means. It was a decree issued by the Popes in peculiar exigencies when some king or subject became willful and disobedient and an interdict was issued against him, the effect of which was to prevent his subjects from obeying him, his soldiers from fighting for him, his wife from living with him, and all trades and classes from supplying his needs or giving him in any way help of any kind, so that he was practically cut off from the world and left to the mercy of the Pope.

9. Finally a hint is given of the name of this system of evil by the number 666. Many interpretations have been given out but the most satisfactory is that which is as old as the days of Irenaeus, a father of the second century, who first suggested that word Lateinos which means Latin and numbers exactly 666, each letter in the name having a certain numerical value. This is

indeed very wonderful, when we remember that Irenaeus lived centuries before the Papacy arose, and yet he foresaw that this system of iniquity would in some way become connected with the Latin language and the Latin race. The Papacy is Latin through and through, using the Latin language and having its constituency among the Latin races. Whatever else this number may mean it certainly is strangely appropriate in connection with this name.

Doubtless there will be important changes in the varied developments of the Papacy and probably before the end there will be some personal embodiment of the anti-Christ, crystallizing in some extraordinary manner that which has been already fulfilled in the system he will represent. But while expecting this let us not commit the fatal error of blinding our eyes to the tremendous facts of the present and the past. As Dr. Bonar has said with such force and wisdom: "It is one of the wiles of the devil so to pre-occupy our minds with the thought of the coming anti-Christ that we shall fail to recognize who is already here."

At the same time let us not forget that the spirit of the Papacy may extend far beyond the Papal organization. There seems to be a marked movement in all the Protestant churches today to gradually return to the things from which the Reformation delivered the Church. The Spirit of formalism and worldliness leads naturally to ritualism, and ritualism finds its only complete satisfaction in Romanism itself. When God's judgment strikes mystical Babylon it will strike all who in any way have shared her spirit, and let us not think that the name of Protestantism will save us from the discriminating and certain judgment of God.

We will come back to this subject again in the 17th and 18th chapters where the same organized and double system of political and ecclesiastical power will meet us under different imagery and in its later developments. But through all the changing figures we will find the same mystery of iniquity, and back of it the same subtle Adversary who has been its supporter and its head, and is at last to become himself its consummate embodiment and final head.

CHAPTER 8

THE FIRSTFRUITS AND THE HARVEST

These are those who did not defile themselves with women, for they kept themselves pure. They follow the Lamb wherever he goes. They were purchased from among men and offered as firstfruits to God and the Lamb. (Revelation 14:4)

Having given us the two contrasting pictures of the Mother Church and the wild beast, her great adversary and oppressor, the revelator now gives us in the 14th chapter of the Apocalypse a series of special visions or pictures of incidents connected with the last days. They are not perhaps consecutive pictures following in precise chronological order, but they are representative scenes taken from the closing events of the Christian age and leading up to the very end, at once to comfort the suffering people of God and to warn the careless and ungodly of coming judgment.

THE FIRSTFRUITS
This is a picture of the company of redeemed and purified ones who are described as the firstfruits from among men, and evidently the first to be caught up to meet the Lord at His coming.

Later we have a picture in the 15th and 16th verses of the full harvest of the earth, which was reaped by the Son of man. But these seem to represent an earlier company caught up to meet Him before the tribulation time had fully developed and at the beginning of the Parousia. Just what the difference between these two companies will be, and how long the interval between the firstfruits and the harvest we are not told; but that there will be a company of prepared ones who, when He comes, will open to Him immediately, and who will be characterized by a peculiar and somewhat nearer fellowship with the Lamb, seems to be very clearly intimated here. It is not an arbitrary distinction but the reward of personal character and holiness. Like the places on the right hand of Christ it is given to them for whom it is prepared, that is, to them who dare to take from God the preparation which it involves, and the separation for which it calls. Let us look more minutely at this wondrous company.

THEIR NUMBER

They were 144,000. This is a covenant number. It is composed of the number 12 multiplied into itself and then into 1,000. Twelve being made up of three and four is the number of God's covenant people and this multiple of 12 denotes a company who stand in peculiar and gracious relations to God. They are an elect people. They do not represent a mass, but a called-out company, who are all known individually, and all numbered. We read of another company of 144,000 in the seventh chapter of Revelation, the called-out and sealed ones among the Jews. These, as we will see later, are not Jews, but they are corresponding people of God, representing the Bride of Christ, the Gentile Church; or perhaps more correctly, the Church of Christ of no particular race or family, but of every race and tongue. God has a people that He is preparing for the coming glory, and of them it is said: "The Lord knows those who are his" (2 Timothy 2:19).

THEIR PLACE

They stand on Mount Zion with the Lamb. Now we are taught by the New Testament Scriptures the spiritual significance of Mount Zion.

> But you have come to Mount Zion, to the heavenly Jerusalem, the city of the living God. You have come to thousands upon thousands of angels in joyful assembly, to the church of the firstborn, whose names are written in heaven. You have come to God, the judge of all men, to the spirits of righteous men made perfect, to Jesus the mediator of a new covenant, and to the sprinkled blood that speaks a better word than the blood of Abel. (Hebrews 12:22–24)

Here Mount Zion is evidently the spiritual center of God's redeemed people. It is not a Jewish Zion; for Zion here is the heavenly Jerusalem contrasted with Mount Sinai. This company therefore represents the elect ones of the Church of the living God, and we may all aspire to a place in their holy ranks and a part in their glorious hope.

IN TOUCH WITH HEAVEN

This company is in very close touch with heaven. They understand the song that is sung before the throne above. They have learned the language of the skies. They are in harmony with the celestial home and none but they can understand the language or the music of the world above. They are heavenly people, and they are waiting for their translation to join that heavenly throng. They are not yet translated, but they are the called-out ones who will have a part in the resurrection from among the dead, and while waiting here they are walking with the Lord, and following the Lamb wherever He goes.

SEPARATED ONES

These are separated ones. They were "redeemed from the earth" (Revelation 14:3), and later it is said, "they were purchased [redeemed, KJV] from among men" (14:4). They were not of the world but had been taken out of it in spirit and in character. God wants a separated people, intrinsically so different from the world that the world will drop them as readily as they drop the world.

PURE AND UNDEFILED

They were pure and undefiled. The word "virgins" (KJV) is used in the masculine here to denote a life severed and separated from all illicit and unholy things. It does not mean that they are necessarily living a strained, ascetic life. The Bible nowhere casts a slur on lawful marriage as a less holy state than celibacy; but the meaning is that they are living rightly, and free from every stain of impurity. It is in this direction that Satan's most insidious and corrupting power has been swayed over human souls, and blessed indeed are they that have been kept undefiled. To them is possible a vision of God and a fellowship with Jesus which belong only to the Bride of the Lamb.

OBEDIENT

They are obedient ones. "They follow the Lamb wherever he goes" (14:4). It is not that they follow Him, but they always follow Him, and they follow Him everywhere. It is uncompromising obedience. It is unqualified submission to His will. It is the acceptance of the test which He Himself has laid down: "You are my friends if you do what I command" (John 15:14).

TRUE ONES

These are true ones. "No lie was found in their mouths; they are blameless" (Revelation 14:5). They are honest, sincere, truthful; free from hypocrisy, deceit and falsehood of every kind. Can such a life be lived below? Only by those in whom Christ lives; for this was the life of the Son of man Himself. "He committed no sin,/ and no deceit was found in his mouth" (1 Peter 2:22); "who is holy, blameless, pure, set apart from sinners" (Hebrews 7:26); and "whoever claims to live in him must walk as Jesus did" (1 John 2:6).

If we fully learn our inability to live this life and surrender ourselves in helplessness to Him, and receive Him, and constantly depend on Him to re-live His life in us, we, too, shall find that "no one who lives in him keeps on sinning" (1 John 3:6), and that He "is able to keep [us] from falling and to present [us] before his glorious presence without fault and with great joy" (Jude 24).

A WORLDWIDE EVANGEL

The next picture is an angel flying in the midst of heaven.

> Then I saw another angel flying in midair, and he had the eter-nal gospel to proclaim to those who live on the earth—to every nation, tribe, language and people. He said in a loud voice, "Fear God and give him glory, because the hour of his judgment has come. Worship him who made the heavens, the earth, the sea and the springs of water." (Revelation 14:6–7)

It is very significant that the Holy Spirit has here grouped together two movements which are the peculiar spiritual features of our days. One is the movement for scriptural holiness and the other the great missionary move-ment to give the gospel as a witness immediately to all nations. It is such a movement which this remarkable passage describes.

1. A Swift and Earnest Message

The angel flying in the midst of heaven is but a symbol of a swift and earnest message speeding over every land and hastening to the coming of the Lord. The peculiarity of the present missionary movement is its rapidity and intensity. It has all been confined within about 100 years, and from present appearances it looks as if within another generation it might reach its cul-mination and give the gospel to every tribe.

2. A Gospel Movement

That it is a gospel movement there can be no doubt. The attempt of some interpreters to apply the term "the eternal gospel" to some special message confined to the last days, and delivered by some literal angel, is very strained and contrary to the analogy of Scripture. The word "angel" is the apocalypti-cal term for the minister of the gospel, and the everlasting gospel can be nothing but the old gospel of which God has said that "the word of God . . . liveth and abideth forever" (1 Peter 1:23, KJV). There is but one gospel and it is everlasting, and the apostle has said that even if "an angel from heaven should preach a gospel other than the one we preached to you, let him be eternally condemned" (Galatians 1:8).

3. For All Nations

This is a message for all nations. "Every nation, tribe, people and language" (Revelation 7:9) is specified. It is the universal proclamation of the message of salvation to all men. That is the peculiar feature of the missionary movement today, that it is confined within no sectional lines but aims at the universal evangelization of the world.

4. Emphasizes the Lord's Coming and Judgment

It is a message that emphasizes the coming of the Lord and the hour of His judgment upon sinful nations and ungodly men. Its message is "the hour of his judgment has come" (14:7). Is not this also a marked feature of the missionary movement of this age? Is there not an increasing and most encouraging tendency toward the premillennial standpoint in the missionary work of our time, and ought not this to be emphasized especially in this crisis of the age? Is there not something in it especially fitted to arouse and awaken the slumbering nations?

When Jonah stood in the streets of Nineveh and proclaimed: "Forty more days and Nineveh will be overturned" (Jonah 3:4), there was something about this message so startling and so authoritative that it forced conviction and awakened the consciences of men. And when the heralds of Christ go forth to heathen lands to declare that the Lord of earth and heaven is about to come, the King of kings is soon to summon to judgment the sovereigns of the earth, One greater than these chiefs and potentates is on His way to set up His throne, there is something in the message that is fitted to arouse the hearts of man. And God will seal it with His quickening power and make it a word of conviction, as solemn as in the days of old.

The time, we are persuaded, is drawing near when the Holy Spirit will lay this burden so heavily upon the missionaries of the cross that the gospel will go forth to the world with a final and authoritative message like this apocalyptic word, "Fear God and give him glory, because the hour of his judgment has come" (14:7).

THE VISION OF THE FALL OF BABYLON

The next picture is a vision of the fall of Babylon: "A second angel followed and said, 'Fallen! Fallen is Babylon the Great, which made all the nations drink the maddening wine of her adulteries' " (14:8). This does not mean that the power represented by Babylon is already fallen, but it is the intimation of its impending fall in connection with the great series of events of which the chapter is a representation. The universal spread of the gospel and the preparation of the Bride of the Lamb are intimately associated with God's final judgments upon the great apostasy. And when the people of Christ are ready, then His providence will not linger behind, but the great panorama of history will move rapidly abreast of the Holy Spirit in the hearts and through the ministry of the Church of God.

THE WARNING

The next picture (Revelation 14:9–12) brings us an awful warning against all those who yield to the power of the apostasy and receive the mark of this system of iniquity in their foreheads or hands. It is apparent that a great conflict is impending. The powers of evil are to break forth in persecuting hate against the people of God, and the martyr spirit is again to be revived and proved, and God encourages His people by this solemn warning to stand true against the terrors of Satan and the system of iniquity in which he has embodied his final assault against the kingdom of God.

A VISION OF THE BLESSED DEAD

Next comes a vision of the blessed dead. This seems specially to apply to the period of persecution just described. Many a faithful witness will seal his testimony with his blood, but " 'Blessed are the dead who die in the Lord from now on.' 'Yes,' says the Spirit, 'they will rest from their labor, for their deeds will follow them' " (14:13). While this is doubtless true of all the blessed dead in every age, it will be especially true of the faithful ones of that tribulation time. Taken from the evil to come they shall enter into rest, and their works shall follow them to claim the great reward which is now so soon to be bestowed.

THE VISION OF THE HARVEST OF THE EARTH

Now comes the vision of the harvest of the earth (14:14–16). This apparently reaches on to the close of the tribulation time and completes the number of God's elect. It differs from the picture of the firstfruits, as the Feast of Tabernacles of old did from the Feast of Pentecost. That was the beginning of the harvest. This is its fullness. "A white cloud, and seated on the cloud was one 'like a son of man' " (14:14) recall all the old imagery associated with the picture of Christ's second coming. He wears upon His brow a golden crown which is the symbol of His reign so soon to begin; and He holds in His hand a sharp sickle with which He is to gather the harvest.

This harvest represents the full number of His people from every age and every land. At the beginning of the tribulation it would appear that a certain number had been caught up to meet Him in the air as the firstfruits; but during these dark and troubled days there were many that have died in the Lord, and there are many living saints who have been true to their testimony and their Lord; and it may be that there are myriads more who were not caught up in the first rapture because they were not ready—foolish virgins, perhaps, with oil in their lamps, but not in their vessels; and now, the whole body of His people is gathered to Him and all the grain is husbanded into His garner. It is the finishing of the number of His elect. It is the culmination of the work of redemption through all the age. It is the great "harvest home" of time.

Ask us not to tell all the minute particulars and details. It looms before us like a mighty vision, vague and indistinct in its finer features, but clear and plain in its great bold outlines. There is to be the reaping; there is to be the harvest. There are some firstfruits; and there is the fullness of the Gentiles and the completing of the Bride, the great multitude that no man can number out of every kindred, and tribe, and tongue, yet to stand before the throne and celebrate the consummation of the great redemption.

THE VINTAGE OF THE EARTH

But there is one picture more. It is the vintage of the earth (14:17–20). This is a very different picture, clothed with lurid light and fearful shadows of wrath and judgment.

The angel who ministers in this scene is a very different angel from the Son of man. He is the angel of judgment, cold and stern as inexorable Justice itself. He, too, has in his hand a sharp sickle, but it is not for the harvest but for the clusters of the vine of the earth. The grapes are hanging rich and purple, and they are ready for the winepress of the wrath of God.

How terribly this suggestive image represents the wickedness of the human heart and the human race. The heavy clusters of purple grapes speak of the passion, the sensuality, the pleasure, the selfishness of a godless world. They remind us of the banquet, the dance, the song, the deep, full draught of earthly indulgence. Yes, drink it with its brimming cup, press out the juice of the clusters of earth's vine, revel in their beauty and luxuriance for life's little day of frivolous pleasure; but remember the winepress of the wrath of God, the treading down of sin and its blind, foolish votaries and victims in earth's last hours of fearful judgment, until the blood reaches to the horses' bridles.

Ah, this is the last picture of the earthly panorama! The crimson wine will yet become crimson blood; the song will end in shrieks of agony, and the winecup of pleasure become the wormwood and the gall of the wrath of God. We are sweeping on to earth's brightest, and yet to time's darkest, saddest hour. Before us opens the vista of glory, but beyond lies the most awful catastrophe of human history. Say to Edom's watchmen, say to earth's sons and daughters as they ask: "What is left of the night?" " 'Morning is coming,' yes, the morning for us, 'but also the night' for you (Isaiah 21:11-12)."

If one had the power to look into the horoscope of life and see you when a few years will have passed and gone in the place to which you are tending, which of these visions would it be? Would it be among the firstfruits with the Lamb, on Mount Zion, and the new song, and the spotless robes?

Would it be with the blessed dead amid their enduring works and eternal rewards? Would it be with the harvest of the earth, when Christ will gather all His own in the great feast of tabernacles in the coming age? Would it be with the loving heralds hastening over land and sea to give the gospel swiftly to all nations? Or, would it be with those who go down to torment with the mark of the beast upon their brow, and those who are ripening for the winepress of the wrath of God? Ask Him who knows, to tell you, and to tell you that you will have your part in the happy company who will meet Him at His coming with joy and not with grief.

CHAPTER 9

THE VIALS AND THE PLAGUES

Out of the temple came the seven angels with the seven plagues. They were dressed in clean, shining linen and wore golden sashes around their chests. Then one of the four living creatures gave to the seven angels seven golden bowls filled with the wrath of God, who lives for ever and ever. (Revelation 15:6–7)

Behold, I come like a thief! Blessed is he who stays awake and keeps his clothes with him, so that he may not go naked and be shamefully exposed. (16:15)

The last of the texts that we have quoted above is the key to the first. It makes it plain and certain that the judgments represented by these seven vials immediately precede and lead up to the coming of Christ as a thief. Exactly what is meant by that coming there can be no question. It is not His public appearing in glory, the grand epiphany which is described in the 19th chapter of the Apocalypse and which has already been hinted at in the vision of the harvest and the winepress and other visions that have gone before. But it is that quiet, solemn, unannounced parousia which will be known only to His waiting Bride, and which will, perhaps, little disturb the ordinary current of human affairs. It is that coming for which His people are waiting every day and which at the farthest cannot now be very far beyond the life of the oldest reader of these lines.

If this be so then it is very plain that the events described, represented by the vials, are not far off future occurrences that are to belong to the Tribulation time, but they are the things which are happening today and ripening fast toward the crisis of the age. With what intense interest therefore, we look around us in the light of these lurid gleams as we follow the white-robed angels of judgment and behold them pouring out the vials of wrath even while we gaze.

THE FIRST VIAL

The first angel poured out his vial upon the earth and immediately there fell a noisome and grievous sore upon the men who had the mark of the beast, and upon those who worshiped his image. This judgment must be looked for among the followers of Papacy and it would seem to mark the first of God's signal judgments upon a people especially connected with this system of iniquity. If one were to ask any impartial historian what people have been most distinctly connected with the Papal power for many centuries, the answer would point us immediately to France. This was the seat of the restored Roman Empire and the foremost supporter of the Vatican. France was always called the eldest son of the Papacy and until the fall of the Pope's temporal power in 1870 the very person of the Pope was guarded by French soldiers.

Now one does not need to look far to find the noisome and grievous sore that fell upon this nation. It is just about 100 years since the most awful political and social catastrophe of modern history fell upon France. The historians who have described the awful events of the French Revolution and its causes and consequences have been led to describe it, with singular appropriateness, as a great political and social disease, some vile and horrid distemper that suddenly struck the body politic with threatened destruction. The wild and fearful scenes of revolution, assassination, outrage, blasphemy and the outbreak of every human passion and every form of hellish wickedness were so unique and unparalleled, that although there have been many French revolutions through many centuries yet there is but one that is known as the French Revolution. It has left its mark forever upon France and Europe, and, more than any other event of the past 500 years, it was a deadly blow at the Papacy itself, for the forces that it set in operation never ceased until the Pope was hurled from his throne and forever despoiled of his temporal sovereignty.

THE SECOND VIAL

The second angel poured out his vial upon the sea and its waters became as blood, and the imagery is that of carnage and death. Following in the line of the French Revolution we come immediately, in the history of modern Europe, to a series of naval wars unequalled in modern history. For eight years from 1797 to 1805 the waters of earth literally ran with blood and it is said that between 500 and 600 fighting ships in the navies of France and her allies were sunk and tens of thousands of lives perished. These terrible naval disasters all fell upon the people who worshiped the beast and were inflicted by the hands of a Protestant power through the influence of Great Britain. It was during this period that the famous battles of Cape Vincent, Copenhagen, the Nile and Trafalgar were fought and won and the maritime ascendancy of England established on every sea. The appropriateness of the prophetic symbol is so obvious that prophecy reads like history.

THE THIRD VIAL

The third angel poured out his vial upon the rivers and fountains of waters, and they ran with human blood until the angel of the waters was forced to acknowledge the justness of the judgment because these very people had shed the blood of saints and martyrs before. This imagery will lead our thoughts at once to some region which had been peculiarly associated with the persecution of God's saints. There are two regions in Europe particularly identified with persecution. One is the low country of the Netherlands and the other the highlands of the Alps and Northern Italy. One feature in the prophetic vision precludes the former and directs us to some region which might properly be called the rivers and fountains of waters. The latter country, Piedmont and Northern Italy, is the fountain-head of all the rivers of Europe running northward and southward in the great streams of the Po, the Rhine, etc. Now it happens that this country was for ages the home of the Waldenses and the Vaudois, the holy and faithful saints of the middle ages, and against these the whole power of the Papacy was directed until their blood ran on every mountain side, and holy martyrs and gentle maidens hurled themselves from the face of the rocks to save themselves from the cruelty of their foes. It was of this that Milton sang with perhaps no thought of this prophecy,

> Avenge, oh Lord, Thy slaughtered saints, whose blood
> Lies scattered on the Alpine mountains cold.

Now following immediately the French Revolution and the maritime wars at the beginning of this century came the most fearful shock of battle which Europe had seen for centuries on these very fields. It was here that Napoleon, suddenly leaping into fame, impelled by a wild devastating ambition, led the armies of the French Republic and fought the famous battles of Lodi, Arcola, Mantua and many others that have given luster to his name. He beat down all resistance and established the French dominion over all these lands, and the people that had drunk the blood of saints so long at last were given their own blood to drink, and heaven recognized the justice of the judgment. All this is very clear and needs but to be traced by a candid mind in the history of our century.

THE FOURTH VIAL

Next the angel of judgment pours out his vial upon the sun, men are scorched with sudden heat and multitudes perish. There is a little uncertainty about the interpretation of this symbol. It may correctly refer to the hotter flame of battle which followed the events already described until the whole continent of Europe was ablaze with war, and men were consumed by the scorching rays and perished by hundreds of thousands. This was true in the first 15 years of the 19th century until at last the very fate of the world seemed to hang in the balance, and the battle of Waterloo in 1815 really saved Europe from the power of a reckless and universal despotism.

But we believe there is another interpretation more strictly in accordance with the simple figure and also in line with the facts of history. The sun is the natural symbol of light, and this stroke upon the sun would seem to suggest a terrible blow at the sources and streams of human knowledge so that some awful cloud came upon the mind of man, some perversion of human reason and conscience, followed by false teachings, wrong principles and monstrous crimes. Now is it not strictly true that since the French Revolution at the beginning of the present century there has been such a scorching stroke upon the mind and conscience of the world? The spirit of wild and reckless license has been let loose and new and destructive phases of infidel thought, bold atheistic materialism, reckless socialism and godless naturalism, with, we may add, gross sensualism have permeated the whole structure of human society and the sad evils are beginning to appear on every side.

Respect and veneration for authority have gone. The home has been invaded and all the holy bonds that held society together are being torn to shreds. Democracy and liberty are becoming demagogism and are the rule of the lowest classes in the community. Socialism is the undermining of human society; Nihilism is threatening the foundations of government; labor and capital are at war, and under every institution there is the muttering of a threatened convulsion and a terrible earthquake. Faith has lost its hold upon the human conscience. Righteousness has been drowned in compromising. Mammon is enthroned above principle and God, and the very Church is almost as broad as the world. The conscience of man has lost its hold and the days have come when men will call good evil and evil good, and the solemn warning of Christ is becoming true, "If then the light within you is darkness, how great is that darkness!" (Matthew 6:23). It is as if the sun of truth and righteousness had been eclipsed, or rather had begun to burn with a fierce and scorching flame and instead of giving its joyful, healthful light was consuming us by its fiercest beams.

THE FIFTH VIAL

The next angel pours out his vial directly upon the seat of the beast. We may now expect some blow upon Rome itself and our expectation is not disappointed. Three times in a century has that blow been struck. The first occasion was in the beginning of the century when the armies of Napoleon, having conquered Italy and Austria, at last besieged Rome, assisted by revolutionary Italian forces, and the Pope was taken prisoner and carried over the Alps in the dead of winter to France where he died neglected and alone; and the Catholic world looked with amazement on the spectacle of him whose person had been considered sacred and inviolate, a helpless and dying prisoner in the hands of his insulting foes.

It was a blow to the prestige and dignity of the Papacy which had never been thought possible.

Again in 1848 the spirit of revolution broke out and once more the temporal power of the Papacy seemed to be departing. The culminating stroke, however, came in 1870, when, after the blasphemous decree of Papal infallibility had been passed, God's forbearance was exhausted and He let loose the dogs of war before which France was crushed in helplessness under the armies of Germany, and Italy took advantage of the fact to claim her freedom while France was helpless to protect the Pope. The Italian troops marched into Rome. The Pope became a prisoner in the Vatican, and the great temporal sovereignty that for ages had ruled the world passed away forever.

The spiritual system did not cease. Indeed, this power was rather intensified and is still spreading and working with all its ancient cunning, but the Papacy as a kingdom has ended and the vial upon the seat of the beast has done its work forever.

Now, how any one can trace these five judgments and read the companion page of the history of the present century and not be deeply moved by the marvelous correspondence and fulfillment we cannot understand. But the progression still advances.

THE SIXTH VIAL

The sixth angel next pours out his vial. But now the scene is changed. The judgment upon the Papal beast has done its work and a new adversary must now be found. There is still another form of organized spiritual wickedness which has not yet appeared in the book of Revelation except for a moment but which now becomes the subject of God's judicial dealing.

It is here described as the River Euphrates, and the "water was dried up to prepare the way for the kings from the East" (Revelation 16:12). The river Euphrates evidently represents some Oriental form of evil power. It is the natural image of the Muslim and Turkish power, the twin apostasy of the ages. It began when the Papacy began and it will pass away at the same time and under corresponding judgments. And so, abreast of the strange movement of God's providence in dealing with Papal lands we have witnessed for half a century His judicial dealing with the Islamic peoples, especially the Turkish empire.

Not suddenly, but like the drying up of an Eastern river has its power been passing away. The beginning of the century was marked by the Greek Revolution and the terrible battle of Navarino by which the Turkish fleet was destroyed and the independence of Greece secured. Then came the rebellion of Mehemit Ali leading to the independence of Egypt, the conquest of Syria and the threatened capture even of Constantinople. Since that time province after province has been slipping from the grasp of the Turk, Moldavia, Wallachia, Bulgaria, Serbia, Montenegro, and section after section in Asia has passed either into independence or into the hands of other powers and but a vestige is left the Turk of his ancient and mighty dominion.

As he disappears another race appears. It is here described as the kings of the East or the kingdom of the East. It is not hard to recognize the Jew, an Oriental people and a people destined yet to rule the world. As the Turk retires the Jew advances. Side by side with the decadence of the Sultan is the marvelous advance of the Hebrew. Today he is the king of finance and European journalism. He is a potent force in politics. He holds the sinews of war. And he has at last become a united people. The heart of the race has revived. The old watchword of Zion has received new meaning. Rich and poor from every land are uniting in a great movement looking to the recovery of Palestine for the Jew, the establishment of a Hebrew state and the return of Israel to the heights of Zion. It is a marvelous movement and the beginning of the end.

But this vial has a further reach. Its force is not spent with mere national and political effects. It also touches the deepest social and spiritual realms. Under it we see three forms of malignant spiritual power going forth among men. They are described as three unclean spirits like frogs that go forth unto the kings of the earth to prepare them for "the battle on the great day of God Almighty" (16:14).

The frogs are natural symbols of evil spirits of impurity, darkness, gloom and evil. They come from three directions. One comes directly from the devil. It is not hard to recognize this unclean spirit. It bears its master's image on its front. It is that fearful system of Spiritualism which has spread its unhallowed influence through every civilized community. It is the devil worship of the beast adjusted to modern civilization and culture. It is undoubtedly supernatural, working miracles not merely by pretence but in reality—miracles like those of Egypt, only inferior to those of the Holy Spirit. And it has gone forth into the kings of the earth. It seems to have had peculiar access to royal palaces and kingly personages. It is infusing into the minds of men the principles of practical atheism and ungodliness which will prepare men for "the battle on the great day of God Almighty" (16:14).

The second of these spirits comes from the beast. It seems to represent some political spirit, perhaps democracy, demagogism, license, the rule of the masses, the rule of the saloon, the rule of the nihilist, the rule that rules to ruin. This spirit is abroad today and already we stand upon the edge of a vortex which at any moment may engulf society.

The third frog comes from the False Prophet. Whether he represents Islam, especially, or all false religions, is not clear. In any event this evil spirit represents some form of false religion, some wild fanaticism, some truth carried to extremes, some frenzied, fiery leader claiming supernatural power, teaching a false spiritism, leading men to call evil good and to claim the sanction and leading of the Holy Spirit for the vilest crimes. We have seen these things in our day as the counterfeits of piety and sanctity.

And we need, in these last times, to watch the voices and the fruits of every religious teaching that bears upon it the stamp of strain or extravagance. "For false Christs and false prophets will appear and perform signs and miracles to deceive the elect—if that were possible" (Mark 13:22). These things have already begun. They are to increase and intensify as the age ripens and they are the most solemn signs of the times in which we live.

AN INTERRUPTION

But there now comes an interruption in the series of vials and judgments. The seventh vial is not immediately poured out, but, while the sixth is still working out its solemn issues, there comes a strange whisper from the air addressed to the saints of God, "Behold, I come like a thief! Blessed is he who stays awake and keeps his clothes with him, so that he may not go naked and be shamefully exposed" (Revelation 16:15).

This is not meant for the great noisy world but it is a sacred whisper intended for His own. It comes as a parenthesis before the sixth vial has done all its work. The great day of God Almighty has not yet come. The forces of earth are gathering for the battle of the ages, but the battle is not on and before it will be on, right in the midst of its preparation, something very strange is to come to pass. It is the translation of the saints of God. It is the coming of the Master as a thief. It is the catching away of the waiting ones from the coming catastrophe, the lifting up of the little flock before the storm.

Therefore you will notice that this whisper comes right in between the 14th and 16th verses. In the 14th verse the battle is preparing and in the 16th verse it is on. But in the 15th we are caught away. Is not this what Christ has intimated in Luke, "When these things begin to take place, stand up and lift up your heads, because your redemption is drawing near" (Luke 21:28)?

There is something unmistakable about this picture of His coming. The thief comes not to take away the house or all its contents. He leaves more than he takes. He comes to take the treasures only and leave the rest. So this coming is for the holy, waiting ones. The morning after He has come the world will still be there—its warehouses, its railroads, its palaces and mansions, its churches and perhaps many of its preachers—but the tried ones, the pure ones, the waiting ones, they will have gone, gone so quietly that they at first will be scarcely missed. "One will be taken and the other left" (17:34).

Is it not all so solemn, so near, so personal? It is to each one that He speaks the gentle warning, "Blessed is he who stays awake and keeps his clothes with him" (Revelation 16:15). That is all.

There is nothing we can do ourselves. We cannot weave the bridal raiment. We cannot glorify ourselves for the ascension. We cannot lift ourselves in spite of the law of gravitation from earth to heaven, but we can be robed and ready and He will do the rest. He will know us by our robes.

Rebekah did not have to prepare her wedding garments. Her husband's servants sent them all and she had but to put them on, and Isaac knew her by her veil and the attire he had sent before. And so of her it is said, " 'His bride has made herself ready./ Fine linen, bright and clean,/ was given her to wear.' (Fine linen stands for the righteous acts of the saints)" (19:7–8). What are these garments? Read back and listen.

> Then I looked, and there before me was the Lamb, standing on Mount Zion, and with him 144,000 who had his name and his Father's name written on their foreheads. . . . And they sang a new song before the throne and before the four living creatures and the elders. No one could learn the song except the 144,000 who had been redeemed from the earth. These are those who did not defile themselves with women, for they kept themselves pure. They follow the Lamb wherever he goes. They were purchased from among men and offered as firstfruits to God and the Lamb. No lie was found in their mouths; they are blameless. (14:1–5)

God help us to watch and keep these garments unto the coming of the Lord.

THE SEVENTH VIAL

Then comes at last the final conflict. Armageddon, it is called. The great battle of the ages in the old field of Megiddo where Josiah fell, where the crusading armies fought, and where at last the kings of the north and the south are to meet in the sanguinary conflict that Ezekiel (38, 39) and

Daniel (11) have described in their sublime visions. Perhaps the forces even now are preparing, the mighty hosts of the north with their eye on Constantinople and Palestine, the Jew and his country, the prize for which they are contending. The ships of Tarshish, of England, and the powers of the south unite under the lion's banner that Ezekiel describes. All this we see dimly in the prophetic foreground, but the event will make it all the more plain. Perhaps we will not see it from the earth for we hope that we will be with Him there.

But now comes the seventh vial which is poured out, not upon the earth, but in the air. The battle scene has changed from the soil of this planet to the clouds of heaven, for Christ has already come into the air and the powers of darkness are meeting Him there and the last vial is the signal that the mighty conflict is about to end. Voices and thunders proclaim along the heavens "It is done!" (16:17) and lo, the judgment of the nations, the fall of Babylon, the convulsion of nature itself and all the attending circumstances of the Great Appearing are around us. The Lord is come and the judgments attending His triumphal march are on their way.

The details of these things will come in the later visions. Meanwhile let us again pause and ask, Are we ready? In which of these comings will we have our first vision of the Lord, the sweet parousia or the awful epiphany? From which side will we look down upon this rocking earth and rending heaven? The earth side or the heaven side? Will it be true of us,

I see earth's last red bloody sunset,
    I see the dread Avenger's form,
I hear the Armageddon onset,
    But I shall be above the storm.

There comes a moaning and a sighing,
    There comes the death clod's heavy fall,
The thousand agonies of dying,
    But I shall be beyond them all.

My hopes are passing upward, onward,
    And with my hopes my heart is gone,
My eyes are turning skyward, sunward,
    Whose glory brightens round His throne.

CHAPTER 10

MYSTICAL BABYLON, THE WOMAN AND THE BEAST

I saw a woman sitting on a scarlet beast that was covered with blasphemous names and had seven heads and ten horns. The woman was dressed in purple and scarlet, and was glittering with gold, precious stones and pearls. She held a golden cup in her hand, filled with abominable things and the filth of her adulteries. This title was written on her forehead:

MYSTERY
BABYLON THE GREAT
THE MOTHER OF PROSTITUTES
AND OF THE ABOMINATIONS OF THE EARTH.
(Revelation 17:3–5)

It will help us to understand the varied imagery of this wonderful book if we pause at this point and fix in our minds the fact that we have four figures in the Apocalypse which stand as two sets of companion pictures. The one is the coming King and the companion picture is His holy Bride. The opposite picture is the earthly kingdom with seven heads and 10 horns and the counterfeit bride, the false church represented by a vile woman. These four figures loom up above every other amid the symbolism of the book: the Lord Jesus Christ, the King of kings and Lord of lords, and the devil's counterfeit of earthly politics and dominion. This is one contrast. The other is the glorious woman clothed with the sun and crowned with the stars, His blessed Bride; and her antithesis is the harlot who represents the false church.

As the Lord Jesus Christ is to be united with His Bride, so Satan's earthly king becomes wedded to the false church and the woman appears therefore seated upon the beast.

483

Once more the holy Bride is designated in the closing vision of the Apocalypse as the glorious city which is to be her home, and so she is described as "the new Jerusalem, coming down out of heaven from God" (Revelation 21:2). In keeping with this the false woman is also associated with the city which is her home, and she is called Babylon. Altogether we have six images: the Lord Jesus, His Bride and the new Jerusalem—a Trinity of blessed and glorious realities; and in contrast with them we have the dragon's kingdom, the false church and the mystic Babylon.

All these images of the evil power are focused in the 17th chapter of Revelation where we see appearing again and again the beast, the harlot and the city of Babylon where all together they establish their dominion and meet their doom.

There are really two powers described, the one a political and the other an ecclesiastical power. We saw them both in the 13th chapter of Revelation as two different beasts. Here they are represented by a beast and a woman and the two become united and are judged and destroyed. Let us look at the special features of this remarkable picture and learn its prophetic and practical lessons.

THE FIGURE OF A WOMAN

This system of spiritual evil is represented under the figure of a woman. This is no new representation. In Zechariah 5:7–11 we behold a woman sitting in the midst of an ephah and then borne by two other women with wings like a stork to her own abode in the land of Shinar—which is just Babylon—and the angel interprets it to the prophet by saying, "this is wickedness" (Zechariah 5:7).

This is God's ancient picture of this false woman.

Again, in the 13th chapter of Matthew we find a woman mixing the leaven in three measures of meal. And again in this same book of Revelation in connection with the church of Thyatira the same evil system is represented as "that woman Jezebel" (Revelation 2:20). How truly it is said that woman can be earth's greatest blessing or bitterest curse! Her power for evil is as boundless as her power for good.

> She raised a mortal to the skies;
> She brought an angel down.

A HARLOT

She is a vile woman, a harlot. It is implied that she was once pure but has committed spiritual adultery with the world. This figure, of course, is to be understood in its highest spiritual meaning. In the book of Hosea we find as the very basis of the prophet's appeal to Israel the figure of the false wife; and in the epistle of James those who become the friends of the world are addressed as adulterers and adulteresses, and the apostle adds, "Don't you know that friendship with the world is hatred toward God? Anyone who chooses to be a friend of the world becomes an enemy of God. Or do you think Scripture says without reason that the spirit he caused to live in us envies intensely?" (James 4:4–5).

SITTING ON MANY WATERS

This woman is represented as sitting on many waters. These waters are explained as "peoples, multitudes, nations and languages" (Revelation 17:15). This represents the wide dominion of the false church over earth's myriads. The Papacy has been eminently successful in her foreign missions because she has adapted herself unscrupulously to the superstitions, prejudices and passions of the various races with whom she has mingled, and today her spiritual sway extends over more than 200 million of the human family.

DWELLING IN THE WILDERNESS

She is represented as dwelling in the wilderness: "Then the angel carried me away in the Spirit into a desert" (17:3). This expression is peculiar and seems to describe with singular propriety the condition of Rome and the surrounding country at the time the Papacy arose. It came out of the wreck of Roman power; and at the time that it first appeared in its supreme claims for ecclesiastical primacy and temporal sovereignty, Gibbon says of Rome she had reached at this time

> . . . the lowest period of her depression by the removal of the seat of empire and the successive loss of the provinces, the sources of private and public opulence were exhausted, the lofty tree under whose shade the nations of the earth had reposed was deprived of its leaves and its branches, and the sapless trunk left to wither in the ground. The Campagna of Rome was reduced to the state of a dreary wilderness in which the land is barren, the waters are impure and the air infectious. The depopulation was constant and rapid and gloomy enthusiasts might expect the approaching fate of the human race.

HER ATTIRE

The attire of this woman is described. She was "dressed in purple and scarlet, and was glittering with gold, precious stones and pearls" (17:4). It is unnecessary to identify these colors with the insignia and adornment of the entire Papal ritual and officiary. The prominent colors in its great ecclesiastical ceremonies are purple and scarlet. The red hood of the cardinal is the most honored gift of the church. Its altars are decked with gold and precious stones so that even silver is scarcely seen. In the single church of St. Paul's at Rome there is altar after altar which has been endowed by kings and princes, each of which is of incalculable value.

HOLDS A GOLDEN CUP

She is represented as holding in her hand a "golden cup . . . filled with abominable things" (17:4). It is strangely significant that one of the official medals of the Papacy struck by Leo XII contains on its face this very picture of a woman holding in her hand a golden cup and with the Latin inscription, "*sedet super universam.*"

THE BLOOD OF SAINTS

This woman is "drunk with the blood of the saints, the blood of those who bore testimony to Jesus" (17:6). She has been a persecuting power and the rage of persecution has become the wild passion of intoxication. It is unnecessary for us to recall that we have already said in this connection in the former chapters to prove that with the Papacy the shedding of the blood of saints has been a passion and a carnival of fiendish delight.

THE NAME ON HER FOREHEAD

Her name is emblazoned on her forehead,

MYSTERY
BABYLON THE GREAT
THE MOTHER OF PROSTITUTES
AND OF THE ABOMINATIONS OF THE EARTH. (17:5)

Here we have the first local mark of identity, apparently at least, but we are prepared to attach a purely figurative meaning to the local name by the word "MYSTERY" which precedes it. We are reminded that the prophet is not speaking about literal but mystical Babylon. Babylon was the head of the whole system of earthly powers described by Daniel's vision, and these represent in prophetic symbolism the whole system of Antichrist. Beginning with the tower of Babel, the first center of man's rebellion against God, it represents the whole series of developments of Satan's kingdom from the beginning to the end. This system is to nominal Christianity what ancient Babylon was to the heathen world.

HER MOTHERHOOD

But what is meant by her motherhood and her children, "THE MOTHER OF PROSTITUTES/ AND OF THE ABOMINATIONS OF THE EARTH" (17:5)? Of course, it first suggests the impure and defiling influence of her teaching and example upon her own children. We do not need to look far to find the degrading effects of Romanism in all the communities that have been steeped in its superstitions. Look at those European countries where it has predominated and you will find all the hallowed restraints of domestic and social life relaxed and destroyed. And when you come to such lands as the republics of South America and the colonies of France and Spain where the priesthood has ruled with unrestricted influence, you find the sanctity of home almost unknown, the rising generation blighted with the stain of illegitimacy and the very ministers of religion detested and abhorred because of their unholy lives.

But more is meant than this. It is meant that this mother church has ecclesiastical children, that there are other churches besides the Papacy that are included in the mystical Babylon. While we condemn the fearful record of the Papacy let us not forget that the name of Protestant does not shield us from her curse if we are sullied with her stain. There is a Romanism of Protestantism just as real as that of the Papacy—a spirit of outward form, of compromise with the world, of ecclesiastical ambition and pride, of gorgeous architecture, splendid ritual and dead works which will bring the same curse upon the daughters as falls upon the mother's head.

Alas! the saddest thing about this woman is that once, she, too, was pure. She seems to be the same woman that the apostle saw in her youth in the 12th chapter, clothed with the sun and trampling upon the darkness of night. But, alas! how changed has she become since she learned to lean upon the arm of flesh and compromise with the spirit of the world! And if the Apostolic Church could sink so low, why may not the church of the Reformation, the church of the Puritans, the church of the Covenanters also become partaker of the guilt and doom of Babylon? Is not this the meaning of that solemn passage which we hear sounding from heaven: "Come out of her, my people,/ so that you will not share in her sins,/ so that you will not receive any of her plagues" (18:4)?

We cannot fail to notice, especially in the 18th chapter which describes the doom of Babylon, the atmosphere of luxury, self-indulgence, commercial enterprise, enormous wealth, aesthetic culture and the pomp and glory of the present world connected with this whole religious system. It seems most aptly to describe the church which seeks to ally itself with the world's wealth, refinement and pleasure. She had lived "deliciously" (18:7, KJV). She said, "I sit as queen; I am not a widow, and I will never mourn" (18:7).

She was full of the merchants of the earth. She was bedecked with gold, silver, precious stones and pearls, and clothed in fine linen, purple, silk and scarlet. Her houses were filled with ivory, precious wood, marble, brass and iron, perfumes, wine, equipage, earth's most precious fruit, luxury, beauty and glory, and the highest aesthetic culture. The voice of harpists and musicians, pipers and trumpeters are all represented there. Surely it describes the church in alliance with the world, embracing it in her membership, compromising with it in her principles, and finding with it her pleasures, her aims and her rewards. Is not this the church which we see taking form on every side of us today? Her name is Protestant but her spirit is that of the woman sitting on the beast. We see her in the third chapter of Revelation as Laodicea. We see her here as Babylon.

Do not let us be misunderstood as including all parts and members of the visible church. It is only in so far as the visible church enters into the spirit of Babylon that she becomes partaker with her of her character and doom. The Papacy is the mother but these are her daughters that share the destiny of her who gave them birth.

THE CITY

In the 18th verse of the 17th chapter and in the verses which follow in the 18th chapter the image changes from the woman to the city and the vision becomes localized in Babylon more than in the woman. "The woman you saw is the great city that rules over the kings of the earth."

There seems no other city on earth with which this can be identified but Rome. Twice already has this vision of wealth, influence and worldwide dominion been realized in the city of the seven hills, and there seems every reason to suppose that it will yet be realized once more in some era of greatness and glory before the end which yet may await this historic place. True, at the present time Rome is not the metropolis of a worldwide commerce such as the 18th chapter describes, but it would not be difficult to restore its ancient preeminence in the last days of the tribulation times, especially if once again the Papal system became the embodiment of earth's combined systems of political and ecclesiastical power. Certainly, at the time that John wrote she was entitled above all other places on earth to this preeminence, and all through the Middle Ages she was the center of the world's wealth, culture, influence and power. The features which are specified in the descriptions which follow leave no doubt of the identity of Rome.

THE MOUNTAINS

Among these are the mountains on which she is represented as sitting. "The seven heads are seven hills on which the woman sits" (17:9). Rome is built on seven hills and has long been known as the seven-hilled city. They are the topographical feature of Rome.

But these mountains are next explained not merely as literal hills but as symbols of seven kings or kingdoms, and they are more fully explained in the 10th verse. "They are also seven kings. Five have fallen, one is, the other has not yet come; but when he does come, he must remain for a little while. The beast who once was, and now is not, is an eighth king. He belongs to the seven and is going to his destruction" (17:10–11).

We have already explained in a former chapter that the seven heads of this world power are the successive empires that have dominated the world: namely, Egypt, Assyria, Babylon, Persia and Greece. These were the five that had fallen in the days of John. The one that was still in existence at that time was Rome. The other that was not yet come was the Papacy. And the eighth head of the beast, who was of the seven and was to head it up as an eighth head and then go into perdition, was the devil himself who had been in all the seven as their master mind and invisible head, and who, at last, it would seem, is to become incarnate as a visible personality and lead the last battle against Jehovah and then go into perdition.

THE WOMAN'S ATTITUDE

Next we come to the attitude of the woman to the beast. She is represented as sitting on him, carried by him and supported by his power. This represents the union of the false church with the world power. We see this through the whole story of the Papacy, and after the church became the state religion of Rome the unity became more intimate until the purity of the church was corrupted and finally the earthly and the spiritual power became identified in their aims, policies and means of aggrandizement. The Papacy used the armies of the world for the propagation of her policy and principles and the punishment of heretics, and she in turn crowned earth's kings and rewarded them with her endorsement.

Charlemagne the Great, who restored the old Roman Empire, was crowned by the Pope as the founder and the king of the whole Roman Empire. Henry of England was called the Defender of the Faith. France was named the eldest son of the Papacy. Her cathedrals and altars were built and adorned by the munificences of princes and they were expected in return to obey her and submit to her supremacy. Thus she committed fornication with the kings of the earth and sat on the beast as her supporter.

THE ATTITUDE OF THE 10 HORNS

We next note a peculiar feature of this vision, the attitude of the 10 horns of the beast to this woman. We know who these 10 horns were: the broken kingdoms which followed the wreck of the Roman Empire. They received power as kings for a season with the beast and they give their strength unto the beast and with him make war against the Lamb, and at last are to be arrayed against the Son of God when He comes.

It is remarkable that these horns appear without crowns at this stage of the vision. It looks as though the monarchical was to give place in the last days to the democratic form of government for earth's nations. They are still to be horns but democratic rather than kingly horns. But the peculiar feature is that toward the last we find these horns in the 16th verse turning against the harlot and making her desolate and naked and eating her flesh and burning it with fire.

Do we find any such strange transformation in the attitude of modern nations toward the Papacy? Surely there is nothing more remarkable than the exact correspondence of the events of modern history with this part of the vision. Was there ever a country more completely under the control of the Papacy than France; and yet, was there ever a country that turned so violently against the Papacy in the French Revolution and the series of events that followed, defiling her sanctuaries, besieging the Pope in his capital, capturing him, carrying him off to die in exile, and setting in operation the long train of events which culminated in the fall of the temporal power of the Papacy?

Scarcely less marked was the next chapter in this drama, the rising up of Italy—long the seat and constituency of the Papacy—driving the Pope from the throne and establishing an independent political power under his very eyes. So we have lately seen the people of Cuba and South America rising against the Spanish power which was practically an instrument of the Papacy, and we know that their hatred of the monks and priests was far greater than of the representatives of the Spanish political power. Thus already have the horns begun to ravage and waste the harlot, and God is fulfilling His precious Word and will still fulfill it in the same direction yet more wondrously.

THE DESTRUCTION OF BABYLON

The destruction of Babylon is the great catastrophe of the 18th chapter. There seems to be a double process of destruction. The cry that echoes through the heavens is twofold. "Fallen! Fallen is Babylon the Great!" (18:2). So we see two processes of destruction going on in the providence of God. One is political. This has already begun through the agency of the 10 horns, earth's political forces. The other is to be the more sudden and terrible destruction of the ecclesiastical system which will be by the personal appearing of the Lord Jesus and the brightness of His coming. The vision of Daniel represents the gradual process culminating in a sudden catastrophe. There the words used are "will be taken away and completely destroyed forever" (Daniel 7:26). What the exact significance of this final catastrophe will be it is premature for us to discuss. It is one of the events of the future connected with the closing days of the great tribulation when so many stupendous and awful judgments are to culminate on this doomed earth.

It is surely becoming for us to judge with modest deference these mighty future possibilities. But out of all these solemn signs the lesson is surely plain. It is the call for these last days, "Come out of her my people,/ so that you will not share in her sins,/ so that you will not receive any of her plagues" (Revelation 18:4). This does not mean come out of the churches, but, come out of the spirit of compromise, the spirit of luxury, the spirit of selfishness, the spirit of a worldly church, the spirit of Babylon, the spirit of indulgence, extravagance and pride, the spirit that seeks its satisfaction here and sits a queen instead of a widow waiting for her absent Lord.

Thank God that while so many even in the churches of Protestantism have fallen into the spirit where we fear they will meet the curse of Babylon, there is a little flock all through the ages that today can be found in all branches of the Church of Christ walking in separation and watching, white-robed and Spirit-filled, for their inheritance when the Bridegroom comes and the true kingdom will be ushered in. God grant that we may be found in that happy company.

CHAPTER 11

THE MARRIAGE OF THE LAMB

Let us rejoice and be glad
  and give him glory!
For the wedding of the Lamb has come,
  and his bride has made herself ready.
Fine linen, bright and clean,
  was given her to wear.
(Fine linen stands for the righteous acts of the saints.)

Then the angel said to me, "Write: 'Blessed are those who are invited to the wedding supper of the Lamb!'" And he added, "These are the true words of God." (Revelation 19:7–9)

The events described in the preceding chapters have produced a profound impression in the heavenly world. As from the battlements of the skies the glorified beings there looked down upon the final destruction of the great system which so long defied God and oppressed His people, watching the smoke of her burning, there arose from the heavenly host a great shout,

"Hallelujah!
Salvation and glory and power belong to our God,
  for true and just are his judgments.
He has condemned the great prostitute
  who corrupted the earth by her adulteries.
He has avenged on her the blood of his servants."

And again they shouted:

"Hallelujah!" (19:1–3)

Next from the four living creatures and the 24 elders came echoing back the same response as they fell upon their faces and cried, "Amen, Hallelujah!" (19:4). And then the chorus was taken up by all the voices of the heavens until, like the sound of many waters and the voices of mighty thunderings, it rolled along the heavens, "Hallelujah!/ For our Lord God Almighty reigns" (19:6).

The special reason for this sublime spectacle of triumph and rejoicing is given in the next verse. It was the undertone of the great organ of the skies thundering forth the notes of the wedding march of the Bride of the Lamb, and the chorus ends with the overture, "Let us rejoice and be glad/ and give him glory!/ For the wedding of the Lamb has come,/ and his bride has made herself ready" (19:7).

A SUPREME EVENT

There is a supreme event in every human life to which affection, hope and memory look forward or backward. It is the climax of life's fondest anticipations and aims. It is not always the winning of a fortune or the attainment of some place of fame and honor, but more often some matter of the heart and the home—perhaps the wedding day when the fond bride at last reaches the accomplishment of her heart's desire or the loving bridegroom comes to claim the one who is dearer to him than all his fortunes or his earthly honors. While this is true in this poor world of imperfect and oft-disappointed happiness, it is more transcendently true in that heavenly world where hope and love are not

> Mere transient fires,
> Whose spark flies upward and expires.

In the story of redemption and the history of heaven the supreme event for which the ages are waiting is the marriage of the Lamb. The Bible is one long love story and redemption a divine romance of the love of God. The picture of ancient Eden opens with a bridegroom and a bride typical of that greater union which our text portrays. Born out of His being and then given to His arms in wedded love, Eve was God's first type of the true Church of Jesus Christ formed out of His heart and then given back to Him in everlasting love. All through the story of redemption the figure constantly appears. We see it in the marriage of Isaac to Rebekah, the one bride chosen from a foreign people and brought home by the faithful servant along that typical journey which foreshadowed at every step the waiting Church and her meeting with her Lord in the eventide. The marriage of Moses to his Midian bride; the story of Ruth and her espousals and the repeated references to this figure in the Psalms and prophets are all in keeping with this thought. The 45th Psalm is a love song for the Bride of the Lamb and the King of glory. The Song of Songs is the celebration of the love of the greater King to His chosen and beloved Church. Isaiah sings of Hephzibah and Beulah which just mean "married" and "beloved." God pleads to Jeremiah for His wayward backsliding bride and cries, "Return, faithless people, . . . for I am your husband" (Jeremiah 3:14). "I remember the devotion of your youth,/ how as a bride you loved me/ and followed me through the desert,/ through a land not sown" (2:2). Ezekiel pictures the foundling girl left naked and friendless on the street and taken up by God's loving heart, nursed and nurtured, clothed and cared for, educated and refined, and at last decked in costly raiment and adorned with richest jewels and then wedded to Him as His beloved, "You became mine" (Ezekiel 16:8); and then becoming unfaithful to her divine lover and Lord. Hosea continues the picture in still more vivid figurative language and brings it to a climax in those beautiful words that have become the very language of our heart's deepest love to Christ,

> I will betroth you to me forever;
>   I will betroth you in righteousness and justice,
>   in love and compassion.
> I will betroth you in faithfulness,
>   and you will acknowledge the LORD.
>   (Hosea 2:19–20)

> "In that day," declares the LORD,
>   "you will call me 'my husband';
>   you will no longer call me 'my master.' "
>   (2:16)

Christ's parables have frequent references to the same figure. He tells us of the marriage of the King's Son and of the 10 virgins who went to meet the Bridegroom; and John the Baptist describes himself as the friend of the Bridegroom, waiting on the Bride, introducing her to her Lord, and rejoicing greatly because of the Bridegroom's voice. And Paul, even in his most logical and practical epistles, falls into the same strain and sees in human love and earthly marriage only the imperfect type of that grander union, the mystery of grace, Christ and His Church. "Husbands, love your wives, just as Christ loved the church and gave himself up for her . . . to present her to himself as a radiant church, without stain or wrinkle or any other blemish, but holy and blameless" (Ephesians 5:25).

> This is the heavenly secret,
>   The love life of the Lord;

The golden chain that bindeth
The story of His Word.

Christ is the heavenly Bridegroom;
To seek His Bride He came;
This is the consummation,
The Marriage of the Lamb.

THE SUPREME EVENT

And so we reach at length in the Apocalyptic vision the supreme event. The obstacles have been removed. The great false church has been destroyed. The counterfeit bride has been put down, and now the true Bride is to receive her diadem of glory and her place by the side of her Lord. All heaven is waiting with suppressed and intense sympathy, while from the grand organ of the skies the mighty notes already begin to swell the wedding march of glory. "Hallelujah!/ . . . The wedding of the Lamb has come,/ and his bride has made herself ready" (Revelation 19:6–7).

There is much about this stupendous event which we cannot explain. Just when and where it is to occur we may not fully know. Some time after the rapture and before the epiphany and glorious appearing of Christ to begin His millennial reign we know it will be. Somewhere in the air to which He has caught up His beloved ones and from which they have been watching the events of the stormy scene below will be the scene. But just what it will mean there is no language, there are no figures, and perhaps there are no sufficient faculties and capabilities in our human nature fully to understand. But this much is plain:

1. A Glorious Union

It will mean some glorious union between us and our Redeemer. It will mean some joy surpassing all that we have ever known or dreamed of rapture and delight. It will mean some tide of love compared with which all human love is but as a drop to the ocean and a taper to the sunshine. Have you ever had even a taste of some exquisite joy? Have you ever had a touch of divine peace and love? Do you remember what it meant to know that you were pardoned and saved? Have you ever been comforted in some hour of sorrow by your Savior's love? Have you ever got so near Him in the hour of prayer that His joy and even His glory perhaps but for a moment filled and comforted your heart until everything was cheap in comparison? Perhaps it has been interrupted. Perhaps it has alternated with doubt and fear and many a sorrow, but can you remember some gleam of heavenly sunshine, some taste of heavenly wine? Oh, beloved, there is at least the alphabet with which to spell out the significance of heaven. That is enough to start with in measuring the meaning of this transcendent ecstasy. Just take the sweetest, brightest, gladdest moment you have ever known of the love of Jesus and multiply it by eternity and you can form some conception of the exquisite and transcendent rapture of the marriage of the Lamb.

2. A Perfect Union

It is to bring us into perfect union with God. It is the pouring into the earthly vessel of all the fullness of His being who is love and joy and blessedness in Himself and must impart it to every soul into which He comes. Union with God is the end and object of salvation. "Now this is eternal life: that they may know you, the only true God, and Jesus Christ, whom you have sent." (John 17:3). "That all of them may be one, Father, just as you are in me and I am in you" (17:21). This is the supreme prayer in the 17th chapter of John. It does not merely mean to be one with each other in some method of Christian union but it means to be one with God as the bridegroom and the bride, as the soul and body, as the branches and the vine.

THE BRIDEGROOM

We know who He is. It is the Lamb, not the Father or the Holy Spirit, although each of these is brought into mysterious and glorious union with us in the experience of redemption. But the marriage of the Bride is with the Lamb because He is the only being that could come into such intimate and perfect union with a human Bride. He is not only the Son of God but He is the Son of man. By His mysterious incarnation He has become one of our race. He has a body, a soul and a nature as perfectly human as ours. He has lived among us in simplicity and perfect oneness with our race. He has left the story of His life, and it is so natural and complete as to win our confidence and attract our sympathy. We see Him as a babe at Bethlehem, as a boy at Nazareth, as the man of Galilee, in the home at Bethany, in all the experiences of human joy and suffering, in all the little touches of a real human life; and it makes us feel that He is bone of our bone, flesh of our flesh and heart of our heart.

If some great prince came down into a peaceful valley of his empire to woo and win a peasant maiden, he could never do it if he stood off in his dignity and majesty. He could only impress her with awe. She might respect and admire him but she could not come near enough to love him. Therefore he must woo her by simple tenderness and meet her on a common plane. He must make her feel that he understands her simpler life and is so within reach and touch of her perfect trust and confidence that she can come to him as freely as to her nearest, dearest friend. Therefore Christ stepped from the throne of His majesty and came to our level that He might woo us and

win us and thus become to us not a Lord but a Lover and a dear intimate
Friend. He is the Bridegroom. There is something in His heart that wants
our love and that is fitted to clasp around His heart the tendrils of our affection. It is not irreverent to sing, "My Jesus, I love Thee, I know Thou art
mine."

The very object of His coming to us in human flesh is to win this closer
confidence and this deeper love expressed by the figure of the bridegroom
and the bride.

THE BRIDE

But who is she? Perhaps this question is not quite so clear. We know in a
general sense she is the Church, but how many in the Church; and how far
is the Church as a whole able to meet and fulfill the place of the Bride in the
intimacy and love of Jesus?

In the first place in the nature of things the relationship of the bride and
the conditions which it requires and expresses are essentially exclusive. A
man may have many friends who are deeply attached to him but the affection he expects from a wife is different from all other. A woman may be
devotedly attached to many of her relatives and associates, but to one her
heart goes out with that tenderness and oneness which every true human instinct recognizes as peculiar and exclusive. Such love cannot be forced by the
will of the subject or object of it. No man can compel it by force or even
persuasion unless it springs spontaneously in the heart of the loved one. No
woman can render it at will. It is part of its very nature that it must be
wooed and won by long processes often of kindness, affection and fellowship.

If the language means anything as applied to Christ it means that there are
those who cherish toward Him a love intensely personal, peculiar and exclusive, and a love which must be won and developed by relationships and
experiences such as all human analogies would suggest. May it not therefore
be true that Christ has friends who love Him sincerely and serve Him faithfully, but who have not yet entered into that closer place of intimacy expressed by this figure of the Bride? Are there not differences among all
Christians as varied as all degrees of human friendship and social life? Are
there not many who know Christ only as a Savior, as a Master, as a Helper,
and in some measure as a Friend but they have never yet come into perfect
touch with His heart? They do not know His voice, they shrink from His
closer communion, they have chambers in their hearts that are shut out
from His eye, they are conscious of things that they know He would not ap-
prove, and there is perhaps as much of fear as there is of love in the respect
they bear to Him. How can they be in any full sense part of the Bride of the
Lamb? They are not harshly excluded by any decree of election or reproba-

tion. They are invited to the innermost chambers of His heart, but they must pass through an experience that will fit them for the place of deepest love. They must receive those spiritual capacities and quickened senses which will know Him, respond to Him, receive Him in all the tenderness of love. They must have not only the bridal garment, but the bridal heart.

Do our Bibles reveal any intimations of these different classes among the friends of Christ? In the 45th Psalm, which is the love song of this theme, we find not only the bride who is brought unto the king in all her beautiful raiment but we also find the Queen Mother who stands at her right hand in the gold of Ophir, and "her virgin companions follow her" (45:14), who are also brought unto the king but not in the same place as she is permitted to enter. May they not represent Christians true to Christ and near to His beloved Bride but who have not come so near as she, while perhaps the Queen Mother may represent the Jewish people, the mother church of Israel, standing in her place in the glorious day of manifestation?

Again, in this very Apocalypse have we not read in one of our recent studies of two classes of people who are to have a part in the coming of the Lord and a blessed part? They are described in the 14th chapter of Revelation. First, there are the 144,000 who are described as the firstfruits unto God and the Lamb. These have been redeemed from among men. They are a called-out company. Their lives are spotless and undefiled. They follow the Lamb wherever He goes and even on earth they have learned the song they sing in heaven. Their ear is quickened to a closer intimacy with the things of God than others.

But later in the same chapter we have a second company described as the harvest of the earth. The others were the firstfruits. These are the full harvest. Surely the figures themselves determine the classes here described. The one represents those caught up first to meet the Lord in the parousia, the second the full harvest finally gathered at His great epiphany as He comes to begin His glorious reign.

If these things be so it may shed a solemn light on the parable of the 10 Virgins in the 25th chapter of the gospel of Matthew, and these represent, not the Bride who is already returning with her Lord, but her friends who go out to meet her and go in to the marriage supper of the Lamb while she goes in to the marriage of the Lamb.

But if further light were needed to confirm this view, it would, we think, be found in our text. It is where we see two distinct parties represented. First, there is the Bride herself described in connection with the marriage and in her beautiful garments of spotless white and surpassing glory. Then, after she has been presented and described in the seventh and eighth verses, in the ninth verse there is an entirely distinct statement: "Blessed are those who are invited to the wedding supper of the Lamb" (Revelation 19:9). This is not the marriage of the Lamb but the supper that follows it. To represent the Bride as called to the marriage supper would be out of keeping with all propriety. The Bride is the one who gives the supper with her Lord. Those that are called to the marriage supper are the friends and companions who are to share with her her joy. But, oh, how different the joy of each! They have the marriage supper. She has the Bridegroom.

Beloved, if these things be so, how tender and sacred is the obligation they lay upon us to emulate the spirit of Paul, who, in speaking of the highest prize of the Hope as something not cheaply won, uses this stirring language,

> What is more, I consider everything a loss. (Philippians 3:8)

> I want to know Christ and the power of his resurrection and the fellowship of sharing in his sufferings, becoming like him in his death, and so, somehow, to attain to the resurrection from the dead.
>
> Not that I have already obtained all this, or have already been made perfect, but I press on to take hold of that for which Christ Jesus took hold of me. Brothers, I do not consider myself yet to have taken hold of it. But one thing I do: Forgetting what is behind and straining toward what is ahead, I press on toward the goal to win the prize for which God has called me heavenward in Christ Jesus. (3:10–14)

God forbid that we should narrow down the blessed company of those who shall sit with Christ upon His throne to any little exclusive circle of our own electing. God give us the largest-hearted Christian love and unity. Does it not speak to all the instincts of our being that it would somehow be impossible for the self-indulgent, time-serving professor of religion—saved perhaps, but saved by the skin of his teeth, wanting only enough of Christ to keep him out of danger, and sacrificing as little as he can for his faith and his Lord—that he should share the place and the same reward with the martyr who lays down his life at the stake or the equally faithful soldier of the cross who lives out a life of self-denial and loving service for Jesus? There is a difference here and there will be an awful difference there. Just what it is all going to mean the day alone can declare. But beloved, let us take no risks, let our watchword be

> I want to stand when Christ appears
>   In spotless raiment dressed;
> Numbered among His hidden ones
>   His holiest and best.

Give me, oh Lord, Thy highest choice,
   Let others take the rest.
Their good things have no charm for me,
   For I have got Thy best.

HER RAIMENT

We have already seen that the imagery of clothing simply represents the character and habit of life. The Bride is therefore described by her garments. First we are told that they are "given her to wear" (Revelation 19:8). She did not have to make them or buy them but they were given unto her by the grace of her Lord, and she simply put them on and wore them in fitting form and becoming style until they became the very habit of her life. Christ will clothe us with all the grace and holiness that we will wear; and as Isaac's bride received her outfit from his generous servant and met him in the veil that he himself had sent her, so we can best please our Lord by being nothing, pretending nothing, claiming nothing, expecting nothing of ourselves, but putting on Christ Jesus and living a life of sweet and constant dependence on His all-sufficient grace. We can have from Him all the grace, all the patience, all the unselfishness, all the gentleness, all the love, all the sweetness that we will wear through the tests and trials of life.

Next, we may notice that her garments were of two classes. They were "clean and white" (19:8, KJV). The word "white" here literally means bright. It is a word used to describe the transfiguration robes of the Lord Jesus. First, our garments must be clean, free from all the defilements of sin, but secondly they must be beautiful, lustrous, glorious. The difference between these two words may be perfectly expressed by the difference between linen when taken from the clothesline and when taken from the laundry. The linen on the clothesline is clean, but the linen that has passed under the hot iron and been rubbed and polished is bright as well as clean and shines with radiant luster. So Christ is preparing His Bride not only to meet Him without blame but to meet Him refined, beautified, glorified by the whole experience of Christian life and the glory that comes from sanctified trial and the tests of life triumphantly borne, through His all victorious grace. To change the figure

Many a hard and biting sculpture
   Polished well those stones elect,
In their places now compacted
   By the heavenly Architect,
Wherewith God hath willed forever
   That His palace should be decked.

In conclusion we notice the other call: "Blessed are those who are invited to the wedding supper of the Lamb!" (19:9). Happy are they who will inherit this blessedness; but far more supremely, eternally blessed are they who will know Him and sit down with Him on His throne as His Bride.

Speaking of the parable of the 10 Virgins and the fact that the Bride does not appear there suggests the beautiful incident in the life of a well-known Christian woman. One of her friends one night dreamt that the Lord had come and that the glorious company of the beloved ones were gathered around Him. She recognized herself as there and many that she knew, but she looked in vain for this dear friend, the sweetest Christian she had ever known. She could not see her. Her heart was very sad and she asked an angel who was standing by where her friend was and how it was that she could not be seen in that company. "Oh," replied the angel, "that is very plain. Why, the rest are all around the Bridegroom but she is hidden in His heart and therefore cannot be seen by other eyes."

Blessed be His name! There is room for us all even in His heart! Let us aspire to the nearest, highest place both while we walk with Him here and when we will sit with Him there.

CHAPTER 12

THE EPIPHANY, THE RESURRECTION AND THE MILLENNIUM

I saw heaven standing open and there before me was a white horse, whose rider is called Faithful and True. With justice he judges and makes war. His eyes are like blazing fire, and on his head are many crowns. He has a name written on him that no one knows but he himself. He is dressed in a robe dipped in blood, and his name is the Word of God. The armies of heaven were following him, riding on white horses and dressed in fine linen, white and clean. (Revelation 19:11–14)

I saw thrones on which were seated those who had been given authority to judge. And I saw the souls of those who had been beheaded because of their testimony for Jesus and because of the word of God. They had not worshiped the beast or his image and had not received his mark on their foreheads or their hands. They came to life and reigned with Christ a thousand years. (The rest of the dead did not come to life until the thousand years were ended.) This is the first resurrection. Blessed and holy are those who have part in the first resurrection. The second death has no power over them, but they will be priests of God and of Christ and will reign with him for a thousand years. (20:4–6)

Five stupendous events are presented in the majestic panorama in the 19th and 20th chapters of Revelation. They are the glorious epiphany of the Lord Jesus Christ; the battle of Armageddon, the binding of Satan, the First Resurrection and the Millennial Reign.

THE EPIPHANY

This is not the coming of Christ for His saints but with His saints. It is

503

that glorious event which Enoch long ago described: "See, the Lord is coming with thousands upon thousands of his holy ones to judge everyone, and to convict all the ungodly of all the ungodly acts they have done in the ungodly way, and of all the harsh words ungodly sinners have spoken against him" (Jude 14–15). This is that glorious coming which sounds as a deep undertone through all the prophecies of the Holy Scriptures. Joel saw it afar when he wrote "Multitudes, multitudes/ in the valley of decision!/ For the day of the LORD is near/ in the valley of decision" (Joel 3:14). Isaiah saw it when he cried "The earth reels like a drunkard,/ it sways like a hut in the wind;/ . . . The moon will be abashed, the sun ashamed;/ for the LORD Almighty will reign/ on Mount Zion and in Jerusalem,/ and before its elders, gloriously" (Isaiah 24:20, 23). Zechariah beheld it afar when he cried:

> A day of the LORD is coming when your plunder will be divided among you.

> Then the LORD will go out and fight against those nations, as he fights in the day of battle.

> The LORD will be king over the whole earth. On that day there will be one LORD, and his name the only name. (Zechariah 14:1, 3, 9)

Christ saw it in vision when He exclaimed, "They will see the Son of Man coming in a cloud with power and great glory" (Luke 21:27).

John beholds Him marching down the ether path as a mighty Conqueror. He is mounted upon a white horse, the symbol of victory and righteousness, for "with justice he judges and makes war" (Revelation 19:11). His eyes are like a "blazing fire" (19:12) and from His mouth there passes a consuming flame like "a sharp sword" (19:15) with which He smites the nations and destroys His foes. His vesture is "dipped in blood" (19:13) as the symbol of victory over His enemies, and He "treads the winepress of the fury of the wrath of God Almighty" (19:15). On His head are many diadems, for He has already conquered sin, Satan and death and He is about to wear the crown of all the world. He wears a number of glorious names. "Faithful and True" (19:11) is one, and it means that all that He has promised and all that He has threatened is about to be fulfilled. The "Word of God" (19:13) is another, and this means that He is acting as the representative of God, fulfilling His will, representing His thought and acting in His name and character. There will be no appeal from His judgment, for behind it is all the majesty and power of the Father's throne. Another lofty name is "KING OF KINGS AND LORD OF LORDS" (19:16). He is coming now to meet earth's confederate powers and sovereignties and He is to be recognized as the only supreme Ruler to whom every knee should bow. Above all these there is another name, known only to Himself, and it means that after all we know of Jesus there is still much we do not know. There is a mystery still hidden in His infinite heart and all that He is yet to reveal to us is far greater than even what we now know of His power and love.

But this mighty Conqueror is not alone. He is simply the Leader of a host who follow in His train, for "the armies of heaven were following him, riding on white horses and dressed in fine linen, white and clean" (19:14). These are His translated saints. These are the souls that have been caught up to meet Him in the air and are coming back with Him along with His mighty angels to witness His public triumph and to share His millennial throne.

Do not fail to notice that these triumphant hosts all come with Him from heaven and not from earth. They have already joined Him in the great rendezvous of the skies. It will be too late then to take your place. It must be taken already. Are you enrolled for the glorious company of the returning ones who are coming back with Jesus when He returns to reign? What language can describe the surpassing glory and splendid majesty of this bright epiphany! How human imagery fails! The simple and sublime description of the Apocalypse leaves us awed and overwhelmed with its silent majesty.

THE ARMAGEDDON CONFLICT

One would have thought that all the world would have been waiting with open arms to receive so glorious and beneficent a King. But lo, we behold earth's armies in battle array to resist His coming. With strange presumptuous fatuity the kings of the earth have allowed themselves to be enrolled under the banner of the Antichrist and his wicked ally, here described as the Wild Beast and False Prophet. These represent on the one hand the godless governments of the earth and on the other her false religion. One is political, the other ecclesiastical sovereignty. Both have usurped the place of Jehovah. Both have gathered into their conflict the forces of an ungodly world. From other Scriptures it is plain that the ostensible object of their campaign is some real objective point on earth. They are not fighting in the air but they are fighting God's people on earth. There seems no reason to doubt that the objective point of their attack will be Jerusalem and the Jews. Both Daniel and Zechariah tell us that this last conflict is to be waged against and around Jerusalem and its decisive battle is to be upon the old field of Palestine known as Megiddo, or Armageddon. The Old Testament prophets tell us that for a time the hosts of the ungodly will seem to prevail. The devoted city will fall and the horrors of a fearful sack will have just begun when the Son of God will appear from heaven delivering His people and destroying His enemies.

The discomfort and destruction of the foe is described by a graphic and sublime picture. Suddenly John beholds an angel standing in the sun and beckoning to all the fowls of heaven to gather and prepare themselves to feast on the carcasses of captains and of kings and of myriads of men both small and great.

We find the same vision in Ezekiel where the birds of the air are summoned to "the sacrifice I am preparing for you, the great sacrifice on the mountains of Israel. There you will eat flesh and drink blood. You will eat the flesh of mighty men and drink the blood of the princes of the earth" (39:17). So terrible shall be that slaughter that it will take seven months to bury the dead after that fearful battle and the great valley of Hamon Gog will be the hideous cemetery where Satan's last victims will leave their lifeless bones.

The soldiers who have been drawn into this fearful and fatal battle will be slain and simply lose their lives, but the leaders will be caught alive and hurled into the lake of fire which now for the first time becomes the actual place of punishment for the ungodly. There is no doubt, therefore, that the actual leaders of this last battle will be living men and that their punishment will be the first awful taste of death eternal. Let us not suppose, however, that earth's inhabitants will all perish. The millions of mankind will still live on and pass under the reign of Christ in the millennial years. It is only those who will be actually arrayed in open conflict against the Lamb who will be slain.

THE BINDING OF SATAN

Next comes the capture and imprisonment of the great Arch-leader of all these hosts of evil. Long has he kept in the background and worked out his deep-laid plans through human dupes and instruments. But now the hand of justice and vengeance reaches the actual head of all the wickedness of the ages and Satan himself is caught in the resistless grasp of Omnipotence. A mighty angel comes down from heaven and lays hold of the dragon, that old serpent, the devil and Satan. One is strongly inclined to think that this mighty angel is no other than the Son of God Himself, who "appeared . . . to destroy the devil's work" (1 John 3:8). Often before had He met him in personal combat. Now He meets him for a last defeat and with the resistless grasp of almighty power He holds him helpless in His hand and binds him hand and foot and then hurls him into the bottomless abyss where he is confined in a sealed dungeon for a thousand years.

What a story the history of Satan is! Even the few lurid gleams we have reflect an awful light upon the tragedy of evil and the author of sin. We behold him in Ezekiel's vision (Ezekiel 28), an anointed cherub standing in

Eden, walking up and down upon the holy mountain of God, and in the midst of the stones of fire, perfect in his ways until iniquity was found in him. We see him decked with every precious stone, the sardius, the topaz, the diamond, the beryl, the onyx, the jasper, the sapphire, the emerald, the carbuncle, and the gold, and his children come honestly by their love of jewelry. We see him with most exquisite aesthetic taste, himself a musical instrument, for the workmanship of His tabrets and pipes was prepared in him the day that he was created, and it would seem that he was just one beautiful creation of self-contained brilliancy, loveliness, melody and transcendent genius. But his heart was lifted up because of his beauty and he corrupted his wisdom by reason of his brightness and he defiled his sanctuary by the multitude of his iniquities; and so Lucifer, "How you have fallen from heaven,/ O morning star, son of the dawn!/ You have been cast down to earth,/ you who once laid low the nations!" (Isaiah 14:12). Now he is the dark-winged angel of eternal night.

And so we see him all through the history of the human race watching for the ruin of others, meeting the first human pair at Eden's gates with the awful insinuation of the temptation and the fearful blight of sin.

Again we behold him rearing on earth a kingdom of human ambition, pride and wickedness with which to rival the very throne of Jehovah. Next he appears meeting the Son of God at the threshold of his ministry and seeking at last to crush Him in the garden and on the cross. And when he found himself unable to destroy the Son of God or defeat His personal work, we see him through the ages assailing His people and seeking either to corrupt or destroy His church, until at last the final crisis has come in the last battle of the ages, and he is vanquished.

And now for a thousand years the world is to be without a devil and the human race put on trial to show what really it will do under the fostering influences of divine love and without the instigations and influences of the great seducer. What a world, what an age that will be when Satan will tempt no more and all his deceitful wiles and dreadful power will be withdrawn from human history and the only influence outside of earth and humanity will be the beneficence and the holiness of Christ and the heavenly world.

THE FIRST RESURRECTION

We are next brought face to face with the resurrection of the dead. This also is one of the transcendent and preeminent truths of divine revelation. It is something the human mind could never imagine or grasp alone. There is no precedent or parallel for it in human experience or history. Death is to reason and sense the end of all. "But it has now been revealed through the appearing of our Savior, Christ Jesus, who has destroyed death and has brought life and immortality to light through the gospel" (2 Timothy 1:10).

"But Christ has indeed been raised from the dead, the firstfruits of those who have fallen asleep" (1 Corinthians 15:20).

But there is a resurrection and a resurrection. Not equally will all the children of our human race partake of this wondrous change, for we read in the passage of "the first resurrection" and this implies that there is another resurrection. We are told "Blessed and holy are those who have part in the first resurrection" (Revelation 20:6). It is therefore for the blessed and holy only and they that do not partake of it are not blessed or holy. We are told that "The rest of the dead did not come to life until the thousand years were ended" (20:5). This solemn and tremendous statement implies there will be a multitude of human beings who will remain under the dominion of death and sleep on in their silent tombs during all the glorious events of the thousand years. They will only awake from the sleep of death to face the awful scenes of the Great White Throne and the judgment of terror and destruction.

Nor is it here alone that we read of the first resurrection. Our Lord Jesus Christ speaks of those who will be "considered worthy of taking part in that age and in the resurrection from the dead . . . and they and can no longer die; for they are like the angels. They are God's children, since they are children of the resurrection" (Luke 20:35–36). Paul himself tells us that he was striving "somehow, to attain to the resurrection from the dead" (Philippians 3:11). It is evidently a partial resurrection, a few from among many. Daniel tells us of a time when "Multitudes who sleep in the dust of the earth will awake" (12:2), not all, but many, and then he adds that those that awake will awake "to everlasting life" (12:2) and for those that do not awake it will be "to shame and everlasting contempt" (12:2). But this 20th chapter of Revelation crystallizes the doctrine of the resurrection in language so simple and direct that, as Dean Alford has forcibly said, if it does not teach the literal resurrection of the saints at the coming of Christ a thousand years before the resurrection of the wicked "then there is an end of all significance in language and Scripture is wiped out as a definite testimony to anything."

Of course, it is presupposed that all the holy dead will not rise at the very moment when Satan is bound and Christ begins His millennial reign. The description is quite in keeping with the fact that these persons had been already raised from the dead for John saw them at this point already raised and seated on thrones. Perhaps there had been several groups of resurrected ones during this period of the end, some caught up just before the tribulation, some caught up at its close but altogether united in the coming of Christ and the glory of His reign and all contemplated in one vision as those that had part in the first resurrection.

The question is, Beloved, will you, will I be there? How can I tell? Thank God the answer is very plain for "If we died with him,/ we will also live with him;/ If we endure,/ we will also reign with him" (2 Timothy 2:11–12). Have you died with Him? Then you will rise with Him. Have you entered into the spiritual resurrection? Do you know Him and the power of His resurrection and the fellowship of His sufferings, and have you been made conformable unto His death in your inner life? Then you will attain unto the resurrection from among the dead.

THE MILLENNIAL REIGN

"I saw thrones on which were seated those who had been given authority to judge. And I saw the souls of those who had been beheaded because of their testimony for Jesus and because of the word of God. They had not worshiped the beast or his image and had not received his mark on their foreheads or their hands. They came to life and reigned with Christ a thousand years" (Revelation 20:4). This is no new doctrine. Peter tells us that "the time comes for God to restore everything, as he promised long ago through his holy prophets" (Acts 3:21). Therefore this is the burden of the prophetic vision; this is the meaning of the highest and sublimest flights of the Psalms and the prophets of the past. It is necessary to recall the visions of Isaiah, of Zechariah, of Joel, of Ezekiel. Our Lord Himself left no doubt of this blessed hope upon the minds of His disciples when He said to them such words as these:

> You are those who have stood by me in my trials. And I confer on you a kingdom, just as my Father conferred one on me, so that you may eat and drink at my table in my kingdom and sit on thrones, judging the twelve tribes of Israel. (Luke 22:28–30)

And again:

> I tell you the truth, at the renewal of all things [*Palingenesis,* as the Greek word expresses it], when the Son of Man sits on his glorious throne, you who have followed me will also sit on twelve thrones, judging the twelve tribes of Israel. And everyone who has left houses or brothers or sisters or father or mother or children or fields for my sake will receive a hundred times as much and will inherit eternal life. (Matthew 19:28–29)

This was what the Master meant when He said "To him who overcomes, I will give the right to sit with me on my throne, just as I overcame and sat down with my Father on his throne" (Revelation 3:21).

Beloved, we have neither language nor conceptions fully to take it in. It will mean a world without a devil, a world without a curse, a world without a prison, a hospital or a criminal, a world without a victim of oppression, the cry of outraged innocence, a tear of sorrow or a shade of night or darkness. It will mean that your mind and spirit will be restored to all the perfection of which human nature is capable and that you will be as holy, as beautiful, as happy, as wise, as strong, as glorious as He. It means that your body will never know again an infirmity or a pain, that your physical form will respond to every thought and wish of your soul and that space and distance will be annihilated and you can go perhaps as rapidly from world to world as your thought can pass today. It means that your loved and lost will be given back to your affection and every trace of sorrow be forever wiped away. It means that this sad world will be restored and all that the philanthropist, the patriot, the missionary has dreamed and longed to see will be at last fulfilled under the beneficent, peaceful government of Jesus Christ. The war drum will throb no longer. The oppressor will cry out no more. Wrong will be no longer upon the throne and right upon the scaffold, but Christ will reign in righteousness, peace and blessing from shore to shore and pole to pole and even earth's rigorous climate, devouring sea and barren wastes will disappear, and this terrestrial scene will "rejoice and blossom" (Isaiah 35:1).

And best of all it means that Christ will be with us in all His glory and in all His grace. "The dwelling of God is with men" (Revelation 21:3) and under His blessed reign and the reign of His saints the glorious gospel will cover the earth and all nations will accept the benignant scepter of the Prince of Peace and the Lord of All.

CHAPTER 13

THE GREAT WHITE THRONE

Then I saw a great white throne and him who was seated on it. Earth and sky fled from his presence, and there was no place for them. And I saw the dead, great and small, standing before the throne, and books were opened. Another book was opened, which is the book of life. The dead were judged according to what they had done as recorded in the books. The sea gave up the dead that were in it, and death and Hades gave up the dead that were in them, and each person was judged according to what he had done. Then death and Hades were thrown into the lake of fire. The lake of fire is the second death. If anyone's name was not found written in the book of life, he was thrown into the lake of fire. (Revelation 20:11–15)

The thousand years have run their course and the earth is bright and glorious with all the blessing of the millennial age, until the awful curse of sin has almost been forgotten, and the idea of a personal devil is but a distant remembrance of long-forgotten ages.

Yet we must not forget that while sin has long been suppressed, and the human race has accepted the scepter of Christ to earth's remotest bounds, yet the elements of man's natural corruption have still remained in the human soul, and human nature in itself is really no better notwithstanding the altered circumstances with which it has been favored through the millennial years.

Therefore God permits one further test. One more dark tragedy must pass over the face of this long-distracted planet before it will finally settle into its eternal orbit of righteousness and blessing.

And so it comes to pass that at the close of the 1,000 years Satan is loosed from his prison and permitted to go back once more to deceive the nations. Perhaps there was a purpose in this for even Satan himself. May it not be that God designed to let him see the difference between good and evil through the glorious object lesson of the millennial world? For 6,000 years he has been permitted to rule, and the result is desolation, sorrow, death and desperate ruin. Now for 1,000 years Christ has reigned and he beholds a prospect of beauty, blessedness and peace. How can he fail to recognize the difference between the evil and the good, and, if there can be one spark of desire in his fallen spirit, to turn toward the light? This is his final opportunity. Who can tell whether, if even he had learned the lesson of his long and dreadful imprisonment, had appreciated the meaning of this blessed object lesson of righteousness, and had turned to Jehovah with repentance and sincerity, even he might have found some place of mercy.

But the result shows that he is incorrigibly bad. The only feeling that seems to animate him is a fiendish hate of God and man, a relentless resolve to blight and wreck the very scene that he beholds, and to use his brief respite not to undo his long career of wrong but to perpetrate the most audacious and desperate climax of his long career of wickedness. This is his last chance and he stakes his all upon it. For a thousand years he has been planning his desperate scheme and now is his opportunity to accomplish it.

Perhaps he has come back to earth in the very form and nature of man. Perhaps he has mimicked the Son of God to the last extreme and been granted the power to become incarnate, a fiend in human form.

And so he presents himself to men in his last disguise, a gifted glorious man, and begins to gather around him the restless spirits, who, with unsanctified natures, have been tolerating the restraints of a holy government and fretting under the restrictions of Christ's authority.

In alluring light and with ingenious disguise he pictures before them, as once he did to the Son of God on the high mountain of the wilderness, the splendors of a universal empire, combining all the power, the wealth, the grandeur of the world in its supreme civilization, all the glorious culture of those days, and promises to them the aid of supernatural power and even the brilliant dream of dethroning the Son of God from the very heavens as well as the earth, and raising humanity to its grandest possibility, even to "be as gods" and sit upon the throne of the Infinite and Eternal.

This was the dream of Eden. This was the proud ambition which prompted the building of Babel's tower. This was the audacious proposal that He made to the Son of God in the wilderness. This, no doubt, will be his last exploit. It was for this that he left his high place in the heavens. This has been the purpose of his grand rebellion from its inception, to take the very place of God and cast Him from His throne. Doubtless he offers to many the alluring bribe, not of boundless power and supreme dominion, but the gratification of every selfish and unholy desire, the allurements which Paganism and Islam have held out to their votaries, the satisfaction of every gross and sinful passion, and an existence of sensual delight; and there will be enough of evil left in human nature to give a ready response.

One by one the restless and unholy spirits of earth gather to his side until at length their numbers are as "the sand of the sea" and as a mighty army of millions, perhaps billions of men, armed not only with the weapons of earth but of hell, and, led by this brilliant archangel, they oppose the camp of the Son of God and besiege the "beloved city" itself.

To human reason and sight it will doubtless seem at first a fearful and formidable assault, but if we are to judge by the dramatic picture of the Apocalypse the suspense will not be long. The tragedy will be swift and terrible.

The fire of God will fall from heaven and in a moment the myriad ranks of earth and hell will melt away, engulfed in devouring flame. Satan will again be caught and cast out in eternal imprisonment not now into the abyss, the scene of his former confinement, but into the Lake of Fire where the Wild Beast and the False Prophet are already suffering torment day and night forever.

Henceforth the devil's career is ended. No more will he return to the earth or go forth to other realms to deceive and to destroy. He has been tested to the uttermost and found to be incorrigibly bad, and human nature has been proved and tried and it also has utterly and signally failed.

Now the story of time is to end. The last of earth's dispensations has run its course, and the Eternal Cycle is about to begin. And so the final scene so long prepared at last appears, and before the vision of the Seer there rises a spectacle of majesty and terror and a tragedy of woe more awful than mortal or angel has ever gazed upon before.

It is the Great White Throne. It is the final judgment. It is the resurrection of the wicked. It is the passing out of the old earth and heaven and the ushering in of the new creation.

THE GREAT WHITE THRONE

It is the symbol of sovereignty and of judgment. Its greatness tells of the importance of this august occasion. It is the greatest day that earth has ever seen. It is the grand assize before which all the millions of the past are to appear. Its whiteness speaks of the immaculate justice and unerring wisdom which are to characterize the Tribunal. There will be no mistakes here. There will be no misunderstandings here. There will be no hasty judgments here. Everything will be right and everything will be final and from this court there will be no appeal.

Where that throne will be erected the boldest imagination can only approximately conceive. Probably it will appear in the air where the New Jerusalem is to descend, hanging suspended from the heavens and towering high above the earth. It will be encompassed with clouds of awful blackness and gleams of terrific light. Myriads of angels will hover round it as the officers of justice and the executioners of judgment, and all the portents of a dissolving universe will add to the sublimity and terror of the scene.

But the grandest of all the objects of that awful day, will be:

HE WHO SITS UPON IT

It is the throne of Jehovah. It is the throne of the Son of God. The form that sits enwrapped in majesty is He who once stood a prisoner before Pilate's judgment hall. Pilate and Jesus meet at last, but, oh, how altered are the circumstances! Poetry has imperfectly tried to paint that scene and write upon our imagination:

> . . . that dreadful Form
> With rainbow wreath and robes of storm,
> On cherub wings and wings of wind,
> Appointed Judge of all mankind.

Well may we ask,

> Can this be He who wont to stray
> A pilgrim on the world's highway,
> Oppressed by power and mocked by pride,
> The Nazarene, the Crucified?

Yes, it is even He, and many will remember in that day how once He said, "A time is coming when all who are in their graves will hear his voice and come out—those who have done good will rise to live, and those who have done evil will rise to be condemned" (John 5:28–29). "The Father judges no one, but has entrusted all judgment to the Son" (5:22). "And he has given him authority to judge because he is the Son of Man" (5:27).

The men of Athens will be there to remember how once a passing missionary stood in the Areopagus and cried, "God . . . commands all people everywhere to repent. For he has set a day when he will judge the world with justice by the man he has appointed. He has given proof of this to all men by raising him from the dead" (Acts 17:30–31).

The Gentiles of Cesarea will remember how Peter said, "He is the one whom God appointed as judge of the living and the dead" (10:42). Yes, it is Jesus. It is He who came to save the world, and they who have rejected the blood of the Lamb are now to realize what is meant by "the wrath of the Lamb" (Revelation 6:16).

Once or twice during His earthly life there blazed from His eye and from His tongue the foregleam of judgment fire, as when He cursed the barren fig tree and it withered at His word; or, as when he uttered those awful woes against the Scribes and Pharisees which we read in Matthew, finishing up at last with the fearful words, "You snakes! You brood of vipers! How will you escape being condemned to hell?" (Matthew 23:33).

Now His mission of mercy is accomplished. His mediatorial work is finished, and He sits down upon the throne of absolute and impartial judgment, and there is something in His countenance and His bearing so awful that the very universe shudders, and from His face the earth and heaven flee away; the sun goes out in darkness; the firmament is rolled up as a scroll; the stars forget to shine, and the earth reels and staggers like a drunken man.

THE RISEN DEAD

"And I saw the dead, great and small, standing before the throne. . . . The sea gave up the dead that were in it, and death and Hades gave up the dead that were in them" (Revelation 20:12–13). Now earth's myriads who had lived and died and slept on through the 1,000 years are ushered back to life again by an awful power which compels them to live. The wretched spirit of the criminal steals back into his more wretched form, his face distorted with agony and his risen body bearing the impress of the soul that abused it and that now comes back to share its doom. Just as truly as the righteous rise so will the wicked come forth from the graves of earth, from the graves of ocean, from the elements into which their bodies have been dissolved by decay, or by cremation. God will know where to find them. Each soul will take on a body absolutely fitted to its nature and reflecting its quality and character and they will cringe before that awful throne and form a spectacle more terrible even than judgment.

Oh, soul, you may for a little season cut the frail cord that binds you to your body; you may suspend for a little the functions of that mortal frame and "shuffle off," as you call it "the mortal coil." But remember you have got to live forever. That soul can never die and that body must come forth to life and judgment to be "judged according to what [he] had done" (Revelation 20:12).

THE JUDGMENT

The "books were opened. Another book was opened, which is the book of life. The dead were judged according to what they had done as recorded in the books" (20:12). The inexorable principle of this judgment is personal merit or demerit. They are judged rigidly according to their works. There is no mercy here. This is the cardinal principle of divine judgment enunciated by Paul in the second chapter of Romans in these solemn words:

So when you, a mere man, pass judgment on them and yet do the same things, do you think you will escape God's judgment? Or do you show contempt for the riches of his kindness, tolerance and patience, not realizing that God's kindness leads you toward repentance?

But because of your stubbornness and your unrepentant heart, you are storing up wrath against yourself for the day of God's wrath, when His righteous judgment will be revealed. God "will give to each person according to what he has done." To those who by persistence in doing good seek glory, honor and immortality, he will give eternal life. But for those who are self-seeking and who reject the truth and follow evil, there will be wrath and anger. There will be trouble and distress for every human being who does evil: first for the Jew, then for the Gentile; but glory, honor and peace for everyone who does good: first for the Jew, then for the Gentile. For God does not show favoritism. (2:3–11)

This is the law pure and simple. The gospel is a subsequent and wholly different principle. But the persons who will stand in this judgment have rejected the gospel, and therefore they will be judged strictly by the law and according to their works.

There are two books. The one is the book of record or remembrance, containing all the actions, thoughts, words, motives—the whole testimony against sinful men.

How can this testimony be preserved? Ah, friends, has not science taught us something of the innumerable ways in which God can register the records of the past by countless automatic processes on the living pages of the universe? What is the telephone but just a little hint of the unseen wires that are passing through the spaces of this universe in every direction, and registering at the other end every whisper and echo of our lives? What is the phonograph but a suggestion that God has a thousand sensitive plates in every part of yonder firmament, and that every word you speak becomes recorded and treasured up yonder to be re-echoed in the judgment day? What is man's photography but a little bit of light discovered by our imperfect minds out of the vaster and grander processes which we have never discovered, by which God, perhaps, is constantly recording and preserving a continuous photograph of every act and attitude of human life, and that someday it will all repeat itself in the awful video of the judgment record? Thus God can preserve a testimony and can make every conscience and soul confess that it is true.

Let us not think that this is to be some hurried, terrified moment of swift and sudden doom. Doubtless it will be calm and long protracted, and time will be given for every testimony, every excuse, every case, and each soul will go forth echoing its own sentence and vindicating even its most terrific judgment. For it is written, "that at the name of Jesus every knee should bow/ . . . and every tongue confess that Jesus Christ is Lord" (Philippians 2:10–11).

Oh, how can sinners stand in that great day! Oh, how can any of us meet that awful test? Beloved, we cannot stand; we cannot meet it; we dare not face that dread tribunal and that holy God.

And we need not, because there is another book that will be opened in that day. It is the Lamb's book of life. It is the record of those names that accepted eternal life as the free gift of the Savior's love and the purchase of His precious blood. It is a book of mercy. It is a record of grace, and for those who are entered there the judgment is past. The Lord bore it Himself in their stead and in that dreadful day they will sit with Him among the justified and among the judges of the world. Beloved, this, the Great White Throne, is no place for a child of God. Alas, for those that enter there! For them mercy is past and for them justice only can mean eternal doom.

It is true that God will adjust the standard of judgment to the light and opportunity that each soul enjoyed. "All who sin apart from the law will also perish apart from the law" (Romans 2:12), and for them the standard will be the law of conscience, the unwritten law of God in their own hearts. And if it will be found that any mortal being has lived up to the law of conscience he will be acquitted in that day. But is it not written "If you, O LORD, kept a record of sins,/ O Lord, who could stand?" (Psalm 130:3).

Beloved, do not venture into the judgment of the Great White Throne, but hasten to the foot of Calvary. Accept His mercy and His precious blood. Tell Him that He has been judged for you in that awful hour when He cried, "Now is the time for judgment on this world; now the prince of this world will be driven out" (John 12:31), and "I, when I am lifted up from the earth, will draw all men to myself" (12:32). Tell Him you accept His judgment instead of yours and ask Him to make you know that your name is written in the Lamb's book of life; and then, for you, this glorious word is true, "I tell you the truth, whoever hears my word and believes him who sent me has eternal life and will not be condemned; he has crossed over from death to life" (5:24).

I will never forget a Christian woman on whom I called many years ago in her last hours, and how this glorious truth of our deliverance from the judgment was used of God to banish her fears and open for her an abundant entrance into the everlasting kingdom of our Lord and Savior, Jesus Christ. I found her near her end and sincerely but timidly trusting in the mercy of her Savior. She had given her heart and life to Him the best she knew, "But, oh," she said to me again and again, "that awful judgment, how I dread it! I believe that somehow God will forgive and take me in, but oh, the judgment! The judgment! My soul shrinks from the terrible prospect!" I sat down by her side with my open Bible and poured into her mind the glorious gospel that had but just before brought to me the perfect peace of God. I said to her, "Dear sister, you are not going into the judgment. You have been judged already in Christ for your sins, and long, long before that dreadful judgment will come to pass you will have been with Jesus in heaven and through the glory of the millennial years. When you come with Him to the judgment you will be seated by His side." As the truth gradually broke in upon her soul and at last filled it, it was beautiful to see the transformation. The darkness and dread melted away and the light of hope and victory passed over her face, and she wept with wonder and gratitude to think it could be true. As she passed through the gates there was not a cloud nor a fear.

Beloved, do you know your full salvation? Will you claim it?

And, oh sinner, will you know your only hope? Keep out of the judgment. Flee to the Savior. Make sure that your name is written in the Lamb's book of life.

THE EXECUTION OF THE SENTENCE AND THE DOOM OF THE CONDEMNED

Our sensitive hearts may shrink from the truth but our weakness will not quench those flames, and our specious reasonings will not close those fiery gates. It is written by the kindest hand that ever sought to bless us, "If anyone's name was not found written in the book of life, he was thrown into the lake of fire" (Revelation 20:15).

This is the dreadful abode prepared not for man but for the devil and his angels. Into it Satan and Antichrist have already been hurled, and now those who have chosen him as their master and rejected the mercy of the Lord are to share his everlasting punishment. What it means it is idle to speculate. It is called the "second death" (20:14). It is spoken of as "forever and ever" and if men may speciously reason that this verse just means age-long, it must be remembered that the age in which it occurs is not one of the pages of time but the mighty aeons of eternity. Oh, let us not deceive ourselves by playing with words, but let us take in all their meaning the earnest faithful warnings by which divine mercy would shut us up to the only way of escape; and let us "flee from the coming wrath" (Matthew 3:7) and "take hold of eternal life" (1 Timothy 6:12).

CHAPTER 14

THE NEW HEAVEN AND EARTH AND THE NEW JERUSALEM

Then I saw a new heaven and a new earth, for the first heaven and the first earth had passed away, and there was no longer any sea. I saw the Holy City, the new Jerusalem, coming down out of heaven from God, prepared as a bride beautifully dressed for her husband. And I heard a loud voice from the throne saying, "Now the dwelling of God is with men, and he will live with them. They will be his people, and God himself will be with them and be their God. He will wipe every tear from their eyes. There will be no more death or mourning or crying or pain, for the old order of things has passed away." (Revelation 21:1–4)

First of all, let us fully understand that the sublime picture of these closing chapters of the Apocalypse is not a description of the heavens into which our beloved ones enter when they pass from us through the gates of what we call death. There is a heaven into which Christ has passed and where, like Stephen, our parted ones who sleep in Jesus are welcomed home. There is a Father's house where they rest in peace and blessedness and doubtless it has in it in embryo the elements of the glorious city and the eternal rapture which this vision describes; but the full glory has not yet come. They are waiting for their crowns and for their everlasting home until we will be gathered with them in the great consummation.

Let us also remember that this is not a description of the millennial earth and the glorious state which Christ's reign for 1,000 years will bring. That is briefly described in the 20th chapter. The scenes in this chapter come after the millennium and the dissolution of all things which it is to lead. This is the eternal state, a new heaven and a new earth. May the Spirit of inspiration give us a vision to see and a heart to understand this glorious Apocalypse of the future.

A NEW HEAVEN AND EARTH

The scenes of this chapter follow earth's final tragedy. There has been a crisis, a catastrophe, a fearful cataclysm. Before the face of Him upon the Great White Throne the earth and the heavens fled away and there was found no place for them. Just as man had to pass from the earthly to the heavenly, from the natural to the supernatural, from the mortal to the resurrection life through the gates of death, so now the material universe itself has to pass through the resurrection by way of death. The old planet is consumed with flame, the firmament and the heavenly bodies pass through a similar convulsion or dissolution, and from the wreck there emerged a new heaven and a new earth.

This did not occur at the commencement of the millennial age. Then undoubtedly great changes in earth's climate and surface took place, but they were only partial. Now it would seem the whole fabric of the universe must pass through the great transition and have its resurrection too. It would seem as if the taint of sin and the touch of Satan had left defilement and pollution upon the very atmosphere of the universe and God must have a great housecleaning and wash out with flames of fire every vestige, every memory of the awful crisis through which nature and the universe have passed.

And so by some mighty process the existing universe is dissolved and out of it emerges a new creation.

Now this is not the first time this doctrine has been revealed in the Holy Scriptures. Back in Isaiah we read,

> Behold, I will create
> new heavens and a new earth.
> The former things will not be remembered,
> nor will they come to mind.
> But be glad and rejoice forever
> in what I will create,
> for I will create Jerusalem to be a delight
> and its people a joy.
> I will rejoice over Jerusalem
> and take delight in my people;
> the sound of weeping and of crying
> will be heard in it no more.
> (65:17–19)

And again in Second Peter 3:7–13, we are told that as the earth was once destroyed by a flood of water it is to be once more destroyed by a sea of fire.

By the same word the present heavens and earth are reserved for fire, being kept for the day of judgment and destruction of ungodly men. (3:7)

Since everything will be destroyed in this way, what kind of people ought you to be? You ought to live holy and godly lives as you look forward to the day of God and speed its coming. That day will bring about the destruction of the heavens by fire, and the elements will melt in the heat. But in keeping with his promise we are looking forward to a new heaven and a new earth, the home of righteousness. (3:11–13)

This is precisely the teaching of the Revelation, and it looks forward not to the millennial reign of Christ but to the great crisis that is to follow it. The apostle's eye is looking on to the end of the panorama and taking it all in the light of final consummation.

In the change which is to come upon the earth it is added that "There was no longer any sea" (Revelation 21:1). Today the ocean covers and renders waste three-quarters of the surface of this planet. The world without an ocean could contain four times as great a population as the present surface of the planet. The ocean is a place of danger and death. There will be a river of delight and, doubtless, a sea of glass in the terrestrial geography of the coming age, but all that is terrific and scourging in the old ocean will have passed away.

THE NEW EARTH, GOD'S ABODE

It will be the personal residence of God. "Now the dwelling of God is with men, and he will live with them. They will be his people, and God himself will be with them and be their God" (21:3). This is a most significant statement. At the present time this earth is not the residence of God in any primary sense. For a little while it was the residence of Jesus Christ, but He was far from home and His Father's throne. At present it is the residence of the Holy Spirit but He is here as a visitor calling out a people to be gathered home. It is a far outlying world. It is a distant sphere that rolls in its orbit of darkness around the central throne; somewhere else today is the personal seat of God and the metropolis of the universe. When Jesus Christ ascended He went home to His Father's throne. He left the realms of earth; He passed through the heavens, He ascended far above all heavens and somewhere yonder in space He rested and sat down at the right hand of God.

The eye of the telescope has not discovered the metropolis of God's empire. The light of inspiration has not told us where; but somewhere, locally and actually, God has His capital where Christ in human form is residing, and where angels and the spirits of glorified men and the bodies of Enoch and Elijah and those that rose from their graves after Christ's resurrection and ascended with Him, are living today in actual physical presence. It is not so far away that we cannot reach it by the telephone of prayer, but that may be farther than the farthest star that rolls in dark immensity.

Science tells us that somewhere in this universe there is a central star around which all the stars and constellations are revolving. Just as the moon moves around the earth, and the moon and earth around the sun, so the sun and all its planets are revolving around some other center and this system round a yet greater. And yonder in the far Pleiades they tell us a mighty sun, Alcyone, far vaster than ours, seems to be at present the center of all the stellar motion. Is it there perhaps that God has His abode? We cannot tell, but this we know that the center of the universe some day will be this little world of ours. God will come down with His retinue and His throne; from earth will go forth the authority and the power that will govern all the material worlds and all the myriad beings that people immensity.

What a glorious prospect! What a stupendous honor! What a majestic hope! It would seem as if God were at last to be avenged for the curse of sin by turning the curse into a blessing and making the very place that had been associated with the bitterest hate of Satan and the cruelest sorrow of Jesus, His own dear Son, the very jewel of the universe, the paragon of creation and the capital of the heavens.

NO DEATH OR SORROW

It will be a world without death, disease or sorrow. There will be no more crying. There will be no more pain. There will be no death; and God will wipe away all tears from their eyes. This does not only mean that there will be no tears shed in that happy world, but that all the tears that were ever shed will be turned into joy, that they will be more than healed and there will be no single memory or shadow of pain or grief to gall the perfect felicity of eternal years. Oh, sorrowing one, be patient. Lift up your heart. Rejoice! "Weeping may remain for a night,/ but rejoicing comes in the morning" (Psalm 30:5). Oh, mourner, some day earth's fairest scenes will not be its cemeteries, and earth's sweetest affections will not be merely the means of making death beds sadder and breaking loving hearts.

NO SIN

The other feature of the renovated earth will be that there will be no sin, and nothing that defiles will enter into the holy city and the happy life of the coming ages. Satan will never tempt again. There will be no more curse or cursed one. Never again will God have to cloud His face and perform the strange work of judgment which He so little loves, but the universe will settle down to everlasting love and uninterrupted joy. We will be established and will know that we will never fall again. Angels will be confirmed in their high and holy state and the very shadow of evil will at last be forgotten. Heaven will be so pure that evil will not be thought, remembered or conceived. The curse of time is to know both good and evil. In the innocence of those happy years man will not know evil but only good. Oh, for that day to come when the crushing, defiling shadow of sin and doubt and fear will never fall again!

THE NEW JERUSALEM

Speedily the vision of the apostle is absorbed with one spectacle. It is the picture of the New Jerusalem, the holy city which he now beholds descending from God out of heaven and which is to be the chief attraction of the heavenly age.

Let us notice that this city is not created for the first time. It is recognized as having been there before, and John sees it descending from God out of heaven and resting finally upon the earth where it becomes the capital of the earth just as earth is the capital of the universe. This encourages us to believe that the New Jerusalem had already been a part of the glorious economy of the millennial age.

As we have already suggested it seems probable that this glorious city, with its blessed inhabitants constituting the Bride of the Lamb, was formed at Christ's coming in the air and became the residence of Christ and His saints during the millennial age. During that period it is not located on earth but seems to be suspended in the air where Christ will come to gather His risen and translated ones. It would seem as if during the millennial age it would be the heavenly home of the saints and so near to earth that they can pass from its gates constantly and instantly on their ministries of service and government over all the earth, but representing a higher life than that which the tribes of earth will live in their terrestrial sphere. Now, however, the glorious city descends to earth and becomes its metropolis.

The description of this city of light and glory is not a mere figure or symbol. God is not playing with words when He gives us the dimensions, the structure, the very colors of the heavenly city. He means that it is an actual fact and not a mere figure of speech. There will be a real world, a real body of physical beings, a real Christ in His risen state and real city with all the glory and splendor of which these vivid descriptions give us but a faint approximation.

1. Its Form

Let us note the form and structure of this glorious city. "The city was laid out like a square, as long as it was wide" (Revelation 21:16). It is a perfect cube like the Holy of Holies in the ancient Tabernacle which was a figure of heaven. The most remarkable feature of this description is that the height was equal to the breadth and length. In so vast a city as this it would either require that the towers should rise to a prodigious elevation or else that the streets should run vertically as well as laterally. There seems no reason why the latter should not be the case because to us up and down are terms entirely dependent upon the center of gravity. The reason it is difficult for us to ascend is because of the attraction of the earth; but in that city earth's attraction will be broken and God will be the center of gravitation, and in the supernatural life we, like Christ, will be invested with a power that will enable us to rise and soar in the heavens as freely as to pass from place to place on earth. Therefore it would seem to be true that the streets of this city will run up and down as well as backwards and forwards and that our material conceptions of space and substance will be transcended by higher laws.

2. The Dimensions of the City

They are colossal and at first we are staggered by its vastness. The entire measurement is 12,000 stadig, that is 1,400 miles. If this is the circuit of the city it would make it 370 miles long, the same width and the same height. Think of a city one side of which would reach from New York to Buffalo, the next from Buffalo to North Carolina, the whole space including the states of New York, Pennsylvania, New Jersey, Maryland, Virginia and West Virginia. And then when we attempt to realize the height we are staggered by the conception of a city whose towers would reach nearly 400 miles into the air, that is almost 100 times as high as earth's most lofty peaks.

This is the Father's house with its many mansions which Christ has been so long preparing. This is the eternal home of all the families of the redeemed. Here are to be the palaces and homes of all the holy that have ever lived on earth. Surely in this mighty city of the skies there will be room for all. Oh, you who are poor and often tried with pinching poverty, lift up your heads, your fortune is coming by and by, your city has foundations and its Builder and Maker is God, your home is prepared where decay and parting will never come. Take in the grandeur of your Master's thought, the beneficence of His resources, the transcendent glory of the hope laid up for you, and remember Him who said, "Everyone who has left houses or . . . fields for my sake will receive a hundred times as much and will inherit eternal life" (Matthew 19:29).

3. The Walls of the City

It is surrounded with a jeweled wall of solid and crystalline jasper. The walls are not so high as the city, being only a little over 200 feet in height. But even this would present a magnificent effect with the turrets of the city rising high above.

The foundations of this wall are described apart from the wall. They consist of various precious stones representing all the tints of the rainbow and the most precious crystals of the mine. They seem to represent the steps that rise to the entrance of the city. There are 12 gates to the city and to each of these gates it would seem there is a grand approach by means of 12 lofty steps. These steps are of all the colors of the rainbow blending in perfect harmony. There is the ruby, the sapphire and the diamond, the emerald, the topaz and the amethyst, all that crystal radiance and tinted beauty can combine to produce the most dazzling effects.

All this will be blended by God's infinite taste, and the city will look like a rainbow of glory even in its very foundations.

4. The Gates of the City

It is entered by 12 gates. Each of these is a single pearl. God will know how to make the materials for this splendid architectural monument if He has to gather all the pearls of the universe and blend them into one of these massive gates of crystalline beauty. And doubtless from these gates there will open broad highways and magnificent avenues into every part of the glorious city.

5. The Streets of the City

They are solid gold and its pavement is described as like transparent glass. This does not represent so much its transparency as its translucency. It is finely polished like a mirror. Glancing up these splendid avenues and these golden palaces shining in the light of God, each reflecting back the glory of the golden pavement and the glorious sky, one can scarcely imagine what a spectacle of dazzling splendor it must be.

6. The River of the Water of Life

This flows from the throne of God and of the Lamb, circling, doubtless, through the city, running down its innumerable avenues and carrying freshness and life to every part. Doubtless it will be in some sense the channel of physical and spiritual life and convey to those who drink of its waters and bathe in its depths the quickening fullness of the blessed Spirit and the living Christ.

7. The Trees upon Its Banks

Upon the banks of the river grows the tree of life. It is not a single tree but a single kind of tree with innumerable trees bearing their fruit anew each month while its leaves are for the healing of the nations who people the earth abroad.

8. The Light of the City

There is no light and there is no sun. If our sun has been renewed in yonder heavens, it is but as a taper compared with the glory of Him who is the Light of heaven. "For the glory of God gives it light, and the Lamb is its lamp" (21:23). God Himself sheds His effulgence through the eternal day and He who is the "light, in him there is no darkness at all" (1 John 1:5) fills the heaven with the glory and brightness of His supernal presence. There is no need for rest. There is no cessation of the song or service. There is no yesterday and no tomorrow. There is no chronology and there is no time, but it is one glad, eternal now, and the happy beings know that their joy can never end, their day can never have a period.

9. The Temple of Heaven

There is no temple there for God is the temple. No outward forms of worship are necessary in our conventional sense, for it is all worship, all love, all fellowship. Perhaps no language will be needed, but knowing as we are known, communing with God in the silent eloquence of the Spirit and undoubtedly knowing each other's hearts as perfectly as God knows ours, heart to heart and soul to soul will flow together like kindred drops of water or globules of air and all will ever breathe out and send forth their adoration unto Him, who is the Source of Life and the Supreme Object of their worship and love.

Yes, this is the city for which Abraham looked, the "city with foundations, whose architect and builder is God" (Hebrews 11:10). This is "the heavenly Jerusalem" of which the apostle wrote where dwell the "thousands upon thousands of angels in joyful assembly . . . the church of the firstborn" (12:22–23). This is the goal of ancient hope, the dream of ancient prophecy and the eternal reward of the sacrifices of the saint, the sufferings of the martyr and the love of those who counted all but loss for Christ. This is the vision that came to the seraphic soul of him who sang with almost inspired cadences,

> Oh, mother, dear Jerusalem
>   When shall I come to thee?
> Then shall my sorrows have an end,
>   When I thy joys shall see.

10. The Inhabitants of the City

Three classes are described:

a. Those that are written in the Lamb's book of life, Christ's redeemed ones (Revelation 21:27).

b. Those who wash their robes. "Blessed are those who wash their robes, that they may have the right to the tree of life and may go through the gates into the city" (22:14). This describes not only the saved ones but the sanctified also.

c. Those that overcome. This is for the conqueror. After we have taken Christ as Savior and as Sanctifier we will be tested and we must withstand in the evil day and having done all, stand. While the Lord has said, "To him who is thirsty I will give to drink without cost from the spring of the water of life" (21:6), He also adds immediately afterwards, "He who overcomes will inherit all this, and I will be his God and he will be my son" (21:7). The palaces and thrones of the New Jerusalem are only for the conquerors.

11. The Outcasts

On the other hand there is a very explicit account of those who are excluded.

a. The cowardly (21:8). This is the Greek translation of the word "fearful" there. The cowardly man is placed in contrast with the conqueror, the man who does not dare to overcome self and sin, but yields with cowardly selfishness and fear to the public opinion of the world and the clamor of his own heart. He cannot stand the tests that are necessary for this glorious prize and is disqualified and excluded.

b. The unbelieving. The very organ and sense by which we will be able to know and understand that heavenly world, is a spirit of faith. A man without faith would be lost in heaven, blind to its life, deaf to its sounds, insensible to its sweetness and delight.

c. The vile. That is those that sin against nature and the very instincts which God has put within us for our purity and protection against sin.

d. The murderers, including all who are controlled by violent passions and the spirit of hate which is essentially murder.

e. The sexually immoral, including all the forms of sensual and gross indulgence in impurity and licentiousness.

f. Those who practice magic arts. Those who play with spiritualism, clairvoyance and all the various forms by which the devil in the present day is getting men to worship him, including Christian Science, theosophy and all kindred forms of spiritism.

g. Idolaters, and this includes not only the worshipers of wood and stone but "greed, which is idolatry," (Colossians 3:5) and "if anyone loves the world, the love of the Father is not in him" (1 John 2:15).

h. All liars are excluded.

i. Everything that defiles. There will be no sin or possibility of sin in that holy place.

j. All that are not written in the Lamb's book of life, all the unsaved ones.
Where do we stand? Looking up at that city of light, gazing down into

that yawning abyss of fiery woe, once more let us hear Him say, "The Spirit and the bride say, 'Come!' And let him who hears say, 'Come!' Whoever is thirsty, let him come; and whoever wishes, let him take the free gift of the water of life" (Revelation 22:17).

CHAPTER 15

EVEN SO, COME

He who testifies to these things says, "Yes, I am coming soon."
Amen. Come, Lord Jesus. (Revelation 22:20)

T he last few verses of the book of Revelation contain a number of concluding messages.

THE SACREDNESS OF THIS BOOK

The first is a solemn assertion of the truth and importance of these prophecies and the announcement of an awful penalty upon all those who will trifle with their integrity by taking from or adding to the words of the prophecy of this book. "The angel said to me, 'These words are trustworthy and true. The Lord, the God of the spirits of the prophets, sent his angel to show his servants the things that must soon take place' " (Revelation 22:6). "I warn everyone who hears the words of the prophecy of this book: If anyone adds anything to them, God will add to him the plagues described in this book. And if anyone takes words away from this book of prophecy, God will take away from him his share in the tree of life and in the holy city, which are described in this book" (22:18–19). This is God's awful seal upon the sacredness and importance of this, His last message to mankind.

THE PROPHETIC MESSENGER

There follows a little incident relating to the messenger by whom the revelation was brought to John. For the moment John seems to have taken him for the Lord Jesus Himself and so fell down at his feet to worship him, but the messenger immediately corrected him and announced that he was not divine and had no right to worship, was but simply one of John's "fellow servants." And he adds with singular significance, "With your brothers the prophets and of all who keep the words of this book" (22:9). This is a little flash of light into the heavenly world which leaves much further light to be desired. This messenger seems to have been a human being employed as an instrument of comfort, help and service for the apostle of the Lord. It is therefore true that the glorified ones whom we call dead are thus employed in the heavenly world. This is not spiritism nor anything approaching it but it gives us the right to believe that those who have passed on are blessedly employed and perhaps know far more of this world that they have left behind than they knew while here.

It may be that this was one of those prophets of the Old Testament who was raised from the dead as we know that many of the Old Testament saints were, immediately after Christ's resurrection. We are told at that time "the tombs broke open and the bodies of many holy people who had died were raised to life. They came out of the tombs, and after Jesus' resurrection they went into the holy city and appeared to many people" (Matthew 27:52–53).

This would afford a clear explanation of the mystery. It may be that there are more than we dream already serving with the ascended Lord as the firstfruits of the coming resurrection. And it may be to these the Scriptures refer when they speak of His having led captivity captive, and ascended on high with the glorious train of the ransomed captives from the reign and realm of death.

THE TIME AT HAND

Next comes a solemn assurance of the urgency of this prophetic message and the fact that it is for the present time and that the crisis of these momentous events is speedily coming on. Daniel was told to seal the vision and leave it for the future ages; but John was told to "not seal up the words of the prophecy of this book, because the time is near" (Revelation 22:10).

THE MORNING STAR

Next comes the personal message of the Lord Jesus Himself identifying Himself with the one who had appeared at the opening of the Apocalypse as the Alpha and Omega, the Beginning and the End, the First and the Last, and announcing Himself as the Root and Offspring of David, the Bright and Morning Star, and the One who was about to speedily and swiftly come.

His reference to His relation to David was a ray of hope for suffering and waiting Israel, letting them know that the promises and covenants made with their ancient king and head were not forgotten, and the still more beautiful figure of the Bright and Morning Star is the assurance to His waiting people that His presence with them in their hearts is the sure foregleam of His speedy and visible coming. It is the same truth expressed by the Apostle Paul in the beautiful words, "Christ in you the hope of glory" (Colossians 1:27). It is a word of comfort and a ray of light to all for whom it still is the dark hour of the night while the sun is yet hidden beyond the distant horizon. But the Morning Star is risen in our hearts. We know Jesus and He in us is the preparation and the pledge of His blessed parousia and His glorious appearing.

But the announcement of His coming is very urgent, emphatic and repeated. Three times He says,

> "Behold, I am coming soon! Blessed is he who keeps the words of the prophecy in this book." (Revelation 22:7)

> "Behold, I am coming soon! My reward is with me, and I will give to everyone according to what he has done." (22:12)

> He who testifies to these things says, "Yes, I am coming soon." (22:20)

The word soon here literally means swiftly. It tells us of an accelerated movement in the final preparations for the Lord's return, and when the signs begin to come to pass He will soon be here. God's chronology is not like ours, rigid and absolute, but adjusted to conditions and preparations; for He has said that, "he will finish the work, and cut it short in righteousness: because a short work will the Lord make upon the earth" (Romans 9:28, KJV).

We are in the days of this shortened work. This is the time when we may hasten the coming of our Lord by sending forth the message of the gospel and seeking to have the Bride prepared to meet her coming Lord. Are we endeavoring to make real His own promise and command, "Behold, I am coming soon" (Revelation 22:12), or more literally, "swiftly"?

A HARDENED AGE

Next we have the intimation of a state of things toward the end in which the hearts of many will grow obdurate and the appeals of the gospel will fall on deaf and unresponsive ears. Surely that is the meaning of the 11th verse. "Let him who does wrong continue to do wrong; let him who is vile continue to be vile; let him who does right continue to do right; and let him who is holy continue to be holy" (22:11). Soon human character will become crystallized. Men and women are settling down to their eternal state. The Lord's coming will stereotype all conditions and there will be no place for change in those dreadful days; but even before the end men will reach the condition, where being past feeling they neither hope nor fear, and the most inspiring vision of the coming glory and the most awful warnings of the dark abyss are equally in vain. Surely the world is reaching this coarse material age and men just live on according to their natural tendency and trend—each hasting to his own place. Oh, how solemn! Oh, how terrible! Oh, let us make sure which way we are settling!

THE SPIRIT'S CRY

Then there follows an ardent and intense cry and prayer from the Spirit and the Bride for Him to come (22:17). This is the meaning surely of this remarkable passage. It is the cry of the Holy Spirit, "Come, Lord Jesus." It is the cry of the waiting Bride, "Come, beloved One." The Holy Spirit has been entrusted with the executive administration of the present age with this one view of leading up to the Lord's return. Oh, how He longs for the consummation! Oh, how earnestly and ardently He has been working to this end! And whenever a human soul enters into the true condition of the Bride, the separation, education, love, fellowship and intimacy which alone can qualify us for Christ's perfect love and eternal fellowship on the throne, the one cry of all our being is, "Come, Lord Jesus" (22:20).

Dear one, you may know by this whether you are of the Bride or not. Are you saying, "Come"?

THE MISSIONARY CRY

Next comes the universal call to all the world, the great evangelistic cry; the sending forth of the message to all the nations before the end. We have it in the 17th verse also. "Let him who hears say, 'Come!'" This is the missionary cry. This is the angel flying in the midst of heaven having the everlasting gospel to preach unto all them that dwell upon the face of the earth, to all kindreds and peoples and tribes and tongues. This is the great movement of our time. This is the great trust committed to our hands. Let us take up the cry and pass it on until "this gospel of the kingdom will be preached in the whole world as a testimony to all nations, and then the end will come" (Matthew 24:14).

THE LAST INVITATION

Once more the Lord Himself now turns to the sinner and makes His last appeal in all the intense and solemn light of the things that have just been passing before our minds. It would seem as if His heart became overwhelmed as once before when He was marching into Jerusalem in triumph and all the grandeur of His surroundings passed swiftly out of His thoughts; and as He gazed upon the city at His feet He could only think of its peril and coming doom, and yielding to an impulse of unutterable compassion He burst out into bitter weeping and addressed to impenitent Israel that plaintive appeal, "If you, even you, had only known on this day what would bring you peace—but now it is hidden from your eyes" (Luke 19:42).

It is said that once a squadron of Austrian cavalry were sweeping in review in front of a great assembly when out from the crowd there stepped a little child in heedlessness who toddled across the way unnoticed until it was just in front of the galloping dragoons. It seemed impossible to save its little life. A moment more and with a mighty thunder those iron heels would dash out its little life. But there was one man equal to the occasion. Leaning forward from his seat, holding himself in the saddle with great dexterity by his feet, he reached in front of his fiery charger until his hands just swept the ground, and by a dexterous movement he caught the little one just in time, lifted it from destruction and recovered his seat without the line for a moment breaking, when a mighty cheer like a thousand thunders told of the joy and admiration of that great multitude.

So the Lord Jesus Christ is Himself marching on to His final triumph and almost at the crisis of His appearing. Suddenly He pauses in these closing messages, bends down from His throne and reaches out His hands in tenderness and love to you, poor lost one, who are standing across His path and must inexorably be crushed beneath the tread of the armies of the judgment unless you are swiftly saved. It is you, dear one, that He is calling now as he cries, "Whoever is thirsty, let him come; and whoever wishes, let him take the free gift of the water of life" (Revelation 22:17). Often before had He said, "Come," but never was there such a "Come" as this. Every barrier is broken down, every difficulty is reduced to the simplicity of trust and love. He does not even demand that you should know much or do much or feel much or attempt anything, but just come. Move toward Him. Let your heart reach out, let your prayer cry out, let your will resolve the best you can to follow Him, and He will count it coming; and has He not already said, "Whoever comes to me I will never drive away" (John 6:36)?

THE LORD'S LAST WORD

Yet once more we cannot resist lingering for a moment to notice the deep and longing desire on the part of the Lord Himself to come. We have heard the Spirit's cry for Him to come. We have felt the Bride's deep longing that He should come; but now behold Him expressing His own intense desire to come. Pressing into language its utmost fullness of meaning He cries, "Yes, I am coming soon" (Revelation 22:20). This is His hour as well as ours. This is the reward of His sufferings, the coronation of His once thorn-crowned head, the joy of His meeting with His Bride and His loved ones, the full fruition of all His suffering and shame. Will we not help the Master's joy and hasten His coming?

THE RESPONSE OF LOVE

Finally the response of His people's heart is, "Amen. Come, Lord Jesus" (22:20).

Is this our amen? Is this our response? And will we take the "even so," and by His grace make our lives agree with our language, evening up everything we say or do to this blessed hope, this simple watchword, "Even so, Come Lord Jesus, Come quickly"?

> Christ is coming; this we know
> Let our lives be "Even so."

"The grace of the Lord Jesus be with God's people. Amen" (22:21).

SCRIPTURE INDEX

HOW TO USE THIS INDEX: This index is divided in sections by book of the Bible. Under each book, a subdivision of chapter is listed. The verses used are listed under the chapter starting from lowest to highest. Following each verse used is the Roman numeral of the volume where the verse appears, and then the pages of that volume it appears on. Many verses appear in several volumes. The information on the appearance of each verse is concluded with a semi colon.

For example: If you were looking up all the times Simpson quoted Genesis 1:3 go to GENESIS, look under the Chapter 1 heading across the paragraph until you see the 3 following the semicolon. This paragraph under Chapter 1 looks like this:

1, I.11, 12, 16, 20; 2, I4, 13, 14, 21; **3, I.4, 14, 14, 16, 21, IV.375, 409;**

You will find that this verse appears in volume 1 once on pages 4, 16 and 21, and twice on page 14, and it also appears in volume 4 on pages 375 and 409.

195, IV.79, V.539, VI.416, 436; 13, III.184, 245, 249, IV.516, V.537, VI.415, 436, 436, 436, 437; 14, VI.437
Referred to: 5, IV.161; 9, I.104

Chapter 6
2, VI.437; 10, VI.437; 16, III.172, 349, IV.112, 123, 343, VI.514; 16-17, VI.438
Referred to: 4, VI.437; 5, VI.437; 8, VI.437

Chapter 7
9, I.212, VI.469; 9-10, VI.438; 10, II.137, III.242, IV.486, VI.413; 12, VI.414; 14, VI.143; 14-15, VI.416; 15-17, III.302; 16, IV.326; 16-17, I.212; 17, III.122, 229, IV.483, VI.419
Referred to: 1-8, VI.466; 1-17, VI.443

Chapter 8
3, VI.108; 5, III.51; 10, VI.441; 13, VI.441
Referred to: 1-11:19, VI.439

Chapter 9
6, VI.442; 21, VI.442
Referred to: 7-11, VI.442

Chapter 10
Referred to: 1-11:19, VI.443; 11, VI.443

Chapter 11
12, VI.443; 15, IV.26, 187, VI.444; 17, VI.434, 445; 17-18, VI.444; 18, VI.445, 445, 445, 445, 445, 445
Referred to: 1-19, VI.434; 17, VI.434

Chapter 12
9, I.33, VI.448; 10, II.344, V.388, VI.451; 11, VI.379, 452, 453; 12, V.388, VI.452; 17, VI.450
Referred to: 1-17, VI.487; 1-18:24, VI.447; 9, I.41

Chapter 13
1, VI.459; 2, V.452; 8, II.22, V.37, 47, 378, 410, VI.279; 11, VI.447

Referred to: 1-18, VI.484

Chapter 14
1-5, VI.480; 2, III.386; 4, VI.413, 467, 467, 467; 4-5, V.484; 5, VI.413, 467; 6, VI.414; 6-7, VI.468; 7, VI.469, 469; 8, VI.447, 469; 13, II.146, VI.215, 470; 14, VI.470; 19, III.122
Referred to: 1-5, VI.499; 1-20, VI.465; 2, V.398; 4, II.147; 9-12, VI.470; 14-16, VI.470; 15-16, VI.465; 17-20, VI.471

Chapter 15
3-4, V.538

Chapter 16
12, VI.477; 13, VI.45; 14, I.202, III.165, VI.45, 478, 479; 15, I.75, III.490, VI.479, 480; 17, VI.481
Referred to: 12, III.350; 14, VI.479, 479; 15, VI.479; 16, VI.479, 479

Chapter 17
3, VI.447, 485; 4, VI.485, 486; 5, VI.486, 487; 6, VI.486; 9, VI.488; 10, VI.457; 10-11, VI.489; 12, VI.457; 14, II.147, 182, III.168; 15, VI.485; 18, VI.488
Referred to: 1-18, VI.484; 11, VI.457; 16, VI.490

Chapter 18
2, VI.490; 4, VI.487, 491; 7, VI.487
Referred to: 1-24, VI.487, 490

Chapter 19
1-3, VI.494; 4, VI.494; 6, III.146, 214, V.379, VI.494; 7, V.484, VI.494, 496; 7-8, I.75, VI.414, 480; 8, III.254, V.73, VI.5, 13, 501; 9, VI.499, 501, 502; 10, IV.176, 347, 354, 399; 11, III.214, VI.413, 504, 504; 11-13, III.445; 12, VI.504; 13, VI.504, 504; 14, V.505; 15, VI.504, 504; 16, III.227, 445, VI.413, 418, 504
Referred to: 1-21, VI.473; 1-20:15, VI.503

Chapter 20
1-3, III.474; 4, VI.509; 5, VI.508; 5-6, V.490; 6, VI.508; 12, VI.515, 515; 12-13, VI.515; 14, VI.518; 15, VI.518
Referred to: 1-10, I.41

Chapter 21
1, III.122, VI.521; 2, III.321, VI.484; 3, I.28, II.149, IV.187, V.437, VI.510, 521; 3-4, III.302; 4, III.122; 5, V.537; 6, VI.527; 7, VI.527; 9, V.442; 16, VI.523; 23, II.95, VI.526; 27, II.4, VI.414
Referred to: 8, I.255, VI.527; 27, VI.526

Chapter 22
5, VI.419; 6, VI.529; 7, VI.531; 9, VI.529; 10, VI.411, 530; 11, III.183, VI.531; 11-12, II.342; 12, VI.531, 531; 14, VI.416, 527; 15, I.348; 16, II.341, III.357, VI.450; 17, I.126, 137, 258, III.231, 292, IV.205, V.383, VI.396, 414, 420, 420, 528, 532, 533; 18-19, VI.529; 20, II.342, III.122, 231, 231, VI.324, 328, 413, 419, 427, 531, 532, 533; 20-21, VI.85; 21, I.152, VI.534
Referred to: 17, VI.532